MCSE: Windows 2000 Network Security Design Study Guide Exam 70-220

OBJECTIVE	PAGE
Analyzing Business Requirements	
Analyze the existing and planned business models. • Anlalyze the company model and the geographical scope. Models include regional, national, international, subsidiary, and branch offices. • Analyze company processes. Processes include information flow, communication flow, service and product life cycles, and decision-making.	12, 19
Analyze the existing and planned organizational structures. Considerations include management model; company organization; vendor, partner, and customer relationships; and acquisition plans. I	54
Analyze factors that influence company strategies. • Identify company priorities. • Identify the projected growth and growth strategy. • Identify relevant laws and regulations. • Identify the company's tolerance for risk. • Identify the total cost of operations.	70, 163
Analyze business and security requirements for the end user.	95, 105
Analyze the structure of IT management. Considerations include type of administration, such as centralized or decentralized; funding model; outsourcing; decision-making process; and change-management process.	95, 105
Analyze the current physical model and information security model. • Analyze internal and external security risks.	153
Analyzing Technical Requirements	
Evaluate the company's existing and planned technical environment. • Analyze company size and user and resource distribution. • Assess the available connectivity between the geographic location of work sites and remote sites. • Assess the net available bandwidth. • Analyze performance requirements. • Analyze the method of accessing data and systems. • Analyze network roles and responsibilities. Roles include administrative, user, service, resource ownership, and application.	201, 209, 215, 220, 224
Analyze the impact of the security design on the existing and planned technical environment. • Assess existing systems and applications. • Identify existing and planned upgrades and rollouts. • Analyze technical support structure. • Analyze existing and planned network and systems management.	258, 266, 272, 279, 283

OBJECTIVE	PAGE
Analyzing Security Requirements	
Design a security baseline for a Windows 2000 network that includes domain controllers, operations masters, application servers, file and print servers, RAS servers, desktop computers, portable computers, and kiosks.	306
Identify the required level of security for each resource. Resources include printers, files, shares, Internet access, and dial-in access.	306
Designing a Windows 2000 Security Solution	
Design an audit policy.	369
Design a delegation of authority strategy.	380
Design the placement and inheritance of security policies for sites, domains, and organizational units.	380
Design an Encrypting File System strategy.	396
Design an authentication strategy. • Select authentication methods. Methods include certificate-based authentication, Kerberos authentication, clear-text passwords, digest authentication, smart cards, NTLM, RADIUS, and SSL • Design an authentication strategy for integration with other systems.	423
Design a security group strategy.	406
Design a Public Key Infrastructure. • Design Certificate Authority (CA) hierarchies. • Identify certificate server roles. • Manage certificates. • Integrate with third-party CAs. • Map certificates.	542, 546, 555, 565, 569
Design Windows 2000 network services security. • Design Windows 2000 DNS security. • Design Windows 2000 Remote Installation Services (RIS) security. • Design Windows 2000 SNMP security. • Design Windows 2000 Terminal Services security.	584, 608, 637, 647
Designing a Security Solution for Access Between Networks	
Provide secure access to public networks from a private network.	677
Provide external users with secure access to private network resources.	686
Provide secure access between private networks. • Provide secure access within a LAN. • Provide secure access within a WAN. • Provide secure access across a public network.	687
Design Windows 2000 security for remote access users.	719
Designing Security for Communication Channels	
Design an SMB-signing solution.	737
Design an IPSec solution. • Design an IPSec encryption scheme. • Design an IPSec management strategy. • Design negotiation policies. • Design security policies.	743, 746, 751, 757
• Design IP filters and security levels.	
• Define security levels.	

Exam objectives are subject to change at any time without prior notice and at Microsoft's sole discretion. Please visit Microsoft's Training & Certification Web site (www.microsoft.com/Train_Cert) for the most current listing of exam objectives.

MCSE:
Windows 2000 Network Security Design
Study Guide

MCSE:
Windows® 2000 Network Security Design
Study Guide

Gary Govanus

Robert King

San Francisco • Paris • Düsseldorf • Soest • London

Associate Publisher: Neil Edde
Contracts and Licensing Manager: Kristine O'Callaghan
Acquisitions & Developmental Editor: Dann McDorman
Editor: Linda Stephenson
Production Editor: Judith Hibbard
Technical Editors: Bob Gradante, Daniel Renaud
Book Designer: Bill Gibson
Graphic Illustrator: Tony Jonick
Electronic Publishing Specialist: Nila Nichols
Proofreaders: Camera Obscura, Erika Donald, Amy Garber, Laurie O'Connell, Nancy Riddiough, Suzanne Stein
Page Layout: Pete Gaughan
Indexer: Ted Laux
CD Coordinator: Kara Eve Schwartz
CD Technician: Keith McNeil
Cover Design: Archer Design
Cover Photograph: Natural Selection

Library of Congress Card Number: 00-106117

ISBN: 0-7821-2758-4

Manufactured in the United States of America

10 9 8 7 6 5 4 3 2 1

To Our Valued Readers:

In recent years, Microsoft's MCSE program has established itself as the premier computer and networking industry certification. Nearly a quarter of a million IT professionals have attained MCSE status in the NT 4 track. Sybex is proud to have helped thousands of MCSE candidates prepare for their exams over these years, and we are excited about the opportunity to continue to provide people with the skills they'll need to succeed in the highly competitive IT industry.

For the Windows 2000 MCSE track, Microsoft has made it their mission to demand more of exam candidates. Exam developers have gone to great lengths to raise the bar in order to prevent a paper-certification syndrome, one in which individuals obtain a certification without a thorough understanding of the technology. Sybex welcomes this new philosophy as we have always advocated a comprehensive instructional approach to certification courseware. It has always been Sybex's mission to teach exam candidates how new technologies work in the real world, not to simply feed them answers to test questions. Sybex was founded on the premise of providing technical skills to IT professionals, and we have continued to build on that foundation, making significant improvements to our study guides based on feedback from readers, suggestions from instructors, and comments from industry leaders.

The depth and breadth of technical knowledge required to obtain Microsoft's new Windows 2000 MCSE is staggering. Sybex has assembled some of the most technically skilled instructors in the industry to write our study guides, and we're confident that our Windows 2000 MCSE study guides will meet and exceed the demanding standards both of Microsoft and you, the exam candidate.

Good luck in pursuit of your MCSE!

Neil Edde
Associate Publisher—Certification
Sybex, Inc.

SYBEX Inc. 1151 Marina Village Parkway, Alameda, CA 94501
Tel: 510/523-8233 Fax: 510/523-2373 HTTP://www.sybex.com

Software License Agreement: Terms and Conditions

The media and/or any online materials accompanying this book that are available now or in the future contain programs and/or text files (the "Software") to be used in connection with the book. SYBEX hereby grants to you a license to use the Software, subject to the terms that follow. Your purchase, acceptance, or use of the Software will constitute your acceptance of such terms.

The Software compilation is the property of SYBEX unless otherwise indicated and is protected by copyright to SYBEX or other copyright owner(s) as indicated in the media files (the "Owner(s)"). You are hereby granted a single-user license to use the Software for your personal, noncommercial use only. You may not reproduce, sell, distribute, publish, circulate, or commercially exploit the Software, or any portion thereof, without the written consent of SYBEX and the specific copyright owner(s) of any component software included on this media.

In the event that the Software or components include specific license requirements or end-user agreements, statements of condition, disclaimers, limitations or warranties ("End-User License"), those End-User Licenses supersede the terms and conditions herein as to that particular Software component. Your purchase, acceptance, or use of the Software will constitute your acceptance of such End-User Licenses.

By purchase, use or acceptance of the Software you further agree to comply with all export laws and regulations of the United States as such laws and regulations may exist from time to time.

Reusable Code in This Book

The authors created reusable code in this publication expressly for reuse for readers. Sybex grants readers permission to reuse for any purpose the code found in this publication or its accompanying CD-ROM so long as all three authors are attributed in any application containing the reusable code, and the code itself is never sold or commercially exploited as a stand-alone product.

Software Support

Components of the supplemental Software and any offers associated with them may be supported by the specific Owner(s) of that material but they are not supported by SYBEX. Information regarding any available support may be obtained from the Owner(s) using the information provided in the appropriate read.me files or listed elsewhere on the media. Should the manufacturer(s) or other Owner(s) cease to offer support or decline to honor any offer, SYBEX bears no responsibility. This notice concerning support for the Software is provided for your information only. SYBEX is not the agent or principal of the Owner(s), and SYBEX is in no way responsible for providing any support for the Software, nor is it liable or responsible for any support provided, or not provided, by the Owner(s).

Warranty

SYBEX warrants the enclosed media to be free of physical defects for a period of ninety (90) days after purchase. The Software is not available from SYBEX in any other form or media than that enclosed herein or posted to `www.sybex.com`. If you discover a defect in the media during this warranty period, you may obtain a replacement of identical format at no charge by sending the defective media, postage prepaid, with proof of purchase to:

SYBEX Inc.
Customer Service Department
1151 Marina Village Parkway
Alameda, CA 94501
(510) 523-8233
Fax: (510) 523-2373
e-mail: info@sybex.com
WEB: HTTP://WWW.SYBEX.COM

After the 90-day period, you can obtain replacement media of identical format by sending us the defective disk, proof of purchase, and a check or money order for $10, payable to SYBEX.

Disclaimer

SYBEX makes no warranty or representation, either expressed or implied, with respect to the Software or its contents, quality, performance, merchantability, or fitness for a particular purpose. In no event will SYBEX, its distributors, or dealers be liable to you or any other party for direct, indirect, special, incidental, consequential, or other damages arising out of the use of or inability to use the Software or its contents even if advised of the possibility of such damage. In the event that the Software includes an online update feature, SYBEX further disclaims any obligation to provide this feature for any specific duration other than the initial posting. The exclusion of implied warranties is not permitted by some states. Therefore, the above exclusion may not apply to you. This warranty provides you with specific legal rights; there may be other rights that you may have that vary from state to state. The pricing of the book with the Software by SYBEX reflects the allocation of risk and limitations on liability contained in this agreement of Terms and Conditions.

Shareware Distribution

This Software may contain various programs that are distributed as shareware. Copyright laws apply to both shareware and ordinary commercial software, and the copyright Owner(s) retains all rights. If you try a shareware program and continue using it, you are expected to register it. Individual programs differ on details of trial periods, registration, and payment. Please observe the requirements stated in appropriate files.

Copy Protection

The Software in whole or in part may or may not be copy-protected or encrypted. However, in all cases, reselling or redistributing these files without authorization is expressly forbidden except as specifically provided for by the Owner(s) therein.

To my wonderful wife, Bobbi, for all her patience, love, and understanding.
Gary Govanus

As always, to Suze.
Bob King

Acknowledgments

Hillary Clinton wrote a book published by Touchstone books, called *It Takes a Village*. That was about raising a child. If her book had been about writing a book, it would have been entitled It Takes a State!

This book started in the fall of 1999, when Neil Edde from Sybex called and asked if Bob and I would like to handle writing a couple of study guides. Along the way, Dann McDorman helped us through the first few chapters, and then turned things over to the unflappable production editor, Judith Hibbard. No matter how crazy things got (and they got really crazy on this book), Judith was always there as a calming influence. Never once did she tell us to get a grip, or to stop whining and get to writing. She has been wonderful to work with, and she tells me she enjoyed the experience so much, she wants to work on another book with us. This just proves that she is truly masochistic!

The person who really wrote the book was Linda Stephenson. Linda's role in this effort was to take the material we wrote and then make some sense out of it. She is the one who put it into complete sentences and made sure that our thought process was linear instead of scattered. That was not an easy task. This book went through several different complete revisions, so I am sure Linda has had to work four or five times harder than she is used to. Linda has already started to work with us again, this time on the Exam Notes book for the Security Exam. Linda is another glutton for punishment that I could not have lived without.

Then there are the technical editors, Bob Gradante and Daniel Renaud, who worked with us to keep us honest during the entire process. They did a great job of checking all the facts, figures, and technical information. Thanks to Scott Beckstrand for contributing to the Case Studies and Bonus Exams.

Then there are all the people who worked on the book that we never even got to deal with. They are Tony Jonick, graphic artist; Pete Gaughan, page layout; Nila Nichols, electronic publishing specialist; and Ted Laux, indexer.

Finally, there is my family. Writing one of these takes a lot of time, time away from wives, children, grandchildren, parents, and all the others that care about us. We would like to thank all of them for their patience, support, and love.

That is really an impressive list, isn't it? We all came together and worked really hard to present you with the best possible information. Our goal was to give you the tools to make your testing experience successful. Good luck!

Gary Govanus

It's funny how life throws you curveballs from time to time. When I accepted this project, I was living just north of Tampa, was self-employed, and planned to use the traditional slow period at the beginning of the year to write. By the time we started working, I was moving to Grand Rapids, had a new job, and ended up using all of my free time trying to keep up! Special thanks go to my little girls, Katie and Carrie, with whom I missed a lot of bedtime stories and Disney videos! And special thanks go to my wife, Susan, who, because of the business I'm in, has experienced single parenting for the last few months (I'll take some time off now—I promise!), and to the management of The Ziemba Group, who cut a new employee some slack so he could finish a prior commitment.

I'd also like to thank my partner, Gary Govanus (this is starting to feel like one of those Oscar acceptance speeches that gets cut off in the middle). Gary is a true friend, a true professional, and someone whom I respect deeply! He also recommended me to Sybex in the first place—thanks Gary.

Thanks also go to the folks at Ingram Micro, who donated a couple of killer Everest computers to my home lab so I could test my theories before I committed them to print! Ingram Micro doesn't sell to the public, but if you're a reseller, I give them two thumbs up for service! (You can visit them at `www.ingrammicro.com`.)

Bob King

Contents at a Glance

Contents

Introduction

Microsoft's new Microsoft Certified Systems Engineer (MCSE) track for Windows 2000 is the premier certification for computer industry professionals. Covering the core technologies around which Microsoft's future will be built, the new MCSE certification is a powerful credential for career advancement.

This book has been developed, in cooperation with Microsoft Corporation, to give you the critical skills and knowledge you need to prepare for one of the elective requirements of the new MCSE certification program for Windows 2000 Security. You will find the information you need to acquire a solid understanding of Windows 2000 Security; to prepare for Exam 70-220: Designing Security for a Microsoft® Windows® 2000 Network; and to progress toward MCSE certification.

Why Become Certified in Windows 2000?

As the computer network industry grows in both size and complexity, the need for *proven* ability is increasing. Companies rely on certifications to verify the skills of prospective employees and contractors.

Whether you are just getting started or are ready to move ahead in the computer industry, the knowledge, skills, and credentials you have are your most valuable assets. Microsoft has developed its Microsoft Certified Professional (MCP) program to give you credentials that verify your ability to work with Microsoft products effectively and professionally. The MCP credential for professionals who work with Microsoft Windows 2000 networks is the new MCSE certification.

Over the next few years, companies around the world will deploy millions of copies of Windows 2000 as the central operating system for their mission-critical networks. This will generate an enormous need for qualified consultants and personnel to design, deploy, and support Windows 2000 networks.

Windows 2000 is a huge product that requires professional skills of its administrators. Consider that Windows NT 4 has about 12 million lines of code, while Windows 2000 has more than 35 million! Much of this code is needed to deal with the wide range of functionality that Windows 2000 offers.

Windows 2000 actually consists of several different versions:

Windows 2000 Professional The client edition of Windows 2000, which is comparable to Windows NT 4 Workstation 4, but also includes the best features of Windows 98 and many new features.

Windows 2000 Server/Windows 2000 Advanced Server A server edition of Windows 2000 for small to mid-sized deployments. Advanced Server supports more memory and processors than Server does.

Windows 2000 Datacenter Server A server edition of Windows 2000 for large, wide-scale deployments and computer clusters. Datacenter Server supports the most memory and processors of the three versions.

With such an expansive operating system, companies need to be certain that you are the right person for the job being offered. The MCSE is designed to help prove that you are.

As part of its promotion of Windows 2000, Microsoft has announced that MCSEs who have passed the Windows NT 4 core exams must upgrade their certifications to the new Windows 2000 track by December 31, 2001, to remain certified. The Sybex MCSE Study Guide series covers the full range of exams required for either obtaining or upgrading your certification. For more information, see the "Exam Requirements" section later in this Introduction.

Is This Book for You?

If you want to acquire a solid foundation in Windows 2000 Security, this book is for you. You'll find clear explanations of the fundamental concepts you need to grasp.

If you want to become certified as an MCSE, this book is definitely for you. However, if you just want to attempt to pass the exam without really understanding Windows 2000, this book is *not* for you. This book is written for those who want to acquire hands-on skills and in-depth knowledge of Windows 2000.

If your goal is to prepare for the exam by learning how to use and manage the new operating system, this book is for you. It will help you to achieve the high level of professional competency you need to succeed in this field.

What Does This Book Cover?

This book contains detailed explanations, hands-on exercises, and review questions to test your knowledge.

Think of this book as your complete guide to Windows 2000 Security. It begins by covering some business concepts that will allow you to configure security to enhance your company's business objectives. You will also learn about the various components of Windows 2000 security, like the different types of protocols and their implementations.

At the end of each chapter, you'll find a summary of the topics covered in the chapter, which also includes a list of the key terms used in that chapter. The key terms represent not only the terminology that you should recognize, but also the underlying concepts that you should understand to pass the exam. All of the key terms are defined in the glossary at the back of the study guide.

Finally, each chapter concludes with 10 review questions that test your knowledge of the information covered. You'll find an entire practice exam, with 40 additional questions and two more case studies, in Appendix A. Many more questions, as well as additional case studies, are included on the CD that accompanies this book, as explained in the "What's on the CD?" section at the end of this Introduction.

The topics covered in this book map directly to Microsoft's official exam objectives. Each exam objective is covered completely.

How Do You Become an MCSE?

Attaining MCSE certification has always been a challenge. However, in the past, individuals could acquire detailed exam information—even most of the exam questions—from online "brain dumps" and third-party "cram" books or software products. For the new MCSE exams, this simply will not be the case.

To avoid the "paper-MCSE syndrome" (a devaluation of the MCSE certification because unqualified individuals manage to pass the exams), Microsoft has taken strong steps to protect the security and integrity of the new MCSE track. Prospective MCSEs will need to complete a course of study that provides not only detailed knowledge of a wide range of topics, but true skills derived from working with Windows 2000 and related software products.

In the new MCSE program, Microsoft is heavily emphasizing hands-on skills. Microsoft has stated that, "Nearly half of the core required exams' content demands that the candidate have troubleshooting skills acquired through hands-on experience and working knowledge."

Fortunately, if you are willing to dedicate time and effort with Windows 2000, you can prepare for the exams by using the proper tools. If you work through this book and the other books in this series, you should successfully meet the exam requirements.

This book is a part of a complete series of MCSE Study Guides, published by Sybex, that covers the five core Windows 2000 requirements as well as the new Design electives you need to complete your MCSE track. Titles include:

- *MCSE: Windows 2000 Professional Study Guide*
- *MCSE: Windows 2000 Server Study Guide*
- *MCSE: Windows 2000 Network Infrastructure Administration Study Guide*
- *MCSE: Windows 2000 Directory Services Administration Study Guide*
- *MCSE: Windows 2000 Network Security Design Study Guide*
- *MCSE: Windows 2000 Network Infrastructure Design Study Guide*
- *MCSE: Windows 2000 Directory Services Design Study Guide*

There are also study guides available from Sybex on additional MCSE electives.

Exam Requirements

Successful candidates must pass a minimum set of exams that measure technical proficiency and expertise:

- Candidates for MCSE certification must pass seven exams, including four core operating system exams, one design exam, and two electives.
- Candidates who have already passed three Windows NT 4 exams (70-067, 70-068, and 70-073) may opt to take an "accelerated" exam plus one core design exam and two electives.

If you do not pass the accelerated exam after one attempt, you must pass the five core requirements and two electives.

The following table shows the exams a new certification candidate must pass.

***All* of these exams are required**

Exam #	Title	Requirement Met
70-216	Implementing and Administering a Microsoft® Windows® 2000 Network Infrastructure	Core (Operating System)
70-210	Installing, Configuring, and Administering Microsoft® Windows® 2000 Professional	Core (Operating System)
70-215	Installing, Configuring, and Administering Microsoft® Windows® 2000 Server	Core (Operating System)
70-217	Implementing and Administering a Microsoft® Windows® 2000 Directory Services Infrastructure	Core (Operating System)

***One* of these exams is required**

Exam #	Title	Requirement Met
70-219	Designing a Microsoft® Windows® 2000 Directory Services Infrastructure	Core (Design)

Exam #	Title	Requirement Met
70-220	Designing Security for a Microsoft® Windows® 2000 Network	Core (Design)
70-221	Designing a Microsoft® Windows® 2000 Network Infrastructure	Core (Design)

***Two* of these exams are required**

Exam #	Title	Requirement Met
70-219	Designing a Microsoft® Windows® 2000 Directory Services Infrastructure	Elective
70-220	Designing Security for a Microsoft® Windows® 2000 Network	Elective
70-221	Designing a Microsoft® Windows® 2000 Network Infrastructure	Elective
Any current MCSE elective	Exams cover topics such as Exchange Server, SQL Server, Systems Management Server, Internet Explorer Administrators Kit, and Proxy Server (new exams are added regularly)	Elective

For a more detailed description of the Microsoft certification programs, including a list of current MCSE electives, check Microsoft's Training and Certification Web site at `www.microsoft.com/trainingandservices`.

The Designing Security for a Microsoft Windows 2000 Network Exam

The Designing Security for a Microsoft Windows 2000 Network exam covers concepts and skills required for the support of security in a Windows 2000 network. It emphasizes the following areas of Windows 2000 security:

- Making sure you can control access to various network resources
- Finding out how to audit access to resources
- Defining and configuring authentication
- Defining and configuring encryption

This exam can be quite specific regarding Windows 2000 Security requirements and operational settings, and it can be particular about how various communications are performed. It also focuses on fundamental concepts relating to Windows 2000 Security. Careful study of this book, along with hands-on experience, will help you prepare for this exam.

Microsoft provides exam objectives to give you a very general overview of possible areas of coverage of the Microsoft exams. For your convenience, we have added in-text objectives listings at the points in the text where specific Microsoft exam objectives are covered. However, exam objectives are subject to change at any time without prior notice and at Microsoft's sole discretion. Please visit Microsoft's Training and Certification Web site (`www.microsoft.com/trainingandservices`) for the most current exam objectives listing.

Types of Exam Questions

In the previous tracks, the formats of the MCSE exams were fairly straightforward, consisting almost entirely of multiple-choice questions appearing in a few different sets. Prior to taking an exam, you knew how many questions you would see and what type of questions would appear. If you had purchased the right third-party exam preparation products, you could even be quite familiar with the pool of questions you might be asked. As mentioned earlier, all of this is changing.

In an effort to both refine the testing process and protect the quality of its certifications, Microsoft has introduced adaptive testing, as well as some new exam elements. You will not know in advance which type of format you will see on your exam. These innovations make the exams more challenging, and they make it much more difficult for someone to pass an exam after simply cramming for it.

Microsoft will be accomplishing its goal of protecting the exams by regularly adding and removing exam questions, limiting the number of questions that any individual sees in a beta exam, limiting the number of questions delivered to an individual by using adaptive testing, and adding new exam elements.

Exam questions may be in multiple-choice or case study–based formats. You may also find yourself taking an adaptive format exam. Let's take a look at the exam question types and adaptive testing, so you can be prepared for all of the possibilities.

Multiple-Choice Questions

Multiple-choice questions include two main types of questions. One is a straightforward type that presents a question followed by several possible answers, of which one (or more) is correct.

The other type of multiple-choice question is more complex. This type presents a set of desired results along with a proposed solution. You must then decide which results would be achieved by the proposed solution.

You will see many multiple-choice questions in this Study Guide and on the accompanying CD, as well as on your exam.

Case Study–Based Questions

Case study–based questions first appeared in the Microsoft Certified Solution Developer program (Microsoft's certification program for software programmers). Case study–based questions present a scenario with a range of requirements. Based on the information provided, you need to answer a series of multiple-choice and ranking questions. The interface for case study–based questions has a number of tabs that each contain information about the scenario. At present, this type of question appears only in the Design exams.

Adaptive Exam Format

Microsoft presents many of its exams in an *adaptive* format. This format is radically different from the conventional format previously used for Microsoft certification exams. Conventional tests are static, containing a fixed number of questions. Adaptive tests change, or "adapt," depending on your answers to the questions presented.

The number of questions presented in your adaptive test will depend on how long it takes the exam to ascertain your level of ability (according to the statistical measurements on which the exam questions are ranked). To determine a test-taker's level of ability, the exam presents questions in increasing or decreasing order of difficulty.

Unlike the previous test format, the adaptive format will *not* allow you to go back to see a question again. The exam only goes forward. Once you enter your answer, that's it—you cannot change it. Be very careful before entering your answer. There is no time limit for each individual question (only for the exam as a whole). Your exam may be shortened by correct answers (and lengthened by incorrect answers), so there is no advantage to rushing through questions.

HOW ADAPTIVE EXAMS DETERMINE ABILITY LEVELS

As an example of how adaptive testing works, suppose that you know three people who are taking the exam: Herman, Sally, and Rashad. Herman doesn't know much about the subject, Sally is moderately informed, and Rashad is an expert.

Herman answers his first question incorrectly, so the exam presents him with a second, easier question. He misses that, so the exam gives him a few more easy questions, all of which he misses. Shortly thereafter, the exam ends, and he receives his failure report.

Sally answers her first question correctly, so the exam gives her a more difficult question, which she answers correctly. She then receives an even more difficult question, which she answers incorrectly. Next, the exam gives her a somewhat easier question, as it tries to gauge her level of understanding. After numerous questions of varying levels of difficulty, Sally's exam ends, perhaps with a passing score, perhaps not. Her exam included far more questions than were in Herman's exam, because her level of understanding needed to be more carefully tested to determine whether or not it was at a passing level.

When Rashad takes his exam, he answers his first question correctly, so he is given a more difficult question, which he also answers correctly. Next, the exam presents an even more difficult question, which he also answers correctly. He then is given a few more very difficult questions, all of which he answers correctly. Shortly thereafter, his exam ends. He passes. His exam was short, about as long as Herman's test.

BENEFITS OF ADAPTIVE TESTING

Microsoft has begun moving to adaptive testing for several reasons:

- It saves time by focusing only on the questions needed to determine a test-taker's abilities. An exam that might take an hour and a half in the conventional format could be completed in less than half that time when presented in adaptive format. The number of questions in an adaptive exam may be far fewer than the number required by a conventional exam.
- It protects the integrity of the exams. Exposing fewer questions at any one time makes it more difficult for individuals to collect the questions in the exam pools with the intent of facilitating exam cramming.
- It saves Microsoft and/or the test-delivery company money by reducing the amount of time it takes to deliver a test.

We recommend that you try the Edge Test Adaptive Exam, which is included on the CD that accompanies this study guide.

Exam Question Development

Microsoft follows an exam-development process consisting of eight mandatory phases. The process takes an average of seven months and involves more than 150 specific steps. The MCP exam development consists of the following phases:

Phase 1: Job Analysis Phase 1 is an analysis of all the tasks that make up a specific job function, based on tasks performed by people who are currently performing that job function. This phase also identifies the knowledge, skills, and abilities that relate specifically to the performance area to be certified.

Phase 2: Objective Domain Definition The results of the job analysis provide the framework used to develop objectives. The development of objectives involves translating the job-function tasks into a comprehensive set of more specific and measurable knowledge, skills, and abilities. The resulting list of objectives—the *objective domain*—is the basis for the development of both the certification exams and the training materials.

Phase 3: Blueprint Survey The final objective domain is transformed into a blueprint survey in which contributors are asked to rate each objective. These contributors may be past MCP candidates, appropriately skilled exam development volunteers, or Microsoft employees. Based on the contributors' input, the objectives are prioritized and weighted. The actual exam items are written according to the prioritized objectives. Contributors are queried about how they spend their time on the job. If a contributor doesn't spend an adequate amount of time actually performing the specified job function, his or her data is eliminated from the analysis. The blueprint survey phase helps determine which objectives to measure, as well as the appropriate number and types of items to include on the exam.

Phase 4: Item Development A pool of items is developed to measure the blueprinted objective domain. The number and types of items to be written are based on the results of the blueprint survey.

Phase 5: Alpha Review and Item Revision During this phase, a panel of technical and job-function experts reviews each item for technical accuracy, then answers each item, reaching a consensus on all technical issues. Once the items have been verified as technically accurate, they are edited to ensure that they are expressed in the clearest language possible.

Phase 6: Beta Exam The reviewed and edited items are collected into beta exams. Based on the responses of all beta participants, Microsoft performs a statistical analysis to verify the validity of the exam items and to determine which items will be used in the certification exam. Once the analysis has been completed, the items are distributed into multiple parallel forms, or *versions*, of the final certification exam.

Phase 7: Item Selection and Cut-Score Setting The results of the beta exams are analyzed to determine which items should be included in the certification exam. Analysis is based on many factors, including item difficulty and relevance. During this phase, a panel of job-function experts determines the *cut score* (minimum passing score) for the exams. The cut score differs from exam to exam because it is based on an item-by-item determination of the percentage of candidates who answered the item correctly and who would be expected to answer the item correctly.

Phase 8: Live Exam As the final phase, the exams are given to candidates. MCP exams are administered by Sylvan Prometric and Virtual University Enterprises (VUE).

Microsoft will regularly add and remove questions from the exams. This is called item *seeding*. It is part of the effort to make it more difficult for individuals to merely memorize exam questions passed along by previous test-takers.

Tips for Taking the Designing Security for a Microsoft Windows 2000 Network Exam

Here are some general tips for taking the exam successfully:

- Arrive early at the exam center so you can relax and review your study materials. During your final review, you can look over tables and lists of exam-related information.
- Read the questions carefully. Don't be tempted to jump to an early conclusion. Make sure you know *exactly* what the question is asking.
- Answer all questions. Remember that the adaptive format will *not* allow you to return to a question. Be very careful before entering your answer. Because your exam may be shortened by correct answers (and lengthened by incorrect answers), there is no advantage to rushing through questions.
- Use a process of elimination to get rid of the obviously incorrect answers first on questions that you're not sure about. This method will improve your odds of selecting the correct answer if you need to make an educated guess.

Exam Registration

You may take the exams at any of more than 1,000 Authorized Prometric Testing Centers (APTCs) and VUE Testing Centers around the world. For the location of a testing center near you, call Sylvan Prometric at 800-755-EXAM (755-3926), or call VUE at 888-837-8616. Outside the United States and Canada, contact your local Sylvan Prometric or VUE registration center.

You should determine the number of the exam you want to take, and then register with the Sylvan Prometric or VUE registration center nearest to you. At this point, you will be asked for advance payment for the exam. The exams are $100 each. Exams must be taken within one year of payment. You can schedule exams up to six weeks in advance or as late as one working day prior to the date of the exam. You can cancel or reschedule your exam if you contact the center at least two working days prior to the exam. Same-day registration is available in some locations, subject to space availability. Where same-day registration is available, you must register a minimum of two hours before test time.

You may also register for your exams online at `www.sylvanprometric.com` or `www.vue.com`.

When you schedule the exam, you will be provided with instructions regarding appointment and cancellation procedures, ID requirements, and information about the testing center location. In addition, you will receive a registration and payment confirmation letter from Sylvan Prometric or VUE.

Microsoft requires certification candidates to accept the terms of a Non-Disclosure Agreement before taking certification exams.

What's on the CD?

With this new book in our best-selling MCSE Study Guide series, we are including quite an array of training resources. On the CD are numerous practice exams and flashcards to help you study for the exam. Also included are the entire contents of the study guide. These resources are described in the following sections.

The Sybex Ebook for *MCSE: Windows 2000 Network Security Design Study Guide*

Many people like the convenience of being able to carry their whole study guide on a CD. They also like being able to search the text to find specific information quickly and easily. For these reasons, we have included the entire contents of this study guide on a CD in PDF format. We've also included Adobe Acrobat Reader, which provides the interface for the contents as well as the search capabilities.

The Sybex MCSE Edge Tests

The Edge Tests are a collection of multiple-choice questions that can help you prepare for your exam. There are three sets of questions:

- Bonus questions specially prepared for this edition of the study guide, including 40 questions that appear only on the CD
- An adaptive test simulator that will give the feel for how adaptive testing works
- All of the questions from the study guide presented in a test engine for your review

A sample screen from the Sybex MCSE Edge Tests is shown below.

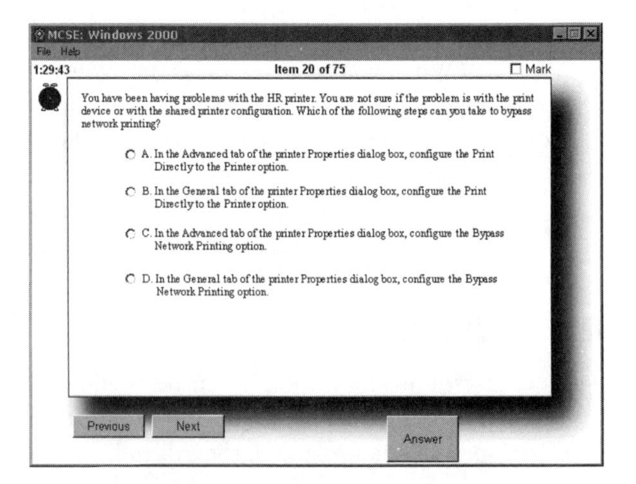

Sybex MCSE Flashcards for PCs and Palm Devices

The "flashcard" style of exam question offers an effective way to quickly and efficiently test your understanding of the fundamental concepts covered in the Designing Security for a Microsoft Windows 2000 Network exam. The Sybex MCSE Flashcards set consists of 150 questions presented in an engine developed specifically for this study guide series. The Sybex MCSE Flashcards interface is shown below.

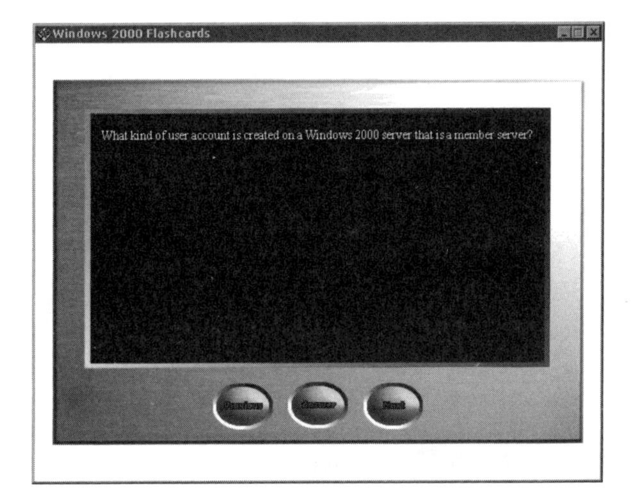

Because of the high demand for a product that will run on Palm devices, we have also developed, in conjunction with Land-J Technologies, a version of the flashcard questions that you can take with you on your Palm OS PDA (including the PalmPilot and Handspring's Visor).

How Do You Use This Book?

This book can provide a solid foundation for the serious effort of preparing for the Windows 2000 Security exam. To best benefit from this book, you may wish to use the following study method:

1. Study each chapter carefully. Do your best to fully understand the information.
2. Answer the review questions at the end of each chapter. If you would prefer to answer the questions in a timed and graded format, install the Edge Tests from the CD that accompanies this book and answer the chapter questions there instead of in the book.
3. Work through the case studies, referring back to the information presented in the chapter to guide you. After you have decided on a course of action, read the suggested answer. Reread the chapter to clarify any differences.

4. Note which questions you did not understand and study the corresponding sections of the book again.
5. Make sure you complete the entire book.
6. Before taking the exam, go through the training resources included on the CD that accompanies this book. Try the adaptive version that is included with the Sybex MCSE Edge Tests. Review and sharpen your knowledge with the MCSE Flashcards.

To learn all of the material covered in this book, you will need to study regularly and with discipline. Try to set aside the same time every day to study and select a comfortable and quiet place in which to do it. If you work hard, you will be surprised at how quickly you learn this material. Good luck!

Contacts and Resources

To find out more about Microsoft Education and Certification materials and programs, to register with Sylvan Prometric or VUE, or to get other useful information, check the following resources.

Microsoft Certification Development Team
`www.microsoft.com/trainingandservices`

Contact the Microsoft Certification Development Team through their Web site to volunteer for one or more exam development phases or to report a problem with an exam. Address written correspondence to:

Certification Development Team
Microsoft Education and Certification
One Microsoft Way
Redmond, WA 98052

Microsoft TechNet Technical Information Network
`www.microsoft.com/technet/subscription/about.htm`
(800) 344-2121

Use this Web site or number to contact support professionals and system administrators. Outside the United States and Canada, contact your local Microsoft subsidiary for information.

Microsoft Training and Certification Home Page
`www.microsoft.com/trainingandservices`

This Web site provides information about the MCP program and exams. You can also order the latest Microsoft Roadmap to Education and Certification.

Palm Pilot Training Product Development: Land-J
`www.land-j.com`
(407) 359-2217

Land-J Technologies is a consulting and programming business currently specializing in application development for the 3Com PalmPilot Personal Digital Assistant. Land-J developed the Palm version of the Edge Tests, which is included on the CD that accompanies this study guide.

Sylvan Prometric
`www.sylvanprometric.com`
(800) 755-EXAM

Contact Sylvan Prometric to register to take an MCP exam at any of more than 800 Sylvan Prometric Testing Centers around the world.

Virtual University Enterprises (VUE)
`www.vue.com`
(888) 837-8616

Contact the VUE registration center to register to take an MCP exam at one of the VUE Testing Centers.

Assessment Test

1. What constitutes a domain restructure?

   A. Domain restructure is sometimes referred to as domain consolidation.

   B. Domain restructure is sometimes referred to as resource domain elimination.

   C. Domain restructure is sometimes referred to as an administrative domain elimination.

   D. The sum total of all the transitive trusts serviced by Kerberos v5.

2. If you find that a CA has been compromised, what must you do?

   A. When a CA has been compromised, you must revoke the CA's certificate and create a new certificate.

   B. Restore from backup.

   C. Revoke only the certificates that the CA has issued.

   D. Start your entire PKI over again.

3. Which of the following would you associate with an alarm?

   A. Traps

   B. MIBs

   C. Agents

   D. Managers

   E. Hosts

4. Secure e-mail systems typically provide the following security functions:

   A. An Exchange Gateway.

   B. Senders can digitally sign e-mail messages to provide data integrity.

   C. Senders can use IPSec to sign e-mail messages.

   D. Senders cannot repudiate signed messages because only the sender has possession of the signing credentials.

5. Analyzing the service and product life cycles is part of which section of the design cycle?

   A. Planning and Design

   B. Implementation

   C. Management

6. Before you can audit the Active Directory, you have to:

   A. Be a member of the Universal Administrators group.

   B. Enable Audit directory service access in Audit Policy.

   C. Disable all other forms of auditing.

   D. Enable the auditing of the Group Policy objects.

7. In the pyramid approach to management, how many levels are there?

   A. 3

   B. 4

   C. 5

   D. 6

8. How can you guarantee that you are using an application that hasn't been tampered with?

   A. Make sure it is approved by the UN Security Council.

   B. Require that application components be digitally signed.

   C. Require that application components are IPSec compliant.

   D. Make sure that applications run on PGP/IP.

9. In a typical VPN setup, what protocol is used between the VPN server and the private network?

   A. FTP

   B. PPTP

   C. TCP/IP

   D. L2TP

   E. DHCP

10. Can SSL be used as part of SSO in a cross-platform environment?

    A. SSL can be used as part of SSO, but only in a homogeneous environment.

    B. SSL can be used as part of SSO in a cross-platform environment.

    C. SSL cannot be used as part of SSO.

    D. SSL cannot be used as part of SSO, but it can be used as part of DPMA.

11. Define tolerance of risk.

    A. The amount a company can afford to lose from an incursion

    B. The amount a company can spend to prevent an incursion

    C. The amount of resources a company can bring to bear to protect information or a resource

    D. The level of risk exposure that an enterprise feels is warranted with any resource or data

12. What is repudiation?

    A. The intruder causes network data to be modified or corrupted. Unencrypted network financial transactions are vulnerable to manipulation. Viruses can corrupt network data.

    B. This term refers to malicious code running as an auto-executed ActiveX control or Java applet uploaded from the Internet on a Web server.

    C. Network-based business and financial transactions are compromised if the recipient of the transaction cannot be certain who sent the message.

    D. Sometimes breaking into a network is a simple as calling new employees, telling them you are from the IT department, and asking them to verify their password for your records.

13. What are the two IPSec communication modes?

A. Transport mode

B. Tunnel mode

C. Subway mode

D. Encrypted mode

E. Plain text mode

14. When documenting a computer, one way is to take screen shots of which screen?

A. The Desktop

B. The Network Settings tab from Control Panel

C. The Registry

15. What Microsoft product can you use to ensure that incompatible applications are not used after the Windows 2000 rollout?

A. Proxy Server

B. IIS

C. SQL

D. RAS

E. SMS

16. How are CAs administered?

A. As a service.

B. Using an MMC snap-in.

C. Using specially installed third-party utilities.

D. They require no administration.

17. Choose the features of Terminal Services security:

    A. Encryption

    B. VPN

    C. PPP

    D. Limit logon attempts and connection time

    E. Password protection

18. RIS cannot be installed to a folder on a volume where the following is present:

    A. NTFS

    B. System Files

    C. A domain controller

    D. Active Directory

19. What is MPPE?

    A. Microsoft's version of TCP/IP

    B. The Ipv6 version of DHCP

    C. Microsoft Point-to-Point Encryption

    D. A new form of MP3

20. As part of the technology review, it is important to map out:

    A. The numbers and locations of each type of dot matrix printer

    B. The types of network cards in each host on the network

    C. The PC serial number and the matching cube location

    D. The network's physical and logical topology

21. Which of the following IPSec default policies is the most secure?

    A. Client

    B. Respond only

    C. Server

    D. Secure Server

    E. IPSec 3DES only

22. What is the make-up of a tiger team?

    A. A tiger team is made up of security experts who attempt to hack their way into a network to show areas of vulnerability.

    B. A tiger team is made up of security experts who attempt to track someone who has hacked their way into a network.

    C. A tiger team is made up of security experts who determine how much damage a hacker has done after an intrusion.

    D. A tiger team is made up of security experts who analyze the preliminary security plan to spot obvious areas of vulnerability.

23. By default, what is the authentication method security protocol?

    A. CA

    B. SA

    C. DES

    D. Preshared key

    E. Kerberos

24. Why use certificate hierarchies? Select all that apply.

    A. Certificates can be issued for a number of purposes

    B. Organizational divisions

    C. Geographic divisions

    D. You can tailor the CA environment to provide a balance between security and usability

    E. Because of the flexibility that the Microsoft PKI provides

25. What is a certificate trust list?

    A. Another name for user certificates

    B. A list of self-signed certificates that are to be trusted by your organization

    C. An enterprise root CA

    D. Certificates only given out by a stand-alone CA

26. Which of the following devices cannot be mapped by a default Terminal Services client?

    A. Drives

    B. Windows printers

    C. LPT ports

    D. COM ports

    E. Clipboard

27. What is a transitive trust?

    A. The relationship between a resource domain and an administrative domain

    B. The relationship between all domains in a Windows NT 4 relationship

    C. Authentication across a chain of trust relationships

    D. Authentication within a domain

28. According to Microsoft, which of the following is not a type of business structure?

    A. International

    B. Local

    C. National

    D. Regional

29. How are uniform security policies used?

    A. They can only be assigned to sites.

    B. They are a feature implemented with Exchange 2000.

    C. They are the same as the Gateway for Netware in NT 4.

    D. They provide consistent security settings for classes of computers.

30. When is IPSec used?

    A. To make the communication links secure, and to keep network data packets confidential

    B. With PGP

    C. With SMTP

    D. With POP3

31. Which of the following has Microsoft targeted for one of the reasons projects fail?

    A. Poor planning

    B. Separation of business goals and technology

    C. Improper upgrade path

    D. Using other NOSs in a Windows 2000 installation

32. What is a social engineering attack?

    A. This term refers to malicious code running as an auto-executed ActiveX control or Java applet uploaded from the Internet on a Web server.

    B. The intruder floods a server with requests that consume system resources and either crash the server or prevent useful work from being done. Crashing the server sometimes provides opportunities to penetrate the system.

    C. Sometimes breaking into a network is a simple as calling new employees, telling them you are from the IT department, and asking them to verify their password for your records.

    D. Network-based business and financial transactions are compromised if the recipient of the transaction cannot be certain who sent the message.

33. If you decide to enforce a Group Policy, you are doing which of the following:

    A. Making sure that all users in an OU will have to use that GPO

    B. Making sure that all users in a site will have to use that GPO

    C. Making sure that all users in a domain will have to use that GPO

    D. Making sure that domains or organizational units at a lower level in Active Directory cannot override the policy

34. Why would you create an organizational unit?

    A. They make perfect areas for delegating authority.

    B. To minimize LAN traffic.

    C. To simplify logon procedures for users accessing the network using either IPSec or RADIUS.

    D. To help keep things organized.

35. IPSec is used in which of the following:

    A. Any implementation of TCP/IP

    B. Only when supernets are required

    C. When VPNs are required

    D. Only with IPv6

36. When is a Service Ticket (ST) granted?

    A. To provide access to a particular resource

    B. To start the authorization process

    C. To start the authentication process

    D. To introduce KDCs

37. Suppose a user is going to attach to a resource within a Windows 2000 network. If that user does not have a domain user account, which security protocol will allow the user to complete the attachment?

A. NTLM

B. Public Key Certificate authentication

C. SLL

D. IPSec

38. In Windows 2000, what keeps track of the certificate information for existing Windows accounts?

A. PCMA

B. SSL/TSL

C. KDC

D. Active Directory

39. How many firewalls are necessary for the screened subnet design?

A. At least one

B. At least two

C. At least three

D. At least four

40. When you document the services your network provides, you should include things like:

A. The SQL applications

B. DNS

C. DHCP

D. RAS

41. None, Notify, Read, and Read Create are examples of what?

    A. DNS security settings

    B. DHCP security settings

    C. DHCP servers

    D. DNS servers

    E. SNMP security settings

    F. SNMP servers

42. Which of the following cannot be associated with SNMP?

    A. Manager

    B. Agent

    C. MIB

    D. Root server

    E. GET

43. Windows 2000 uses two types of key encryption. They are ____________ and ____________.

    A. Public Encryption

    B. Secret Key Encryption

    C. Double Kerberos 5

    D. PGP

44. If you wanted to distribute DNS administration, which group could you use?

    A. Domain Admin

    B. DNS Admins Group

    C. DHCP Admin

    D. Enterprise Admin

    E. Local Admin

45. If you are designing a network that is going to use a VPN and NAT with Windows 2000, which tunneling protocol(s) can you use?

A. L2TP

B. TCP/IP

C. IGMP

D. PPTP

E. PPP

46. Which port is used with L2TP?

A. 1677

B. 7100

C. 50

D. 25

47. Pick two of the following that are parts of the basic design criteria.

A. Planning and Design

B. Functionality

C. Performance

D. Implementation

E. Management

48. What is one of the things you must do when migrating domains to Windows 2000?

A. Assure that SID history is compatible with Windows NT 3.51, NT 4, and Windows 2000 Professional

B. Upgrade the primary and backup domain controllers immediately

C. Upgrade the member servers immediately

D. Plan the restructure of the Windows 2000 domains

49. What are the levels of encryption in Terminal Services?

A. Low

B. Medium

C. High

D. All of the above

50. What protocols are used to support trust relationships in Windows 2000?

A. Kerberos v5 protocol and NTLM authentication

B. NetBIOS and WINS

C. TCP and IP

D. IPX and IP

51. Certificate mapping can be done at what levels of the Active Directory Forest?

A. Local user account

B. Global group

C. Domain local group

D. Domain user account

E. Organizational unit

F. Site

Answers to Assessment Test

1. A. A domain restructure can also be referred to as a domain consolidation.

2. A. When a CA has been compromised, you must revoke the CA's certificate.

3. A. A trap is a kind of an alarm in SNMP.

4. B, D. Secure e-mail will allow senders to digitally sign messages and they cannot repudiate signed messages.

5. A. Analyzing the service and product life cycles is part of the Planning and Design phase.

6. B. Before you can audit the Active Directory, you have to enable auditing of the Directory Server Access Event object.

7. D. There are six levels: shareholders, chairman of the board, board of directors, senior management, middle management, and staff.

8. B. You can require that application components are digitally signed. Applications that use Authenticode make use of digital signing.

9. C. The protocol that is used between the private network and the VPN server is just TCP/IP.

10. B. SSL can be used as part of SSO in a cross platform environment.

11. D. Tolerance of risk is the amount of exposure that an enterprise feels it can endure for a particular resource or set of information.

12. C. If a transaction cannot be certain of the sender, it can be repudiated.

13. A, B. The two IPSec communication modes are tunnel mode and transport mode.

14. B. Screen shots of the Network Settings tab from Control Panel will save a lot of note-taking!

15. E. You can use SMS to ensure that incompatible applications are not used after the rollout.

16. B. The Certification Authority console is an MMC snap-in.

17. A, D. Terminal Services security is made up of encryption and the ability to limit logon attempts and connection time.

18. B. RIS cannot be installed on the same volume as the system files.

19. C. MPPE is the Microsoft Point-to-Point Encryption method.

20. D. Some of the answers above may actually appear in the map of the network's physical and logical topology.

21. D. Secure Server is the most secure.

22. A. A tiger team tries to break into a network to show areas of vulnerability.

23. E. Kerberos is the default authentication method security protocol.

24. A, B, C, D. You can configure hierarchies to use certificates for a number of purposes, provide certificates for organizational divisions, geographic divisions and to provide a balance between security and usability.

25. B. A certificate trust list, as the name implies, is just a list of self-signed certificates for the CAs whose certificates are to be trusted by your organization.

26. A. Tough question! The default Terminal Services client cannot map drives. In order to map drives, you need the Citrix ICA–based clients.

27. C. A transitive trust is authentication across a chain of trust relationships.

28. B. Microsoft recognizes International, National, and Regional.

29. D. Uniform security policies allow consistent security settings to be applied and enforced on classes of computers in the enterprise, such as the domain controller class.

30. A. To make the communication links secure, and to keep network data packets confidential, you can use Internet Protocol security (IPSec).

31. B. Separating the business goals and technology is one way to make a project fail.

32. C. A social engineering attack is a simple attack by an intruder who calls and says he belongs to the IT team, in order to gain access to usernames, passwords, and other information about the network.

33. D. Options exist that allow you to enforce the Group Policy in a specific Group Policy object so that domains or organizational units lower in Active Directory are prevented from overriding that policy.

34. A. An organizational unit is one of the ways to designate authority.

35. C. IPSec is the suite of security protocols that can be used for Virtual Private Networks.

36. A. A service ticket (or session ticket) is granted to provide access to a particular resource.

37. B. Public Key Certificate authentication in Windows 2000 allows client applications to connect to secure services on behalf of users who do not have a Windows 2000 domain account.

38. D. The Active Directory is used to map certificate information to existing Windows accounts.

39. B. The screened subnet requires two firewalls.

40. B, C, D. The services will be things like DNS, DHCP, routing, e-mail, SMS, RAS, or any one of a dozen other things to keep the network responsive to a user's needs. The SQL application will be documented as part of the applications.

41. E. None, Notify, Read, and Read Create are all examples of SNMP security settings.

42. D. A root server is associated with DNS.

43. A, B. Windows 2000 uses both Public and Secret Key Encryption.

44. B. You would use the DNS Admins Group.

45. D. While both PPTP and L2TP are tunneling protocols, only PPTP can be used in an environment that uses NAT.

46. C. Port 50 is used with L2TP.

47. B, C. Functionality and performance are parts of the basic design criteria.

48. D. When you are migrating domains, you have determined that you are going to merge some of the domains. This is how you would plan the restructuring of the Windows 2000 domains.

49. D. There are three levels of encryption in Terminal Services: Low, Medium, and High.

50. A. Trust relationships in Windows 2000 are supported by Kerberos v5, and NTLM is along to provide backward compatibility.

51. D. You can map a certificate to a domain user account.

Analyzing the Company Model and Processes

MICROSOFT EXAM OBJECTIVES COVERED IN THIS CHAPTER:

✓ **Analyze the existing and planned business model.**

- Analyze the company model and geographical scope. Models include regional, national, international, subsidiary, and branch offices.
- Analyze the company processes. Processes include information flow, communications flow, service and product life cycles, and decision-making.

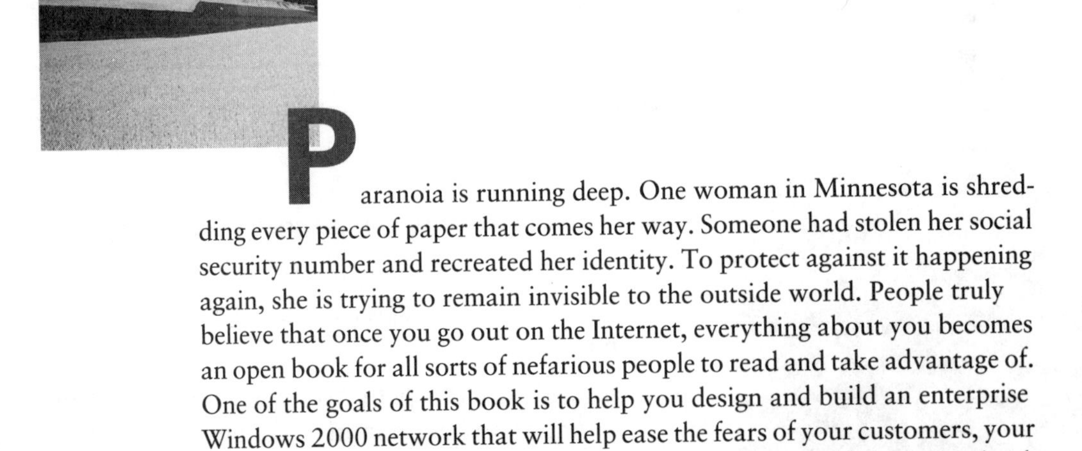

Paranoia is running deep. One woman in Minnesota is shredding every piece of paper that comes her way. Someone had stolen her social security number and recreated her identity. To protect against it happening again, she is trying to remain invisible to the outside world. People truly believe that once you go out on the Internet, everything about you becomes an open book for all sorts of nefarious people to read and take advantage of. One of the goals of this book is to help you design and build an enterprise Windows 2000 network that will help ease the fears of your customers, your superiors, your end users, and other members of your information technology team. That is one of the goals of this book, but not the main goal.

Our main priority in this book is to help you pass Exam 70-220, "Designing Security for a Microsoft Windows 2000 Network." After all, that is why you picked up this book in the first place, isn't it? You really want to become a Windows 2000 Microsoft Certified System Engineer, MCSE, and that is where we begin to discuss the Microsoft Windows 2000 paradigm.

With earlier versions of Microsoft's networking products, the order in which you took the tests was suggested, but for the most part, unimportant. Granted, the NT Server, NT Workstation, and NT in the Enterprise exams were all very similar, but the order in which you took the exams had little bearing on whether you passed or failed.

When Windows 2000 came out, Microsoft decided that there were too many paper MCSEs and made some strides to eliminate the phenomenon. Now, candidates for the coveted MCSE credentials are put through a track that is, in Microsoft's words, "designed for information technology professionals working in a typically complex computing environment of medium to large organizations. A Windows 2000 MCSE candidate should have at least one year of experience implementing and administering a network operating system."

To earn your MCSE, you must pass four core exams; you must also pass one of the following core exams:

70-219	Designing a Microsoft Windows 2000 Directory Services Infrastructure
70-220	Designing Security for a Microsoft Network
70-221	Designing a Microsoft Windows 2000 Network Infrastructure

After you get by that exam, you must pass two others, choosing from the three just listed and Exam 70-222, "Upgrading from Microsoft Windows NT 4.0 to Microsoft Windows 2000." Sound rigorous? It is and it is intended to be.

Now, we certainly don't want to talk you out of buying or reading this book, but if you have not taken the first four exams, some of the concepts in this book may seem very unfamiliar. As we get into the book, we will discuss things like the Active Directory Service (ADS) that was introduced with Windows 2000. If you are not familiar with ADS, you may have a difficult time with some of the concepts discussed here. If you are coming over from a NetWare NDS environment, many of the concepts will be familiar, though the terminology and usage will be different. Our suggestion to you would be to get the first four exams out of the way before tackling this one. It will just make your life easier, because from now on, we are going to assume that you know that stuff. It is the only way we can work!

The Analysis Process

In this chapter we are going to start the analysis process. This means taking a close look at what you currently have. Normally, when we start a new IT project, we look at the components of the network and decide how those components will be impacted by the changes that are being proposed. Because upgrading or migrating to Windows 2000 is such a large project that is going to impact the entire organization, we will start looking at the organization level. In the next several sections, it would be wise to put yourself in the frame of mind of a consultant. You are going to engage a new customer and try to plan the customer's migration to Windows 2000; you will want to make sure that your area of expertise—security—will be well represented. Before you can do anything, though, you need to know where the starting points are.

To arrive at those starting points, imagine you are just coming into an organization for the first time. You have absolutely no idea what the company does, or how large it is, but you know that those things impact the type and levels of management the company has, and how management gathers information. Once the information has been gathered, management must make decisions to determine how best to exploit that information. In that regard, you as a consultant are going to try to find out how the company gathers information and how communications flow throughout the organization. That is the work we have cut out for us in this chapter.

The Network Design Process

If you are an MCSE for NT 4, you know there was some carryover between exams. For example, if you knew about the differences between disk striping and disk striping with parity, you knew you had a couple of questions nailed on the Workstation exam, the Server exam, and the Enterprise exam. For the elective exams you will take for the Windows 2000 MCSE, you must know the network design process cold. Each of the electives starts out with the Analyze and Design phase, so getting a handle on it early will be very helpful.

As you may have guessed, designing a network is a very subjective thing. There are several different ways to evaluate business need and design networking solutions. In each case, though, there is a process that can be broken down into three parts: the design phase, the implementation phase, and the management phase. Figure 1.1 illustrates the process.

FIGURE 1.1 Network design process to evaluate business needs and plan networking solutions

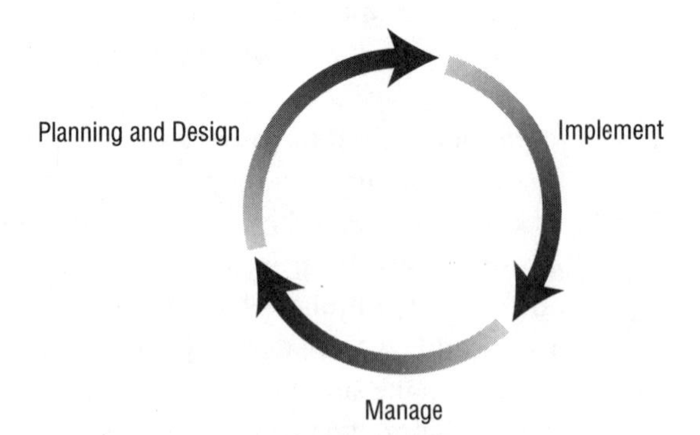

You can see this is a never-ending process—you start with designing, move to implementing, and while you are managing, you are designing again. Let's look at what happens in each stage.

Phase 1: Planning and Design

During the planning and design part of the process, your focus will be a high-level overview of the company, its processes, and its goals. This phase includes the following tasks:

- Determining the company model and its geographical scope
- Analyzing how information flows through the company
- Analyzing how communications flow through the company
- Analyzing the service and product life cycles
- Analyzing the corporate decision-making strategy
- Determining the business needs
- Evaluating and selecting network services
- Determining the technological and security configurations that affect those business needs
- Assessing the existing network infrastructure and usage
- Developing the network design
- Evaluating the costs versus benefits

Once the planning and design phase of the project is complete, you can move on to the implementation phase.

Phase 2: Implementation

In implementation, you complete these tasks:

- Test pilot design
- Installation
- Configuration

Finally, the new system or process is in place and it is time for utilization.

Phase 3: Management

After the network infrastructure has been altered and the new security plan put in place, it is time for the day-to-day stuff to take over. This includes vigilance in the following areas:

- Determining whether the network infrastructure continues to meet the original business need
- Monitoring performance and planning for future network capacity
- Troubleshooting to resolve any problems that arise

In the remainder of this chapter, we'll focus on the initial steps involved in the planning and design phase, namely, understanding your company model and how it operates (including communication and decision-making). But first, let's examine some of the basic concepts involved in network design.

Understanding Basic Design Criteria

As you begin the network design process, one of the first things you must accomplish is getting a firm handle on the business goals of the organization. The business goals drive the design. The design criteria are then broken down into four aspects:

- Functionality
- Security
- Availability
- Performance

Functionality

When the design is deemed *functional*, the design fulfills the reason for implementing the technology. For example, the business goal may be to connect the company to the Internet. The design may be to install an ISDN router utilizing a single 64k channel. That being done, the design is deemed functional. We have met the business goal. *Functionality*, however, is independent of other business goals. A design may be functional but not be secure or highly available or achieve performance criteria. In the example of our ISDN line, that solution may meet all the business goals of a single-person office, or of a small home-based business. If we are trying to meet a business goal of having high-speed Internet access for a company of 5,000, the ISDN line is not going to fill the bill. Function should be evaluated first when reviewing any design. If the design is not functional, the remaining business goals are irrelevant, and the project stops.

Security

This is going to be the major area we look at in this book. Secure design ensures the confidentiality and safety of data. A design is *secure* when authorized users are provided access to data and unauthorized users are prevented access to data. This is one of the deceptive business goals. It sounds so darn easy! It should take your crack security team about an afternoon to get this done. Wouldn't that be nice? It would certainly make studying for this exam a whole lot easier. When we start looking at the business goal for *security*, suddenly the cut and dried becomes much more nebulous. Let's take a simple example. First of all, you have decided that everyone on your network needs a password to log on, and that there should be some basic default standards about the length of the password and how long it will be valid. (Don't snicker, there are probably a lot of smaller companies out there who are avoiding adding passwords to computer accounts for a variety of reasons.) Once you start looking at the password issue, though, you begin to realize that using passwords to establish front line security is just not that simple. Some people may have access to data that needs to be kept more secure than the data that other people have access to. Therefore, their passwords should be longer and be changed more frequently. How do you identify these people and manage the passwords?

We can take our security example several steps deeper. Besides needing a business goal for internal security, we have users with laptops who are roaming the country and need to access the network. You must provide security that will let them log on and also verify that they actually are authorized users, not someone who has stolen a laptop and found the password taped to the bottom.

What about users from outside your company that are very important partners, who need to access your network from their own, but don't need any rights or capabilities to manage the network? An example would be the virtual private network (VPN) that allows one of your partners access to certain areas of your intranet, but does not give him access to other areas. Who is going to set up and manage the VPN? What types of security and auditing are going to be in place to make sure that it is not being abused and used as an unauthorized portal to your company's most valued secrets?

Remember, this is just skimming the top. We haven't even started to look at the protocols necessary to make all this happen yet, or the new technology that can be instituted with things like smart cards. Now you see why we have our work cut out for us, and now you see why it was worth it to lay out your hard-earned money to buy this book.

Availability

A design is *available* to the extent that users can get to the technology and use it in a meaningful fashion. *Availability* is determined by measuring the percentage of time that users have access to the technology, or *up-time*. The higher the percentage of up-time, the higher the availability.

This is especially true of e-commerce solutions. This part of the process can make or break a project, or even a bottom line. A candy maker in the United States took a serious hit with an enterprise resource planning (ERP) implementation. These problems translated to a 19 percent drop in third-quarter profits and a 12 percent drop in sales.

Meanwhile, an appliance manufacture wanted to institute an SAP R/3 implementation in time for Labor Day. Because the project did not work as advertised, the manufacturer suffered from backed-up inventories and delayed shipments.

Finally, how would you like to be the IS manager who decided to relaunch a Web site for a major toy store, just in time for the holidays. The company grossly underestimated its I-commerce capacity needs, resulting in locked-out customers. I am betting that there were some very tense moments in that person's life (to put it politely!).

Performance

The *performance* part of the design is based on response time specified by business needs. The performance of technology is typically driven by events that must occur within a period of time. Acceptable performance minimizes the end-user whine, "God, the network is slow today!" We don't mean to imply that performance is solely about speed. Performance also means things like network up-time. Let's say, for example, that you work for a company that has discovered the Midas touch, and everything the company does turns to gold. Money is no object, so all of the computers on your network are connected to the main server room using gigabit Ethernet over fiber optics—we are talking a screaming network. That is just fine, as long as the servers are there to serve and the switches, concentrators, and routers are there to switch, concentrate, and route. If any piece of the network infrastructure is down, the performance of the whole suffers.

The extent to which the design meets or exceeds the requirements of the real world determines its performance aspect. Performance is based on functionality and availability, but is usually independent of security. If your network has all the speed you need to get the corporate database, and if that database is available, then the access to the database can be achieved and searches performed. You have performance, but you do not necessarily have security. The extent to which the lack of security affects the functionality of the design depends on the purpose of the design. Before you say "Huh???" work with me on this one. Say you have a stand-alone server dedicated to making files or white papers available to the outside world. You have designed a system with great throughput that will answer people's requests in a split second. You have the latest and greatest server designed with every type of redundancy developed, so after a year, the server has achieved 100% up-time. But there is no security—anyone who can access the server can download files or upload papers without authenticating to the system. Is it functional? Absolutely, if all you are doing is hosting the server that provides the "Joke of the Day" and you don't care what is put up there or what is copied from there.

Are there circumstances under which that server would not be deemed functional? Certainly. Suppose that server was used to provide information to a financial institution on funds transferred from one bank to another. Now is it functional? No, absolutely not. With no security, it does not meet the business goal of moving money safely and securely.

Each of the four criteria—functionality, security, availability, and performance—must be satisfied to have a truly successful design. They should be uppermost in your mind as you begin to analyze your company's business model.

Designing with these four criteria in mind is also vital to your success on the exam. An extremely secure design with extremely poor performance is unlikely to be the correct solution to a Microsoft exam problem!

Is This an MCSE Exam or an MBA Exam?

Good question! Since this chapter's objectives center around analyzing the business requirements, you may get the impression it is time to trade in your pocket protector for a standard industry issue blue suit! As an MCSE+I, MCT, MCP, CNE, Master CNE, and Master CNI, I have taken more than my share of tests. As you can see by all the letters, I don't know when to stop taking tests! Since I sometimes take an exam for informational purposes only (that means the line doesn't turn green at the end of the exam), I have spent more than my share of time with objectives. I started out by looking at these objectives and thinking, "What the heck is this all about?"

As I began to research this book, I found some of the material for this chapter in *Business @ the Speed of Thought*, by Bill Gates (Warner Books, 1999). Now, while much of Gates's book simply restates the desire for a paperless office, Gates reemphasizes his commitment to what he calls the "corporate Digital Nervous System." Gates's Digital Nervous System is simply a way to put all sorts of useful information in the hands of all employees. Of course, it is up to the IT department (that means the person who smiles back at you from the mirror every morning) to make this Digital Nervous System work! (After Gates lays out the Digital Nervous System, he subtly shows how Microsoft products can make it all happen.)

Now, before you blow Gates's book off as more marketing hype, look closely at the underpinnings of the Microsoft corporate culture. It all revolves around the preaching and teaching of Bill Gates. Gates has built Microsoft in his own image, and the MCSE program is beginning to show the effects. Look at what Gates says in Chapter 2, "Can Your DNS Do This?":

"A Digital Nervous System gives its users an understanding and an ability to learn what would not be possible otherwise. A good flow of information and good analytical tools gave us insight into new revenue opportunities among volumes of potentially impenetrable data. It maximized the capabilities of human brains and minimized human labor.... To begin creating a Digital Nervous System, you should first develop an ideal picture of the information you need to run your business and to understand your markets and your competitors. Think hard about the facts that are actionable for your company. Develop a list of the questions to which the answers would change your actions. Then demand that your information systems provide those answers. If your current system won't, you need to develop one that will—one or more of your competitors will."

As you look at the objectives and look at all the tests you have to take between now and your MCSE, be assured that when you are finished, you will be very well versed in the design and operation of many of the components of the DNS—and I don't mean Domain Name Service! Many of the objectives are designed to help you design a Digital Nervous System, whether you know it or not. If you get a chance, pick up a copy of the book at the library and look it over. It may help you get a handle on where Microsoft is coming from with all this discussion that does not seem to revolve around technology. Like it or not, the ideas espoused in Gates's book are at the foundation of the Windows 2000 MCSE program.

Business Model Analysis

Understanding your company's business model is the very first step in the very first phase of network design. All businesses are affected by the environment in which they operate. Factors like economic conditions, government regulation, changing customer buying habits, differences in technological enhancements, and competition may impact business performance. If business is going to be impacted, your network model will be impacted.

What does it mean to look at the environment in which your business or company operates? For a frame of reference, let's look at Figure 1.2.

FIGURE 1.2 Forces that affect the environment of any business

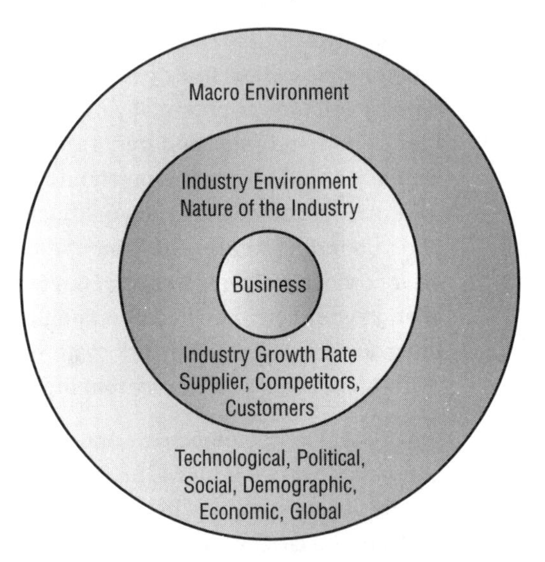

Analyzing the Company Model and Geographical Scope

As you can see from Figure 1.2, the broadest set of variables comprise those technological, political, social, demographic, economic, and global variables that affect the business in a broad way. The next set of variables includes items that will make an impact at the industry level. Each of these needs must be addressed to get a feel for the dynamics of the industry and the players in it.

For the sake of Windows 2000 security, all of these variables may not seem like they apply, but they do. When you begin to analyze your company model and geographic scope, there are many items that need to be taken into consideration.

Microsoft Exam Objective

Analyze the existing and planned business model.

- Analyze the company model and geographical scope. Models include regional, national, international, subsidiary, and branch offices.
- Analyze the company processes. Processes include information flow, communications flow, service and product life cycles, and decision-making.

International Company Model

When designing a secure network for an international company, you certainly must be aware of the impact of these variables. For example, anyone who has attempted to connect two offices on two different continents knows the challenges that technology can present. While there are "standards" that apply to the technology, some of these standards change when you cross international boundaries. Talking about leased lines and capabilities in Minneapolis, Minnesota, may have an entirely different slant when the conversation occurs in London or Paris. For one thing, the nomenclature may be completely different. Speeds may vary. While a T1 in the United States may seem like great speed at 1.544 Mbps, if you were trying to order one in Europe they would hopefully know you wanted an E1 line that transfers data at 2.048 Mbps. Things are just different. That is just technology.

Political and economic solutions will have to be tailored to the countries your offices are operating in. Security solutions that make sense in one area may not be economically feasible in another, or may be outlawed because of treaty or agreement. Encryption technology is just one small example.

Even the social aspects may affect the security model. Recently, I was doing some work for a large law firm in Chicago. This firm had international offices, and many of the people I was working with had been given opportunities for overseas travel. Some of the challenges they faced were to be expected.

There's an old joke going around—maybe you've heard it. What do you call someone who speaks three languages? Trilingual. What do you call someone who speaks two languages? Bilingual. What do you call someone who speaks only one language? American.

Being American, and speaking only one language (just like me), they automatically had the language barrier to overcome. They were fortunate, because most of the people they dealt with did speak English. The other unexpected social challenge they faced involved the sense of urgency that went along with the project. These people were only in the country for two weeks. They had several tasks that needed to be accomplished immediately so the project could proceed on schedule. They found that their European counterparts did not share the sense of urgency they had. It brought to mind the other old saying: Poor planning on your part does not constitute an emergency on my part.

National Company Model

The problems faced defining a security model for a national company, rather than an international company, are not easier or harder, they are just different. The problems crop up in some interesting areas. On a national level, the planning you do will involve a variety of different governmental units, utilities, and regulatory commissions. It may be difficult to ferret out the agencies or companies that you need to complete a given task.

Economic and demographic considerations will play other roles in decisions you make on a corporate level. The industry environment may change dramatically from one geographic location to another. Depending on the location of your offices, you may run into a shortage of trained, competent employees, or if there is a sufficient labor pool, the cost of hiring an employee may be higher than expected. For example, if you work in an industry that designs and manufactures auto parts for resale to the major automakers in the United States, you probably would not have a problem finding a consultant that understood the industry in the area around Detroit, Michigan. The same could not be said if you were working in Marquette, Michigan. Same state, same industry, different climate.

Other determinations to keep in mind include growth rate. If you are in an explosive industry, you will need to plan your security for resources that are currently getting accessed heavily, but may experience even more traffic in the future. An example of this is a company that specialized in making reservations for bed and breakfast inns around the United States. Potential customers would call this clearinghouse for reservations rather than call the B&B directly. When the company first started, they were receiving about 10 calls a day. This was a very comfortable pace for a home-based business run by someone who may not have wanted to work that hard. The owner of this business decided to put up a Web page. The Web page was successful beyond the owner's wildest dreams, to the point that the number of calls went from 10 a day to 50 the first morning. The number of calls climbed from there. The owner did not have the infrastructure or security built into the Web page to handle reservations over the Web. It was a very interesting period while the company ramped up to meet their level of success.

Regional Company Model

The first question that comes to mind is what is *regional*? This calls for my favorite answer to any question. It depends. Regional can be defined as a small clustering of offices reporting to a management office that is not the central office. So, for example, regional insurance offices would be managed by district offices, which would be managed by the corporate office. It can be described as having offices in more than one state or province. So how does designing security for a regional company differ from designing security for a national company? Again, it is not harder or easier, it is just different.

For example, I was recently tasked with designing a solution to interconnect three small offices of the same company. The goal was to have real-time connections to a shared database that could be centrally maintained at the corporate office. Response time was an issue in the current configuration. The present solution was dial-up, and that just wasn't making it. Where I live, there would be several relatively low-cost ways to handle that problem. Unfortunately, the three offices were not located in the area where I live, but were in an area of rural Wisconsin not served by a major telephone company. In fact, there were two very small cooperative-type phone companies involved. The area was small enough where it was not economically feasible for the telephone companies to upgrade to the latest digital technology. It became apparent quickly that while a solution could be found, it would not be cost effective given the technology available in these areas at that time. This was both a technological function and an economic function.

Branch Office Model

The branch office model may be the most difficult to define. Of all the models, this one can be the hybrid. Take a look at Figure 1.3. This may give you some idea of the branch office model.

FIGURE 1.3 Branch office model

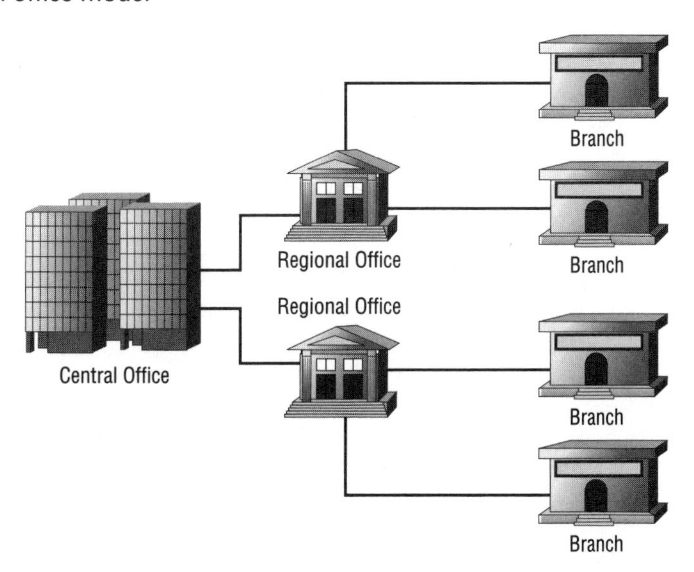

As you can see, the branch office model is more removed from the corporate headquarters. There are layers between what happens in the mahogany row and what happens in the central office.

In the case of a branch office model, the driving factor for communication may move from politics to *information flow*. You will need to look at how information moves between the branches and the regional offices and between the regional offices and the home office. How much raw information do the branches need to share? Will most of the information be moved to a central location before being processed or made available, or will the information be made available directly from the branch office? In *Business @ the Speed of Thought*, Bill Gates describes the data warehouse that Microsoft calls MS Sales. MS Sales gives everyone in the organization the ability to look at all sorts of information about the way Microsoft products are being sold anywhere in the world. This would be an example of where a single database, stored in a single location (or mirrored in several locations), could be accessed from anywhere in the company. The branch office data would move to the data warehouse where it could be processed and queried. Queries would not have to traverse the network to go to the smaller branch offices.

For IT management, this would be advantageous because many of the branch offices may not have the staff to manage and oversee the security of the network. Having many different sites where the information could be accessed would also make auditing much more challenging.

Subsidiary Company Model

When is a company part of a company, but at the same time not part of a company? When it is a subsidiary. There are a variety of issues that fall into the category of challenges when you discuss subsidiaries.

The majority of the challenges involve internal politics. In a large company, there are two kinds of IS people: those who work in the central office, and those who don't. Those who work in the central office cannot understand why the people who do not work in the central office cannot comprehend the corporate computing culture vision. The people who don't work in the central office cannot understand why the people who do work in the central office feel it is absolutely necessary to meddle in affairs they do not understand. After all, what can the people who live and work in the ivory tower possibly know about the stresses and strains of working in the trenches? When everyone works for the same company, with the same general management, the two factions can be directed to common goals, so that at times something can be accomplished. Upper management may step in and say, "This is the way it is going to be," and the dictum has been passed. But the model of a subsidiary confuses the picture somewhat.

Subsidiaries are more autonomous than other forms of corporate structure. They usually have their own form of senior management, who report back to the holding company at only the highest levels. Because they are so autonomous, convincing them to follow the home office corporate policy may be a difficult sale. In this case, you may end up treating the subsidiary as if it were a most favored partner. You may need to look at the security links between the companies, make sure your security is in place, and let the subsidiary take care of its own problems.

This autonomy may be the result of a conscious decision, or it may be the result of acquisition. For example, one company that I dealt with was an OEM for auto parts for many of the major auto companies. One of the things that surprised me was their list of customers. They were not only supplying standard parts to U.S. automakers, but also to a variety of automakers that were not headquartered in Detroit. This company had offices all over the world, from Ireland to Japan and back again. While each plant was a subsidiary of the home office, each plant was treated as a separate, unique entity. They were all tied together by the network infrastructure, but each location was treated independently. It was not the prettiest network design I have ever seen, and it was an administrative and security nightmare, but it worked for that company. In this case, the network infrastructure was designed around the autonomy of the subsidiary.

It is important to keep in mind how the security concerns of each of these entities will impact your security design, not only in the real world, but also in the testing world. For example, it is important to remember that an international company based in the United States may have to watch what security technology it exports, because some encryption can be legally exported and some can't. As this book is being written, the laws and treaties on what the U.S. can export are changing.

Different suppliers in different areas may impact national security. Regional offices may bypass that aspect, but may face problems delegating management responsibilities from the central office. Branch offices may range in size from very small to large, and therefore security concerns will vary with the expertise at each location. In any case, communication between locations will be something that has to be taken into consideration.

When you go into that little exam room, expect to be given questions that are based on case studies. The case studies will present you with tons of information. Some of the information will be beneficial and useful, some of the information will be for background, and some of the information will be just smoke designed to cloud the issue. You will be expected to know the difference and sort through the smoke.

Design Scenario: Understanding the Corporate Model and Security

It's Monday morning at 9:00 and you have just walked into the weekly corporate management meeting. You carry the title of Senior Vice President in Charge of Technology. The title sounds really impressive, but in reality, you are just the computer person working for a small company of about 40 people. Not a bad gig, certainly not in Boise, Idaho.

When you walk into the meeting, you are surprised to see the owner of the company sitting at the head of the table, waiting. Not only is she there, but there are several people you have never seen before. The owner is smiling. Not just smiling, but *really* smiling. When the meeting kicks off, the owner makes an announcement. Over a game of golf that weekend the new folks in the room had made a very generous offer to buy your company. The offer was to purchase the company for $25 per share of outstanding stock. The deal is contingent upon several key factors, not the least of which is your getting the corporate-wide network ready to be integrated with the new company. In addition, the new owners will be absentee owners, leaving the corporate management in place.

For a moment you are taken aback. Then you remember that when you were hired six months before, you insisted on 10,000 shares of stock. At the time, since the company was private, the stock was worth anything the owner wanted to pay for it, and since she was notoriously frugal, you hadn't given it a second thought. Now, however, you are giving it second and third thoughts. It is time to go work and find out how to get your corporate network attached to the new company.

You suddenly realize that you will soon be a member of a larger organization. When you start questioning, you discover that the company has its home office in Athens, Greece. There are other offices in Lisbon, Paris, Istanbul, and Tel Aviv. You are now a potential member of a larger international organization. What kinds of decisions are necessary to make this deal become a reality?

First of all, you are quick to grasp the enormity of things you don't know. When working with your own little company, you knew the network backwards, forwards, inside, and out. Now, suddenly, you are thrust into a situation where there are a multitude of questions and not enough answers. When your boss finally wipes the large grin off her face, she asks what you are going to do to make this work?

After pausing for a minute with a pensive look on your face, you decide to approach this like any network design. You start by laying out the four phases of the design project:

- Functionality
- Security
- Availability
- Performance

After questions are raised and answered, you find that things are not all that different between Boise and Athens. You are actually looking forward to your first meeting at the new corporate headquarters.

Analyzing the Company Processes

Designing a secure network is all about protecting data. But before you can protect the data, it is essential to know where it comes from and who needs it. This is where you begin to analyze who needs access to what and how in the world do they get to it. Let's start with the raw material of any business decision, from hiring an employee to releasing a new product—information.

Microsoft Exam Objective

Analyze the existing and planned business model.

- Analyze the company model and geographical scope. Models include regional, national, international, subsidiary, and branch offices.
- Analyze the company processes. Processes include information flow, communications flow, service and product life cycles, and decision-making.

Information flow is the lifeblood of any company. Many companies have so much information they are drowning in it. It has become an industry in itself. Information comes in so many different formats that it can be more frustrating than useful. Sometimes it is hard to remember how excited you are to have the information at your fingertips when the stack of papers reaches the sky. When you begin to analyze information flow, you are going to put it into the context of the Digital Nervous System. That means figuring out how to make it easier, more cost effective, and more efficient to get access to the information your company needs.

Let's take a look at an example that was almost universal a few years ago, and which unfortunately is still common today. If your company is like most companies, it is constantly looking for new people. Let's assume that the manager of the Information Technology department is so excited about the job you are doing that he wants to hire someone else, and find someone who is just like you. Under the traditional method of locating potential employees, the process would usually begin with the IT manager filling out a paper requisition for a new slot in the IT department. Once the requisition was filled out, it would be forwarded to the Human Resources department, where the requisition would be logged and forwarded, in the inter-company mail, to whomever is in charge of signing off on new positions. Once the sign-off has occurred, the requisition would be placed back in the inter-company mail, where it would arrive back on someone's desk. That someone, probably a lower echelon clerk, would review the requisition, and place an ad in the local Sunday paper and wait for the resumes to come pouring in. Once the flood of paper resumes had abated, the same lower echelon clerk would compare the information in the requisition to the information in the resumes, and finally make a determination about whom to interview. All those selected for interviews would be called and all those who were not selected would be sent a personalized letter or post card telling them that their resume would be kept on file for at least a year.

As for the lucky ones, the interviews would be scheduled, memos would be sent out, resumes would be forwarded, and finally, at long last, the potential candidate would show up for an interview. The interviewer would probably have a long list of questions made up, just to be sure that every candidate for this job was asked the same questions. When the interview was complete, the clerk would generate a summary sheet for each of the candidates, with a recommendation, and forward those on to the head of IT. At this point, the head of IT would look over the paperwork, make notes, and send back a request for schedules of interviews of those candidates who appeared most qualified. Candidates who didn't make the cut would receive the personalized "thanks but no thanks" letter.

During the second interview, more question sheets would be generated, more summaries written up, and more memos would fly through the office. If this hiring is a team decision, meetings would probably have to be held, with memos going out to schedule the meetings and agendas drawn up to make sure everyone knew what was going to be discussed. Now, once the second round of interviews was complete, the remaining candidates would have to be screened by another committee, or still others would be involved in the decision-making process. Finally a decision would be made, the final candidate and new hire would receive an offer letter, and the remaining candidates would receive another letter telling them, "Thank you very much but no thank you."

As you can see from this all too typical scenario, by the time someone was actually hired, at least a dozen trees had been killed and several cases of paper were used to effect the hiring. Once the person was hired, the real paperwork began! Now, employment forms needed to be filled out, security badges requested, office supplies requisitioned, as well as office space and office furniture obtained. There are computers to order, software to load, cables to be run, and network IDs to be obtained. There are manuals to print and the human resource manual to obtain. There are samples of forms to be provided, so the new hire knows how to request sick time, vacation time, or overtime. For everything there is a reason, and for every reason there is at least one piece of paper, put in one inter-office envelope and delivered to someone's desk by some hardworking mailroom person. The cost of this effort is staggering. Surely there has to be a better way.

Here comes that Digital Nervous System again. What if, when you analyzed the way that information flowed through your company, you were able to simplify it, speed it up, and minimize the number of fingers in the pie? Do you think you could convince management that it would speed things up?

Now, let's take a look at the same process using an intranet designed to assist people in making intelligent decisions in an efficient manner. Suppose your manager was reviewing the results of the digital report you filed on your activities for the past week. While doing that, your manager was able to cross-reference your report and compare it to the number of outstanding requests for service that were in the helpdesk database. By running the cross-reference, your boss could see the average amount of time it took you to close a service request. Judging from the backlog of service requests, it does not take a rocket scientist or math major to figure out that if you worked from now until you were 250 years old, non-stop, without a vacation, you might be able to clear the backlog. A light goes on, and someone figures out that another body, just like you, is required to speed up the work.

At this point, your boss can go out and fill out a digital form on the intranet that will be forwarded to the Human Resources department via e-mail. Using the information gathered from your report, your boss can even justify the hire with cold, hard facts. Facts usually go a long way toward convincing the people on mahogany row that another employee is really needed, and this is not the request of a middle level manager trying to increase the size of the fiefdom. Once Human Resources checks the request over, it is forwarded, again by e-mail, to the powers-that-be that need to sign off on it. When they approve the electronic form with a digital signature, it is then returned to HR for action.

At this point, HR can codify the characteristics that are needed in the new employee. This can be done for a variety of reasons. First of all, the information can be compared to the current database of resumes that your company has filed over the past year. Secondly, the information can be forwarded to the Web designers, so it can be included on the employment section of the company Web page. Once the priorities and characteristics are completed, an ad can be generated and e-mailed to the local newspapers for inclusion in the "Help Wanted" section for those potential employees who may still read the paper, or have the ad included on the paper's Web page. It can also be forwarded to whatever online employment search engines your company uses. Instead of having to wait until Sunday for results to start coming in, the HR department is already examining resumes on file, and new applications may start arriving almost immediately.

When an electronic resume arrives that meets the criteria, the e-mail can be forwarded to those people who will be doing the initial interview, with copies immediately sent to other people who may be interested. After all, one candidate may be right for several different jobs. The others can add comments to the resume or suggest questions, and e-mail the information back to the Human Resources department. The interview can be requested and scheduled via e-mail or pager, with a minimum of hassling with voicemail and waiting for a response.

During and after the interview, notes can be taken and impressions given via e-mail. Electronic meetings can be held to discuss the candidate. If necessary, the interview can be conducted using a Web cam so others can watch. At the very least, chat software could be configured so people could forward appropriate questions.

When the first round of interviews is complete, those candidates who are not being considered can receive an e-mail. In some cases, you may want to assign all the rejected candidates an individual logon id so they can check the status of their resume and whether it has been checked out of the electronic database. In addition, you may give them the rights necessary to update their resume in your database whenever anything changes. After all, computer people are constantly going to training, passing tests, getting certifications, and being exposed to new products.

If the candidate is hired, using a mail merge function will begin the process of generating an offer letter (or e-mail) and any forms that are mandated to be saved as paper documents. Once the job has been accepted, forms can be filled out electronically, and office furniture, office space, and technology can all be requisitioned electronically. Basically, everything can be done without killing any trees, and it can be done today.

Is it being done this way in most offices? The simple answer is "no." Would this be a more efficient way of handling the process? Certainly. There are some key questions that can be asked about the information flow of any company to see if it is making the most of the Digital Nervous System:

- Do you have the information flow that enables you to answer the hard questions about what your customers and partners think about your products and services, what markets you are losing and why, and what your real competitive edge is?
- Do your information systems simply crunch numbers in the back room or help to directly solve customer problems?
- Is important data culled only for special one-time use, or can employees get access to it on a daily basis?
- Make a list of the questions about your business that demand action. Does your information system provide the data to answer them?

Communication Flow

What is the difference between information flow and *communication flow*? I must admit, it is a very fine line. Let's look at it this way. Say that you and I had to make a decision on what colors of widgets our company was going to produce next year. First of all, we would go out and gather sales figures to find out what colors of widgets sold this year, which were the most popular, and what trends were exhibited, if any. After all, the red and green widgets may have started out slow at the beginning of the year, but may have come on strong during the holiday season at the end of the year. Once we have processed all the information, we can begin to discuss it, either face to face or by electronic means. That discussion would be communication flow. The acquiring of information would be information flow.

Now, while this processing of information is all fine and good, how can it be used to make large companies more efficient? Well, we just looked at how it would impact the hiring process, but how could this Digital Nervous System help reduce costs, increase efficiency, and help bring products to market?

Let's take a look at how an integrated information retrieval Internet presence can help a manufacturer be more efficient. Let's suppose that our company, SuprComputers-'R-Us, is in the business of making all sorts of computers—for home use, for business use, for use as servers, and for use in ways that we haven't even dreamed up yet. Now, SuprComputers-'R-Us does not have a brick-and-mortar sales presence anywhere. Everything is done over the Web. SRU has targeted none but the super-savvy computer user. The company doesn't want the customer who is out to look at the color of the computer case—it wants the customer who demands the *super-duper* 5000 MHz processor that can handle 6 or 7 terabytes of RAM, standard. Don't ask what it can do—design it just the way you want it and then ask what the darn thing costs. That is how SRU makes its money.

Now, how does communication impact the decision-making process? If SRU has its stuff together, the company management can make instantaneous decisions on what the customers want. All they have to do is look at the sales figures coming off the Web. Those figures will tell management if their customers are buying tower cases or desktops, CD-ROMs or DVDs. Whenever a customer inputs an order, the parts are automatically allocated from current inventory to that computer. That allocation reduces inventory and increments the order that is going to be placed with all the SRU suppliers.

Those orders to the manufacturers of memory, motherboards, cases, and drives are all automatically e-mailed out each afternoon at 4:00. By the time the e-mail arrives at 4:05, each of the manufacturers is expecting it. When the e-mail comes in to the sales person, a rule on the account forwards it to the order desk. The order is pulled, sent to shipping, and packaged. The order is picked up by the overnight delivery service by 6 p.m., and SRU has the parts necessary to build lots more computers the very next day by 10 in the morning.

This system is an accountant's dream come true. SRU's accountant doesn't have to do much work. After all, when a customer places an order, he has to give a credit card number to release the computer to manufacturing. The credit card number is automatically verified while the customer is online. As soon as the customer approves the order, the amount is tallied and electronically sent to the bank that evening. The deposited funds show up in the account the next day. SRU has the same type of arrangement with its suppliers. When it receives an order and verifies it, the supplier's invoice is brought up in the accounting software and marked for payment. That evening, the accounting software sends instructions to the bank to electronically transfer funds to the supplier. The supplier does not have to wait 30, 60, or 90 days to get its money. If the wait is 7 days, payment may be overdue!

Communication Flow at the Coffee Shop

While the SuprComputers-'R-Us scenario may seem to be far-fetched, it is being used today in companies large and small. Your company is certainly using some aspects of the Digital Nervous System, even if you never knew it was called that.

If you work for a small company, you may be convinced that this is not for you: After all, it is just not cost effective for a company that sells items with small price points. Think again!

It was a beautiful Minnesota Saturday morning. It was winter (hey, this is Minnesota—winter sometimes feels like a year-round state of mind!), the sky was blue, and the air was crisp. Unfortunately, I was on my way to my office, because I had to work. It seems that the development editor was sending notes out asking when Chapter 1 was going to be complete.

Now, when I rented my office space, I had some stringent criteria in mind. It had to be close to home, quiet, and private. It had to be small enough for one person, but large enough to hold all my computer equipment. Most of all, there had to be certain facilities near by. Like most computer people, I exist on the two major food groups—sugar and caffeine. Therefore, there had to be a convenience store and a coffee shop nearby—in the same building would be better, but my budget wouldn't allow for a building that fancy.

My office is strategically located. It is 1.5 miles from home and two blocks from the local Caribou Coffee. I have to pass one to get to the other. It is *perfect*!

Now, on this beautiful Saturday morning, every person from a 5-mile area seemed to be in my Caribou. I had to wait an extended period of time to get my latte, but I put that time to good use and observed the way things worked.

I have always been amazed that these little coffee shops can make enough money to survive, much less thrive. After all, there are usually two or three people working at any time of the day or evening, and while retail salaries are never high, they have to be high enough to entice people away from other things. These storefronts are usually pretty large, with plenty of room to sit and read or talk to friends. They don't seem to be interested in turning tables over to increase customer flow, so the ratio of square footage to revenue has to be considerable when your highest-priced item in the store is under $20. How do they do it?

The only explanation I can figure is volume and communication. Usually, when I stop at Caribou, there are several people working behind the counter. No one comes out from behind the counter to wait tables like in a "conventional" diner or coffee shop. There are no little green pads where the orders are written down and no one is yelling the orders back and forth. Everything is geared toward electronically processing the order, getting the money, filling the order, and moving on to the next customer.

When I came in that fine Saturday morning, one person behind the counter took my order for an extra large latte and a blueberry muffin. Okay, not very original, but filling just the same. Once the order was placed, he entered it into the computerized cash register and took my money. I got out of the ordering line and went into the receiving line, where I got to watch Jenny, the world's best coffee person, do her thing. Jenny would individually prepare each cup of coffee. Whether it was mocha, a turtle, a latte, or a cappuccino, Jenny was on top of things. First, she would check the computer screen in front of her to find out what was ordered. The computer would track the order to make sure that the customers were handled on a first in first out basis. When she received the information from the computer, she would make the coffee and deliver the order. No matter what, from the time your order came up on Jenny's screen until the time you were out the door, it was less than two minutes.

> Now, I am not sure, but I would bet that computer system is smart enough to know how much coffee is being used every day. I would also bet that computer system is smart enough to know when to order more coffee, more mugs, or more blueberry muffins. I will also bet that a good manager can check that information and find out that blueberry muffins sell better on a cold Saturday in Minnesota than, for example, a summer Saturday in Arizona.
>
> Digital Nervous Systems are at work, in your neighborhood, right now. You just may not know it.

Service Life Cycle Management

What is the service life cycle and how do you manage it? Does this have anything to do with the help desk having to support the SRU computer that was sold today for the next five years? Well, sort of. The service life cycle differs from the life cycle of the service. Let me give you another example. The *service life cycle management* is based on the principle that the importance of the Information Technology department is the delivery of services to its customers. Services are the tools IT customers use to do their jobs.

These services can include keeping secure track of sales and accounting transactions, as well as the output generated from spreadsheet and word processing programs. It also provides for measurement information used to prioritize resources. Service management can be divided into three segments:

- Planning for a Highly Available System
- Deploying the Highly Available System
- Managing the Available System

Planning for a Highly Available System

When you start planning for your highly available system, you start by looking at what you have available today. This includes the people, processes, and technology that are serving the company today. If you don't have up-to-date documentation, you need to get it. You also need to define the services that have to be available. That is the first step to designing an available system.

Deploying an Available System

Once the planning and design phase have been completed, the first step in deploying the actual changes is a dry run. Set up and run a pilot installation. After all, isn't that why the company hired all those IT people—to have built-in test subjects? The pilot's main purpose is to test the people, processes, and technology planned and designed. The design of the test phase must include mock disasters, mock attacks, and mock invasions from hackers.

The pilot also must run long enough to produce a sample of the desired audit reports and measurements necessary to maintain the security of the network and to plan for the future of the system.

When the pilot has been deemed a success, then it is time to bite the bullet and implement. When you deploy, consider these points:

- When designing your deployment strategy, be sure to include things like the goal of the design, how the design will be used, any constraints that come into play, and how your customers' expectations need to be considered.
- Once the master project plan is completed, make sure that the entire project team has access to it.
- Your final deployment plan should list any system management tools that will be implemented, as well as any processes that should be followed.

Operations Management for a Highly Available System

An available secure system does not exist without constant vigilance. The tools, teams, and processes involved with maintaining the system are integral to its function. All the fancy security audits, password schemes, logon requirements, rights and permissions, group policies, and more, mean absolutely nothing if the people using the system have not been trained. These people also have to be committed to the security of the network and be proactive in reporting any potential security breach.

Product Life Cycles

SRU's Digital Nervous System takes out all the guesswork in ordering, help desk operation, and order fulfillment. It also provides the product designers and management a unique insight into the buying patterns of their customers. The data is right there for the crunching. By trending, management can see what options are hot and what options are cooling off. Since all ordering is done off the Web and all computers are custom built, adding a new feature or a new peripheral is simply a matter of updating a few Web pages and including the new features in the database. Decisions are simplified because risk is minimized. If the new peripheral does not sell, it is not purchased, so there is not a large inventory sitting on a shelf somewhere gathering dust.

As a matter of fact, many companies have this down to a science. It is called *just-in-time* (JIT) *ordering*. JIT ordering has been around for years. During the Y2K scare, one of the theories that called for the economic world to collapse and riots to ensue had to do with JIT ordering. The thought process went like this: Companies in the technologically developed countries would handle the Y2K issue. Countries that were not as developed would not have the resources to deal with Y2K. When a manufacturer in the developed world was used to ordering something from a manufacturer in a less developed country, chaos would ensue if that supplier could not deliver. When the supplier could not deliver, the manufacturer would close, laying off employees, who would be without funds. They in turn would need to eat, so they would riot. Needless to say, that is just another example of someone reaching way out there for an *end of the world* scenario.

Not only are peripherals not sitting on the shelves, the decision to end the life cycle of products becomes a no-brainer. If the product is advertised on the Web and is not selling a certain predetermined number of units over a predetermined amount of time, it is simply removed from the catalog. Because SRU's manufacturing cycle is so close to real time, the amount of inventory left to dispose of should be minimal. The business decision to kill a particular product should be automatic. The emotional decision may not be so easy.

You are probably wondering about the emotional decisions. After all, does emotion have any part in the cut-and-dried world of decision-making for big business? Certainly. No matter how much the process has been digitized, sanitized, and computerized, someone has to make a yea/nay decision on the project. Many companies have suffered setbacks because of emotional decisions. One of Microsoft's key competitors in the networking market, Novell, suffered because of decisions made to purchase the WordPerfect Corporation. The decision was made on emotion, to challenge Microsoft on the desktop while Microsoft was challenging Novell for the network. The merger of Novell and WordPerfect did not last long, but there are still some former employees of WordPerfect worldwide wondering where in the heck that plan came from.

Making the Decisions

Up until this point in the chapter, we have taken a broad overview of the business model process and the way Bill Gates thinks the Digital Nervous System should operate. Unfortunately, you probably don't work in an environment that is structured this way. Since most people resist change, it may take some convincing just to get management to see that this truly is the wave of the future and something they should be working towards. This section will take a look at how you work with the corporate infrastructure to make it more efficient and cost effective.

Network Infrastructure vs. Process Flow

Throughout the first chapter, we have looked at some of the common tasks performed by generic companies all over the world. Things like hiring, production, ordering, scheduling, and shipping are worldwide phenomena that occur in every company, no matter the size. For the exam, you have to be aware of ways to automate or digitize those processes.

Separate the Way the Company Uses the Network from the Way the Processes Flow within the Company

No one ever said the migration to Windows 2000, or its implementation, was going to be easy. There is going to be a lot of work involved and much of that work will revolve around planning.

Look at Figure 1.4 for an example of the way some decisions will have to be made.

FIGURE 1.4 Decision-making flowchart

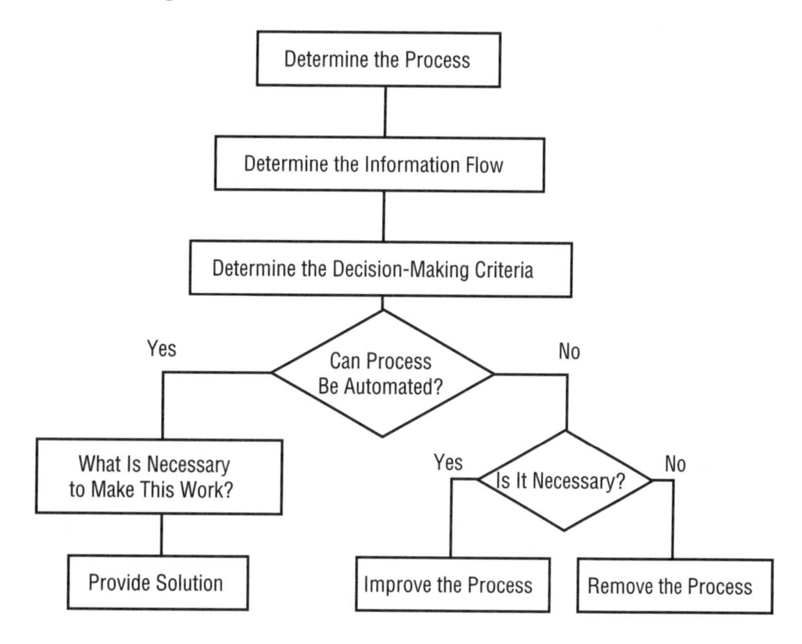

When you start your planning, define the major processes that your company uses. You can start with a high-level overview, like hiring an employee or designing a widget. Chances are, once you get into this, you will find that your company has hundreds of areas that can be defined as a process or a subprocess. I mentioned a process of hiring an employee. Subprocesses could be things like tracking resumes and interviews; hiring; providing resources; and tracking reviews, vacation, sick time, salary negotiations, benefits, and termination. You can see how the list can grow rapidly.

Once you have the process defined, you can look at how information is gathered as part of that process. For example, how does the system of providing an annual review work? Look at Figure 1.5 and we can examine the process.

FIGURE 1.5 Annual review flowchart

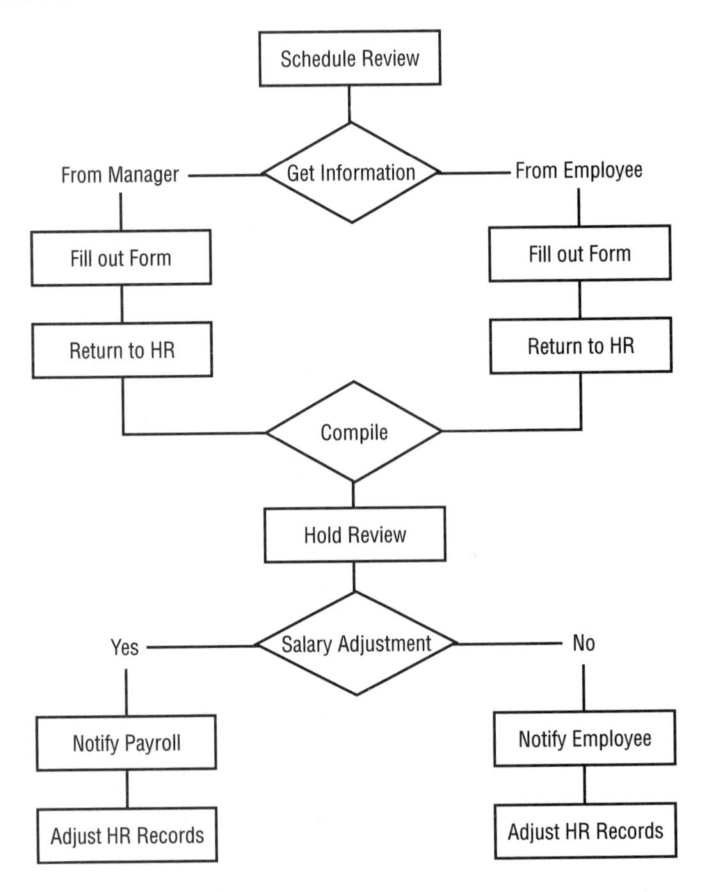

In this case, the first thing that has to be done is to schedule the review. Once the review is scheduled, forms need to be completed by both the manager/supervisor and the employee. After the forms are filled out, they need to be returned to Human Resources, where the information is compiled and provided to both the manager/supervisor and the employee during the review. When the review is completed, a decision on a salary adjustment must be made. If there is going to be a salary adjustment, the size needs to be determined, and the adjustment needs to be approved by the powers that be. If there is not going to be an adjustment, again, Human Resources needs to notify Payroll and the employee, and a note needs to be placed in the employee's file.

As you look at this process, figure out the ways the network is currently used to make this process more streamlined. Are the forms currently available in paper or electronic format? If the forms are available in electronic format, what type of electronic format is available? Here is where we start picking nits. Is the form available as an attachment to an e-mail that can be filled out and e-mailed back in a word processing format? Or is the form available so that it can be filled out online, with that information being entered immediately into a database?

By analyzing these processes, you are beginning to make a list of the things that can be improved in your Digital Nervous System.

Divisional Information Flow

In the case of the annual review, we took a rather mundane process (as long as it is happening to someone else) and thought of ways to improve the flow of information through the company, making it available to more key people sooner. We are going to take that process and look at it from a larger scope, this time between divisions of the same organization.

First let's define terms. When I say divisions, I am not talking about the Human Resources department and the IT department. I am talking more like Chevrolet and Pontiac are divisions of General Motors.

Here again, we are in the planning process. Somewhere a decision has to be made as to when to address cross-divisional procedures. Is it before or after handling internal processes? Whenever the exploration begins, you are going to find that the flow of information will certainly be more complicated. For example, for the annual review of a senior manager, chances are information has to be passed both internally in the division as well as externally back to the corporate headquarters. Again, setting up flowcharts of the way the information is processed, from inception to final filing, will clarify the steps needed to improve the process.

Communication between Levels of the Organization

Any time now, things are going to become tricky. Talking to someone in Human Resources about how an annual review is handled is much more straightforward than talking with someone about how communications flow between levels in an organization. When you start asking about how well upper management communicates with middle management and how well middle management communicates with the staff, there may not be many clear and distinct lines. In addition, you may begin to see personal bias come into play. After all, most upper level managers pride themselves on their communication skills. The opinions come in when you talk to the people that upper management communicates with.

The other part of this examination that may be tricky is the necessity of breaking down certain stereotypes. In the past, in the paper-oriented corporate environment, there was usually a well-defined hierarchy for *need to know*. For example, a senior vice-president in charge of widget manufacturing may be able to request a month-to-date report of how well the super-sized blue widgets are selling on Wednesdays in states with names ending in *S* in the Eastern time zone of the United States. While this report is perfectly okay for a Senior VP to call up, there may be guidelines prohibiting a mere sales representative from getting the same information. The tricky part is to determine why the salesperson is prohibited from getting the information. Is it need to know? Or is it based on the fact that in the old days, generating that report would require programming resources and the resources of the mainframe, all of which were really expensive? Today, that same information may be available from within a standard database application query window at no charge. Does that change the level of communication? More and more companies are breaking down the old need to know boundaries because the information is more freely available and can be used to provide more solutions to more problems more efficiently.

Design Scenario: Corporate Information Flow

It's just another day in the neighborhood for a consultant. There you sit, waiting in traffic, thinking about this new client you are about to see. You have done some homework on the firm; you know that it is an old-line law firm. The company is international, with offices in Berne, Washington, London, and Chicago. It has different divisions, dealing primarily in corporate law, contract law, and merger and acquisitions. You also know the firm has about 1,500 lawyers working for it worldwide, with a support staff that averages about 4 support folks to each lawyer. So you are looking at a company that has 7,500 employees. You didn't want to get too much more information, because you'd rather hear the whole story from the client.

When you get to the client site, you announce yourself to the receptionist and he points you to the conference room on the top floor of the building. It's where the senior partners hang out. When the meeting starts, you find that one of the senior partners has read Bill Gates's book and wants a Digital Nervous System, but the law firm is concerned about how it works. That is why you are there. Where do you start?

You start by asking all those insightful questions you had while sitting in traffic:

How do you manage information now?

What types of information do you want to make available?

How is that information gathered?

How is the information shared?

How is the information secured?

How is data transferred from one area of the company to another?

Then you begin to explore the international aspects of the project. How are the separate offices and divisions defined? Once you have the answers you realize that you are dealing with an international company that is segregated by divisions. Each division operates in a different city. The business goal is to make information about various cases available on line. This information may be available to any lawyer in the company, regardless of specialty, or it may be available only to those folks dealing specifically with the client at any given time. The information will have to be protected; certain people will have the ability to change the data, but most of the company will only be able to see and read the data.

Currently, each division's active clients are discussed at a morning meeting. These meetings are becoming longer and longer, and although they provide an interesting revenue stream, there has to be a better way. Security, of course, is key.

It's your turn. You stand up and begin talking about corporate intranets, and how each division can have its own intranet with information on its cases immediately available. You also begin talking about how e-mail will help to pass information about each client without the partners having to be in a meeting all morning. For those face-to-face meetings, there is videoconferencing. For the meetings that require a dialog, but where no one really wants to leave his desk, there are private chat functions. By plugging your laptop into the wall, you dial in to your corporate intranet and show the partners how you can immediately access information about their firm from your files, as well as from the Internet. You open a chat session with your administrative assistant, checking on the whereabouts of your passport, because you hear that Berne is beautiful this time of year, and hey, you have to start the project somewhere. The partners begin to smile, and all that remains is haggling over your fee.

Summary

Analyzing the company model and the processes does not seem like it would normally fall into the IT bailiwick. As we move toward the institution of a Digital Nervous System, the primary goal will be to make information immediately available to those people who need it, while protecting the information from those people who don't. As you analyze the business, do it with an eye toward taking things that are traditionally in paper format and turning them digital. Also look at how decisions or procedures can be simplified by the proper application of the Digital Nervous System.

Before you can take advantage of the Digital Nervous System, you have to have one in place. That requires a full-blown project. Any time we deal with network projects, they are in three stages: design, implementation, and management.

To design the new project, you first have to figure out a starting point. This involves discovering the type of company you are working for, the types of management they employ, and how they are currently dealing with information flow and communication flow. Information flow and communication flow are all interrelated with the network design and infrastructure. When the management staff has the information, and has discussed the ramifications, they will make decisions based on that information. A firm understanding of the process and of the underlying influences are necessary to pass the test.

Key Terms

Before you take the exam, be certain you are familiar with the following terms:

functionality

security

availability

performance

information flow

communication flow

service life cycle management

Review Questions

1. According to Microsoft, the network design process consists of three phases:

   A. Purchase, Install, Manage

   B. Planning and Design, Implementation, Management

   C. Installation, Configuration, Administration

   D. Setup, Installation, Configuration

2. What is the method of providing information instantaneously to anyone attached to a corporate network called?

   A. Paperless office

   B. Digital Nervous System

   C. Office 2000 scenario

   D. Office implementation

3. A regional office differs from a branch office in what way?

   A. The regional office implies some form of management responsibility.

   B. The branch office implies some form of management responsibility.

   C. Neither office has any form of management.

4. When is a network design considered *available*?

   A. When the first PDC is installed and users are added

   B. When users can get to the technology and use it in a meaningful fashion

   C. Whenever the network is considered *up*

   D. Whenever a new resource is added

5. What is the performance part of a design based on?

   A. Response time specified by business needs

   B. Bandwidth

   C. Business needs

   D. Equipment needs

   E. The speed of the processor in each of the domain controllers and the speed of the network infrastructure

6. In IT, what constitutes a service life cycle?

   A. How long it takes to restore data after a server has crashed.

   B. How long a server can remain in service

   C. The principle that the importance of the Information Technology department is the delivery of services to its customers.

   D. The service contract you have with an outside vendor.

7. What is communication flow?

   A. The way the telephone answering system is set up

   B. Message flow in any electronic messaging system

   C. The organizational chart

   D. The way communications are handled through the levels of the organizational chart

8. What is information flow?

   A. The accessibility of information

   B. The way information is made available

   C. All of the above

Answers to Review Questions

1. B. Microsoft divides the network design process into three phases: Planning and Design, Implementation, and Management. The three are interconnected and all seem to lead back into each other.

2. B. An office where information is immediately available is referred to as the Digital Nervous System. This seems to be Microsoft's vision for the future.

3. A. A regional office implies some form of management, while a branch office does not have the same connotation.

4. B. A design is available to the extent that users can get to the technology and use it in a meaningful fashion.

5. A. The performance part of the design is based on response time specified by business needs.

6. C. The service life cycle management is based on the principle that the importance of the Information Technology department is the delivery of services to its customers.

7. D. In this context, communication flow is the way communications are handled through the levels of the organizational chart.

8. C. All of the above

The Multinational Startup

You should give yourself 10 minutes to review this case study, diagram as needed, and complete the questions for this testlet.

Background

Your consulting firm has been hired to assist in the Windows 2000 migration and integration for a company based in Minneapolis, Minnesota. Until the start of this year, the company had 1,000 employees, all based throughout the Twin Cities of Minneapolis and St. Paul. Just before the end of the year, the owner of your company purchased two companies of roughly the same size, which will need to be connected to the enterprise network. The total number of users when the project is completed is estimated at 3,500. In addition, each of these companies comes with various strategic partners that will need to access the information on your enterprise network. The companies that have been acquired are located in Athens, Greece, and in Orlando, Florida. You are joining the process as the discussions begin on how to merge the companies.

Current System

Minneapolis Located on the shores of beautiful Lake Calhoun, the company occupies a sprawling campus that includes four floors in a six-story building. When the company started out five years ago, it had just part of one of the floors and about 100 people. Since that time, the company has grown, and every time a tenant has moved out of the building, the company has taken over the office space. This grow-as-you-go philosophy has left members of the same departments scattered throughout the building.

All of the floors are connected to the Windows NT network. No one in the IT department can give you a real firm picture of the network infrastructure. The network has been growing so quickly that the prime directive has been to throw more hardware at it. You can ascertain that there is an Exchange e-mail system in place. Several groups are using different database applications to perform different tasks, but the development of these applications has been outsourced and no one is exactly sure how they work. In the discussions, you do hear frequent mention of servers running Microsoft SQL Server, so you know those are around somewhere. Users are running a mish-mash of computing gear, relative to the kind of vendor the purchasing people could obtain equipment from at the time. You have a 40% laptop/60% desktop mix. You have a small enterprise fax software program running on a Windows 95 computer that allows about 10 marketing people to send faxes out from their desktops. The majority of the staff are basic users that are non-power-user types. The other users vary in skill level from needing to know how to turn the computer on to the tech weenie wannabees on the fourth floor who trade shareware programs they download from the Web. The IT department handles the doling out of Internet connectivity. Only certain people have access to the Internet, and that is through a dual-channel ISDN line. Others in the office have managed to scam an extra telephone jack and are dialing in from their workstations, accessing the Internet through MSN, AOL, FreeInet, and a variety of others. At present, there are no network connections between the offices in Athens and the offices in Orlando.

Orlando The Orlando office actually has more people working in it than there are in Minneapolis. It is located in northern Orlando, away from Disney and the tourists. Many of the services in Minneapolis are mirrored in Orlando—things like marketing, accounting, and human resources. Confusion seems to run rampant right now, because the people in Orlando don't know about the products that Minneapolis and Athens have to offer, and no one knows who should be doing what, when, or how. The company is all on NT 4, with a variety of applications; some of the applications are compatible with the Minneapolis corporate standards and some aren't. The Orlando office does have a fractional T1 connection to the Internet. The office is using Lotus Notes as its e-mail package.

Athens Not much is known about the Athens office. The company was purchased because it had developed a great add-on product to your product. When senior management discovered that 80 percent of the customers from the Minneapolis office also owned the product developed by the Athens subsidiary, the boss ran out and bought the company. This discovery took senior management four years. The sales department knew about it almost from the start of the company. The Athens office has about 1,300 users, most of which are salespeople, marketing types, and support staff. The manufacturing plant is located on the island of Rhodes, and due to local customs, manufacturing occurs only between March and

October. The rest of the time, the plant is closed. The office has several Windows NT 3.51 servers running SP3, which is used predominantly for file and print sharing. There is an Internet connection and a Linux box that is only used to provide POP3 e-mail. According to folks in the Minneapolis and Orlando office, the folks in Athens are definitely not overworking the e-mail system.

Because this has been a stand-alone company, all of the normal accounting, purchasing, and human resources functions are there. It has been agreed that management will remain with the company. At present, there is little or no communication between the offices.

Fortunately, most of the people in the office speak and read English.

Problem Statement

Your consulting company has been brought in to assure that the integration of all three of the offices will occur flawlessly. At the very first meeting, several main problems became apparent: There was no secure communication between offices and no safe information sharing, and there was duplication of effort on a variety of levels.

Envisioned System

Overview The CEO and owner of your company has said—and the senior management have concurred—that it's paramount that your company become one intact entity instead of several distinct units that don't communicate with one another very well. The owner is a big proponent of efficiency and therefore the fact that there are so many people doing the same things in different ways is making him crazy. The CEO envisions a system wherein all users participate on what looks to them like one big universal network.

CEO "I have probably bitten off more than I can chew right now. These three offices need to communicate now! There has to be a relatively easy way to create a secure network where information can be made available to anyone in the organization instantly. Is that too much to ask? Oh, and by the way, I am sick and tired of getting phone calls in the middle of the night from Athens. Surely there must be a way to get them the ability to communicate with us some way other than the phone."

Security

Overview Because the product you develop is constantly undergoing research and development, and because the industry is highly competitive, security must be maintained at a very high level.

CFO "With the merger going on and with all the systems with highly sensitive data on them, it's paramount that security is maintained at an extremely high level. I cannot emphasize this enough."

Availability

Overview Because the network will span several different time zones, the availability of the network must be 24x7x365.

Orlando and Athens operations managers "One of the biggest problems we have is finding someone in to talk to. It is not that difficult between Minneapolis and Orlando but between Athens and anywhere it is a nightmare."

Maintainability

Overview There are two problems here. First of all, you will be dealing with an international company, meaning you will not be able to utilize the same vendor for maintenance. Secondly, information will have to be available from all levels of the organization, all day every day. The information must be up-to-date in real time. Because this could possibly tell your competition exactly what you are doing and for whom, the information must be secure.

CEO "These new products we're developing are *so* revolutionary and will have such an impact, that it's important for us to make sure everyone has the same information at the same time."

Athens operations manager "My understanding is that our product will now be bundled with the products developed in Minneapolis. That means we have to know how many to produce. Given the limitations of Rhodes' manufacturing cycle, there may have to be some offloading of responsibilities to other areas of the company."

Performance

Overview Some users have complained of slow performance. The CEO has made it very clear that you are to find the cause of the performance issues and rectify as needed.

Orlando branch manager "It is *so* difficult for us to try to communicate with anyone in this company. My god, half the people in the home office don't even have e-mail addresses! When is this company going to be dragged kicking and screaming into the '80s?"

Funding

Overview While you have not been given *carte blanche* by the CEO, he has made it clear that money isn't necessarily an issue, within reason of course. The problems need to be solved so that the company can safely continue to manufacture their products in the most efficient manner possible.

CEO & CFO "Look, we don't think that we need the Rolls Royce of installations, *but* we can tell you that everything is riding on our ability to ship our combined products in a timely manner, and the network we're asking you to build is going to be a big part of that. We think the company will continue to grow, though not as rapidly as in the last several months. So, that being said, give us a network that makes sense."

Questions

1. What is the business problem?

   A. Users are not all on one network.

   B. The company's software versions are not consistent.

   C. Everybody needs an e-mail account on the Minneapolis server.

   D. You shouldn't have that much confusion in any one company.

2. What solution(s) should you implement to solve the customer's business problem?

   A. Ensure that each location has a secure connection to the Internet.

   B. Set up secure wide area connections between all of the sites. Wide area bandwidth should be adjusted according to the size of the site and its needs.

   C. Up-version all servers to Windows 2000.

   D. Assure that there is an Exchange server at each site and that directory replication is taking place between all servers.

   E. Set up some form of IIS Server in a central location for the sharing of information.

   F. Assure that all users are on a uniform O/S desktop, and that service pack and service release levels are current.

   G. Establish a plan to up-version the existing Exchange servers to Exchange 2000 by Q1 of next year.

3. What solution(s) should you implement to meet all of the customer's needs?

   A. Ensure that each location has a secure connection to the Internet.

   B. Set up secure wide area connections between all of the sites. Wide area bandwidth should be adjusted according to the size of the site and its needs.

   C. Up-version all servers to Windows 2000.

   D. Assure that there is an Exchange server at each site and that directory replication is taking place between all servers.

   E. Set up some form of IIS Server in a central location for the sharing of information.

   F. Assure that all users are on a uniform O/S desktop, and that service pack and service release levels are current.

   G. Establish a plan to migrate all e-mail to the latest version of Exchange.

4. You need to explain to management why you want to up-version to Windows 2000 on the servers. In what ways will this upgrade positively affect this scenario?

   A. Increased security in the form of Kerberos will enhance the protection that the company needs to avoid being hacked.

   B. Active Directory will ensure that new users coming on board in foreign countries will quickly show up in the overall list of users.

   C. Windows 2000 works better with Exchange 5.5 and enhances its functionality.

   D. Windows 2000 provides increased support for Linux servers.

   E. RAS support is greatly increased in Windows 2000.

   F. You can begin investigating virtual private networking for trouble spots like Athens. Permanent connections to the states are prohibitively expensive but they could utilize a high-speed connection to their ISP to arrive at the same goal using a VPN.

5. Given the following table, rank the sites, in the order of importance, according to the amount of attention you think they'll require in order to facilitate your upgrade. For each site listed on the right, write in the order in the left column in which you think the site deserves attention.

Rank	Site
	Athens
	Minneapolis
	Orlando

Answers

1. A. The *main* business problem is that users are not all connected together even though they should be. The very act of connecting everyone together via some methodology would clear up the majority of your communications problems.

2. B. You would start with B, setting up wide area connections in order to assure that everybody's on the same playing field and can begin to share information. The links between the different organizations must be secure.

3. A, B, C, D, E, F, G. All of the above are good starts, but not quite good enough. You have not addressed security needs, for example, nor have you addressed the planning necessary to make this project run smoothly. For example, the servers may also have a problem, hardware-wise, supporting Windows 2000, or there may be issues involved in moving some information between the United States and Greece. You don't have enough information yet. More work needs to be done in the planning areas!

4. A, B, F. There should be a strong business case to be made for linking Athens with the United States using a VPN rather than a leased line. The VPN security embedded in Windows 2000 will be a big help making this happen.
   AD will also aid in security management and ensure that administration is done in an efficient manner.
   On a side note, your Exchange 2000 upgrade planned for Q1 of next year is a good bet because Exchange 2000 interfaces with AD, Exchange 5.5 does not.

5. See table

1. Minneapolis
2. Athens
3. Orlando

The first couple of choices are obvious. Minneapolis, being the main site, is the first candidate for upgrade, especially given their status as the home office and the poor condition of their Internet connectivity. Since all information will flow from here, you will need to get Minneapolis on line and secure first. Once that has been accomplished, you will have to begin to work on connecting Athens. From the sounds of the setup in Orlando, they at least have some of the infrastructure building blocks in place, much more so than the other two. If you were to create a secure Website to start the information sharing process, you could work toward the 24x7x365 network. You have to take baby steps first!

Analyzing the Business Plan

MICROSOFT EXAM OBJECTIVES COVERED IN THIS CHAPTER:

- ✓ **Analyze the existing and planned organizational structures. Considerations include the management model; company organization; vendor, partner, and customer relationships; and acquisition plans.**
- ✓ **Analyze factors that influence company strategies:**
  - Identify company priorities.
  - Identify the projected growth and growth strategy.
  - Identify the relevant laws and regulations.
  - Identify the company's tolerance to risk.
  - Identify the total cost of operations.

Probably everyone has heard the old expression, "Plan the work and work the plan." What this all boils down to is that we have to know where the company is before we can look at where it's going. So, in this chapter we are going to take a look at the business side of things. There are going to be several chapters in this book that will make you think you are pursuing your MBA instead of your MCSE, but they will definitely make you a better person, increase your chances for staying awake during company meetings, and provide another career opportunity as a management-speak translator should you ever decide to get out of information technology.

This is one of the foundation chapters. In later chapters we will focus on things like planning, risk analysis, and risk management. Now it is time to lay the groundwork for those pieces and start to form a business plan. Once the business plan is in place, we can find out how the business will be affected by Windows 2000.

Analyzing Corporate Operations

You are probably thinking, "Here we go with more management speak," and you are right. We are also going to spend a lot more time talking about planning. After all, to quote another old saw, proper planning prevents pretty poor performance. We are doing all this planning to minimize our chance of failure for this security project. When you start analyzing why projects fail, technology is rarely the root cause of failure. Usually people, processes, and organizational constraints lead to project failures. Through its case studies, Microsoft has determined that projects fail for a number of reasons:

Separation of *goal* and *function* A problem must be understood in terms other than simply function, or *how* something works. You also have to understand the underlying goal or purpose of the solution—in other words, *why* you need it to work. Functionality must exist to help achieve a particular goal or to solve a particular problem.

Often, functionality is created without understanding the goal it serves. To make matters worse, those of us in IT have been doing this for years! Think about it, when was the last time you (or your company) bought something because it was a bigger, faster, prettier model with more bells and whistles. Not that the company really needed it, or in some cases even wanted it, but we bought it because it was new.

Separation of business and technology If your business goals and your technology goals don't match, there is no way the technology goals can support your business needs. An example of this would be when the IT department is all jacked up to install the latest and greatest Web site and intranet, and no one in the company really believes it is needed. The business goal (to gather information) must match the technology goal (to provide immediate access to information through an intranet).

Lack of common language and process To communicate effectively, people need a common language and common process. When those are missing, confusion and unrealistic expectations result. Here again, we in the IT industry are very guilty of this. How many times have you been in a meeting with management types and started talking geek? You probably didn't even know you were doing it, but as soon as a suit comes up with an idea, and you start mumbling about bandwidth, 100Mb Ethernet, and Pentium III 500 with 4 terabytes of RAM, the blue suits are sleeping. They feel the same way about that stuff as you do about paradigm shifting, ROI, cost of operations, product life cycles, and margins. Yawn! I've got to quit this—I am putting myself to sleep!

Failure to communicate and act as a team Obviously, moving people beyond individual effort and getting them to work effectively as a team is critical to the success of a project.

Processes that are inflexible and difficult to change The computer industry is often a confusing environment. Teams must be able to adapt to meet the ever-changing needs of their customers and users.

To minimize the chance of failure, you can approach projects like upgrades, migrations, or installations by adhering to the following solutions:

Customer-focused projects *Customer-focused project* actions are determined by the goal of solving a particular business problem rather than for the sake of interesting technology. This focus helps to align business and technology, because technology is being used to support the needs of the business.

User-centric designs Products have to be designed based on how the consumer will use the system. When you have this type of *user-centric design* focus, you keep what the system does aligned with what it needs to do. The only reason to put a feature in the design is to make it easier for someone to use the product.

Common language and terminology By working as a cohesive team, you can develop a common language and terminology. Too often, the IT department uses technology speak, while the business department uses management speak—and neither understands the other. By working together, this wall can be broken down.

Microsoft has a special set of courses to handle project management. The courses are part of the Microsoft Solutions Framework. For more information look at http://www.microsoft.com/msf.

Microsoft Exam Objective

Analyze the existing and planned organizational structures. Considerations include the management model; company organization; vendor, partner, and customer relationships; and acquisition plans.

Organizational Structures

Enterprise organizations can be defined and structured in various ways. In this section we will take a look at company organization as defined by the management model. You will notice that many of the terms used in this discussion will reappear in the discussion of IT management, which sometimes (but not always) is a mirror of the company's organization as a whole.

The Pyramid Approach Management Model

If you have taken any of the Microsoft Official Courseware on Windows 2000, you have run into the proper way to design an ADS implementation. It all starts out with the pyramid approach. Just in case you think Microsoft has come up with a new and groundbreaking concept, take a look at Figure 2.1. If this were a management class, the diagram would be called the scenario for Management 101. That would give it a fancy name to hide the fact that it is pretty much made up on the spot.

FIGURE 2.1 Pyramid approach to management

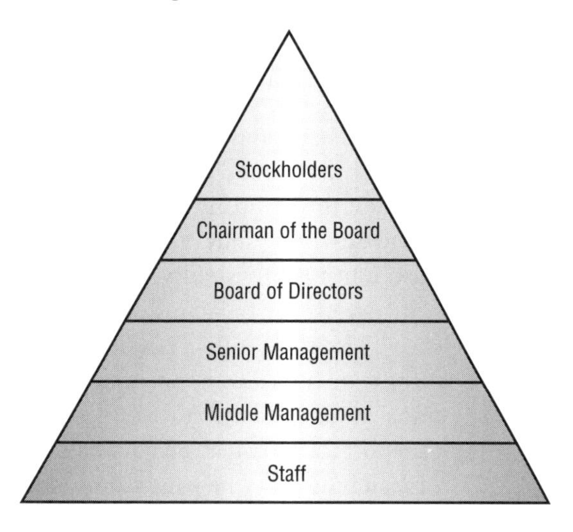

Way back in the '90s it was all the rage to talk about employee-run organizations, but when you really and truly break it down, companies with more than five or six people usually follow some variant of the pyramid approach to management. The titles may change somewhat, but that is pretty much the way it works.

This chart of the organizational structure is important to you, because somewhere down the line, you (or your boss, or your boss's boss) are going to have to answer for the decisions you make as part of the Windows 2000 security project. This is a great way of identifying who you are going to have to please, and what their unique needs are.

As each level is examined, keep in mind the picture of the pyramid and the effects of gravity. When there are problems within a company, the pressure to fix those problems may start at the top and roll downhill. The momentum may grow, as well as the amount of flack someone is going to have to take at the bottom.

Shareholders

Now, unless your title is Chief Information Officer, your chances of being called in front of the shareholders is probably slim to none, and Slim left town. While you may not have to answer to the shareholders directly, you may have to answer to them indirectly. If the security plan that you put in place is deficient and if something of consequence is impacted, the company as a whole may suffer. If the company suffers, profits may go down. If profits drop, or if the company suffers a loss, the value of the stock may go down, and literally thousands of people could be impacted. You didn't realize you had so much responsibility on your shoulders, did you?

Now, you may be saying, wait a minute, what about privately held companies? There are still "shareholders," even if they aren't called that. Let's say that you own a company that employs 25 people. You own 100% of the company and hold the title of president and CEO. There are still people that you report to. They may be your customers, they may be the vendors you buy from, and they may be your wife and family, but someone other than you is going to be interested in how well that company does.

Chairman of the Board

The board of directors will usually elect the chairman, but the COB is the one ultimately responsible for the operations of the company. In many companies, the title of chairman is symbolic, but in others, the opinion of the chairman carries a lot of weight (isn't that right, Mr. Gates?). The chairman of the board may be a majority stockholder in the firm, which makes the position even more important.

Board of Directors

Depending on the size of your company, your title, and who you report to, the board of directors may be a tremendous resource, or as unreachable as putting a human on Venus before the end of the year. The board of directors is usually appointed. The members, in most large organizations, are not now employed by the enterprise, though individual members may once have been. The board is usually very diversified, with members who are successful leaders in their own right—otherwise they would not have been invited. If you have access to the board, and can position yourself to use them as a resource, do it. Their goal is the same as yours—to make your company more successful than it is today.

The board of directors sets broad policies for the company and is interested primarily in one thing: profits. If the company is doing well, the board is happy. If the company slips, the board may begin to put pressure on the next level down.

Senior Management

Finally, we are getting to a level where the rubber hits the road. This is where real work starts getting done. Honest! Now, the work may not look like the work we do, but it is real work nonetheless. This is where policy is decided, money is allocated, and high-level decisions are made. *Senior management* may not be there to decide what the user-naming conventions will be for the Windows 2000 implementation, but it will be there to decide if there will be a Windows 2000 implementation at all. These are the people who are led by someone with a lofty title like chief executive officer.

Senior management (unless you work for a company like Microsoft) will usually have just a rough idea of what the IT department does. If you think about it, when it comes to senior management, the IT department may be in a no-win situation. If your network works perfectly every day and everyone can access all the stuff they need to access without a hitch, why does the company need IT? If the network is not operating according to expectations, that means IT is not doing its job, so why do we need IT?

Senior management is important to the security process at several levels. One of the primary levels is to have a member of senior management be active in planning security for the network. Senior management speaks in language that most IT people find mystifying, talking about ROI, inventory turns, and other business concepts. Meanwhile, senior management may find your talk of forests, trees, sites, and domains just as mystifying. Having someone on the security team who can go back to Mahogany Row where senior management works and explain the security plan in words that managers can understand is a very important resource.

Middle Management

These are the people you may deal with on a day-to-day basis. They have titles like operations supervisor, sales manager, or shift supervisor. They are the hard-working people right smack dab in the middle of every issue. On one side are the staff-level folks complaining about working conditions, low pay, poor equipment, and understaffing. On the other side, you have senior management pushing for a higher efficiency rating, more *return on investment*, less expenses, and more output. Middle management gets paid more than the staff, and earns every penny of it.

Staff

This is where all the policies, right and wrong, and all the decisions, right and wrong, get carried out. These are the people who do all the nitty-gritty work. These are the ones who make it happen. As you will notice in the pyramid, this level is at the bottom. Without a firm foundation, companies will fail. Unfortunately, when stuff ends up rolling downhill, this is usually where it lands.

Types of Managers

We will look at three management styles: Management by Empowerment, Micromanagement, and the Peter Principle at Work.

Management by Empowerment

Scott Adams, the creator of Dilbert, wrote in one of his books that if you have to be told that you are empowered, you're not. I think that is really true.

Authors' Disclaimer: Everyone has different hot buttons. Ours is management style. If we seem to make one style seem more attractive than another, it is because we work better under that style and we are far too shortsighted to see how anyone could work under any other style. If you really love to be micromanaged, more power to you!

With *management by empowerment*, the staff member is given a task to do and the ability to make the decisions necessary to do the job. The employee then carries out the task until completion. This was explained by one of the best managers we know, Bill Haas. Bill had been a colonel in the

U.S. Air Force. Retired military officers have a reputation as somewhat rigid and dictatorial; Bill wasn't. He used what he referred to as the "monkey theory of management." Each task was a monkey. When you were presented with a monkey, you could feed the monkey, give the monkey to someone else, or put the monkey back on its perch when you were done playing with it. The trick was, the monkey must never starve to death. It always had to be fed, meaning you had to be working on your task and making progress.

Empowerment management means the manager is there to provide the staff with resources to do the job, but not to act as a roadblock. The staff member is trusted to make decisions, based on corporate-approved criteria and guidelines, and then report back when the task is completed. This can also be described as the "no news is good news" approach. This approach works best with the Digital Nervous System.

Micromanagement

The *micromanagement* style is just the opposite of the empowerment style. The micromanager wants to know what is going on every minute of the day with every one of the people who report directly to him. This is the manager who holds so many meetings to check on the progress of various projects that nothing gets done. When the MM finally calls a meeting to complain about the lack of progress, your pointing out that the problem is the number of meetings you have to attend can be a career-limiting proposition. Many hands-on managers fall into this category. Hands-on managers would rather do the task, because they know they can do it right the first time. That does not exhibit trust in the staff, does it?

The Peter Principle at Work

The Peter Principle states that people are promoted until they reach their level of incompetence. I am sure you have bumped into people like this. They started out like the rest of us, lowest part of the food chain, the bottom feeders. For whatever reason, they excelled and were driven to accept a management post. Once they were promoted, they excelled again, and were promoted again; the cycle continued until they were put in a position where their skill set did not meet the job requirements and they were destined for failure.

Let's look at an example of the Peter Principle at work—we'll call him John. John came in and managed the technical staff in a midsize, value-added-reseller consulting company. John was a great technical manager. He knew tech weenies, he spoke our language, and he understood how we thought and worked. It was a match made in heaven. John was promoted and put in charge of the consulting group. Better tech weenies. More experienced tech weenies. Another match made in heaven. John succeeded again and became the CEO's brightest star. John was then promoted to manage a technical education center. Instead of managing a group of tech weenies, John managed a group of sales weenies. Now, just in case you have not noticed, sales weenies are a lot different than tech weenies. They don't think, act, react, or live the same way tech weenies do. This was a match made in hell. John, due to his superior management skills, did manage to last two years, but it was not pretty. He started getting frustrated after about day three. He went from empowerment to micromanagement to Peter Principle at Work without moving his desk.

Design Scenario: Types of Managers

On this, yet another day in the life of a consultant, you have two customers to see. Both are old-line clients you have worked with for years. Your first stop will be to see the CEO of Acme Computer Warehouse and Bar Supply. He has a project that he wants to discuss with you. Every time his employees talk about him, they use phrases like "laid back." His favorite management word is "empowerment," and he takes it to the max. When you first started consulting, he set a budget for the number of hours you would spend on a project. The next time he needed to see you was when you reported the project was completed. If the project wasn't completed and money ran out, you had to go see him and tell him that, and explain where you were with the project and the roadblocks you encountered. Once that was done, you would work to allocate more money, and the project was back under way.

The next stop was at another old-line company, World Wide Web Resources. At WWWR, things were handled a little differently. In this case, the CEO wanted to see you in regard to a past project. He has your billing sheets and would like to see your time sheets and project notes to determine if you spent an appropriate amount of time on each phase of the project. You have been through several projects with this company, and it is always the same thing. You get approval for a project after months of meetings, the CEO is constantly checking up on you as work on the project, and then you are challenged on each and every bill submitted.

As a consultant, you learn each of the CEOs' hot buttons. When you discuss projects with the CEO at ACWBS, you have learned to use terms like "delegation of authority," and "project team leads." Meanwhile, at WWWR, you talk about oversight, reporting, and supervision. You are just making sure to talk with the respective managers in a language they can relate to.

The Company Organization

In the next chapter we will discuss some of the ways companies can be structured, based primarily on location. In this section, we are going to look at ways the company may be divided up that could have a major impact on security. Let's start at the simplest and work up to the most complex. Since we are supposed to be dealing with organizations of over 5,000 users, we will skip the home-based businesses and the small- to medium-sized companies.

Single Entity

In a single entity company, you have one corporate structure. The corporate structure may involve multiple divisions, but all come under the single corporate entity. An example of this, at least at the time this book was written, would be a company like Microsoft. Although Microsoft goes out and acquires other entities, they soon come under the Microsoft corporate entity. All products developed and distributed by Microsoft bear the unique Microsoft logo, and all management flows directly down from the chairman of the board, Bill Gates.

Umbrella Organization

No doubt the MBA programs of the world give this a more elegant name, but for discussion's sake, "umbrella organization" works. When you think of an umbrella organization, picture one central company that owns several relatively smaller companies or divisions. These smaller companies operate semi-autonomously, contributing profits back to the parent. There are usually several more levels of management involved in this type of organization.

An example is General Motors. Everyone always talks about GM, but the real work is done in the Chevrolet, Pontiac, Buick, and Cadillac divisions, as well as the truck divisions, the parts divisions, etc. The difference between an umbrella company and a holding company is that in the former the link between the companies or divisions is more visible. In addition, the smaller business units usually contribute directly to the finished product of the parent company.

Holding Company

A holding company is like an umbrella organization, only different. With a holding company, the products produced by the downstream entities may not contribute directly to the final product of the parent. An example of this would be a company like Anheuser-Busch, the brewery folks. Actually, although A-B is usually thought of, and quite fondly, for their beer, they are into so much more. The company owns a snack food division and several theme parks, and formerly owned the St. Louis Cardinals National League baseball team. While the Busch name is usually prominent, in this type of scenario it doesn't have to be.

Nonprofit

You might think of nonprofit organizations as being somewhat technologically deprived due to a lack of cash flow. In many cases, that is true. However, one of the authors rethought his stance after seeing the plans for a storage area network configuration for a regional office of a church.

Nonprofit organizations may look to the money-saving advantages of a new network over and above other features.

Governmental and Educational Institutions

Who better to form a Digital Nervous System than government branches and educational institutions? These are certainly two of the primary purveyors of paper. In addition, they are two of the primary purveyors of chaos and confusion.

Consider the case of a couple who own some rental property. They have the property managed, and the local county government was contending that the management company wasn't paying an occupancy tax for the property. One of the owners contacted the rental manager, who said it was being paid; then he called the county, who said it wasn't. Since the property is 1,500 miles from the couple's home, they didn't find it the easiest dispute to mediate. One of the owners finally flew down, found the clerk's office, found out what piece of paper the county was missing (because that is all that it was), drove over to the management company and got the paper filled out, and then drove back to the clerk's office with the paper. While he was at the management company, he was shown copies of the four forms the property manager had already sent the county. Anyway, within about an hour, the problem was resolved. Of course, that hour required a $350 airline ticket, time off work, loss of rental of the house for the week, and a rental car and per diem. That was at least a $4,000 piece of paper. It would have been wonderful if the form could have been filed electronically, online, so it would have been immediately available to the clerk. Then the owner could have handled the entire thing over the Internet and never left his office.

Governments and educational institutions are all moving to the Digital Nervous System. In many localities, routine licenses and permits are applied for online. Forms that used to take days to get via snail mail and phone-in requests can be downloaded, filled out, and e-mailed back in a matter of minutes. Tasks that used to require hours standing in line are accomplished from your chair. We recently heard about a woman getting her Master's degree in Education. When she started the Master's program at a small private college, she was shocked when she was told she had to personally be there to register for her classes. During her undergraduate years, that was handled via the Web.

Vendor, Partner, and Customer Relationships

How does your company interact with those people with whom it does business? What impacts will that have on your security concerns? How can your vendors, your partners, and your customers access your enterprise network? Is it tough to define what your digital network is going to be like in the future?

All right, here is what we are going to do. Create a large circle of candles, light them, dim the lights, and look into the crystal ball to see what the future holds. We could do it that way, or you could base your business plan analysis on something a little more scientific. It will still be a best guess scenario, but it will help shape the future of your network.

First of all, we have to get just a bit MBA-ish here. It's likely that everyone reading this book has heard of Andy Grove, the CEO of Intel. Grove has written a book called *Only the Paranoid Survive* (Bantam Doubleday Dell, 1996), and in it he describes something called a *strategic inflection point.* According to Grove, "A strategic inflection point is perhaps an engineer's description of what those who went to liberal arts school call a paradigm shift. It's a moment in time when circumstances shifted on you and you have a choice to make between two alternatives. At that moment two alternatives are very close to each other but in time they will take you very far apart, they will diverge. That moment in time is what I call a strategic inflection point." What we are doing with this section of the analysis is attempting to predict some of those strategic inflection points.

This can be done by asking some questions and trying to come up with rational answers. These inflection points will be things that will affect all types of industries. If your company believes these kinds of things will happen, then you have to start preparing for them as part of this process.

- Does your company believe that in the future, people at work will use computers every day for most of their jobs? There are many people who will use computers occasionally, but many people use their computers only a few times a day. Some people still go days without using a computer.

- Does your company believe that one day most households will have computers? About half the households in the United States have computers. Some countries have a higher percentage; most are much lower than the United States. It has been predicted that before long computers will be as common as television sets.

- Does your company believe that one day most businesses and most households will have high-speed connections to the Internet and the World Wide Web?

- Does your company believe that e-mail will become as common a method of communication among people in business and homes as the telephone or paper mail is today? Currently, not everybody uses e-mail, even if they have a computer.
- If your company believes that most people will have computers and will use them every day, do they also believe that most information will start arriving in digital form?
- Is it in the future of your company to send bills to their customers electronically?
- Is it in the future of your company to receive payments electronically?

If you answered "yes" to the majority of these questions, you have defined the way your network will be put to work to interact with your vendors, partners, and customers. Now it remains to define exactly how extensive you will want that interaction to be.

Vendor Access

So what would be the best practice of allowing vendors access to your enterprise network? How extensive would that access have to be?

Certainly, if your company currently has e-mail accounts, many of your vendors are already accessing your network by sending messages concerning their latest sales events to your purchasing department. If your e-mail box is typical, it fills up daily with messages from people who have sold you something in the past, companies that want to sell you something in the future, and from companies that just want to let you know they are still around.

Using Active Directory, or using distributed security with the public key infrastructure, lets you set up trusted communications between two networks. Suppose you have a trusted vendor. Suppose this vendor has been supplying widgets to your company for years. Imagine that you use those widgets as part of a just-in-time manufacturing system—you only want enough widgets on hand to complete two days' worth of production. You know that amounts to 5,000 widgets. In the past, your company would have to contact the vendor on a daily basis to order the appropriate number of widgets. If your vendor had trusted access to your network, the vendor could check the inventory daily, ship you the appropriate number of widgets, and be out of your system in minutes.

Partner Access

Imagine the amount of information that could be shared if you could set up security so members of your key partner staff could access the appropriate parts of your intranet? Say, for example, that you are working on building a new prototype of the world's finest vertical ferblitzer. Now, you have tried and tried to explain to your partner exactly how this new prototype will set the world on its ear, but to no avail. You need to show your research to your partner. You have several choices: You can print it out and send it Fed-Ex or snail mail. You can attach 8 or 10 megabytes of information to e-mail and hope the partner isn't using a dial-up POP3 account with size limitations. Or you can point the members of your key partner staff to the information on your intranet and let them see for themselves. You can share documents and data on a routine basis.

Customer Access

This is a whole book in itself. If people need a product, they will usually buy that product in the easiest, most cost-effective way possible. Now, this doesn't necessarily mean everyone. After all, there are people like Tim, who will drive an hour to a store 45 miles away because that store advertised a product for $10 less than the store two blocks from Tim's house. We will all admit that Tim is an exception.

How can you make buying your product easy on the customer? Well, if half the homes in America are on the Internet, put your product where they can find it. Put up a Web site. Give them secure access, allowing them to pay electronically. Put up a page of comparisons to your competition. Make sure you have pages dedicated to support, a page to show off all your latest products, and links to an ordering system that will let your customers buy your products when it is convenient for them. They don't have to wait for a salesperson to call. They don't have to call and be put on hold. They don't have to drive to their store. They enter the information and before they know it, the product is delivered.

This has been a relatively successful concept. Just ask Amazon.com, which in two years surpassed the annual revenues of Barnes and Noble.

If your company is going to make an e-business commitment, this is the time to know that.

Design Scenario: Access to the Keys of the Kingdom

You are back on the road again, off to see a new client. All you know about this client is the name of the company, "FYI Training Solutions."

When you arrive, you meet with the President and CEO of the company, Bobbi. She invites you into her office, and you begin to discuss her networking needs. This company is a startup and Bobbi is truly one of the world's best entrepreneurs. She has a vision; she just is not sure how to implement the vision. The vision is to provide online customizable training to customers via the World Wide Web. She wants to make some forms of training available 24x7 and some forms of training available on an appointment basis, where a certified trainer would be available to answer questions via chat sessions. The certified trainers will all be contractors or partners of her firm. The total number of her employees will be low, but she will need to protect her system and provide access only to those people she wants into the system. She ends her part of the meeting with the question, "How do I do this?"

You respond with some questions of your own. Just who is going to get access to the system? If you sell your product to a customer, how do you envision that customer getting access from the Web? How will contractors or trainers get access to areas where the chats will take place? Will this be hosted internally or externally? Will people be able to download or print course materials, or just access them from your private site?

Bobbi tells you that you have raised some very good questions and she is not sure of the answers. She says she will find out, and get back to you. It may even happen in other design cases later in this book!

Plans for Acquisitions

Any plan for a businesses future has to take into account the unexpected—such as acquisition of another company. In the case study at the end of Chapter 1, "Analyzing the Company Model and Processes," our semi-hapless CEO decided that the best way to expand was to go out and buy other companies. It worked. We will be following that scenario through the first four chapters of the book, to see how we can continue to analyze the way business operates and the impact of some rash decisions.

Now, don't get the idea that acquisitions are rash ideas. Most are well thought out. There are issues for the IT security department to consider, especially because it will be up to that department to make the transition as easy as possible. Acquisitions take place in four phases: pre-acquisition, acquisition, post-acquisition, and managing the combined systems. Security is impacted in several ways.

Pre-Acquisition

In the pre-acquisition phase, the companies begin the dance that will lead to the eventual marriage. Someone calls someone else, a hint is dropped at a meeting, or a rumor is circulated. Let the games begin. For our sake, let us assume that we are the company doing the acquiring (not that it matters), and that this is a friendly takeover, not an angst ridden, guilt ridden, and unfriendly takeover.

First of all, the call comes into IT that we are looking to take over the ABC Company, and our suits want to access their network to get information on the state of the company. You have to make that happen. If the target firm has a corporate intranet, and the other IT department is willing to share the information, this could be a task as simple as an e-mail or two, saying let us in.

As the talks heat up and begin to get serious, now it is necessary to view what kind of network the target has, how it is configured, and what security policies it has in place. How does the current network match your network standards? What types of information will you need to get the new combined systems to talk to each other in the most secure way possible?

This may involve adding another tree to your forest!

Acquisition

The big day comes; the suits are celebrating with champagne and congratulating themselves on what they have just done to the value of their stock options. Meanwhile in the trenches, the feelings may be running more to subdued, just-under-the-boiling-point panic. After all, the company you know and love has two full-time, fully staffed IT departments. Even though everyone is saying there will be no layoffs, you know deep in your heart-of-hearts that it could be you.

Enough self-pity, there is work to be done; it is time to link the two networks together fully, finding out exactly what you have just bought. It is time to truly test security and find out if there are holes and how to patch them.

Post-Acquisition

The tests are run, the analysis has been completed, and now it is time to work with the *new* IT team to bring their network up to your standards, or your network up to theirs. This is an entire project unto itself, obviously, fraught with security concerns. Every time something gets upgraded, it has to have its security tested and certified. The work continues, and finally it is impossible to tell where the two old networks left off and the combined network starts.

Management

Once the task of merging the networks is complete, the task of management begins. There is twice as much to audit, and there is twice as much to secure. And you thought you might be out of a job. You are busier now than you have ever been.

Now that we have looked at how the company is organized, it is time to start looking at how the company goes about its day-to-day business.

Design Scenario: You Are Doing What?

You have just walked onto another customer's site—this time it is Total GroupWide Health Plan Systems of Montana, a health maintenance organization with eight offices spread all through the state. Carried tucked neatly away in your briefcase are the rollout plans for the new Windows 2000 network that will link all eight offices together. As you are waiting in the foyer, you overhear some excited conversation about Florida and Arizona. You can't catch all of it, but something interesting is in the air. You are finally ushered into the CEO's office. As Brandice gets up from behind her desk, she has a big smile on her face. You start the conversation by saying, "Just think, if we agree to terms here today, within three months your 8 facilities will all be linked together into one large Windows 2000 network." Just as you pause for a breath, she says "25 facilities."

Somewhat taken aback, you erase the look of shock on your face, and say, "Excuse me?" Brandice replies that as of 10 o'clock that morning, TGWHPS now has 25 locations in Montana, Florida, and Arizona. She has just signed the papers completing the acquisition of the Really Healthy Old People Health Plan that covers those two states. She says that your plans need to take into account the acquisition.

After congratulating her, you ask her how long she has been working on this, and she says about a year. You follow up with a question about why this is the first you have heard of it. She replies that she didn't think it would impact your project, and besides, you never asked.

You silently mutter an epithet that sounds like "shoot" and start asking more questions so you can start the plan over again.

Analyzing Company Strategies

This part of the chapter could be subtitled, "Why Are We Doing This Anyway?" Switching to Windows 2000 is a major undertaking. The planning alone is a daunting process (just think, you still have a couple chapters of business analysis to go before we even get to any technical stuff!), not to mention the actual rollout. So, in this section, we will analyze the factors that influence your company's strategies to roll out Windows 2000.

Microsoft Exam Objective

Analyze factors that influence company strategies:

- Identify company priorities.
- Identify the projected growth and growth strategy.
- Identify the relevant laws and regulations.
- Identify the company's tolerance to risk.
- Identify the total cost of operations.

The Company Priorities

What drives your company to do what it does and how it does it? Is it the strategic inflection point that Andy Grove talked about? A major upheaval in the way your business is conducted? Is it the vision of corporate CEO and board of directors? What is the big-picture business problem here and how are you going to address it?

Customers Drive the Business

More and more companies are getting onto the Internet. In 1998, brick and mortar stores far outpaced online stores in sales volume. The sales volume of online stores in 1998 was only .5 percent of the total retail sales of the seven largest economies. In 1999, Forrester Research predicted that more than 50 million households will make online purchases over the next five years. Additionally, there will be a hefty increase in online spending per household—growing from $1,167 in 1999 to $3,738 in 2004.

What does this mean for your company? If you don't have a strong Internet presence now, you will in the near future. Most senior management may be slow on the technology uptake, but they are always quick to spot a new revenue stream. If they haven't spotted it yet, maybe it's time for you to bring it to their attention? Now, it is time to examine your *company's priorities* and see where senior management wants to take the company.

Identifying the Priorities

What are the priorities of your business and, what's more important, how do you identify them? Ideally, this would be a very simple task. You know that your company wants to do a better job of serving its customers. I am pretty sure there is no company in the world that wants to do a worse job of serving its customers. Even nonprofit and governmental agencies have customers, and these customers are demanding more and more service.

Now we have the obvious stuff out of the way, how do you locate the real priority of the company? If you go out into the front entryway of your corporate headquarters, is there a vision statement? Taking a close look at the vision statement may give you an idea of where your company wants to go.

No, as we write this, we are not wearing rose-colored glasses. We understand that many companies in business today do a great job of writing a very ethereal-sounding vision statement that just makes you wonder where the boss's halo went. Once the vision statement is written and hung on the wall, many companies leave it there and forget about it. We did say "*may* give you an idea of where your company wants to go."

Once you have read the vision statement, take a few steps back from the day-to-day grind of getting up and going to work and try and determine if that vision statement is valid. Is your company really trying to provide better customer service, or are they just giving that lip service? You can tell. Say, for example, you work for a technical company. The company is constantly harping on its commitment to customer service, meanwhile cutting back the tech support department by 50%. It would appear the reality does not meet the stated goal.

As you read this, you might be struck by how cynical it sounds. That is because the authors have worked for some really terrible employers who were only out to acquire the customer's money, not the customer's loyalty. We have also unfortunately done business with companies like that. On the other hand, we have worked for companies where the owner's word was his bond. Since we have had the opportunity to work for a variety of businesses in a variety of industries, we can tell you from experience that when viewed from the day-to-day, the bad stuff stays the same with each company. The faces change, but the problems stay the same. There are always one or two incompetent middle managers making bad decisions. There are always new product announcements that fall flat. There are employees you wouldn't necessarily invite to dinner every Friday night. But if you step back and look at a company from a broad perspective, you can get a good idea of the commitment to the vision statement.

For example, one company we know had a vision statement that made all the usual points about employee empowerment, customer satisfaction, and stockholder *return on investment*. Then it said something about being a good corporate citizen. All of a sudden, all those e-mails about contributing to the United Way, matching contributions for Habitat for Humanity, the sponsorship for 10K walks for Breast Cancer, and the paid day to work at the food shelf made sense. The employees were empowered. Although it sometimes seemed that management neglected staff and didn't understand the things they were working on, the truth was they *did* understand, and realized that left to do their own thing, they would produce the desired results: happy, satisfied customers. Management was there for staff—every time they had a problem, management helped solve it. Sometimes the solution was not exactly what staff would have wanted, but maybe the workers weren't always right the first time either. So the vision statement is a place to start.

Take a look at the direction the company is going. As an insider, you probably have a better idea of the company's real priorities. People on the outside have to listen to what the company says. You get to see what the company does. If the company says it is heavy into new product development, you should ask, "is it?" Do you have company-wide meetings where the CEO gets up and gives one of those rally-round-the-flag-boys speeches? Does the CEO follow through? These are some of the ways to judge the priorities of the company.

Design Scenario: Determining the Company's Priorities

As someone who has achieved most favored consultant status with Acme Computer Warehouse and Bar Supply, you are invited to the annual company event. The annual company event is known to be a great time of golf and good food, interrupted by speeches over dinner.

Although you are not usually one to attend other companies' galas, you decide that you may just as well attend this one. You are currently working on their plans for the Windows 2000 rollout and you would kind of like to know what makes upper management tick.

After the great round of golf, everyone adjourns to the clubhouse. Let the mandatory meetings begin. The first part of the meeting involves presenting all the gag gifts that seem to be a part of every golf outing. Once the last crying towel has been dispensed, the meetings begin. You are really trying to figure out why senior management seems to be so against the Internet.

The first item of business is the awarding of the annual charity donation. The chairman of the board stands up and makes the announcement that the employees of this company have raised $5,000 to be given to the company founder's favorite charity, Parents against Pornography. The Chairman then announces that the board of directors has voted to match the contribution on a two for one basis.

Next on the agenda are the reports of annual sales. You begin to nod off. You find that ACWBS has a 5% market share in the city and the company is beginning to look at ways to sell their products to a broader base than just the City of San Antonio. They are exploring opening offices in Houston, Dallas, and Amarillo; however, office space is expensive in all those areas and the company is trying to find a way to minimize the cost.

In addition, the bar supply business would improve greatly if the company had offices in New Orleans and San Francisco. Once again, the office space problem is holding back the expansion. Finally, the discussion turns to how to make ACWBS more accessible to their customers. It would be wonderful if customers had some form of 24x7 support options, but that would just be too expensive. The CEO vows to continue to search for solutions to these weighty issues over the next year.

On Monday, you sit down and put together a rough strategy designed to provide ACWBS employees with Internet usage. To protect against company employees going to sites they shouldn't be going to, you have instituted a firewall and a program like Net Nanny. You also design a strategy that will let the company offer a knowledge base for their customer support needs as well as providing online ordering for both the bar supply business and computer business.

Once you have the company's priorities covered, you go see the CEO to reaffirm your most favored consultant status.

Growth Strategy

Here again, look around and you will be surprised what you can find out. If you work for a company that does planning, and most do, somewhere around the company there is a business plan. Now, if you work for a smaller company, that business plan may be accessible in the boss's office simply by asking. The business plans are usually updated on a yearly basis and point to where the company thinks it is going.

If you work for a large company, you may need to look at the annual report, or perhaps at statements made to the financial community by senior management. In this case, you should get an idea of ways to identify the projected growth and *growth strategy*. Remember that the annual reports or the business plans are the goals for the company. Some companies set goals that are conservative. When goals are based on past performance, they are routinely met and exceeded. When those goals for growth are published, they cause the knowledgeable employee to think, "We can do better than that."

Other companies take an aggressive goal-setting approach. These companies publish goals that challenge the people who have to reach them. When a knowledgeable employee looks at these goals, she thinks, "What are they, nuts?" History may show that the company doesn't always reach its goals. But perhaps it does better than expected because the bar was raised so high.

What kind of corporate growth is your company going through? Growth can be measured in a variety of ways. First of all, growth can be measured in sales. These figures are usually pretty easy to get. Talk to one of the salespeople. He will know. Walk through the sales office and look at the big thermometer chart on the wall. That will also tell you.

Hiring practices can also project corporate growth. If your manager is saying that your department is going to double in size over the next two years, you have a pretty good idea of the growth plans. These facts and figures are well known within the company, and can be found in annual reports, business reports, or internal communications. The goal is laid out, and the strategy to make those goals should be defined also.

If your company is planning on doubling sales over the next 12 months, what types of initiatives is that driving? First of all, the number of salespeople will have to increase. If the number of people selling your product increases, the number of sales support people will also have to increase. If corporate sales increase, that means manufacturing, shipping, and receiving will have to increase as well. In each case, this will present more nodes on the network with potentially more sites and more security hassles for you to deal with.

Relevant Laws and Regulations

By this time you have a good idea of where the company wants to go. You have looked at acquisition plans, growth plans, and growth strategies. You have examined the direction the company is going to take and how it is going to get there.

As you look at this from the perspective of security, are there any laws and regulations that will need to be taken into consideration as part of the security process? The law that immediately jumps to mind is the one that used to prohibit exporting any 128-bit software technology from the United States. That regulation has now been overturned and the worry has lessened.

How would you determine if there are any laws and regulations that you have to look at from a security perspective? If you can, check with the corporate legal department. If you are expanding into foreign countries that have never been dealt with before, look for some outside help. This may come in the form of suppliers who have sold goods in those countries or have offices located there.

Identify the Company's Tolerance to Risk

How much is your company willing to pay or willing to do to protect the information and resources that it has? In the United States, this is an ongoing issue as more and more Web sites and networks are being attacked by a variety of cyber terrorists. The popular denial of service attacks are creating massive headaches for purveyors of Web pages everywhere.

Recently major Web sites, including newsgathering organizations, auction houses, and others, have been hacked. Congress is getting involved and the president of the United States has started taking notice. These are not your ordinary small-business, small-budget, little-or-no-IT-department sites. These are major players on the Internet.

If it can happen to those sites, it can certainly happen to yours. In Chapter 4, "Enterprise Risk Assessment," we will discuss the ways of establishing and analyzing the risk to the network. In this chapter, we are broaching the question of how committed senior management is to security.

How Bad Is It?

Every day, intruders break into Web sites. How do they do it? There are dozens of ways. In most cases, someone failed to establish adequate security controls, and an intruder was able penetrate the network. Now, that may seem obvious, but malicious users can use methods to subvert a normally functioning system without actually penetrating that system's security. As a matter of fact, attacks take many forms.

In a recent edition of the *Windows 2000 Magazine* "Security Update," there were no fewer than six different security risks identified in third party products. These risks included:

- A Denial of Service condition in Netopia's Timbuktu Pro software. By performing a specific series of connections and disconnections, an intruder can cause the authentication protocol to misbehave, thereby causing the software to hang.
- SNMP Trap Watcher Denial of Service. By sending a trap string of more than 306 characters to the SNMP Trap Watcher 1.16 monitoring system, an intruder can crash the software.
- True North Software's Internet Anywhere 3.1.3 mail server had two problems reported. By sending a specific string of characters as the

parameter of the RETR POP3 command, an intruder can crash the server. In addition, if an intruder opens 3,000 or more connections on the SMTP port, the server will respond with an error reporting too many connects. By establishing a second large set of connections (800 or more) immediately after the 3,000 connections, the intruder can crash the service.

- Checkpoint Technologies' Firewall-1 software could be tricked by an intruder using particular techniques. Once tricked, the firewall will open TCP ports to an FTP server behind the firewall.
- MYSQL Server had a vulnerability reported that allows a remote user to bypass password checking. The problem is a result of faulty string checking.
- Novell's GroupWise Web Access was vulnerable to a specific URL being sent to the interface. By sending the URL, a malicious user can crash the server.

In each of the cases listed, the company was aware of the problem and had either issued the patch or was working on the patch.

This is one week's worth of issues, reported by just one publication. There are more that go unreported, or reported in a different forum. If your digital nervous system is going to be hooked to the Internet, your organization will be vulnerable to these kinds of attacks. During this stage of the process, it is important to know what type of risk prevention your company is willing to fund.

Identify the Total Cost of Operations

A favorite method of closing a sale is to discuss how the proposed piece of office equipment will affect the total *cost of operations* of the organization. It goes something like this: Well, Ms. Customer, I know you are really anxious to get started using the Super Whiz-Bang 6000 copier. I also know that as a good businessperson you are concerned with keeping costs to a minimum. What would you say if I told you that you could begin to enjoy the benefits of the 6000 for as little as $5 per day per location?

When phrased like that, it sounds as if anyone could afford a copier that might retail for $5,000. It makes it sound so cheap!

Why is the identification of the total cost of operations important? You are now entering the realm of management speak. Two of the things managers love to talk about is lowering the total cost of operations and increasing the return on investment. If you are convinced that Windows 2000 improvements in security are needed on your network, these are the two catch phrases that are needed to sell it to management.

In this case, you can take a look at the total cost of operations for the entire company, or for a particular department. An example of this was when Compaq rolled out Windows 2000. When Compaq was discussing upgrading its network to Windows 2000, one of the obvious concerns was how much this was going to cost the company.

After doing a preliminary study, the company found that as part of the rollout, it could significantly reduce the number of servers (by over 75%) needed to handle the network. The hardware cost alone was enough to reduce the cost of operations to where the project became feasible.

Okay, we did not take these Compaq figures at face value. We asked some serious questions. First of all, the replaced servers were older model machines that probably would not have fit the Windows 2000 hardware compatibility list or had the horsepower to run the operating system and handle large volumes of requests. The servers that replaced the older machines were the super servers. So cost alone was not a factor.

When figuring the cost of operations, managers love it if you can be specific. As an example, say you can tell management that the budget for the hardware repair team for 2000-2001 fiscal year is $X divided by Y number of servers, for a cost of operations of $Z just for repairs. If the company were to consolidate hardware, repair costs would go down. If the cost of repairs stayed the same for one year to the next and you reduced the number of servers by 300, you would save 300 x $Z. Here you are dealing in hard and fast dollar amounts that people can get their hands around. You are not using the phrases "I think" and "I am sure that we could." You have done your homework and can back it up. Managers love that stuff.

Design Scenario: Cost of Operations

Your consulting firm has been called in to take a look at a potential Windows 2000 upgrade at the site of your largest client. You have been asked to go in and start laying some groundwork for the planning of the project.

When you arrive, you start by meeting with the chief information officer and also the chief financial officer. They say that one of the driving forces behind the upgrade is the cost of doing business. The network infrastructure is aging and they know that their 750 servers are going to have to be upgraded. In addition, having 90 domains is creating an administrative nightmare. In the last year alone, the IT department's budget was $10 million to manage the worldwide network. The CFO is concerned that the costs are out of line for a company of 75,000 people. After all, the company's total revenue last year was only $65 million. The CFO wants to increase the return on investment by decreasing the cost of operations. They have to do better than the $5 million in profit they declared this year.

You decide to take these figures and go back to your office and do some of the math. First of all, you figure the total cost of operations. If the company had $65 million in revenue and a $5 million profit, that means the cost of operations was $60 million. Since the IT department amounted to 1/6th of the total cost of operations, that may indicate the costs are out of line.

Also, you recognize that the cost of maintaining each server on the network is running about $13,300 a year. This would indicate that there should be further study done to determine if that can be minimized by reducing the number of servers.

Summary

This chapter really ran the gamut, didn't it? We started out talking about the different ways a company could be organized. As part of that we examined the different types of managers and how each managerial type interacted with staff.

Company organization was next. This is important from the long-term planning and architecture strategy point of view because the architect will need to know how the various layers interact to be able to spot potential problems. When we got into vendor, partner, and customer relationships, we began to gather the seeds for our security layout. Here we can decide if we have to concern ourselves only with internal security, or if we have to protect ourselves from the outside world. Protecting the enterprise network from the outside is difficult enough, but the task may be made more challenging if we purposely have to leave openings for customers, partners, and vendors to access parts of the network. Then we examined a scenario where the company suddenly decides to acquire another company and the other company's network.

When that objective was completed, we had a broad overview of how the company operated. Then we needed to look at the *why* of the operation. Why exactly is the company in business? What are its business strategies? If these business strategies work, how rapidly will the company grow and how will that growth be managed? As you analyze security, it is imperative to know if there are any laws, regulations, or treaties that you have to watch out for.

The final two parts to the second objective will be discussed in different areas of this book. They will become somewhat of a recurring theme. What are the company's tolerance levels for risk, and how much does this cost? What is the cost of operations? As you begin to design the foundation of the security plan, you really have to know how secure to make it. You can design a really secure network, with firewalls in place, matching all the requirements for C2 security compliance. You can design it, but if the company isn't ready to pay the bill, it is not going to happen. If the company does not want to pay the bill, then the company has to accept some responsibility for risk, and understand that some of its information may be compromised.

The "how much does it cost?" aspect is important for a variety of reasons. Later in the book a security plan will be developed and put in place. When the plan is developed, someone is going to have to sign off on it, and that sign-off is going to involve discussions of dollars. If you know the current cost of operations, you can make some comparisons to determine if the changes make fiscal sense.

Key Terms

Before you take the exam, be certain you are familiar with the following terms:

company priorities

cost of operations

customer-focused project

function

goal

growth strategy

management by empowerment

micromanagement

return on investment

senior management

user-centric design

Review Questions

1. In the management pyramid, the chairman of the board reports to which entities?

   A. Staff

   B. Middle management

   C. Senior management

   D. Board of directors

   E. Stockholders

2. A manager who gives his employee an assignment and then asks about each step along the way is using which management style?

   A. Empowerment

   B. Micromanagement

   C. Hands-off management

   D. Hands-on management

3. To find out the company's priorities, you can look in these places:

   A. The corporate mission statement

   B. The annual report

   C. The company newsletter

   D. Company meetings

   E. Management briefings

   F. All of the above

4. Cost of operations is determined by which of the following:

   A. Gross sales less gross expenses

   B. Net profit less gross expenses

   C. Gross expenses

   D. Net expenses plus net profit

5. Cost of operations can be determined on which level/s?
   - A. Company level
   - B. Department level
   - C. Management unit level
   - D. Employee level
   - E. All of the above

6. What are the outside influences driving most companies?
   - A. Quest for profit
   - B. Customers
   - C. Quest for power
   - D. Quest for recognition

7. How can tolerance to risk best be described?
   - A. Ability to sustain a loss
   - B. Definition of an acceptable loss
   - C. Decision based on facts as to what risks can and should be prevented and what risks are acceptable given the current imperfect security setup

8. A line supervisor is traditionally considered a member of which level?
   - A. The board of directors
   - B. Senior management
   - C. Middle management
   - D. Staff

9. Any manager can practice hands-on management.
   - A. True
   - B. False

10. Managers who give their direct reports tasks to do and then allow them to complete the assignments unencumbered are using which management style?

A. Empowerment

B. Hands-on

C. Micromanagement

Answers to Review Questions

1. D, E. In publicly held companies, the board of directors appoints the chairman of the board. The shareholders elect members of the board of directors.

2. B. A micromanager is a manager who wants to know what every one of his direct reports is doing at every minute of every day.

3. F. When you are trying to locate information on what would be important to the company, you can look to each of these locations.

4. C. The cost of operations is the cost of doing business. It comprises all expenses associated with the company. Once you determine what your cost of operations will be, you can figure out how to sell enough stuff to pay for that.

5. E. You can determine the cost of operations for each of these units, down to and including the employee level. The company can figure out what it costs every day to keep you employed. Items that would make up the cost of operations are things like salary, vacation, taxes, benefits, rent cost involved in cube, computers, training, office supplies, and office furniture. A percentage of management's salary could also be put into the equation, since each manager has to spend a certain part of her year making decisions that affect you.

6. B. Customers drive the business.

7. C. Tolerance to risk is a company's conscious decision, based on a factual assessment of the amount of risk it is equipped to take for any given resource or piece of data. Resource and data protection come at a cost; when the cost of protection exceeds the value of the data; it is no longer cost effective to provide security.

8. C. A line supervisor would be considered a middle manager.

9. A. Any level of management can practice hands-on management or any other management type.

10. A. This type of manager empowers his or her reports to do their tasks with minimum management interference.

CASE STUDY

The Multinational Startup

You should give yourself 10 minutes to review this case study, diagram as needed, and complete the questions for this testlet.

Background

Your consulting firm has been hired to assist in the Windows 2000 migration and integration for a company based in Minneapolis, Minnesota. Until the start of this year, the company had 1,000 employees, all based throughout the Twin Cities of Minneapolis and St. Paul. Just before the end of the year, the owner of your company purchased two companies of roughly the same size that will need to be connected to the enterprise network. The total number of users when the project is completed is estimated at 3,500. In addition, each of these companies comes with various strategic partners that will need to access the information on your enterprise network. The companies that have been acquired are located in Athens, Greece, and in Orlando, Florida. At this point, the buyouts are complete. It is your job to analyze the company to discover the starting point for the Windows 2000 rollout.

Current System

Minneapolis Located on the shores of beautiful Lake Calhoun, the company occupies a sprawling campus that includes four floors in a six-story building. When the company started out five years ago, it had just part of one of the floors and about 100 people. Since that time, the company has grown, and any time a tenant has moved out of the building, the company has taken over the office space. This grow-as-you-go philosophy had left members of the same departments scattered throughout the building.

All of the floors are connected to the Windows NT network. The decision has been made to move to Windows 2000, although no one is sure why. The current network setup seems to be a shambles. For example, there is one NT 4 server on a Compaq Proliant Series 6000 computer that just seems to *be there*.

Communication between offices is currently being done using just e-mail, snail mail, and the phone.

One recent change has been that the owner of the company has turned over the reins to a new chief executive officer. When she was asked about the Proliant, she replied, "That is why I am hiring you, to find these things out."

Orlando The Orlando office actually has more people working in it than there are in Minneapolis. It is located in northern Orlando, away from Disney and the tourists. Many of the services in Minneapolis are mirrored in Orlando: things like marketing, accounting, and human resources. The site is all on NT 4, with a variety of applications; some of the applications are compatible with the Minneapolis corporate standards, and some aren't. The Orlando office does have a fractional T1 connection to the Internet. The office is using Lotus Notes as its e-mail package. The office has been notified that Windows 2000 is coming and by this time next year Lotus Notes will be a thing of the past. When asked for a reason, the answer was that the corporate network is going that route. The firestorm that developed was one of the reasons the owner decided to hire a CEO. While this office has not participated in hosting Web services, it does have an Internet connection.

Athens The Athens office has about 1,300 users, most of whom are salespeople, marketing types, and support staff. The manufacturing plant is located on the island of Rhodes, and due to local customs, manufacturing occurs only between March and October. The rest of the time, the plant is closed. The office has been upgraded to Windows NT 4 servers running SP5. It is predominantly used for file and print sharing. There is an Internet connection and a Linux box that is providing for only POP3 e-mail.

The decision had been made to upgrade the 3.51 servers directly into Windows 2000, but after it became obvious the planning was going to take awhile, the company went ahead and upgraded to NT 4. In addition, the people in Athens know that Exchange is coming. Due to the increase in communication between the United States and Greece, the Athenians are getting more used to e-mail.

Because this has been a stand-alone company, all of the normal accounting, purchasing, and human resources functions are there. It has been agreed that management will remain with the company. Communication between sites remains by e-mail, snail mail, and phone.

Problem Statement

- There is a new CEO on the scene and she needs some answers and she needs them quick. The basic structure of the company puts the owner, who currently owns 100% of the stock, at the top of the pyramid. He has agreed to stock options amounting to 20% of the company if first-year goals are met. The options were offered to the CEO and the two senior vice presidents she brought with her.
- Senior management has tasked you with studying the current company and preparing a white paper laying out the strengths and weaknesses of the current IT structure.

Envisioned System

Overview The new CEO says that she has three offices that she needs to communicate with now. She has read about this Digital Nervous System, and she wants one. She wants you to determine where the company is now. The next phase will be to determine what needs to be done to move forward.

CEO "I just came to this company and I have the owner breathing down my neck every day, checking on what it is I am doing. I am spending so much time in meetings with him, I am having trouble getting anything else done. Luckily, I have a strong team in place. Both my senior vice presidents have been with me for years, and know the way I operate.

"I want a study done on the company. Analyze it from an IT perspective and get back to me in 30 days with the results. If you have any problems, see the senior vice president in charge of finance. You will be a direct report to him."

Availability

Overview Because the network will span several different time zones, the availability of the network must be 24x7x365.

CEO "I truly believe that we must have the ability to communicate with our outlying branches as quickly as possible. We should have e-mail or a Web site or something to make that happen. That should be a major priority."

Maintainability

Overview There are two problems here. First of all, you will be dealing with an international company, meaning you will not be able to utilize the same vendor for maintenance. Secondly, information will have to be available from all levels of the organization, all day, every day. The information must be up-to-date in real time. Because this could possibly tell your competition exactly what you are doing and for whom, the information must be secure.

CEO "These new products we're developing are *so* revolutionary and will have such an impact, that it's important for us to make sure everyone has the same information at the same time."

Athens operations manager "My understanding is that our product will now be bundled with the products developed in Minneapolis. That means we have to know how many to produce. Given the limitations of the Rhodes manufacturing cycle, there may have to be some offloading of responsibilities to other areas of the company."

Performance

CEO "This company is customer driven. We have to provide service to the customer. That means establishing an electronic presence and beginning to offer our goods and services online."

Orlando branch manager "It will be wonderful to communicate with anyone in this company. How are you going to do that? What type of e-mail package are you going to use? You know, I think we should hold a meeting to discuss how I can be a part of that project, because it really interests me."

Athens branch manager "You know, the RAS system we have built up is just wonderful! Now our employees can work from home!"

Funding

Overview While you have not been given *carte blanche* by the CEO, she has made it clear that money isn't necessarily an issue, within reason of course. The problems need to be solved so that the company can safely continue to manufacture their products in the most efficient manner possible.

CEO & CFO "Look, we don't think that we need the Rolls Royce of installations *but* we can tell you that everything is riding on our ability to ship our combined products in a timely manner, and the network we're asking you to build is going to be a big part of that. We think the company will continue to grow, though not as rapidly as the last several months. So, those points being said, give us a network that makes sense."

Questions

1. What is the current business problem?

A. The new CEO is not sure where she is starting.

B. Each of the units has a different type of manager.

C. E-mail needs to be installed.

D. Lotus Notes needs to be removed from the systems.

2. What suggestion(s) should you give to solve the customer's business problem?

A. The manager in Orlando is a hands-on type manager who may need to be reined in.

B. There needs to be a set of goals set up that provide functionality with the technology.

C. Lotus Notes should be removed immediately.

D. The owner needs to define the business goals that must be met to secure the 20% stock options for the new management team.

3. As you begin the study, you start out looking at the company priorities as expressed by the new CEO and her management team:

A. Rid the company of Lotus Notes.

B. Roll out Windows 2000.

C. Establish an Internet presence so the customers can more easily access the sales team.

D. Establish an Internet access presence so the offices can communicate.

E. Make sure the Orlando manager and the owner are involved in all decisions.

4. How should the Compaq Proliant server that is not being used be mentioned in the report?

   A. As a surplus piece of equipment

   B. As a thing to do in the future

   C. As a technology goal

   D. As a function of the technology goal

5. What is the management type of the new CEO?

   A. Hands-on

   B. Micromanaging

   C. Entrepreneurial

   D. Empowering

Answers

1. A, B. The CEO is brand new to the company and she knows little if anything about the outlying areas. She is tasking you with trying to find out where the company is currently so she can begin to move forward. One of her challenges will be to "manage" the owner and also the manager from Orlando who already wants a meeting.

2. A, B. Your report should be written to provide the owner of the company and the manager in Orlando with the information that they require, thus encouraging them to keep their hands off the project.

   The report should also stress the business goals of the company and how the functionality of the technology in place or available will help realize those goals.

3. C, D. The CEO has made it plain that she wants the company to be able to communicate and she wants her customers to be able to access the company online.

4. D. The Compaq server can be mentioned as a functional part of the technology goal. It can be used as the foundation for the corporate Internet or intranet.

5. D. She exhibits all the classic styles of an empowering manager.

Analyzing the Management Model

MICROSOFT EXAM OBJECTIVES COVERED IN THIS CHAPTER:

✓ **Analyze the business and security requirements of the end user.**

- Analyze the structure of the IT management. Considerations include type of administration, such as centralized or decentralized; funding model; outsourcing; decision-making process; and change-management process.

Now that we have some concept of the Digital Nervous System, and have considered the business plan, it is time to take a closer look at things that will affect making that a reality. First of all, we look at an overview of how the end user is going to be affected by the deployment. This overview will take a two-pronged approach: how the requirements of the end user will be affected from a business perspective, and how the requirements of the end user will be affected from a security perspective.

Once we finish with the end user, it is time to look *very* close to home, examining the structure of the information technology management team. Here we are looking at several different types of management, how management can make decisions, and how change is managed.

Evaluating the Business Requirements of the End User

Sometimes we love 'em and sometimes we hate 'em, but we always keep in mind that end users are our customers and we wouldn't have jobs without them. In this section, we are going to start looking at how these people do their jobs and what kinds of things need to be in place to make sure they can continue to do their jobs in the future, like after we roll out Windows 2000.

Microsoft Exam Objective

Analyze the business and security requirements of the end user.

- Analyze the structure of the IT management. Considerations include type of administration, such as centralized or decentralized; funding model; outsourcing; decision-making process; and change-management process.

One of the traits exhibited by the really good IT teams is the ability to make it look like they are not doing much. Think about it, and I think you will agree that if the IT team does its job right, disturbance to the customers will be minimal and they will think that nothing is being done. Meanwhile, you are working your tail off nights and weekends to make sure they are not disturbed. After all, that is why you make the big bucks, right?

What will the impact of the Windows 2000 rollout be on the end user? Like many answers in the technology field, it depends. It depends on how they do their jobs and what types of things they require. It can also depend on how you have laid out your Active Directory.

Types of End Users

End users can be grouped into five types, and their business requirements will vary by type. The types are the external authenticated user, Internet user, regular user, roaming user, and traveling user.

External Authenticated User

This user is someone who does not work for your company but requires access to your network. Examples would be the consultant who routinely works on your network and needs to access resources on your network from her office. It might also be a vendor or partner, as we saw in the last chapter, who needs to access information on orders that have already been placed or on orders that they would like to place. Let's take a look at an example.

The Govanus Design Scenario: The Lazy Consultant

As a consultant, I am a firm believer in keeping the nice leather chair that I have in my office warm as much as possible. If I am in my car or at someone else's office, I may not be as efficient as I am at my own office, where I know where everything is located. I can rationalize this several ways: The usual rationalization is that if I can do the task you require from my office, I am not charging you travel time, which saves you money. It rationalizes well and it accomplishes my primary business goal of being able to wear jeans and T-shirts to work every day.

My current consulting project is to lay out and plan the Windows 2000 migration for ACME Accounting and Bar Supplies. Now, I have been their consultant for years and have been able to solve many of their problems, but it usually involves a trip to the client site. When I design their network, I am going to design it so that I can get access to their system by creating a Virtual Private Network from my office to theirs on the fly. That way I have access to the resources of their network, and can do what I need to do and get out without ever leaving my chair. This is a win-win situation for both sides.

Internet User

What is the corporate policy toward Internet users? Are you the kind of a company that provides only an informational Web site? Or are you the kind of company that provides things like driver downloads or downloads of brochures of your company's products? These are also people that will be accessing your network. The trick when you analyze this user is to figure out exactly how much access they will need and only provide them that much!

Regular User

You know all about this type of user. You probably have to walk by dozens of them every day to get to your cube. These are the people who are going to show up for work in the morning, do what they have to do, and then head home. These are the types of people that will need access to printers, file services, application services, e-mail, maybe some database access and, of course, access to the Digital Nervous System. These users will also need to access the Internet, but that access should be controlled and monitored to make sure they are not stealing company time by frittering away time looking at CNN or the Cindy Crawford Web site or some other pursuit that is not in the immediate best interest of the company.

When it comes down to analyzing the regular users, you are going to have to look at how they are grouped and what access to resources they require. Also, be sure to keep in mind the challenges that come with teams formed across location boundaries.

Roaming User

The roaming user is the user who may provide a challenge. This is the person who travels from location to location within your company and needs access to the same resources no matter where he is. For example, this would be the company executive team that travels all over the world from company location to company location. In the example of the case study we used at the end of the first chapter, the company had offices in Minneapolis, Athens, and Orlando. In this case, an executive headquartered in Minneapolis would need to access her resources even if she was accessing the network from Athens.

Traveling User

The traveling user also provides unique challenges, especially in terms of security. A traveling user will need to access the enterprise network for a variety of reasons. There may be reports to fill out and file, there will be e-mail to access, and there may be specialized applications that need to be accessed. The problem is that you never know where the user is going to try to access the network. The only thing you can be sure of is that it will not be from within your corporate network. In this case, you will have to make decisions on how you are going to provide access. Are you going to create a portal through the Internet Web page to the corporate intranet? Are you going to make a separate Web server available, or are you going to use a dial-up remote access solution, or terminal server? Depending on the requirements placed on your network by the traveling user, any or all of these may be an option.

Impact of End User Security Requirements

Another of the buzzwords for Windows 2000 is *distributed security*. Distributed security is the coordination of many security features on a computer network to implement an overall security policy. It allows users to access appropriate computer systems, get the information they need, and use that information. It also involves making sure the users who access the information have the appropriate levels of access. Many may be able to read the data, but few may be able to alter it. By the same token, if the information is sensitive or private, only authorized individuals or groups are allowed to read the files. Protection and privacy of information transferred over public telephone networks, the Internet, or even segments of the private network, can also be a concern.

Table 3.1 lays out some of the security features available in Windows 2000.

TABLE 3.1 Security Features

Feature	Explanation
Security groups	Security groups gives you the flexibility to cluster users and other domain objects into groups for easy administration of access permissions. This means you can assign the same security permissions to large numbers of users in one operation, making you much more efficient. It also ensures that when you do apply permissions they are consistent across all members of group. In addition, assigning permissions to a group means access control on resources does not change and therefore it is easy to control and audit.
Security policy	In Windows 2000, the security policy defines the security behavior of the system. This is done using Group Policy objects (GPOs) in Active Directory. Through the appropriate use of GPOs, administrators can apply the exact same security profiles to various classes of computers with predictable results. For example, Windows 2000 comes with a default Group Policy object called the Default Domain Controllers Policy that controls the security behavior of domain controllers. Once this has been defined for one Domain Controller, all Domain Controllers can receive the same policy.

TABLE 3.1 Security Features *(continued)*

Feature	Explanation
Domain model	The domain model has changed somewhat in Windows 2000. A domain is still a grouping of network objects that share a common security directory database. A domain defines the security authority and forms a boundary of security that has the ability to deploy consistent internal policies and explicit security relationships to other domains.
Trust management	If you are familiar with trust relationships from Windows NT 4, the basic concept has not changed much. A trust is still a logical relationship defined between domains to allow pass-through authentication. In this way, trusting domain honors the logon authentications of a trusted domain. There is a term that may be new to you. The term *transitive trust* refers to authentication across a chain of several trust relationships. In Windows 2000, all trust relationships support authentication across domains by using Kerberos v5 protocol and *NTLM* authentication for backward compatibility.
Symmetric key encryption	Symmetric key encryption is also called secret key encryption. In symmetric key encryption same key is used to encrypt and decrypt the data. Its benefit is the speed with which it can process data.
Public key encryption	If symmetric key encryption is called secret key encryption, public key encryption can be called asymmetric. With public key encryption, instead of there being just one key, there are two keys. One of the keys is public, while one key is private. This is also referred to as the Public Key Infrastructure, or PKI.
Single sign-on	With single sign-on, users can authenticate to multiple servers and applications at the same time. While each of these other servers or applications may require authentication, the system takes care of the authentication process and all the events are transparent to the end user.

TABLE 3.1 Security Features *(continued)*

Feature	Explanation
Smart card logon	Smart card logon is an optional method of authentication provided with Windows 2000. Smart cards give a secure way to manage user authentication, interactive logon, code signing, and secure e-mail.
Remote access policies	Remote access policies can determine if a server will accept requests for remote access and then set the criteria for the access. Criteria can include during what hours of what days, using what protocols, and using what types of authentication.
Encrypting File System	In Windows 2000 the Encrypting File System lets a user encrypt certain files or folders stored on a local computer for added protection. EFS automatically decrypts the file for use and encrypts the file when it is saved. Security is insured because no one can read these files except the user who encrypted the file and an administrator who has an EFS recovery certificate.
IP Security (IPSec)	Windows 2000 also incorporates the Internet Protocol security (IPSecurity, or IPSec) for data protection of network traffic. IPSec is actually a suite of protocols that allows for secure, encrypted communications between two computers over an insecure public network, like the Internet. IPSec is one of the building blocks of a virtual private network.

Security combines some of the most advanced technologies with good business practices to ensure the safety of the information on a network. This does not come by chance. Good security involves a security team developing and working a network security plan. This plan should include sections like those shown in Table 3.2.

TABLE 3.2 Sections of a Security Plan

Plan Section	Description
Security risk section	The security risk section lays out the types of security hazards that can potentially affect your enterprise.
Security strategy section	The security strategy section lays out the general security strategies necessary to meet or exceed the potential for risk.
Public Key Infrastructure strategy section	The PKI strategy section should include your plans for deploying certification authorities to make use of Windows 2000's internal and external security features.
Security group descriptions section	This section includes descriptions of all the security groups and their relationship to one another. This section is also used to map GPOs to security groups.
Group Policy section	The group policy section includes how you have configured the security Group Policy settings. An example of this would be the network password policy.
Network logon and authentication strategies section	The network logon and authentication strategies section includes the authentication strategies put in place to control the logging on to the network and for using remote access and/or smart card to log on.
Information security strategies section	The information security strategies section includes data on how you plan to implement the information security solutions. This would include things like secure e-mail and secure Web communications.
Administrative policies section	The administrative policies section includes policies that apply to the delegation of administrative tasks. In addition these policies cover the monitoring of audit logs that will help administrators detect suspicious activity.

As you look over the table above, remember your network security plan can contain more levels than this. These are just suggested as a minimum.

To determine how the security plan will impact your end users, it is important to apply each of the eight procedures laid out in Table 3.2 to each of your end user business needs. An example of this would be the need of making the application for employment process available on the Internet. Table 3.3 shows the results.

TABLE 3.3 Results of the Employment Process

Plan Section	Description
Risk analysis section	Define the risk. In this case, potential employees will be entering the corporate Web site. Someone must decide if the user will be actually filling out an application online or if the user will be using the corporate network to facilitate e-mailing in a resume.
Security strategy section	Now we have an either/or type of decision. If the user is filling out an online application, there must be some type of secure channel provided. Perhaps you can provide the user with a login and password so the applicant can update the application or check on the application's status. That decision leads to others—for example, what rights or permissions will the user need to have to be able to save information to your server, access the information again, and edit it. There are also privacy issues involved, because no one else should be able to make changes to this resume. If the user is accessing the corporate mail servers to allow for e-mailing the resume, a Messaging Application Programming Interface (MAPI) must be provided on the Web page. In this case, the internal network and the person receiving the e-mail provide the security.

TABLE 3.3 Results of the Employment Process *(continued)*

Plan Section	Description
Public Key Infrastructure section	The PKI section is really devoted to internal network security. This section deals with what happens to the application or resume once it hits Human Resources.
Security group descriptions section	The security group descriptions section is really devoted to internal network security. This section deals with what happens to the application or resume once it hits Human Resources.
Group Policy section	The Group Policy section is really devoted to internal network security. This section deals with what happens to the application or resume once it hits Human Resources
Network logon and authentication strategies section	The network logon and authentication strategies section is designed for the scenario where the applications being used over the Internet actually authenticate users and establish security channels for confidential encrypted communications. This can be done using Internet Authentication Service (IAS), the Secure Socket Layer (SSL), and the Transport Layer Security (TLS) process. For the application that is e-mailed, you will have to provide the Secure/Multipurpose Internet Mail Extensions (S/MIME) server such as Exchange Server.

As you can see, planning to secure each transaction for each of the corporate business cases can be a rather daunting task. This is only half the process. What happens to the information when the clerk in Human Resources receives it? How is security impacted here?

We will be discussing each of these sections in more detail. We will start with risk assessment in Chapter 4, "Enterprise Risk Assessment." Since these will be broken down and discussed in depth later, what follows is a very limited discussion.

Design Scenario: Developing a Security Plan

This week, you have been called in to help a company develop a security plan. You start the day meeting with the CIO and her top assistant. They tell you that they have been reading all these horrible stories about companies getting all their information ripped off over the Internet, and since most of their business comes from the Internet, they are really concerned. When it is your turn to speak, you say that you have to figure out where the company stands, security-wise. You start by asking for information, and the first piece of information you ask for is the current security plan. The CIO glances nervously at the aide and asks if the company has one of those. The aide glances back and says he always thought that was a management document, and not one that he would be concerned with. What do you do next?

Suggest to the customer that a security plan would be a very good thing to have. Explain the different sections of the security plan, including *security risk*, security strategy, the Public Key Infrastructure strategy, security group descriptions, group policies, network logon and authentication strategies, information security strategy, and administrative policies.

Suggest also that you would be able to start the risk analysis section immediately, since that is apparently what they are asking for.

Analysis of IT Management Structure

Let's start our analysis of the information technology team at the top and ascertain how this model can be spread out over an Active Directory Services (ADS) tree. If it is designed well and can expand, it will work to provide the best and most efficient network management possible.

Microsoft Exam Objective

Analyze the business and security requirements of the end user.

- Analyze the structure of the IT management. Considerations include the type of administration, such as centralized or decentralized; funding model; outsourcing; decision-making process; and change-management process.

Evaluating the Current Network Management Model

If you have previously studied the Infrastructure design elective, or the ADS Tree design elective, you know the flexibility that comes from the decision to install a Windows 2000 network. In Windows NT, that flexibility was lacking. You had a domain, and Domain Administrators administered each domain. This could be one person, or a group of people, and they took care of one domain. If you wanted access to a different domain, you had to be given access to that domain. This was usually done by adding a global group to a local group. As you may have heard, things are different with Windows 2000.

Centralized or Decentralized Management?

Because of the flexibility of Windows 2000, there is flexibility in the management—much more so than in Windows NT. When you start looking at a large ADS tree, comprising several sites and dozens of domains, the thought of having to administer that can be daunting. Of course, the thought of administering a large NT network with dozens of domains all having different trust relationships was nothing to sneeze at either. NT administrators, ever creative, found some ways around the complexities of managing a multidomain model. First of all, it comes down to administrative management philosophy. When managing a network, there are two schools of thought.

The first school says, "The IT group are the network gods and goddesses; therefore we shall rule our dominion and be masters of all that we see." As you will see in the next section, this can be a very effective style of management. This is called *centralized management*. In a centrally managed system, a single person, or a small clustered group of people, manages every phase of the network operation. In the case of the multidomain model, one group of people would administer every domain.

The other school of thought starts out just like centralized management, but adds a little something to it. In this school, called *distributed management*, the thinking goes, "The IT group are the network gods and goddesses. We shall rule our dominion and be the masters of all that we can see...except, we recognize that this could get out of hand. We are the rulers, and therefore cannot be bothered with the routine, mundane tasks of everyday life. We shall delegate."

This network management delegation can take several forms. The first form is to delegate by responsibility. Look at Figure 3.1 to see what I mean.

FIGURE 3.1 Distributed management by responsibility

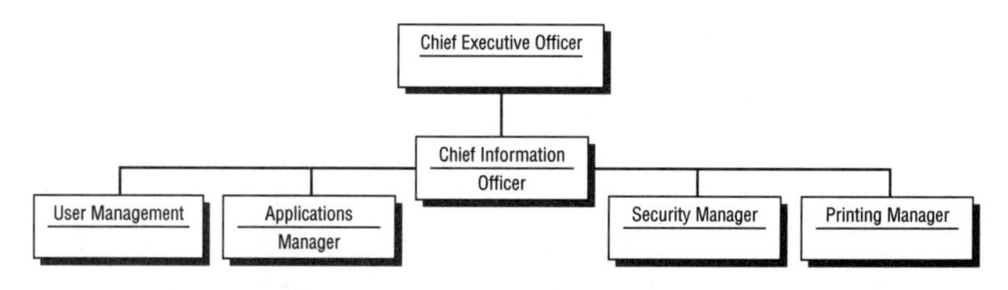

In this case, you have specialists managing different aspects of your network. You may have one person or a group of people in charge of configuring application support, or adding new users. You may also have a security specialist whose only responsibility it is to make sure the network is secure.

The other type of distributed management is distribution by location. Take a look at Figure 3.2 to see what I mean.

FIGURE 3.2 Distributed management by location

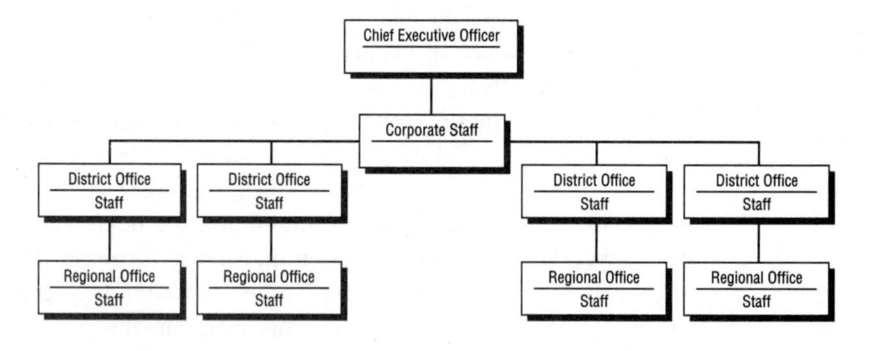

There are few networks that are set up as a true *centralized administration* model or a true distributed model. As a matter of fact, even within the *distributed administration* segment, there are fluctuations. We will refer to these as the *hybrids*. Figure 3.3 shows a kind of hybrid model.

FIGURE 3.3 Hybrid model of management

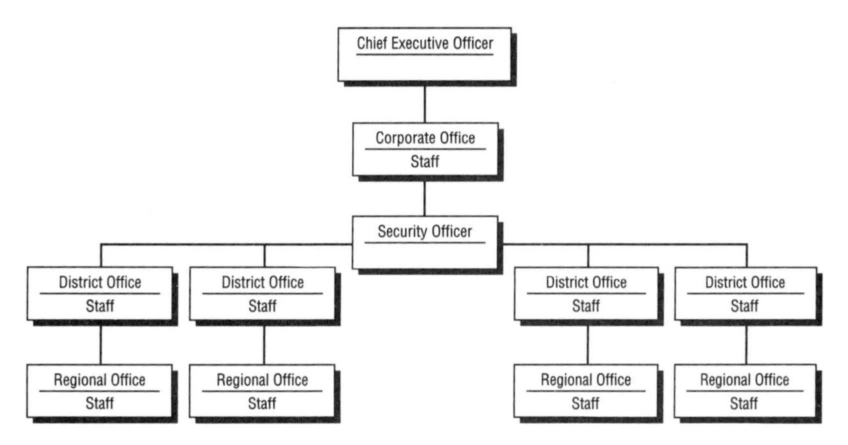

Strengths and Weaknesses of Each Type of Management Model

There are plusses and minuses to each type of management model. In addition, most of the mature network management teams were not designed, they just kind of happened.

Centralized Management

The three major strengths of centralized management are ease of communication, the ability to maintain and foster a clear vision, and a more streamlined decision-making process.

If we are just dealing with a small group of network managers all located in the same place, communication is much simpler because these people will be seeing each other every day. Not only will they each have the benefit of the normal written and verbal forms of communication, but they will be able to experience the nonverbal communications as well. You know the type I am talking about—kind of like, "Don't ask the boss for that new $100,000 file server today because she is really in a bad mood." Knowing some of the background or politics that goes into everyday life in the big company can also ease communication. For example, if you happen to be around when the big boss goes on a rampage about being fiscally conservative, and it is the night before your boss submits a new budget calling for a 25% increase, you may understand why your boss is just a little bit testy.

Because a small group of people manage the network, and the group members are all centrally located, it will be easier to maintain the vision of how the network should be managed. Not only will there be peer support in management decisions, but there will be peer pressure to contend with as well. Consider this real-world example of a successful small company: In the department made up of system engineers, the philosophy was to get the job done right, no matter what it took. This sometimes meant working long hours, well over the 15 or 20 minutes the salesperson had quoted. The job was finished and finished the right way. The company would be billed according to quote, and it would be up to the sales manager and the salesperson to work out the differences. The philosophy wasn't ever verbalized, not even when a new staff member came on board. It just was there, permeating the department structure. The system engineers took pride in what they did, and they made sure that other members of the team did also. That would have been difficult to convey over long distances.

Finally, there is the streamlined decision-making process. If there are few people involved, there is less discussion and a quicker resolution. If there are large numbers of people involved, each with a different agenda, the decision-making for major projects can be a long and drawn out process involving meeting, after meeting, after meeting. This is where your boss really earns his money!

The issues with centralized management feed off the advantages. If you have very few people involved, there is no outside point of view that can be helpful. In addition, the group may suffer from inbreeding. All the employees have their own specialty, and they are not exposed to other areas, so they stagnate. Finally, a problem arises in the fact that the corporate IT team, located in the ivory towers of the home office, cannot possibly know all the problems that are faced in the field. Some of these problems may require unique and individual solutions that the corporate IT team will be unaware of.

Distributed Management

Distributed management gives the local offices the attention they deserve. If there are unique solutions required, the people in the field are much more able to respond in an appropriate manner.

Distributed management also gives the end users in the field a feeling of being important. There is someone on site to take care of a problem. They don't have to call a faceless person, miles away, for an answer. There is someone right here to understand. Sometimes, visibility goes a long way toward acceptance.

Distributed management also promotes specialists, either in their own particular field, like security, or in their own office. Even though we all strive for standardization, we know that it is a goal and not usually a reality. There is always something just a little special about every network segment, and the only way to know that is to be there.

Distributed management does have its problems. Communication is much more difficult when spread out over distance. There can be times where there is not a clear feeling of what is expected. Working in IT carries with it a two-edged sword: On one side is the joy of working in IT because there is always some new challenge to face. The other side of the sword is that there are always more new challenges to face than time to face them. That usually makes effective communication difficult. You just may not feel you have the time to communicate exactly what you want. You simply expect the person in the other location to know.

Decisions take longer. There are more people involved; and they all have their own ideas about the ways things should be done, so it requires more time to reach a consensus. The problem with consensus is that most people did not get their own way. That means hard feelings and decrease in morale.

None of these problems are insurmountable. They just need to be recognized and efforts made to make sure they do not undermine the effectiveness of the IT team.

Hybrid Management

It seems that in most companies today the hybrid form of management is the one in place. It follows the military dictum that "all battle plans are fine until the first shot is fired." IT departments tend to be reorganized more often than any department but Sales. The department structure just kind of *evolves* from one day to the next, and pretty soon someone decides that they had better figure out who goes where and who does what within the organization.

You know how this works. Someone is hired as a network specialist (or whatever the fancy buzzword title is in your company for the network grunt) and this network specialist starts off doing the routine, mundane jobs that network specialists do all over the world. Now, we fast forward into the future. After six or eight months, the network specialist seems to have picked up more and more information on Exchange. She just seems to get it, and doesn't take nearly as long fixing problems and issues as other people do. Meanwhile, the corporate Exchange specialist gets a new position at a company down the block. When he leaves, the network specialist gets absorbed into the Exchange role without a title change or organizational move. Management loves it when stuff like that happens, mostly because there are no raises involved! Anyway, multiply this scenario by a dozen and pretty soon you have an organizational chart that has no basis in reality, and people cannot figure out who is supposed to give annual reviews to whom.

Hybrid management is probably the most common and the most effective. It provides specialists where they're needed, distributed administration based on location where it is needed, and is flexible enough to handle the change.

Analyzing the Funding Model

As you begin to plan the rollout of your new network, one thing will become clear very quickly. This sucker is gonna cost a bunch of money. First there is the analysis of every part of the network, from the desktop to the longest link between facilities. Everything will have to be examined, planned, tested, implemented, and managed. Each step along the way there will be hours designated to that project that will not be available to do other things. The question now facing the group is, how do we fund this?

Funding models come in various types and are as unique as the companies utilizing a Digital Nervous System. But there are some similarities in the basic decision-making process—for example, deciding whether to do the task in house or to outsource it.

Using In-House Resources

If you are a manager looking to fund a long-term project, using in-house resources can be very attractive. First of all, the cost has already been allocated somewhere in the budget. Now, granted, it may require some budgetary sleight of hand to move a person from the help desk or user administration to the new security rollout, but budgetary sleight of hand is the IT Manager's stock in trade, isn't it?

With in-house resources, the IT Manager already knows the strengths and weaknesses of each team member. They can budget for specialized training and usually pay for a week of training at about what a consultant will charge for two or three days of work.

The other obvious advantage is little or no corporate learning curve. People already in the organization understand how the organization works and probably have a good idea what button to push to get something accomplished. Outside folks need some time to learn those corporate idiosyncrasies.

The disadvantage of in-house resources may be that they have never done this particular task before. There may be some on-the-job training, and with any OJT, there are usually some first-time mistakes that can cost downtime or frustration. It is a cost that must be factored in. Also, people learning on the job don't work as quickly as people who have done this before. In each task, there are some tricks and shortcuts that can be picked up. Learning these tricks and shortcuts while several hundred people sit on their hands waiting for the network to be available again can be costly.

Outsourcing Resources

Hiring consultants is another way to fund the rollout. Just like in-house people, outside consultants have certain advantages. Some of these benefits are visible; others are well hidden, but there just the same.

First of all, when you hire a consultant, you don't usually have to train him. Usually his company has already taken care of that. Depending on the task you want the consultant to do, you can hire a specialist to come in and do one thing very well, and very quickly, and leave. Because this person has done this before, if something goes awry, he has a better understanding of the underlying processes and can usually solve the abnormality much faster.

There are also some benefits that may not be readily apparent. First of all, consultants are disposable. You hire them to do a job, they come in and do the job, and then they leave. There are no hard feelings, no lawsuits, no unemployment compensation claims, no prorated vacation/sick time, exit interviews or anything else. Just a goodbye, send me the check, and I will see you later. Another hidden advantage of a consultant is that they can get away with a lot more than a real employee. It comes with the consultant mystique and also the knowledge that the consultant cannot really be fired. Here is an example.

CJ is a consultant and an independent trainer. He goes into people's businesses for a short period of time, does a job, and leaves. If he is there consulting on security or consulting on another topic, he can tell people things they don't want to hear, and have them listen. It seems that, in many companies, experts can only come from outside the front door. CJ may be telling senior management something the IT staff has been saying for months, but the fact that they are paying CJ large amounts of money to tell them these things gives him instant credibility. He can also say things in ways that a real employee may not be able to get away with. Corporate politics being what they are, some senior managers don't want to listen to staff members. If a staff member were to suggest that a member of the management team needs to rethink a position or reexamine a position, it may be career limiting. Since CJ works for himself, and already holds the title of CEO, there is not much that someone from outside CJ's company can do to throw a roadblock in his career path.

The final thing that makes consultants so viable is that they are always easy to blame. There are always two things people can blame for a problem and get away with it. The first is the network and the second is a consultant. If you tell anyone the problem is a network gremlin, or the consultant did it, they will nod knowingly and the subject will be closed. There's a story about the consultant who did a job for a customer that was perfectly capable of carrying out the task without the consultant's help. Since this job involved airfare, rental car, per diem, hotels, and an hourly rate for a weekend full of work, the consultant thought it wise to point out that they really didn't need him. This was a simple task, and one their staff had the training and expertise to pull off without the consultant's presence. The head of the upgrade team was a longtime friend of this fellow, and he said in his slow Southern drawl, "Yep, but if you are here and we screw up, we can blame you and keep our jobs. The peace of mind is worth the money."

Getting Senior Management on Your Team

In every large project, it is necessary to have massive amounts of management support. Someone on the team has got to be able to look at the rollout and make those go/no go decisions. Someone has got to be able to go back to senior management and explain why more money, more time, or more resources are needed.

Having someone rather high up on the management team to be a part of the project always tends to grease the wheels a little bit. Let's face it, one of the laws of network computing states that the higher up the corporate ladder you go, the less you know about network computing. That usually doesn't stop this person from having really fine equipment. Now, if you go back to senior management and explain that you need more money because a newer, faster, better gizmo came out to make your job, the project, and life in general much better, there may be some frowns on the other side of the table. Those frowns may not be because you want more money; those frowns may be because senior management has no clue what you are talking about. If there is someone from the management team on your team, that person can go in and explain to them what it is you need and why, in management-speak, so they will understand. Trust us, it works.

Another reason it helps to have someone high up the corporate ladder on your side is that people hate change. Overworked, underpaid, and underappreciated middle managers hate change worse than most. When you are working on projects, some of these people may come up and try to get in your face about the change you are instituting. The conversation usually starts out something like, "I don't know what fool thought this idea up, but. . . ." The conversation usually ends rapidly and agreement is forthcoming if you point out that the "fool" is the superior of the person she reports to.

Understanding the Decision-Making Process

When it comes to security, there are some difficult decisions to be made. Most of these decisions are costly, either in real terms like the money necessary to institute the security plan, or in terms of potential loss to the organization.

When you begin to look at how decisions are made, sometimes it helps to have a guidepost. In 1996, there was an article in the *Journal of Information Technology* written by Pat Finnegan and Lynda O'Mahony on the problem solving/decision-making process. Finnegan is from University College Cork, in Ireland, and O'Mahony was with Apex Systems, Hinckley, Leicestershire, U.K.

In their model of group problem solving, they found that the process consisted of group activities supplemented by individual or small group assignments. The model is shown in Figure 3.4. Although the stages are put in some sequence, much of the work takes place in processes that are not nearly as rational. It must all be noted that it is the group processes that occur at each stage that are considered important rather than the nature of the stages themselves.

FIGURE 3.4 The group problem solving/decision-making process

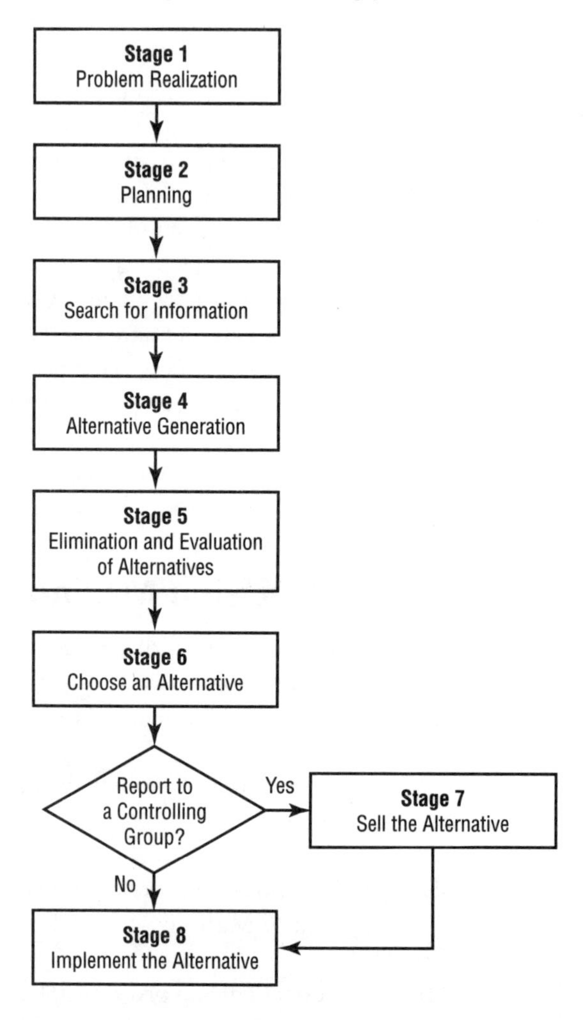

The decision-making process was more difficult for ad hoc groups than for permanent groups. With an ad hoc group, there was an additional stage added to the process, because the final choice of the alternatives was usually taken away from the group.

Stage 1: Problem Realization

The process begins here. Hopefully, the problem realization is that you may have security issues, and not that someone has hacked his way into the system. Meetings are held on a regular basis to set security policy, review the implementation, and audit the network to make sure changes have not occurred that were not planned for.

Stage 2: Planning

IT security planning in a large company is always a group effort. Whenever you work with a group dedicated to solving a security problem, the planning stage was found to be a formal part of the process. The group may be broken up into subgroups, like the group responsible for the delegation of group security policies, or the Internet group, or the firewall group. If the security group is broken down into subgroups, those subgroups need to be coordinated. Normally, the full decision-making body decides on the level in the group where the decision should be made and whether or not to delegate this to a permanent or ad hoc group. A *contract* is normally drawn up between the two groups, which outlines the group's objectives, budget, and time frame. The contract may or may not be formal. For example, the security group may tell the firewall subcommittee to investigate the latest firewall software and come up with a recommendation and cost estimate by the next meeting. As soon as the chairman of the firewall subcommittee nods his head, a contract has been established. Inter- and intra-group communication, coordination, collaboration, and cooperation patterns are also established at this stage.

Stage 3: Search for Information

The purpose of the search for information is to gain a deeper understanding of the security problem. The task of searching for information is normally distributed among group members. Depending on the size and scope of the network, the internal and external environment will be scanned. The information gathered is then brought back to the group. The group compares its problem task in the light of the new information, and as a result the group may sometimes reformulate its task. This is a crucial step in the group decision-making process as it is unlikely that the group will drastically reformulate the task after this.

Stage 4: Creation of Alternatives

This is the stage where the group operates as more than a collective of individuals. Although individuals often generate ideas, alternatives are very much the result of group interaction, which generally takes place in a face-to-face environment, or as the result of *electronic meetings*. Here is where the security committee starts to discuss how to solve the problem. For example, earlier in the chapter we mentioned the challenges posed by a roaming user. In this section, the alternatives may be discussed including locations of Global Catalog servers, terminal services, or remote access. Some of these alternatives may be standard, straightforward kinds of ideas. Others may be out-of-the-box ideas that may or may not prove to be useful. These could also be described as discussion generators.

Stage 5: Evaluation of Alternatives

The evaluation stage is very much of an iterative process. During this stage the group cycles between discussions and individual tasks. Not all alternatives are evaluated to the same extent: some are dismissed early on while others require greater study. Each alternative is compared with the others to determine how far each goes toward filling the gap between the desired and current situation. External advisors are often brought in at this stage and their activities have to be coordinated. "External advisors" usually equates to *contractors*. This may be the case where the group is discussing implementing new types of firewalls. You have narrowed the choice down to three, but since your group does not have any experience with the three choices, you bring in contractors to discuss the pros and cons of each type.

Stage 6: Choose an Alternative

The evaluation process and choices are closely tied. In this stage, the group makes choices on whether to accept or reject an alternative. In most of the groups studied, the final act of choice was made by consensus with considerable negotiation taking place.

Stage 7: Selling the Alternative

This stage is the tricky stage. Now, the technical side has to turn into sales folks. For a technical person, using the "because it is better" approach to the question of why we are doing this makes perfect sense. Unfortunately senior management doesn't really think that is a valid reason. They need to be sold, with things like risk analysis and return on investment. For the security group, this means they must be able to justify their choice and it is on the quality of this alternative that the work of the group will be judged. The senior management will either accept their recommended alternative, choose another, ask for clarification, or reject the alternative. Where clarification is sought, the security group, depending on the issues raised, will begin again at either Stage 3, 4, or 5.

Stage 8: Implement the Alternative

The implementation stage is the final step in the problem solving process because the means to solve the problem has been established and just has to be implemented. The same group can do this or, more often, it is given to an existing lower-level group.

Now that the decision has been made and the alternative decided upon, it has to be instituted. This requires change. When it comes to network security, that change will be wide ranging and will impact all levels of the organization chart. This change must be managed to have the buyoff from the people it will affect.

Understanding the Change-Management Process

All you have to do to cause chief information officers to get really nervous is to start talking about enterprise-wide changes. You know the kind, the ones that will affect every person that authenticates to your network, from the people at the desktop, to the trusted partners coming in over virtual private networks (VPNs), to the people coming in from the Internet. It is a simple fact of life that complex systems that have to work together require intelligent management.

The fundamental building blocks to managing change are standards. Standards have to be a policy. The bevy of hardware and software choices currently available requires a clear view of what is available and what is acceptable to this network. There are organizations like the Distributed Management Task Force (DMTF) that are helping to establish those standards for vendors that are building solutions. Having these standards in place should go a long way to helping companies manage change. One group of change-management experts, IT Service Management Forum, Ltd. (ITSMF, Ltd.) suggests creating a Change-Management Board with a chairperson and members from the following groups:

- Customers
- Developers
- IT service providers
- Problem solvers
- Others affected by changes

The project team has first reviewed changes submitted to the governing body. Once submitted, the governing body is responsible for prioritizing requests for consideration. It then decides which changes are to be implemented. So there are three main phases in the change-management process: planning and design, implementation, and management.

Planning and Design Phase

During the planning phase, the study showed that the senior management sponsors should undertake the following:

- Explain why the change is happening; discuss the business reasons for the change and the costs or risks of not changing.
- Define and communicate the project objectives and scope; tell employees what they can expect to happen and when.
- Help select the right people for the team and ensure adequate time availability of these resources; provide the needed budget for the design phase.
- Enlist the support of other senior managers and stakeholders in the project objectives and scope; provide a channel for key managers to provide direction at key decision points in the process.
- Help the project team select their approach and timeline, and resolve startup issues for the team.

The responsibilities shift somewhat during the design phase. They are:

- Reinforce why the change is happening; help employees understand the business reasons for the change.
- Listen and respond to feedback from the organization; actively seek input from all levels of management.
- Create a positive network of conversation about the project with peers and managers at all levels.
- Provide updates on the project's progress; let employees know what they can expect and when.
- Stay engaged and up-to-date on the project; attend key project meetings and training sessions.

- Keep other senior managers and stakeholders informed on project status and issues; help clear calendars for key decision-making meetings with these stakeholders.
- Enable employees to attend change-management training; personally attend as well.
- Remove obstacles encountered by the team.

Sounds good, but how does it work? Say for example that you are working with a large company that has never had full-time Internet access. Those employees that needed access were given a separate phone line and given a dial-up account. At some point, the IT Committee has determined that to meet the business goals of e-mail access, customer support, and information retrieval, access to the Internet is a good thing. So the change starts when the decision is made to add Internet access.

At this point the *change-management* planning takes over. The management representative can go to the other members of the senior management team and validate the decision. The manager can then go to the employees and tell them they are going to have Internet access and begin to set expectations about when the access will arrive and what it means to the individual. If there is training mandated about how to surf the Web or how to use a particular e-mail package, the manager helps arrange for that to happen. As is the case with most change, there will be a group of people who will not like the change. Having management support will facilitate these people being heard by those in charge. After the airing of the dissenting views, management can also reiterate the decision, giving it credence.

A long, long time ago, there was a consultant named Courtney. Now, Courtney was working as a consultant for a small network. The company was getting ready for expansion, and the network in place was kind of home grown. There was no security, because after all, each of the employees was like "family." When Courtney pointed out to the CEO and CFO that there were several temporary people that were only members of the family for one day, suddenly security became an issue. When she started to institute logon names with passwords, she had a member of middle management that thought it was the dumbest thing he had ever heard of, and he proceeded to tell Courtney that. Loudly. With a finger in her face. Courtney was not pleased. The manager finally put his foot in it when he said something on the order of, "I don't know what damn fool thought this up. . . ." At that point, Courtney calmly picked up the phone and started dialing. When the manager asked Courtney who she was calling, she gave the CEO's name. Courtney's antagonist asked her why she was calling Mahogany Row, and she told him that since he wanted to question the damn fool that made the decision, she was going to get him on the phone right away. The conversation ended as quickly as it had begun and the middle manager became a big supporter of passwords. That illustrates a very valuable consulting lesson. To paraphrase an American president, "Speak softly and carry a large management stick."

Why in the World Do All This Planning?

One of the first implementations of Windows 2000 was at Barnesandnoble.com. As a matter of fact, the rollout occurred months before the actual release of the product. An article in *Information Week* magazine of January 24, 2000, had the following to say about the conversion: "The company converted to Windows 2000 Release Candidate 3 during a weekend in November. Barnesandnoble.com's six-month testing period—which covered Windows 2000's use of the processors, failover in cluster configurations, scalability, and performance—proved helpful in the deployment. It took less than two days to make the switch with no hiccups." Later in the article it was noted that B&N benefited from being a member of Microsoft's early-adopter program.

Laura DiDio, a senior analyst with Giga Information Group, was quoted as pointing out, "I think some organizations will have a rough ride for a combination of reasons: bugs, unfamiliarity with the new operating system, improper trainers, and the complexity of Windows 2000."

Implementation Phase

As the project moves into the stage where it is actually impacting people's lives, the management team can assist in the project by doing the following:

- Reinforcing why the change is happening; explaining the business reasons and the priority for the business.
- Sharing the change with all levels in the organization.

- Providing answers to "What does this change mean to me?" and "What is expected of me?"
- Listening to resistance and responding to feedback from the organization.
- Creating a positive network of conversation about the project with peers and project stakeholders.
- Actively participating in implementation planning; staying involved with the project; monitoring progress and removing obstacles.
- Ensuring that adequate resources are available or adjusting the implementation plan to fit available resources.
- Engaging middle managers in transition planning; defining their role for the transition and setting clear expectations.
- Keeping other senior managers and stakeholders informed on project status and issues.
- Recognizing behavior and results that are consistent with the change and rewarding role models.
- Expecting results and measuring performance toward results.

Management Phase

As part of the management phase, the management team member would be in charge of communication, letting people both above and below know how the project affected the company in a positive way.

In addition, the manager would also be responsible for making sure all the auditing and checking promised in the design phase was being carried out.

Design Scenario: Enter the Consultant

Once again, your consulting company has been contacted to do a job for a large local firm. As you enter the front door, you are provided a visitor's pass and an escort to the conference room. While passing through the hall, you notice an old friend of yours. You haven't seen Bonnie since she left your company to go to work for a competitor. A smile and a wave, and you are off to the conference.

When you enter the conference room, you meet the head of IT, and the system administrators from five of the company's six locations. The sixth administrator is out sick; otherwise she would have been in the meeting.

The project is laid out, and the IT director keeps saying things like, "Senior management has instructed us to do this." Or, "The CEO wants it done this way." He also said, "...while you are working with my staff."

Soon the talk turns to things like deliverables, and when they will be provided. Soon after, the meeting is over and you leave knowing much more about the company than what the CIO has told you. What kinds of things did you learn?

First of all the company uses distributed management. After all, there are the CIO and system administrators from each of six locations. Secondly, the company is happy to use both in-house resources as well as outsourcing projects that are unique in nature and beyond the skill set of the current staff. The company has already started the planning process, because they have recognized the problem and are taking steps to remedy the issue. They apparently have some level of sign-off from the CEO and it sounds like the CIO is in touch enough with senior management to keep them apprised of the situation. The project is either closing in on the end of the planning stage or moving on into the design stage.

To think you gathered all that information from just listening to what was being said. Scary, isn't it? Who knows, next they may even want you to start reading the manuals! Nah!

As you read through the early chapters in this book, you are probably asking yourself how in the world this material is going to apply to the test. For example, are they really going to ask me a question about the different types of end users, or the different phases of the change design process? The answer, quite simply, is "no." Then why cover it? The reason is simple, the test writers expect you to know this information so that you can apply it to other questions. The Microsoft testing model for the architecture exams is based on very long, very detailed, very drawn out scenarios. Each test is based on three or four of these scenarios and you are supposed to read them and make decisions based on the information given. Some of the information may be design related. Some of the information may be protocol or security policy related. If you don't recognize the unique needs of the remote user, you may not be able to fully understand the question. So, don't despair, we are laying the foundation.

Summary

In this chapter, we took a close look at the structure of the IT management team. In a way, we dissected it to look at how it made and carried out its decisions. In addition we looked at the way those decisions were funded. The role of outsourcing was discussed from a variety of angles and we looked at what has to happen to make sure that people will accept any change that is decided on.

Once we finished taking apart the IT team, we went to the desktop and began to look at the end user. How could we determine the type of business and security requirements that the end users need to give them access to the information they need to do their jobs. What we came up with through all this was that the planning process was far from over. As a matter of fact, now we have started putting things on project management charts and started to assign timelines to some of the tasks. This is starting to sound serious.

In the next chapter, we will begin to get more granular and take an in-depth look at the risk analysis process.

Key Terms

Before you take the exam, be certain you are familiar with the following terms:

centralized administration

change-management

distributed administration

distributed security

Encrypting File System

Group Policy

IP Security (IPSec)

NTLM

public key encryption

security group

security risk

smart card logon

symmetric key encryption

transitive trust

Review Questions

1. In a multiple domain Windows NT environment, it was possible to have one-way trust relationships. In Windows 2000, by default, all trust relationships within a forest are termed:

   A. One-way

   B. Two-way

   C. Either way or two-way

   D. Transitive

2. Public key encryption depends on:

   A. Two keys, one public and one private

   B. Two keys, both public

   C. Two keys, both private

   D. One private key that is sent with the message

3. Smart card logon requires:

   A. Nothing, it is included with Windows 2000

   B. The use of third party solutions

   C. An encrypted password

4. IPSec is which of the below:

   A. The next generation of the Internet Protocol, otherwise referred to as IP Version 6

   B. Used exclusively on proxy servers and Web servers

   C. A suite of protocols that will allow for secure communications across an insecure network like the Internet

   D. Still in development

5. Why is it necessary to have a Windows 2000 pilot before the rollout and implementation of a Windows 2000 enterprise network?

   A. It's not

   B. To get the bugs out of the rollout process

   C. To test security before it is implemented

   D. To make sure the last remaining bugs are out of the production release

6. Symmetrical encryption is another name for:

   A. Kerberos 5

   B. Secret key encryption

   C. PKI

   D. IPSec

7. When using EFS, an encrypted file can only opened by which of the following:

   A. A system administrator

   B. A system administrator with a recovery certificate

   C. Anyone who has permissions to the directory the file is in

   D. Anyone who has been given an explicit permission assignment to that file

   E. The user who encrypted the file

8. Security Policies can be assigned to:

   A. Users

   B. Groups

   C. Systems

   D. Trees

   E. Sites

9. Somewhere on your network, there is a folder that contains all the information on the ultra-top-secret U200-X project. As you design your security, you spend extra time planning the permissions and access restrictions to this folder. You also make sure you know who may be attacking this folder and how they may try and get in. This is an example of:

   A. Proper planning

   B. Job protection

   C. Public Key Infrastructure design

   D. Kerberos 5 integration

   E. Risk analysis

10. Your company has an enterprise network that serves users in 10 different locations. The chief information officer and the security administrators are housed at the corporate office. Each of the 10 locations has a staff of at least three administrators to handle the day-to-day operations of the local site. The infrastructure team is located in Chicago, while the ADS team is located in Michigan. This is an example of:

    A. Centralized administration

    B. Distributed administration based on location

    C. Distributed administration based on specialty

    D. A hybrid approach to distributed administration

Answers to Review Questions

1. D. In Windows 2000 all trust relationships are transitive. This means that a user logging on to one domain will have the ability to access resources in the other domains.

2. A. With public key encryption, there are two keys; one is privately held and the other is publicly held.

3. B. While support for smart card logon is included with Windows 2000, third-party vendors provide the actual hardware.

4. C. IPSec is a suite of protocols that allows for secure communications across an insecure network like the Internet. IPSec allows for things like Virtual Private Networks (VPNs).

5. B, C. Pilots are an important part of any upgrade or migration project. They help the rollout team find the problems before trying to put the new operating system or security plan in place for the rest of the company. It helps to make sure the transition is as painless as possible.

6. B. Symmetrical encryption is another name for secret key encryption.

7. B, E. When a file has been encrypted, the person who has done the encryption has the key, so obviously they can decrypt the file. To protect against data loss when a user leaves the company, there is a recovery certificate that will allow the designated account to decrypt the file.

8. C. Security Policies are designed to be used with systems, not individual users, groups, trees, or sites.

9. E. Risk analysis is the procedure of determining the potential risk to information or resources. Using this information to design the security package helps to ensure protection.

10. D. This is an example of a hybrid approach to distributed administration.

The Multinational Startup

You should give yourself 10 minutes to review this case study, diagram as needed, and complete the questions for this testlet.

Background

Your consulting firm has been hired to assist in the Windows 2000 migration and integration for a company based in Minneapolis, Minnesota. Until the start of this year, the company had 1,000 employees, all based throughout the Twin Cities of Minneapolis and St. Paul. Just before the end of the year, the owner of your company purchased two companies of roughly the same size that will need to be connected to the enterprise network. The total number of users when the project is completed is estimated at 3,500. In addition, each of these companies comes with various strategic partners that will need to access the information on your enterprise network. The companies that have been acquired are located in Athens, Greece, and Orlando, Florida. At this point, the buyouts are complete and some minor changes to the infrastructure have been finalized. The time has come to start looking at security.

Current System

Minneapolis Located on the shores of beautiful Lake Calhoun, the company occupies a sprawling campus that includes four floors in a six-story building. When the company started out five years ago, it had just part of one of the floors and about 100 people. Since that time the company has grown and any time a tenant has moved out of the building, the company has taken over the office space. This grow-as-you-go philosophy has left members of the same departments scattered throughout the building.

All of the floors are connected to the Windows NT network. While the infrastructure is chaotic, it is getting better. The decision has been made to move to Windows 2000. Active Directory Services will be used extensively. So far that is as far as the discussions have gone. The network continues to grow quickly. While in many cases you are still throwing hardware at the problem, you are at least throwing corporate standard hardware and documenting its existence. You have verified the Exchange e-mail system and made sure all users were utilizing it. Several groups are using different database applications to perform different tasks, but the development of these applications has been outsourced and no one is exactly sure how they work. In the discussions, you do hear frequent mention of the SQL Server servers, so you know those are around somewhere.

Users are running a mish-mash of computing gear, relative to the kind of vendor the purchasing people could obtain equipment from at the time. You have a 40% laptop/60% desktop mix. You have a small enterprise fax software program running on a Windows 95 computer that allows about 10 marketing people to send faxes out from their desktops. The majority of your users are basic users—not power-user types. The other users vary in skill level from needing to know how to turn the computer on to the tech weenie wannabees on the fourth floor. You have managed to stem the tide of shareware with threats of firing.

Since you have come into the picture, the Internet connectivity has been upgraded to a T1 status. Everyone in the company has access to the Internet and has an Internet mail address. Communication between offices is currently being done using just e-mail, snail mail, and the phone.

Orlando The Orlando office actually has more people working in it than there are in Minneapolis. It is located in northern Orlando, away from Disney and the tourists. Many of the services in Minneapolis are mirrored in Orlando—things like marketing, accounting, and human resources. The confusion from the last chapter has abated somewhat, but it is still lurking just under the surface. The site is all on NT 4, with a variety of applications; some of the applications are compatible with the Minneapolis corporate standards and some aren't. The Orlando office does have a fractional T1 connection to the Internet. The office is using Lotus Notes as their e-mail package. As you can tell, not much has been done here. The users have all had their Internet e-mail addresses changed to the corporate DNS name, and there is a connector in place between Lotus Notes and Exchange, so people can communicate and share appointments and things. The office has been notified that Windows 2000 is coming and by this time next year Lotus Notes will be a thing of the past. This decision was sent out by memo without any input from the Orlando office. Rumor has it they weren't smiling and morale took a hit.

Athens If there have been major strides made, they have been made in the Athens office. First of all, people in Minneapolis now know something about it! To refresh you, Athens is the location of the company that was purchased because it had developed a great add-on product to your product. When senior management discovered that 80% of the customers from the Minneapolis office also owned the product developed by the Athens subsidiary, the boss ran out and bought the company. This discovery took senior management four years. The sales department knew about it almost from the start of the company. The sales department couldn't get the information to management. The Athens office has about 1,300 users, most of which are salespeople, marketing types, and support staff. The manufacturing plant is located on the island of Rhodes, and due to local customs, manufacturing occurs only between March and October. The rest of the time, the plant is closed. The office has several Windows NT 3.51 servers running SP3. It is predominantly used for file and print sharing. There is an Internet connection and a Linux box that is providing for only POP3 e-mail.

The decision has been made to upgrade the 3.51 servers directly into Windows 2000. In addition, the people in Athens know that Exchange is coming. Due to the increase in communication between the United States and Greece, the Athenians are getting more used to e-mail. However, since the mail being sent is still SMTP/MIME, there is concern that plain text is flying over the Internet.

Because this has been a stand-alone company, all of the normal accounting, purchasing, and human resources functions are there. It has been agreed that management will remain with the company. Communication between sites remains by e-mail, snail mail, and phone.

Problem Statement

Now that the integration of the company is at least moving along, security is becoming more and more of a concern. The senior management has tasked you with beginning the security planning process. You must provide secure connections between sites and secure access to information and resources. Secure access is needed to accounting, personnel, manufacturing, and development information. You also need to establish one e-mail standard at all sites. You must provide a plan for change-management to ensure that the memo-to-Orlando debacle will not occur again. And finally, you need to provide a security plan that will make sense as the company continues to merge.

Envisioned System

Overview Now that it is becoming obvious that these three locations can in fact work together and communicate, the CEO wants to make sure that it is done securely. She has read about this Digital Nervous System, and she wants one. She has also read about other companies that have been hacked, and she wants to make sure that it doesn't happen to this company. Of course, like most CEOs, she is not really sure what a hack is, but she knows she is against it.

CEO "The change in the company over the last several weeks has been remarkable. We are finally communicating! Now we have to get cracking on the second part of the plan, to make sure the communications are secure. There has to be a relatively easy way to create a secure network where information can be made available to anyone in the organization instantly. Is that too much to ask? One thing, though: I want to make sure we do this in a sensible, efficient manner. Let's not run off willy-nilly trying to get this done."

Security

Overview Because the product you develop is constantly undergoing research and development, and the industry being what it is, security must be maintained at a very high level. As you can see from the statements made by the CEO, it is taking a higher priority.

CFO "With the merger going on and with all the systems with highly sensitive data on them, it's paramount that security is maintained at an extremely high level. I cannot emphasize this enough. On the other hand, we have to be careful not to step on any toes, and also to make sure that the security we do install is not too intrusive into people's lives. Our senior management has heard about all those systems where people have to remember dozens of passwords and we certainly don't want anything like that here."

Availability

Because the network will span several different time zones, the availability of the network must be 24x7x365.

Maintainability

Overview There are two problems here. First of all, you will be dealing with an international company, meaning you will not be able to utilize the same vendor for maintenance. Secondly, information will have to be available from all levels of the organization, all day every day. The information must be up-to-date in real time. Because this could possibly tell your competition exactly what you are doing and for whom, the information must be secure.

CEO "These new products we're developing are *so* revolutionary and will have such an impact, that it's important for us to make sure everyone has the same information at the same time."

Athens Operations Manager "My understanding is that our product will now be bundled with the products developed in Minneapolis. That means we have to know how many to produce. Given the limitations of Rhodes manufacturing cycle, there may have to be some offloading of responsibilities to other areas of the company."

Performance

Overview The CEO is thrilled to death with the new connection to the Internet. Her stock quotes just come flying into her machine. The increased use of e-mail has been a godsend. Just yesterday, the CEO received several new pictures of her grandchildren, so she is truly thrilled.

Orlando Branch Manager "It is *wonderful* now that we can communicate with anyone in this company. Some of the people in the home office are still a little shaky using e-mail, but at least they have it. It is a great improvement."

Funding

Overview While you have not been given *carte blanche* by the CEO, she has made it clear that money isn't necessarily an issue, within reason of course. The problems need to be solved so that the company can safely continue to manufacture its products in the most efficient manner possible.

CEO & CFO "Look, we don't think that we need the Rolls Royce of installations, *but* we can tell you that everything is riding on our ability to ship our combined products in a timely manner, and the network we're asking you to build is going to be a big part of that. We think the company will continue to grow, though not as rapidly as in the last several months. So, that being said, give us a network that makes sense."

Questions

1. What is the current business problem?

A. The e-mail systems are not the same.

B. The company's software versions are not consistent.

C. Management is suddenly concerned with security.

D. You shouldn't have that much confusion in any one company.

2. What solution(s) should you implement to solve the customer's business problem?

A. Ensure that each location has a secure connection to the Internet.

B. Set up secure wide area connections between all of the sites. Wide area bandwidth should be adjusted according to the size of the site and its needs.

C. Up-version all servers to Windows 2000.

D. Begin the planning process to provide a secure network.

E. Set up some form of IIS Server in a central location for the sharing of information.

F. Assure that all users are on a uniform O/S desktop—that service pack and service release levels are current.

G. Establish a plan to up-version the existing Exchange servers to Exchange 2000 by Q1 of next year.

3. As you begin the planning process, what steps should you immediately take?

   A. Begin forming a study committee, including a member of senior management.

   B. Gather in all the network documentation that has been located to this time.

   C. Begin establishing a high-level overview of the needs of the end users; i.e. how many are there in each location, what are their unique needs as a group, how can they be divided by groups.

   D. Talk with ADS design committee to find out how the network is being integrated into Active Directory Services.

   E. Talk with the infrastructure group to determine how the infrastructure will be affected by the migration to Windows 2000.

   F. All of the above.

4. Which of the following best describes the Windows 2000 security group feature?

   A. Users can authenticate to multiple servers and applications at the same time.

   B. A suite of protocols that allows secure encrypted communication between two computers over an insecure network.

   C. Allows you to organize users and other domain objects into groups for easy administration of access permissions.

   D. Optional method of authentication that involves an interactive logon, code signing, and secure e-mail.

   E. A logical relationship established between domains to allow pass-through authentication.

5. Which best describes the Windows 2000 security policy feature?

   A. There are two keys. One of the keys is public and the other key is private. This technology opens up numerous security strategies and is the basis for several Windows 2000 security features.

   B. Called secret key encryption.

   C. A logical relationship established between domains to allow pass-through authentication.

   D. Can be used to determine what hours of the day a server can be accessed, what protocols can be used, and what types of authentications are required.

   E. Defines the security behavior of the system. Administrators can use this to centrally apply explicit security to various classes of computers in the enterprise.

6. Which best describes the Windows 2000 domain model feature?

   A. Optional method of authentication that involves an interactive logon, code signing, and secure e-mail.

   B. A collection of network objects that share a common directory database with respect to security.

   C. Users can authenticate to multiple servers and applications at the same time.

   D. Lets a user encrypt designated files or folders on a local computer for added protection of data stored locally.

   E. A logical relationship established between domains to allow pass-through authentication.

7. Which choice best describes the Windows 2000 trust management feature?

   A. A logical relationship established between domains to allow pass-through authentication.

   B. Allows you to organize users and other domain objects into groups for easy administration of access permissions.

   C. Called secret key encryption.

   D. Users can authenticate to multiple servers and applications at the same time.

   E. Lets a user encrypt designated files or folders on a local computer for added protection of data stored locally.

8. Which best describes the Windows 2000 public key encryption feature?

   A. Defines the security behavior of the system. Administrators can use this to centrally apply explicit security profiles to various classes of computers in the enterprise.

   B. There are two keys. One of the keys is public and the other key is private. This technology opens up numerous security strategies and is the basis for several Windows 2000 security features.

   C. A suite of protocols that allows secure encrypted communication between two computers over an insecure network.

   D. Called secret key encryption.

   E. A logical relationship established between domains to allow pass-through authentication.

9. Which best describes Windows 2000 remote access policies?

   A. A suite of protocols that allows secure encrypted communication between two computers over an insecure network.

   B. Users can authenticate to multiple servers and applications at the same time.

   C. A logical relationship established between domains to allow pass-through authentication.

   D. Can be used to determine what hours of the day a server can be accessed, what protocols can be used, and what types of authentications are required.

   E. Called secret key encryption.

Answers

1. C. At this stage of the process, management has suddenly discovered security and wants to make sure that everything in the network is as it should be. Notice, however, that there are comments and statements made to show that this change should be planned and managed, not just instituted.

2. D. You would start with D, setting up the planning process for security. You should begin by enlisting either the CEO or the CFO to be on the committee, since they both feel so strongly about the topic. It will also help "sell" your alternatives to senior management when the time comes.

3. F. In this case, it is time to do some serious planning, and do it in a hurry. You are going to need to get input from a variety of sources, including the group tasked with designing the ADS and the group tasked with laying out the infrastructure. Grab it all and grab it quick.

4. C. A security group allows you to organize users and other domain objects into groups for easy administration of access permissions.

5. E. A security policy defines the security behavior of the system. Administrators can use this to centrally apply explicit security to various classes of computers in the enterprise.

6. B. In Windows 2000, the domain model is a collection of network objects that share a common directory database with respect to security.

7. A. Trust management is a logical relationship established between domains to allow pass-through authentication.

8. B. With public key encryption there are two keys. One of the keys is public and the other key is private. This technology opens up numerous security strategies and is the basis for several Windows 2000 security features.

9. D. Remote access policies can be used to determine what hours of the day a server can be accessed, what protocols can be used, and what types of authentications are required.

Enterprise Risk Assessment

MICROSOFT EXAM OBJECTIVES COVERED IN THIS CHAPTER:

- ✓ **Analyze the current physical model and information security model.**
  - Analyze internal and external security risks.
- ✓ **Analyze factors that influence company strategy.**
  - Identify the company's tolerance for risk.

Isn't this what security is all about? Trying to figure out who will be trying to get into your network and stopping them before they get access to sensitive data? Of course, you also have to consider *internal security risks* as well as *external security risks*. After all, how do you know that every one of your 5,000+ employees is a happy camper and not just out to steal the company secrets?

In this chapter we are going to address questions like, "What is at risk?" and, "What are the potential threats to the network?" We will look at how to determine internal security of applications and information and then we will look outside the company. We need to know how to protect against people trying to get in, and also, how to let people into the network who are supposed to be in the network.

Where Are the Hackers?

Before you can protect against or even identify risk, you have to analyze where your network is vulnerable.

Take a look at Figure 4.1. This graph represents companies that have detected unauthorized use over a 12-month period. The largest abuse was "Insider Abuse of Net Access." That checked in at 97% of the companies surveyed. I will just bet that if you sit and ponder for a while, you will be able to figure out what types of sites accounted for that abuse. Yep, seems there are lots of folks out there who like to look at pictures of people with their clothes off. Now, if you have really sharp eyes, you will notice that the percentages add up to more than 100%. That is very much okay, because companies can report more than one type of intrusion.

FIGURE 4.1 Percentage of companies reporting various unauthorized computer uses

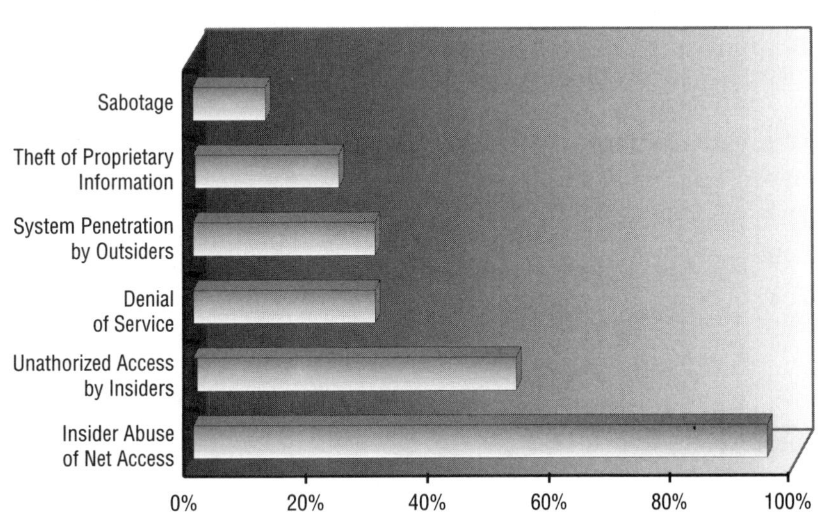

While the statistics do not show anything you probably haven't already figured out, it is interesting to note that the 1999 CSI/FBI Computer Crime and Security Survey showed that the largest dollar amount of loss came from the loss of proprietary information. "Proprietary information" sounds rather research-and-development-ish, doesn't it? I mean, you can understand how a company would be harmed and suffer a huge monetary loss if the new X-15 super-duper top-secret development notes all went to their major competitor. But that is not even the beginning of losing proprietary information.

Suppose your company was a marketing company. Your company had all sorts of studies done to show how your client's products stacked up against the competition. That would be proprietary information. If that information was leaked or if it was obtained by the competition, that would be devastating. What would happen to a company if a group of their top salespeople got together and decided to form their own company? Not a problem, unless they took the corporate customer list and lead list with them. The number of examples can go on and on.

Physical security is one of the puzzle pieces necessary for information security. The physical security model is what protects your hardware or servers from attack. The information security model is what protects the information stored on those servers from attack. For example, from a security point of view, physical security would be putting the server in a locked room and then only giving certain members of the IT staff access to that room. Applying the appropriate rights and permissions to folders and files would be information security.

Evaluating the Physical Security Model

In previous chapters, it has been mentioned several times that the process of analyzing your network would be greatly enhanced with a network map showing where things are and how they are attached to the outside world. Once you get the network map, the things to look at include the placement and use of firewalls and the ways that domains are connected.

One of the considerations of a Windows 2000 network is the placement and use of domains. The days of the Windows NT Resource Domain are over, and these domains should be merged into your Active Directory tree. Since the handling of domains is covered so well in *MCSE: Directory Services Design Study Guide* (Sybex, 2000), by Bob King and Gary Govanus, I will not cover that topic as part of the physical structure.

Even if you are new to the field of network architecture and security, you have probably heard terms like *firewall* and *demilitarized zone* bandied about. If you have never worked with a firewall, now may be the time to explore them.

Start by closely examining Figure 4.2.

FIGURE 4.2 Basic (bastion host) firewall

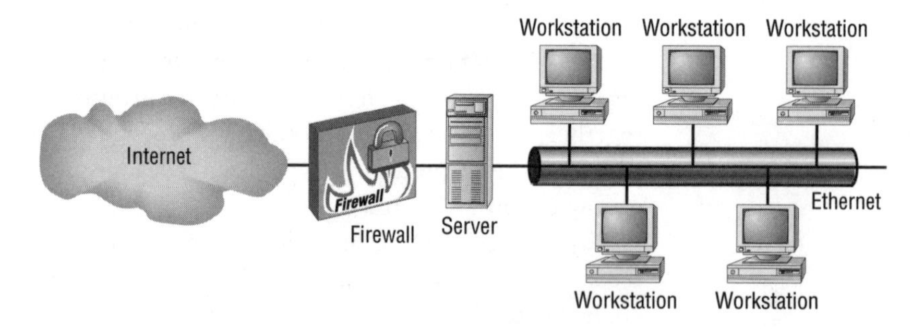

This is a firewall setup at the most basic. You have a corporate network, large or small, connected to the Internet. In this case, a firewall separates the corporate network from the Internet. A firewall is simply a boundary between the Internet and the internal network.

Firewall Basics

How is the boundary constructed and what actually does it do? If you think of a firewall that is used in construction of an apartment building, it is a fireproof divider between two units. If a fire starts in your neighbor's apartment, yours is protected. If your home is the unlucky one to have the fire, your neighbor's is protected. A network firewall monitors traffic coming into the network from the outside, and can also be used to monitor traffic leaving the enterprise and going to the Internet. So all traffic that moves between the internal network and the external network has to pass through the firewall for it to be viable.

How can the firewall make the decision to let the traffic through? That is up to the system administrator to configure. When a firewall looks at a packet coming from or going to the network, the firewall software makes a decision to deny the packet or to allow the packet to go through. The administrator should configure the firewall so that only authorized traffic can pass, and everything else is denied.

This is another of those topics we will cover in more depth during the design and implementation phases of the book. For the analysis section, it is just important that you know that you need firewalls and that you understand the basics of how they operate.

The firewall must be basically immune from penetration. That is a difficult process and certainly an ongoing process. The people who are trying to break in know about firewalls too, and they know the strengths and weaknesses of firewalls and how to exploit them. You have to stay one step ahead of the game.

Firewall Configurations

There are really only two basic kinds of firewall configuration. Microsoft refers to these configurations as the *bastion host* model and the *screened subnet* model. The *bastion host* model is shown in Figure 4.2. It is usually used for smaller networks and its only purpose is to protect the internal network from the external network.

The *screened subnet model* (otherwise referred to as the demilitarized zone or DMZ model) is much more common.

If you have never heard of the screened subnet model, don't feel bad. The way it was explained to me was that because Microsoft Official Courseware is localized (meaning it is translated for countries all over the world), the courseware developers have to be careful to use terms that translate easily. Screened subnet translates easily. DMZ does not, and is not politically correct in several areas of the world. Throughout this book, there will be a screened subnet rather than a DMZ.

Bastion Host

Figure 4.2 is a perfect example of the bastion host approach. There is a single firewall protecting the network. All traffic coming in or going out travels through the firewall. A bastion host approach is perfect for the small business that requires access to the Internet, but may not need much of Internet presence—perhaps just a Web access e-mail server or a POP3 mail server.

Screened Subnets

A screened subnet places all Internet-accessible resources in a separate network segment that can be controlled from the firewall. All traffic, in or out, is screened by administrator-defined rules. In addition, rules are defined for the interaction between all network segments.

Figure 4.3 can be referred to as a *three-pronged screened subnet.* Notice there is only one firewall required. In essence, this could be one host with three network cards attached to three different network segments.

FIGURE 4.3 Three-pronged screened subnet

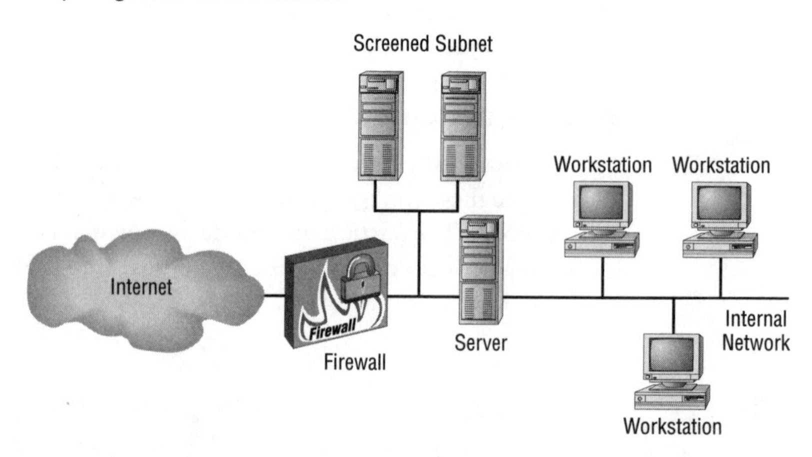

The other type of screened subnet would be referred to as the *mid-ground screened subnet*. In this type, shown in Figure 4.4, there are two different firewalls between the Internet and the internal network. The hosts that serve the Internet, like the corporate Web servers or e-mail servers, are definitely in a no-man's-land. This approach is more costly, but can be more secure.

FIGURE 4.4 Mid-ground screened subnet firewall deployment

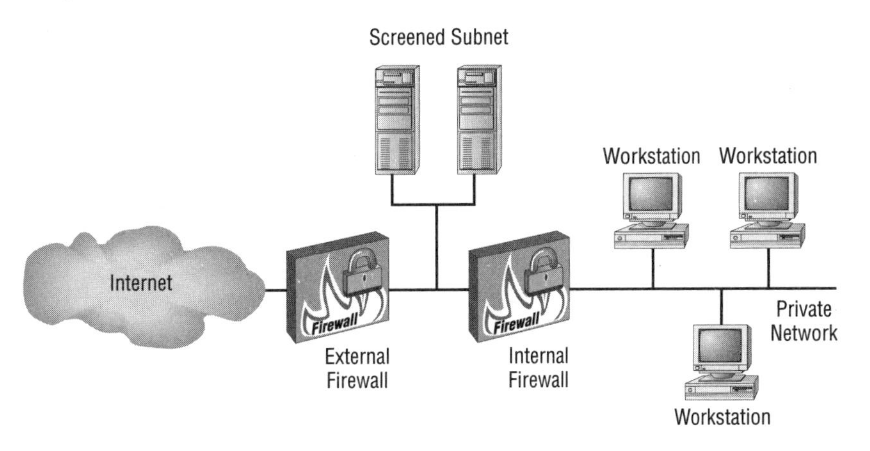

For best results when implementing the mid-ground screened subnet, use two different firewalls. It is still not a guarantee that you will keep people out, but it is making it tougher for them to get in!

These firewall models are presented here for some background as you check your network physical structure. Other things to look for include the unintentional *back door* to your network. For example, look at Figure 4.5.

Figure 4.5 may look an awful lot like Figure 4.4. There is a difference. In this case, someone has put up a remote access server with four modems on it. If these numbers are valid to the outside world, someone has just opened up a potential hole in the network security. Obviously, this is something to be avoided.

FIGURE 4.5 Mid-ground screened subnet firewall deployment with a problem

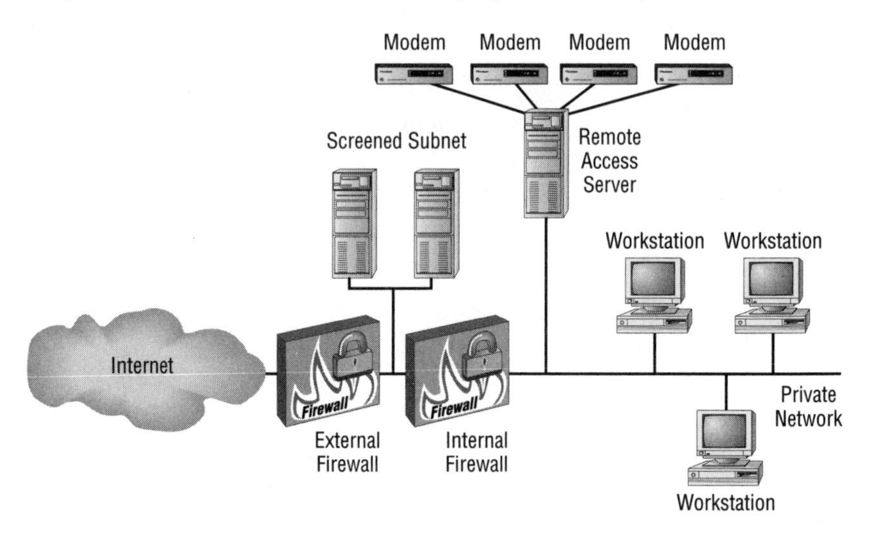

Which Should You Choose?

As you are looking over this information, if you are new to security, you are probably asking yourself which one of these configurations to choose. The answer depends on the breadth and depth of your checkbook, and the size of your network.

If you have a relatively small network, or if the company Internet presence is hosted at your ISP, you may not need much more than a bastion firewall. If your network is larger and you are lacking cash, the three-pronged screened subnet would make sense. In the three-pronged attack, you have one machine acting as the firewall. The machine has three cards in it, one providing access to the outside world, one providing access to the corporate network, and one that provides access to the Internet Web servers or mail servers. Because one machine and one firewall are providing all the protection, this system will be less expensive than the mid-ground screened firewall.

If you have a large, very busy network and deep pockets, the best way to go is the mid-ground. In this case there are two separate machines acting as the firewalls, and each machine is using a different type of firewall software. Any attack from the outside has to penetrate the first firewall, and then work to find a chink in the second firewall. This is usually a very secure, though very costly, solution.

You really do need to know about firewalls. We will be spending some more time with firewalls in later chapters, but before proceeding make sure that you have a firm grasp of the basic concepts. The test is made up of scenario-based questions, and many of the scenarios revolve around what happens to information coming into the screened subnet or DMZ.

Evaluating the Information Security Model

Although looking at an up-to-date network map will help you with the physical model, the information security model may require a bit more effort. In this case, you will be determining how users are getting access to information on your network. There is that generic term *users* again, too. In the age of the Digital Nervous System, the user is anyone who can access information off your network, including internal users, remote users, trusted partners, and even the general public. This can be called the Digital Nervous System or, when opened up to the outside world, you suddenly have an Internet-based enterprise.

Windows 2000 security supports this enterprise in many ways, all of which impact the information security model.

Internal Users

When you institute Windows 2000 and the Active Directory in multiple domain models, the domains are managed as a part of a multilevel hierarchy of domains. The trust relationship between each of these domains is transitive, meaning that every domain trusts every other domain. This will help to open up information stored in other areas of the enterprise, and will also eliminate the hassle of administering one-way trusts.

Windows security includes new authentication based on the Internet standard security protocols Kerberos v5 and Transport Layer Security (TLS). For backward compatibility, Windows 2000 also uses Windows NT LAN Manager (NTLM) authentication protocols. With the advent of Kerberos and the public key infrastructure technology, relationships can be built with other services on other networks or other platforms to allow for access to information. The credentials necessary to accomplish this are done behind the scenes, so the end user never knows how much work is actually being done.

If you decide to use secure channel security protocols (SSL 3.0/TLS), you will find that they support strong client authentication. They do this by equating user credentials in the form of public key certificates to existing network user accounts. This information is managed using the administration tools that you normally use to manage account information and access control. This information is in place, whether the network is making use of shared secret authentication or public key security.

In addition, Windows 2000 has enhanced its support for the use of smart cards. Smart cards provide for an interactive logon that can be used in addition to passwords. These smart cards provide support cryptography and provide secure storage for private keys and certificates. This allows the network administrator to enable strong authentication from the desktop to the domain controller. This all means that, as we plan our internal security, we will have multiple tools in our toolkit to handle all those unique situations. It also means that we will be able to communicate more easily across company boundaries.

External Users

What about those network users who may not be employed by your company? This can include trusted partners, suppliers, consultants, or even the auditor. To make their authentication and access easier, Windows 2000 provides the Microsoft Certificate Server. The certificate server will issue X.509 version 3 certificates to whomever is determined to need it. The certificate server process includes the introduction of the Microsoft CryptoAPI. The CryptoAPI is there to provide certificate management and to handle public key certificates. These certificates include a variety of options including a standard format certificate issued by either a commercial Certificate Authority (CA), a third-party CA, or the Microsoft Certificate Server included in Windows 2000. It is up to the system administrator to define which CAs are trusted in their environment and which certificates are accepted for client authentication. By using these certificates, administrators can provide access to external users who do not even have Windows 2000 accounts. These users can be granted authentication for using a public key certificate while they are mapped to an existing Windows account. The accounts access rights are defined for the Windows account. These rights determine which resources the external users can use on the network.

Secure Information from the Internet

Windows 2000 users can also use tools to manage the private/public key pairs and whatever certificates that they have to use to access Internet-based resources.

Traveling and Remote Users

Remote users have always had special problems. For the system administrator, remote users have usually created unique opportunities. When it comes to the Information Security model, they are truly a headache. First of all, they will usually use standard Simple Mail Transfer Protocol (SMTP)/Post Office Protocol 3 (POP3) to access their Internet mail. It is quick and simple to be sure, but also very open. All that information, including things like passwords, is flying over the network in plain text, just waiting for someone to use a sniffer and grab it.

By the very nature of traveling users, you can almost see the laptop being lugged from airport to airport. For the system administrator, the laptop is a security nightmare. Not only are you expected to provide access to your network from anywhere this person decides to go, but you also have to ensure the security of the information transmitted from the laptop to the central location and from the central location to the laptop.

To make matters worse, laptops get left in rental cars, hotel rooms, airports, and at client sites. Sometimes, laptops get stolen. When a laptop gets stolen, the problem is not replacing a laptop—that is the easy part. The problem is replacing the data that was on the laptop and making sure that data cannot be accessed by anyone else.

As you analyze the information security model, keep in mind that Windows 2000 offers the ability to create VPNs and also can encrypt sensitive files. This means that if the remote user makes use of these tools, the communication between hotel and office can be controlled and secured. By teaching the remote user to encrypt sensitive information, you are guarding against the stolen laptop giving the thieves access to even more sensitive information. All of these issues and the training involved to include the end user should be a part of your plan.

Now that we have looked at the physical and information model, it is time to look at how to determine exactly what your risk is, and how to manage it.

Design Scenario: Keeping the Bad Guys Out

You have just gotten a panic call from one of your best customers, Acme Computer Warehouse and Bar Supply, Inc. It appears that the ACWBS intranet site has been hacked. Suddenly the corporate Web page resembles something from a cartoon show. The page has been created and uploaded to your site, and it is signed by a notorious group of hackers, but the boss isn't sure if the work came from inside the network or from outside the company.

When you arrive, you glance at the network map and determine that a few things have been added to the network since the last time you were there. First of all the bastion host firewall is still in place, such as it is. The firewall came absolutely free for download from the Internet, so you weren't expecting much. The customer may have gotten what they paid for.

The next thing you notice is a RAS server. This wasn't there the last time you were here. When you ask about it, you learn that the RAS server gives customers access to the intranet so they can get access to the corporate catalog. Where do you go from here?

First of all, you can't be sure whether the corporate intranet site was hacked internally or externally. Auditing isn't mentioned and we can't assume. So the best thing to do is protect it from both sides. In this case, go for the mid-ground screened subnet with two firewalls. The customer is currently convinced that its network is vulnerable. Now is a good time to reinforce that conviction and do the job right. Also, lose the RAS server. There are better ways to give customers access to catalogs than by publishing the phone number and logon information for your network.

Once the firewalls are in place, move the corporate Web page to the Internet. You can also move the intranet Web server to the screened subnet to give you more control over who can access it and what they can do it once they are there, and to let you audit access.

The Basics of Risk Management

When you have looked at how your physical network is laid out and you have determined what information you have to protect, it is time to look at how you are going to protect it. Almost everything can be protected. All it takes is time and money. The problem with really secure information is that it is really secure and not very accessible. Somewhere between *locked in a vault* and *open to the world* is where you want your information. Now you have to assess the risks that your network faces.

Microsoft Exam Objective

Analyze the current physical model and information security model.

- Analyze internal and external security risks.

There are four steps to assessing and managing risks, and effective risk management requires all four of them:

1. Identify risks
2. Quantify risks
3. Plan for risks
4. Monitor and manage risks

To adequately analyze risk, you'll need a detailed plan. So, the best time to perform an initial risk analysis is as part of the early planning process.

You shouldn't make the mistake of thinking that risk analysis is a one-time thing. As you are going to see, you will be reevaluating your plan and your risk analysis from time to time throughout this project and by checking things after the project has been completed. With network security, risk analysis is a never-ending process, simply because people are coming up with new ways to put your network at risk each and every day.

Identify Risks

In this book, we will define *risk* as the possibility of suffering a loss due to an internal or external breach in security. For any network, the loss mentioned in the definition could come in the form of what could be called a diminished quality to end product or a denial of service. It might also show up as an increased cost; it could be missed deadlines or even the complete failure to achieve the business goals of the network. In other words, risk is a problem waiting to happen.

There are numerous ways to identify risks. If you have a limited amount of time, the best ways to identify risks may be to brainstorm and talk with the experts. Who are the experts? The experts are the people who use your network.

In order to identify risks, you obviously have to know what the various risks *are*. This means categorizing possible threats, from denial of service attacks to Trojan horses.

You also have to review your current security setup and spot the possible holes. This is an involved topic that we'll be exploring more in the next two chapters, but here we'll discuss some general methods of uncovering your security problems.

Brainstorm and Talk with the Experts

All of your risks may not be apparent from just meeting with the project team or meeting with the IT staff. It's probably worth your time to call a brainstorming meeting with key resources throughout your company. If you can look at a particular part of the company and wonder if there is something there that may need to be protected that you don't know about, you should probably get that part of the company involved somehow. Ask these people where they see the most risk to their data or to their resources. You may be surprised at what you uncover.

Don't forget to solicit outside opinions. Take your risk assessment studies to people around the company and have them look at it. They may have valuable input on things that need to be protected that you may never have thought of.

Categorize Potential Threats

There are all sorts of different risks that a network can face. Table 4.1 outlines some of the risks. It also helps to give us a starting point for the discussion of the threats we need to protect against.

TABLE 4.1 Common Types of Security Risks in an Organization

Security Risk	Description
The threat of identity interception	In this case someone discovers the username and password of a valid user. This discovery can come in a variety of ways.
The threat of a masquerade	In this case, an unauthorized user pretends to be a valid user. The user may spoof the IP address of a system that is normally trusted and use that address to gain the access rights to the impersonated device or system.
The threat of a replay attack	In this case, the intruder records a network exchange between a user and a server and plays it back at a later time to impersonate the user.
The threat of data interception	By using a sniffer, it is easy to spot if data is moved across the network as plain text. If it is, an unauthorized person can monitor the network segment and capture the data.
The threat of manipulation	Here, the intruder causes network data to be modified or corrupted.
The threat of repudiation	In this case, the e-business financial transactions are in question if the recipient of the transaction cannot be certain who sent the original message.
The threat of macro viruses	This is very popular, especially with applications such as Outlook. In this case, a user writes an application-specific viruses that could exploit the macro language and cause damage.

TABLE 4.1 Common Types of Security Risks in an Organization *(continued)*

Security Risk	Description
The threat of denial of service	In this case the intruder floods a server with requests that simply overwhelm system resources and crash the server.
The threat of malicious mobile code	This threat of malicious code refers to dangerous code that is running as an automatically executed ActiveX control or Java applet that has been uploaded from the Internet on a Web server.
The threat of misuse of privileges	This is an all-time favorite. A person with the ability to administer a system knowingly or mistakenly uses their privileges over the operating system to obtain private data.
The threat of a Trojan horse	This is a generic term for a malicious program that masquerades as a desirable and harmless utility.
The threat of social engineering attack	Sometimes breaking into a network is as simple as telephoning new employees, telling them you are from the IT department, and asking them to verify their password for your records.

Obviously there are different risks for different environments. If you're working for a small company that has a dial-up connection to the Internet so you can get your e-mail from AOL, your risks are much different than a multinational corporation dealing in billion-dollar weapons contracts, with multiple portals into the Internet and into other companies. In addition, the concerns of the small-business owner, a college or university, some governmental agencies, and other organizations, will differ. Some companies want access strictly limited, while others want a more open and free atmosphere.

In each case, there are different assets that need to be protected. In some cases, the primary concern might be interruption of service to users on the Internet. In other cases, it might be the revelation of sensitive financial data of all your customers. If a company's Internet presence is interrupted or its "information only" Web site changed, the actual effect may be one of annoyance, but the real impact may be minimal. For the company with thousands of customers' financial records hanging out for everyone to see, the risk is tremendous.

When analyzing the types of security that you are going to need, take it from the point of view of the attacker. Potential attackers are probably not going to waste a lot of time going after an individual PC connected to the Internet for casual use. Corporate networks, financial institutions, and governmental bodies have long been looked at as attractive targets for intruders.

Later in this chapter we will look at something called the *risk matrix*. You can use the matrix to estimate the risks to an area of the network by considering the relationship between the importance of the assets being protected and the likelihood that someone can attack your environment. This means that as the importance of your assets increases, so does the security risk. As the likelihood of an attack increases, so does the security risk.

Many times, the importance of an asset is determined subjectively, not objectively. It is simply not black and white. The final decision often rests on estimates of how the safety of individuals or organizations, their health and well-being, their financial status or their reputations, would be affected by an attack. Corporate politics may even play a part. For example, a senior manager in the organization may be storing information of a personal nature on the network. The information may not be business related, but it would cause this executive embarrassment or loss if it were discovered. Now, you may not see the severity of the risk, but someone else may.

You know the golden rule, "Them that's got the gold make the rules." There is an IT axiom supporting that rule. It states that the higher up the corporate ladder you climb, the less you know about computing. Of course, the higher up the corporate ladder you climb, the better computer you get. This means many CEOs have computers that would rival servers in the computer room for performance, memory, and disk space. All so the CEO's secretary can come in and print out his e-mail for him to read!

The likelihood of an attack depends upon the motivation of the attacker, the resources available to the attacker, and the nature of the adversarial environment. All of these conditions are fluid and change at a moment's notice. For example, Thursday night at 5 everyone in the IT department goes out after work to a softball game. After the game, they head to the local watering hole to quaff a few frosty cold beverages. Morale is high, camaraderie and esprit de corps are running rampant, and the motivation of the potential attacker is minimal. Friday afternoon, the entire starting lineup is laid off due to cutbacks corporate-wide. The manager who the evening before was a wonderful person for buying drinks and playing softball with the troops is now a pariah to the people who are leaving and to the people who are staying. After all, how could this manager go out the night before and party with the very people that were going to be fired the next day and not say anything? Motivation for a potential attacker has skyrocketed, as has the nature of the adversarial environment.

This is actually a worst-case scenario. Now, you have some of the same people who are charged with protecting the network angry enough to be considered potential threats. Those who are staying may have the motivation and the skills, and they certainly have the opportunity. How are you going to protect against that?

For a fascinating story of computer espionage, check out *The Cuckoo's Egg: Tracking a Spy Through the Maze of Computer Espionage,* by Clifford Stoll. It was published by Pocket Books and reprinted in 1995. It will give you a whole new appreciation for network auditing and why every 75 cents counts.

Review Current Security Standards

How secure is your network? That may be a difficult question to answer. There are several ways of finding out. If you are a manager, the simplest (though perhaps not the best) way is to ask. Ask your IT people for the current security standards. Are they posted on the intranet? Are they written down? How specific are they? Once you have the security bible, the next logical step is to see if the IT team followed through. Try to access stuff you are supposed to be able to access. Can you? More importantly, try to access stuff you are *not* supposed to access. That will probably be the telling tale.

If you are not satisfied with that approach, you may decide to do a formal risk assessment. These are usually comprehensive and have a habit of showing up serious areas of vulnerability. A formal risk assessment by a third party is an excellent way to identify enterprise-wide security risks. It may also reveal some hidden issues that will help you redefine the way you use your network, or the way you connect your network to the outside world.

Threat assessment can be done in one of three ways. There is the *tiger team* approach, the corporate *think tank* method, and the *system security engineering process*.

Tiger Teams

The tiger team approach puts together a team of professionals whose job it is to break into your network. These folks get together and start a concentrated attack on your systems. The results of the attacks are then documented and the protection strength of the system is estimated based on their relative success. This system is helpful if the members of the tiger team have been doing this for a while. Giving this task to a group of people who have never tried to break into a network will probably not realize the results you desire.

Think Tanks

With a think tank approach, a group gets together for a period of time and tries to assess the risks to the network. This group can be formed from within the company, or you can go to various groups of consultants to have the service performed for you. The assessments require some preparation of those people who are involved, and mostly revolve around discussions. This is a worthwhile process for the corporate environment because it will foster the collective understanding of the need for security. There are obviously inherent shortcomings. These sessions may not be enough, because there may not be checks to find if the suggestions were followed through properly. These sessions also require that all the right people participate with the right information. People to include in the think tank include system and network administrators, developers of custom products your company uses, and managers with a strong technical background.

System Security Engineering Process

Here, a formal threat assessment, management, and mitigation process is defined. The primary advantage of this is that all the basic steps in a good risk analysis are generally included in the process. An example would be that as part of the formal risk assessment, network maps and architecture designs would be gathered and reviewed. Then there would be a detailed and rigorous engineering-based identification of threats based on available assets and other data. This is followed by safeguard integration and iterations through the process for a new architecture.

The disadvantage of this formal approach is that it is usually expensive and time-consuming. To do a proper engineer analysis for most environments costs more than most security budgets will allow.

When you look at the basic philosophy involved in this approach, it almost seems just like the brainstorming session. That is really not the case. In this scenario, the teams are more investigative, taking more time and effort to examine threats. This still does not make sure that everything that needs to be identified is identified, but the structure gives it a better chance.

The other major difference is that system security engineering efforts usually involve assigning a number value to estimate the risk and the factors that affect risk. There is even a military standard available to show you how it is done, MIL-STD-1785. The problem with assigning a numerical value to a risk is that the assignment is still subjective. The group decides the numerical value. It certainly goes a long way to help establish priorities, but it still can be arbitrary.

So, You Think You Are Having a Bad Day

MSNBC Reporter Bob Sullivan published this online article on January 19, 2000:

> The link was sent to MSNBC by a concerned technology worker who found it searching for flaws in Web site security. It pointed to a rather obvious location on `www.globalhealthtrax.com`.
>
> Merely clicking on the link brought up a plain text file of customers, their home phone numbers, and in about 1,000 cases, bank account information—including account numbers, routing numbers, and even bank names. The records date from Nov. 19, 1998, through this month, though there are only a handful of new entries dated after May of 1999.

GlobalHealthtrax, which sells health products using the multilevel marketing method, allows customers to pay for their monthly subscription of products by automatically deducting from bank accounts or through automatic charges to a credit card. But when that information was entered by customers into the Web site, the site spat it back out on another page.

The file was viewable because the Web designer had set up the site to allow anyone the ability to view files in the `cgi` subdirectory, which is meant to be hidden from view.

"I don't know what to say. We pay a lot of good money for that site to be secure," said president Everett Hale. He said his company switched Web sites last year, and its active Web home is now `www.ghtonline.com`. He said he thought all the data and scripts from the old site had been removed from the Internet. "We're going to have to have some quick meetings today."

The company's vice president, Lorin Dyrr, said she suspected a former associate from the company had posted the personal information to the site as an act of corporate sabotage. That associate had provided assistance developing the older version of the company's Web site and might have dropped the customer list as an act of revenge.

"We are going to pursue this. This is a felony," she said. "I'm pretty angry that anybody would want to put people at risk."

Dyrr said her company had been in the process of deleting all information from the older site, and believed it to be essentially empty before MSNBC's call.

"But we are going to investigate, and if it's our fault we'll take the responsibility."

GlobalHealthtrax was told about the MSNBC story in advance of publication so the company had time to remove the customer account information. The data was deleted by 3 p.m. ET Tuesday.

> But that might not have been soon enough. Some of the customers MSNBC contacted said they'd noticed peculiar activity connected to their accounts in recent months.
>
> Jim Manuel of Phoenix, Ariz., said he recently received a surprise overdraft notice from his bank, and discovered about $200 was missing from his account.
>
> "Their site was supposed to be secure," Manuel said.
>
> Another customer who requested anonymity said there were consistent unauthorized withdrawals from her bank account last year, although she initially believed that to be a billing dispute with the company. She has since closed the account.
>
> Another customer who also requested anonymity said there was a mysterious $70 charge on his credit card last year.
>
>

Pretty scary, huh? Aren't you glad it didn't happen to you? First of all there would be the shock of finding out that you were that vulnerable. Secondly, there would be the humiliation of having the security breach published on MSNBC, not to mention having it brought up as an example of "what not to do" in a best selling study guide on Windows 2000 security.

Obviously, there are parts of your network that need more security than others. But you may not be aware of what is on your network and needs to be protected without doing a *security analysis*. The security analysis takes the risk analysis one step further. It looks at what is at risk and the security in place to meet the risk. Then it makes the determination of whether the security is adequate to meet the risk. Once this determination has been done, levels of security can be assigned to areas of the network, to certain job descriptions, and to certain levels of the organization tree, and it can all be worked out so that everyone can agree.

Having the security analysis is also a good idea so that you can go in and try to break into places where you are not supposed to be. After the Web designer left GlobalHealthTrax, I wonder if anyone did that? I am kind of betting that someone on the IT staff was sending out resumes in the middle of January of 2000.

Quantify Risks

Quantifying risks is a discipline unto itself. Your options range from sophisticated probability analysis to the simpler techniques outlined below. Obviously, the accuracy of your results is commensurate with the techniques you use. Later in this chapter we will take a look at several ways to quantify risks. All of the methods do boil down to some simple concepts:

- Determine your tolerance levels
- Assign a probability to each risk
- Assign a cost to each risk
- Assign a priority to each risk

Microsoft Exam Objective

Analyze factors that influence company strategy,

- Identify the company's tolerance for risk.

Determine Your Tolerance Levels

Risk tolerance may vary, depending on the area of the enterprise or the size of the organization. If you work for a small company, someone causing an additional cost of $250,000 or a delay of two weeks to a rollout may put your entire company at risk. If you work for a large organization, these overruns may be acceptable for certain areas of the company, and not acceptable for others. Write down some hard numbers. How much cost and delay is acceptable? Remember that this isn't your preference, it's just the bottom-line numbers you can tolerate.

So what kinds of things do you take into consideration? Let's look at two extreme examples. In the first, we have a very small company, maybe a one- or two-person shop. In this case, both the employees are mobile users, and they both travel much of the time. Their Internet presence amounts to an e-mail server that provides Exchange access when they are on the road, but that is about it. There is some information stored on the server, but it is not of a sensitive nature. Everything that is sensitive is either on the laptops or stored on Zip or Jaz disks and kept offline. In this case, the risk tolerance for the server would be very high. The company could stand to lose the server and there would not be much information that could potentially harm the company. The risk tolerance on the laptops would be low. The company could ill-afford to lose the laptops since much of the company information would be stored on them. The security plan would have to take into account how to make sure they were secured.

In the next scenario, let's go to the opposite extreme. Let's look at a bank. Certainly the majority of information and hardware on this system would be required to be secure 24 hours a day, 7 days a week. With millions of dollars at stake, everything they do has a low tolerance to risk. They just can't afford it. If someone breaks in through Internet banking, they could transfer funds all around and never be traced. If that happened, the lawsuits alone could bankrupt the bank. In this case, everything must be secured to the maximum degree affordable.

Assign a Probability

For each risk, determine how likely it is to occur. Unless you're using statistical methods, you'll assign a probability based on your team's knowledge of the risk. Assess their confidence level. If the resources that will do the work aren't comfortable with the current technology, then the risk is more likely to occur.

You can also use an analysis tool to help identify more likely risks. For example, Microsoft has a program called IT Advisor for Risk Management, which is freely available for download from Microsoft's Web site at `http://www.microsoft.com/cio/building/advisor/risk/download.htm`. The IT Advisor includes a *risk matrix model*, which can help you identify and minimize the exposure to risks associated with any project.

In case you're interested, Microsoft has a series of IT Advisor tools, all available from the `http://www.microsoft.com/cio/itadvisor.htm` Web site. The tools include an IT Advisor for Database Consolidation, Security, Knowledge Management, Governance, and Commerce. They come in two flavors: one available off the Web, and the other a stand-alone desktop edition. Each desktop edition is about a 5MB download.

Look at Figure 4.6. It is a diagram of the risk matrix.

FIGURE 4.6 Risk matrix

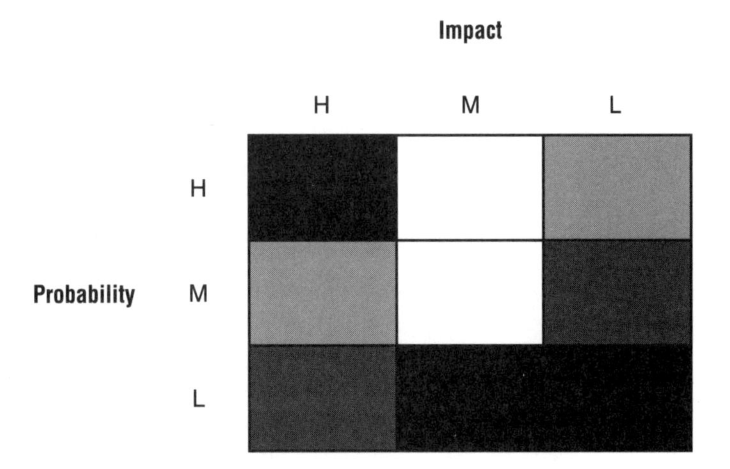

Your risk assessment results will place you in one of four positions on the risk matrix. The four major positions fall within the three-by-three matrix, which covers two areas: probability and impact.

Risk Matrix Positions

The four positions on the risk matrix are shown in Table 4.2.

TABLE 4.2 Risk Matrix Positions

Position	Description
Highly exposed	Items judged as highly exposed involve significant risks that have a high likelihood of becoming losses. Without a great deal of close management, the overall outcome of the project may have a major negative impact on the business.
Significantly exposed	Items assessed as significantly exposed involve moderate to significant risks that have a moderate likelihood of becoming losses. With proactive leadership and an effective risk management strategy, potential negative consequences of the attack can be lessened or avoided altogether.

TABLE 4.2 Risk Matrix Positions *(continued)*

Position	Description
Moderately exposed	Items assessed as moderately exposed involve either significant risks that have a low likelihood of becoming losses, or minor risks that have a high likelihood of becoming losses. Both accepting some minor risk as is and implementing some basic risk management procedures will help maintain the generally positive outlook.
Slightly exposed	Items assessed as slightly exposed involve minor risks that have a low likelihood of becoming losses. This has a good chance of a positive impact on the business, and risk-management efforts may play a lesser role in managing the project.

For more information on the IT Advisor, see the "Using the IT Advisor for Risk Management" section at the end of the chapter.

Assign a Cost

The cost of a risk can be measured in dollars, lost time, lost quality, or all three. Try to quantify the cost of a risk, even as a range such as $25,000–$50,000. One way to evaluate costs is to perform a what-if analysis and see the impact if a risk does occur. Many companies have this down to a science, calling it a disaster plan.

Most disaster plans start out with the obvious and move out to the borderline absurd. For example, let's take a look at a company that has its corporate headquarters in St. Louis. In this case, the disaster planning team would start out by saying, "What happens if we have a fire in the computer room that destroys everything?" Once the disaster has been stated, they could look at the options. This would include going online from another location, buying all new equipment, replacing the computer room, and restoring from tape backup. Costs would include all of the equipment and people hours, plus lost productivity of employees, lost sales revenue to customers, etc.

The absurd would be something like this: How long would it take us to recover if the New Madras fault gave way and the company headquarters and the off-site storage location were completely destroyed by fire? How long would it take us to be back online and working, and what would be the cost entailed?

Assign a Priority

Based on your tolerance level, the potential cost of the risk, and the probability of it occurring, assign a priority to the risk. For example, if the cost of a risk is beyond your tolerance level and it is very likely to occur, assign a high priority to the risk. Use these priorities to determine which risks to focus your security efforts on first.

Plan for Risks

Once you've identified and quantified risks, you need to plan for them. Because risk planning can take a lot of time and energy, you may want to plan for only the high-priority risks or the medium- to high-priority risks. Planning entails:

- Identifying triggers for each risk
- Identifying proactive, contingency, or mitigation plans for each risk

Identify Triggers

Triggers are indicators that a risk has occurred or is about to occur. The best triggers tell you almost as soon as a problem has occurred.

To identify triggers, talk with the people who are most likely to cause the risk to occur and those who are most likely to feel its impact. Ask them how they would know that the problem is occurring. Start with listening to how they would know that the problem has already occurred, and then work backward to determine how you would determine the problem actually occurred without their telling you.

As the security manager, consider how the risk would be reflected in the plan. Would the plan show increased levels of auditing?

For each risk you're addressing, create a watchlist that shows the possible triggers, when they are likely to occur, and who should watch for the trigger.

Identify Plans

Once you've identified triggers, you need to create action plans. You can plan for risks in one of four basic ways:

- Be proactive. Identify the risk and take steps to avoid it by taking actions ahead of time, thereby decreasing the likelihood of the problem occurring.
- Work to lower the consequence of the risk. When you do that, you are basically just reducing the risk's impact. For example, if you have a very sensitive project, is there a way the data can be stored in several locations or on removable media that can be safely locked away at the end of the day?
- Plan ahead. Develop a contingency plan, so you know what you will do if the problem does occur. This falls under disaster planning. Make sure that there is a way to react to a threat or defeat the intruder before the intruder can access sensitive data.
- Keep in mind that risk management plans can have unexpected ramifications. Look for new risks that occur as a result of the plan and address them in it.

All of these plans require that you be *proactive* in how you think about possible risks.

Proactive Risk Management

Since security and risk assessment is an ongoing, never-ending process, there should be a way to be somewhat proactive. To be proactive you have to assess risks continuously and use these assessments whenever decisions have to be made. When decisions are made, the risks are carried forward and dealt with until they are resolved or until they turn into actual problems and are handled.

The proactive risk management process is shown graphically in Figure 4.7.

FIGURE 4.7 Proactive risk management process

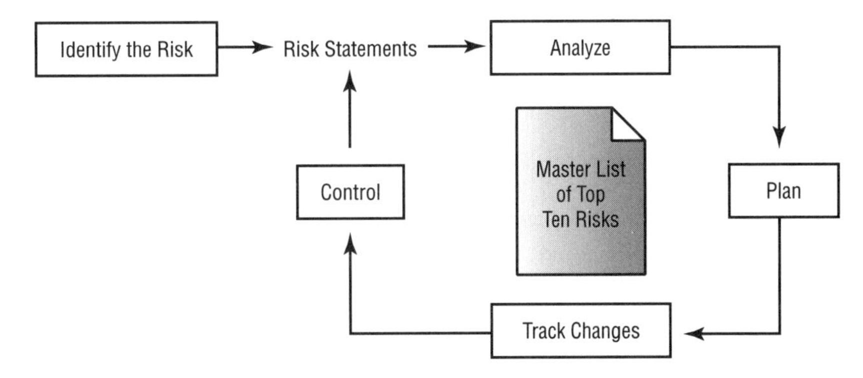

We have already covered ways to identify the risks. We have also covered how to analyze the impact of the risks. These risks are then put on a risk hit list, or the master list of top-10 risks.

Top-10 Risk List

The top-10 risk list is a grouping of the threats that warrant immediate action. Managing security risks takes time and effort, so it is important that the security team remains focused on the risks that can do the most damage. Once a limited number of major risks have been identified, plans can be made for how to meet them.

Risk Action Planning

With risk action planning, the risk information is turned into decisions on how best to handle the risk and what actions are necessary. Planning involves developing actions to address individual risks, prioritizing risk actions, and creating an integrated risk management plan.

The four key areas that should be addressed as part of the risk action planning are:

Research What is known about the risk? What can you do to learn more about the potential risk, and where can you find information to determine where the risk is emanating from?

Accept Can you live with the consequences of the risk? Can you accept the risk and take no further action?

Manage Can the security team do anything to mitigate the impact of the risk should it occur?

Avoid Can the security team do anything to avoid or block the risk?

Risk Contingency Planning

In the world of risk management, it is called *contingency* planning. In the IT world, it is called disaster recovery planning. No matter what you call it, the basics are the same. What happens if everything goes to heck in a hand basket? What do you do then?

A contingency plan is put into place when all else fails. For example, you have secured some highly sensitive information. You have auditing enabled to find out who is accessing the information, from where, and when. You are so paranoid about this, you have the system audit the information two different ways, and you compare the audit trails. Most days, the security team views the audit trail with a sigh—after all, they always match. Today, however, the audits don't match. One shows that a user whom you have never heard of compromised the information. As a matter of fact, this user was so good, he even covered his tracks with the one auditing program he could find. He just didn't know how good you were at *intruder detection*. What now? How do you track the intruder? Or, do you let the intruder in and watch for him, so you can see if he has any back door accounts? All of this information should be decided before it happens, not after.

Part of the contingency plan should also be a notification tree or a notification list. Suppose the Human Resources department notices an irregularity in the payroll program. Who do they call and when? All of that information should be decided beforehand.

Risk Action Form

This is one of those things that can be included as part of your Digital Nervous System. You can put the form online, so that whenever someone sees a potential threat, she can report it immediately. Of course, since some of the information on the form may be compromising in one way or another, you are going to have to make sure the database is really secure. That is just one more thing to worry about. Some of things the team will need on the form include:

Risk identifier The *risk identifier* name would refer back to a risk statement that identifies the known risks.

Risk statement The *risk statement* describes the condition that exists that could lead to a loss for the company. This is basically a description of the risk.

Risk management strategy A *risk management strategy* is the description of what is going to happen if the risk occurs.

Risk management strategy metrics These are the criteria that will be used to determine whether the countermeasures are working.

Action items A list of things the team can do to manage the risk. These items will be logged into the risk tracking system.

Due dates When action is expected to be taken.

Personnel assignments The people who have been assigned to handle the action items.

Risk contingency strategy A *risk contingency strategy* is a paragraph or two describing the team strategy in the event that the actions planned to manage the risk don't work. The team would execute the risk contingency strategy if the risk contingency trigger were reached. The *risk contingency trigger* is defined as that point when it is obvious the contingency strategy did not work.

Monitor and Manage Risks

Your risk management plan is in place. Now your job is to make sure you and others on the project team act on it. Take any actions necessary according to your proactive, mitigation, and contingency plans. Monitor your watchlist to see if triggers are occurring, and implement contingency plans as needed. Be sure to reassess your risks regularly. You might find the following ideas useful for monitoring your risks:

- Include a Risks section in status reports and request that resources identify any assumptions they are making, as well as any new risks they see.
- Set up regular meetings with team members to reevaluate the risk management plan and to identify new risks to the project.
- Each time something changes significantly on the network, reassess the risks and reevaluate your risk management plan.

We refer to these various tasks as *risk tracking* and *risk control*.

Risk Tracking

It is critical that the security team monitors the status of risks and the actions it has taken to mitigate them. Risk tracking is essential to an effective action plan implementation. This also means that a constant surveillance of the compromised area must be implemented to make sure the solutions implemented solved the problem. This is a basic watchdog function.

Risk Status Reporting

For the security team to make the most of risk tracking, there has to be some form of reporting. This is critical, if for no other reason than to be able to notice trends developing in attacks or potential compromises. Risk status reporting can identify four major risk management situations:

- If the risk is resolved, the risk action plan can be completed.
- Risk actions are checking things off the list of things to do known as the risk management plan.
- If some risk actions are not successful, the risk management plan should be reevaluated and an alternate plan should be implemented.

As the security team takes actions to manage the risks, the total risk exposure for the project should begin to approach acceptable levels.

Risk Control

After the security team has chosen the risk metrics and the triggering events, there is nothing fascinating about risk management. It falls under the "patience" guidelines of sitting back and waiting for something bad to happen. As you respond to reports, you can control the action plans if you find something that works better than your original procedure. You may also reset the triggering levels and generally tweak the risk management process. Risk management works with project management to accomplish these four goals:

- Control risk action plans
- Correct for variations from plans
- Respond to triggering events
- Improve the risk management process

If this process is not integrated into the day-to-day function of the network administration, it may soon become a background activity that may not get completed in a timely fashion.

Design Scenario: How Much Is Too Much?

The life of a consultant never ends, does it? Today you are tasked with talking to the CEO of ACWBS again. It seems the shock of being hacked has worn off and now he is screaming about the size of the bill to set up the midground screened subnet.

When you walk in, he begins sputtering. After patiently listening to him, you finally end the discussion of cost by doing a risk analysis. You start by identifying the risks to the company. He understands the company is at risk. Then you start asking him to rate various pieces of the ACWBS information structure to criticality and when you get to things like inventory and accounts receivable, he begins to understand how much his company could be hurt by an intrusion.

Finally, after showing him all the steps that you have put in place to identify the risk, categorize the risk, and manage the risk, he starts smiling again and signs the contract. You leave with a smile on your face, pondering when in the world you went from being a great computer consultant to being a great salesperson.

Using the IT Advisor for Risk Management

The IT Advisor for Risk Management is an interview-based tool. When you start it up the first time, you are asked to enter a username and password to be used for later sessions. If you look at the screenshot in Figure 4.8, you will see that to get started, you have to start a new project.

FIGURE 4.8 Opening screen of IT Advisor for Risk Management

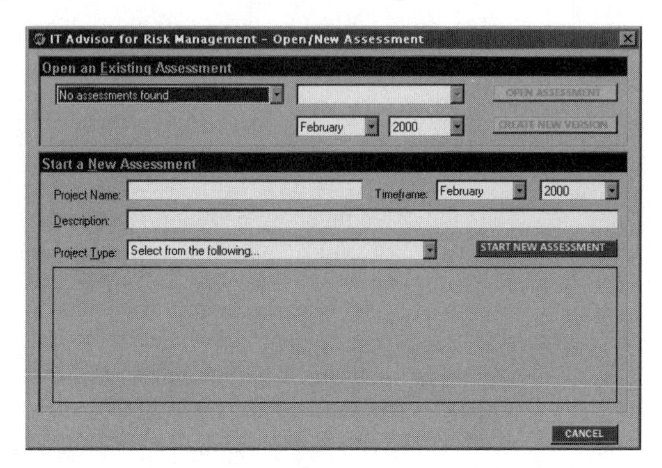

In this case, we will call the project Acme. It is also looking for a type of project. There are four to choose from:

- Application development
- Infrastructure deployment
- Enterprise architecture
- Total cost of ownership

The security project we are working on does not involve application development, and no one has started to make noise about the total cost of ownership, so that leaves either infrastructure deployment or enterprise architecture. Infrastructure deployment is defined as projects involving those resources that support the enterprise-computing environment. These resources include technologies and enterprise architecture standards; operational processes such as policies, operating procedures and services; and people and organizational resources such as skill sets and management. The infrastructure can affect the success of business projects, the adoption of new technology, end user mobility, and project deployment schedules.

The enterprise architecture projects are defined as a framework for developing enterprise systems based on an integrated model of multiple views of the enterprise. An enterprise strategic architecture consists of data architecture, applications architecture, technology architecture, and business architecture. The integration of these four perspectives provides the underlying structure for directing the development of the enterprise's information system and computing environment.

Judging from these definitions, the appropriate choice would be the infrastructure deployment. Once that has been chosen, it brings up the brainstorming screen shown in Figure 4.9.

FIGURE 4.9 Brainstorming opening screen

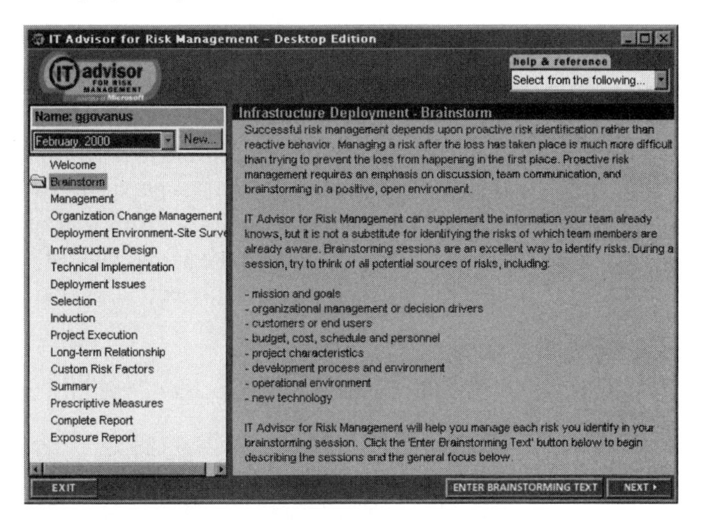

This will help you start the risk assessment process. When you click brainstorm, it brings up a text box where you can simply free-flow ideas. While this is helpful in the overall scheme of things for a real project, here it doesn't do much for us. Let us move on to the next setting, Management, shown in Figure 4.10.

FIGURE 4.10 Management screen

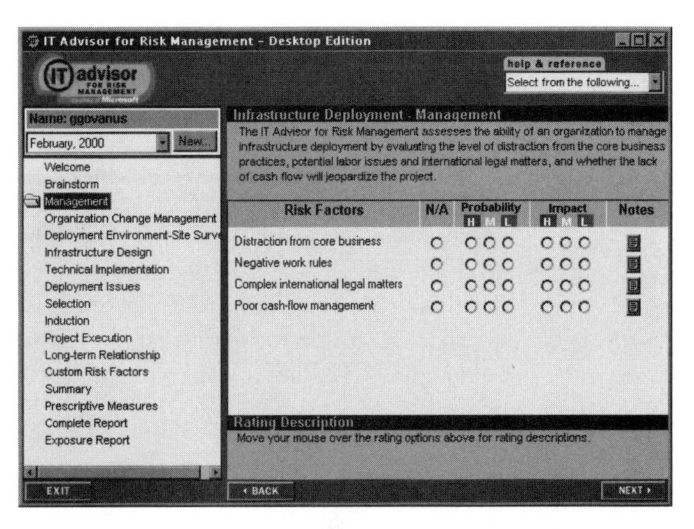

Here is where you would start inputting information, trying to evaluate the level of distraction caused by various activities. These activities include distraction from core business, negative work rules, complex international legal matters, and poor cash flow management. You judge the risk factors using probability and impact, and there is a section for notes on your decisions.

Next look at Figure 4.11, which covers organization change-management. As you can see, the options here are much more granular, covering all aspects of change-management, from lack of management support to the disruption caused by moving employees around. In looking at this screen, you can tell that the people who designed this tool have actually done this kind of thing before: that is obvious with the choices for negative effect of the political power distribution and the lack of a sane schedule. And here we thought that we were the only people on earth who have worked on major network redesigns that had to be done tomorrow.

FIGURE 4.11 Organization change-management risk factors

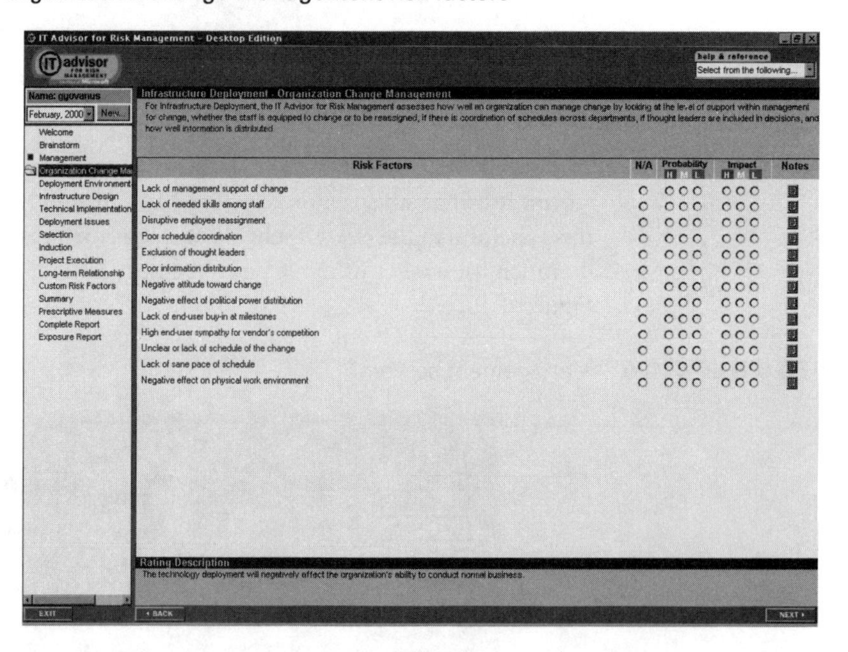

Let's skip down to the choice for Induction. This is where some of the material that we covered in the first few chapters comes into play. As you can see in Figure 4.12, the Advisor wants to know how well you feel you know the organization's business structure and what effect that will have on the project as a whole.

FIGURE 4.12 Your understanding of the organizational business structure and its impact on the project

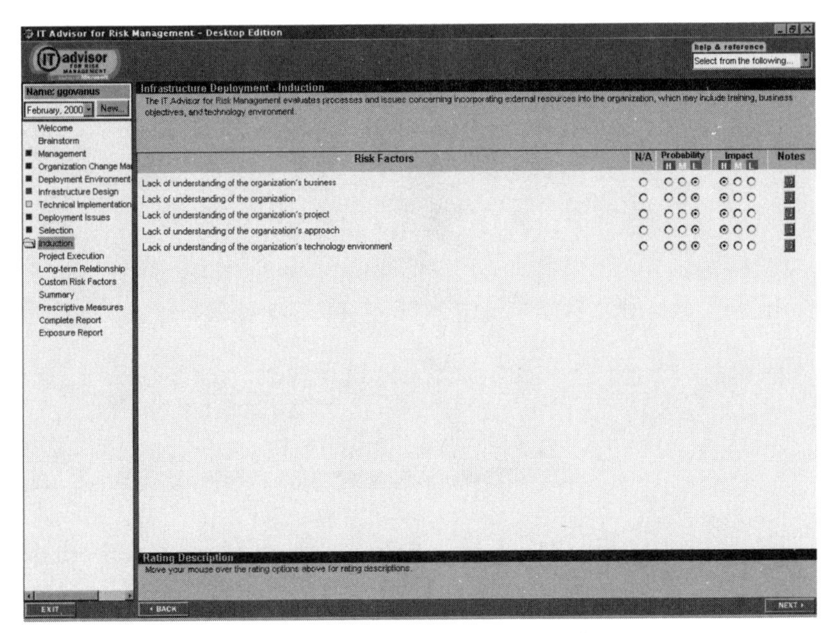

When you have gone through all the questions and have rated all the scenarios, IT Advisor will present you with a graphical overview report (see Figure 4.13). Since most of the choices we made as we went through the selection process were not ultracritical, Acme came out right smack in the middle where you would expect.

FIGURE 4.13 Overview report with recommended prescriptive measures

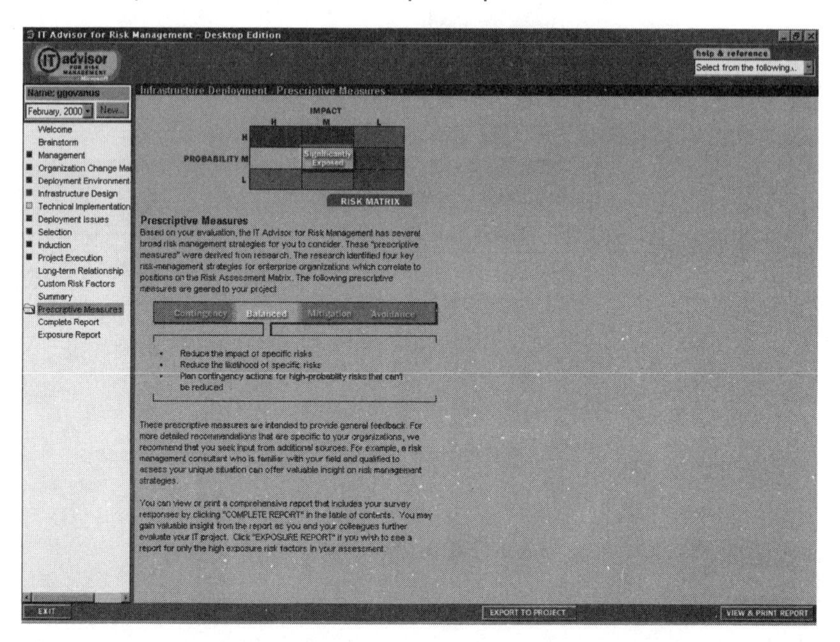

There were, however, areas of major concern that had to be viewed as high priority. There was a separate report for those issues (Figure 4.14).

FIGURE 4.14 Report highlighting areas of high exposure risks

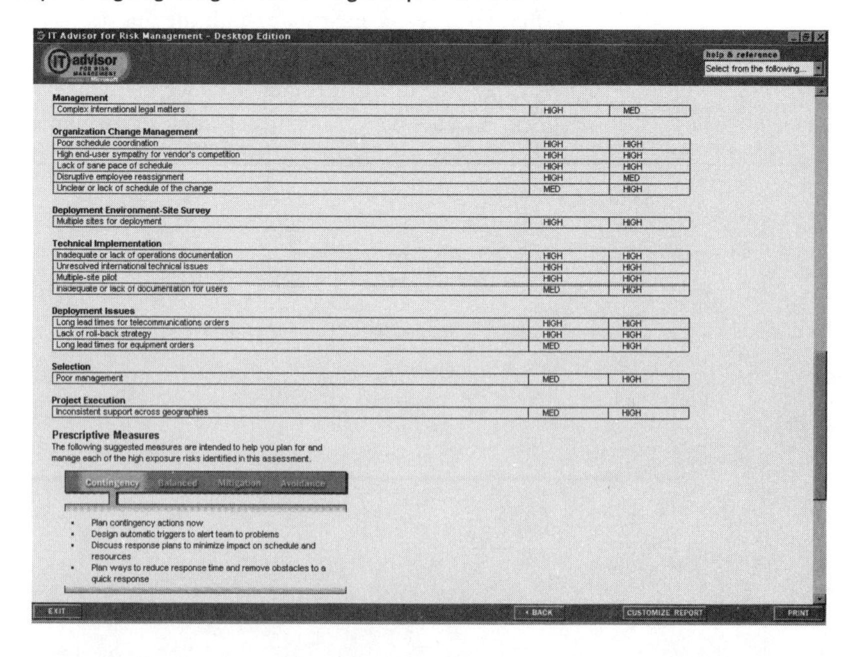

As you can see, this report is not designed to help you come up with specific solutions: It is designed to help you quantify your thinking and find out where the problem areas may be before the project even starts. You can even take the results of this and export it into Project Manager.

If the exam you take is anything like the exam we took, you will probably see at least one question on risk assessment. While the questions we saw did not go into the depth to which we have taken the process, it is important to be cognizant of the degree of risk that companies are comfortable accepting. Be sure to read the questions carefully and make sure you look for the telltale signs for risk tolerance. For example, companies that want to be on the bleeding edge of technology are aware they are more susceptible to risk and accept that as an effect of the decision to be the first on the block with the new toys. Staid, conservative firms that are the last to institute new technology would not generally be considered prime candidates for risk acceptance.

Summary

In this chapter we started out looking at how the physical design of your network can affect information security. Internal security is controlled with concepts like rights and permissions, while physical security is controlled by the judicious use of tools like firewalls and virtual private networks.

When you have established the way into and out of the network, the next step is to gauge how much effort should be involved in protecting the data. This is called risk management. First you determine how badly the organization would be harmed if something were compromised, and then you take the appropriate steps to protect it. Once it has been protected, you continue to watch it to make sure that your efforts are not being circumvented by methods you hadn't planned on.

Key Terms

Before you take the exam, be certain you are familiar with the following terms:

bastion host

external security risks

firewall

internal security risks

intruder detection

mid-ground screened subnet

risk

risk contingency strategy

risk contingency trigger

risk identifier

risk management strategy

risk statement

screened subnet model

security analysis

system security engineering process

think tank

three-pronged screened subnet

tiger team

Review Questions

1. In looking over the firewall configuration for your company, you notice that all traffic has to go through two firewalls to get outside the company, and all your company's Web-servers and e-mail servers are located between the firewalls. This is an example of what kind of design?

   A. Bastion host

   B. Dual firewall

   C. Default for Cisco routers

   D. Screened subnet

2. You are called in to consult for a small company. They are concerned with the recent outbreaks of hacking on major Web sites. When you arrive, you ask how they connect to the Internet, and they say by dial-up access to a local ISP. They only use the Internet sparingly, so there are no plans for a full-time connection. The company is a transcription service, typing the transcripts of what went on in a local open court the previous day. At the end of the day, all information is forwarded to the client by courier and the files are deleted from the computers. All modems are set to not auto-answer. They ask what type of firewall you suggest for this organization?

   A. Bastion host

   B. Screened subnet

   C. None

3. A small company with a light Internet presence should probably use which of the following:

   A. No firewall

   B. Bastion host type firewall

   C. Microsoft Proxy Server

   D. Screened subnet configuration

4. A risk contingency trigger is defined as which of these:
   A. An event that causes the risk contingency plan to go into effect
   B. An intrusion from the Internet
   C. Finding someone has accessed files they should not have accessed
   D. The monthly meeting of the risk committee

5. The purpose of a tiger team is to do which of the following:
   A. Take up one of the three rings at the circus
   B. Act as an emergency response team at the time of attack
   C. Clean up the mess after an attack
   D. Test the system before the attack

6. A good rule of thumb is (choose two):
   A. All firewalls can be easily hacked; that is why it is best to have two.
   B. The more features and security the firewall offers, the more expensive it is.
   C. After you have allowed everything you want to flow through the firewall, deny everything else.
   D. All data is precious, therefore spare no expense on the firewalls.

7. What is a replay attack?
   A. An unauthorized user pretends to be a valid user. In one case, a user may assume the IP address of a trusted system and use it to gain the access rights that are granted to the impersonated device or system.
   B. The intruder records a network exchange between a user and a server and plays it back at a later time to impersonate the user.
   C. The intruder causes network data to be modified or corrupted. Unencrypted network financial transactions are vulnerable to manipulation. Viruses can corrupt network data.
   D. The intruder floods a server with requests that consume system resources and either crash the server or prevent useful work from being done. Crashing the server sometimes provides opportunities to penetrate the system.

8. What is referred to as a denial of service attack?

   A. The intruder causes network data to be modified or corrupted. Unencrypted network financial transactions are vulnerable to manipulation. Viruses can corrupt network data.

   B. The intruder floods a server with requests that consume system resources and either crash the server or prevent useful work from being done. Crashing the server sometimes provides opportunities to penetrate the system.

   C. This is a generic term for a malicious program that masquerades as a desirable and harmless utility.

   D. Sometimes breaking into a network is as simple as calling new employees, telling them you are from the IT department, and asking them to verify their password for your records.

9. Which is *not* one of the four parts of quantifying risk?

   A. Determine your tolerance levels

   B. Assign a probability to each risk.

   C. Assign a cost to each risk

   D. Assign a priority to each risk

   E. Ask the tiger team

10. To have a really safe screened subnet firewall, the two firewalls should be:

    A. Set to allow everything

    B. Set so that each firewall allows different types of packets to flow through

    C. From different manufacturers

    D. Run on machines that have minimum amounts of memory

Answers to Review Questions

1. D. Also known as a Demilitarized Zone or DMZ, the screened subnet puts two firewalls between the internal network and the outside world.

2. C. There are three things that go into making this decision. First, and foremost, there is no connection to the Internet. The modems can be a concern because someone could theoretically find the numbers and dial in, but since the modems are set to not auto-answer, you have a mini-firewall right there. Finally, all the critical data for the organization is moved offsite every evening, and the transcripts are public record anyway, so the risk is low.

3. B. Oh man, this is a toughie. Answers B or C could be right. Why is it B? Because this is a security course on firewalls, and the official Microsoft stand now is that Proxy Server is not a true firewall. So, small companies with a light Internet presence that want to use a firewall should opt for a bastion host type design.

4. A. This is another tough one. The question is asking for a definition of a risk contingency trigger. That is the event that causes the risk contingency plan to be put into effect. Both B and C could be triggers, but they are not the definition of the trigger.

5. B. The tiger team is tasked with attempting to break into a system to test the security. Once the tiger team has attacked the system, if it finds an intrusion, it reports back to the risk management team, which decides what action to take.

6. B, C. Basically, the more features a firewall will offer, the more expensive it is. Some can get *very* pricey. Also, when defining what traffic can come through the firewall, after you have allowed all the appropriate traffic, deny everything else.

7. B. A replay attack is when an intruder records a network exchange between a user and a server and plays it back at a later time to impersonate the user.

8. B. A denial of service attack is when an intruder floods a server with requests that consume system resources and either crash the server or prevent useful work from being done.

9. E. A, B, C, and D are the four things used to quantify risk.

10. C. In a screened subnet environment, having two firewalls from different manufacturers increases the security.

CASE STUDY

The Multinational Startup

You should give yourself 10 minutes to review this case study, diagram as needed, and complete the questions for this testlet.

Background

Your consulting firm has been hired to assist in the Windows 2000 migration and integration for a company based in Minneapolis, Minnesota. Until the start of this year, the company had 1,000 employees, all based throughout the Twin Cities of Minneapolis and St. Paul. Just before the end of the year, the owner of your company purchased two companies of roughly the same size that will need to be connected to the enterprise network. The total number of users when the project will be completed is estimated at 3,500. In addition, each of these companies comes with various strategic partners that will need to access the information on your enterprise network. The companies that have been acquired are located in Athens, Greece, and in Orlando, Florida. At this point, the buyouts are complete and some minor changes to the infrastructure have been finalized. The time has come to start looking at forming an Internet presence and security.

Current System

Minneapolis Located on the shores of beautiful Lake Calhoun, the company occupies a sprawling campus that includes four different floors in a six-story building. When the company started out five years ago, it had just part of one of the floors and about 100 people. Since that time, the company has grown and any time a tenant has moved out of the building, the company has taken over the office space. This grow-as-you-go philosophy had left members of the same departments scattered throughout the building. However, recently the company signed a long-term contract with a local moving and storage company and has been systematically relocating departments in an orderly manner. Communication has improved and morale has picked up.

All of the floors are connected to the Windows NT network. While the infrastructure was chaotic, it is getting better. The decision has been made to move to Windows 2000. Active Directory Services will be used extensively. Security is now the hot topic, and the CEO wants to know if the company's information is at risk, and what steps are being taken to protect that information. So far, that is as far as the security discussions have gone. Since you have come into the picture, the Internet connectivity has been upgraded to a T1 status. Everyone in the company has access to the Internet and has an Internet mail address. Communication between offices is currently being done using just e-mail, snail mail, and the phone. When the final plan is in place, there will a corporate intranet, and you will be responsible for securing those Web servers as well as the Web servers that will make up the publicly accessible Web pages.

Orlando The Orlando office actually has more people working in it than there are in Minneapolis. It is located in northern Orlando, away from Disney and the tourists. Many of the services in Minneapolis are mirrored in Orlando, things like marketing, accounting, and human resources. The site is all on NT 4, with a variety of applications; some of the applications are compatible with the Minneapolis corporate standards and some aren't. The Orlando office does have a fractional T1 connection to the Internet. The office is using Lotus Notes as their e-mail package. As you can tell, not much has been done here. The users have all had their Internet e-mail addresses changed to the corporate DNS name, and there is a connector in place between Lotus Notes and Exchange, so people can communicate and share appointments and things. The office has been notified that Windows 2000 is coming and by this time next year Lotus Notes will be a thing of the past. While this office will not participate in hosting any of the Web services, they do have an Internet connection and a lot of information that must be protected.

Athens The Athens office has about 1,300 users, most of which are salespeople, marketing types, and support staff. The manufacturing plant is located on the island of Rhodes, and due to local customs, manufacturing occurs only between March and October. The rest of the time, the plant is closed. The office has been upgraded to Windows NT 4 servers running SP5. It is predominantly used for file and print sharing. There is an Internet connection and a Linux box that is providing for only POP3 e-mail.

The decision had been made to upgrade the 3.51 servers directly into Windows 2000, but after it became obvious the planning was going to take a while, the company went ahead and upgraded to NT 4. In addition, the people in Athens know that Exchange is coming. Due to the increase in communication between the United States and Greece, the Athenians are getting more used to e-mail. However, since the mail being sent is still SMTP/MIME, there is concern that plain text is flying over the Internet.

Because this has been a stand-alone company, all of the normal accounting, purchasing, and human resources functions are there. It has been agreed that management will remain with the company. Communication between sites remains by e-mail, snail mail, and phone.

Problem Statement

Now that the integration of the company is at least moving along, security is becoming more and more of a concern. The senior management has tasked you with beginning the security planning process. You will need to provide secure connections between each of the sites and the Internet. You must put in place a plan to establish the risk each location faces and how they are managing the risk. And finally, you need a security plan that will make sense as the company continues to merge.

Envisioned System

Overview Now that it is becoming obvious that these three locations can in fact work together and communicate, the CEO wants to make sure that it is done securely. She has read about this Digital Nervous System, and she wants one. She has also read about other companies that have been hacked, and wants to make sure that it doesn't happen to this company. Of course, like most CEOs, she is not really sure what a hack is, but she knows she is against it.

CEO "Why, I just read in *Forbes Magazine* and *The Wall Street Journal,* about all the trouble some of these companies is having from hackers. Surely that can't be happening here, can it? Why, we have really important stuff on our network and we need it protected. There is another problem here too; I want to make sure that this company is not sued for sexual harassment or anything like that. Keep the hackers out, and make sure to keep the employees away from those sex sites I hear so much about."

Security

Overview Because the product you develop is constantly undergoing research and development, and because the industry is what it is, security must be maintained at a very high level. As you can see from the statements made by the CEO, it is taking a higher priority.

CFO "With the merger going on and with all the systems with highly sensitive data on them, it's paramount that security is maintained at an extremely high level. I cannot emphasize this enough. On the other hand, we have to be careful not to step on any toes, and also to make sure that the security we do install is not too intrusive into people's lives. Our senior management has heard about all those systems where people have to remember dozens of passwords and we certainly don't want anything like that here."

Availability

Because the network will span several different time zones, the availability of the network must be 24x7x365.

Maintainability

Overview There are two problems here. First of all, you will be dealing with an international company, meaning you will not be able to utilize the same vendor for maintenance. Secondly, information will have to be available from all levels of the organization, all day every day. The information must be up-to-date in real time. Because this could possibly tell your competition exactly what you are doing and for whom, the information must be secure.

CEO "These new products we're developing are *so* revolutionary and will have such an impact, that it's important for us to make sure everyone has the same information at the same time."

Athens operations manager "My understanding is that our product will now be bundled with the products developed in Minneapolis. That means we have to know how many to produce. Given the limitations of the Rhodes manufacturing cycle, there may have to be some offloading of responsibilities to other areas of the company."

Performance

CEO "I'm just thrilled to death with our new connection to the Internet. My stock quotes just come flying into my machine. The increased use of e-mail has been a godsend. Just yesterday I received several new pictures of my grandchildren."

Orlando branch manager "It is *wonderful* now that we can communicate with anyone in this company. Some of the people in the home office are still a little shaky using e-mail, but at least they have it. It is a great improvement. Did you know some people have told me that they can see information on our network from their home? How do they do that? Are they supposed to do that?"

Athens branch manager "You know, the RAS system we have built up is just wonderful! Now our employees can work from home!"

Funding

Overview While you have not been given *carte blanche* by the CEO, she has made it clear that money isn't necessarily an issue, within reason of course. The problems need to be solved so that the company can safely continue to manufacture its products in the most efficient manner possible.

CEO & CFO "Look, we don't think that we need the Rolls Royce of installations, *but*, we can tell you that everything is riding on our ability to ship our combined products in a timely manner, and the network we're asking you to build is going to be a big part of that. We think the company will continue to grow, though not as rapidly as in the last several months. So, that being said, give us a network that is secure and makes sense."

Questions

1. What is the current business problem? Choose all that apply.

   A. The e-mail systems are not the same.

   B. Each of the units is connected to the Internet with no firewalls in place.

   C. Management is suddenly concerned with security.

   D. There has not been any risk assessment, security assessment, or risk management.

2. What solution(s) should you implement to solve the customer's business problem? Select all correct responses.

   A. Ensure that each location has a secure connection to the Internet by instituting a bastion host firewall solution.

   B. Set up secure wide area connections between all of the sites. Wide area bandwidth should be adjusted according to the size of the site and its needs.

   C. Up-version all servers to Windows 2000.

   D. Begin the risk management process to provide a framework for the internal and external security plans.

   E. Set up some form of IIS Server in a central location for the sharing of information.

   F. Assure that all users are on a uniform O/S desktop, and that service pack and service release levels are current.

   G. Establish a plan to up-version the existing Exchange servers to Exchange 2000 by Q1 of next year.

   H. Plan and deploy screened subnet firewalls at each location.

   I. Plan and deploy a combination of bastion host and screened subnet types of firewalls.

3. As you begin the risk assessment and management process, what step(s) should you immediately take? Choose the best answer.

   A. Begin forming a study committee, including a member of senior management, and members from all three locations.

   B. Gather in all the network documentation.

   C. Begin taking a high-level overview of the Internet connectivity and intranet plans of the organization.

   D. Talk with the ADS design committee to find out how the network is being integrated into Active Directory Services.

   E. Talk with the infrastructure group to determine how the infrastructure will be affected by the implementation of the firewalls.

   F. All of the above.

4. What is an example of *identity interception*?

   A. This term refers to malicious code running as auto-executed ActiveX control or a Java Applet uploaded from the Internet on a Web server.

   B. This is a generic term for a malicious program that masquerades as a desirable and harmless utility.

   C. The intruder floods a server with requests that consume system resources and either crash the server or prevent useful work from being done. Crashing the server sometimes provides opportunities to penetrate the system.

   D. Someone discovers the user name and password of another valid user. This can occur by a variety of methods, both social and mechanical.

   E. An unauthorized user pretends to be a valid user. In one case, a user may assume the IP address of a trusted system and use it to gain the access rights that are granted to the impersonated device or system.

5. What is an example of *manipulation*?

A. The intruder floods a server with requests that consume system resources and either crash the server or prevent useful work from being done. Crashing the server sometimes provides opportunities to penetrate the system.

B. The intruder records a network exchange between a user and a server and plays it back at a later time to impersonate the user.

C. This is a generic term for a malicious program that masquerades as a desirable and harmless utility.

D. This term refers to malicious code running as auto-executed ActiveX control or a Java Applet uploaded from the Internet on a Web Server.

E. The intruder causes network data to be modified or corrupted. Unencrypted network financial transactions are vulnerable to manipulation. Viruses can corrupt network data.

6. What is an example of a *denial of service*?

A. Network-based business and financial transactions are compromised if the recipient of the transaction cannot be certain who sent the message.

B. This is a generic term for a malicious program that masquerades as a desirable and harmless utility.

C. The intruder floods a server with requests that consume system resources and either crash the server or prevent useful work from being done. Crashing the server sometimes provides opportunities to penetrate the system.

D. Application-specific viruses could exploit the macro language of sophisticated documents and spreadsheets.

E. This term refers to malicious code running as auto-executed ActiveX control or a Java Applet uploaded from the Internet on a Web server.

7. What is an example of a *macro virus*?

   A. The intruder records a network exchange between a user and a server and plays it back at a later time to impersonate the user.

   B. Application-specific viruses could exploit the macro language of sophisticated documents and spreadsheets.

   C. This is a generic term for a malicious program that masquerades as a desirable and harmless utility.

   D. An administrator of a computing system knowingly or mistakenly uses full privileges over the operating system to obtain private data.

   E. Network-based business and financial transactions are compromised if the recipient of the transaction cannot be certain who sent the message.

8. What is *repudiation*?

   A. Network-based business and financial transactions are compromised if the recipient of the transaction cannot be certain who sent the message.

   B. An unauthorized user pretends to be a valid user. In one case, a user may assume the IP address of a trusted system and use it to gain the access rights that are granted to the impersonated device or system.

   C. The intruder causes network data to be modified or corrupted. Unencrypted network financial transactions are vulnerable to manipulation. Viruses can corrupt network data.

   D. This is a generic term for a malicious program that masquerades as a desirable and harmless utility.

   E. If data is moved across the network as plain text, unauthorized persons can monitor and capture the data.

9. What is an example of *misuse of privilege*?

A. Application-specific viruses could exploit the macro language of sophisticated documents and spreadsheets.

B. If data is moved across the network as plain text, unauthorized persons can monitor and capture the data.

C. Sometimes breaking into a network is as simple as telephoning new employees, telling them you are from the IT department, and asking them to verify their password for your records.

D. An administrator of a computing system knowingly or mistakenly uses full privileges over the operating system to obtain private data.

E. The intruder records a network exchange between a user and a server and plays it back at a later time to impersonate the user.

10. What is a *Trojan horse*?

A. If data is moved across the network as plain text, unauthorized persons can monitor and capture the data.

B. The intruder records a network exchange between a user and a server and plays it back at a later time to impersonate the user.

C. Sometimes breaking into a network is as simple as telephoning new employees, telling them you are from the IT department, and asking them to verify their password for your records.

D. This term refers to malicious code running as auto-executed ActiveX control or a Java Applet uploaded from the Internet on a Web Server.

E. This is a generic term for a malicious program that masquerades as a desirable and harmless utility.

Answers

1. B, D. At this stage of the process, management has suddenly discovered security and wants to make sure that everything in the network is as it should be. This is especially true of the connections to the Internet, which at this point in time are exposed. In addition, no one has assessed exactly what risks exist in the company—and before you can protect something, you have to know what to protect.

2. D, H. This calls for a two-pronged attack. You should begin with the risk assessment and risk management process while making plans to implement firewalls at each site. If you look closely at the answers, you will see several that call for the implementation of different types of firewalls. Microsoft says that the bastion host method should be used for small implementations. Over 1,000 in each location does not constitute "small," so go with the recommendations of the screened subnet deployment.

3. F. Again, you have some serious analysis to do, and while that is going on, there are some open connections to the Internet to contend with. Risk assessment should start with the open connections and solve that problem first.

4. D. Identity interception is when someone discovers the user name and password of another valid user. This can occur by a variety of methods, both social and mechanical.

5. E. Manipulation is when an intruder causes network data to be modified or corrupted. Unencrypted network financial transactions are vulnerable to manipulation. Viruses can corrupt network data.

6. C. A denial of service attack (DoS) is when the intruder floods a server with requests that consume system resources and either crash the server or prevent useful work from being done. Crashing the server sometimes provides opportunities to penetrate the system.

7. B. A macro virus is when application-specific viruses could exploit the macro language of sophisticated documents and spreadsheets.

8. A. Repudiation is when network-based business and financial transactions are compromised if the recipient of the transaction cannot be certain who sent the message.

9. D. An example of misuse of privilege is when the administrator of a computing system knowingly or mistakenly uses full privileges over the operating system to obtain private data.

10. E. A Trojan horse is a generic term for a malicious program that masquerades as a desirable and harmless utility.

Technology Review

MICROSOFT EXAM OBJECTIVES COVERED IN THIS CHAPTER:

✓ **Evaluate the company's existing and planned technical environment.**

- Analyze company size and user and resource distribution.
- Assess the available connectivity between the geographic location of work sites and remote sites.
- Assess the net available bandwidth.
- Analyze performance requirements.
- Analyze the method of accessing data and systems.
- Analyze network roles and responsibilities. Roles include administrative, user, service, resource ownership, and application.

Just in case you have forgotten the purpose of the book, it is *security*. Trust us, we are getting closer to talking almost exclusively about security. So far, this has seemed like more of a business primer than an MCSE study guide. We just wanted you to know that we feel for you! At least in this chapter, we get to start talking about technology instead of profit and loss, cost of operations, and information flow. In this chapter, we are still not talking a whole lot about security, but at least we are getting closer. As a matter of fact, Chapter 6, "Evaluating the Impact of the Security Design on the Technical Environment," starts examining and analyzing the current security strategy and the plans for the future. Hey, we didn't make up the objectives—we're just the messengers!

In this chapter we are going to start looking at the infrastructure of the network. We are going to figure out what the size of the company is, where its resources and users are, and how that is going to affect the way that Windows 2000 will impact the network bandwidth. Once we can figure out how much bandwidth there is available, we can figure out if what we have will be sufficient for what we will need to do the job. When we look at what types of bandwidth we will need to do the job, we will need to figure out how we are actually going to get to the data and systems.

Finally, we are going to go back and review some network roles and responsibilities. Some of this has been covered in the previous four chapters. Some of this will be covered again before the book is finished. You may ask why, but Microsoft is nothing if not thorough!

Documenting the Current Environment

From a technology point of view, the quickest way to analyze the company size, user count, and resource distribution is to document your current environment. This will give you a better feel for your existing network's physical and logical topology.

Microsoft Exam Objectives

Evaluate the company's existing and planned technical environment.

- Analyze company size and user and resource distribution.

Having that inventory of the hardware and software that your organization uses is very important for the planning of the Windows 2000 infrastructure.

For an in-depth look at planning a Windows 2000 infrastructure, check out the *MCSE: Infrastructure Design Study Guide* (Sybex, 2000), by Bill Heldman. The discussion in our book will pale by comparison, but should be enough to get you through the security exam.

The area of the network you will need to document includes things like:

- Hardware and software
- Network infrastructure
- File, print, and Web servers
- *Line-of-business applications*
- Directory services architecture

Sounds like a rather daunting task, doesn't it? There are some tools available to help. The NT network diagnostic applications like Network Monitor may be useful for documenting part of your network. If you have access to System Management Server, that will provide some insights also. Finally, there may be some utilities provided by the manufacturer of your WAN equipment that may provide help.

Hardware and Software Inventory

If you haven't already done this, it is time to conduct a hardware and software inventory of all the servers and client computers on the network. In addition, you will have to document all routers, printers, modems, and any other hardware, such as *Redundant Arrays of Independent Disks (RAIDs)* and Remote Access Servers (RASs). As part of the inventory, be sure to include information on the *Basic Input/Output System (BIOS)* settings and the configuration of peripheral devices, like printers, scanners, and input devices. Document the driver versions and other software and firmware information.

Your *software inventory* should list all applications found on all computers, and include version numbers, or date and time-stamp data, of dynamic link libraries (DLLs) associated with the applications on your system. Also remember to document any service packs that you might have applied to either the operating system or applications. This task does not need to be as large as it sounds. You can obtain this information using scripts and a variety of third-party applications that will get the information from Windows and Windows NT networks that use Windows Management Instrumentation (WMI).

If you don't already have it, Systems Management Server may be a wise investment at this point. It can produce detailed reports on hardware, system software, and applications in use in your organization.

For more information on using SMS to provide this information, look at Chapter 8, "Using System Management Server to Analyze your Network Infrastructure," in the *Windows 2000 Server Resource Kit, Deployment Planning Guide*.

An example of the documentation for a network configuration of a server or a client computer should include information from the network settings section of control panel. Include things like Identification, Services, Protocols, Adapters, and Bindings tabs. If you have some software that will allow you to take some screen shots, the documentation is relatively painless. Check out the identification page shown in Figure 5.1.

FIGURE 5.1 Sample server identification page

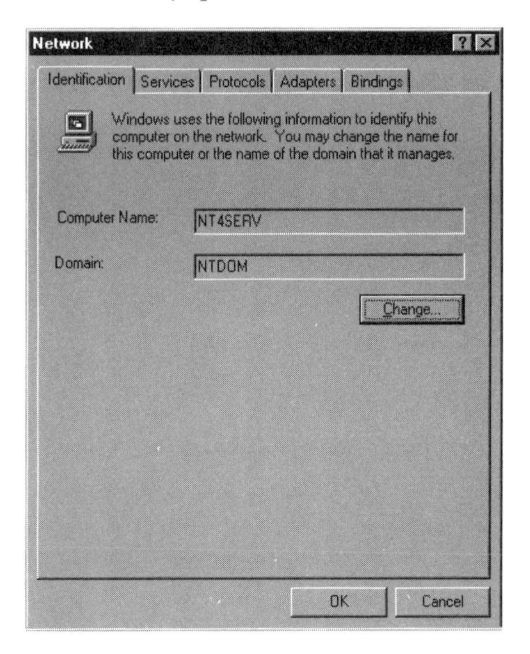

By continuing to use the screen shot program, we can show the services for this server (see Figure 5.2).

FIGURE 5.2 Sample server services page

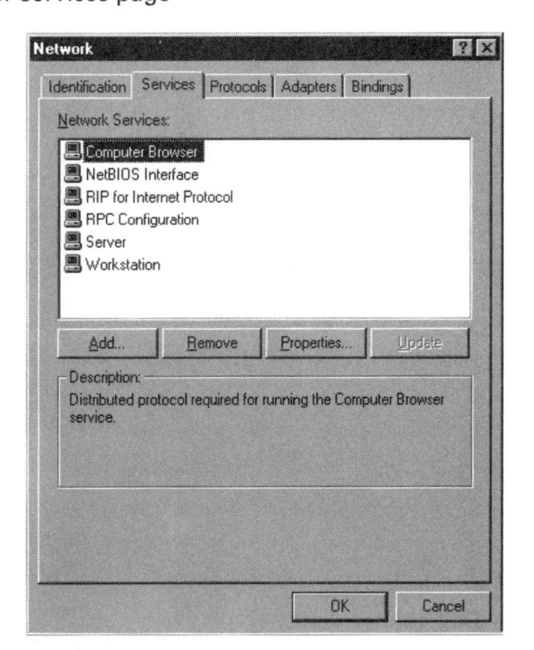

One more tab, one more screen shot, and the protocols page comes to life (see Figure 5.3).

FIGURE 5.3 Sample server protocols page

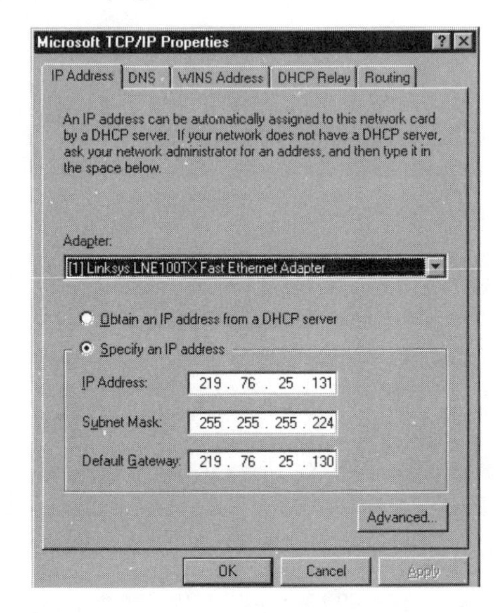

To get a look at where this server goes to look for DNS resolution, we simply took another screen shot, which is shown in Figure 5.4.

FIGURE 5.4 Sample server page showing source of DNS information

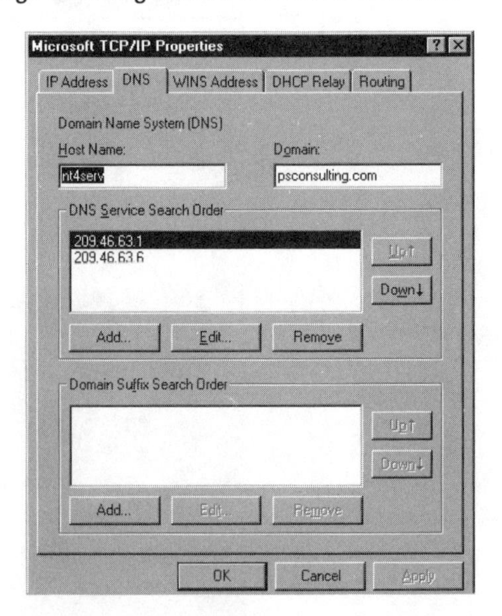

We also needed to document the number and types of adapters (see Figure 5.5).

FIGURE 5.5 Sample server page showing adapter information

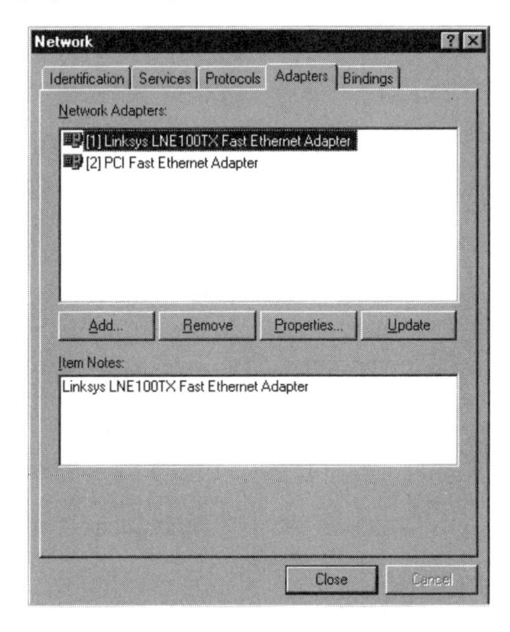

Finally, we needed to document the protocol bindings, as shown in Figure 5.6.

FIGURE 5.6 Protocol bindings information

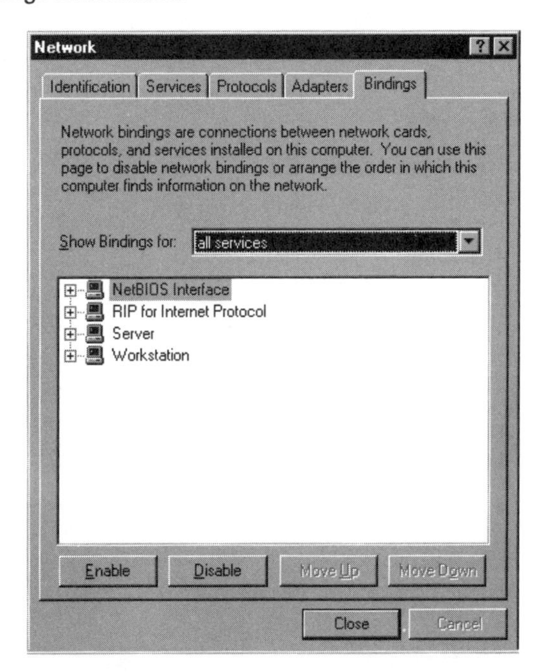

There was some more information that we needed. It included information on the TCP/IP configuration of the two network cards. Here, we went out to a command line and issued an `IPCONFIG /ALL >A:\IP.TXT` command.

Govanus here. Yep, I am an old DOS kind of guy, working at the command line if for no other reason than to confuse all the icon-users out there and stay one step ahead. We old guys have to use every resource at our disposal to stay ahead of you young pups!

That command took all the IP information and sent it to a text file on the A:\ drive. At that point we can put the documentation into a folder, a document management system, or even print it out and put it in an old-fashioned three-ring binder. Our hardware documentation would be close to complete, and it would be relatively painless.

Here is the output from the `IPCONFIG` command:

```
Windows NT IP Configuration
   Host Name . . . . . . . . . : nt4serv.psconsulting.com
   DNS Servers . . . . . . . . : 209.46.63.1
                                 209.46.63.6
   Node Type . . . . . . . . . : Broadcast
   NetBIOS Scope ID. . . . . . :
   IP Routing Enabled. . . . . : Yes
   WINS Proxy Enabled. . . . . : No
   NetBIOS Resolution Uses DNS : No
Ethernet adapter FET2:
   Description . . . . . . . . : PCI Fast Ethernet Adapter
   Physical Address. . . . . . : 00-A0-0C-C0-19-19
   DHCP Enabled. . . . . . . . : No
   IP Address. . . . . . . . . : 223.146.115.132
   Subnet Mask . . . . . . . . : 255.255.255.224
   Default Gateway . . . . . . : 223.146.115.130
Ethernet adapter Lne100tx1:
   Description . . . . . . . . : Linksys LNE100TX Fast
Ethernet Adapter
   Physical Address. . . . . . : 00-A0-CC-35-79-A7
```

```
DHCP Enabled. . . . . . . . . : No
IP Address. . . . . . . . . . : 219.76.25.131
Subnet Mask . . . . . . . . . : 255.255.255.224
Default Gateway . . . . . . . : 219.76.25.130
```

Why Do I Need This Stuff?

The hardware and software inventories will be useful to you. They can be used for these purposes:

- To make sure that the current network infrastructure, the server hardware, computer BIOS, and the software configurations are all compatible with Windows 2000 Server. You can do this by comparing your inventory to the *Hardware Compatibility List* (*HCL*). Better to do it before you start an upgrade than to discover halfway through that something isn't going to like Windows 2000.
- To determine how much you are going to have to upgrade each server and client computer. This will allow you to draft specifications and purchase orders for acquiring new equipment.

After you have finished the inventory, you should have a really good idea of the company size and the user and resource distribution.

Design Scenario: Surely There Must Be an Easier Way?

The last project just ended, and the next one hasn't been signed yet, so you are in that contractor state of limbo fondly referred to as "on the bench." This is the time when you get to study for your next certification test, play with new technology, or be available to do whatever the dispatcher has for you to do.

Today, when you come into the office, the dispatcher calls you over and asks you to help out one of the new PC techs. It seems that this tech was asked to document network and IP settings for three dozen computers and after two days, he reports that he is about half done. People are beginning to talk. When you get to the client site, the PCT shows you the extensive notes he takes on each system. He has his laptop sitting next to the system he is inventorying and he goes to a screen on the computer to inventory, and then enters all the information into documents on his laptop in his best two-finger, one-word-per-minute typing style. You ask politely if he might like to find an easier way. He is all for that—this typing is not why he joined the ranks of the IT professionals.

At this time, you break out a handy-dandy screen shot utility, and write some batch files for the lad to use. He can install the utility, take screen shots of the network configuration tabs, and run two or three batch files that export the information to a text file. Once that is done, the floppy can be copied into a directory on the laptop, the utility can be uninstalled, and the tech is on to the next system. Between the two of you, 20 systems are inventoried before lunch, and now both of you can go back and ride the bench!

Document Network Infrastructure

While you are documenting the network environment, step back and look at the big picture. Besides noting all the specifications of each piece of equipment, take a minute to make notes about areas that need to be stabilized before the upgrade can successfully happen. If you solve current problems before deploying the new operating system, deployment and troubleshooting will be much easier. Setting up a test lab to duplicate problems and configurations is a good way to evaluate the impact of deploying Windows 2000 with a given set of protocols, hardware drivers, and client/server configurations.

Microsoft Exam Objectives

Evaluate the company's existing and planned technical environment.

- Assess the available connectivity between the geographic location of work sites and remote sites.

When documenting the infrastructure, you are getting both the hardware data to document your infrastructure's physical structure and software data to document the existence and configuration of protocols in use on your network. You also need to document the *logical organization* of your network, name and address resolution methods, and the existence and configuration of services that are used. Documenting the location of your network sites and the connection speeds between them will also assist you in deciding how to upgrade to Windows 2000.

Physical Network Diagram

When you create, modify, or upgrade your physical network diagram, you are checking the information that you have about your existing network. This can include the following:

- How the physical communications links are configured. This may be as simple as copying your wiring diagram or network map.
- All your different types of servers. Be sure to include computer name, IP address (if static), the server's role in the network, and what function it serves in the domain membership scheme of things. A server can operate in many roles other than as a primary domain controller (PDC) or backup domain controller (BDC). It can be a *Dynamic Host Configuration Protocol (DHCP)* server, a *Domain Name System (DNS)* server, a *Windows Internet Name Service (WINS)* server, a print server, a database server, a router, an application server, or a file server.
- Document the locations of devices, such as printers, hubs, switches, modems, routers and bridges, and proxy servers, that are on the network. Be sure to document the real location. For example, if a print server is located under someone's desk, make sure you make a note of

that. Too many hours have been wasted trying to find equipment that you know should be there, only to discover it was hiding behind a dozen pairs of shoes.

- Wide Area Network (WAN) communication links (analog, ISDN, or other) and the available bandwidth between sites. This could be just an approximation or an actual measured capacity.
- Number of users at each site, including mobile users.

Figure 5.7 is an example of a physical network.

FIGURE 5.7 Sample physical network map

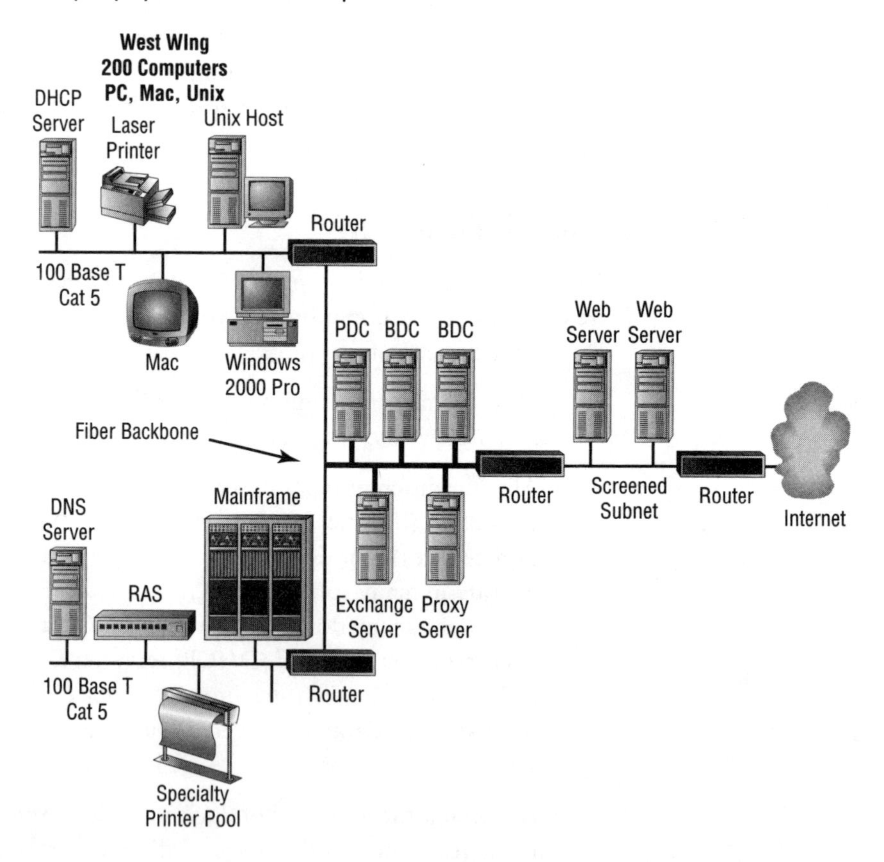

If you can, document any special configuration information like firmware revisions, throughput, or anything else out of the ordinary. You can also document the connections between remote locations and combine some of that information, as shown in Figure 5.8. This is another example of a physical network diagram, just taking a different form.

FIGURE 5.8 Sample physical network map illustrating remote connections

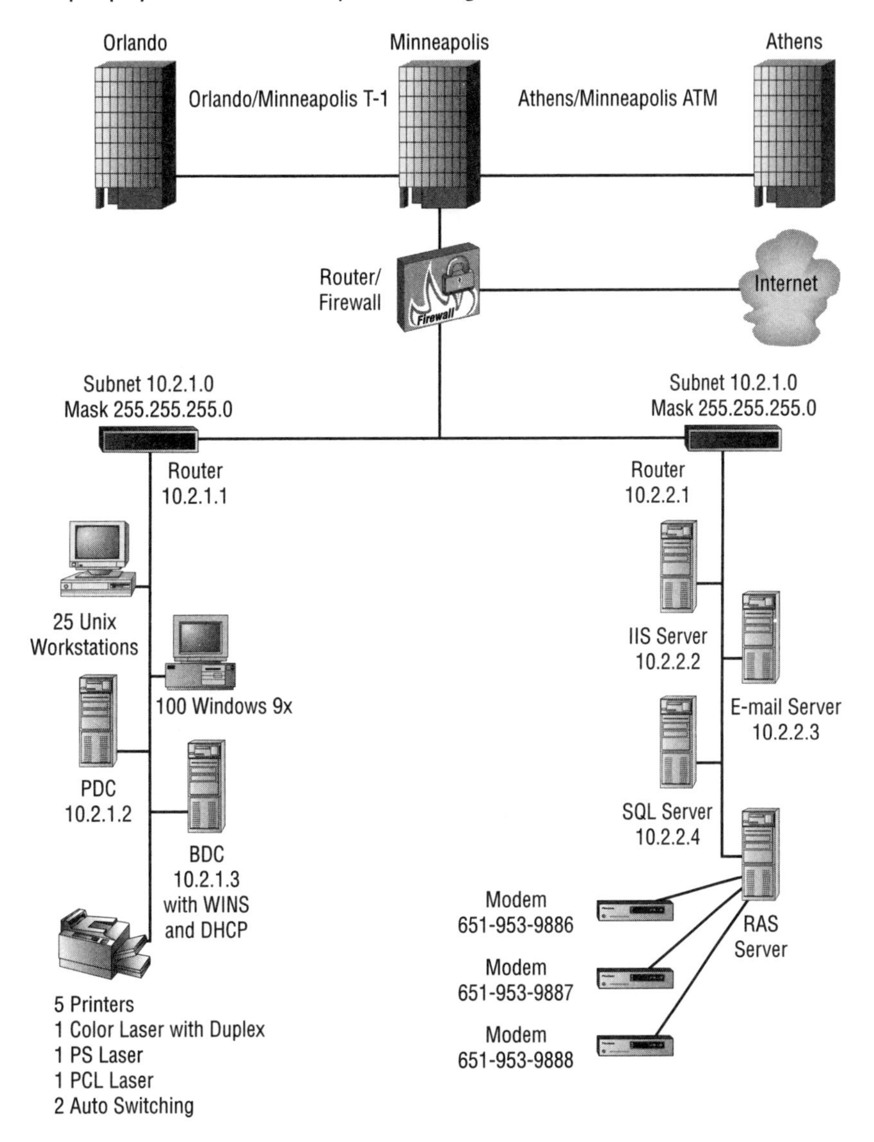

Logical Network Diagram

The difference between the logical network diagram and the physical network diagram is one of granularity. The logical diagram is like taking a step back and, rather than looking at each PC on each desktop, just looking at the management or configuration pieces. Figure 5.9 shows the difference.

FIGURE 5.9 Logical network diagram

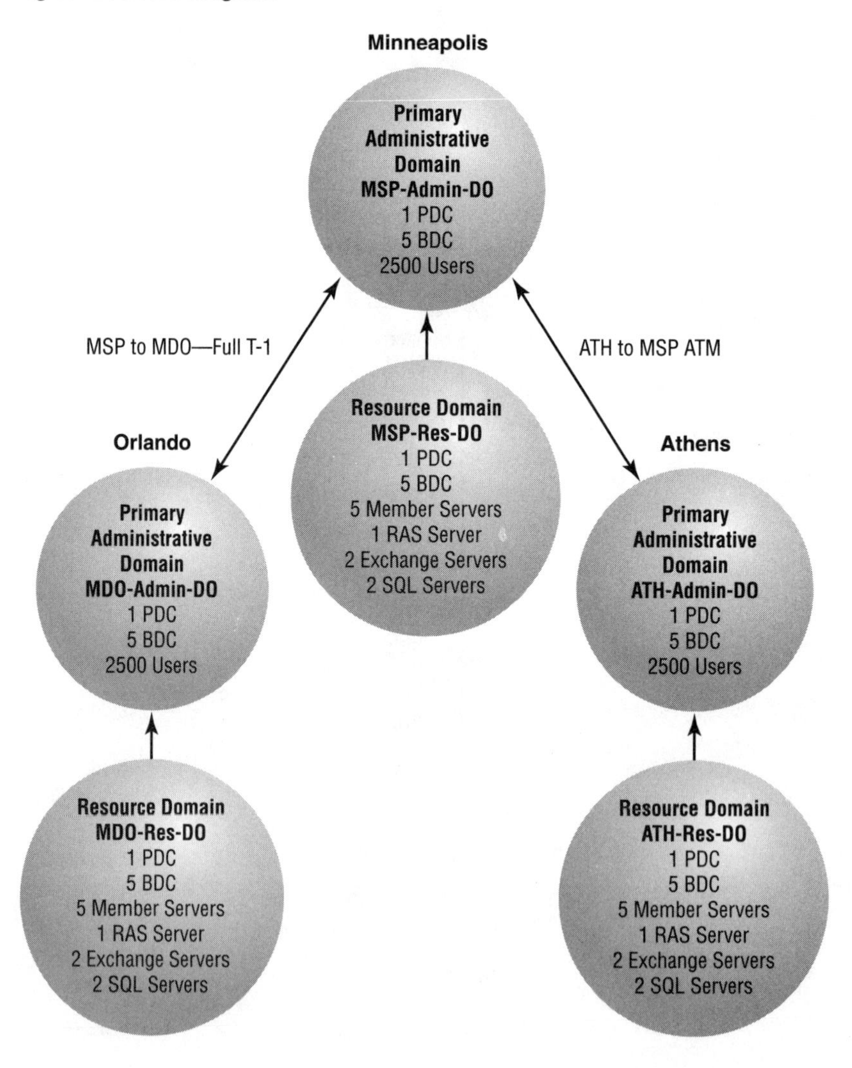

A logical network diagram should show things like these:

- *Domain architecture*, including the domain trust relationships, how they are named, and if there are any special subnet addressing schemes.
- Server roles, including primary or backup domain controllers, DHCP Service servers, or WINS servers.
- Trust relationship details, including whether the trust is *transitive*, one-way, or two-way.
- This would be a good place to include operating systems as well: NT 4, Windows 2000 Professional, Windows 2000 Server, Unix, Unix-like, Novell, etc.

These diagrams, as you can no doubt tell, serve multiple purposes. Besides showing the location and number of users and resources, they also serve to assess the available connectivity between the geographical location of work sites and remote sites.

Other Network Considerations

Besides the diagrams of the networks, there are some other things that need to be documented. This will help in your planning by providing you with a baseline to improve on.

Name Resolution Services

Make sure that you document all DNS and WINS servers that are on your network. Make sure the configuration information and version information are included as well as hardware details. If any of the DNS servers are not running Windows NT, check to make sure the version of DNS can support dynamic updates and service (SRV) resource records. If the version of DNS you are using does not currently support dynamic updates, you will have to determine if there are upgrades available from the software.

Most networks are a combination of different operating systems. If the hosts on your network are not running NT, document the services they use and the services they provide, like Unix BIND, Berkeley Internet Name Domain, and DNS. If your network does have BIND present, it may cause a problem because versions earlier than 4.9.7 or BIND 8.1.2 are not compatible with Windows 2000. Other things to note include the presence of Service

Advertising Protocol (SAP) and the Routing Information Protocol (RIP) services.

Before you go into the exam, make sure you know about BIND, RIP, and SAP, and their coexistence in a Windows 2000 environment—not that there would be test questions on this, but you never know!

IP Addressing Configuration Methods

The documentation process should also cover all DHCP service servers on your network, including information like the following:

- IP addresses that you have statically assigned to servers or client computers
- DHCP settings, such as default gateways and DHCP relay agents, as well as other DHCP options
- Subnet details and how they relate to the overall network map
- The number of subnets and hosts on your network, including a complete list of the IP addresses and subnet masks on the network
- Lease durations for DHCP addresses

Remote and Dial-Up Networking

Are there remote or mobile users on your network? More documentation! In this case, you have to document how they access the network and what the dial-up configurations look like at various locations. If you use third-party software for mobile users, review and document the configuration of those products. If you use virtual private networks (VPNs), document the configurations of your VPN with the goal of evaluating whether you can replace it with a Windows 2000 VPN.

Bandwidth and Performance

Have you ever heard the complaint, "God, the network is slow today"? Let me rephrase that, have you ever gone through a day when you

Design Scenario: Network Maps

When you finally get another new client, you find it is an international company with three locations. In your meeting with the IT director, she tells you that she has just taken the job and the last IT person kind of left things in the lurch. When she starts asking the staff questions about the network, she tends to get some blank looks. She would like you to put together a plan of the network. Where do you think you should start?

You start by asking questions about the network layout. About all she can tell you is the location of the offices and the names of the IT administrative contacts in each location. AT&T Worldnet handles all communications between sites. Immediately after the meeting, you put a call in to the AT&T representative and get a copy of AT&T's network map of the WAN infrastructure. By the end of the day, you have sent e-mails to each of the IT contacts, and your logical map of the network is almost complete. After that is done, you will begin working on a proposal to create a detailed physical and resource map of the network.

didn't hear the complaint, "God, the network is slow today"? If your company is planning on upgrading to Windows 2000, this is the perfect time to start to do something about that problem.

Microsoft Exam Objectives

Evaluate the company's existing and planned technical environment.

- Assess the net available bandwidth.
- Analyze performance requirements.

Start by documenting your network's current *bandwidth utilization*. You should do this to establish a baseline from which changes can be measured. If you are wondering how you are going to do this, there are a variety of third-party and Microsoft tools to measure bandwidth metrics, such as bytes and packets sent or received, transmit and receive errors, and packets per second. Document the speed of the network links between your organization's network segments and the geographical locations.

Once this has been accomplished, look at the logical and geographical dispersion of your organization in terms of bandwidth considerations. Take a close look at the amount and types of traffic that move over your organization's communication links. As an example, are your Wide Area Network (WAN) links periodically slowed by domain replication between domain controllers at different sites? Make sure the net available bandwidths of all the WAN links and network segments are documented. Try to record the available bandwidth during the course of low, normal, and high network utilization.

If you are an NT 4 MCSE, this should not be a new concept. There were several questions on your exams about the ways to study bandwidth. Each of the questions pointed to the fact that you should sample the network traffic at different times of the day, and different days of the week.

Bandwidth in the Planned Environment

Now it is time to look at how you think your upcoming change to Windows 2000 will affect your network infrastructure. Consider the quality and the bandwidth of your existing network. This includes questions like these:

- What kind of network wiring are you using?
- What are the speeds and throughput of your hubs and cabling, and are these fast enough for your purposes?
- How fast are the links to your remote sites?
- How much traffic is generated on your network internally?
- How much traffic is generated over the external links?

Again, we arrive at the question of what does this have to do with the price of tea in China? When you upgrade to Windows 2000, there is going to be an impact on bandwidth usage. If you have a remote office that uses just a word processor or a spreadsheet as its main desktop application, that is not going to generate much network traffic to the branch server. In this case, Category 3 twisted pair, 10 Mbps network cabling would be adequate. In the main office, you might have shared applications with shared data, like databases and accounting systems, as the main desktop applications. These applications will generate far more network traffic and require faster network devices and cabling.

All through this book, we have been talking about the Digital Nervous System. The Digital Nervous System makes use not only of the corporate intranet, but also of the Internet, and any time you connect an enterprise network to the Internet, bandwidth will be taking a serious hit. Ethernet networks running shared applications might now require a Category 5 cabling and infrastructure that can operate at 100 Mbps.

Start by evaluating your bandwidth in the test lab for a specific configuration. If your organization plans to use voiceover IP, or video-over IP, your hardware must be capable of handling the bandwidth demand of those services.

The next question would be, how could I tell how much bandwidth that would take? If you are working in the lab, there are built-in Windows diagnostic tools that can help you determine how much the bandwidth demand will increase if, for example, you decide to institute real-time videoconferencing over your network's WAN links. In a test lab, you can test several possible configurations of your equipment and operating parameters to figure out the lowest demand.

Depending on the Windows 2000 features you decide to use in your deployment, your bandwidth will be affected. For example, if you have a distributed file system (dfs) in a branch office that replicates over a slow link to another dfs volume, you may be faced with a decision to upgrade the link to improve bandwidth or place the alternative volume in the branch office to reduce the amount of network traffic on the slow link.

In addition, there are some features of Windows 2000 that do require specific configurations. One of these would be placing a VPN server at one end of a WAN connection as part of establishing a secure VPN connection. You will need to include configuration considerations, such as how you plan to integrate the VPN with proxy servers, in your plan. Look closely at the existing infrastructure of your network and the anticipated benefits and features that you expect to deploy.

You will also have to check out your network devices for compatibility with Windows 2000. The hardware compatibility list is an important part of any Windows 2000 deployment. Check it for network cards, modems, and any other peripherals. You may be surprised at the ways that Windows 2000 can make use of hardware. For example, it can offload TCP checksum calculations onto network adapter cards that support this Windows 2000 feature.

If performance is still an issue, take a closer look at all that Windows 2000 does support. For example, it does support Asynchronous Transfer Mode (ATM). If you are wondering how to get to ATM from a traditional infrastructure, Windows 2000 eases the transition by offering *LAN emulation* (LANE) services. Windows 2000 also supports IP over ATM. If you are going to take advantage of these features, make sure the ATM vendor supplies updated drivers for the operating system and make sure your adapters are listed on the HCL.

Windows 2000 and Bandwidth

You already know about the Active Directory Service. There will be some increased overhead between domains, organizational units (OUs), sites, and forests as more and more organizations are attached to your network. There are other internal uses for bandwidth also.

Windows 2000 makes heavy use of dynamic DNS and of DHCP. Now, dynamic DNS is simple in concept, but seriously cool in implementation. As you know from your intimate knowledge of TCP/IP, DNS is the name resolution protocol that allows your browsers to resolve the name `www.microsoft.com` to an IP address. You also know that Dynamic Host Configuration Protocol (DHCP) is used to automatically assign IP addresses to hosts on your network, including information on things like gateways, proxy servers, WINS servers, and the location of those DNS servers.

The way names like `www.microsoft.com` get resolved to IP addresses is to have the name registered in the first place. Traditionally that required human intervention at some point along the way. With dynamic DNS, the human intervention has been removed. Now, if you bring up a Web server, it can go out and request an IP address from a DHCP server, lease an address, and then register itself with DNS. This way, hosts like servers do not require a static IP address. That is just one more stride for the system administrator not having to work as hard, but it is also one more load on the bandwidth.

When you plan your network, consider the placement of your DHCP servers in regard to the number and size of the geographical sites on your network and the speed and reliability of its WAN links. DHCP traffic between remote sites requires an improvement in the bandwidth and reliability of the links between.

Some Windows 2000 networks may still have to support clients that resolve IP addresses using NetBIOS requests. This requires WINS, and generally works with Windows version 3.2 and earlier, Windows 95, Windows 98, and

Windows NT. As you plan your network, this is a very good time to begin eliminating WINS on your network. It was originally designed to handle smaller networks and its bandwidth use does not scale well to the enterprise.

If you are going to be installing Windows 2000 Routing and Remote Access servers for LAN-to-LAN and secure VPN links, keep in mind that it does support a variety of protocols including IPX/SPX and AppleTalk.

If your Windows 2000 network is also going to be integrated with Unix systems, note the version of BIND that exists on your system. While Windows 2000 is fully compatible with earlier versions of BIND, there is increased DNS functionality with BIND versions 4.9.7 or BIND 8.1 and later.

Again, this is an important section of the book. On the exam, you may be asked to make some decisions based on WAN connectivity or the placement of various services. We will be covering some of these topics in more depth later in the book, but you need to assure yourself that you have the foundation laid before we get there.

Design Scenario: "God, the Network Is Slow!"

One of your customers has just decided to make the move to Windows 2000. Like most customers, he decided that he would just make the change, so he has four or five domain controllers, several member servers, several resource servers, and about 1,000 users all operating on Windows 2000. They have configured the dynamic DNS and have the DHCP thing going. Everything is working—it is just not working as quickly as they would have liked. When the customer asks you about it, you ponder knowingly, and then ask several questions. "First of all, what type of network infrastructure do you have?"

The answer comes back, "We have just finished rewiring the building with the finest Category 3 cabling on the market. I got one heck of a deal on Category 3 cabling. Sometimes, it really pays to go against the grain. Why, I managed to save thousands over buying that Category 5 stuff and moving to 100 Mbps Ethernet. Even the concentrators were on sale!"

At this point, you slowly move your chair back toward the wall, back where you can make a quick getaway if necessary, and suggest to the client he check his available bandwidth. Your best bet is that the Category 3, 10 Mbps Ethernet just isn't carrying the load, and the client will have to do it again, this time the right way!

Accessing Data, Systems, and Resources

When we start talking about accessing data, systems, and resources, this says "servers." That translates into domain controllers; member servers; and file, print, and application servers. How are you going to make all these things available during the upgrade process?

Microsoft Exam Objectives

Evaluate the company's existing and planned technical environment.

- Analyze the method of accessing data and systems.

Domain Controllers

If you work in a large company, you will be using an incremental deployment of Windows 2000 into the production environment. There is no way around it. Once you get Windows 2000 installed on a few servers in your organization, you can use the Windows 2000 utilities to manage the network.

Windows 2000 is designed to be backwardly compatible with Windows NT. Windows NT 4 workstations using the NTLM protocol can send network authentication requests to any Windows 2000 domain controller acting as a domain controller in a Windows NT domain. Trust relationships are easily established between Windows 2000 domains and Windows NT 4 domains, supporting authentication between domains. Basically this translates into the fact that you do not have to upgrade all of your NT 4 domains to Windows 2000 at the same time.

When you do upgrade an NT 4 domain to a Windows 2000 domain, you need to upgrade the primary domain controller in the given domain first. Once that has been upgraded, then you can upgrade the backup domain controllers in that domain to Windows 2000 at your own pace. When all the controllers are upgraded, the domain can be added to the ADS tree. Then member servers and client computers can be upgraded independently from your domain upgrade strategy.

When you do upgrade a domain controller, as in most network-related operations, make sure to have a plan in place to cover your anatomy. Find a way to make sure that you can roll things back if something goes wrong. In the case of the Compaq computer rollout, they made sure that they had all domain controllers synchronized and backed up before doing a rollout. They would then pull a BDC offline and put it in a closet. That way, if anything did go wrong, they could at least reestablish the domain. Microsoft refers to this process as bringing a BDC current and then isolating it.

Hmm. A process. One that is definable. Knowing the process and what goes on when would seem to be an easy target for a test writer. What do you think?

Member Servers

Member servers are servers that function as a member of a Windows NT or Windows 2000 domain, but whose role is not that of a domain controller. Member servers serve the network by providing functions like these:

- File, print, and application services
- Web, proxy, and remote access servers
- Database servers
- Certificate servers

Before upgrading, make sure to check the hardware compatibility list and consider the role of the server after the upgrade. Microsoft has not issued any rigid specifications for estimating the hardware components required for a particular function. You will need to test the computer in its role (preferably in the test lab rather than on the production network) to determine whether it is adequate in terms of CPU speed, RAM, and hard disk space, and whether it performs adequately while running the drivers, applications, and protocols of its intended role.

The Security Infrastructure

Windows 2000 has been designed with security in mind. It features things like IPSec, Kerberos authentication, and public keys to offer a higher level of security than was previously available in Windows NT.

Because 2000 is designed to be backwardly compatible with Windows NT, it is easy to introduce Windows 2000–based servers into an existing network security structure. However, as you migrate or upgrade your NT network to 2000, the security-specific features that you plan to deploy will affect your security strategy.

A big part of the distributed security services of Windows 2000 is its support for Public Key Infrastructure (PKI). PKI is an authentication method employing digital certificates, certification authorities (CA), and certificate management software. You can use the CA to secure e-mail clients and Internet communication, as support for smart card technology, and to secure communication with non-Kerberos clients. The use of PKI and how to deploy it will be discussed in greater detail later in this book.

When you are looking at bandwidth, performance, and access, this is a good time to define your certificate requirements, practices, and strategies. If you are thinking of implementing a third-party PKI, make sure it is compatible with Windows 2000. In this case, compatibility means support of rooted certification hierarchies as implemented in Windows 2000. Note that the Windows 2000 PKI will not replace the existing Windows domain trusts and authorization mechanisms, such as the Kerberos protocol. The PKI features of Windows 2000 are integrated with the domain controller and Kerberos authentication services.

PKI can be implemented in stages, to support particular goals. These goals may be to support e-mail or to support authentication to existing systems, depending on your priorities.

Design Scenario: Who's on First?

You have been called in to oversee a Windows 2000 rollout. The on-site staff has done all of the planning work, and, to be honest, you are quite surprised that this company is ready to roll out already. Several weeks ago, the head of the IT department called with some questions about Windows 2000 that showed the staff needed training. You suggested it, but you weren't sure they would carry through. The company is notoriously closefisted.

When you arrive, you immediately enter a meeting with the head of IT and his staff. They are reviewing the rollout scenarios. The conversation starts out with a brief overview of the network. It appears the company has one administrative domain and two resource domains. The appropriate trust relationships are in place, and the logical network map appears to be in place. When the head of IT starts talking about the physical map, it appears your fears may be groundless. He lists all the servers, key problem areas, what servers provide what service, and even covers applications that will have to be upgraded. You are impressed.

Now comes the discussion of the rollout. The head of IT lays out an elaborate plan where all the application servers and member servers will be upgraded first. After all, he doesn't want to make the changes too traumatic for the users.

When it is your turn, you compliment the head of IT on the fine job he has done mapping out the network, and suggest that you start rewriting the rollout schedule so the primary domain controllers can be upgraded first, the backup domain controllers next, and then, when you have time, the application servers.

Analyzing Network Roles and Responsibilities

As you continue to evaluate the company's existing and planned technical environment, you have to consider more than the hardware and wiring. You have to consider who currently cares for and uses the hardware and software, and what, if any, impact the upgrade will have.

Microsoft Exam Objectives

Evaluate the company's existing and planned technical environment.

- Analyze network roles and responsibilities. Roles include administrative, user, service, resource ownership, and application.

Earlier in the chapter we discussed having maps of the network that actually went several layers deep. First of all, there is the granular map that shows how many computers of what type are available at each location. Then you would take a step back and look at how these computers were organized into domains, and how the domain model would be impacted by the implementation of Active Directory Services. Then, we took another step back and looked at how the various locations were integrated and how the communications occurred between different sites. Now we have to take another step back and find out who is taking care of all these things and how are they doing it. The roles would include administrative, user, service, resource ownership, and managing applications.

Identifying Administrative Roles

We need to make the distinction between centralized and distributed management. Centralized management or administration says, in a small network, "I am the network god or goddess and I control all in my world. No one else shall venture here." With distributed management, the network administrators say, "We are the network gods or goddesses and we control all in our world. Because we are so important, we have to delegate the minor stuff so we won't be disturbed." Obviously, centralized administration is usually found in smaller companies. In this section, we take a look at how the administration is decentralized and what must be done to get the administration team up to speed on Windows 2000. As you can see from Figure 5.10, this could lead to a type of a network map all its own.

FIGURE 5.10 Summary identifying administrative roles

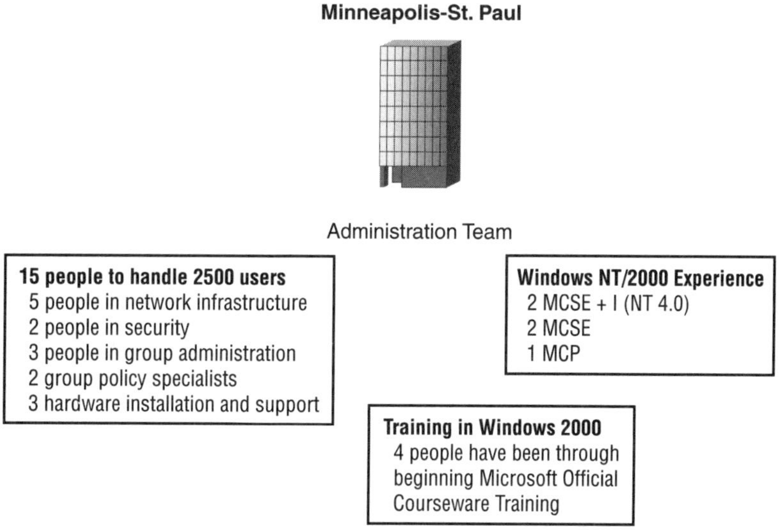

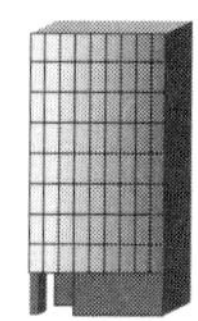

Here you see that the network map shows the number of admin team members and their location, experience, and training. In this scenario, you are trying to locate where your administrative specialists are, to determine if there are any shortcomings throughout the network. For example, in Minneapolis-St. Paul, there are no Internet specialists, Web page specialists, or e-mail specialists. When it comes time to roll out Exchange 2000, a specialist may have to be imported from other areas of the company, or you may have to train current staff members to make up the shortfall.

Also, looking at the breakdown, you see that less than 30% of the staff have been through Windows 2000 training. Since the company is going to be migrating from the traditional domain trust environment, having the remainder of the staff trained on Windows 2000 would be a definite benefit. The terminology alone is enough to cause the most hardened NT-bigot to cringe and scratch in places where it is usually not polite to scratch!

Identifying User Roles

Since this chapter is about the technology involved in your network, what in the world would the role of users have to do with that? After all, users are the reason for the network to be there. Users tend to be that faceless, nameless mass of humanity that we deal with on a day-to-day basis. They just use the technology we provide.

It is in that *use* of technology that we have to pay particular attention as we plan taking the enterprise network to the next level. Because we deal with users so often, sometimes we take them for granted. This is not the time to have that occur.

Normal Users

Normal users are the vast majority of the users on our network. They don't really require anything special, they just require everything to work. In addition to wanting it to work, they want it to work consistently. That may be where the rub comes in. What defines "consistently"? Is it the fact that the network has an up-time of 99%? Or is it that the bandwidth is sufficient to provide an adequate level of response 99% of the time?

Normal users are the ones who need the day-to-day applications, need access to the Internet, need access to the intranet, and need to be protected from themselves.

Secure Users

Secure users are the users who may require a higher degree of security for one reason or another. Each and every industry has some of these, and most companies do, also. For example, network administrators often hate it when there is a problem in the payroll department. No matter what the task, the network weenie often feels like he is intruding into some high-level, top-secret stuff, and that he might accidentally see what the great high mucketymucks were taking home, and that would corrupt him somehow.

Increased security may be as simple as making sure the patient health records are not accessible to those people who are in charge of collecting past due accounts. It may be as complex as working with financial institutions that require C-2 compliance, or handling computer issues on warships of the United States Navy. Each case requires special care, and if your network has users like this, be sure to include them in your plan.

Power Users

The power user may be a software developer with a test system hooked to your network, or even a Web designer with a test Web server included in the corporate system. Imagine the issue if your company was responsible for discovering and testing computer viruses. In that case, you may have to design an entirely separate room just for the virus detection team.

Specialty Users

Specialty users are the people with high-level demands. They may be users of nonstandard operating systems, or they may be users of applications that eat bandwidth for lunch. These are the people with the special needs that should be considered as part of the testing process.

Users who fall into this category may be a group of Mac users who have their own little AppleTalk segment that feeds into the main network, or may be the CAD/CAM operators. In some environments, it may be digital imaging that takes up terabytes of disk space and requires instant access to the data.

Identifying Service Roles

As you continue to look at the network, you will see how important the services you provide are. Now, the services we are discussing have nothing to do with delivering a new desktop to the new person in Accounting. These services will include DNS, DHCP, routing, e-mail, SMS, RAS, or any of a dozen other things to keep the network responsive to a user's needs. Each of these services may have special bandwidth needs that must be recognized and accounted for.

Earlier in the chapter we looked at the ways DHCP and DNS had to be carefully integrated to maintain backward compatibility and yet provide the functionality of Windows 2000. Previously we also looked at how firewalls could protect the network from intrusion and also from abuse. Each of these services needs to be designed and implemented after significant testing in your Windows 2000 environment.

What about other services? In a large enterprise environment, certainly as envisioned by the developers of Windows 2000, remote connectivity becomes a major player. Another diagram that can be created, or integrated into the others, will show how a remote client and remote networks will connect to the corporate network.

In this case, Microsoft has come up with a flowchart for determining the network connectivity strategies. Take a look at Figure 5.11.

FIGURE 5.11 Network connectivity strategies

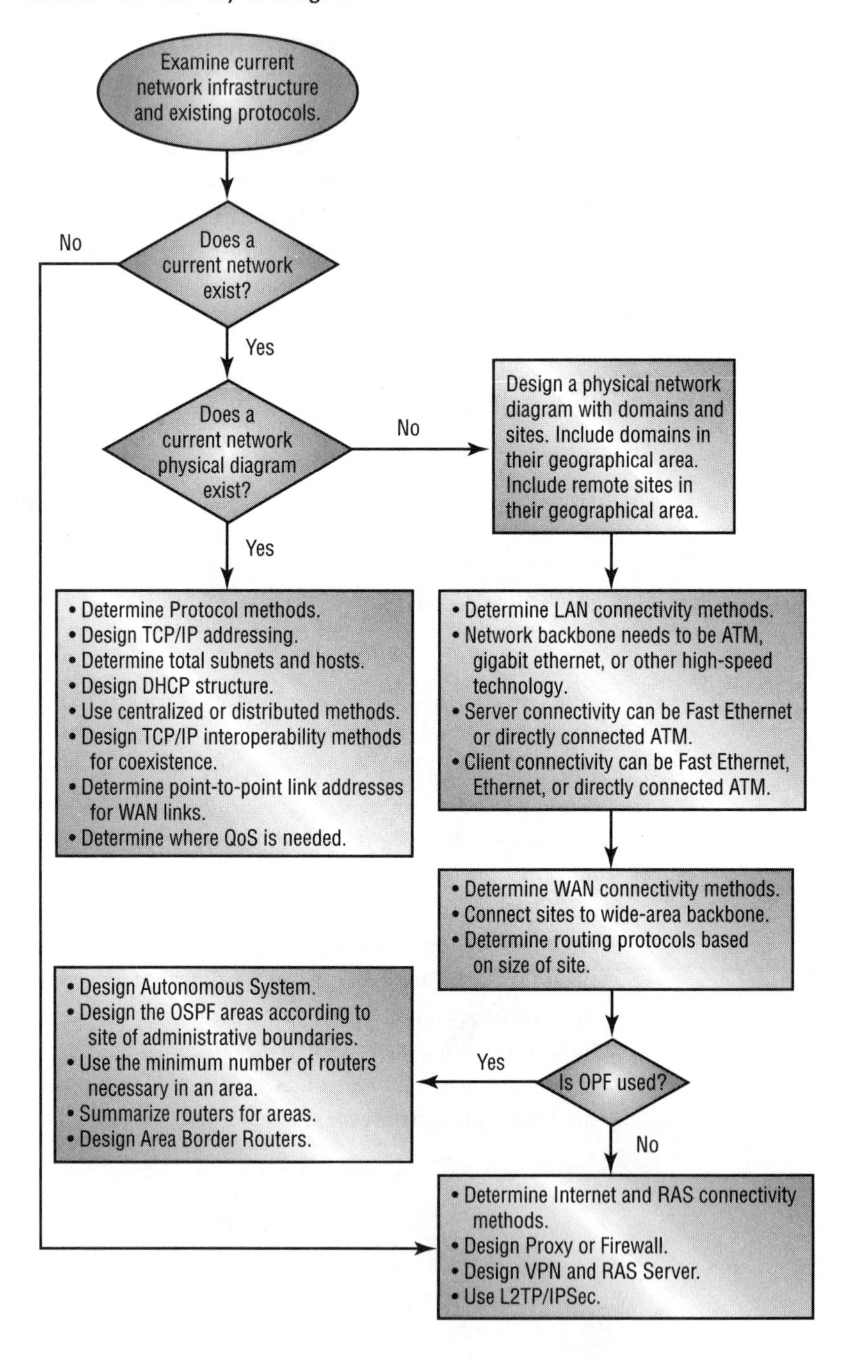

In this case, the design involves many of the small parts of a network that form the overall infrastructure. The sections that follow will look at some of the different aspects of the Wide Area Network and some of the procedures and design considerations. In this case, we are looking at either Virtual Private Networks or remote access connectivity.

Identifying Resource Ownership

What are the critical resources within your organization that must be accounted for? You know the types: There is that super-spiffy specialty printer that costs $10 every time someone fires it up. There are also permissions that must be assigned to whoever has to control all the routers that have to control the communication over the backbone.

Types of Resources

Resource objects include computers and network resources such as IP networks, routers, peripherals, user groups, and individual user accounts. Four of these types of resources can be identified using SMS.

System Computers and other hardware devices on the network, such as routers and Simple Network Management Protocol (SNMP) devices

User group Windows 2000 user groups

User Individual user accounts

IP Network IP subnets as reported by the Network Discovery Agent

Identifying Critical Applications

When you are looking at the technology providing the underlying support for your network, it is critical to remember some of the specialty applications or network-wide applications that are used. Once again, this is an opportunity to make sure that when the rollout is completed, users have access to everything they need, with the performance and reliability they require.

Suppose your company has committed to a Digital Nervous System. Now you and your rollout team are tasked with making that information immediately available to everyone within the enterprise, whether their offices are in Minneapolis, Minnesota, or in a small town outside of London. The information must be up-to-date and consistent, and performance and reliability must be such that the users will want to use the system. This will surely call for some advanced planning.

Applications are designed to gather information and provide knowledge. One case of application envy would be in educational institutions. Students are the ultimate knowledge workers, since learning is all about gathering knowledge. If you are designing your network for a school or a school system, you have to give teachers the ability to use the Internet and the enterprise network to share with each other, and to let students explore the subject matter in a variety of ways.

For example, in one school district, the Western Heights Independent School District in Oklahoma, PCs have become a way of life. This is a small seven-school district with a moderate industrial tax base. Its student population is culturally diverse. Fully 65% of the kids qualify for free or reduced-cost lunches, so this is not the richest school district in the United States. In a recent three-year period, though, the school district voted to spend $6.8 million in local funds to create a technology-driven curriculum.

The PC has been integrated into the classroom as a teaching tool. One civics teacher starts his class each day with fresh news gathered from the Internet. First there is a science photo from NASA, then news clips from `abcnews.com`, and then a story that leads into whatever he is going to talk about that day.

If you were the administrator or network architect of this school system, it would be important to understand how the teachers and students use the applications you provide to do their daily jobs.

We hate to harp, but there is a lot of good stuff in this chapter that you may see again when you have money on the line. Know the concepts and we will expand on them in later chapters.

Summary

Finally, we have gotten to talk about technology! We started out looking at how the network was laid out. First we looked at the size of the company and where the employees were. Once that had been established, it was necessary to document how all these distant offices were able to communicate with one another, as well as how access was provided to remote users.

Once we documented how people were able to access the network, the terms *performance* and *reliability* came into play. An application is not much use to a user if the performance is so slow that the user feels the application is not responding. For an application to be an important part of someone's work life, it must be responsive and also available at all times.

Finally, we examined who was going to take care of all that: where were the administrators, where were the specialty applications, the services, and the resources to make the network something the users would use.

This chapter didn't have much on security. That will start to change in the next chapter. We are still going to be analyzing, but we will be analyzing the impact of the security design on the existing and planned technical environment. This will include assessing the existing systems and applications, identifying existing and planned upgrades and rollouts, analyzing the technical support structure, and analyzing existing and planned network and systems management.

If you are wondering how many times you are going to have to analyze and assess the existing systems and applications, have patience: this time, we will be looking at security and determining if the systems and applications are consistent with Windows 2000 security.

Key Terms

Before you take the exam, be certain you are familiar with the following terms:

bandwidth utilization

Basic Input/Output System (BIOS)

Dynamic Host Configuration Protocol (DHCP)

Domain Name System (DNS)

domain architecture

Hardware Compatibility List (HCL)

LAN emulation (LANE)

line-of-business applications

logical organization

Redundant Array of Independent Disks (RAID)

transitive

Windows Internet Name Service (WINS)

Review Questions

1. As you do your technology review, things to document include:

   A. Hardware and software

   B. Network infrastructure

   C. File, print, and Web servers

   D. Line-of-business applications

   E. Directory services architecture

   F. All of the above

2. When you inventory hardware and software, you should include:

   A. BIOS

   B. Serial numbers from hard drives

   C. Configuration settings

   D. Driver versions

   E. Manufacturer of memory

3. From a Windows 2000 command line, the command to output all of the TCP/IP configuration information to a text file named `IP.TXT` is:

   A. `WINIPCFG /ALL >> IP.TXT`

   B. `IPCONFIG > IP.TXT`

   C. `DHCP /ALL`

   D. `IPCONFIG /ALL >IP.TXT`

4. What is the difference between a logical network design and a physical network design?

   A. A logical network design shows all the hardware and software; a physical network design shows the locations of domains and sites.

   B. The physical network design shows the locations of hardware and domains. The logical network design shows the locations of sites and software.

   C. The difference between the logical network diagram and the physical network diagram is one of granularity. The physical network design shows all hardware and software, and the logical network design shows domains with necessary and important servers.

   D. There is no difference. The two are interchangeable.

5. What versions of BIND are compatible with Windows 2000 Dynamic DNS?

   A. All versions.

   B. Any version prior to version 5.3.1.

   C. BIND is not compatible with Windows 2000.

   D. Versions after 4.9.7 or after 8.1.2.

6. After the migration to Windows 2000, Ethernet networks running shared applications should be configured for which of the following?

   A. Cat 3 cabling running 4MB Token Ring

   B. Category 5 cabling that can operate at 100 Mbps

   C. Category 5 cabling that can operate at 16 Mbps

   D. Fiber optics as a backbone and ATM to the desktop

7. As you plan to upgrade an NT 4 domain, it is mandatory to upgrade which level of servers first?

   A. PDC.

   B. BDC.

   C. Member Servers.

   D. There is no preferred order.

8. When upgrading an NT 4 domain to Windows 2000, when should member servers be upgraded?

   A. Immediately after PDCs.

   B. Immediately after BDCs.

   C. Before the routers but after the RAS servers.

   D. The need to upgrade member servers is not pressing.

9. SMS can help in the documentation phase with these tasks:

   A. Identifying computers that do have sufficient or compatible hardware

   B. Identifying computers with software that is not compatible or that will not operate properly with Windows 2000

   C. Identifying applications most often used, so that compatibility testing is done on all of the most important applications

   D. Analyzing network usage to determine network capacity availability, protocols in use, and which computers are being used as servers

   E. Upgrading incompatible applications

   F. Ensuring that incompatible applications are not used

   G. All of the above

10. When you document the network roles, they should include these:

A. Owners of resources

B. Members of the Domain Admin Group

C. Line-of-business applications

D. Number of users

E. All of the above

Answers to Review Questions

1. F. When a technology review is completed, everything should be documented: hardware and software; the network infrastructure; file, print, and Web servers; line-of-business applications; and the directory services architecture.

2. A, C, D. As part of the inventory, be sure to include information on the basic input/output system (BIOS) settings and the configuration of peripheral devices like printers, scanners, and input devices. Document the driver versions and other software and firmware information.

3. D. From a Windows 2000 command line, the command is `IPCONFIG /ALL; >IP.TXT. WINIPCFG` is used with Windows 9x versions.

4. C. The difference between the logical network diagram and the physical network diagram is one of granularity. The physical network design shows all hardware and software, and the logical network design shows domains with necessary and important servers.

5. D. If your network does have BIND present, it may cause a problem because versions earlier than 4.9.7 or version 8.1.2 are not compatible with Windows 2000.

6. B. Ethernet networks running shared applications might now require Category 5 cabling that can operate at 100 Mbps.

7. A. When you do upgrade an NT 4 domain to Windows 2000, you need to upgrade the primary domain controller in the given domain first.

8. D. The need to upgrade to Windows 2000 is not as pressing as the need to upgrade domain controllers.

9. G. SMS will allow you to do a computer inventory that will show which computers have sufficient or compatible hardware, identify computers running software that is not compatible with Windows 2000, identify applications that are most often used, analyze network usage, upgrade incompatible applications, and ensure that incompatible applications are not used.

10. E. The roles would include administrative, user, service, resource ownership, and application.

The Multinational Startup

You should give yourself 10 minutes to review this case study, diagram as needed, and complete the questions for this testlet.

Background

Your consulting firm has been hired to assist in the Windows 2000 migration and integration for a company based in Minneapolis, Minnesota. Until the start of this year, the company had 1,000 employees, all based throughout the Twin Cities of Minneapolis and St. Paul. Just before the end of the year, the owner of your company purchased two companies of roughly the same size that will need to be connected to the enterprise network. The total number of users when the project is completed is estimated at 5,500. In addition, each of these companies comes with various strategic partners that will need to access the information on your enterprise network. The companies that have been acquired are located in Athens, Greece, and in Orlando, Florida. At this point, the buyouts are complete and some minor changes to the infrastructure have been finalized. The time has come to start looking at beginning to plan the actual Windows 2000 rollout.

Current System

Minneapolis Located on the shores of beautiful Lake Calhoun, the company occupies a sprawling campus that includes four floors in a six-story building. When the company started out five years ago, it had just part of one of the floors and about 100 people. Since that time, the company has grown, and any time a tenant has moved out of the building, the company has taken over the office space. This grow-as-you-go philosophy had left members of the same departments scattered throughout the building. However, recently the company signed a long-term contract with a local moving and storage company and they have been systematically relocating departments in an orderly manner. Communication has improved and morale has picked up.

All of the floors are connected to the Windows NT network. While the infrastructure was chaotic, it is getting better. The decision has been made to move to Windows 2000. Active Directory Services will be used extensively. Security is now the hot topic, and the CEO wants to know if the company's information is at risk, and what steps are being taken to protect that information. To date, that is as far as the security discussions have gone. Since you have come into the picture, the Internet connectivity has been upgraded to a T1 status. Everyone in the company has access to the Internet and has an Internet mail address. Communication between offices is currently being done using just e-mail, snail mail, and the phone. While some things about the physical network are known, there are still many mysteries. The remote offices of Orlando and Athens are certainly pretty much of a black hole as far as the corporate IT department is concerned.

Orlando The Orlando office actually has more people working in it than there are in Minneapolis. It is located in northern Orlando, away from Disney and the tourists. Many of the services in Minneapolis are mirrored in Orlando—things like marketing, accounting, and human resources. The site is all on NT 4, with a variety of applications; some of the applications are compatible with the Minneapolis corporate standards and some aren't. The Orlando office does have a fractional T1 connection to the Internet. The office is using Lotus Notes as their e-mail package. As you can tell, not much has been done here. The users have all had their Internet e-mail addresses changed to the corporate DNS name, and there is a connector in place between Lotus Notes and Exchange, so people can communicate and share appointments and things. The office has been notified that Windows 2000 is coming and by this time next year Lotus Notes will be a thing of the past. While this office will not participate in hosting any of the Web services, they do have an Internet connection and a lot of information that must be protected.

When the buyout happened, much of the Orlando IT department bailed out and went to work in other areas. The help desk folks have stayed and many of the PC techs are still there. There are two-way trusts between domains, so the administration of the network is working; there just isn't much information available about the network.

Athens The Athens office has about 1,300 users, most of whom are salespeople, marketing types, and support staff. The manufacturing plant is located on the island of Rhodes, and due to local customs, manufacturing occurs only between March and October. The rest of the time, the plant is closed. The office has been upgraded to Windows NT 4 servers running SP5. It is predominantly used for file and print sharing. There is an Internet connection and a Linux box that is providing for only POP3 e-mail.

The decision had been made to upgrade the 3.51 servers directly into Windows 2000, but after it became obvious the planning was going to take a while, the company went ahead and upgraded to NT 4. In addition, the people in Athens know that Exchange is coming. Due to the increase in communication between the United States and Greece, the Athenians are getting more used to e-mail. However, since the mail being sent is still SMTP/MIME, there is concern that plain text is flying over the Internet.

Because this has been a stand-alone company, all of the normal accounting, purchasing, and human resources functions are there. It has been agreed that management will remain with the company. Communication between sites remains by e-mail, snail mail, and phone.

The Greek IT department remains intact and ready to help.

Problem Statement

Now that the integration of the company is at least moving along, it is time to start the Windows 2000 rollout. Everything starts with the rollout and everyone in the company is anxious to have it finished. The issue right now is where to start.

Envisioned System

Overview Now that it is becoming obvious that these three locations can in fact work together and communicate, the CEO wants to make sure that it is done securely. She has read about this Digital Nervous System, and she wants one. She understands that the basis for the Digital Nervous System and the instantaneous access to information is Windows 2000. She has been through major IT shifts before and she isn't really excited to have any bad experiences.

CEO "It is time to upgrade to Windows 2000. Our current NT 4 network, while stable, isn't providing us with the features that Windows 2000 will give us. Now that we are international in scope and have all these partners who need to access our network, we need the functionality. Now that I have said that, I have to tell you the last time I went through a major operating system change, *everything* went wrong and our network was hosed up for months. There will not be a repeat of that performance, is that understood?"

Security

Overview Because the product you develop is constantly undergoing research and development, and because the industry is what it is, security must be maintained at a very high level. As you can see from the statements made by the CEO, it is taking a higher priority.

CFO "With the merger going on and with all the systems with highly sensitive data on them, it's paramount that security is maintained at an extremely high level. I cannot emphasize this enough. On the other hand, we have to be careful not to step on any toes, and also to make sure that the security we do install is not too intrusive into people's lives. Our senior management has heard about all those systems where people have to remember dozens of passwords and we certainly don't want anything like that here."

Availability

Because the network will span several different time zones, the availability of the network must be 24x7x365. The 24x7x365 uptime must be maintained during the rollout. According to the IT director, "Everything has to be checked and double-checked to make sure that it will work with Windows 2000 and that it will continue to work on our network while we upgrade. We cannot afford downtime."

Maintainability

Overview There are two problems here. First of all, you will be dealing with an international company, which means that you will not be able to utilize the same vendor for maintenance. Secondly, information will have to be available from all levels of the organization, all day, every day. The information must be up-to-date in real time. Because this could possibly tell your competition exactly what you are doing and for whom, the information must be secure.

CEO "These new products we're developing are so revolutionary and will have such an impact that it's important for us to make sure everyone has the same information at the same time."

Athens operations manager "My understanding is that our product will now be bundled with the products developed in Minneapolis. That means we have to know how many to produce. Given the limitations of Rhodes' manufacturing cycle, there may have to be some offloading of responsibilities to other areas of the company."

Performance

Overview The CEO is thrilled to death with the new connection to the Internet. She has been able to communicate with the remote offices in a more efficient manner, and she is glad to have all the functionality she had at her last job. She received the monthly reports from the general managers in Greece and Orlando and she was able to review the reports and formulate questions for both managers and for the managers' staff.

Orlando branch manager "It is *wonderful* now that we can communicate with anyone in this company. Some of the people in the home office are still a little shaky using e-mail, but at least they have it. It is a great improvement. I understand that Windows 2000 will make things even better. We have so many remote users that are running around with vital information on their laptops—it will be great to get that encrypted."

Athens branch manager "Will the Windows 2000 rollout mean we will have to buy a new server? Can we still keep our Unix hosts?"

Funding

Overview While you have not been given *carte blanche* by the CEO, she has made it clear that money isn't necessarily an issue, within reason of course. The problems need to be solved so that the company can safely continue to manufacture their products in the most efficient manner possible.

CEO & CFO "Look, we don't think that we need the Rolls Royce of installations, *but* we can tell you that everything is riding on our ability to ship our combined products in a timely manner, and the network we're asking you to build is going to be a big part of that. We think the company will continue to grow, though not as rapidly as in the last several months. So, that being said, give us a network that makes sense."

Questions

1. What is the current business problem?

   A. The e-mail systems are not the same.

   B. Each of the units is connected to the Internet with no firewalls in place.

   C. Management is suddenly concerned with rolling out Windows 2000 without having any idea of what they currently have.

   D. There has not been any risk assessment, security assessment, or risk management.

2. What solution(s) should you implement to solve the customer's business problem?

   A. The company appears to have the makings of a logical network map. Begin by putting that on paper.

   B. Set up secure wide area connections between all of the sites. Wide area bandwidth should be adjusted according to the size of the site and its needs.

   C. Up-version all servers to Windows 2000.

   D. Begin having the IT departments in Orlando and Athens physically and logically map their networks.

   E. Set up some form of IIS Server in a central location for the sharing of information.

   F. Assure that all users are on a uniform O/S desktop, and that service pack and service release levels are current.

   G. Have the application development team begin to inventory line-of-business applications and test their compatibility with Windows 2000.

   H. Plan and deploy screened subnet firewalls at each location.

   I. Plan and deploy a combination of bastion host and screened subnet types of firewalls.

3. As you gather in the network information, what kinds of things are you looking for in these maps?

   A. Numbers and types of users

   B. Documented DHCP scopes for each server

   C. Printouts of routing tables

   D. Location of domain controllers and description of who they serve

   E. Location of SQL applications

   F. Hardware, software, and operating system inventory

   G. All of the above.

Answers

1. C. Management has suddenly discovered Windows 2000, and it appears that the management team would like it in place right now. The problem seems to be that no one knows exactly what the enterprise network really looks like.

2. A, D, G. The business case calls for the Windows 2000 upgrade, but no one is sure where to start. They appear to have a high-level overview about the network, so start by putting that on paper. While that is being done, the various IT departments can be putting together their physical inventory and network maps, so these can be merged into an enterprise map. Because this is a physical inventory, the PC techs in Orlando can do most of it. When it comes to the network layer inventory, someone from Minneapolis will have to be dispatched to Orlando to handle the problem.

3. G. All of the information you gather at this point will be beneficial later.

Evaluating the Impact of the Security Design on the Technical Environment

MICROSOFT EXAM OBJECTIVES COVERED IN THIS CHAPTER:

✓ **Analyze the impact of the security design on the existing and planned technical environment.**

- Assess existing systems and applications.
- Identify existing and planned upgrades and rollouts.
- Analyze technical support structure.
- Analyze existing and planned network and systems management.

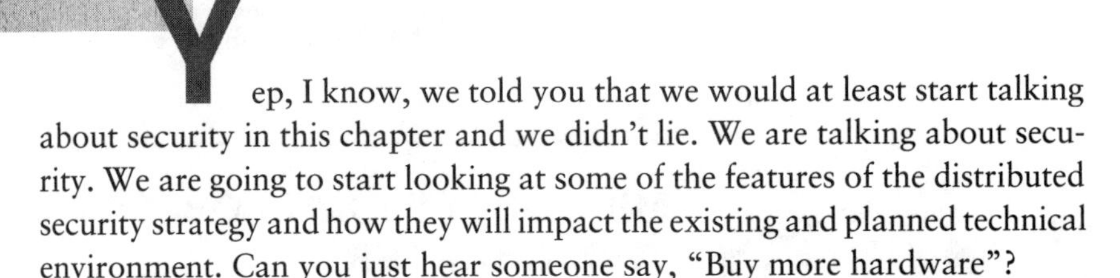

Yep, I know, we told you that we would at least start talking about security in this chapter and we didn't lie. We are talking about security. We are going to start looking at some of the features of the distributed security strategy and how they will impact the existing and planned technical environment. Can you just hear someone say, "Buy more hardware"?

In this chapter we are going to take a break and do a better analysis of the new security features of Windows 2000 and what the impact of each will be on the technical environment. Then we can take that information and put it to use to figure out how the existing applications can be enhanced with Windows 2000 security. If there were parts of the security structure that don't quite measure up, they would fall into the existing upgrades and rollouts category.

Since this all implies massive amounts of change, you know that technical support will be busy, and the analysis of the technical support structure will determine if it is ready to handle the load. Finally, we will look (again) at analyzing the existing and planned network and systems management. This is a look at how the security configuration tool can make system management an easier task.

So that is the task ahead of us. It may seem pretty daunting, but at least we are dealing with security and not return on investment! In the next chapter, we start the design phase, where we begin looking at the Windows 2000 security baseline. That is just a little teaser to help you through the hard work ahead.

Windows 2000 Security Concepts

Before we can discuss a new security plan intelligently, we have to make sure that we are operating on a level playing field. Since some of the people reading this book may be long-term security professionals, and some people may be security newbies, we should probably spend some time defining terms. These terms will even be helpful when you write your security plan. They will go a long way toward helping you familiarize yourself with distributed security. In as many cases as possible, we will try to compare and contrast the NT 4 system with the Windows 2000 system or point out how the concept applies to the upcoming migration or upgrade.

Windows 2000 Security Model

Windows 2000 security is based on a simple model of authentication and authorization that uses Microsoft Active Directory directory service. *Authentication* identifies the user when the user logs on and when the user makes network connections to services. Once the user has been identified, the user is *authorized* to access a specific set of network resources based on permissions. Authorization takes place through the mechanism of access control, using *access control lists* (*ACLs*) that define permissions on file systems, network file and print shares, and entries in Active Directory.

Domain Model

In Windows 2000, a domain is a collection of network objects, such as user accounts, groups, and computers, that share a common directory database with respect to security. A domain identifies a security authority and forms a boundary of security with consistent internal policies and explicit security relationships to other domains.

Migrating Domains to Windows 2000

Before you can migrate Windows NT domains to 2000, there are certain steps that must be accomplished:

1. Complete the design of the Windows 2000 forest.

2. Plan the migration of Windows NT domains to Windows 2000 native domains and deploy new features of Windows 2000 Server.
3. Plan the restructure of the Windows 2000 domains.

If you were to put this into a flowchart, it would look like Figure 6.1.

FIGURE 6.1 Domain migration flowchart

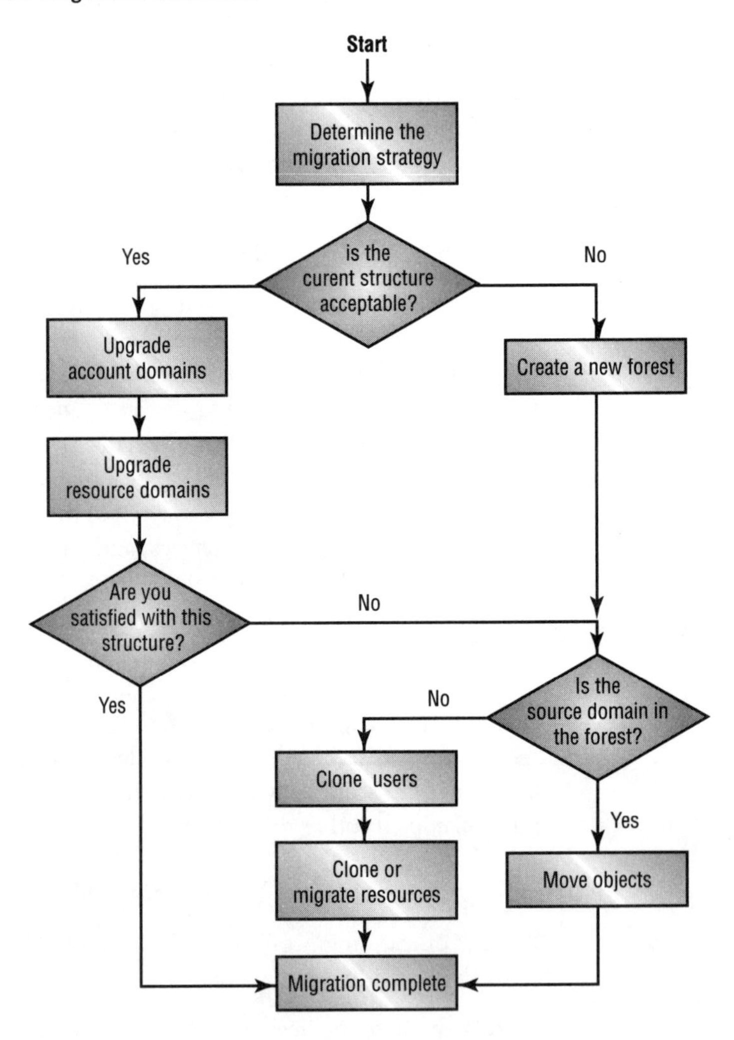

When you start analyzing your current domain environment and begin looking at migrating to Windows 2000, you want to make sure that the migration is as painless as possible. The migration should meet certain goals, as laid out in Table 6.1.

TABLE 6.1 The Path to a Perfect Migration

The Goal Should Be	Which Means You Will Need to Do This
A seamless transition to Windows 2000 causing little or no disruption to the production network.	You must make sure that you have planned for all eventualities to make sure that the users can access their data, the resources are available, and applications are accessible during the migration process. Since most people hate change, strive to make sure the users' familiar environment is maintained during and after the migration.
To maintain the current levels of system performance or improve response time.	You must make sure that you have planned for all eventualities to make sure that the users can access their data, the resources are available, and applications are accessible during the migration process. Since most people hate change, strive to make sure the users' familiar environment is maintained during and after the migration.
To eliminate network downtime, or increase the average mean time between failures.	You must make sure that you have planned for all eventualities to make sure the users can access their data, the resources are available, and applications are accessible during the migration process. Since most people hate change, strive to make sure the users' familiar environment is maintained during and after the migration.
To minimize the administrative overhead.	You must make sure that every effort is made to minimize the number of times a member of the IT staff needs to touch a user's computer after the upgrade. Keeping the number of user contacts to a minimum means your upgrade was seamless.

TABLE 6.1 The Path to a Perfect Migration *(continued)*

The Goal Should Be	Which Means You Will Need to Do This
To maximize the number of *quick wins.*	Getting a quick win means to have some feature of the new network available at the earliest opportunity so people can see how they will benefit from the upgrade.
Above all, you should maintain system security.	There should be little or no negative impact on the current security policy. Make sure the security of the network is maintained or is strengthened after the upgrade.

As you analyze your current domain trust structure, your goal should be to migrate the NT domains and move the Windows 2000 domains to native mode as soon as possible. *Native mode* is the final operational state of a Windows 2000 domain, and is enabled by setting a switch on the user interface. While the procedure for the switch is relatively simple, the implications are extensive. Switching to native mode means all the domain controllers in the domain have been migrated to Windows 2000. Native mode is one of those things that once you do it, you can't go back!

Domain Migration Concepts

Domain upgrade is sometimes referred to as "in-place upgrade" or "upgrade." A *domain upgrade* is the process of upgrading the Primary Domain Controller (PDC) and the Backup Domain Controllers (BDCs) of a Windows NT domain from Windows NT Server to Windows 2000 Server.

Domain restructure is sometimes referred to as "domain consolidation." A *domain restructure* is a complete redesign of the domain structure, usually resulting in fewer, larger domains. This choice is for those who are dissatisfied with their current domain structure or who feel that they cannot manage an upgrade without serious impact to their production environment.

Upgrade and restructure are not mutually exclusive; some organizations might upgrade first and then restructure, while others might restructure from the start. Both require careful thought and planning before choices are implemented.

Trust Management

A trust is a logical relationship established between domains to allow *pass-through authentication,* in which a trusting domain honors the logon authentications of a trusted domain. In Windows 2000, you will hear the term *transitive trust. A transitive trust* refers to authentication across a chain of trust relationships. In Windows 2000, trust relationships support authentication across domains by using Kerberos v5 protocol and NTLM authentication for backward compatibility.

To start the examination of a domain structure of an enterprise network, look at Figure 6.2. It is fairly indicative of a common multiple master domain design found in many organizations.

FIGURE 6.2 Common domain design

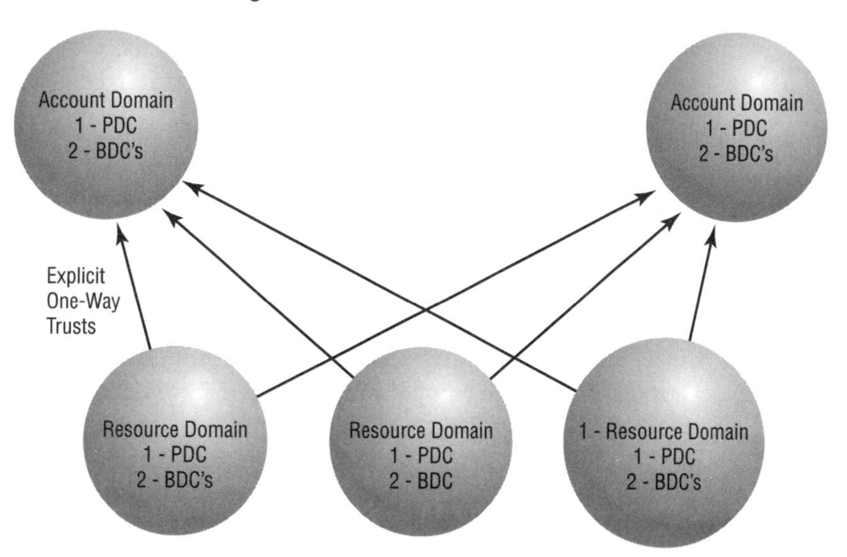

As you look at your existing NT domain structure, ask yourself the following questions about each domain:

- What purpose does this domain serve? This can help you set a priority for the upgrade.
- Can this domain be collapsed into another domain, eliminating an administrative center?

- How many domain controllers will be needed to manage this domain, and where will they be physically located?
- What DNS namespace(s) exists within your organization? (Once domains are named in Windows 2000, they cannot be renamed. You need to know the existing naming conventions and what additional namespaces your organization requires so that you can create a unique namespace for the forest.)

Account Domain Upgrades to Windows 2000

After you have looked at the logical design of your domains, you can set your upgrade priorities. As you upgrade from NT 4, you can bring the domain into the forest.

- Remember the point made above about forest naming. Make sure the forest name space is defined just the way you want it. If it is not, the entire forest will need to be restructured just to correct the namespace.
- Since the root domain is the first domain in a forest, create it carefully. After the root domain has been created, the name cannot be changed. There is that naming thing again.
- When you create other domains, they are referred to as *child domains*. Be careful when adding a child domain. If it is added to the wrong part of the forest, you will have extra work to do to get the domain configuration the way you want it. The amount of work will depend on the number of objects in the misplaced domain.
- When you set up policies for the use of groups and access control lists, make sure the policies will not obstruct the way you plan to do things in the future.

Resource Domain Upgrades to Windows 2000

Resource domains were commonly used in Windows NT to hold the computer accounts of resources such as servers and client computers. Resource domains existed primarily to limit the size of the account database. If you are working in a smaller environment, you may not have had any need for resource domains. In large organizations, with thousands of computers, the resources simply overwhelmed the security database. By creating a resource domain, the system administrator, in effect, partitioned the database to make authentication easier and faster. With Windows 2000, this is no longer a problem, so now you have to plan for a way to get rid of the resource domains.

NT Limits on the Size of the Account Database

In Windows NT, the maximum size recommended for the Security Account Manager (SAM) account database is 40MB. In a domain containing user accounts, security groups, and Windows NT client and server computer accounts, this might equal fewer than 20,000 user accounts. If you work for a very large company and you want to scale an organization with more than this number, user and computer accounts need to be stored in separate domains. In design terminology, that meant that account domains were created for user accounts, and resource domains were created for computer accounts. If the resource domain was created as a holding area for servers and computer accounts, they were usually created with explicit one-way trusts to either a single account domain (master domain model) or a number of account domains (multiple-master domain model). With Windows 2000, some of these domains may be eliminated.

Provide Local Administrative Capability

There were times when having administration carried out from one location was not feasible. In that case, the organization utilized decentralized administration. In a decentralized organization with geographically disparate facilities, it is often desirable to have local personnel authorized to administer resources. After all, what administrator wants to travel potentially hundreds of miles just to add user accounts? To allow this kind of decentralized responsibility in Windows NT systems, it was recommended that resource domains be created with their own administrative structure. As with scaling beyond SAM size limits, this resulted in master or multiple-master domain structures with explicit one-way trusts to the account domains in the organization. The administrators in the remote locations were not usually given administrative responsibility to the account domain. In other words, imposing one-way trusts ensured that resource domain administrators had only administrative scope over the resource domain.

As part of your upgrade plan, your administrative model must reflect the implications of upgrading a resource domain. If you have already upgraded the account domain, and then you upgrade the resource domain as a child of the account domain, a transitive trust is established between them. For this reason, you need to consider how this transitive trust affects local administration of resources.

If you do not want administrative permissions to extend beyond the resource domain, you might consider other options, which include:

Restructuring Resource Domains into Organizational Units

You might redesign your domain structure. You could consider merging your resource domains into the upgraded account domain as organizational units (OUs). This option would obviously influence your thinking on the order of domain upgrade.

Upgrading a Resource Domain within the Existing Forest and Using Windows 2000 Delegation of Administration Features

Another approach would have you upgrade your resource domain to be in the same forest as the account domain(s). In this way you would use Windows 2000 delegation of administration features to limit the capabilities of the local administrators. Before you do this, check the administrative groups in the resource domain and remove all administrators who are not administrators in the account domains. If there are only local resource domain administrators, add one or more of your account domain administrators. These administrators will be able to administer the domain while it is being upgraded. As a further precaution, make sure that resource domain administrators do not have administrative access to the domain controllers through local computer accounts.

After the PDC is upgraded, you might even create a new domain local group to hold your resource administrators, and use Windows 2000 delegated administration to grant them sufficient privilege to carry out their roles.

Upgrading a Resource Domain as a Tree in a New Forest

Finally, you can upgrade your resource domain and make it a tree in a new forest, linking the tree to the account domain through an explicit one-way trust. This would effectively mirror the structure that existed before the upgrade.

Design Scenario: What a Trusting Relationship!

Your customer has just presented you with a high-level map of the corporate network. The company is medium to large. It is not General Motors to be sure, but it is not a Mom and Pop grocery store either. Well, it may have started out as a Mom and Pop grocery 75 years ago, but now it is a national food chain with stores all over the country.

The network map just shows the way the distribution points are connected. Each regional distribution point has a master administrative domain, with several resource domains. The resource domains are connected to the master domains with one-way trust relationships. The multiple master domains are all linked with two-way trust relationships.

The head of IT looks at you and begins to whine (again) about the administrative cost of keeping up this system. There are dozens of domains scattered all over the country, and keeping straight why each one was created is a nightmare. That doesn't include keeping straight what domain trusts what other domain and why. He shrieks that surely there has got to be a better way.

At this you begin to smile, and once the customer has settled down, you begin to take him on a mental walk through the forest. At least it will be a forest, once the Primary Domain Controller in the central IT department is upgraded to Windows 2000 and the rollout begins.

Know the difference between authentication and authorization. It will be important when we start talking about protocols. Also know the information on the proper process to upgrade an NT 4 network to a Windows 2000 network—which controllers get upgraded first, and how things get merged into the directory tree.

Security Policy

Security policy settings define the security behavior of the system. Through the use of Group Policy objects in Active Directory, administrators can centrally apply explicit security policies to various classes of computers in the enterprise. For example, Windows 2000 comes with a default Group Policy object called Default Domain Controllers Policy that governs the security behavior of domain controllers. Let's take a look at some of the components and the way they work together to provide security.

Microsoft Exam Objectives

Analyze the impact of the security design on the existing and planned technical environment.

- Assess existing systems and applications.

Access Control Components

When the PDC is upgraded to Windows 2000 and Active Directory Services are installed, the security principals are integrated with ADS. What effect does that move have on access to resources?

Security Identifiers

Keep in mind that Windows 2000 is built on Windows NT technology. After all, Microsoft makes sure you know that by printing it on every Windows 2000 CD. Since the basis for 2000 is NT, the developers took every precaution to make sure that security would be backwardly compatible to the NT security model. In the Windows NT security model, resources are identified as security principals. Security principals include objects such as users, groups, and computers. Each of these objects is uniquely tracked by security identifiers (SIDs). SIDs are domain-unique values, built when the user or group is created, or when the computer is registered with the domain.

When describing a SID, Microsoft says, "The components of a SID follow a hierarchical convention. A SID contains parts that identify the revision number, the authority that assigned the SID, the domain, and a variable number of sub-authority or Relative Identifier (RID) values that uniquely identify the security principal relative to the issuing authority." Now I realize that sounds incredibly geeky, but let's break it down into the smallest parts.

Basically, this says that SIDS have built-in pieces. The first piece is the revision number of the SID. It is the revision number that helps to provide the uniqueness of the SID. Then there is a piece that identifies which authority actually assigned the SID to the object. Obviously, the SID was provided by a PDC. There should also be a piece of the SID that identifies which domain the controllers were a part of. Finally there is the RID in the SID. Since these SIDs can be assigned to hundreds of users and hundreds of computers, there has to be a way to ensure they are unique. That is where the RID comes in. The variable number that uniquely identifies the security principal relative to the issuing authority means that somewhere, some authority gave this computer or user another unique number, just to be sure that the previous unique number was really a unique number. Better to be safe than sorry.

Keep in mind there are some well-known SIDs that identify generic groups and users across all systems; the security principals discussed are identified in the context of a domain. These security principals cannot be moved between domains without their SIDs changing. If SIDs are altered in any way, resource access is affected. During an upgrade, however, security principals remain in the same domain in which they were created, so the SIDs identifying the security principals remain unchanged. As a result, resource access is unaffected by upgrade.

Security Configuration and Analysis

Have you ever had the experience of having to configure dozens of computers exactly the same way? There were times when the only way to do that was by clicking your way through each individual setting, making the appropriate changes in the appropriate spots. It was very inefficient, and definitely unscientific.

With Windows 2000 you can use the *security configuration and analysis* tool. With this tool, you take a machine that you have configured just the way you want it, and then you can compare the security settings to a standard template. Once the comparisons are finished, you can view the results, and resolve any discrepancies revealed by the analysis. You can also use the tool to import a security template into a Group Policy object and apply that security profile to many computers at once. To make your life even easier, Windows 2000 has several predefined security templates to mirror various levels of security and to configure different types of clients and servers on the network.

Symmetric Key Encryption

Symmetric key encryption is also called secret key encryption. Symmetric key encryption uses the same key to encrypt and decrypt the data. It provides rapid processing of data and is used in many forms of data encryption for networks and file systems.

Public Key Encryption

Public key encryption, also called asymmetric key encryption, has two keys, one public and one private. Either key can encrypt data that can only be decrypted by the other key. This technology opens up numerous security strategies and is the basis for several Windows 2000 security features. These features are all dependent on a Public Key Infrastructure (PKI).

Authentication

Authentication confirms the identity of any user trying to log on to a domain or to access network resources. Windows 2000 authentication enables *single sign-on* to all network resources. With single sign-on, a user can log on to the domain once, using a single password or smart card, and authenticate to any computer in the domain. Authentication in Windows 2000 is implemented by using Kerberos v5 protocol, NTLM authentication, or the Windows NT logon feature to Windows NT 4 domains.

Access Control

How is authorization implemented? It is done through *access control*. After a user has been authenticated to a domain, the next step is to access a resource. When the attempt is made, there must be a decision made whether the action should be permitted or denied. This decision is determined by the permissions that are associated with the resource; in the case of a file, the permissions may be read or read/write. To control the access, Windows 2000 uses object-specific access control lists (ACLs). How does this compare with the way NT used to do the same thing?

Authentication and Access Tokens in NT 4

Just as with Windows 2000, *authentication* is the means by which a user is *identified* to the domain. The user, in effect, is presenting credentials, usually in the form of a user name and password. Assuming these credentials are acceptable, the security subsystem creates an access token for the user. The access token includes the primary SID (the SID of the user) as well as the SIDs of all the domain and local computer groups of which the user is a member.

The user access token can be thought of as the form of user ID presented to the system. When the user wants to access a resource, the user presents the access token. This is a lot like a key opening a door: If the key fits, the door opens. If the access token is correct, the user can access the resource.

Authorization and Security Descriptors

What if the object that needs access is not a user? In that case, it is called a security descriptor, which is attached to resources like files or printers. Just like the user access token, a security descriptor contains an access control list (ACL). This list consists of access control entries (ACEs). An ACE is made up of a SID, as well as an indicator that the security principal is granted or denied some sort of access to the resource. This access would be in the form of permissions such as read, write, and execute. The system then performs an access check verification by simply comparing the SIDs in the access token against the SIDs in the ACL to determine whether to grant or deny requested permissions.

Single Sign-On

Users dislike having to authenticate separately to multiple network servers and applications. A user might have to provide separate passwords to log on to the local computer, to access a file or print server, to send e-mail, to use a database, and so forth. Different servers can demand a change of passwords at different intervals, often with no reuse permitted. In this case, a typical user might be required to remember half a dozen passwords. Not only is authentication tedious for the user, but also at some point, users begin to write down a list of current passwords. In this way, a multiple-authentication network can become vulnerable to identity interception.

The *single sign-on* strategy makes a user authenticate interactively once and permits authenticated sign-on to other network applications and devices. These subsequent authentication events are transparent to the user.

Two-Factor Authentication

Two-factor authentication requires users to present some form of physical object that encodes their identities, plus a password. The most common example of two-factor authentication is the automated teller machine (ATM) card that requires a personal identification number or PIN.

Biometric identification is another form of two-factor authentication. A special device scans the user's handprint, thumbprint, iris, retina, or voiceprint, in place of an access card. Then the user enters the equivalent of a password. This approach is expensive but it makes identity interception and masquerading very difficult.

For business enterprises, the emerging two-factor technology is the *smart card*. This card is not much larger than an ATM card and is physically carried by the user. It contains a chip that stores a digital certificate and the user's private key. The user enters a password or PIN after inserting the card into a card reader at the client computer. Because the private key is carried on a chip in the user's pocket, the private key is very hard for a network intruder to steal.

Data Integrity

If you were to ask your boss about the priority of your job, these next two points would be very high on the list. When you talk about ensuring *data integrity,* you are talking about how to protect the data on your network from becoming corrupted. This corruption may come from a malicious attack or just from some accidental modification or deletion. When you are talking about stored data, this means that only authorized users can edit, overwrite, or delete the data. For network communication, this means that a data packet must contain a digital signature so that the recipient computer can detect if the packet has been tampered with.

Data Confidentiality

Data confidentiality means making sure only the right people can actually read or see the data. This strategy of data confidentiality means to encrypt data before it passes through the network and to decrypt it afterward. This strategy stops data from being read by someone sniffing on the network (data interception). A packet of nonencrypted data that is transmitted across a network can be easily viewed from any computer on the network by using a packet-sniffing program downloaded from the Internet in about 15 minutes or less.

Nonrepudiation

Nonrepudiation means that the packet cannot be denied by the person sending it. There are two parts to nonrepudiation. The first part is to establish that a specific user, who cannot disavow the message, actually sent the message. The second part is to ensure that the message could not have been sent by anyone else who might have been masquerading as the user.

This is another application for the Public Key Infrastructure. The user's private key is used to place a digital signature on the message. If the recipient can read the message using the sender's public key, then only that specific user and no one else could have sent the message.

Code Authentication

Code authentication requires that code downloaded from the Internet be signed with a digital signature. In order for this digital signature to be accepted, it must come from a trusted software publisher. You can configure Web browsers to avoid running unsigned code. Note that software signing proves that the code is authentic, meaning it has not been tampered with after publication. It does not guarantee that the code is safe to run. You have to decide which software publishers to trust.

Audit Logs

Auditing user account management as well as access to important network resources is an important part of a security policy. Auditing leaves a trail of network operations, showing what was attempted and by whom. Not only does this help to detect intrusion, but the logs become legal evidence if the intruder is caught and prosecuted. Finding and deleting or modifying the audit logs poses an additional time-consuming task for the sophisticated intruder, making detection and intervention easier for you.

Physical Security

It should go without saying that the critical enterprise network services need to reside in locked rooms. If intruders can sit down at the network server console, they may be able to take control of the network server. If critical network servers are not physically secure, a disgruntled employee can damage your hardware by using something exceptionally accessible, like a cup of coffee! Your data is also open to physical attack. In this case, anyone with access to Explorer can do some serious damage by just indiscriminately using the delete key. Damage from these kinds of intrusions can result in just as much loss of data and downtime as you can have from a more sophisticated, external attack to your network. Attacks on the network do not have to be sophisticated to be effective. One of the easiest forms of a denial of service attack for someone to master is simply turning off or unplugging a server. Locking up the server will make that harder to accomplish.

Think This Is Common Sense??

Several years ago, when Brandice was a hardware tech, she stopped in a law office. The senior partners had decided that it was important to show their clients and potential clients how advanced they were, so they wanted to demonstrate that they were part of the digital age. In this case, sitting right in the middle of the waiting room was the only server in the single-server environment. It even had a keyboard and a monitor, so people could play solitaire. This was not a pretty picture.

The other case that makes you begin to wonder if these people should be contributing to the gene pool almost got Brandice thrown out of a client site. She was sent to the site to check out the network to see if the company she worked for wanted to provide 7x24 support. When she met the secretary, who was doubling as the network administrator, she asked where the server was, and was taken into the corporate break room. She patiently thanked the person for the offer of coffee, but said she really needed to see the server. The secretary said, "Have at it," and pointed to a space under the cabinets. Sure enough, there was the server, taking up an empty space in cabinets of the break room, directly under the coffeepot.

At that point, Brandice said something brash, like, "Surely there has got to be a better place for this server than here. My God, one tipped cup of coffee and you are out of business." Granted, she may have also said something about "what damn fool would put the server there?" Since Brandice apparently was talking to the damn fool, the administrator took umbrage. Brandice went back to the office laughing, and thankfully, her boss said he really didn't want that company as a client anyway!

User Education

The best defense against a social engineering attack is to educate your users about keeping their passwords confidential and secure. Business policies about distribution of critical information need to be clearly stated. Publish a security policy and require everyone to follow it. One way to educate is by example: Make sure that the IT staff protect their passwords and that they encourage users to protect theirs too.

Design Scenario: Oops!

You have just entered a customer site for the very first time. The customer has decided that he may want your firm to do a security audit of his network, but he has questioned your salesperson about the company's reputation and how he would know whether you are really any good. During this meeting, you are doing your best to put on the happy face and prove what a bright, knowledgeable, affable person you are.

The customer seems to be impressed. As a matter of fact, he wants to show you around the company. The first stop is the newly upgraded accounting department. As you walk around, you poke your head into cube after cube, oohing and aaahing over the bright shiny new computers. As you are about to enter one cube, you look at the nameplate on the cube, and see CJ Carpenter. You think to yourself, hmmm, that is the same name as my best friend, but she doesn't work here. While you are admiring the new computer, the client tells you that this is the cube of an up-and-coming new auditor who specializes in IT matters. As you glance at the monitor, you happen to gaze upon a Post-it note with the words "PW-Cardinals" on it. Hmm, that is the name of your favorite baseball team.

When you get back to the client's office, he is talking about how he is not really sure he needs to have a security check run. After all, each of the 200 users in this company are just like family and no one would ever do anything to damage the network. As an aside, you start talking to the client and asking rather generic questions, like, "what kind of policy do you have for logon names?" He proudly boasts that he has come up with a masterstroke. The naming convention is the first letter of the person's first name, the first letter of his middle name, and the first four letters of his last name.

As you continue to talk, you walk over to a conference table and ask if you can use the laptop on the credenza. The client says sure, but adds that it won't do you much good since it is not logged in. At that point, you smile, and log on as CJCARP, with a password of Cardinals. You then show the client how you can now go in and rename some very sensitive documents. Needless to say, you get the job.

The Effect on Existing Systems and Applications

All through this chapter and actually all through the book, we have been talking like the only systems you were going to upgrade would be the server side. What about the client upgrades and the application upgrades? When do these need to be done? Do you need to wait until a domain is upgraded to Windows 2000 before you can upgrade the client? Absolutely not.

Microsoft Exam Objectives

Analyze the impact of the security design on the existing and planned technical environment.

- Identify existing and planned upgrades and rollouts.

Upgrading Client Systems

Just as Windows 2000 Server products are backwardly compatible to NT 4, you can use Windows 2000 clients and servers with Active Directory in your existing Windows NT environment. As a matter of fact, if you do upgrade, your life may actually be easier. Table 6.2 lists some of the reasons you may decide to upgrade clients to Windows 2000.

TABLE 6.2 Features of a Simple Client Upgrade

Feature of Simple Client Upgrade	Benefit of Simple Client Upgrade
Simplified manageability	Makes use of plug and play. Makes use of the hardware wizard with device manager. Provides support for universal serial bus (USB). Administration with the Microsoft management console. Windows 2000 has a new backup utility.
More advanced setup and troubleshooting tools	For those systems that are working on networks with an Active Directory domain controller and properly configured Group Policy objects, the automatic application installation allows an administrator to specify a set of applications that are always available to a user or group of users. If a required application is not available when needed, it is automatically installed in the system.
Improved file system support	NTFS has changed. NTFS 5 enhancements include support for disk quotas, the ability to defragment directory structures, and FAT32.
Improved application services	Windows 2000 makes use of the Win32 driver model. Uses DirectX 5. Windows 2000 also uses the Windows script host.

TABLE 6.2 Features of a Simple Client Upgrade *(continued)*

Feature of Simple Client Upgrade	Benefit of Simple Client Upgrade
Improved information sharing and publishing	The Microsoft distributed file system (dfs) for Windows 2000 Server makes it easier for users to find and manage data on the network.
Improved print server services	Provides for easier location of printer through Active Directory.
Increased scalability and availability	Windows 2000 improves symmetric multi-processor support.
Encrypted data security for laptops or sensitive information	Windows 2000 uses the encrypting file system.

Client and Server Interoperability Requirements

Again, it seems that so far we have been talking about the perfect world, where all servers are Windows 2000 and all clients are Windows 2000 Professional. That just doesn't happen much anymore. That, of course, means more work for you. You will have to consider the extent to which your Windows 2000 system needs to interoperate with both Windows legacy systems and non-Microsoft operating systems. If you plan to maintain a heterogeneous environment that includes network operating systems other than Windows 2000, you need to determine which legacy applications and services must be retained or upgraded to maintain acceptable functionality across all platforms.

What are the interoperability requirements with respect to operating in a heterogeneous environment? This takes a look at the degree to which the migrated environment will need to interoperate with other operating systems like Novell and Unix, as well as other network services.

Important considerations might include:

- The need to support pre–Windows 2000 clients, which means that you have to plan to maintain services such as Windows Internet Name Service (WINS) to support name resolution.
- The need to maintain pre–Windows 2000 domains, which means that you need to maintain and manage explicit trusts.

- The need to interoperate with non-Microsoft operating systems, such as Unix. This could be a reason for rapid migration to enable widespread use of the Kerberos authentication.
- What are the interoperability requirements with respect to the source environment (where you are migrating from)?

Utilizing Kerberos to interoperate with non-Microsoft operating systems may require some third-party solutions.

This section may not take up a lot of pages, but it is really important. Any time you upgrade or migrate to a new network operating system, the developers of the operating system put wizards or utilities in place that will help you move from one environment to another. Although the wizards and utilities are wonderful, the developers can't thing of everything. They also can't think of every possible scenario for upgrades. This is another case where testing before rollout or just exploring before rollout will pay *huge* dividends. There are few things worse than having to kludge together a solution in the middle of a major rollout. You probably have scheduled your rollout to take place during downtime (or at least slack time), and although there is certainly a fudge factor, the fudge factor won't usually cover the time needed to redo a legacy operating system!

Application Compatibility

So, by now you have figured out how you will perform the domain migration. A big question remains: When you upgrade to Windows 2000, will all the business applications still work? Before going any further, this is a good time to make a list of all your strategic applications and then test them. Some important questions you need to ask about your applications include the following:

- Will the application run on Windows 2000? Don't just assume that because the application runs on Windows NT, it will certainly run on Windows 2000. That is not necessarily the case. If, after testing, the answer is "no," you are going to have to decide how important the application is to the business. You may have to scrap the application or scrap the upgrade.

- Does the application need to run on a BDC? If the answer is "yes," and the application will not run on Windows 2000, it will be impossible to switch the upgraded domain to native mode.
- Do you have contacts with your application software vendors? If you experience problems running the application on Windows 2000, you need to be aware of how the application vendor plans to provide support for Windows 2000. Again, this is a dangerous area for assumption. Don't assume the vendor will have an application upgrade—check to be sure.
- If the application was internally developed, do the company programmers have plans to develop a Windows 2000 version? If the application cannot run on Windows 2000, and there are no plans to upgrade, you are facing the decision of scrapping the application or scrapping the upgrade.
- What operating systems do you have deployed on your clients and servers? The answer to this has implications for your migration path. Certain software upgrade paths to Windows 2000 are not supported (for example, from Windows NT 3.5).

You may ask, so just how backwardly compatible is Windows 2000? Well, let's put it this way: you might not want to maintain Windows NT 3.51 servers in your resource domains, because Windows NT 3.51 does not support universal or domain local group membership.

Knowing the answers to these questions will help you formulate a test plan covering the important test cases. It will also help you develop a project risk assessment. This risk assessment spells out the implications of various applications that are not functioning correctly. If a really important, corporate-wide application isn't going to work in a Windows 2000 environment, that could have massive repercussions on any proposed migration. It is obviously important to find that out before you start the rollout, not after. That scenario could be described as a serious, "Oh, shuckey darn!" or words to that effect.

Some application services designed for Windows NT, such as Windows NT Routing and Remote Access Service (RRAS), assume unauthenticated access to user account information. The default security permissions of Active Directory do not allow unauthenticated access to account information. The Active Directory installation wizard gives you the option of configuring Active Directory security for compatibility by granting additional permissions. If you feel that loosening the security of Active Directory to allow the use of RRAS servers would compromise your security policy, you need to upgrade these servers first. If you are using LAN Manager Replication Service to replicate scripts within the domain, then you need to upgrade the server hosting the export directory last.

Design Scenario: Fearless Fosdick to the Rescue

There is a serious panic phone call to your office. It appears that one of your customers has done something he shouldn't. He *pleads* with you to go over and help straighten things out. It's Saturday morning and you had some serious downtime planned, but because he is a friend as well as a client, you decide to drive down.

When you get there, the customer tells you that he decided he wanted to surprise the IT department on Monday and have the Windows 2000 upgrade started. He came early this Saturday morning to show them how easy it could be. After all, how hard can it be? You put in the CD, it comes back and tells you that there is a new version of Windows available, you click OK a couple of times, and away you go. Anyway, he did this to the PDC of the Master Domain and now when he tries to run a DOS application that the company *must* have, it doesn't work. What is he going to do?

First, you notice that the tape backup unit still has a tape in it. You check the host and find that a full backup of the PDC ran on Friday night. Things are looking up. First, you send the customer for coffee. You temporarily upgrade one of the BDCs to a PDC, and then start the restore on the former PDC. While the restore is running, the customer comes back with the coffee. While you sip your latte, you patiently explain that the reason he pays his IT department so much money is to let them handle things like the upgrade. You point out to him that his forte is management stuff, and although he has an envelope with the name and password of the administrator account, he shouldn't use it.

When the restore is completed, you test the apps, and everything works. The machine is re-promoted to the PDC, and the client is happy. He makes the comment that now the IT department will never know what he has done. You point out that their ignorance will last only as long as it takes your accounting department to bill his company for 10 hours of time-and-a-half, noncontract time. Chances are, when the head of IT sees the bill, she may ask some questions.

Upgrade or Restructure and the Effect on the Rollouts

At this point in the planning process, you will be making the decision to either maintain your current domain relationships and upgrade the PDCs and BDCs or, in many cases, restructure the domain structure to take advantage of the flexibility of Windows 2000. Why would you restructure your entire domain structure just to accommodate a new operating system?

Microsoft Exam Objectives

Analyze the impact of the security design on the existing and planned technical environment.

- Identify existing and planned upgrades and rollouts.

Why Restructure Domains?

In a word, the number one answer is money. Here your company has spent all this money on studies, planning, and analysis to determine that you are going to upgrade to Windows 2000. As the upgrade planning progresses, your primary responsibility is to make sure that you make full use of whatever features Windows 2000 has that your company needs. If not, if the company thinks even for a minute that you are upgrading for the sake of upgrading, you have gone from a career fast-track to the slow lane during rush hour in Los Angeles. Here are some of the features that may be applicable:

Windows 2000 has greater scalability You might have designed your previous Windows NT domain structure around the size limitations of the SAM database, leading you to implement a master or multiple-master domain model. With the improved scalability of Active Directory, you could restructure or collapse your current Windows NT domains into fewer, larger Windows 2000 domains. Windows 2000 domains can scale to millions of user accounts or groups.

Windows 2000 and delegation of administration We have already talked about resource domains that allow administrative responsibility to be delegated. Windows 2000 OUs can contain any type of security principal, and administration can be delegated as you require.

Windows 2000 offers finer granularity of administration Depending on the scope of the network, your domain map may look like a complex mesh of trusts. Now is the time to consider implementing some of these domains as OUs to simplify administration, or you might simply redesign your domain model to benefit from fewer explicit trusts.

The question to ask now is when do you upgrade a domain and when do you restructure your entire network?

The difference between an upgrade and a restructure is simple. With an upgrade, you keep the domain configuration that you have now, and just upgrade the PDC and BDCs of each domain to Windows 2000, while moving the domains into the Windows 2000 forest.

Restructuring says that you are not satisfied with the way the current domain structure is laid out. You may want to merge some domains because their functionality has changed. You may want to eliminate domains and move the users or resources into another domain. In any case, if this calls for a reconfiguration of your domain architecture, you are looking at restructuring, and you should consider the following questions when determining whether and how to restructure your domains:

- Do you need to restructure? You will probably answer "yes" if some or all of the following conditions are true:
  - You are happy with much of your domain structure and can carry out a two-phase migration: upgrade to Windows 2000, then restructure to fix any problems.
  - You are unhappy with your current domain structure.
  - You feel you cannot manage the migration without impacting your production environment.
- When do you need to restructure? The answer depends on the reason you are restructuring:
  - If you can solve your migration requirements by doing a two-phase migration, then you need to restructure after upgrade.
  - If you feel your domain structure cannot be salvaged (for example, if you decide you need to redesign your directory services infrastructure to take advantage of the enhanced capabilities of Active Directory), you need to restructure at the beginning of the migration process.
  - If you feel you cannot avoid impacting your production environment, you need to restructure at the beginning of the migration process.

It is recommended that you restructure after completing the upgrade but before using features such as application deployment or the new Group Policy. If you restructure after some of these features have been used, it can create more difficulties than if the restructure had taken place at the beginning of the migration process.

When to Restructure Domains

Depending on your migration plan, you might choose to restructure your domains immediately after upgrade, in place of an upgrade, or as a general domain redesign some time in the future. These options are described as follows:

After the Upgrade

The most likely time for domain restructure is after an upgrade, as the second phase of migration to Windows 2000. The upgrade has already addressed the less complex migration situations and the network should be stable.

When you choose to restructure after upgrade, most likely you will be reworking the domain structure to reduce the complexity or just to bring resource domains into the forest in a secure way.

Instead of Upgrade

You might feel that your current domain structure cannot be salvaged (for example, if you need to redesign your directory services infrastructure to take advantage of Active Directory), or that you cannot afford to jeopardize the stability of the current production environment during migration. In either case, the easiest migration path might be to design and build a *pristine forest*: an ideal Windows 2000 forest isolated from the current production environment. This ensures that business can carry on normally during pilot project operation and that the pilot project eventually becomes the production environment.

After you have built the pilot project, you can begin domain restructuring by migrating a small number of users, groups, and resources into the pilot. When this phase has been completed successfully, transition the pilot project into a staged migration to the new environment. Subsequently, make Windows 2000 the production environment, decommission the old domain structure, and redeploy the remaining resources.

After the Migration

At this stage, domain restructure takes place as part of a general domain redesign in a pure Windows 2000 environment. This might occur several years down the line, when, for reasons such as organizational change or a corporate acquisition, the current structure becomes inappropriate.

The Implications of Restructuring Domains

After you have determined why and when you need to restructure domains, you need to examine the implications of such a restructure. The following sections describe the implications of these changes:

- Moving users and global groups, workstations, and member servers and other security principals
- Establishing trust relationships
- Cloning security principals

Moving Security Principals

What makes domain restructure fundamentally possible is the ability to move some of the security principals between domains in Windows 2000. While you can move some types of security principles, there are a number of implications—for example, how security principals are identified by the system and how access to resources is maintained. Some of these implications can affect how you approach a domain restructuring.

Effect on SIDs

If you remember our discussion of SIDs from earlier in the chapter, you remember that the SID is partly made up of a domain identifier. This domain-centric nature of SIDs will have the some consequence when you move a security principal, such as a user or a group, between domains. Obviously, if part of the SID identifies the domain and the domain changes, the security principal must be issued a new SID for the account in the new domain.

In the Windows NT security model, the way a user can access resources is affected by the way the operating system looks at the user access token and compares the primary SID of the user, as well as the SIDs of any groups the user is a member of, to the access control list (ACL) on the resource security descriptor. Because the lists of SIDs contained in the ACL have information that can cause access to be granted or denied to the security principals identified by the SIDs, changing the SID is going to require changing or updating the ACL.

Effects of Moving a Security Principal on Global Group Membership

Because a global group can only contain members from its own domain, moving a user account to the new domain would cause the new account to be excluded from some of the access to resources in the old location.

Assuming appropriate trust relationships exist between the new domain and the resource domain, it would seem that this situation could be fixed in a number of ways.

Adding the New SID to Resource ACLs

Access to resources could be maintained by adding the new SID for the user to the ACLs on all the resources the user formerly had access to. This fix would be a real pain because it would time-consuming and overly complicated.

Moving the Group

Because some security principals can be moved in Windows 2000, entire groups could be moved to the new domain. However, the ACLs referencing the group also reference the group SID, so the resources would have to be repermissioned to refer to the new SID—more of that time-consuming and overly complicated stuff.

Creating a Parallel Group in the Target Domain

If the group is moved to another domain, a problem would occur if all the group members are not moved in one fell swoop. This would mean that the group would have to be maintained in the old domain, and a new group would have to be created in the new domain. Resource access would be maintained for the original group and its members, but resources would need to be repermissioned to grant access to the new group. Again, repermissioning would have to continue while the groups existed in both domains.

Moving Users and Global Groups

Because a global group can contain only members from its own domain, when a user is moved between domains, any global groups of which the user is a member must also be moved. This has to occur just to maintain access to resources protected by ACLs that refer to global groups. In addition, if a global group is moved, its members must also be moved.

- This means that for each user being moved, all the affected global groups are also moved.
- For each group being moved, all of its members are also being moved.

If the source domain is a native mode domain, global groups can also contain other global groups. This means all of the members of each nested group and all of the global groups that have members in that nested group must be moved. Sounds complicated, doesn't it? Just be sure you know the implications of moving users and groups.

This is just an example of what happens when you decide to move a security principal. For further information on the impact of moving principals, check out the *Microsoft Windows 2000 Resource Kit* and the published white papers.

What About Technical Support?

How can your Help desk adapt to the new environment? As a network administrator, you are faced with a multitude of challenges, not the least of which is delivering an appropriate business computing environment to your user community, but maintaining this environment and keeping the costs associated with it down. You have to deliver the right applications and environment for the user to do the job and deliver a level of administrative control to ensure that the quality of service and uptime provided for the enterprise as a whole is high.

Microsoft Exam Objectives

Analyze the impact of the security design on the existing and planned technical environment.

- Analyze technical support structure.
- Analyze existing and planned network and systems management.

In order to help lower management and support costs, most organizations have three distinct groups of administrators. Each group has its own unique set of management tasks and requirements and the common need for remote management tools and services.

Desktop Support Management

The goal of the desktop support management group is to ensure that people have the computing resources they need. This is a challenge because of the multiple desktop configurations that are the norm in each organization. You know how it goes: The IT department sets a *standard* desktop machine that will be rolled out to all new users and all users that require an upgrade. By the time the information gets to Purchasing, it has been changed from "standard" to "suggestion," and you end up with desktops from whatever clone manufacturer has the lowest price on machines designed to run 2000 on any given day.

No matter what the computer type or desktop standard, desktop support management usually involves repetitious work—installing and upgrading applications, moving users, and so forth. Accordingly, desktop support managers are often the front line for finding, troubleshooting, and resolving problems. In addition, because users may be spread across a large physical space, people doing desktop support try to resolve as many problems as possible without actually visiting every desktop. This leads to a demand for management tools that work well remotely. When a desktop visit is unavoidable, it is necessary to have accurate configuration information before the technician arrives.

Network Management

One step up the food chain is the network management team. They are tasked with making sure the network is up and running, 24 hours a day, seven days a week. That means providing on-demand bandwidth.

The network support team also has to contend with multiple points of failure. The network design may be perfect, but if a router goes out, life turns ugly, quickly. To make matters worse, it doesn't even have to be your router. Suppose the router belongs to your ISP? If that is the link to your gateway to the outside world, your customers will not care that it was not under your direct control—they just want access. It is now up to you to make sure your ISP's equipment is protected, and that there is some semblance of fault tolerance.

Network management involves two sometimes-conflicting goals. The first is to move as many bits as possible, while maintaining excellent uptime, availability, and security. Second, you must spend the least amount possible on plant costs, maintenance, and support. Even more than data center or desktop management, network management depends on simultaneously monitoring the health of hundreds, thousands, or tens of thousands of network devices. Ideally, tools will predict problems, automatically flag them when they occur, and escalate warning notices if necessary.

Data Center Management

Finally, there is the management of the data center. Here, the goal is simple. Make sure the data and the services are available on demand. The service levels must remain consistent and critical data must be preserved.

Data center managers typically provide application services to large groups of users and are therefore most concerned with overall uptime for applications delivered to users. Because of this focus on providing robust application services to many users, and because those services are usually run from a small number of servers, data center managers tend to be more interested in data integrity, security, and accounting than desktop support managers are. In addition, data center managers typically spend more time on maintenance and upgrades, per server, than desktop managers.

Design Scenario: Definition of an Expert

Your consulting company has been working off and on with a local company for about 10 years. In that time, you have been able to provide a variety of services, ranging from server installations, router configurations, and security consulting. Every time you show up at the center, you are amazed at the ability of the department to get anything done. Due to the explosive growth of the company, people have been thrown at problems, and as a result, the proper people are not in the proper place. The IT department is under the direction of the chief financial officer. The CFO loves to tell anyone who will listen that the only thing he knows about IT is that it costs too much!

The CEO and the CFO had a meeting with the local Microsoft representative, and she started them thinking about Windows 2000. The CEO has called you in to get your feel for the situation. You are brought in because you know the strengths and weaknesses of the parties involved, and you are a neutral observer. The CEO wants to know what they can do to institute Windows 2000 in a timely and forthright manner. You look at her and—calling on your long relationship—you ask, "Do you really want to know or do you want me to tell you what you want to hear?" She acts offended at first, and then says, no, be honest. You figure, what the heck, you were looking for clients when you found this one, so go for broke.

You start by telling her to tell the CFO to stick to finances. Turn the IT department over to the de facto manager, CJ. Everyone comes to CJ for advice anyway, and he seems to know all the answers. Whenever something goes wrong, people ask CJ and CJ steers them to the appropriate resource within the department.

At this point you break out a piece of paper and divide it into thirds. The first third is labeled desktop, the middle third network, and the last third, data center. Then you place all the employees where they will do the most good, moving them all around from their current positions into positions they really want to be in. The CEO is amazed. She thinks this an amazing idea, and is so glad to have an expert like you to call on.

She immediately calls CJ into the room, and proceeds to lay out "her" plan. At the end she does give you credit for being the expert behind the idea. When the meeting is over, it's 7 p.m., and CJ wants to celebrate with a cold beverage. You agree, and when you get to the local watering hole, CJ pulls out a memo, addressed to the CEO four months ago, laying out a department almost exactly the way you had. He looks puzzled and asks why the heck you are the expert and his memo was ignored.

You smile, and point out that experts never work for the company! The definition of an expert is someone who charges far more than the company really wants to pay!

Security Requirements

How does security play a role in this? The goal of infrastructure, applications, and service management has shifted from the monitoring and control of properties of managed objects to assurance of service levels as perceived by the user. The users do not care what the security implications are, they just want access to the data they are supposed to have access to. At a minimum, it is necessary to provide a single flexible security model that embraces networks, systems, middleware, applications, and user services. The following are some Windows 2000 tools that can make this possible.

Group Policy Infrastructure

Administrators create Group Policy by using the Group Policy MMC snap-in, either as a stand-alone tool or as an extension to the Active Directory Users and Computers tool and the Active Directory Site and Services tool via Manage Group Policy. All Group Policy settings are contained in Group Policy objects (GPOs) that are associated with Active Directory containers (sites, domains, or OUs), thus using the Active Directory.

Administrators can filter the effects of Group Policy on computers and users by using membership in Security Groups and setting ACL permissions.

Administrative Templates

Group Policy requires a source template that is used to create the user interface settings. The Group Policy can use either an MMC extension snap-in to the Group Policy snap-in, or an ASCII file referred to as an administrative template (`.adm`) file. The `.adm` file consists of a grouping of categories and subcategories that together define how the options are going to be displayed through the Group Policy user interface. The file also indicates the registry locations where changes should be made if a particular selection is made, as well as specifies any options or restrictions for the selection. In some cases, a default value will be specified.

Analyze Existing and Planned Network and Systems Management

What kinds of management tools do you have and what kinds are you going to need? In previous chapters we talked about how SMS (Systems Management Services) could help draw the network map and provide information that would make decisions easier. Windows 2000 has some management tools that will help the security teams to better manage the network. They include tools for managing change and configuration, protecting data, managing the users' environment, and helping install and deploy applications.

Microsoft Exam Objectives

Analyze the impact of the security design on the existing and planned technical environment.

- Analyze existing and planned network and systems management.

Change and Configuration Management Tools

When you start talking about system management, you are usually talking about a very big job. This includes things like managing configurations and also deploying applications. System administrators everywhere are trying to find easy ways to install applications, standardize a desktop, and also lock down the desktop configuration. One way that can be done with Windows 2000 is to use the tool *IntelliMirror*.

IntelliMirror Basics

IntelliMirror is another one of those cases where the name fits the function. You can use it to mirror users' data, applications, and customized operating system settings to a Windows 2000 Server–based server, using intelligent caching and centralized synchronization. This means that users have access to all of their data and applications. This is true even if they are not connected to the network. The user has the peace of mind of knowing the data is safely maintained on the server, where it can be backed up. IntelliMirror provides users and administrators with the following functionality:

- Managing the users' data
- Assisting with software installation and maintenance
- Assisting with the management of user settings

User Data Management

As the name suggests, data is mirrored. The data can be mirrored from the local system to the network, or network data can be cached locally. The data can reside on the local laptop or workstation for offline use while a copy of the data resides on the server for protection. In this case, the data does not reside in only one location; it can be configured to follow the user if the user moves to another computer.

Software Installation and Maintenance

Windows 2000 Server has some software installation technologies that have been designed to simplify the installation of applications, as well as updates, repairs, and even uninstalls of applications.

System administrators can use the Software Installation and Maintenance tool that will assign applications to users. When properly configured, all users that need the applications will automatically have the application on their desktops.

Administrators can make available applications that the users may not need, but may want. In this case, it will be up to the users to decide whether to install the application.

Advertised Applications

When administrators assign an application to users, the application is advertised to users during logon at a workstation. Basically, this process works almost like having the application installed on the local computer. Shortcuts for the application magically appear in appropriate locations (including the Start menu or the Desktop), and the appropriate registry entries for the application are added to the local computer registry.

As opposed to advertising, when an application is published, the application is advertised to the Active Directory directory service. In this case, the application has no shortcuts on the user's Desktop or Start menu, and no changes are made to the local computer registry. Published applications are available for users to install by using the Add/Remove Programs control panel tool or by clicking a file associated with the application (for example, by clicking a `.dot` file for Microsoft Word).

User Settings Management

IntelliMirror also includes ways for administrators to manage user and computer settings. With IntelliMirror, user settings are mirrored to the network, and administrators can define specific computing environments for users and computers. Administrators can do the following:

- Add new users and computers remotely
- Define settings for users and computers
- Apply changes for users
- Restore a user's settings if the user's computer fails
- Ensure that a user's Desktop settings follow the user if the user moves to another computer

Remote Operating System Installation

Now, another problem that faces network administrators and desktop support personnel is the installation of the operating system. When you are looking at installing a new operating system on a computer, you know you have to allocate a substantial amount of time for the task. It is especially onerous because you know much of the time will be spent waiting. The remote operating system installation allows remote install–capable clients like Net PCs and computers with a Net PC–compatible floppy boot disk to install the operating system files automatically from a Windows 2000 remote install server.

The remote installation process installs an operating system on the local computer's hard disk using a remote source like a CD image on a server. Normally, a workstation that is participating in the remote installation model is set to boot off the local disk. However, the workstation first boots from the network (remotely) to get the operating system installed on the local hard disk. The network boot is initiated either by the BIOS (Basic Input Output System) or by a special boot floppy. In either case, the network boot is controlled by boot code that adheres to the Net PC specification. The preferred BIOS boot model for this environment is one in which the BIOS gives the user a small window prior to booting off the disk, in which a special keypress causes a *service* boot off the network.

In a Net PC–compatible network boot, the boot code uses dynamic host configuration protocol (DHCP) and boot information negotiation layer (BINL) to get an IP address for the workstation and to find a Remote Installation Service (RIS) server. Then the boot code uses trivial file transfer protocol (TFTP) to download a boot program from the RIS server. It then transfers control to the boot program.

Security Management Tools

Windows 2000 Server includes tools that support the ability to define a corporate-wide default security configuration, as well as to quickly check that the operational system adheres to the corporate standard.

Security Configuration Manager

Administrators use the Security Settings extension of the Group Policy MMC snap-in to define security configurations for computers within a Group Policy object. A security configuration consists of the security settings that are applied to each security area supported for the Windows 2000 Professional or Windows 2000 Server.

This security configuration is included within a GPO. The GPO is then applied to computers as part of the group policy enforcement. The Security Settings extension reads a standard security configuration and performs the required operations automatically. These security areas can be configured for computers:

Account policies Account policies include computer security settings for the password policy, the account lockout policy, and Kerberos policy in Windows 2000 domains.

Local policies Local policies include the security settings for the Audit policy, any of the standard user rights assignment, and other security options. The Local policy also allows administrators to configure who has local or network access and how local events are audited.

Event log The event log controls security settings for the Application, Security, and System event logs. Administrators can access these logs using the Event Viewer.

Restricted groups Computer security settings are included for built-in groups that have certain set standards. Restricted Group policies affect the membership of these groups. Examples of restricted groups are local and global groups.

System services The system services policies control the configuration settings and security options for system services such as network services, file and print services, telephony and fax services, Internet/intranet services, and so on.

Registry The registry policies are used to configure and analyze settings for security descriptors, the access control list (ACL), and auditing information for each registry key.

File system The file system policy is used to configure and analyze settings for security descriptors (including object ownership), the access control list (ACL), and auditing information for each object (volume, directory, or file) in the local file system.

Once again, you are facing a problem. There is a ton of material in this chapter that is testable material. Make sure you are comfortable with the concepts and how to apply them. You may not want to spend the vast majority of time on the really granular stuff, but know the materials. There are questions on the exam from every topic covered in this chapter.

Summary

Do you feel like you have really been pounded? There is a lot of material in this chapter, isn't there? First of all, we reviewed some of the security concepts that go along with working with Windows 2000. In order to put them into perspective, we looked at the concepts not only in how they applied to 2000 but how they compared and contrasted to Windows NT 4. All in all, it might make you think you were back in a freshman literature class again, taking yet another essay test on the *Red Badge of Courage* or *Animal Farm*.

I used the comparisons between Windows 2000 and NT to lead into how to assess what problems or challenges you were going to have with security when you upgraded the existing systems and the existing applications. That led into how to decide if you were going to upgrade or roll out, and if you rolled out, what you were going to have to do to consolidate domains into a forest.

The discussion of the tech support structure was a toughie. In this case, we looked at how some of the tools in Windows 2000 could be used to ease the job of the tech support team. Finally, there was how you currently manage your network and how you plan on managing your network in the future. All in all, there was a lot of material to cover as we finally start getting into security. The next chapter really gets into security, as we look at establishing baselines and auditing policies. Hurry and get the review questions and the case study finished, so you can start getting into the real meat of the exam.

Key Terms

Before you take the exam, be certain you are familiar with the following terms:

access control lists (ACLs)

auditing

authentication

authorized

code authentication

data confidentiality

data integrity

domain restructure

domain upgrade

native mode

nonrepudiation

pass-through authentication

pristine forest

public key encryption

security configuration and analysis

single sign-on

smart card

symmetric key encryption

transitive trust

two-factor authentication

Review Questions

1. What is authentication?

    A. Once the user is identified, he has authentication to access a specific set of network resources based on permissions.

    B. Authentication identifies the user when the user logs on and when the user makes network connections to services.

    C. Rights and permissions granted only to files and folders.

    D. Rights and permissions granted only to computer objects and leaf objects in the tree.

2. What is authorization?

    A. Once the user has been identified, the user is authorized to access a specific set of network resources based on permissions.

    B. Authentication identifies the user when the user logs on and when the user makes network connections to services.

    C. Authorization is what provides the user with the permissions to log on from a particular computer using a particular password on any particular day.

    D. Authorization is provided only through biometrics or smart cards.

3. What is a trust?

    A. A trust is what distinguishes an administrative domain from a resource domain.

    B. A trust allows users in a resource domain to access resources in the administrative domain.

    C. A relationship built up between two people after many years of being together.

    D. A trust is a logical relationship established between domains to allow authentication in which a trusting domain honors the logon authentications of a trusted domain.

4. Why were resource domains used in Windows NT? (Pick two.)

   A. To limit the size of the account database

   B. To provide local administrative capability

   C. To keep user accounts separate from the computer accounts

   D. To provide easy manageability

5. What is a function of IntelliMirror?

   A. When installed on a system with two hard drives and one controller, it provides for a minimum value of RAID.

   B. A built-in synchronization function for use with Exchange 2000 and Windows CE devices.

   C. Remotely installing Historic SIDs on BDCs in a Windows 2000 forest.

   D. Automated software installation and maintenance.

6. When is an application advertised?

   A. The application is advertised to users during logon at a workstation.

   B. The application is advertised after an extensive period of beta testing and a large, boisterous marketing campaign.

   C. The application is advertised using Group Policy objects.

   D. When a user finally upgrades the computer to Windows 2000.

7. How are applications published?

   A. Applications are usually published on CD-ROM.

   B. Administrators can publish applications to Group Policy objects associated with users in these Active Directory containers.

   C. The application is published after an extensive period of beta testing and a large, boisterous marketing campaign.

   D. Usually late.

8. What is security configuration?

A. The set of rights and permissions granted to the user on a given file or folder.

B. Security configuration consists of security settings applied to each security area supported for the Windows 2000 Professional or Windows 2000 Server.

C. Kerberos v5.

D. NTLM.

9. How are group policies created? (Choose two.)

A. With the support configuration tool.

B. With MS-Admin.

C. Administrators create Group Policy by using the Group Policy MMC snap-in as a stand-alone tool.

D. By using an extension to the Active Directory Users and Computers and the Active Directory Site and Services via Manage Group Policy.

Answers to Review Questions

1. B. Authentication is what identifies the user when the user first logs on and when the user makes network connections to services.

2. A. After a user has been authenticated, the user is authorized to access a specific set of network resources based on the permissions the user has been granted.

3. D. In the world of Windows NT/2000, a trust is defined as a logical relationship established between domains to allow authentication in which a trusting domain honors the logon authentications of a trusted domain.

4. A, B. Resource domains were used in large organizations to limit the size of the account databases and also to allow for local administrative capability.

5. D. IntelliMirror will allow for automated software installation and maintenance.

6. A. An application is advertised when a user logs on to a workstation.

7. B. Applications are published to GPOs associated with users in Active Directory containers.

8. B. A security configuration consists of security settings applied to each security area supported for the Windows 2000 Professional or Windows 2000 Server.

9. C, D. Group Policies are created with the Group Policy MMC snap-in as a stand-alone tool or as an extension to the Active Directory Users and Computers.

CASE STUDY

The Multinational Startup

You should give yourself 10 minutes to review this case study, diagram as needed, and complete the questions for this testlet.

Background

Your consulting firm has been hired to assist in the Windows 2000 migration and integration for a company based in Minneapolis, Minnesota. Until the start of this year, the company had 1,000 employees, all based throughout the Twin Cities of Minneapolis and St. Paul. Just before the end of the year, the owner of your company purchased two companies of roughly the same size that will need to be connected to the enterprise network. The total number of users after the project is completed is estimated at 5,500. In addition, each of these companies comes with various strategic partners that will need to access the information on your enterprise network. The companies that have been acquired are located in Athens, Greece, and in Orlando, Florida. At this point, the buyouts are complete and most of the changes to the infrastructure have been finalized. The time has come to explore the impact of the Windows 2000 rollout and its effect on the current network security.

Problem Statement

Now that the integration of the company is at least moving along, it is time to start the Windows 2000 rollout. Everything starts with the rollout and everyone in the company is anxious to have it finished. The issue right now is where to start. When you arrive on the scene, you are presented with a domain map that looks like…well, to be perfectly honest…looks pretty bad. As a matter of fact, spaghetti junction would be more like it. There are probably two dozen domains, with two-way trusts between most of them and one-way trusts between the rest. The people in IT have no idea why some of them exist: some just magically appeared on the network. It is obvious, though, that there are at least two resource domains for each administrative domain.

Current System

Minneapolis Located on the shores of beautiful Lake Calhoun, the company occupies a sprawling campus that includes four floors in a six-story building. When the company started out five years ago, it had just part of one of the floors and about 100 people. Since that time, the company has grown, and any time a tenant has moved out of the building, the company has taken over the office space. This grow-as-you-go philosophy had left members of the same departments scattered throughout the building. However, recently the company signed a long-term contract with a local moving and storage company, and they have been systematically relocating departments in an orderly manner. Communication has improved and morale has picked up.

All of the floors are connected to the Windows NT network. While the infrastructure was chaotic, it has stabilized. Communication between NT domains is reliable, even across the WAN links to the other offices. The decision has been made to move to Windows 2000. Active Directory Services will be used extensively. Security remains the hot topic, and the CEO wants to know how much impact the rollout of Windows 2000 will have on the way the network is operating at this point.

The remote offices of Orlando and Athens have recently been mapped and documented. As far as the corporate IT department is concerned, the motto seems to be, "Hey, it ain't pretty, but it works."

Orlando The Orlando office actually has more people working in it than there are in Minneapolis. It is located in northern Orlando, away from Disney and the tourists. Many of the services in Minneapolis are mirrored in Orlando: things like marketing, accounting, and human resources. The site is all on NT 4, with a variety of applications; some of the applications are compatible with the Minneapolis corporate standards and some aren't. The Orlando office does have a fractional T1 connection to the Internet. The office was using Lotus Notes as their e-mail package, but the decision was made to upgrade them to Exchange. It is a temporary step until the final upgrade to Exchange 2000, but at least everyone is using the same e-mail package now. The users have all had their Internet e-mail addresses changed to the corporate DNS name. The office has been notified that Windows 2000 is next on the horizon. While this office will not participate in hosting any of the Web services, they do have an Internet connection and a lot of information that must be protected.

When the buyout happened, much of the Orlando IT department bailed out and went to work in other areas. The Help desk folks have stayed, and many of the PC techs are still there. There are two-way trusts between domains, so the administration of the network is working. The implementation in Orlando matches the current corporate standard of "it ain't pretty, but it works!"

Athens The Athens office has about 1,300 users, most of whom are salespeople, marketing types, and support staff. The manufacturing plant is located on the island of Rhodes, and due to local customs, manufacturing occurs only between March and October. The rest of the time, the plant is closed. The office has been upgraded to Windows NT 4 servers running SP5. It is predominantly used for file and print sharing. Again, the decision was made to upgrade immediately to Exchange from their POP3 server, so everyone in the company has Exchange.

The decision had been made to upgrade the 3.51 servers directly into Windows 2000, but after it became obvious the planning was going to take awhile, the company went ahead and upgraded to NT 4. Due to the increase in communication between the United States and Greece, the Athenians are getting more used to e-mail. As a matter of fact, several people in Greece have become expert at creating forms.

Because this has been a stand-alone company, all of the normal accounting, purchasing, and human resources functions are there. It has been agreed that management will remain with the company. Communication between sites remains by e-mail, snail mail, and phone.

The Greek IT department remains intact and ready to help.

Envisioned System

Overview Now that it is becoming obvious that these three locations can in fact work together and communicate, the CEO wants to make sure that it is done securely. She has read about this Digital Nervous System, and she wants one. She understands that the basis for this Digital Nervous System and the instantaneous access to information is Windows 2000. She has been through major IT shifts before and she isn't really excited to have any bad experiences.

CEO "It is time to upgrade to Windows 2000. Our current NT 4 network, while stable, isn't providing us with the features that Windows 2000 will give us. Now that we are international in scope and have all these partners who need to access our network, we need the functionality. Now that I have said that, I have to tell you the last time I went through a major operating system migration, *everything* went wrong, and our network was hosed up for months. There will not be a repeat of that performance: is that understood?"

Security

Overview Because the product you develop is constantly undergoing research and development, and because the industry is what it is, security must be maintained at a very high level. As you can see from the statements made by the CEO, it is taking a higher priority.

CFO "With the merger going on and with all the systems with highly sensitive data on them, it's paramount that security is maintained at an extremely high level. I cannot emphasize this enough. On the other hand, we have to be careful not to step on any toes, and also to make sure that the security we do install is not too intrusive into people's lives. Our senior management has heard about all those systems where people have to remember dozens of passwords and we certainly don't want anything like that here."

Performance

Overview The CEO is thrilled to death with the new connection to the Internet. She has been able to communicate with the remote offices in a more efficient manner, and she is glad to have all the functionality she had at her last job. She received the monthly reports from the general managers in Greece and Orlando, and was able to review the reports and formulate questions for the managers and their staff.

Orlando branch manager "It is *wonderful* now that we can communicate with anyone in this company. Some of the people in the home office are still a little shaky using e-mail, but at least they have it. It is a great improvement. I understand that Windows 2000 will make things even better. We have so many remote users that are running around with vital information on their laptops, it will be great to get that encrypted."

Athens branch manager "Will the Windows 2000 rollout mean we will have to buy a new server? Can we still keep our Unix hosts?"

Maintainability

Overview There are two problems here. First of all, you will be dealing with an international company, which means that you will not be able to utilize the same vendor for maintenance. Secondly, information will have to be available from all levels of the organization, all day, every day. The information must be up-to-date in real time. Because this could possibly tell your competition exactly what you are doing and for whom, the information must be secure.

CEO "These new products we're developing are so revolutionary and will have such an impact that it's important for us to make sure everyone has the same information at the same time."

Athens operations manager "My understanding is that our product will now be bundled with the products developed in Minneapolis. That means we have to know how many to produce. Given the limitations of Rhodes' manufacturing cycle, there may have to be some offloading of responsibilities to other areas of the company."

Availability

Because the network will span several different time zones, the availability of the network must be 24x7x365. The 24x7x365 uptime must be maintained during the rollout. According to the IT director, "Everything has to be checked and double-checked to make sure that it will work with Windows 2000 and that it will continue to work on our network while we upgrade. We cannot afford downtime."

Funding

Overview While you have not been given *carte blanche* by the CEO, she has made it clear that money isn't necessarily an issue—within reason, of course. The problems need to be solved so that the company can safely continue to manufacture its products in the most efficient manner possible.

CEO & CFO "Look, we don't think that we need the Rolls Royce of installations—*but* we can tell you that everything is riding on our ability to ship our combined products in a timely manner, and the network we're asking you to build is going to be a big part of that. We think the company will continue to grow, though not as rapidly as in the last several months. So, that being said, give us a network that makes sense."

Questions

1. What can you ascertain will have to be done with the domains?

   A. They will have to be upgraded.

   B. They will have to be restructured.

   C. There isn't a lot of information, but it sure seems like some restructuring may be in order.

   D. There has not been any risk assessment, security assessment, or risk management, so you are jumping the gun.

2. What solution(s) should you implement to solve the customer's business problem?

   A. The company appears to have the makings of a logical network map. Begin by completing the layout on paper.

   B. Start looking at the members of the IT department to see where they will fit in the new network order.

   C. Up-version all servers to Windows 2000.

   D. Immediately institute Kerberos v5 across the network and institute transitive trusts everywhere.

   E. Have the applications team begin to inventory line of business applications and test their compatibility with Windows 2000.

   F. Plan and deploy screened subnet firewalls at each location.

   G. Plan and deploy a combination of bastion host and screened subnet types of firewalls.

3. As you gather in the network information, what kinds of things are you looking for in these maps?

   A. Numbers and types of users

   B. Documented DHCP scopes for each server

   C. Printouts of routing tables

   D. Location of domain controllers and description of who they serve

   E. Location of SQL applications

   F. Hardware, software, and operating system inventory

   G. All of the above

4. If the migration goal is to minimize administrative overhead, what is the implication for the migration process?

   A. There should be little or no impact on the current security policy.

   B. There needs to be seamless migration of user accounts from Windows NT to Windows 2000. This means, if possible, users need to be able to retain their passwords. Administrators should only have to visit the client computer a minimum number of times. There needs to be minimal setup of new permissions for resources.

   C. Plans must be in place to make sure that the users' access to data, resources, and applications is maintained during the migration process. The users' familiar environment needs to be maintained during and after the migration.

   D. The enterprise needs to obtain earliest access to key features.

5. If the migration goal is to maximize the number of quick wins, what is the implication for the migration process?

   A. There should be little or no impact on the current security policy.

   B. There needs to be seamless migration of user accounts from Windows NT to Windows 2000. This means, if possible, users need to be able to retain their passwords. Administrators should only have to visit the client computer a minimum number of times. There needs to be minimal setup of new permissions for resources.

C. Plans must be in place to make sure that the users' access to data, resources, and applications is maintained during the migration process. The users' familiar environment needs to be maintained during and after the migration.

D. The enterprise needs to obtain earliest access to key features.

6. If the migration goal is to maintain system performance, what are the implications for the migration process?

A. There should be little or no impact on the current security policy.

B. There needs to be seamless migration of user accounts from Windows NT to Windows 2000. This means, if possible, users need to be able to retain their passwords. Administrators should only have to visit the client computer a minimum number of times. There needs to be minimal setup of new permissions for resources.

C. Plans must be in place to make sure that the users' access to data, resources, and applications is maintained during the migration process. The users' familiar environment needs to be maintained during and after the migration.

D. The enterprise needs to obtain earliest access to key features.

7. If the migration goal is to maximize the average mean time between failures, what are the implications for the migration process?

A. There should be little or no impact on the current security policy.

B. There needs to be seamless migration of user accounts from Windows NT to Windows 2000. This means, if possible, users need to be able to retain their passwords. Administrators should only have to visit the client computer a minimum number of times. There needs to be minimal setup of new permissions for resources.

C. Plans must be in place to make sure that the users' access to data, resources, and applications is maintained during the migration process. The users' familiar environment needs to be maintained during and after the migration.

D. The enterprise needs to obtain earliest access to key features.

8. If the migration goal is to maintain system security, what are the implications for the migration process?

A. There should be little or no impact on the current security policy.

B. There needs to be seamless migration of user accounts from Windows NT to Windows 2000. This means, if possible, users need to be able to retain their passwords. Administrators should only have to visit the client computer a minimum number of times. There needs to be minimal setup of new permissions for resources.

C. Plans must be in place to make sure that the users' access to data, resources, and applications is maintained during the migration process. The users' familiar environment needs to be maintained during and after the migration.

D. The enterprise needs to obtain earliest access to key features.

9. What security feature of Windows 2000 can be used to protect the data on laptops?

A. Universal groups

B. NTLM

C. EFS

D. CDFS

E. NTFS

10. Can the network in Athens keep their Unix hosts?

A. Possibly. It depends on what version of BIND they are running.

B. Absolutely not.

C. Yes, Windows 2000 has features that will let it coexist with Unix hosts.

Answers

1. C. Management has suddenly discovered Windows 2000, and it appears that the management team would like it in place right now. The network map, however, sounds like it truly is a hodgepodge. With so many resource domains and administrative domains, there are probably areas available for consolidation.

2. A, B, E. The business case calls for the Windows 2000 upgrade, but still more needs to be known about the domains, the line-of-business applications and their integration with Windows 2000, and how the current IT staffs can be best utilized.

3. G. All of the above. Any information you can gather at this point will be beneficial later.

4. B. There needs to be seamless migration of user accounts from Windows NT to Windows 2000. This means, if possible, users need to be able to retain their passwords. Administrators should only have to visit the client computer a minimum number of times. There needs to be minimal setup of new permissions for resources.

5. D. The enterprise needs to obtain the earliest possible access to key features of the new operating system.

6. C. There must be plans in place to make sure that the users' access to data, resources, and applications are maintained during the migration process. In addition, the users' familiar environment needs to be maintained during and after the migration.

7. C. There must be plans in place to make sure that the users' access to data, resources, and applications are maintained during the migration process. In addition, the users' familiar environment needs to be maintained during and after the migration.

8. A. There should be little or no impact on the security policy.

9. C. The network administrator will have to establish an encrypted file system policy to meet the needs of the traveling or remote user.

10. C. Yes, Windows 2000 has features that will let it coexist with Unix hosts.

Security Baselines

MICROSOFT EXAM OBJECTIVES COVERED IN THIS CHAPTER:

- ✓ Design a security baseline for a Windows 2000 network that includes domain controllers, operations masters, application servers, file and print servers, RAS servers, desktop computers, portable computers, and kiosks.
- ✓ Identify the required level of security for each resource. Resources include printers, files, shares, Internet access, and dial-in access.

In the last chapter we went over some of the security terms and how some of the Windows 2000 security worked. In this chapter we are going to look at how to start laying out security baselines for many of the resources on your network. This chapter is going to be a little different than previous chapters. In those chapters it was easy to break the information down into chunks that matched the objectives. In this chapter things will be a little different. Here we are going to present the strategies and you are going to have to apply them to the specific situation. You will see this clearly as we get into it.

Now you may be asking why we are not going to lay out for you the required level of security for each resource, or develop a *security baseline* that includes domain controllers, operations masters, application servers, and file and print servers. The answer is simple. Not only is there no right answer to these questions—there may be several right answers for each scenario. Each scenario will be unique, so there simply is no little green pill that says, "Do it this way."

Microsoft Exam Objectives

Design a security baseline for a Windows 2000 network that includes domain controllers, operations masters, application servers, file and print servers, RAS servers, desktop computers, portable computers, and kiosks.

Identify the required level of security for each resource. Resources include printers, files, shares, Internet access, and dial-in access.

Now some of this may be pretty straightforward. For example, take the case of the operations master. As you know from your previous tests, the operations master must be available when a server attempts to join an existing tree by creating a new domain. Therefore, you should make sure that operations masters are placed in areas where they are readily accessible by Active Directory.

On the other end of the spectrum are kiosk machines. These are the standalone workstations that you see in places like malls and airports. They are important to your security plan because you are going to have to lay out your group policy to install the exact applications they need to operate.

To wax philosophical here for a second, we really do wish that we could lay out the perfect scenario for a Windows 2000 network, because then we would implement it on our networks. The fact remains that the largest security hole in any network is usually the interface between the chair and the keyboard. If the system administrator does something stupid, or forgets to do something smart, the system is vulnerable.

Distributed Security Strategies

Finally, we get to start looking at how security will affect the enterprise. In Microsoft-speak, we are talking about distributed security, and that refers to the logical security features that operate primarily within the network. Microsoft identifies seven primary security strategies that you should pursue in making the enterprise network secure:

- Authenticate all user access to system resources.
- Apply appropriate access control to all resources.
- Establish appropriate trust relationships between multiple domains. (This was covered in depth in Chapter 6, "Evaluating the Impact of the Security Design on the Technical Environment.")
- Enable data protection for sensitive data.
- Set uniform security policies.
- Deploy secure applications.
- Manage security administration.

As you begin to lay out your network security matrix (otherwise referred to as your network security plan), you should make these seven themes central to the distributed security plan. Why don't we start by examining each of these concepts?

Authenticating All User Access

Probably the first tenet of security that everyone learns is, "Make sure that the people who need to get into the network can have access and the people who should not have access to the network are blocked (or at least hindered) from entering." So, to provide security for your Windows 2000 network, you must provide access for legitimate users but screen out intruders who are trying to break in. This means you must set up your security features to authenticate all user access to system resources. Authentication strategies set the level of protection against intruders trying to steal identities or impersonate users.

In Windows 2000, authentication for domain users is based on user accounts in Active Directory. Administrators manage these accounts using the Active Directory Users and Computers snap-in to the Microsoft Management Console (MMC). User accounts can be organized into containers called *organization units,* which reflect the design of your Active Directory namespace. The default location for user accounts is the Users folder of this snap-in. Check out Figure 7.1 to see this demonstrated.

FIGURE 7.1 MMC with organization unit and Users folder

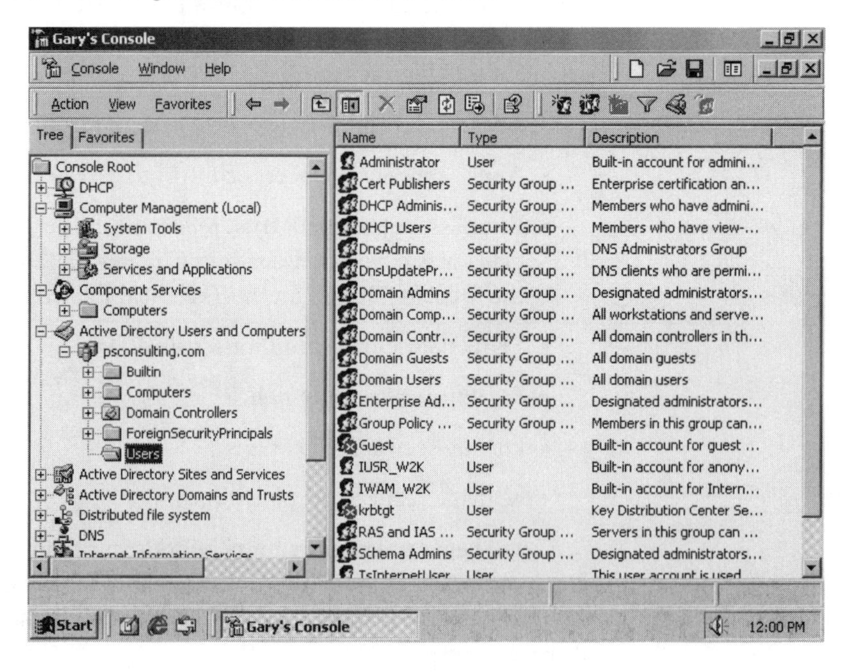

When someone new joins the company, the administrator creates only a single account for that user, rather than having to create half a dozen or more separate accounts on different servers and application databases. With the domain authentication service integrated with the enterprise directory, that single user account is also a directory entry for global address book information, and a way to provide access to all network services. The user can log on at different client computers or laptops in the domain, using only one password.

Windows 2000 automatically supports single sign-on for users within a forest. Domain trust relationships in the forest are transitive or two-way by default, so authentication in one domain is sufficient for referral or pass-through authentication to resources in other domains in the forest. The user logs on at the beginning of a session, after which network security protocols like the Kerberos v5 protocol, NTLM, and Secure Sockets Layer/Transport Layer Security protocols transparently prove the user's identity to all requested network services.

If your installation needs an even more secure way of authentication, Windows 2000 also supports logging on with *smart cards*. The smart card is an identification card carried by the user that is used instead of a password for interactive logon. It can also be used for remote dial-up network connections and as a place to store public key certificates used for Secure Sockets Layer (SSL) client authentication or secure e-mail.

When you use Active Directory, authentication is not limited to users. Computers and services are also authenticated when they make network connections to other servers. For example, Windows 2000–based servers and client computers connect to their domain's Active Directory for policy information during startup. They authenticate to Active Directory and download computer policy from Active Directory before any user can log on to that computer. Services also have to prove their identity to clients that request mutual authentication. Mutual authentication is a " you-show-me-yours-and-I-will-show-you mine" kind of thing. Both parties to the communication have to be assured they are communicating with the right host. Mutual authentication works to prevent an intruder from adding another computer as an impostor between the client and the real network server.

Computers and services can be *trusted for delegation,* which means services can make other network connections "on behalf of" a user without knowing the user's password. The user must already have a mutually authenticated network connection to the service before the service can make a new network connection to another computer for that user. This feature is particularly useful in the context of an Encrypting File System (EFS) running on a file server. To use a service to delegate a network connection, use the Active Directory Users and Computers MMC snap-in. Then select the Trust computer for delegation check-box on the property sheet. This is shown in Figure 7.2.

FIGURE 7.2 Trust computer for delegation part of the MMC

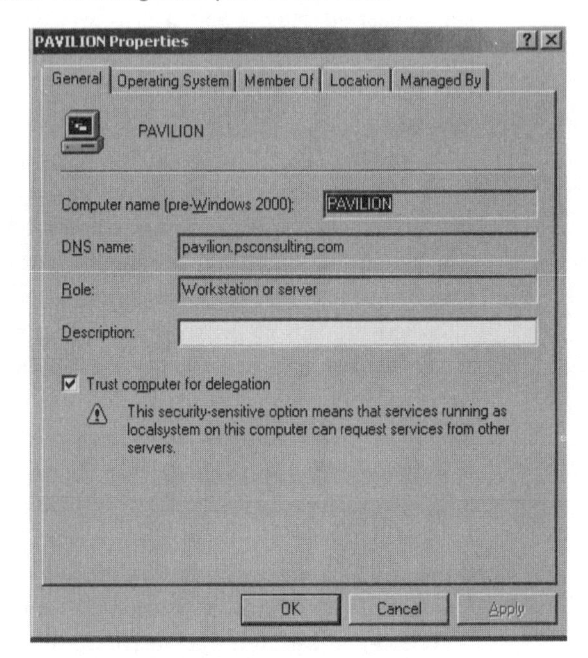

Trust computer for delegation is a very powerful capability. It is not enabled by default and requires Domain Administrator privileges to enable for specific computers or service accounts.

Computers or accounts that are trusted for delegation need to be under restricted access to prevent introduction of Trojan horse programs that would misuse the capability of making network connections on behalf of users.

Some accounts might be too sensitive to permit delegation, even by a trusted server. You can set individual user accounts so that they cannot be delegated, even if the service is trusted for delegation. To use this feature, go to the Active Directory Users and Computers MMC snap-in and open the property sheet for the account. Look for the Account is sensitive and cannot be delegated check-box on the Account tab of the property sheet. This is shown in Figure 7.3.

FIGURE 7.3 Account cannot be delegated

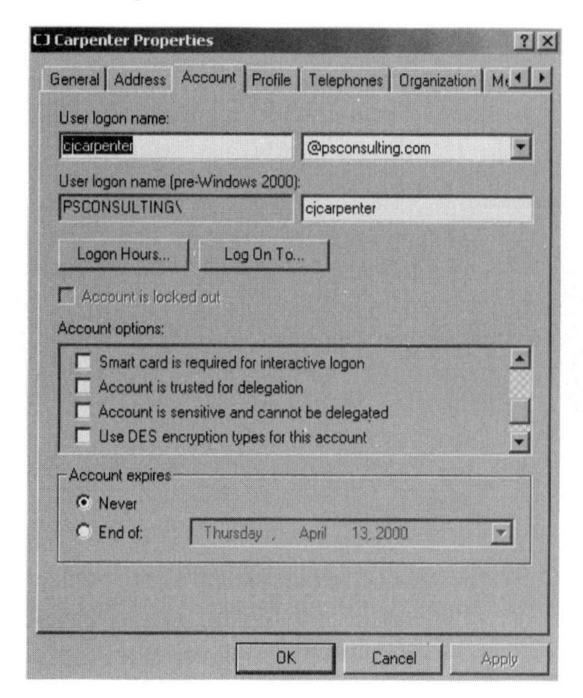

Security Matrix Considerations

As you look at the network and put together your security matrix, there are some considerations that you should be sure to address. These are the best practices that Microsoft recommends when planning your authentication policies.

The first issue is passwords. Now, the discussion on passwords is long, philosophical, and borderline religious. You know about religious discussions. These are the kind that start out, "Which is better, NetWare or Windows 2000?" These are the discussions you cannot win, and you just state your case and get the heck out of the discussion. Now, as far as passwords go, you have some password zealots that say your users should have long and complex passwords. You have other zealots that think that passwords,

> **Hardened Systems**
>
> One of the first questions that security professionals get asked is how to harden a domain controller, a domain, or even a network. After all, we are all looking for that little green pill to make everything safe and secure, aren't we? In this case, though, it probably would not come in the form of a pill, it would come in the form of a list of step-by-step procedures to take to make sure that the network was secure. It is a great concept, but has lousy follow-through.
>
> Finding the answer to the question, "How do you harden a network?" requires that you first determine how hard you want it. If you are administering a small network and the only connection to the outside world is an e-mail server hosted by your ISP, where POP3 mail is stored, your "network hardening" tasks are going to be minimal. If, however, you are working diligently to harden the network of a power company with nuclear plants, your efforts will be much more focused. If you were looking to this book for the key to the perfectly secure network, I think you will probably be out of luck.

while not useless, are darn close—as long as 3M keeps selling Post-it notes. We have all seen too many passwords taped to monitors or under keyboards to swear by passwords as the last line of security.

No matter where you stand, the facts remain that the simplest way to defend against brute force or dictionary password cracking tools is to establish and enforce long, complex passwords. Windows 2000 lets you set policy to govern the complexity, length, lifetime, and reusability of user passwords. A complex password has 10 or more characters, including upper- and lowercase, punctuation, and numerals. An example of a complex password is *CJ,will,be,3,on2,15,01*. Why are you shaking your head incredulously and thinking, "I can just see forcing that on my users—they would hang me"? You can always try. Stranger things have happened!

If complex passwords are out of the question and you are still looking for a strong front line of security, there are other ways, but all of the other ways are somewhat costly. For example, smart cards provide much stronger authentication than passwords, but they also involve extra overhead. Smart cards require configuration of the Microsoft Certificate Services, smart card reader devices, and the smart cards themselves.

There are third-party vendors that offer a variety of security products, besides smart cards, that are Windows 2000 compatible. Many of these provide two-factor authentication, including *security tokens* and *biometric* accessories. These accessories use extensible features of the Windows 2000 graphical logon user interface to provide alternate methods of user authentication.

So, what is the trick? How do you determine what is the appropriate password length and what your users will stand? There are some examples that you may want to follow.

The Windows 2000 MMC has a section for *security templates*. These are intended to be sample templates for various types of network resources. For example, there are templates for high-security domain controllers and high-security workstations. There are also templates for basic domain controllers and workstations that have the password functions listed as "not defined."

In the high-security templates, password history is enforced with up to 24 passwords remembered. That means that users cannot re-use the password until the password has been changed 24 times. As far as how often the user must change the password, the maximum age is 42 days and the minimum age is 2 days. Placing a minimum age means that the creative user cannot simply change her password 25 times in the same day to keep the same password. Now, your users wouldn't do a thing like that, would they?

In addition, you can enable only passwords that meet complexity requirements. This is similar to installing the `Passfilt.dll` implementations in Windows NT 4, SP2, which instituted a password policy with the following requirements:

1. Passwords must be at least six (6) characters long.
2. Passwords must contain characters from at least three (3) of the following four (4) classes:

Description	Example
English uppercase letters	A, B, C, ... Z
English lowercase letters	a, b, c, ... z
Westernized Arabic numerals	0, 1, 2, 3, ... 9
Non-alphanumeric	Special characters, such as punctuation symbols

3. Passwords may not contain your username or any part of your full name.

Finally, passwords may be stored using reversible encryption for all users in the domain.

So, now it comes down to, "How secure do you want to make it?" As I have said through the entire book, before you make decisions that will affect the entire enterprise, not to mention your annual review, it is always best to involve serious levels of management. If you decide to start instituting the complexity policy, you can bet that you will be a very popular person—your phone will just start ringing off the wall with people who want to talk to you. Unfortunately, they will mispronounce your first name. If this happens to you, your first name may suddenly become "You S.O.B." Having a management sponsor will help alleviate some of that.

Design Scenario: The Case of the Improper Password

It is a normal Monday morning and you are just going about your business of being the best consultant in the whole darn town. You decide to stop in at a client site and see how an upgrade went that weekend. You had pretty much laid the groundwork for the upgrade, but it was up to the staff to pull it all together. You figure a courtesy call wouldn't hurt.

When you come in, you are invited into a meeting that has apparently been going on for a while. As a matter of fact, the discussion has gotten somewhat heated. The IT manager is trying to get a password policy passed, and the IT staff is fighting the change, not because they don't want a secure network, but just because they feel it won't do any good. After all, people are people and they will tape their passwords to the monitor, no matter what you do.

Once again, in the middle of the meeting, someone turns to you and asks what should be done. First of all, you ponder for a moment, and then recognize that each side has a very valid point. It is difficult to get users to use passwords that are difficult to crack, without having them tape them to the monitor. You start by suggesting, since the IT department is in its own domain, that it start the process by requiring secure passwords. You point out that with templates, it is possible to require secure passwords without too much problem. Once the IT department has lived with secure passwords for a month or so, they can begin the sales job necessary to roll them out to the rest of the company.

You also mention that it is going to be a sales job, and there has to be some thought put into how to handle that. If the users believe it is important, they will be more likely to follow through. Just in case, however, you suggest preparing a demonstration on how easy it is to hack into a short password. You also suggest showing how the security staff will be randomly checking accounts to make sure there is compliance. What the hey, for those that don't buy into the importance of it, you can stress the embarrassment they might feel when they are busted for a noncompliant password.

Apply Access Control to All Resources

By the time you have reached this stage working with Windows 2000, you realize how much more of an enterprise approach Microsoft has taken with the product. Instead of examining small (figuratively speaking) islands of the network, suddenly everything is put together so it can be managed from one location. That makes it awfully nice for the administrator, but it also means that users will be able to access resources in the far-flung reaches of the network. This is done through Kerberos authentication.

Kerberos Authentication and Trust

In the last chapter we briefly mentioned Kerberos technology. Kerberos is one of the Windows 2000 buzzwords, so expect to see lots of questions about it on the test. The Kerberos authentication protocol is a technology that provides for single sign-on to network resources. Windows 2000 uses the Kerberos v5 protocol to provide single sign-on to network services within a domain, and also to provide services residing in trusted domains. Kerberos protocol verifies both the identity of the user and of the network services, and it provides mutual authentication. So what does this mean to the system administrator? Take a look at Figure 7.4.

FIGURE 7.4 An example of how Kerberos can be used

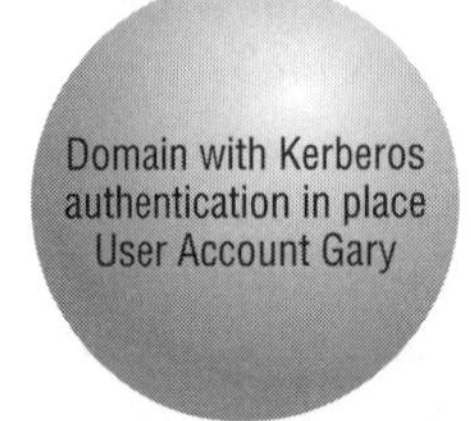

In this case, you have a domain with a user Gary. If Gary is authenticated into that domain and needs to access an application in another domain, the other domain accepts the fact that Gary really is who Gary says he is, just because he is Kerberos authenticated.

How Kerberos Authentication Works

When Gary enters *domain credentials* (by username and password or smart card logon), Windows 2000 locates an Active Directory server and the Kerberos key distribution center (KDC). The Kerberos KDC issues a *ticket granting ticket* to the user Gary. This is a temporary ticket containing information that identifies the user to network servers. After the initial interactive logon, the first ticket granting ticket is used to request other Kerberos tickets to log on to subsequent network services. This process is complex and involves mutual authentication of the user Gary and the server to one another, but it is completely transparent to the user.

The Kerberos v5 protocol verifies both the identity of the user and the integrity of the session data. That means that not only is the user who they say they are, but also the session the verification comes from is the actual communication session. In Windows 2000, Kerberos v5 services are installed on each domain controller, and a Kerberos client is installed on each Windows workstation and server. The Kerberos v5 service stores all of the encrypted client passwords and identities in the Active Directory. Therefore, a user's initial Kerberos authentication provides the user a single sign-on to enterprise resources, using Active Directory.

Users are enthusiastic about Kerberos, because Kerberos authentication reduces the number of passwords they need to remember. Since there are fewer passwords, there is less reason to write them down. That reduces the risk of identity interception. Also, users may have access to more stuff. The trust relationships between all the domains in a forest can extend the scope of Kerberos authentication to a wide range of network resources.

Kerberos Authentication in Action

As you design your security matrix, remember there are no prerequisites for implementing Kerberos authentication. The Kerberos protocol is used pervasively in Windows 2000. You do not need to install or initiate it. It just *is*.

Kerberos security policy parameters, however, can be set in the Group Policy snap-in to MMC. Within a Group Policy object, the Kerberos settings are located under Account policies. The settings are shown in Figure 7.5.

FIGURE 7.5 Kerberos settings in a security MMC

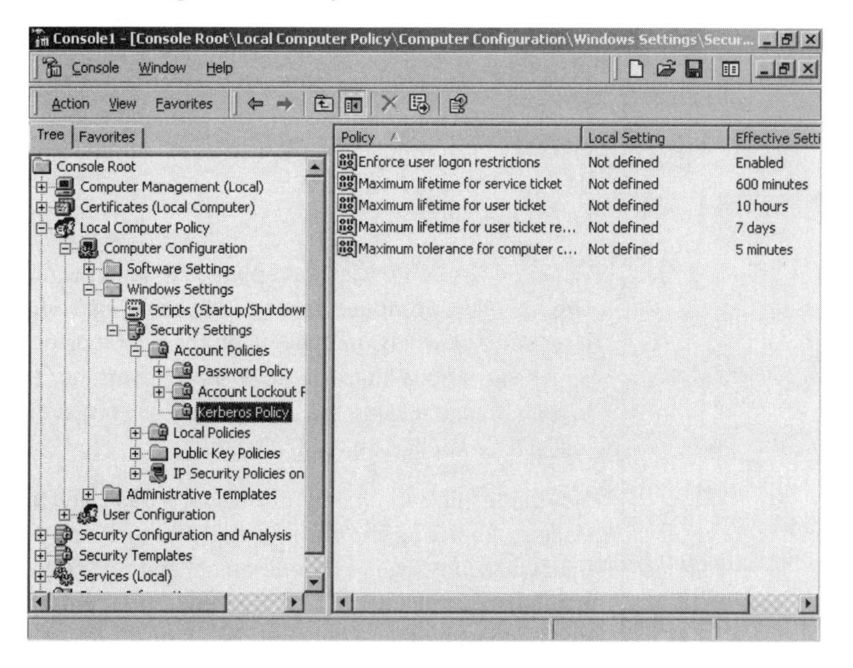

As you can see in the graphic, you can use Kerberos security to enforce user logon restrictions. By default, the maximum lifetime for a service ticket is 600 minutes, while the maximum lifetime for a user ticket is 10 hours. Finally, the maximum lifetime for computer clock synchronization is 5 minutes.

Group Policies: The Security General's Warning

Group Policies are applied to computer accounts or to user accounts. They are stored in Group Policy objects that can work at the domain level, the site level, or the OU level. Now, the thing to keep in mind when you start messing around with Group Policies is that they only work with Windows 2000 clients; they are not backwardly compatible to Windows NT or Windows 9x systems.

Windows 2000 still maintains compatibility with the NTLM authentication protocol to support backward compatibility with previous versions of Microsoft operating systems. You can continue to use NTLM for Windows 95, Windows 98, Windows NT 4 Server, and Windows NT 4 Workstation clients. NTLM authentication is also used on Windows 2000 by applications designed for previous versions of Windows NT that specifically request NTLM security.

When do Group Policies get applied? It depends on what is defined in the Group Policy. Computer settings will be applied when the computer starts. User settings will be applied when the user logs on. Policies will also be applied at various intervals, so leaving a computer on all the time or staying logged on and locking the workstation will not avoid Group Policies. They will still be applied on the fly.

Now, let's think about that for a minute. Basically, that is saying that Group Policies are live as soon as you apply them. Since Group Policies can really limit what computers or users can do, and since Group Policies affect all the computers or users in a site, domain, or OU, these are not things to be deployed willy-nilly. (Willy-nilly is a high-level, technical, geek term that means *without extensive testing.*) Misapplying a Group Policy can cause chaos on a network. Causing chaos on a network can be career limiting, sometimes limiting the career to the close of business. Just a word to the wise: Test these puppies in the lab before rolling them out, and roll them out carefully!

This is called anticipating a question. The maximum lifetime for service tickets is configurable in one-minute increments, while the maximum lifetime for user tickets is configurable in one-hour intervals. The defaults just happen to be equal to the same time period.

Why Use Kerberos Security?

If you want to take advantage of the performance improvements and the security that Kerberos authentication provides, you may want to consider using the Kerberos sign-in as the only network logon protocol in your enterprise. The design of the Windows 2000 version of Kerberos implements the IETF standard version of the Kerberos v5 authentication protocol for supposedly improved cross-platform interoperability. For example, users on Unix systems can use Kerberos credentials to log on to Unix systems and to securely connect to Windows 2000 services for applications that are enabled by Kerberos authentication.

At the time that Windows 2000 was released, Microsoft had not released the specifications of its implementation of Kerberos to OEMs. That meant that Unix systems could not talk with Windows 2000 networks without the benefit of a third-party solution. About four months after release, Microsoft did release the specifications with the intention of making sure that its implementation of Kerberos would allow Unix systems to interoperate with Windows 2000. Since this book was being written as this process was taking place, we can only assume (and hope) they were successful.

Enterprise networks that already use Kerberos authentication based on Unix realms can create trust relationships with Windows 2000 domains and integrate Windows 2000 authorization for Unix accounts using Kerberos name mapping, with the aid of third-party products.

One issue with Windows 2000 is that Windows 2000 Professional computers can receive tickets from Kerberos KDCs running on Windows 2000 servers. At this time, there is a problem getting the certificates from machines that are not KDCs running Windows 2000.

Now, all that glitters is not gold. Kerberos is not the be-all, end-all of security. It does have some things that may make it difficult to use. For example, when you institute Kerberos, make sure that all computers on a Kerberos-authenticated network must have their time settings synchronized with a common time service. (Note the time synchronization setting above!) Not only that, but enterprise network communication must keep that time service on all machines within five minutes, or authentication fails. Windows 2000 computers automatically update the current time using the domain controller as a network time service. Domain controllers use the primary domain controller for the domain as the authoritative time service. This is just something else for you to worry about.

If you are worried about time zones, don't be. Even if the current time is different on computers within a domain, or across domains, Windows 2000 automatically handles time zone differences to avoid logon problems.

Domains in a Windows 2000 tree, by default, use transitive trusts. With Kerberos, when using transitive trusts between domains in a forest, the Kerberos service searches for a trust path between the domains to create what is called across-domain referral. In large trees it might be more efficient to establish cross-links of bidirectional (or two-way) trusts between domains where there is a high degree of cross-domain communication. This permits faster authentication by giving the Kerberos protocol *shortcuts* to follow when generating the referral message.

Kerberos authentication uses transparent transitive trusts among domains in a forest, but it cannot authenticate between domains in separate forests. To use a resource in a separate forest, the user has to provide credentials that are valid for logging on to a domain in that forest.

We are now getting into those areas where the test writers take a great interest. The terms *Kerberos* and *NTLM* will be coming up a lot in future chapters, so it is a word to the wise to pay attention and understand the differences. Kerberos is integrated neatly into Windows 2000 implementations. NTLM is for backward compatibility. Understand the differences and when they are used!

Smart Card Logon

As mentioned earlier, Windows 2000 supports optional smart card authentication. Smart cards provide a very secure means of user authentication, interactive logon, code signing, and secure e-mail. However, deploying and maintaining a smart card program requires additional resources and costs.

How Smart Cards Work

The smart card, which is usually the size of a common credit card, contains a chip that stores the user's private key, logon information, and public key certificate for various purposes. The user inserts the card into a smart card reader attached to the computer. The user then types in a *personal identification number (PIN)* when requested. Yep, this is basically an ATM card on steroids.

Smart cards are designed to provide a form of tamper-resistant authentication through onboard private key storage. The private key stored on the smart card is used in turn to provide other forms of security related to things like digital signatures and encryption.

Smart cards use what is called a *two-factor authentication policy,* and indirectly that permits things like data confidentiality, data integrity, and nonrepudiation for multiple applications, including domain logon, secure mail, and secure Web access.

Smart Card Prerequisites

Smart cards rely on the Public Key Infrastructure (PKI) of Windows 2000. For a full discussion of Public Key Infrastructure, see Chapter 11, "Enhancing Security Using Public Keys."

Implementing Smart Cards

First, you need to implement a PKI and then purchase the smart card equipment. In addition to PKI and the cards themselves, each computer needs a smart card reader. Set up at least one computer as a smart card enrollment station, and authorize at least one user to operate it. This does not require special hardware beyond a smart card reader, but the user who operates the enrollment station needs to be issued an Enrollment Agent certificate.

For detailed procedures on implementing smart cards, see Windows 2000 Server Help. In addition, there will be a more detailed discussion of smart cards in Chapter 9, "Choosing an Authentication Strategy."

Considerations about Smart Cards

You need an enterprise certification authority rather than a stand-alone or third-party certification authority to support smart card logon to Windows 2000 domains.

Microsoft supports industry standard *Personal Computer/Smart Card (PC/SC)*–compliant smart cards and readers—and if you check the hardware compatibility list, you will see Windows 2000 provides drivers for commercially available Plug and Play smart card readers. Smart card logon is supported for Windows 2000 Professional, Windows 2000 Server, Windows 2000 Advanced Server systems, and Windows 2000 Data Center.

Microsoft Windows 2000 does not support non-PC/SC-compliant or non–Plug and Play smart card readers. Some manufacturers might provide drivers for non–Plug and Play smart card readers that work with Windows 2000; nevertheless, it is recommended that you purchase only Plug and Play PC/SC-compliant smart card readers that are on the HCL.

Smart cards can be combined with employee card keys and identification badges to support multiple uses per card.

Now, since cost is always a factor, you should know that the overall cost of administering a smart card program depends on several factors, including:

- The number of users that use the smart card program and where they are located.

- How you decide to issue smart cards to users. This should include stringent requirements for verifying user identities. For example, will you require users to simply present a valid personal identification card or will you require a background investigation? Your policies affect the level of security provided as well as the actual cost. Depending on your industry, some of these decisions may be made for you, by law.
- Your practices for users who lose or misplace their smart cards. For example, will you issue temporary smart cards, authorize temporary alternate logon to the network, or make users go home to retrieve their smart cards? Your policies affect how much worker time is lost and how much Help desk support is needed.

Your network security deployment plan needs to describe the network logon and authentication methods you use. Include the following information in your security matrix:

- Identify the network logon and authentication strategies you want to deploy.
- Describe all the smart card deployment considerations you have identified and the issues with each.
- Describe the PKI certificate services that are required to support your implementation of smart cards.

Applying Access Control

No matter how the users get on to the network, it is what happens once they have been authenticated that counts. This is when they have access to all the resources and this is when they can do the damage.

After a user logs on, the user is authorized to access various network resources, such as file servers and printers that grant permissions to Authenticated Users. As you plan your matrix, you will have to make certain you restrict a user's view of network resources to the devices, services, and directories that are job related. This limits the damage that an intruder can do by impersonating a legitimate user.

Think of this as the domino effect of security. As one security expert put it, "Don't think of it as *if* you will be compromised, just think of it as *when* you will be compromised." In this case, assume the resource has already been accessed and try to figure out what will be the next thing to fall. Once that has been determined, you can figure out what you can do to protect it.

Access to network resources is based on permissions. These permissions serve to identify the users and groups that are allowed to pérform specific actions by using specific resources. For example, the Accounting Group has been given the read/write permission to access files in the Accounting Reports folder. Meanwhile, the Auditor Group has only been granted the read-only access to files in the Accounting Reports folder. In this case, the Accounting Group can actually make changes to the files in the folder while the Auditor Group can just look at them.

Using an access control list that is associated with each resource enables permissions. You can find the ACL on the Security tab of the property sheet. An ACL is a list of the security groups (and rarely the individuals) who have access to that resource. If you look at Figure 7.6, you will see that the group Everyone has the ability to read and execute files, list folder contents, and read the information contained in the TechNet folder.

FIGURE 7.6 Example of the rights given to the group Everyone

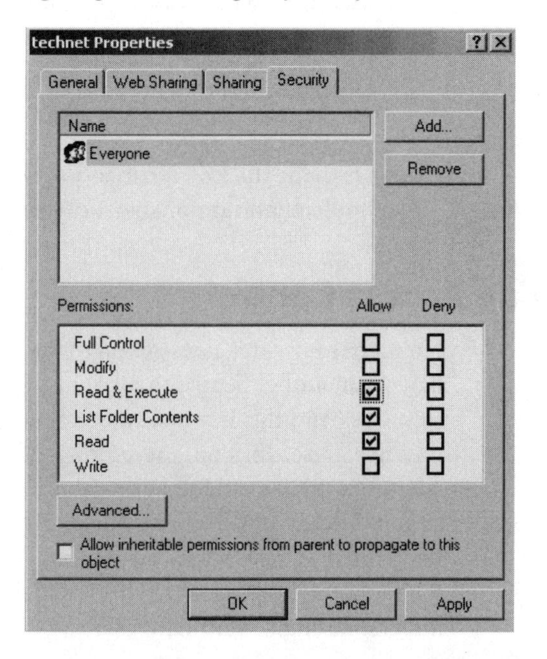

As you plan your matrix, remember to be democratic. Security groups are the most efficient way to manage permissions. Since you are assigning permissions to large groups, instead of individuals, you don't have to work as

hard. Now, if you are inclined to work too hard, you can assign permissions to individuals. Trust me, though, it really is easier to grant permissions to a group and then add or remove users as members of the group.

Windows 2000 has a security group called Everyone, which appears on network-share ACLs by default when they are created. To restrict access to network shares, you must remove the Everyone group and substitute a more appropriate group or groups. Do not assume the default permissions for a resource are necessarily appropriate permissions.

Here is an example: When a new share is created, full control permissions are granted by default to the security group called *Everyone*. Any user authenticated to the domain is in the group called *Authenticated Users*, which is also a member of Users. Look at what the resource is used for and determine the appropriate permissions. Some resources are public while others need to be available to specific sets of users. Sometimes a large group has read-only permission to a file or directory, and a smaller group has read/write permission.

Access Control Lists

ACLs describe the groups and individuals who have access to specific objects in Windows 2000. The individuals and security groups are defined in the Active Directory Users and Computers snap-in to MMC. All types of Windows 2000 objects have associated ACLs, including all Active Directory objects, local NTFS files and folders, the registry, and printers. The granularity of ACLs is so fine that you can even place security access restrictions on individual fonts.

Prerequisites for Implementing ACLs

Access control lists show up throughout Windows 2000. The only prerequisite is that ACLs are lists of security groups and users. As part of your security matrix, you must decide which groups best fit your organizational needs. Project teams or business roles may define the groups. You may look to the company organization chart for inspiration, or you may start grouping by location. The flexibility is amazing!

ACL Implementation

The access control list for an object is generally found in the Security tab of the property sheet. This tab shows the list of groups that have access to this object, plus a summary of the permissions enjoyed by each group. As mentioned above, there is an Advanced button that displays the group permissions in detail so that users can use more advanced features for granting permissions, such as defining access inheritance options.

For example, to view the access control list for a printer, click Start ➤ Settings ➤ Control Panel ➤ Printers. Right-click a printer and select Properties. The access control list for that printer is in the Security tab and is shown in Figure 7.7.

FIGURE 7.7 Printer access control list

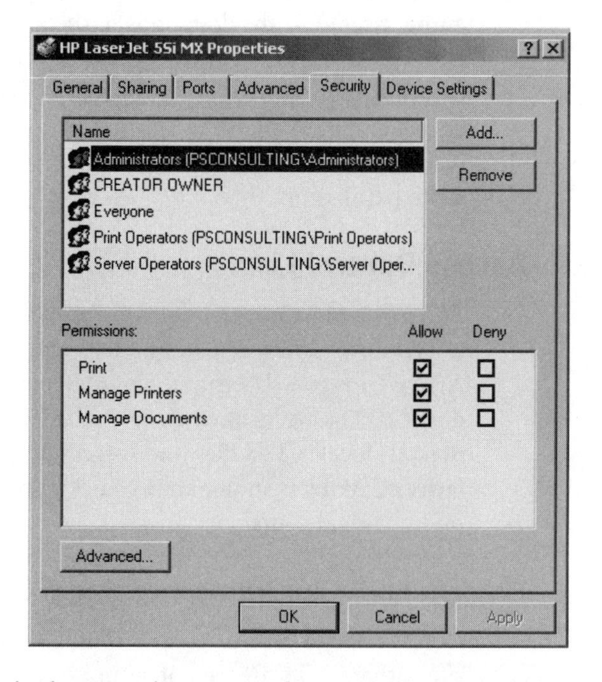

You can do the same thing to see the access control list for a local folder. Simply open My Computer and use Explore to navigate to the folder. Right-click the folder. Point to Properties, and click the Security tab.

To view the access control list of an organizational unit in the Active Directory Users and Computers MMC snap-in, you must open the View menu and select Advanced Features. Otherwise, the Security tab is not visible in the Properties dialog box.

Security Groups

It has been mentioned several times in this book that the best way to make sure that your users can get access to information is through the use of security groups. Windows 2000 allows you to organize users and other domain objects into groups for easy administration of access permissions. Defining your security groups is a major task when you are planning your security matrix.

The Windows 2000 security groups let you assign the same security permissions to large numbers of users in one operation. This ensures consistent security permissions across all members of a group. Using security groups to assign permissions means the access control lists on resources remain fairly static. "Fairly static" means they are easy to control and audit. Users who need access are added or removed from the appropriate security groups as needed, and the access control lists change infrequently. It all falls under that democratic principle mentioned above, to do unto as many others as possible without doing too much work.

How Security Groups Work

There are two *types* of groups in Windows 2000: security groups and distribution groups. Security groups can have security permissions associated with them and can also be used as mailing lists. The distribution group is used simply for the creation of mailing lists. There are no security functions associated with the distribution group.

When you create a new user, you add the user to existing security groups to completely define the user's permissions and access limits. To get you started defining groups, Windows 2000 comes with several predefined security groups.

Security Group Types

Windows 2000 supports four kinds of security groups, and these groups are set apart by *scope*:

Domain local groups are best used for granting access rights to resources. Resources can be defined as file systems or printers that are located on any computer in the domain where common access permissions are required. *Domain local groups* are also known as resource groups. The advantage of using domain local groups to protect resources is that members of the domain local groups can come from both inside the same domain and outside the domain.

Global groups are used for combining users who share a similar resource access profile based on job function or business role. These permissions can be assigned to *global groups* in any domain in the forest. In addition, global groups can be made members of domain local and universal groups in any domain in the forest. Typically, organizations use global groups for all groups where membership is expected to change frequently. These groups can only have as members user accounts defined in the same domain as the global group or global groups from the same domain in native mode. Global groups can be nested to allow for overlapping access needs or to scale for very large group structures. The most convenient way to grant access to global groups is by making the global group a member of a domain local group that is granted access permissions to a set of related project resources.

Universal groups are used in larger, multidomain organizations where there is a need to grant access to similar groups of accounts that are defined in multiple domains. Permissions can be assigned to *universal groups* in any domain in the entire forest. It is better to use global groups as members of universal groups to reduce overall replication traffic from changes to universal group membership.

Users can be added and removed from the corresponding global group within their domains, and a small number of global groups are the direct members of the universal group. Universal groups are easily granted access by making them a member of a domain local group used to grant access permissions to resources. Universal groups are used only in multiple domain trees or forests. A Windows 2000 domain must be in native mode to use universal security groups.

Membership in universal groups is included in the global catalog. Membership in global groups is not. Therefore, using global groups for members of universal groups will make them more stable than including individual user accounts (whose membership in groups is more dynamic and numerous, thus causing more global catalog—forest wide—replication).

Computer local groups are security groups that are specific to a computer and are not recognized elsewhere in the domain. If a member server is a file server and hosts 100 gigabytes (GB) of data on multiple shares, you can use a *computer local group* for administrative tasks performed directly on that computer or for defining local access permission.

For the test, be sure to know these four types of groups and how they are used. Be especially wary of the proper use of universal groups, computer local groups, and domain local groups. These are new, different, and interesting in Windows 2000 and therefore new, different, and interesting to the test writers.

Default Permissions of Security Groups

For member servers and client computers, the default Windows 2000 access control permissions provide the following levels of security:

Members of the Everyone and Users groups (normal users) do not have broad read/write permission as in Windows NT 4. These users have read-only permission to most parts of the system and read/write permission only in their own profile folders. Users cannot install applications that require modification to system directories, nor can they perform administrative tasks.

Members of the Power Users group have all the access permissions that Users and Power Users had in Windows NT 4. Power Users have read/write permission to other parts of the system in addition to their own profile folders. Power users can install applications and perform many administrative tasks.

Members of the Administrators group have the same level of rights and permissions as they did for Windows NT 4.

For servers configured as domain controllers, the default Windows 2000 security groups provide the following security:

Members of the Everyone and Users groups do not have broad read/write permission as in Windows NT 4. Normal users have read-only permission to most parts of the system and read/write permission in their own profile folders. Normal users can only access domain controllers over the network—interactive logon to domain controllers is not granted to regular users.

Members of the Account Operators, Server Operators, and Print Operators groups have the same access permissions as in Windows NT 4.

Members of the Administrators group have total control of the system as in Windows NT 4.

Prerequisites for Implementing Security Groups

Security groups are a built-in feature of Active Directory. No special installation or prerequisite is required.

Implementing Security Groups

To create new users and place them in Security groups, use the Active Directory Users and Computers snap-in of MMC. Figure 7.8 shows the New Object—Group dialog box.

FIGURE 7.8 New Object—Group dialog box

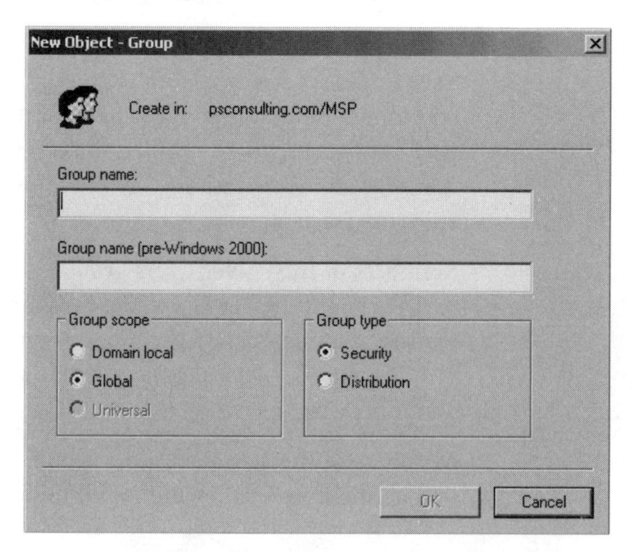

As you can see, defining the group as Domain Local, Global, or Universal, as well as setting the Group Type as Security or Distribution, is as simple as clicking radio buttons.

Considerations About Security Groups

When designing your security matrix and deciding on security groups, a good strategy is for project or resource owners to define their own domain local groups based on required access permissions. This is a part of the distributed administrative principles. In this case, you allow the owner or the manager of a resource to manage the group memberships. That is a permission of groups. This strategy allows the resource owners or project leads to manage access by updating the appropriate group. It also means that the enterprise administrators don't have to become involved in the day-to-day lower-level decisions.

Microsoft says that members of global security groups should have similar job function. Members of domain local security groups should have similar access needs.

A security group is composed of people with similar jobs or roles in the company. The group is often named after the role, such as the Windows 2000 built-in groups for Account Operators, Administrators, and Backup Operators. Personnel who naturally belong on the same project or department mailing list probably belong in the same security group in Active Directory. As mentioned above, these Windows 2000 security groups have a secondary role as mailing lists.

Using groups that correspond to project teams or responsibilities is an effective way to grant access appropriately. Usually, everyone in a department needs access to the department printers. The engineers on a software project need access to the common source directories. These are natural groups.

The system has to determine all of a user's universal and global security group affiliations at logon time. When a user is a member of many groups, this has some impact on performance while the system determines all the group memberships.

One of the NT security theories that have migrated over to Windows 2000 is the idea of nested groups. Now in Windows NT, we said that we put global groups into local groups. In Windows 2000, the technology and the verbiage have been upgraded. Now we use nested groups. You can use nested groups to make it easier to manage group membership for large groups. In this case, a large group might have 5,000 members in it. It would be very difficult to list every employee individually in your whole company in a single group. The whole-company group would be easier to administer if it was defined as the group that contains each of your department groups. The department groups can then be nested within the whole-company group.

Using Groups for Bandwidth Conservation

Using departmental groups is especially important if your whole-company group is a universal group. If you are working in an organization that has a single local area network (LAN) site, you can use universal groups with no performance degradation. However, if your organization has a wide area network (WAN), now you need to consider the impact of frequent changes to universal group membership on replication traffic across links between sites. If a universal group contains only other groups as members, it does not change very often and replication traffic is essentially nothing. A universal group containing thousands of individual users is likely to require frequent updates across multiple WAN links as each change replicates to all Global Catalog servers in the enterprise. Defining universal groups as groups of groups reduces this network activity.

You might find that your Windows 2000 Server implementation does not permit nested groups. Windows 2000 Server initially operates in *mixed mode,* which means that Windows 2000 and Windows NT 4 Servers can interoperate in the same network. Mixed mode places some restrictions on security groups. When all domain controllers in the domain have been upgraded to Windows 2000, you can switch to *native mode*. This is a one-way transition that enables advanced features such as nesting of security groups.

There are some other holdovers from the NT 4 days. For example, on a specific computer, the users in the local administrator security group have full rights and permissions for that computer. When a Windows 2000 computer is joined to a domain, the Domain Admins group is added as a member of the local administrator group. Local users of the computer generally do not need to be members of the administrators group. The full-privilege administrators group must be used for local administration activities, such as changing the system configuration.

Applying Uniform Security Policies

Uniform security policies allow consistent security settings to be applied and enforced on different classes of computers. A class of computer would be something like the domain controller class. This is a simple matter of creating an organizational unit in Active Directory, collecting appropriate computer account objects into the organizational unit, and then applying a Group Policy object to the organizational unit. The security policies specified in the Group Policy are then enforced automatically and consistently on all the computers represented by the computer accounts in the OU.

Windows 2000 comes with a selection of default Group Policy objects that are automatically applied to domains and to domain controllers. There is also a selection of security templates representing different levels of security for various types of enterprise computers. These templates can be used to create a Group Policy for a group of computers or to analyze the security settings on a specific computer.

Group Policy Objects

A Group Policy object contains a detailed profile of security permissions that apply primarily to the security settings of a domain or a computer (rather than to users). A single Group Policy object can be applied to all of the computers in an organizational unit. Group Policy gets applied when the individual computer starts up, and periodically is refreshed if changes are made without restarting.

How Group Policy Works

Group Policy objects are associated with domains and organizational units (containers) in the Active Directory Users and Computers snap-in to MMC. The permissions granted by the Group Policy are applied to the computers stored in that container. Group Policy can also be applied to sites using the Active Directory Sites and Services snap-in.

Group Policy settings are inherited from parent folders to child folders, which might in turn have their own Group Policy objects. A single container could have more than one Group Policy object assigned to it.

For more information on Group Policy precedence and how conflicts are resolved among multiple Policy objects, see Windows 2000 Help.

Prerequisites for Implementing Group Policy

Group Policy is a feature of the Windows 2000 Active Directory. Active Directory must be installed on a server before you can edit and apply Group Policy objects.

Case Study: What To Do?

Okay, enough of the SuperConsultant already. If you wanted to be a consultant, you wouldn't have a real job.

So, in your real job you are tasked with making sure that users will be able to securely access resources all over the network. Sounds like a piece of cake, but when you start looking at the network, you see that you have all sorts of different operating systems and you begin to wonder if perhaps the company is paying you enough. Then you seem to remember something called Herby, Kirby, Furby, or something like that. After doing some research, you find that there is a protocol that comes with Windows 2000 called Kerberos v5, and you find that this is a standard. After a little exploring and poking around, you find that you can institute Kerberos as part of the Windows 2000 rollout and use it to authenticate users across platforms, across domains, across sites, and even across trees. Life is beginning to look a whole lot better, though they still should be paying you more!

Providing Data Protection for Sensitive Data

Information security strategies are designed to protect data on your servers and client computers. They also must conceal and protect packets traversing insecure networks. That is usually obvious. One danger that occurs may not be so obvious. In this day and age of the home-based office, the traveling user, and the remote user, your company has a lot of data that is on the road. We have all heard horror stories about laptops being stolen. While I am sure that occurs with great regularity, another problem is laptops being lost. If you spend much time in airports or working with rental cars, you know that people leave the darndest things in the strangest places. As an IT administrator, your distributed security matrix needs to identify which information must be protected in the event this computer equipment is lost or stolen. You also have to realize that there are types of network traffic that are sensitive or private and need to be protected from network sniffers. This information must be included in the security matrix also.

In terms of users on your enterprise network, access control, which was discussed earlier, is the primary mechanism to protect sensitive files from unauthorized access. However, since the computers themselves are portable, they are subject to physical theft. Access control is obviously not sufficient to protect the data stored on these computers. To address this problem, Windows 2000 provides the Encrypting File System (EFS).

To make the communication links secure, and to keep network data packets confidential, you can use *Internet Protocol Security (IPSec)*. This works to encrypt network traffic among some or all of your servers. IPSec provides the ability to set up authenticated and encrypted network connections between two computers. For example, you could configure your e-mail server to require secure communication with clients and thereby prevent a packet sniffer from reading e-mail messages between the clients and the server. IPSec is ideal for protecting data from existing applications that were not designed with security in mind.

Network and Dial-up Connections (remote access) should always protect network data transmitted over the Internet or public phone lines. Remote access uses a virtual private network that uses the PPTP or L2TP tunneling protocol over IPSec.

Encrypting File System

The Windows 2000 *Encrypting File System* (EFS) lets users encrypt designated files or folders on a local computer for added protection of data stored locally. EFS automatically decrypts the file for use and re-encrypts the file when it is saved. No one can read these files except the user who encrypted the file and an administrator with an EFS Recovery certificate. Since the encryption mechanism is built into the file system, its operation is transparent to the user and extremely difficult to attack.

EFS is particularly useful for protecting data on a computer that might be physically stolen, such as a laptop. You can configure EFS on laptops to ensure that all business information is encrypted in users' document folders. Encryption protects the information even if someone attempts to bypass EFS and uses low-level disk utilities to try to read information.

EFS is intended primarily for protection of user files stored on the disk of the local NTFS file system. As you move away from this model (remote drives, multiple users, editing encrypted files), there are numerous exceptions and special conditions to be aware of.

How EFS Works

EFS encrypts a file using a symmetric encryption key unique to each file. Then it encrypts the encryption key as well, using the public key from the file owner's EFS certificate. Since the file owner is the only person with access to the private key, that person is the only one who can decrypt the key, and therefore the file.

To protect against the SEU trick, there is a provision for the original encryption key to be encrypted using the public key of an administrator's EFS File Recovery certificate. The private key from that certificate can be used to recover the file in an emergency. It is highly recommended that an organization establish an independent recovery agent.

SEU is an acronym sometimes used by tech support personnel. It means roughly the same thing as an "ID-Ten-T error" or a "carbon-based-unit interface error" between the chair and the keyboard. Let's just say the last two words are "end user" and the first word could be "stu ... silly." Yeah, that's it!

File encryption provides great security, because even if the file can be stolen, it cannot be decrypted without first logging on the network as the appropriate user. Since it cannot be read, it cannot be surreptitiously modified. EFS addresses an aspect of a policy of data confidentiality.

Prerequisites for Implementing EFS

To implement EFS, a Public Key Infrastructure must be in place and at least one administrator must have an EFS Data Recovery certificate so the file can be decrypted if anything happens to the original author. The author of the file must have an EFS certificate. The files and folders to be encrypted must be stored on the version of NTFS included with Windows 2000.

Once the PKI has been established, to implement EFS, you would open Windows Explorer and right-click a folder or a file. Select Properties. On the General tab, click Advanced. Then select the Encrypt Contents to Secure Data check-box. The contents of the file, or of all the files in the selected folder, are now encrypted until you clear the check-box.

For more information on this, be sure to check out Chapter 11, "Enhancing Security Using Public Keys."

Considerations about EFS

Once again, before you get all excited about using EFS, remember it is only supported for the version of NTFS used in Windows 2000 (NTFS5). It does not work with any other file system, including previous versions of NTFS.

EFS can also be used to store sensitive data on servers. This will allow for normal data management—otherwise known as backups. The servers must be well protected and must be trusted for delegation. In the case of data saved to a server, EFS services will impersonate the EFS user and make other network connections on the user's behalf when encrypting and decrypting files.

If, for some reason, the user who owns the data loses the key, EFS uses a Data Recovery policy that enables an authorized data recovery agent to decrypt encrypted files. EFS requires at least one *recovery agent*. Recovery agents can use EFS to recover encrypted files if users leave the organization or lose their encryption credentials. You need to plan to deploy the PKI components and issue one or more certificates for EFS data recovery. These certificates need to be securely stored offline so they cannot be compromised. This usually involves a safety deposit box, a vault, or a large safe. You don't have to make use of any other kind of certificate generation service, because EFS can generate its own certificates for both EFS users and EFS recovery agents.

By default, EFS issues EFS *recovery certificates* to the Domain Administrator account as the recovery agent for the domain. For stand-alone computers that are not joined to a domain, EFS issues EFS recovery certificates to the local Administrator user account as the recovery agent for that computer.

Many organizations might want to designate other EFS recovery agents to centrally administer the EFS recovery program. For example, you can create organizational units for groups of computers and designate specific recovery agent accounts to manage EFS recovery for specific organizational units.

You can deploy Microsoft Certificate Services to issue certificates to EFS recovery agents and EFS users. When certificate services are available online, EFS uses the certificate services to generate EFS certificates.

As you plan your security matrix, be sure to include strategies for EFS and EFS recovery. As an example of EFS strategies, you might include the following kinds of information:

- File system strategies for both laptops and other computers
- How EFS recovery agents are to be handled
- What the recommended EFS recovery processes are
- What the recommended EFS recovery agent private key management and archive processes are
- Which certificate services are needed to support the EFS recovery certificates

Design Scenario: The Case of the Missing Laptop

It's Thursday and life is looking good. After all, starting tomorrow, the company shuts down for its annual 30-day December holiday. You and the rest of the IT team are figuring that once you get everyone out of the building, you will be able to finish up your work of cleaning up the servers and adding hardware to the network in about 7 days, giving you 23 glorious days of vacation.

Your vacation fantasy is suddenly broken by the appearance of Fred. Fred is commonly known as the "techno-weenie wannabe" of the organization. He knows enough to be dangerous, and more than enough to make the life of the IT department miserable. Fred comes with a signed authorization to check out a laptop. He works for the research and design department and is taking some highly confidential material home with him to work on over the shutdown. You start to shudder, and then remember the encrypting file system. It is not used much, but it is used, so you dig around and find the security matrix. In this case, the encryption is justified. You encrypt all the appropriate files and make sure that Fred can decrypt them and work on them. The system administration team keeps the EFS recovery agents locked away in a safe, so you figure you are covered. Fred walks out smiling and your day still hasn't dimmed that much!

Later. . . .

The shutdown is over. Everyone comes back to work, and because the IT team had to make sure everything was ready, you have been at work since early, early morning. About 10:00 you begin to notice some whispers going around the building. By 10:15 the whispers are louder, and you find out that Fred is currently in with the R and D management team. They have just called for the head of IT and the head of Security. You start to be concerned about the things that could have gone wrong over the holiday. You can't be too concerned, though, because you are knee-deep in planning for the next project. The big meeting breaks up. The security manager and the IT manager are seen going into the IT manager's office. Your pager goes off, and the message is to report to the IT manager's office immediately. With a lump in your throat, you start reviewing everything that you have ever had to do with Fred in your head. You walk into the meeting, wondering if they will give you 30 days to find a new job, or if you will be canned immediately. The stern look on the faces of the managers doesn't bode well.

Finally, your boss speaks. He tells you that Fred went to the beach one last time yesterday, and stopped there before driving home. The laptop was on the front seat. When Fred returned, the window was broken and the laptop was gone. That laptop contained all the plans for the SuperWhizBang project, the next great iteration to come out of your company. The boss wanted to talk with you because you checked the laptop out. At that point, you have mentally composed your resume. If your throat were any drier you would be in the desert. If your hands were any wetter, you would be swimming. Your boss continues, and says that the only thing that saved the company from being out more than the price of the laptop was your following procedure and making sure all the critical files were encrypted. You saved the day. By the way, you have been nominated for the employee of the year award, and the $250 gift certificate that goes along with it.

As you leave, you say thanks, and think to yourself, "I knew I was good!"

IP Security

Windows 2000 incorporates Internet Protocol Security (IPSec) for data protection of network traffic. IPSec is a suite of protocols that allow secure, encrypted communication between two computers over an insecure network. The encryption is applied at the IP network layer, which means that it is transparent to most applications that use specific protocols for network communication. IPSec provides end-to-end security, meaning that the IP packets are encrypted by the sending computer, are unreadable en route, and can be decrypted only by the recipient computer. Due to a special algorithm for generating the same shared encryption key at both ends of the connection, the key does not need to be passed over the network.

This section is planned as a high-level overview of IPSec. We will be looking at it in more depth as part of Chapter 15, "Securing Communication Channels."

How IPSec Works

So, at a high level, here is how the process works:

1. An application on Computer A generates outbound packets to send to Computer B across the network. In this case, the network can be anything from a dial-in connection to connections across the Internet.
2. Inside TCP/IP, the IPSec driver compares the outbound packets against IPSec filters, checking to see if the packets need to be secured. The filters are associated with a filter action in IPSec security rules. Many IPSec security rules can be part of one IPSec policy that is assigned to a computer.
3. If a matched filter has to a negotiate security action, Computer A begins security negotiations with Computer B, using a protocol called the *Internet Key Exchange (IKE)*. The two computers exchange identity credentials according to the authentication method specified in the security rule. Authentication methods could be Kerberos authentication, public key certificates, or a pre-shared key value (much like a password). The IKE negotiation establishes two types of agreements, called *security associations,* between the two computers. One type (called the *phase I IKE SA*) specifies how the two computers trust each other and protects their negotiation. The other type is an agreement on how to protect a particular type of application communication. This consists of two SAs (called *phase II IPSec SAs*) that specify security methods and keys for each direction of communication. IKE automatically creates and refreshes a shared, secret key for each SA. The secret key is created independently at both ends without being transmitted across the network.
4. The IPSec driver on Computer A signs the outgoing packets for integrity, and optionally encrypts them for confidentially using the methods agreed upon during the negotiation. It transmits the secured packets to Computer B.

Firewalls, routers, and servers along the network path from Computer A to Computer B do not require IPSec. They simply pass along the packets in the usual manner.

5. The IPSec driver on Computer B checks the packets for integrity and decrypts their content if necessary. It then transfers the packets to the receiving application.

IPSec provides security against data manipulation, data interception, and replay attacks. As part of your security matrix, IPSec is important to strategies for data confidentiality, data integrity, and nonrepudiation.

Prerequisites for Implementing IPSec

The computers in your network need to have an IPSec security policy defined that is appropriate for your network security strategy and for the type of network communication that they perform. Computers in the same domain might be organized and have IP security policy applied to the set of computers. Computers in different domains might have complementary IPSec security policies to support secure network communications.

Considerations for IPSec

The overhead that IPSec requires may be enough to push it out of range on your security matrix. Since IPSec provides encryption of both outgoing and incoming packets, there is a cost of additional CPU utilization. This is especially true when the encryption is performed by the operating system. For many installations, the clients and servers might have considerable CPU resources available, so that IPSec encryption will not have a noticeable impact on performance. For servers supporting many simultaneous network connections, or servers that transmit large volumes of data to other servers, the additional cost of encryption is significant. The cost of the hardware and bandwidth capable of carrying the load will be a factor to be considered in your plan.

Another offshoot of this consideration is testing. You will need to test IPSec using simulated network traffic before you deploy it. Testing is also important if you are using a third-party hardware or software product to provide IP security.

Windows 2000 provides device interfaces to allow hardware acceleration of IPSec per-packet encryption by intelligent network cards. Network card vendors might provide several versions of client and server cards, and might not support all combinations of IPSec security methods. Be sure to check out the product documentation for each card to be sure that it supports the security methods and the number of connections you expect in your deployment.

You can define Internet Protocol Security (IPSec) policies for each domain or organizational unit. You can also define local IPSec policy on computers that do not have domain IPSec policy assigned to them. You can configure IPSec policies to handle these tasks:

- Set the level of authentication that is required between IPSec clients.
- Set the lowest security level at which communications are allowed to occur between IPSec clients.
- Decide whether to allow or prevent communications with non-IPSec clients.
- Require all communications to be encrypted or allow communications in plain text.

So, that means you should consider using IPSec to provide security if your security matrix calls for the following applications:

- Peer-to-peer communications over your organization's intranet
- Client-server communications to protect sensitive (confidential) information stored on servers
- Remote access (dial-up or virtual private network) communications
- Secure router-to-router WAN communications

That takes care of how people can securely access your network, even over an open data communication line. What about accessing secure applications off the network?

Hmmmm. Rumor has it that some of the questions on the test revolve around designing networks and planning security. So it might be a good idea to know when IPSec and L2TP are used and how. Just an answer to a rumor is all. We will talk more about it in the section on VPNs in Chapter 10, "An Integration and Authentication Strategy."

Deploying Secure Applications

It is not enough to set up distributed security and then just go back to business as usual. A secure enterprise network also needs software that has been designed with security features in mind. For example, you may have an exceptionally secure network in most regards, but if your most business-sensitive application transmits passwords over the wire in plain text, much of your security could be compromised. A secure environment needs *secure applications*.

When evaluating software for your enterprise, look for applications designed with these security-enabled features. Look for integration with single sign-on capabilities for authenticated network connections, and the ability to run properly in secured computer configurations. The software need not require administrator privileges if it is not an administrator tool or utility.

One way to check an application's compliance is to look for the Certified for Microsoft Windows logo. This can be used just as the hardware compatibility list is used for hardware. The *Application Specification for Windows 2000* defines the technical requirements that an application must meet to earn the Certified for Microsoft Windows logo. The document identifies the minimum requirement areas that secure applications must support:

- Run on secured Windows 2000 servers.
- Single sign-on by using the Kerberos authentication for establishing network connections.
- Use impersonation of the client to support consistent Windows 2000 access control mechanisms using permissions and security groups.
- Application services run by using service accounts rather than a local system (which has full system privileges).

These requirements are a minimum.

One approach to making sure your users are running "safe" applications is to require that application components be digitally signed. Microsoft *Authenticode,* through Microsoft Internet Explorer, lets users identify who published a software component and verify that no one tampered with it before downloading it from the Internet.

Also, regularly remind users not to run programs directly from e-mail attachments if they are unfamiliar with the sources or if they are not expecting to receive e-mail from the source. This is also a great form of proactive virus protection.

Authenticode and Software Signing

Since the beginning of time, IT people have recognized that software downloaded from the Internet can contain unauthorized programs or viruses that are intended to wreak havoc on the system or even provide access to intruders. As networks become more interconnected, the threat of malicious software and viruses has extended to the intranet.

How Authenticode Works

Microsoft's *Authenticode* was developed to enable software developers to digitally sign software using a standard X.509 public key certificate. That way, users can verify the publisher of digitally signed software as well as verify that the software has not been tampered with, because the publisher signed the code.

Implementing Authenticode Screening

You can enable Authenticode-based screening of downloaded software in Internet Explorer by doing the following: Choose the Tools menu ➢ Internet Options ➢ Security tab. Higher levels of security set from this tab screen software components for trusted digital signatures.

The question for the security administrator is, "Can you trust your users to increase their levels of security?" In each case, increasing the level of security tends to decrease response and functionality. That will probably lead to a minor insurrection when it comes to increasing security. You can bypass the user intervention and take control of these Internet Explorer security settings through Group Policy. Open the Group Policy snap-in to MMC and navigate to the Internet Explorer container. Start by choosing Computer

Configuration ➢ Administrative Templates ➢ Windows Components ➢ Internet Explorer. If you look at Figure 7.9, you will see the result of the default template, with nothing altered.

FIGURE 7.9 Default template

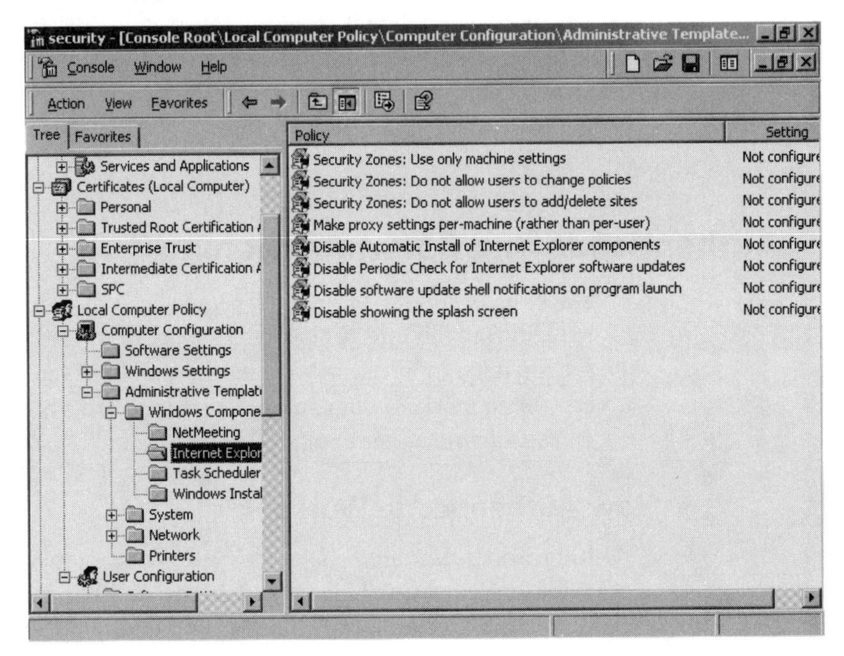

Internet Explorer policies permit you to lock down security settings so that users cannot change them, and to require that all downloaded components have trusted signatures.

Considerations for Authenticode and Software Signing

When it comes time to set your strategy for software signing in your security matrix, it might include the following information:

- Which internal and external groups need the capability of signing software
- What the strategies should be for signing software intended for internal distribution

- What the strategies should be for signing software intended for external distribution
- How the certification authority deployment and trust management strategies should be modified to support the new software signing strategies
- What processes and strategies are needed to enroll users as software signers
- What education plan will be implemented to inform users they are not to run unsigned or untrusted components

Secure E-mail

Information comes into your enterprise from a wide variety of digital sources. One of the most popular ways to transfer information is with e-mail. In today's business, e-mail messages containing sensitive personal information and proprietary business information are routinely sent over the intranet or even the Internet. Hackers or crackers or black hats or whatever you want to call them can easily intercept plain text e-mail messages. People can easily intercept and modify e-mail messages, or spoof the IP address of an e-mail sender and send false messages. Many of today's secure e-mail solutions are based on the open *Secure/Multipurpose Internet Mail Extensions (S/MIME)* standard.

How Secure E-mail Works

Secure e-mail systems based on S/MIME use industry standard X.509 digital certificates and public key technology to provide e-mail security between senders and recipients of e-mail messages. Secure e-mail systems typically provide the following security functions:

- Senders can digitally sign e-mail messages.
- Recipients can verify the identity of the message sender and verify that the message has not been tampered with en route.
- Senders cannot repudiate signed messages because only the sender has possession of the signing credentials.

- Senders can encrypt e-mail messages to provide confidential communications.
- Intended recipients can decrypt the message using private credentials, but others cannot decrypt and read the message.
- Administrators can centrally store users' private credentials in a secure database. If a user's private credentials are lost or damaged, administrators can retrieve the private credentials necessary to decrypt messages.

Considerations for Secure E-mail

To address strategies for secure e-mail, consider including the following information in your deployment plan:

- Make sure that the e-mail server and client applications are secure.
- Make sure to plan for the number of e-mail servers and user groups needing to upgrade or migrate to secure e-mail.
- Define general policies for using secure e-mail organization-wide.
- Research and define the encryption technology to be used, including international export restrictions and limitations.
- Research and define the certificate services needed to support secure e-mail.
- Set up strict enrollment processes and strategies to enroll users in the secure e-mail program.
- Set up the key recovery database backup capabilities and recommended backup and restore practices.
- Set up and define the key recovery capabilities and recommended general recovery practices.
- Define and publish e-mail policies. Make sure your users know that e-mail is owned and operated by the company, and therefore their mail box may be opened at any time by authorized members of management or the IT staff.

Secure Web Sites and Communications

The Web site and the browser have become tools for information exchange both on organizations' intranets as well as on the Internet. While all this information is being moved, standard Web protocols such as *HyperText Transfer Protocol (HTTP)* provide limited security. Now, there are ways you can configure most Web servers to provide directory- and file-level security based on usernames and passwords. Or you can also provide Web security by programming solutions using the *Common Gateway Interface (CGI)* or *Active Server Pages (ASP)*. While these are solutions, they are not really great. They have proven to be susceptible to compromise on more than one occasion. You can use *Internet Information Services (IIS)*, included with Windows 2000 Server. IIS will give you the ability to provide a certain level of security for Web sites and communications using standards-based secure communications protocols and standard X.509 certificates. You can use IIS to provide the following security for Web sites and communications:

- By using the *Secure Sockets Layer (SSL)* and *Transport Layer Security (TLS)* protocols you can authenticate users and establish secure channels for confidential communications.
- If you need secure channels for confidential encrypted financial transactions, you can use the *Server Gated Cryptography (SGC)* protocol.
- Map user certificates to network user accounts to authenticate users and control user rights and permissions for Web resources based on users' possession of valid certificates issued by a trusted certification authority.

Considerations for Secure Web Sites

Consider including the following information in your deployment plan:

- Make sure that you extend your deployment plan to define the Web sites and user groups that must be upgraded or migrated to secure Web sites.
- Be sure to lay out your strategies for using SSL or TLS.
- See to it that you have defined the strategies for using certificate mapping to control user rights and permissions to Web site resources.

- Make sure that you have set up the certification authority deployment needed to support Web sites.
- Document and define the enrollment process and strategies to enroll users in the secure Web sites program.

Case Study: Secure Applications

You have a problem. This is one of those security problems that is staring you in the face, and you have missed it. Your company is very secure. *Very* secure. As a matter of fact, you are just beginning to explore how to hook the company up to the Internet and provide Internet mail to everyone in the system. At the present time, the company naming conventions are such that the users' logon name and e-mail name are the same. No problem, that is the way Windows 2000 likes it. The problem begins to show itself when you notice that people are sending messages to the Everyone group of their departments. You notice that when you look in properties of the address list, you can suddenly see all the e-mail addresses of all the users in that department. Hmmm ... if that e-mail message had been sent outside the company, someone would have had all the logon names for an entire department, whether they knew it or not. That is not a good thing.

In this case, there are a couple of solutions. You can educate the users in the proper use of the blind copy box. This will help some, but will certainly not alleviate the problem. You can also work on a new e-mail naming standard where the e-mail address and the logon name are not the same.

Remember back in the early chapters when we talked about Bill Gates's vision for the Digital Nervous System? Secured Web applications will make it easier for the network to be shared among partners, enhancing the business of e-business. Since it is Bill's vision, the test writers may share that vision. Knowing the information on securing Web sites may be crucial to some of the scenario-based questions.

Managing Administration

Some of the policies in your security plan will involve the daily duties of your IT department staff. Windows 2000 supports delegation of administrative permissions, allowing specific personnel limited rights to administer their own groups and files. Windows 2000 also supports audit logs of system activity, with a fine degree of granularity about which types of events will be logged and in what context.

If you are interested in learning more about auditing, be sure to check out Chapter 9, "Choosing an Authentication Strategy."

It is also extremely important that your plan describes how you intend to protect your Domain Administrator accounts from penetration by an intruder. It is recommended that you set up your domain account policies to require all accounts to use a long and complex password that cannot be easily cracked. This is common sense but it needs to be explicitly stated in your plan.

It is not as obvious that security will be compromised if too many people know the administrator password. The administrator of the root domain of a domain tree is also automatically a member of the Schema Administrators group and the Enterprise Administrators group. This is a highly privileged account where an intruder can do unlimited damage. Your plan needs to state that access to this account is limited to a very small number of trusted personnel. Think about establishing a long and complex password and then sealing it in an envelope and putting the envelope in a safe. In some cases where PKI is implemented, the CA server is actually a stand-alone system that is locked away in a safe. If the safe is there, you can use it to store the administrator password as well!

The Domain Administrator account must be used only for tasks that require administrator privileges. It must never be left logged on and unattended. Encourage your administrator staff to use a second, real-person account for their non-administrative activities (reading e-mail, Web browsing, and so on). Basically there should be one network god or goddess account, and each and every network god and goddess should use his or her own personal account unless absolutely necessary.

Server consoles used for domain administration must be physically secured so that only authorized personnel have access to them. Your security plan needs to state this and list the personnel who might use the consoles. It is not as obvious that users of the Administrator account must never log on to client computers managed by someone who is not equally trusted. The other client computer administrator might introduce other code on that computer that will unknowingly exploit the administrator privileges. There are many hack utilities that will trap information being typed so it can be reviewed later.

Delegation

The delegation of administrative tasks is a practical necessity in a Windows 2000 enterprise environment. It is common to delegate authority not only to members of the IT group but to human resources personnel and various managers for tasks related to their duties. Delegation distributes the administrator's workload without granting sweeping privileges to every assistant. This is an expression of the security concept of *principle of least privilege*: that is, granting only the permissions necessary for the task.

Through various means, Windows 2000 allows you to delegate to groups or individuals a prescribed degree of control over a limited set of objects. The only prerequisite is that the appropriate delegation elements (users, groups, Group Policy objects, files, directories, and so forth) must be in place before delegation can be performed. One of those various means is by using the Windows 2000 built-in security groups.

Built-in Security Groups

Windows 2000 has predefined security groups with special permissions already delegated to each group. Open the Active Directory Users and Computers snap-in to MMC. Start by moving to the View menu and selecting Advanced Features. Once that has been done, the predefined security groups show up in the Builtin and Users folders. Some of these Builtin groups will seem familiar to Windows NT administrators. They carry names like Account Operators, Administrators, Backup Operators, Guests, Print Operators, Replicators, Server Operator, and Users. There is even a Pre–Windows 2000 Compatible Access. This is a backward compatibility group that allows read access on all users and groups in the domain.

To directly delegate control of one of these groups, open the property sheet of the group and click the Security tab. Add the group's manager to the access control list and check the appropriate privileges. As you know, this is done using the MMC.

Delegation of Control Wizard

Open the Active Directory Sites and Services snap-in to MMC. Right-click a site and select Delegate Control. This wizard sets up user group permissions to administer specific sites and services.

Delegate Administration Wizard

Open the Active Directory Users and Computers snap-in to MMC. Right-click an organizational unit and select Delegate Control. This wizard sets up user group permissions to administer organizational units containing computers and user groups. An example would be the delegated right to create new user accounts.

Delegating Control of Group Policy Objects

Delegating administration via Group Policy involves the following three tasks, which can be performed one at a time or all together:

- Managing Group Policy links for a site, domain, or organizational unit
- Creating Group Policy objects
- Editing Group Policy objects

Summary

These last two chapters have been killers, huh? There is definitely a ton of material in this chapter, even if we never did get to lay out the sample security plan for the generic network the way you wanted! We did take a look at several ways that you can authenticate all user access to system resources. As a matter of fact, we looked at ways that involved single sign-on, and even ways where there was double and triple verification. That led to the discussion of how to apply appropriate access control to all those resources.

Case Study: Administrative Control

When you came to work for this company, you always thought of yourself as kind of laid back, the kind of person who could handle just about anything and anyone. Then you met your boss. You found that this person did everything in her power to make you crazy, checking up on your every move. She was the epitome of the micromanager. When you found out there was going to be a huge desktop rollout you began to shudder. Visions of you and Ms. Wonderful hitting every one of 21,000 desktops began to run through your head. You could just hear her, "Why did you do it that way? Are you sure that is the way you did it on the last one?" You figure there has to be a better way of doing this, or you will be sentenced to prison for murder after a very short time.

As you begin to look at the rollout, you begin to examine Group Policies. Now things are beginning to clear up and look better. One Group Policy, to the computer folder, and you are in business.

Since Windows 2000 is an enterprise-wide solution, there had to be ways to establish appropriate trust relationships between multiple domains. In this section, we looked at some of the buzzwords for Windows 2000, including things like Kerberos v5.

Protecting data has always been an issue with any network operating system. Now, using the technology of encrypting file systems, the sensitive data can be protected within the enterprise network and while that data is being carried around on the road. We even looked at ways that the files could be decrypted if the owner left the company.

One of the problems with security is the ability to replicate it, workstation after workstation after workstation. In the past, once you set how you wanted a computer to be protected, there were not a lot of successful methods to push that security out to hundreds of workstations simultaneously. With security policies, you can define how you want something to be handled and then attach the Group Policy object to a site, domain, or OU that contains the computer; in other words, every system in the container would then have identical settings.

Networks were designed to provide multiple users access to the same resources, both hardware and software. Since hardware is an inanimate object, it is relatively easy to provide security policies that will hold. Software, on the other hand, may not be so easy. While you may secure access to the applications, making sure that only those people who need access to them get it, you do not usually have the code. If there are holes in the code, you may have no way of knowing until it is too late.

Finally, we allayed some fears about the amount of work you were going to have to do. In a large network, managing security administration is a full-time job for a department. In this chapter, we discussed how to deploy those responsibilities over several users or groups.

Key Terms

Before you take the exam, be certain you are familiar with the following terms:

Active Server Pages (ASP)

Authenticode

Common Gateway Interface (CGI)

computer local group

domain credentials

domain local groups

Encrypting File System

global groups

HyperText Transfer Protocol (HTTP)

Internet Information Services (IIS)

Internet Key Exchange (IKE)

Internet Protocol Security (IPSec)

mixed mode

native mode

Personal Computer/Smart Card (PC/SC)

personal identification number (PIN)

recovery agent

recovery certificates

secure applications

Secure/Multipurpose Internet Mail Exchange (S/MIME)

Secure Sockets Layer (SSL)

security baseline

security templates

Server Gated Cryptography (SGC)

smart cards

Transport Layer Security (TLS)

trusted for delegation

two-factor authentication policy

uniform security policies

universal groups

Review Questions

1. A user in an Active Directory forest needs to access resources in another tree. The best practice is to have this user take advantage of single sign-on. Single sign-on is instituted through:

   A. Start ➢ Settings ➢ Control Panel ➢ Single Sign On.

   B. Start ➢ Settings ➢ Control Panel ➢ Security.

   C. Start ➢ Settings ➢ Control Panel ➢ Add/Remove Services.

   D. Windows 2000 automatically supports single sign-on for users within a domain forest.

2. *CJ,will,be,3,on2,15,01* is an example of what?

   A. A complex password

   B. A proud grandparent bragging about his grandson

   C. An invalid password

   D. An insecure password

3. A username and password are examples of what?

   A. The minimum requirements to create a Windows 2000 account

   B. Domain credentials

   C. The foundations for Kerberos 5 authentication

   D. A two-tiered security plan

4. How are Kerberos security policy parameters set?

   A. By right-clicking the folder that represents a site and choosing properties and security.

   B. Start ➢ Settings ➢ Control Panel ➢ Security.

   C. Start ➢ Settings ➢ Services ➢ Kerberos.

   D. Kerberos security policy parameters are set in the Group Policy snap-in to MMC.

5. What can implement a two-factor authentication policy?
   - A. Username and passwords
   - B. Smart cards
   - C. Biometrics combined with a smart card
   - D. ADS

6. Before you can use smart cards, what must be in place?
   - A. ADS
   - B. NDS
   - C. IKE
   - D. PKI

7. In Windows 2000, smart cards must be _____________ compliant.
   - A. Unix
   - B. PC/SC
   - C. ASCII
   - D. IETF

8. How many advanced ACL properties are there?
   - A. 5
   - B. 8
   - C. 13
   - D. 26

9. What are the types of groups in Windows 2000?
   - A. Domain and forest
   - B. Forest and trees
   - C. Global and local
   - D. Security and distribution

10. How do the groups Everyone and Users relate to their NT 4 counterparts?

A. Members of the Everyone and Users groups do not have broad read/write permission as in Windows NT 4.

B. Members of the Everyone and Users groups have the same rights and permissions as in NT 4.

C. They are just like their NT 4 counterparts: They are default groups that are normally disabled.

D. They are just like their NT 4 counterparts: They are default groups that are enabled, but they have not been given any rights.

Answers to Review Questions

1. D. Windows 2000 automatically supports single sign-on for users within a domain forest.

2. A. That is an example of a complex password. (Although B would also be considered a correct answer in the context of this book!)

3. B. A username and password are examples of domain credentials.

4. D. Settings for Kerberos security are contained in the Group Policy objects, which are configured using the Group Policy snap-in to the Microsoft Management Console.

5. B. Smart cards provide a two-factor authentication policy. You must have the card and the appropriate PIN.

6. D. Smart cards rely on the Public Key Infrastructure (PKI) of Windows 2000.

7. B. Microsoft supports industry standard Personal Computer/Smart Card (PC/SC)–compliant smart cards and readers and provides drivers for commercially available Plug and Play smart card readers.

8. C. There are 13 advanced parts to the ACL.

9. D. There are two types of groups in Windows 2000: security groups and distribution groups.

10. A. Members of the Everyone and Users groups do not have broad read/write permission as in Windows NT 4.

The Multinational Conglomerate

You should give yourself 10 minutes to review this case study, diagram as needed, and complete the questions for this testlet.

Background

Your consulting firm has been hired to assist in the Windows 2000 migration and integration for a company based in Minneapolis, Minnesota. Until the start of this year, the company had 1,000 employees, all based throughout the Twin Cities of Minneapolis and St. Paul. Just before the end of the year, the owner of your company purchased two companies of roughly the same size that will need to be connected to the enterprise network. The total number of users when the project is completed is estimated at 3,500. In addition, each of these companies comes with various strategic partners that will need to access the information on your enterprise network. The companies that have been acquired are located in Athens, Greece, and in Orlando, Florida.

The three companies can now be considered one, and the preparation for the Windows 2000 rollout is in full swing. At this time, the company is examining various methods of rolling out security across the network.

Current System

Minneapolis Located on the shores of beautiful Lake Calhoun, the company occupies a sprawling campus that includes four floors in a six-story building. When the company started out five years ago, it had just part of one of the floors and about 100 people. Since that time, the company has grown, and any time a tenant has moved out of the building, the company has taken over the office space. This grow-as-you-go philosophy had left members of the same departments scattered throughout the building. However, recently the company signed a long-term contract with a local moving and storage company and they have been systematically relocating departments in an orderly manner. Communication has improved and morale has picked up.

All of the floors are connected to the Windows network. The network is nowhere near native mode yet, but it is getting closer. Active Directory

Services have been deployed to the main campus, and the rollout is continuing in the branch offices. Security is now the hot topic, and the CEO wants to know how in the world you are going to provide secure access to a bevy of remote users, as well as dozens of managers running around with laptops. The CEO wants to know if the company's information is at risk and what steps are being taken to protect that information. Everyone in the company has access to the Internet and has an Internet mail address. Communication between offices is currently being done using e-mail, snail mail, and the phone. The corporate intranet is coming closer to a reality, but there are still problems with accessing resources throughout the enterprise.

Orlando The Orlando office actually has more people working in it than there are in Minneapolis. It is located in northern Orlando, away from Disney and the tourists. Many of the services in Minneapolis are mirrored in Orlando: things like marketing, accounting, and human resources. The site is all on NT 4, with a variety of applications; some of the applications are compatible with the Minneapolis corporate standards and some aren't. The Orlando office does have a fractional T1 connection to the Internet. In addition, the company is looking at creating a virtual private network between the Orlando site and the Minneapolis site.

Athens The Athens office had about 1,300 users, most of whom are salespeople, marketing types, and support staff. Since the merger, the company has hired another 100 people and is looking to hire another 100. The manufacturing plant is located on the island of Rhodes, and due to local customs, manufacturing occurs only between March and October. The rest of the time, the plant is closed. The office has been upgraded to Windows NT 4 servers running SP5. It is predominantly used for file and print sharing. There is an Internet connection and a Linux box that is providing for only POP3 e-mail.

Because this company was in relatively good shape, it was easy to upgrade this company to Windows 2000. The Athens branch is now a domain in the ADS tree, with several OUs. Due to the nature of the beast, Athens had some really old computers and is now getting ready to deploy 1,500 hosts, all running Windows 2000 Professional. The Athens IT director has stressed time and time again how these machines must be alike, for the sake of inter-company politics and to ease the burden on the Help desk.

Because this has been a stand-alone company, all of the normal accounting, purchasing, and human resources functions are there. It has been agreed that management will remain with the company. Communication between sites remains by e-mail, snail mail, and phone.

Problem Statement

Now that the integration of the company is complete, security is becoming more and more of a concern. The senior management has tasked you with making sure the network is secure, and you must provide secure connections between each of the sites and the Internet. You must also provide access to resources. Your security plan has to make sense to individual users, remote users, and remote sites. While passwords need to be secure, users should not have to remember a dozen of them.

Envisioned System

Overview Now that the three locations are working together and communicating, the CEO wants to make sure that it is done securely. She still wants the digital nervous system, but she understands there are other things that have to come first.

CEO "I don't know about anyone else, but I am damn sick and tired of passwords. I must have a million of them. Surely something can be done. Also, I really want you to talk to the CFO—the phone bill for remote users has been absolutely horrendous."

Security

Overview Because the product you develop is constantly undergoing research and development, and because the industry is what it is, security must be maintained at a very high level. As you can see from the statements made by the CEO, it is taking a higher priority.

CFO "What the heck is it with the remote phone lines? The dozen lines we have for users to dial in are accounting for a huge portion of our overall phone costs. How are we going to protect against that happening? Oh, by the way, Fred lost a laptop. He didn't have anything of any value on it, but it could have been a lot worse. Can you make sure that doesn't happen again? Thanks!"

Availability

Because the network will span several different time zones, the availability of the network must be 24x7x365.

Maintainability

Overview There are two problems here. First of all, you will be dealing with an international company, meaning you will not be able to utilize the same vendor for maintenance. Secondly, information will have to be available from all levels of the organization, all day every day. The information must be up-to-date in real time. Because this could possibly tell your competition exactly what you are doing and for whom, the information must be secure.

CEO "These new products we're developing are *so* revolutionary and will have such an impact that it's important for us to make sure everyone has the same information at the same time."

Athens IT Manager "So let me see if I have this right. I am getting a shipment of 1,500 new computers, which all have to have the exact same security settings. According to the security experts in Minneapolis, there are about 200 separate settings that have to be changed on *each computer*! I am supposed to have these 1,500 systems out by what year? Come on, people, get real! You have been out in the cold too long!"

Performance

The network is running along at a fairly decent clip. You need to have great security but to try not to mess around with the bandwidth.

Funding

Overview While you have not been given *carte blanche* by the CEO, she has made it clear that money isn't necessarily an issue, within reason of course. The problems need to be solved so that the company can safely continue to manufacture its products in the most efficient manner possible.

CEO & CFO "Look, we don't think that we need the Rolls Royce of installations, *but* we can tell you that everything is riding on our ability to ship our combined products in a timely manner, and the network we're asking you to build is going to be a big part of that. We think the company will continue to grow, though not as rapidly as in the last several months. So, that being said, give us a network that makes sense."

Questions

1. What is the current business problem?

   A. The e-mail systems are not secure.

   B. Each of the units is connected to the Internet with no firewalls in place.

   C. Management is suddenly concerned with security.

   D. Remote and traveling users need to connect securely.

   E. Users need to access resources all over the tree.

   F. Single sign-on is an issue.

   G. Performance is an issue.

2. What solution(s) should you implement to solve the customer's business problem?

   A. Ensure that each location has a secure connection to the Internet by instituting a bastion host type firewall solution.

   B. Institute Kerberos KDC so that users can access network resources all through the tree.

   C. Up-version all servers to Windows 2000.

   D. Begin the risk management process to provide a framework for the internal and external security plans.

   E. Make sure secure passwords are in place.

   F. Assure that all users are on a uniform O/S desktop, and that service pack and service release levels are current.

   G. Establish a VPN and an EFS security policy.

   H. Plan and deploy a combination of bastion host and screened subnet types of firewalls.

Answers

1. D, E, F. Now that the network is up and working, everyone is starting to want everything. While the e-mail system may or may not be secure, at this point it doesn't seem to be a major problem. Because the firewalls were not mentioned, we can again discern that issue has been addressed. Remote and traveling users are creating a financial burden that must be addressed. It was stressed by several people that users need to access resources all over the tree. Passwords seem to be a hangup also. There is also the issue of the 1,500 new computers, but that is not mentioned here.

2. B, E, G. It looks like you have a big task ahead of you. First of all, you have to make sure that Kerberos KDCs are in place, so that users can be authenticated through the tree. That will help solve the single sign-on issue. To maintain your password security, you want to make sure that complex passwords are required.

   Next, you have to help the poor person in Athens. Any computer that is a part of that domain will have the security policy applied to it.

   Finally for the traveling users, there are VPNs and EFS. With a VPN your user can attach to your network from anywhere and still maintain security. With EFS, if a laptop is stolen, the data can be secure.

Designing the Security Solution

MICROSOFT EXAM OBJECTIVES COVERED IN THIS CHAPTER:

- ✓ Design an audit policy.
- ✓ Design a delegation of authority strategy.
- ✓ Design the placement and inheritance of security policies for sites, domains, and organizational units.
- ✓ Design an Encrypting File System strategy.
- ✓ Design a security group strategy.

In every book we have ever written, there has always been one chapter that could be described as the catchall chapter. Now, if a catchall chapter were a drawer in your kitchen, it would be the junk drawer. For those of you who may not be familiar with the concept of a junk drawer, it is a simple concept. Basically, this is the one area of the house where all the important stuff that doesn't go anywhere else goes. That is pretty much the philosophy behind this chapter.

In Chapter 8 we are going to be talking about a whole long litany of things that are really important, but they just don't fit well in other categories. So we address them here, understanding from the start that transition from one topic to another may be a bit abrupt, and the continuity between objectives may be missing. Does that seem to make sense?

One other thing: Several of these subjects have already been broached. For example, you should pretty much know the basics of how and why to use security groups, so we will just touch on a security strategy for the groups. The same is true for just about all the topics in this chapter. The only objectives listed above that may not have been discussed so far in this book are audit policies. We will solve that problem right now.

Audit Policies

An *audit policy* is a policy that determines which security events should be reported to the administrator. So *auditing* is the process of tracking the activities of users by recording selected types of events in the security log of a server or workstation.

Microsoft Exam Objective

Design an audit policy.

If you look at these definitions as they apply to Windows 2000, you will see that what we are talking about here are basically local events. By local, we mean that you can turn auditing on for a server and record all the comings and goings of the access to a certain file. But you can only do that on that server, and to be able to access the information, you have to have access to the security log of that server or workstation. Auditing can be turned on for a Domain Controller, a member server, or just on a mission-critical workstation.

This is a tricky concept, because while auditing runs on the local machine, it can also be set through a *local security policy*. The local security policy is used to configure security settings for the local computer. These settings include the *password policy, account lockout policy, audit policy, IP Security security policy, user rights assignments, recovery agents for encrypted data,* and other security options. If the computer is a member of a domain, these settings may be overridden by policies received from the domain.

Establishing an Audit Policy

Keeping with the premise of this book that it is always better to plan before implementing, before you implement auditing, you must decide on an auditing policy. An auditing policy simply specifies the categories of security-related events that you wish to audit. As you will see in a few paragraphs, when Windows 2000 is first installed, all auditing categories are turned off. By turning on various auditing event categories, you can implement an auditing policy, one that suits the security needs of your organization.

Auditing Categories and Computer Management

If you choose to audit access to objects as part of your audit policy, you must turn on either the *audit directory service access category* (for auditing objects on a domain controller) or the *audit object access category* (for auditing objects on a member server or Windows 2000 Professional system. Once you have turned on the correct object access category, you can use each individual object's properties to specify whether to audit successes or failures for the permissions granted to each group or user. The phrase "successes or failures for the permissions granted to each group or user" is kind of ethereal, bordering on management-speak. That means that we can set up auditing for a file (say `resume.doc`) or a resource (say the check printer in the payroll department). Auditing will report that Billy Bob successfully accessed the file `resume.doc`, but when he tried to print something out on the check printer in payroll, he was unsuccessful. It is important to note that auditing can be considered nonjudgmental. Auditing just tells you that Billy Bob got into the file. You (or someone like you) have to determine if Billy Bob was supposed to get into that file!

How to Implement an Audit Policy

Audit policies are implemented from the Local Security Policy selection of Administration tools. If you choose Start ➤ Programs ➤ Administrative Tools ➤ Local Security Settings ➤ Local Policies ➤ Audit Policy, you get the screen shown in Figure 8.1.

FIGURE 8.1 Blank audit policies box

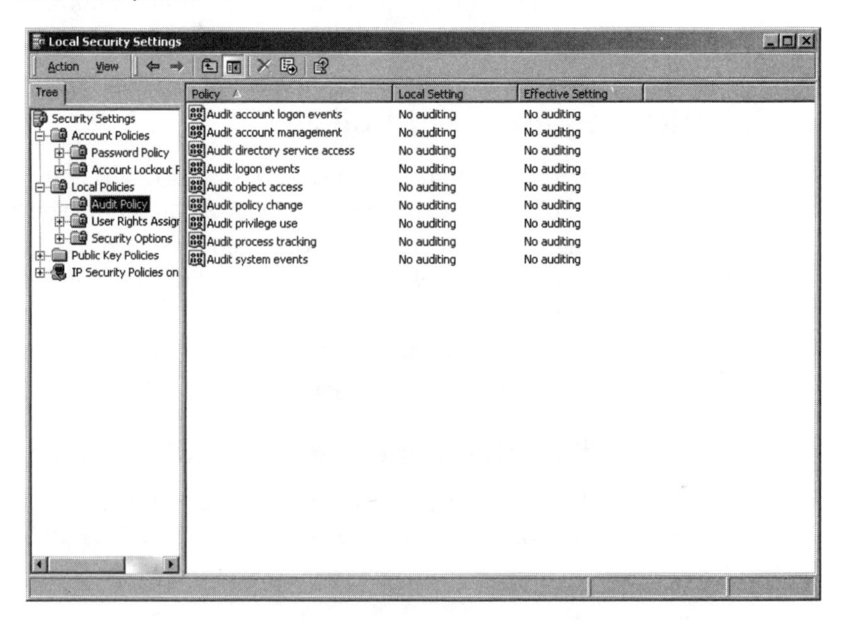

Options, You Always Have Options!

As with most things in computing, there are several ways to arrive at this screen. Another way is through Microsoft Management Console. To accomplish the task this way, you would:

1. Click Start, click Run, type **`mmc /a`**, and then click OK.
2. On the Console menu, click Add/Remove Snap-in, and then click Add.
3. Under Snap-in, click Group Policy, and then click Add.
4. In Select Group Policy Object, click Local Computer, click Finish, click Close, and then click OK.
5. Select Local Computer Policy ➢ Computer Configuration➢ Windows Settings ➢ Security Settings ➢ Local Policies ➢ Audit Policy
6. In the details pane, right-click Audit Object Access, and then click Security.
7. In Local Security Policy Setting, click the options you want, and then click OK.

There are a variety of things that I can choose to audit on this machine. For example, I can audit account logon events, access to Active Directory, or even account management. Table 8.1 shows what each of the auditing events entails.

TABLE 8.1 Auditing Features and Functions in Windows 2000

Event	Description
Audit account logon events	Triggered when a logon request is received by a domain controller. An account logon event is recorded on the computer where the account is validated. For a domain logon, this is the domain controller. For a local account, this is the local computer.

TABLE 8.1 Auditing Features and Functions in Windows 2000 *(continued)*

Event	Description
Audit account management	An entry is made in the log when a user or group account is created or modified.
Audit directory service access	An entry is made in the log when an object in Active Directory is accessed. This audit event needs to be further defined at the object level.
Audit logon events	An entry is made in the log when a user logs on or off a computer. A logon event is only located on the computer where the logon actually occurs. This is always the local computer.
Audit object access	An entry is made in the log when an object such as a file, directory, or printer is accessed. This can mean a file is opened or someone attempted to print to a printer.
Audit policy change	An entry is made in the log when the security options, the user rights, or the audit policies are altered.
Audit privilege use	An entry is made in the log when a user right is used to perform a specific action.
Audit process tracking	An entry is made in the log when an application performs an action that is being tracked by a programmer.
Audit system events	An entry is made in the log when an event occurs that matches the system events criteria.

Think of this event section as a portal to the rest of auditing. For example, if you want to audit access to folders and files, you have to have object access auditing on. Basically, by making changes to this page, you are opening up other auditing opportunities elsewhere on the network. The first opportunity we will look at is auditing the access to objects in Active Directory.

Auditing Active Directory

Auditing the events that happen on a network can be useful, but there are other things that can be learned. Auditing access to objects in ADS can be useful for establishing the usage trends or tracking access to certain objects for security reasons. Before you can audit any objects in Active Directory on a domain controller you have to enable auditing of the Audit directory service access by going to Start ➢ Programs ➢ Administrative Tools ➢ Domain Controller Security Policy ➢ Security Settings ➢ Local Policies ➢ Audit Policies. Once there, you can double-click Audit directory service access and audit the success or failure to directory service access. Once that is done, all of the events in Table 8.2 are available.

TABLE 8.2 Events That Can Be Audited in Active Directory

Events	Description
Full control	An entry is made in the audit log when any level of access is made to the object.
List contents	An entry is made in the audit log when the contents of the object are just listed.
List object	An entry is made in the audit log when the object is viewed.
Read all properties	An entry is made in the audit log when any of the object's properties are read.
Write all properties	An entry is made in the audit log when any of the object's properties are changed or written to.
Create all child objects	An entry is made in the audit log when any child object is created.
Delete all child objects	An entry is made in the audit log when any child object is deleted.

TABLE 8.2 Events That Can Be Audited in Active Directory *(continued)*

Events	Description
Read permissions	An entry is made in the audit log when the object's permissions are read.
Modify permissions	An entry is made in the audit log when the object's permissions are modified.
Modify owner	An entry is made in the audit log when the owner of an object is changed.

So now we have looked at how to activate the auditing of several events, and also how to control auditing for Active Directory activity. One of the things that many managers want to keep track of is the auditing of information on the network. This is a useful tool to make sure that only those people who are supposed to access a file or folder actually access it.

Auditing the File System

Auditing file system events can help simplify administration. To audit any of these events, you first must enable auditing of the Object Access event. You can set this event to *on* using the Group Policy Editor. After enabling the auditing for the object access event, you can audit the events listed in Table 8.3 to track usage trends or to monitor who is accessing files and folders on your networks.

TABLE 8.3 Auditing File System Events

Event	Description
Open a folder or execute a file	An entry is made to the log when a folder is opened or an application is run.
List a folder or read data	An entry is made to the audit log when a file or folder is listed.
Read attributes	An entry is made to the audit log when just the attributes of a file or folder are read.

TABLE 8.3 Auditing File System Events *(continued)*

Event	Description
Read extended attributes	An entry is made to the audit log when the extended attributes of a file or a folder are read.
Create files or write data	An entry is made to the audit log when a file is simply modified or created.
Create folders or append data	An entry is made to the audit log when a folder is simply modified or created.
Write attributes	An entry is made to the audit log when an attribute is modified.
Write extended attributes	An entry is made to the audit log when an extended attribute is modified.
Delete subfolders and files	An entry is made to the audit log when a file or subfolder in a folder is deleted.
Delete	An entry is made to the audit log when a specific file or folder is deleted.
Read permissions	An entry is made to the audit log when the permissions of a file or folder are read.
Change permissions	An entry is made to the audit log when the permissions of a file or folder are modified.
Take ownership	An entry is made to the audit log when a user takes ownership of a file or folder.
Synchronize	An entry is made to the audit log when a file or folder is synchronized with an offline copy.

Auditing at the file or folder level has to be enabled at the file or folder level.

Just a reminder that you can only audit a file or a folder if it resides on an NTFS partition.

How do you actually specify which file or folder to audit? To set, view, change, or remove auditing for a file or folder:

1. Open Windows Explorer, and then locate the file or folder you want to audit.
2. Right-click the file or folder, click Properties, and then click the Security tab.
3. Click Advanced, and then click the Auditing tab.

Auditing Best Practices

When an item is audited, any time there is an event, it is written to the security log. Because the security log is limited in size, you should carefully select the files and folders to be audited. You don't want the security log to fill up. In addition, auditing requires read/write I/O to the disk, taking resources that could be used to do important server stuff. Make sure to carefully consider the amount of disk space you are willing to devote to the security log. The maximum size is defined in Event Viewer.

To view the security log:

1. Open Computer Management by clicking Start ➤ Settings ➤ Control Panel. Once in Control Panel, double-click Administrative Tools, and then double-click Computer Management.
2. In the console tree, click Event Viewer. Double-click Security Log, and in the details pane, examine the list of audit events.

The Auditing List of Things to Do

Microsoft has proposed a best practices list to minimize the risk of security threats. Check out Table 8.4, which shows various events that you should audit, as well as the specific security threat that the audit event monitors.

If you want to prevent files and subfolders within the tree from inheriting these audit entries, select Apply These Auditing Entries.

TABLE 8.4 Identifying Potential Network Threats

Audit Event	Potential Threat
Audit for the failure of a logon.	Auditing this event helps you recognize random-password hacks.
Audit for the success of a logon/ logoff.	By comparing this information to instances when a user may actually be using the account, it will be a check for stolen password break-in.
Audit for the successful change to user rights, user and group management, security change policies, restart, shutdown, and system events.	This audit helps prevent the misuse of privileges.
Set up a success and failure audit for file-access and object-access events. File Manager success and failure audit of Read/Write access by suspect users or groups for the sensitive files.	This audit checks for improper attempts to access sensitive or restricted files.
Set up an audit for the success and failure for file-access printers and object-access events. Print Manager success and failure audit of print access by suspect users or groups for the printers.	This audit helps the network support team check for improper access to printers.
Set up an audit for the success and failure of write access for program files (`.EXE` and `.DLL` extensions). Set up an audit policy for the success and failure of auditing for process tracking. Run suspect programs; examine security log for unexpected attempts to modify program files or create unexpected processes. Run only when actively monitoring the system log.	This audit helps to keep track of a virus outbreak.

Design Scenario: Auditing the Auditors

As you are sitting in your cube pondering the day's list of things to do, you begin to realize that if you worked 24 hours a day, 7 days a week, for the next 6 months, you may be able to make a significant impact on the list. That is, of course, if nothing is added to the list. Just at that moment, the phone rings, breaking your contemplation. The chief financial officer would like to see you.

When you get to the office of the CFO, he looks concerned. In his usual bean-counter manner, he starts right off, "Someone who was not authorized to be there has apparently gotten into the database and has made changes." Now this gets your attention. As you begin to probe deeper, you find that it is not actually a database that has been accessed but an Excel spreadsheet that was out on the network share. The share was designed to share information between members of the Accounting department. The Accounting department has undergone some changes in the past few months, with several contractors being let go and several new employees added to the company. It is certainly possible someone has been messing with the files.

When you ask for specifics, the CFO says it appears some percentages were changed in the file. Since the file is a list of all raises that employees will be getting for the next year, the CFO immediately suspects the people who have had their raises increased. You point out that it might be a simple mistake, or it might be someone trying to make you think it was the people involved, or it might be the ... Martians for all you know at this point. You point out that there are ways of checking, and you start by setting up auditing on the file. You start by auditing all the people who will access the file. You ask if there are any other files that might be vulnerable and set up auditing on those as well. Now it is time to keep watch and check access to the files. The CFO has copies of the files on his local drive so he can make spot checks to see if they have been altered. In addition, you tell the CFO that when the audit results are in, you will check with him to see if there is any suspicious behavior.

Delegation of Authority and Security Groups

Our friend Courtney is constantly wondering what it is that she wants to do when she grows up. Since she is probably older than most of you, it would probably be a good time of life to decide, wouldn't it? Actually, she has always known what she *wanted* to do. She has always wanted a job where people threw large amounts of money at her and required her to do very little work. I guess that is why she teaches. She at least has half the scenario right.

As an administrator, Courtney has always had several tenets that she lives by. The first is that all her network users should think that she is omnipotent. They should think that she knows everything that is going on every minute of every day. The second thing is that she should be able to slough off many of the jobs that she doesn't want to do. Now, you may have thought that was just to get out of work, but actually, this is called *delegating authority*. It's cool!

Because Courtney is a Novell weenie, besides being a Microsoft person, she has been working with directories for years. There is no better way of sloug … ooops, delegating authority than by making proper use of the Active Directory. All kidding aside, take a look at Figure 8.2.

FIGURE 8.2 Domain model with OUs

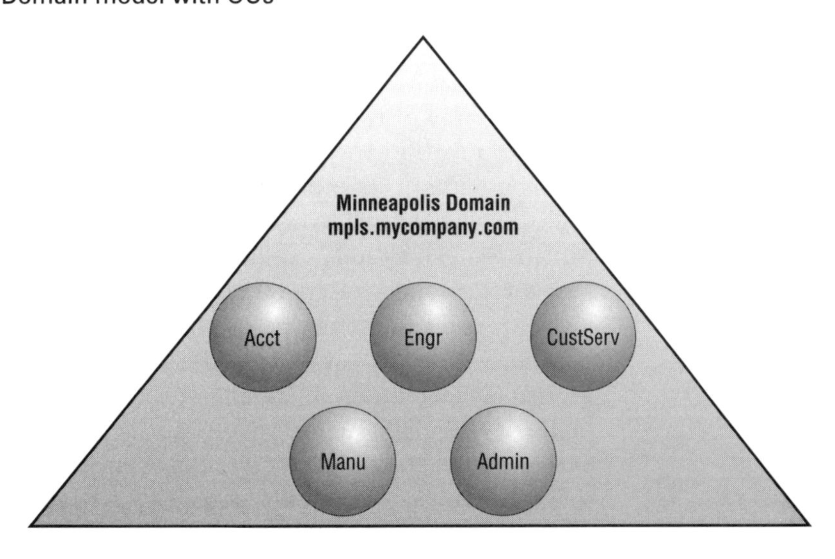

In Figure 8.2, you can see a domain called Minneapolis. Inside that domain, there are five organizational units. Now, we are sure that you have read, or at the very least have purchased, the exceptional study guide written by Bob King and Gary Govanus, called *MCSE: Windows 2000 Directory Services Design Study Guide* (Sybex, 2000). That book goes into great detail about the whys and wherefores of adding OUs to an Active Directory, so I won't re-cover ground you have already studied.

Microsoft Exam Objectives

Design a delegation of authority strategy.

Design the placement and inheritance of security policies for sites, domains, and organizational units.

Needless to say, one of the advantages of creating *organizational units* is that they make perfect areas for delegating authority. You can delegate authority down to the lowest level of your organization by creating a tree of organizational units within each domain and delegating authority for parts of the organizational unit subtree to other users or groups. Now, let's face it, you probably wouldn't be reading a book on architecting a security structure for an enterprise network if you were *just* the type of administrator who added and managed user accounts. You have "been there, done that," got the T-shirt, and moved on to bigger and better things. As a security person, you know that it is not a good thing to have dozens of people logging into your network with the sweeping authority of an administrator. By delegating administrative authority, you can eliminate the need to have people with sweeping authority over an entire domain regularly logging on to accounts. Although you will still have an Administrator account and a Domain Admins group with administrative authority over the entire domain, you can keep these accounts reserved for occasional use by a very limited number of highly trusted administrators.

When you decide how to structure your organizational units and in which organizational units to put each user, consider the hierarchy of administration. For example, you may want to create an organizational unit tree that enables you to grant to a user the administrative rights for all branches of a single department, such as an Accounting department. Alternatively, you may want to grant administrative rights to a sub-unit within an organizational unit, such as the Accounts Payable unit of an Accounting organizational unit. Another possible delegation of administrative rights would be to grant to an individual the administrative rights for the Accounting organizational unit, but not to any organizational units contained within the Accounting organizational unit.

Administration Delegation

Because of the size of the Microsoft designated sample network, the delegation of administrative tasks is a practical necessity in a Windows 2000 enterprise environment. You may have designed a situation where administration was divided along OU lines. That is not the only way that it can be divvied up. You don't even have to make administration IT specific. If you have some tech-weenie wannabes out there who are technically savvy and have a reason for needing rights to administer certain types of objects, go for it. For example, why not delegate authority to human resources personnel and various other manager-types for tasks related to their duties? With careful planning you can distribute the administrator's workload without granting sweeping privileges to every assistant. This is one of the ways of practicing the security concept of "principle of least privilege." In other words, you can grant the tech-weenie wannabes the permissions necessary to accomplish their particular tasks, and no more.

Using various methods in Windows 2000, you can delegate a prescribed degree of control over a limited set of objects to specific groups or individuals. Just keep in mind that the appropriate Active Directory objects (users, groups, Group Policy objects, files, directories, and so forth) must be in place before the administration delegation can be performed. Let's take a look at several of the ways to accomplish these tasks.

Security Groups, Group Policy, and Access Control Lists

These things have been described in previous chapters, so we are not going to go into extensive detail here. They help to form the mechanisms for distributed administration.

Built-in Security Groups

Windows 2000 has a set of built-in *security groups* that come with permissions in place, already delegated to each group. Open the Active Directory Users and Computers snap-in to MMC. Open View ➤ Advanced Features. The predefined security groups are in the Builtin and Users folders. If you want to directly delegate control of one of these groups, open the property sheet of the group and click the Security tab. Once there, all you have to do is add the group's manager to the access control list and check the appropriate privileges. This is shown in Figure 8.3.

FIGURE 8.3 MMC showing delegation of control over groups

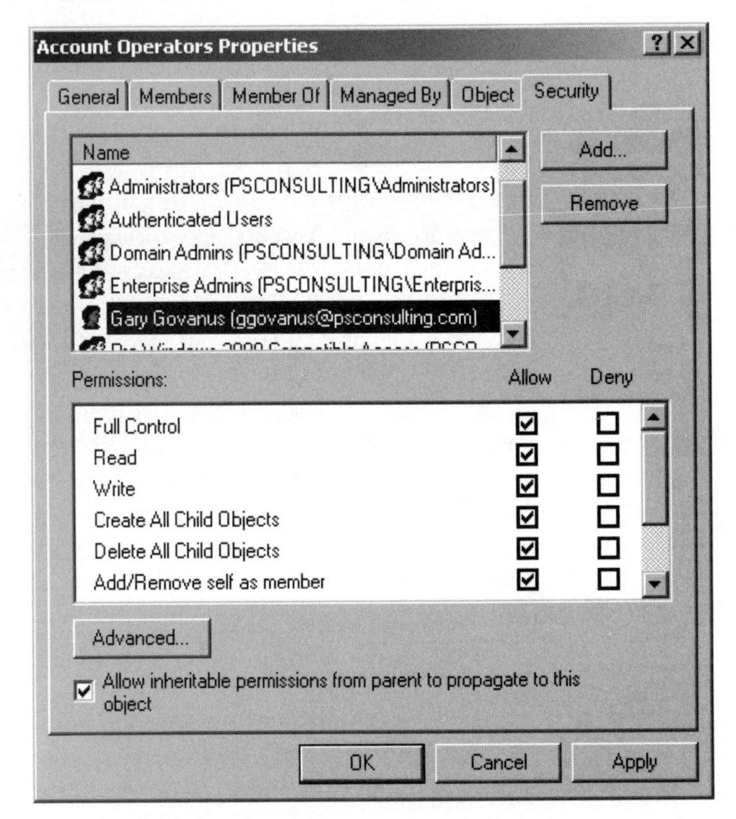

There are other ways of handling this. One of the ways is to use the *delegation of control wizard.*

Delegation of Control Wizard

Again, go into the Active Directory Sites and Services snap-in to MMC. From AD Sites and Services, click Action and then Delegate Control (see Figure 8.4).

FIGURE 8.4 MMC showing the delegation of control wizard getting ready to delegate the Manage Group Policy links

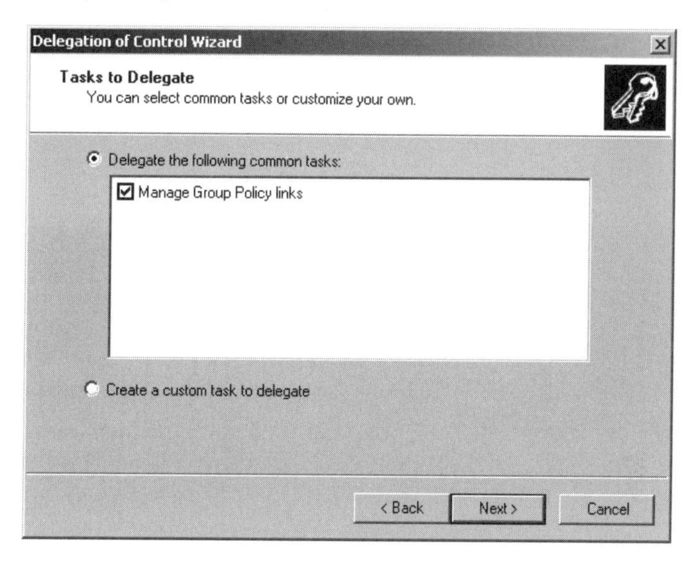

Using the Delegation Wizard to Distribute Administration

This time you will start by opening the Active Directory Users and Computers snap-in to MMC. Right-click an organizational unit and select Delegate Control. The delegation of control wizard sets up user group permissions to administer organizational units containing computers and user groups. An example would be the delegated right to create new user accounts (see Figure 8.5).

FIGURE 8.5 MMC for delegation of administration over users

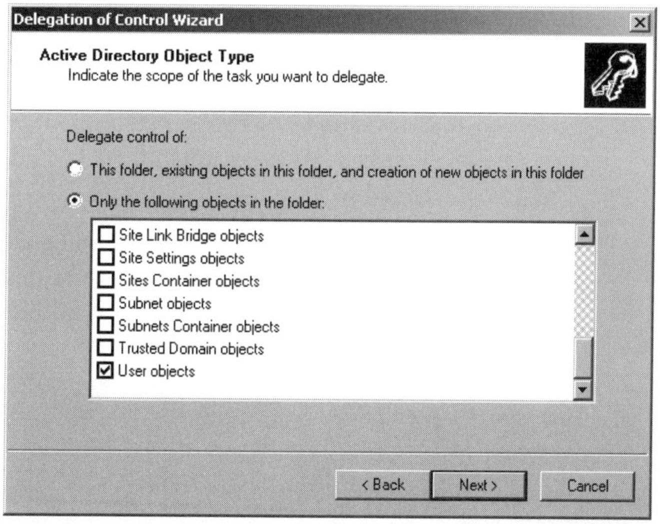

Delegating Control of Group Policy Objects

To delegate administration using Group Policies, you must deal with the following tasks. These three tasks can be performed together or separately, as needed:

- Managing Group Policy links for a site, domain, or organizational unit
- Creating Group Policy objects
- Editing Group Policy objects

Let's take a look at how this would work.

1. For example, you can create an organizational unit (OU) and then create a new Group Policy object (GPO) linked to it: Click Properties on the OU context menu, click the Group Policy tab in the Properties dialog box, and then click the New button. After creating the GPO, launch the Delegation Wizard. The Delegation Wizard provides a clear sequence of steps for delegating specific functionality.
2. You can also directly access the security settings for the GPO itself by clicking Properties on the specific GPO's context menu and then clicking the Security tab. Add your non-administrator user to the list of users for whom security is defined.
3. You can give your user Full Control—Allow privilege. Full Control lets the user write to the GPO, and also to change security permissions on the GPO. To prevent this user from setting security, you may decide to give the user only the Write—Allow permission. If you decide that the user should be exempt from the application of this policy, you can clear the Apply Group Policy—Allow privilege.
4. Finally, to simplify administration for the user, you can launch the management console and add the Group Policy snap-in. Browse for and add the GPO that you are configuring for delegation. After properly configuring this MMC session, save the session and give it to the user. The user can now utilize and administer his GPO with no additional setup.

Since we keep talking about Group Policies and the Group Policy MMC snap-in, this would appear to be a good time to examine Group Policies in a little more depth.

Design Scenario: Mumble, Mumble, Grumble, Grumble

It just has not been a great day. You have just come from a Windows 2000 planning meeting, and you have been the fortunate person who gets to decide how to group people together for your domain. Now, in most cases this does not sound like too difficult a task, but your company has 3,000 people working in this domain. Other than the people who work on your floor, and maybe some folks that eat lunch at the same time you do, you have no clue who most of these people are and what it is they do for a living. To be honest, right now, you couldn't care less, either! You go back to your cube mumbling about the unfairness of life and you start thinking about the actual project you were given. In this case, the CIO tasked you with "using the capabilities of Windows 2000 to the utmost to create groups that make sense within the organization." Hmmmm, that is an interesting piece of management speak, isn't it? Just as you are getting your hands around this concept, it is time to go to another meeting. This one is a full-blown production, announcing a reorganization of some new teams. You are simply not in the mood for rah-rah speeches right now, but it is mandatory, so you go.

Once you get there, you notice that all of senior management is on the stage, and you are impressed. You haven't seen this many suits in one place since you stumbled into a Hart Shaffner and Marx store by mistake! When the meeting kicks off, you begin to realize that what is happening here is going to have a direct impact on your life. They start out introducing the executive vice presidents, who introduce their vice presidents. Each vice president then announces the team leaders that will be their direct reports. It is made clear that each of the team leads will pick their people, and some people will be on several different teams. As you begin to think what a nightmare this is going to be for you, you glance down at the handout and notice the list of team leaders. Suddenly, a light comes on. Look, these people are doing all the picking and choosing anyway, why don't you just create the groups that match with the teams, and give the team leaders the ability to figure out what people go where. That would sure simplify your life a lot. At that point, you truly begin to appreciate the phrase "capabilities of Windows 2000 to the utmost" and the delegation of authority.

Implementing Group Policy Security Settings

By this stage of your MCSE track, you know that implementing a Group Policy consists of creating a new Group Policy object (or modifying an existing one), enabling appropriate settings within the object, and then linking the Group Policy object to an organizational unit, site, or domain that contains computers or users in the domain.

Let's take a look at a sample organizational unit and its associated Group Policy. We are going to get a feel for the nine security policy settings. So, start by opening the Active Directory Users and Computers MMC snap-in, and right-click the Domain Controllers OU. Open the property sheet and click the Group Policy tab. Select the Default Domain Controllers Policy and click Edit. This opens the Group Policy snap-in to MMC. In this module, navigate to the Security Settings container by choosing Computer Configuration ➤ Windows Settings ➤ Security Settings. Your screen should now look like Figure 8.6.

FIGURE 8.6 Security Settings Group Policy

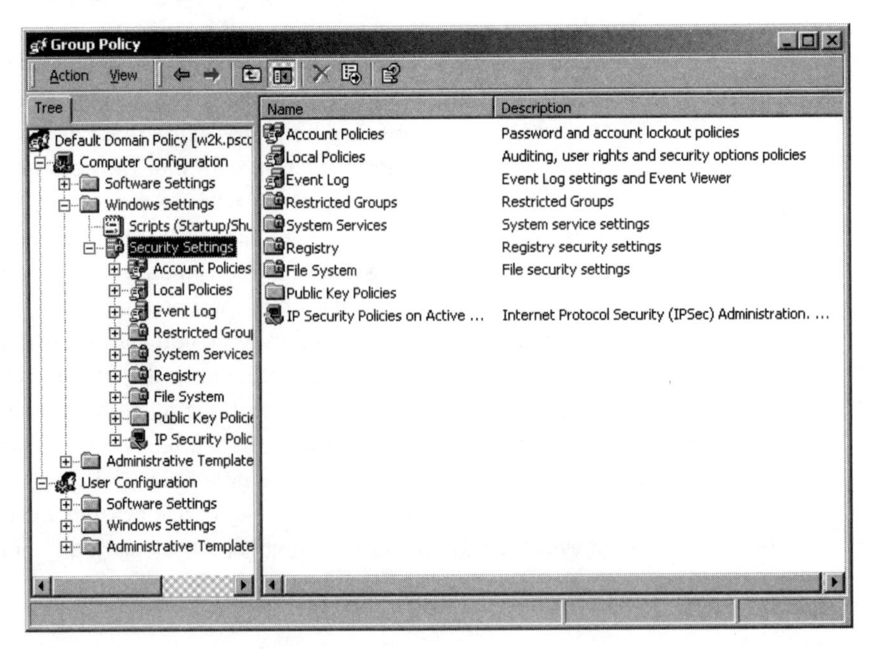

Under Security Settings, there are nine security policy subsettings:

- Account policies
- Local policies
- Event log
- Restricted groups
- Systems services
- Registry
- File system
- Public key policies
- IPSec Security Policies on Active Directory

Some of these policy areas can be applied domain-wide only. Account policies, for example, are applied to all the user accounts in the specific domain. That means that you cannot define different account policies for different organizational units in the same domain.

Of the security policy areas, account policies and public key policies are domain-wide. The other policies can be specified at the organizational unit level.

Defining Account Policies

Table 8.5 shows the scope of the *account policies* and what they can do.

The policies you choose affect the level of Help desk support required for users as well as the vulnerability of your network to security breaches and attacks. For example, specifying a restrictive account lockout policy increases the potential for denial of service attacks, and setting a restrictive password policy results in increased Help desk calls from users who cannot log on to the network. In addition, specifying restrictive password policy can actually reduce the security of the network. For example, if you require passwords longer than seven characters, most users have difficulty remembering them. They might write their passwords down and leave them where an intruder can easily find them.

TABLE 8.5 Account Policies

Policy	Description
Password policy	With a password policy, you can set parameters such as the minimum length of a user's password. You can also define how long a user can use the same password by setting the maximum password age. If you are working in a highly secure environment, make sure you require complex passwords. This will help prevent users from reusing the same password or a simple variation of their password.
Account lockout policy	To protect your network against brute attacks, where someone tries the same logon name and different passwords, over and over again, you can force users to be locked out after a specified number of failed logon attempts. Not only that, but you can specify the amount of time that accounts are locked.
Kerberos authentication policy	You can also modify the default Kerberos settings for each domain in your network, if you desire. This would include things like setting the maximum lifetime of a user ticket.

Defining Local Computer Policies

The second category of security settings that we are going to look at is *local computer policies*. Table 8.6 summarizes tweaks that you can make to local computer policies.

TABLE 8.6 Defining Local Computer Policies

Policy	Description
Audit policy	By setting the audit policy, Windows 2000 can track a variety of security event types. These event types can be system-wide, like a user logging on, or more specific, like a particular user attempting to open and read a specific file. You can have auditing track both successful and unsuccessful attempts.
User rights assignment	You can also use local policies to control the rights assigned to user accounts and security groups for local computers. In this case, you can set which users or security groups have rights to perform tasks that may affect your network security. An example would be controlling who can gain access to computers on the network, who can log on locally to a domain controller, or even who can shut a computer down. You can also use policies to define who can back up and restore files or who can take ownership of files.
Security options	The security options policies allow the administrator to control settings that would force users to log off when logon hours expire or prohibit the use of the Alt+Ctrl+Delete keys to get access to the Windows logon dialog. That would force users to use a smart card for logging on to the local computer.

Event Log Policies

You can use *event log* policies to control the settings of the application, system, and security event logs on local computers. For example, you can specify how large logs can grow, how long logs are kept, and how logs are retained.

Defining Restricted Groups Policies

Restricted group policies can be defined to let the IT team manage the membership of the built-in Windows 2000–defined groups or the user-defined groups. All of these groups will have special rights and permissions. The Restricted groups policies contain a list of members of specific groups whose membership is defined as part of the security policy. The enforcement of the restricted groups policies forcibly sets any computer local group membership to match the membership list settings defined in the policy. If a local computer administrator would try to change the membership, any changes would be overwritten by the policy.

Restricted groups are usually used to manage membership in the built-in groups. These built-in groups include local groups such as Administrators, Power Users, Print Operators, and Server Operators, as well as global groups such as Domain Admins. You can see that the central IT team may have an interest in making sure only certain users can belong to these groups. If you have other groups that you consider sensitive, they can be added to the restricted groups list, along with their membership list. In this way, you are enforcing the membership of these groups by policy and are making sure there will not be local variations on each computer.

Defining Systems Services Policies

Systems services can be a potential entry point for intruders. If a service is running, it may have a default service account with a default password that can open a door. For example, there have been a bevy of articles written on ways that an intruder can try to exploit weaknesses in various Web servers to gain access to a computer's operating system or files. To try to prevent this, you can configure systems services policies to do the following:

- Define the startup mode for Windows 2000 services, either manual or automatic—or, if you know the service is not going to be used, just disable it. One way this works to your advantage is to configure system services to prevent any unnecessary services from running. This can provide security for special servers like domain controllers, DNS servers, proxy servers, remote access servers, and certification authority servers.

- Define the exact rights and permissions that are granted to each of the system services when they run. In this case, you would configure system services to operate with the minimum rights and permissions needed. That would go a long way toward limiting potential damage that could be caused by intruders who try to exploit the service.
- Define security auditing levels for system services. Make sure that you specify the exact types of events to be logged for both failed and successful events. In the example of using auditing to protect against a compromised service, refine auditing to monitor for any inappropriate actions taken by running the susceptible services.

Defining Registry Policies

Registry policies can be used to configure the security audit policy. Because Windows 2000 can record a range of security event types, this can be a useful way of detecting intrusion. These policies are summarized in Table 8.7.

TABLE 8.7 Defining Registry Policies

Policy	Description
Security options	In this case, you are controlling security auditing for registry keys and their subkeys. For example, to make sure that only administrators can change certain information in the registry, you can use registry policies to grant administrators full control over registry keys and their subkeys and to grant read-only permission to other users. You can also use registry policies to prevent certain users from viewing portions of the registry.

You can use registry policies to audit user activity in the registry of the computer when auditing is enabled. You can specify which users and which user events are logged for both failed and successful events.

File System Policies

File system policies are used to provide data on your network. This includes giving you the ability to control security auditing of files and folders. One way this can be used effectively would be to make sure that only users with administrator capabilities can modify system files and folders. In this case, you can use file system policies to give the administrators full control over these areas and grant just read-only permissions to other users. There may be some areas of the network you don't want users accessing at all; in that case, you can use file system policies to prevent certain users from even looking at the files or folders.

For those users who can access files and folders, you can use file system policies to audit their activity. In this case, you are specifying which users and which events are logged for both failed and successful events.

Public Key Policies

To add things like a new Encrypted Data Recovery Agent or set up an Automatic Certificate request, you can use the public key policies area of security settings. You can also use this to manage the list of trusted Certification Authorities.

IP Security Policies on Active Directory

What about setting up IP Security Policies (IPSec)? The information in this area tells the workstation or the server how to handle a request for IPSec communication. For example, the server may require that any communications between the server and a client be secure, it may just permit secure communications, or it may not even require it.

If you decide to use IPSec, it is a good idea to make sure these policies are redefined for your implementation. As always, test, test, and test.

Design Scenario: You Work Too Hard!

As the CIO of a company with a major enterprise network, you know that the best thing you can do for the company is to come up with a good plan to delegate authority down to the people who really do the work. You are a manager, not a technical person.

You also know that there are things that you want out of your Windows 2000 network. In the past, one of the major problems of networking has always been the inconsistency. Even when you had "corporate standards," sometimes they didn't get met. Other times, the major vendors whose products you decided on changed the products, or worse yet, stopped making the products. In the case of Windows 2000 and security, there are just too many things that need to be set on each and every workstation to bring it into compliance with your standards. You are really concerned about ensuring that the machines will be rolled out properly and each setting will be duplicated across the entire domain.

You call in your most trusted assistant and begin to run the problem by her. She commiserates with you for a while and then remembers Group Policies. In this case, she suggests appointing one member of your team to be the Group Policy wizard. She suggests that you appoint Jeff to be the Group Policy wizard, simply because he is the most detail oriented person on the team. In this case, giving Jeff the power and the ability to test Group Policies will be right up his alley. At this point, you congratulate her on a brilliant idea and call for Jeff.

Jeff agrees to the plan and is all excited about his new challenge. After the meeting, you think, it is another great day in the neighborhood.

The Placement and Inheritance of Security Policies

Security policies are implemented at the site, the domain, or the OU. Since multiple Group Policy objects can be linked to any single site, domain, or OU, multiple security policies can be installed at any level. The policies are applied in a specific order: site, domain, and OU. Therefore, there can be multiple inherited policies applying to any level. In addition, due to the hierarchy of the ADS, it is important for troubleshooting to understand what takes priority over what.

Group Policy Hierarchy

By default Group Policy is inherited and cumulative, and it affects all computers and users in an Active Directory container.

Group Policy is processed according to the following order: site, domain, and OU. By default, remember, if there are conflicting policies, the closest policy to the computer or the user wins. To say it another way, the default inheritance method is to evaluate Group Policy, starting with the Active Directory container furthest away from the computer or user object. The Active Directory container closest to the computer or user can override Group Policy set in a higher-level AD container. If there are no conflicts, then the policies are cumulative.

Enforce and Block Policy Options

Options exist that allow you to *enforce* the Group Policy in a specific Group Policy object so that GPOs in lower-level Active Directory containers are prevented from overriding that policy. For example, if you have defined a specific GPO at the domain level and specified that the GPO be enforced, the policies that the GPO contains apply to all OUs under that domain; that is, the lower-level containers (OUs) cannot override that domain Group Policy.

You can also *block* inheritance of Group Policy from parent Active Directory containers. For example, if you specify a particular policy for a domain or OU, and then mark that policy as *block policy inheritance,* this prevents policy in higher-level Active Directory containers (such as a higher-level OU or domain) from applying. However, *enforced* policy options always take precedence.

Block Policy Inheritance can only be set at the domain, or OU level. It cannot be set on individual Group Policies. No Override can be set on individual policies.

Defining Group Policy Links for a Site, Domain, or Organizational Unit

As we have said before, administrators can configure Group Policy for sites, domains, or organizational units. Using the Active Directory tools and setting properties for the specified site, domain, or OU does this. The Group Policy tab in the SDOU's Properties page allows the administrator to specify which Group Policy objects are linked to this site, domain, or OU. This property page stores the user's choices in two Active Directory properties called *gPLink* and *gPOptions*. The gPLink property contains the prioritized list of

Group Policy objects, and the gPOptions property contains the *block policy inheritance* policy setting.

The Active Directory supports security settings on a per-property basis. This means that a non-administrator can be given read and write access to specific properties. In this case, if non-administrators have read and write access to the gPLink and gPOptions properties, they can manage the list of GPOs linked to that site, domain, or OU. To give a user read and write access to these properties, use the Delegation Wizard and select the *Manage Group Policy links* predefined task.

Design Scenario: Surely There Has Got to Be a Better Way

It is time to go into the video meeting talking about the way Group Policies are going to be implemented across the enterprise. You are anticipating a long drawn out affair, where there could be tons of squabbling about territorial rights and access. This may not be the most fun you have ever had.

Once the meeting kicks off, the Group Policy experts from the different divisions come on the screen smiling and joking. It appears they have this under control. When the meeting starts, the team leader stands up and starts talking about the way the team has come up with an enterprise-wide plan for the implementation of security policies. They start by explaining how security policies are, for the most part, cumulative, and how they can be inherited. Then they bring up a shot of the forest and show how certain policies can be implemented high up in the tree. As other policies need to be implemented, they can be implemented specifically for the domains, for the sites, or even down to the organization-unit level.

Rather than the bickering you expected, everyone seemed in perfect harmony. Then it came down to implementation. You asked the fateful question, "How long is it going to take to put these things in place?" You were expecting the request for more time and money to come about this point in the conversation. Once again, the answer surprised you. The Group Policies had been tested in the lab environment. Once the go-ahead has been given, the policies will be rolled out over the weekend. They should be in effect, tested and approved, Monday morning when the regular workweek starts.

Strategy for an Encrypting File System

Encrypting file system basics: A user decides to save a file that needs to be secure. He chooses to save it using the encrypting file system (EFS). EFS is part of the Public Key Infrastructure, so a key is obtained and used to encrypt the file. The de-encryption key is controlled by the user and by a recovery agent. If someone attempts to attack the file, that person will be unable to open it. If the computer is stolen, the information remains in a secure state. If the end user loses the decryption key, the information remains in a secure state.

Microsoft Exam Objective

Design an Encrypting File System strategy.

Before we start getting into how to use the EFS, let's look at some of the prerequisites to using it.

EFS Prerequisites

EFS only works on the Windows 2000 NTFS file system. That means EFS does not work on any NTFS partitions from previous versions of Windows NT.

EFS has some built-in protection. For example, EFS does not run if there is no recovery agent certificate. It will, however, designate a recovery agent account by default and generate the necessary certificate. It will do this even if you don't.

You can use EFS to encrypt or decrypt data on a remote computer, but you cannot use it to encrypt data sent over the network.

Windows 2000 helps prevent some catastrophes in the making. It makes sure that you cannot encrypt system files or folders.

You cannot encrypt compressed files and folders until you decompress them.

Encrypting an entire folder ensures that the temporary copies of encrypted files that it contains are also encrypted.

Copying a file into an encrypted folder encrypts the file, but *moving* it into the folder in the same partition leaves the file encrypted or unencrypted, just as it was before you moved the file.

Moving or copying EFS files to another file system removes the encryption, but backing them up preserves the encryption.

Other file permissions are unaffected. An administrator, for instance, can still delete a user's EFS file even though the user cannot open it.

Encrypting File System and the End User

How does the end user work with EFS? Actually, it is pretty transparent. Users work with encrypted files and folders just as they do with any other files and folders. As long as the EFS user is the same person who encrypted the file or folder, the system automatically decrypts the file or folder when the user accesses it later. However, an intruder is prevented from accessing any encrypted files or folders. To encrypt a file, all the user has to do is go into Windows Explorer and browse to the file. The user highlights the file, right-clicks Properties ➤ General Tab ➤ Advanced button, and gets the screen shown in Figure 8.7.

FIGURE 8.7 Encrypting a file

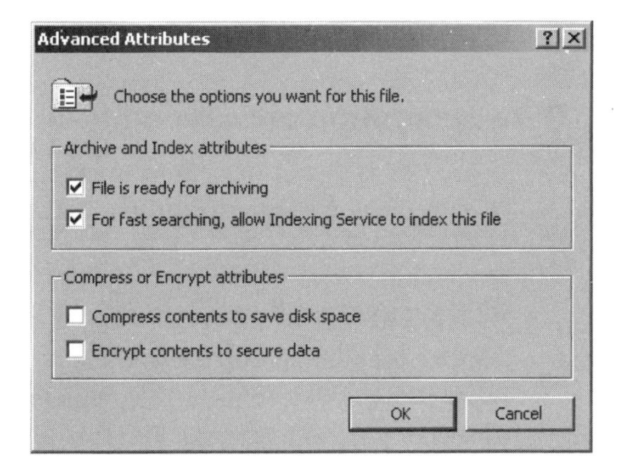

Once the little check-box is clicked, the file is encrypted if it is in a folder that holds encrypted files. Folders themselves are not encrypted—only the contents of the files within a folder. Like folders, subfolders are not encrypted; however, they are marked to indicate that they contain encrypted file data. If the folder is not designated to handle encrypted files, the user receives a warning to encrypt the entire folder. Check out Figure 8.8.

FIGURE 8.8 Encryption warning

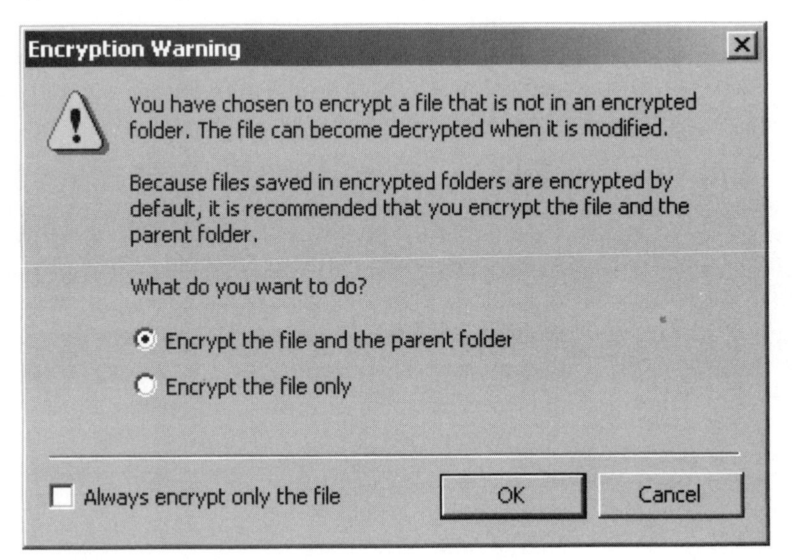

Any file that is saved in an encrypted folder is encrypted by default. Any file that is not saved in an encrypted folder can be decrypted if it is modified.

Data Encryption and Decryption

Since this is so transparent to the user, you have to figure there is a lot of work going on in the background. It all starts when a user wants to encrypt a file.

EFS Encryption Keys

Once a user has specified that a file be encrypted, the actual process of data *encryption* and decryption is completely transparent to the user. The user does not need to understand this process. For the sake of the security administrator, it might be good thing to understand the process.

When you are talking about encryption and decryption, you are talking both per file and for an entire folder. The encryption for a folder is transparent. All the files and subfolders created in an encrypted folder are automatically encrypted. Each file has a unique encryption key. The file does not have to be decrypted to use it—EFS automatically takes care of that for you.

EFS will go out and locate the user's file encryption key from the systems key store and apply it.

Storing Encrypted Files on Remote Servers

There are some caveats to file encryption that should be included in your file encryption strategy. For example, it is perfectly okay for a user to store an encrypted file on a remote server. Just because the file is stored on the remote server, though, is not an indication that there is support for sharing the file with multiple users. As a matter of fact, storing encrypted files on a remote server can actually make them vulnerable to sniffer attacks. Encrypted data is not encrypted when it is in transit over the network—only when it is stored on disk. The exception to this rule is if your system is using Internet Protocol Security security (IPSec). In that case, IPSec encrypts the data while it is transported over a TCP/IP network.

Microsoft also suggests that users should never store highly sensitive data on servers where physical security might be at risk. Finally, if there are any Macintosh clients on the network, you may want to think about encryption. Encrypted files are not accessible to Macintosh clients.

There is some other preliminary work that has to be done before users can encrypt files will be stored on a remote server. First, that server must be designated as *trusted for delegation*. This allows all users with files on that server to encrypt those files.

To designate a remote server for file encryption, open Active Directory Users and Computers. Once that is open, highlight the remote server name and right-click and choose Properties. Select the Trusted for Delegation check-box.

Data Recovery

This is one of those steps that is really obvious! Data recovery is very important when you need to be able to recover data encrypted by an employee after the employee leaves, or when the user's private key is lost. When we first heard about this feature in Windows 2000, we thought about all the damage a disgruntled employee could do. Imagine the problems if someone could go out to the Accounting area and encrypt all the data files so no one could read them! Without proper planning, that could be a very real nightmare. Even if the employee was *not* disgruntled, there are ways that keys can be lost. Imagine if you will what would happen to someone whose hard disk failed?

Through no fault of her own, she would have lost her file encryption certificate and private key. To protect against this, there is a designated recovery agent.

Mandatory Recovery Policy

EFS provides for built-in data recovery by enforcing a recovery policy requirement. The requirement is that a recovery policy must be in place before users can encrypt files. The recovery policy provides for a person to be designated as the recovery agent. Again, this is a transparent process. The default recovery policy is automatically put in place when the administrator logs on to the system for the first time (during installation), making the administrator the recovery agent.

What is the *recovery agent*? Well, the recovery agent is the account that has a special certificate and associated private key that allow data recovery for the scope of influence of the recovery policy. In other words, if you are the recovery agent for the domain, any time someone loses his key or leaves the company without being polite enough to decrypt his files, you will be called on.

How secure is the system if there is a master certificate and key floating around? That is a good point. You need to protect your recovery certificate and private key. So, if you are the recovery agent, you should be sure to use the export command from Certificates in Microsoft Management Console (MMC) to back up the recovery certificate and associated private key to a secure location. After backing up, you should use Certificates in MMC to delete the recovery certificate from the recovery agent's personal store, not from the recovery policy. Then, when you need to perform a recovery operation for a user, you would start by first restoring the recovery certificate and associated private key to the recovery agent's personal store, using the Import command from Certificates in MMC. After recovering the data, you should again delete the recovery certificate from the recovery agent's personal store. You do not have to repeat the export process. Deleting the recovery agent's recovery certificate from the computer and keeping it in a secure location apart from the computer is an additional security measure for the protection of sensitive data. In this case a secure location would be a safe.

The default recovery policy is configured locally for stand-alone computers. For computers that are part of a network, the recovery policy is configured at either the domain, organizational unit, or individual computer level, and applies to all Windows 2000–based computers within the defined scope of influence. Recovery certificates are issued by a Certificate Authority (CA) and managed using Certificates in MMC.

In a network environment, the domain administrator controls how EFS is implemented for users for all computers in the domain. In a default Windows 2000 installation, when the first domain controller is set up, the domain administrator is the specified recovery agent for the domain. The way the domain administrator configures the recovery policy determines how EFS is implemented for users on their local machines. The domain administrator logs on to the first domain controller to change the recovery policy for the domain.

Types of Recovery Policies

Administrators can define one of three kinds of policies: *no recovery policy*, *empty recovery policy*, or *recovery-agent policy* with one or more recovery agents.

No recovery policy When an administrator deletes the recovery policy on the first domain controller, a *no recovery policy* at the domain level is in effect. Because there is no domain recovery policy, the default local policy on individual computers is used for data recovery. This means that local administrators control the recovery of data on their computers.

Empty recovery policy When an administrator deletes all recovery agents and their public-key certificates, an *empty recovery policy* is in effect. An empty recovery policy means that no one is a recovery agent, and that users cannot encrypt data on computers within the scope of influence of the recovery policy. The effect of an empty recovery policy is to turn off EFS altogether.

Recovery-agent policy When an administrator adds one or more recovery agents, a *recovery-agent policy* is in effect. These agents are responsible for recovering any encrypted data within their scope of administration. This is the most common type of recovery policy.

There are a variety of recovery options available. Table 8.8 summarizes them.

TABLE 8.8 Effect of Recovery Policies

Recovery Policy	Effect	Recovery Agent	Tasks
Empty recovery policy	EFS cannot be used.	There is no recovery agent.	You will have to delete every recovery agent.
No recovery policy at the domain level	EFS is available on a local computer.	The default recovery agent is set to the administrator of local computer.	You can delete the recovery policy on first domain controller.
Recovery policy is configured with designated recovery agent(s)	EFS is available locally.	The default recovery agent is set to the domain administrator.	This is the default configuration in a network environment.

Because the Windows 2000 security subsystem handles enforcing, replicating, and caching of the recovery policy, users can implement file encryption on a system that is temporarily offline, such as a portable computer (this process is similar to logging on to their domain account using cached credentials).

Modifying the Recovery Policy

To modify the default recovery policy for a domain, you must log on to the first domain controller as an administrator. Then, start the Group Policy MMC through the Active Directory Users and Computers snap-in, right-click the domain whose recovery policy you wish to change, and click Properties. At this point, you click the recovery policy you wish to change and click Edit. In the console tree, click Encrypted Data Recovery Agents. Finally, you right-click the details pane and click the appropriate action you wish to take.

Encrypting File System: Best Practices

As you plan your EFS policy, remember that you have the option to disable EFS if you feel that it will not benefit your enterprise. You can (and should) designate alternate recovery agent accounts, just in case. You should also make sure that you protect the recovery keys from misuse. Just for safety's sake, make sure that you keep archives of obsolete recovery agent certificates and private keys.

Disabling EFS for a Set of Computers

If you want to disable EFS for a domain, organizational unit, or stand-alone computer, you can do it by simply applying an empty Encrypted Data Recovery Agents policy setting. Until Encrypted Data Recovery Agents settings are configured and applied through Group Policy, there is no policy and the default recovery agents are used by EFS. However, EFS must use the recovery agents that are listed in the Encrypted Data Recovery Agents Group Policy. If the policy that is applied is empty, there is no recovery agent, and therefore EFS does not operate.

Designating Alternate Recovery Agents

You can configure Encrypted Data Recovery Agents policy to designate alternative recovery agents. For example, you may want to distribute the administrative workload in your organization, so you can designate alternative EFS recovery accounts for categories of computers grouped by organizational units. You might also configure Encrypted Data Recovery Agents settings for portable computers so that they use the same recovery agent certificates when they are connected to the domain and when they are operated as stand-alone computers.

Securing Recovery Keys

Because recovery keys can be misused to decrypt and read files that have been encrypted by EFS users, it is recommended that you provide additional security for private keys for recovery. The first step in providing security for recovery keys is to disable default recovery accounts by exporting the recovery agent certificate and the private key to a secure medium and to select the option to remove the private key from the computer. When the recovery certificate and key are exported, the key is removed from the computer. You then store the exported certificate and key in a secure location to be used later for file recovery operations. Securing private keys for recovery ensures that nobody can misuse the recovery agent account to read encrypted files. This is especially important for mobile computers or other computers that are at high risk of falling into the wrong hands.

Maintaining Archives of Recovery Keys

For EFS encrypted files, the recovery agent information is refreshed every time the file system performs an operation on the file (for example, when the file is opened, moved, or copied). However, if an encrypted file isn't used for a long time, the recovery agents can expire. To make sure that encrypted files that have not been accessed for a long period of time can be recovered, you should maintain backups of the recovery agent certificates and of all the private keys. In order to create the backup, simply export the certificate and its private key to a secure medium like a floppy disk or a Zip disk and then store the disk in a safe location. A safe location should be something like a safe or safety deposit box, preferably offsite. When you export the private keys, you must provide a secret password for granting access to the exported key. The secret key is then stored in an encrypted format to protect its confidentiality.

What happens if you have to recover some files that have expired recovery agent information? In that case, import the appropriate expired recovery agent certificate and private key from the backup to a recovery account on a local computer and then perform the recovery.

EFS: Quick Tips

Now, you have seen the best practices. This can be considered a section on "if you were going to do it our way, this is the way it would be done."

- Make sure that you encrypt the entire folder where you save most of your documents. This will make sure that your personal documents are encrypted by default.
- Take the precaution of encrypting your Temp folder. That way, all the temporary files on your computer are automatically encrypted.
- Be sure to take the precaution of encrypting folders rather than individual files. That way, when a program creates temporary files during editing, they are encrypted.

- Remember, to make archives, you can use the Export command from the Certificates snap-in to back up the file encryption certificate and associated private key on a floppy disk, and then make sure you keep it in a secure location like a safe or safety deposit box.

Design Scenario: EFS for the Masses

You have to admit, when you first heard about EFS, you thought this was pretty much of a nightmare waiting to happen. Imagine allowing end users the ability to encrypt files so that *no one* else can get into them. The whole premise was absurd. Now, however, you are beginning to rethink your position. In fact, EFS may have some great implications for the laptop users who seem to propagate like rabbits all over the enterprise. This would be the simplest way to protect data in the case of laptop theft.

The final clincher, at least in your mind, was the fact that you can have an alternate recovery agent. It's not that you don't trust end users, it's just that you always like to have a back door, just in case!

Your Security Plan: Best Practices

This section falls under the *best practices* part of the Group Policy security setting implementation. Suggestions include things like these: When you lay out your Active Directory, create organizational units that will contain computers that have similar roles in your network. Create another organizational unit that will be specific to application servers. You may also decide to create an organizational unit that could contain all your client computers. Once this has been done, you can apply a single Group Policy object to each of these organizational units, and that would implement consistent security settings.

Number one rule in using Group Policies is to test, test, and test some more. Limit the number of administrators who can edit GPOs, and limit inheritance modifications, filtering, and loopbacks. Also, it is a very good idea to limit the number of GPOs that apply to any site, domain, or organizational unit.

Microsoft also recommends that you keep the number of Group Policy objects that apply to users and computers to a minimum. Because the user and computer Group Policy objects have to be downloaded to a computer at logon time, having multiple Group Policy objects increases computer startup and user logon time. Also, applying multiple Group Policy objects can create policy conflicts that are difficult to troubleshoot.

In general, Group Policy can be passed down from parent to child sites, domains, and organizational units. If you have assigned a specific Group Policy to a high-level parent, that Group Policy applies to all organizational units beneath the parent, including the user and computer objects in each container. If you have multiple GPOs, trying to figure out which one is causing the problem can be difficult.

Microsoft Exam Objective

Design a security group strategy.

It is time now to lay out your network security deployment plan. This plan needs to itemize all the important policy choices in each policy category. When you create your plan, be sure to cover the following details:

- Specify the Group Policy settings that you want to change from the default settings, and how they will be changed.
- Be sure to describe all the issues that may be related to changing the settings for the Group Policy. This will assist the Help desk by giving them a heads-up to potential problems.
- Be sure to document any special security requirements and also how you configured Group Policy to meet them.

When you are developing your deployment plan, it's helpful to have a checklist to refer to. The following could serve as a guide:

Deployment Planning Checklist

Decide which security risks affect your network. List all risks and provide enough detail to clarify the problems.

Fill in enough background information to help your readers understand the issues.

Describe the security strategies you are employing to deal with the risks.

Decide who needs to use strong authentication for interactive or remote access login.

Make sure that all network access is authenticated through domain accounts.

Define the complexity, length, and lifetime of passwords for domain user accounts; determine the best way to convey these requirements to your users. Inform staff of the company's policy prohibiting transmission of plain text passwords. Enable single sign-on or protect password transmission.

If strong authentication is indicated, deploy public key security for smart card logon.

With reference to broad security access to enterprise-wide resources, describe the top-level security groups you plan on using (probably enterprise universal groups).

Describe your strategy for providing necessary remote access; convey your plan to those who need to know, and include details such as connection methods.

Identify how your company uses groups and establishes conventions for group names and how group types are used.

Describe how your access control policies support consistent use of security groups.

Define procedures for creating new groups and decide who is responsible for managing the groups.

Determine which existing domains belong in the forest, and which domains use external trust relationships.

Describe your domains, domain trees, and forests and describe the trust relationships between them.

Identify which servers are likely to carry sensitive data and therefore to need network data protection to prevent eavesdropping.

Outline your policy for identification and management of sensitive data.

Describe how IPSec will be used for protecting data or sensitive applications in remote access situations.

If EFS is part of the plan, describe the data recovery policy involved, and define the role of the recovery agent in your company. Describe how you will implement a data recovery process, and be sure it works.

If you are using IPSec, identify how it will be used in your network and explain the performance implications.

Define domain-wide account policies and tell your users what they are.

List the local security policy requirements and Group Policy settings for all system categories: desktops, file servers, print servers, and mail servers.

Identify application servers where security templates can simplify the management of security settings. Consider managing them through Group Policy.

For systems that will get an upgrade from NT 4 instead of a clean installation, describe an effective security template.

For different classes of computers, use security templates to describe the intended security level.

Plan testing to verify that existing applications will run properly under newly implemented security design.

List any additional applications needed to meet security objectives.

Describe the security level required for downloaded code.

Deploy code signing for all publicly distributed software that has been developed within the organization.

State the policies regarding security of the administrator account and the administration consoles.

Identify your policies regarding auditing, including staffing.

Describe any situations where you might delegate administrator control for specific tasks.

Summary

This chapter did cover a lot of ground, didn't it? The first thing we looked at was the way that an IT department could use audit policies to determine who was accessing what on the network. It didn't matter if it was a file, an application, or a resource, we could track who accessed it. In addition, there were several audit policies that could be set up to check on who was accessing the network and how they were getting in.

The next section touched on how to delegate authority. One really popular concept that came out of that section was the idea of letting team leads manage the team group. IT security will set up the group and give it all the permissions it needs, but as far as adding or removing members from the group, heck, let the team lead take care of it. The fact that there were several tools available to help with the delegation of administration was a real plus, too.

Next, we touched on security groups, how to implement them and how to best use the default groups. We looked at how to design and configure security policies and where to place them within the forest so you get the most bang for your buck.

Finally, we looked at how to manage your users and encrypting file system. We pointed out several safety features built in and how best to use those.

Key Terms

Before you take the exam, be certain you are familiar with the following terms:

Account Operators

account policies

auditing

audit directory service access category

audit object access category

audit policy

block

decryption

delegation of control wizard

domain local groups

empty recovery policy

encryption

event log

file encryption key

global groups

IP Security Policies (IPSec)

local computer policies

local security policy

organizational units

Print Operators

Power User

public key policies

recovery agent

registry

restricted groups

system services

trusted for delegation

universal groups

Review Questions

1. Why would you configure your system to audit for the success of a logon/logoff?

   A. To protect against a virus outbreak

   B. To protect against the misuse of privileges

   C. To protect against a random password hack

   D. To protect against a stolen password break-in

2. Under security settings there are nine subdirectories of security policy settings. Which of the following are included?

   A. Account policies

   B. Local policies

   C. Event log

   D. Registry

   E. Public key policies

   F. IP Security Policies on Active Directory

   G. All of the above

3. Why would you encrypt the folder in which you save most of your documents?

   A. The folder is encrypted by default.

   B. To ensure that your personal documents are encrypted by default.

   C. To give you the option of encrypting files or not.

   D. You cannot choose. It is up to the system administrator to choose where you can store encrypted files.

4. If there is no recovery policy specified at the domain level, who is the default recovery agent?

   A. The creator of the file.

   B. The first member added to the Administrators local group.

   C. Any member of the Administrators local group.

   D. The Administrator of the local computer.

   E. If there is no recovery policy specified, there is no EFS capability.

5. There is some other preliminary work that has to be done before users can encrypt files that will be stored on a remote server. What is the first step?

   A. First, that server must be designated as trusted for delegation.

   B. First, the users must be trained in encryption.

   C. All the folders on the server must be encrypted.

   D. The server must be a Windows NT server, SP6 or later.

6. How are group policies processed?

   A. Organizational unit, domain, site

   B. Domain, organizational unit, site

   C. Site, organizational unit, domain

   D. Site, domain, organizational unit

7. IP Security Policies are designed to:

   A. Establish a set of guidelines for communication between the user and the workstation.

   B. Establish a set of communication guidelines between RADIUS and the Server.

   C. Establish a method of screening a subnet.

   D. The policies in this section tell the server how to respond to a request for IPSec communications.

8. Which choices are part of account policies?

   A. Password policy

   B. File system policy

   C. Account lockout policy

   D. Kerberos authentication policy

   E. Account delegation policies

9. Delegating control via Group Policy involves which three of the following tasks:

   A. Managing user policies for the organizational unit

   B. Managing Group Policy links for a site, domain, or organizational unit

   C. Creating Group Policy objects

   D. Deleting Group Policy objects

   E. Editing Group Policy objects

Answers to Review Questions

1. D. You audit for the successful logon and logoff to see if someone is using a password and logon name that you think may be compromised.

2. G. All of the choices are found under security settings.

3. B. You would encrypt a folder to ensure that your personal documents are encrypted by default.

4. D. The Administrator of the local computer is the default recovery agent.

5. A. First, the server must be designated as trusted for delegation.

6. D. Group Policy is processed according to the following order: site, domain, and OU.

7. D. The policies in this section tell the server how to respond to a request for IPSec communications.

8. A, C, D. Account policies are made up of password policies, account lockout policies, and Kerberos authentication policies.

9. B, C, E. The three tasks involved in delegating administration are managing Group Policy links for a site, domain, or organizational unit; creating the actual Group Policy objects; and editing the Group Policy objects as needed.

The Multinational Conglomerate

You should give yourself 10 minutes to review this case study, diagram as needed, and complete the questions for this testlet.

Background

Your consulting firm has been hired to assist in the Windows 2000 migration and integration for a company based in Minneapolis, Minnesota. Until the start of this year, the company had 1,000 employees, all based throughout the Twin Cities of Minneapolis and St. Paul. Just before the end of the year, the owner of your company purchased two companies of roughly the same size that will need to be connected to the enterprise network. The total number of users when the project is completed is estimated at 3,500. In addition, each of these companies comes with various strategic partners that will need to access the information on your enterprise network. The companies that have been acquired are located in Athens, Greece, and in Orlando, Florida.

The three companies can now be considered one, and the preparation for the Windows 2000 rollout is in full swing. At this time, the company is examining various methods of rolling out security across the network.

Current System

Minneapolis Located on the shores of beautiful Lake Calhoun, the company occupies a sprawling campus that includes four floors in a six-story building. Since the merger, the Lake Calhoun facility has become a model of efficiency. Besides being linked to all of the other offices, everyone is finally moved and the company seems to moving forward steadily.

All of the floors are connected to the Windows 2000 network. The Minneapolis location is a site in the tree. The network is getting closer to native mode. Active Directory Services have been deployed to the main campus and the rollout is continuing in the branch offices. Security is still the hot topic, and the CEO has just signed off on the purchase of hundreds of new desktops that are Windows 2000 Professional–compatible, as well as new laptops for dozens of managers. The CEO wants to know what the IT team is doing to streamline configuration and management of all these machines. In addition, she is concerned that some of the managers are carrying around information vital to the company. If one of the laptops is lost or stolen, that information could devastate the company.

Orlando The Orlando office has become a site in the corporate tree. The Orlando manager has coordinated with the Minneapolis team to order new computers. Desktops are all going to be running Windows 2000 Professional with NTFS. There is concern about some of the GPOs being discussed at the Minneapolis level. Also, the IT folks in Orlando are getting worried that they will be outsourced or laid off as the rollout continues.

Athens The Athens office is now fully staffed at 2,300. The location has discovered that the business is doing well, and the extra folks are justified. The office has been upgraded to Windows 2000 servers and Athens is now its own domain in the tree.

Athens has always been ahead of the curve. They have already rolled out their new 1,500 hosts, replacing all the old computers. All the replacement machines, and all the machines for the new people, are running Windows 2000 Professional. The Athens IT director has stressed time and time again how these machines must be alike, for the sake of intercompany politics and to ease the burden on the Help desk. The Athens IT director has also said that the Athens domain has created and implemented several GPOs.

Problem Statement

Now that the integration of the company is complete, security is becoming more and more of a concern. The senior management has tasked you with making sure the network is secure. You must provide consistent security to the desktop and controlled access to resources, including an accounting of who is accessing certain sensitive areas. You will need to provide a security plan that will protect the company in case a laptop is compromised. Although users should not be unnecessarily imposed on, you must protect the company against users losing encryption information. Senior management wants the IT department to be lean and mean. While no layoffs are planned, management feels that there are more efficient ways of administering networks.

Envisioned System

Now that the three locations are working together and communicating, the CEO wants to make sure that it is done securely. She still wants the Digital Nervous System, but she understands there are other things that have to come first.

The CEO has some issues she would like to have addressed: First, why does the IT team spend so much time trying to figure out who works with whom on what? Second, how do I know unauthorized users are not accessing my sensitive information on the network? Third, why in the world did you give a laptop to Fred? He can't keep track of his own car keys. If he loses that thing, this company could be severely compromised. And fourth, just so you know, the Athens manager reports that he is going to make sure that policies that you institute from the corporate site will not be accepted.

Problem Statement

The issues that you are going to have to contend with include delegation of authority, auditing, encrypted file systems, and GPO inheritance.

Questions

1. How can you solve the delegation problem?

   A. Assign a corporate IT staffer to oversee each site.

   B. Delegate control of each site to a local IT staffer.

   C. Delegate control of groups to division heads and team leaders.

   D. Maintain all management from the Minneapolis site.

2. What can you do about auditing?

   A. Encrypt everything.

   B. Establish auditing for selected files and resources.

   C. Audit everything.

   D. Audit logon success and failures.

   E. Determine which files and resources are deemed critical.

3. How do you handle the problem of Fred?

   A. Make sure the laptop is running Windows 2000 Professional.

   B. Make sure the file system is NTFS.

   C. Make sure the My Documents folder is encrypted.

   D. Make sure you have exported the recovery key.

   E. Make sure Fred saves everything to the My Documents folder.

4. How can you solve the problem of the Athens manager?

   A. Make sure all site policies match Athens; therefore you do not have to worry about inheritance.

   B. Agree that the Athens manager knows best, and don't try to override his policies.

   C. Decide that if there are critical corporate policies, they will be instituted at a high level in the tree, and they will be configured so they cannot be blocked.

   D. There is no way currently to solve the problem. This is expected to be fixed in SP3.

Answers

1. C. Delegate control of groups to the appropriate team leader or division head. That will remove the burden from the IT teams.

2. B, E. First determine which files and resources the CEO considers critical and then set up auditing to make sure you know who accesses them when.

3. A, B, C, D, E. While this will not ensure that Fred never loses the laptop, it will ensure that if anyone gets access to the laptop, that person will have a difficult time accessing the information. The exporting of the recovery key ensures that someone will be able to access the data if Fred leaves the company.

4. C. You can configure a GPO where the Athens manager cannot stop it from being implemented.

Choosing an Authentication Strategy

MICROSOFT EXAM OBJECTIVES COVERED IN THIS CHAPTER:

✓ **Design an authentication strategy.**

- Select authentication methods. Methods include certificate-based authentication, Kerberos authentication, clear-text passwords, digest authentication, smart cards, NTLM, RADIUS, and SSL.
- Design an authentication strategy for integration with other systems.

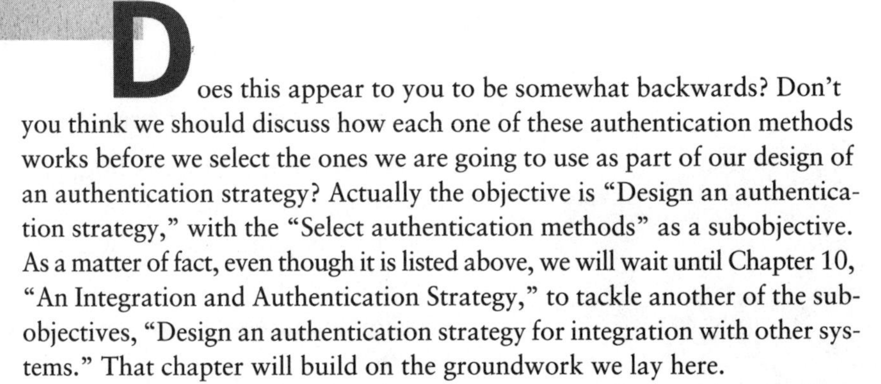

Does this appear to you to be somewhat backwards? Don't you think we should discuss how each one of these authentication methods works before we select the ones we are going to use as part of our design of an authentication strategy? Actually the objective is "Design an authentication strategy," with the "Select authentication methods" as a subobjective. As a matter of fact, even though it is listed above, we will wait until Chapter 10, "An Integration and Authentication Strategy," to tackle another of the subobjectives, "Design an authentication strategy for integration with other systems." That chapter will build on the groundwork we lay here.

So, we are going to flip-flop things here. We are going to take a look at each of the types of authentication, starting with certificate-based. We will look at how it works, how to implement it, and when you would want to use it. Once we have finished with all eight of those, we should have a pretty good foundation to move to Chapter 10 on integration with other systems. Combine the two chapters and you will be able to design a cross-platform, cross-system authentication strategy.

As you can tell, Windows 2000 is exceptionally flexible when it comes to authentication methods. It has to be. Networking has grown to the point where security is a difficult thing because the boundaries are breaking. Up until a short time ago, we all looked at a firewall as protection from the baddies on the outside. Everything on the inside of the firewall was where the people in the white hats hung out, and the people who were determined to do evil were on the far side of the firewall. Now, it has suddenly dawned on people that not only are the bad guys on the outside of the network, but our customers and are partners are out there too. We need to find a way to let the good guys in and still keep the bad guys out. And you thought your job was easy!

Certificate-Based Authentication

This is the basis from which most of the other authentication methods draw. While we will be mentioning *Public Key Infrastructure* in this chapter, we will discuss it in more detail as part of Chapter 11, "Enhancing Security Using Public Keys." This chapter is going to start examining some of the building blocks of the Public Key Infrastructure (PKI). Both certificate-based services and PKI are included with Windows 2000.

Microsoft Exam Objectives

Design an authentication strategy.

- Select authentication methods. Methods include certificate-based authentication, Kerberos authentication, clear-text passwords, digest authentication, smart cards, NTLM, RADIUS, and SSL.
- Design an authentication strategy for integration with other systems.

So why are we spending so much time talking about PKI? Well, it provides the framework of services, technology, protocols, and standards that gives you the ability to lay out a strong security system. The Windows 2000 Public Key Infrastructure includes Certificate Services for issuing and managing digital certificates and Microsoft CryptoAPI version 2 for secure cryptographic operations and private key management. The Public Key Infrastructure is fully integrated with the Active Directory directory services in Windows 2000, and with distributed security services. While PKI provides some of the building blocks that make up Windows 2000 security, certificate services are the core of PKI. So, we are going to start at the bottom of the food chain.

Active Directory and Certificate Services

Take a look at Figure 9.1. This shows the way that enterprise certificate services are integrated with Active Directory and with the entire distributed security services.

FIGURE 9.1 Diagram of Certificate Services in Windows 2000

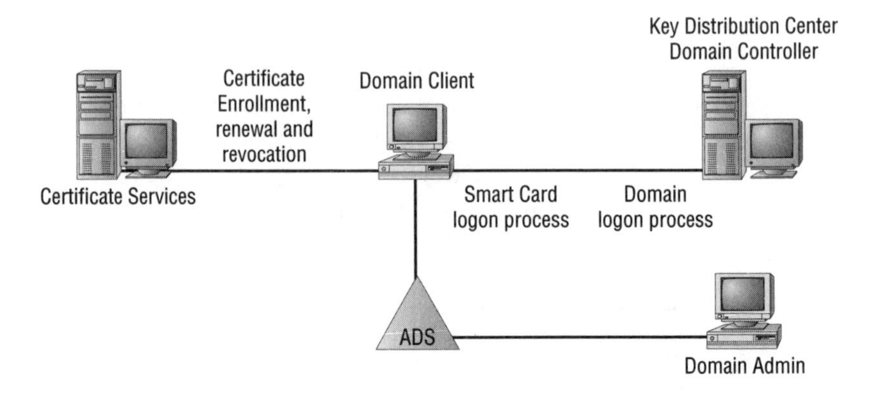

There was a time where if you wanted to use public key technologies, you could. All you had to do was turn to a company like VeriSign or Netscape and contract with them for the use of their certificates. Now, when you install Windows 2000 Certificate Services, you can create *enterprise certification authorities (CAs)*. These CAs are used for issuing and managing the digital certificates. The CAs get the information directly from Active Directory—things such as user account names, security group memberships, and certificate templates. Active Directory also contains information about each enterprise CA that is installed in the domain. Certificate requests are usually sent to enterprise CAs that process the requests to either deny or approve them. Issued certificates are distributed to Active Directory and to the requestor's computers. CAs also publish certificate revocation lists to Active Directory.

So in the graphic above, when the domain client authenticates into the network, it will receive a certificate from the certificate server. Once the system has the certificate, it can go on using the PKI to gain access to network resources. Basically, it works like this. The goal here is to have a public key certificate that can be used on our network, or on other network systems, that proves you are who you say you are. Well, before you can issue a public key certificate, you have to be able to trust the issuer. When you trust the CA, you are saying that you have faith in its security policies. You are basically saying that you trust the CA to determine whether a certificate request is authentic or not. Once the certificate is delivered, Active Directory supports mapping certificates to network user accounts and controlling access to network resources.

Types of Certificate Authorities

When you use Microsoft's Certificate Services, you can create four types of CAs. They are:

- *enterprise root certificate authorities*
- *enterprise subordinate certificate authorities*
- *stand-alone root certificate authorities*
- *stand-alone subordinate certificate authorities*

Enterprise Root Certificate Authorities

This is usually the top-level certificate authority in your PKI. It demands the services of Active Directory in order to verify a certificate requestor's identity. Because the *enterprise root CA* is the top level, it signs its own CA certificate. Once it has signed off on itself, it then publishes that certificate to the Trusted Root Certification Authorities store on every server and workstation in the Windows 2000 domain.

An enterprise root CA uses certificates that are based on certificate templates. These templates ease the process of issuing and requesting certificates for common purposes, including things like code signing, smart card logon, and Internet Protocol Security (IPSec). The enterprise root certificate authority can verify user credentials during certificate enrollment. An Access Control List (ACL) secures each template and the ACL is evaluated to determine whether or not the user requesting the certificate is authorized to receive it.

An enterprise CA issues only the certificate types that are specified by its certificate issuing policy. By default, Windows 2000 enterprise CAs are installed so that they are ready to issue several types of certificates.

You can modify the default configuration by using the Certification Authority console in MMC to specify the types of certificates that are to be issued by each CA.

Enterprise Subordinate Certificate Authorities

Now, an enterprise root certificate authority is an interesting thing. It can be used for issuing certificates directly to end users. A more efficient use of the process, however, is to have the enterprise root certificate authority certify one or more enterprise subordinate CAs. An enterprise subordinate CA will then issue certificates directly to users. These certificates are then used to support services like smart card logons, IPSec, and encrypting the file system. The enterprise subordinate CA also uses certificate templates, so the process of issuing and requesting certificates is simplified. The enterprise subordinate CA must get its certificate from another CA.

Stand-Alone Root Certificate Authorities

The stand-alone root certificate authority is similar to the enterprise root CA. Both are usually the top-level CA in your PKI, but the stand-alone root certificate does not require the Active Directory or membership in a Windows 2000 domain. If a stand-alone root CA is trusted, an administrator must explicitly publish its certificate to a domain member's trusted root certificate authorities store. Any other requests that are sent to the stand-alone root CA are automatically set to a pending status. To fulfill a certificate request, an administrator has to intervene and verify the identity of the requesting entity. As the name implies, a stand-alone root certificate authority has no way to verify a requester's credentials itself.

Stand-alone CAs do not use certificate templates. Therefore, certificate requests to them must include all of the information that is necessary to define the type of certificate that is to be issued. When Windows 2000 services submit certificate requests to stand-alone CAs, the requests include the information that is necessary to define the type of certificate that is being requested. You can use the Web Enrollment Support pages for stand-alone CAs to submit certificate requests to stand-alone CAs for a variety of types of certificates.

Stand-Alone Subordinate Certificate Authorities

The stand-alone root certificate authority is capable of issuing certificates directly to users, but usually the hierarchies are designed so that it will certify one or more stand-alone subordinate CAs. Just like the enterprise subordinate CA, the stand-alone subordinate CA typically is configured to issue certificates directly to users. To issue these certificates, it does not need to be a member of a Windows 2000 domain, or to have access to Active Directory. Like an enterprise subordinate CA, a stand-alone subordinate CA must obtain its CA certificate from another CA. Certificate templates, which simplify the certificate enrollment process, are not supported.

Certification Authority Trust Model

As you may have noticed, in both the enterprise and the stand-alone model, there are root CAs and subordinate CAs. That implies that there is some sort of hierarchy built into the Windows 2000 infrastructure. Windows 2000 supports a hierarchical CA trust model and makes use of *certificate trust lists (CTLs)*.

How does this work? Well, to control what certificates are trusted in the enterprise, you can deploy Windows 2000 Certificate Services to create CA trust hierarchies. Then you can create CTLs.

The Hierarchies

The marketing folk say that the Windows 2000 Public Key Infrastructure supports a hierarchical CA trust model, called the *certification hierarchy,* to provide scalability, ease of administration, and compatibility with a growing number of commercial third-party CA services and public key–aware products. If you are like me, you are not sure you care *why* they included, you just want to know how to make the best use of it.

If you are operating in a very small network, your certification hierarchy may consist of a single CA. If you are working in a larger enterprise network, the hierarchy will usually contain multiple CAs that have clearly defined parent-child relationships. Take a look at Figure 9.2 and you can see this demonstrated.

FIGURE 9.2 Certification hierarchies

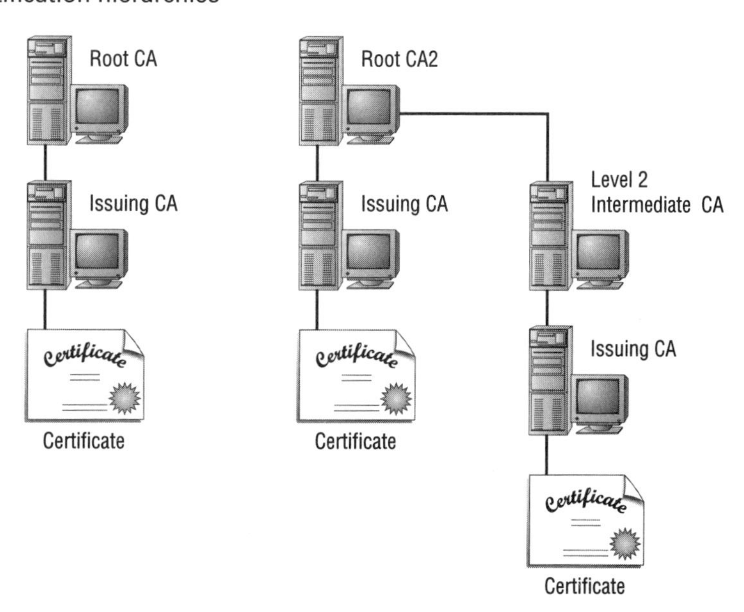

As you can see, the self-certified root CA will certify the subordinate or issuing CA. This can also be referred to as a child CA. The child is certified once the parent CA issues and signs the subordinate CA certificate. A subordinate CA can be either an intermediate or an issuing CA. An *intermediate CA* issues certificates only to subordinate CAs. An *issuing CA* issues certificates to users, computers, or services.

There is no restriction with regard to how deep the certification hierarchy can be. However, for many organizations, a three-level certification hierarchy (root CA, intermediate CA, and issuing CA) meets most needs.

What is the benefit of using a certificate services hierarchy? Now there is single point of enterprise-level control and management of certificates. For example, if an issuing CA is compromised somehow, the root CA can revoke its certificate. Revoking the subordinate CA's certificate voids each certificate that has been issued by the subordinate. Every other certificate, however, is unaffected.

If you are going to be employing the Microsoft Certificate Services, you should make sure to establish strict, comprehensive standards for public key certificate use and management. Be sure that you define what type of root CA suits your requirements. If you are looking for a tight integration into Active Directory, the enterprise root CA is the one to use. If you are working in a heterogeneous environment, a stand-alone root CA can provide comparable services without any dependence on Windows 2000 domains or Active Directory.

Certificate Best Practices

After you have made the decision as to which root CA you are going to employ, you should determine what each of the other CA's functions will be. This should include the primary role of the CA, the type of certificates the CA can issue, and the individuals who can receive each certificate type. If you are working in a small organization, the root level CA may do it all. In a large organization, you will have a number of CAs and each will have a defined function. For example, one CA might be responsible for smart card logon, while another might work with IP Security, code signing, or other types of services.

Once you have the roles defined, it is important to establish standards for certificate revocation and renewal. The certificate revocation standard has to define procedures to revoke certificates that are inappropriately used, or that have simply expired. This can include establishing the *certification revocation list (CRL)* and CRL publishing standards.

The standards for renewal should cover whether or not to renew certificates at all. If you do renew them, you should specify which certificate types are safe for renewal. Finally, you establish when it is appropriate to renew each type of certificate.

Certificate Validation Process

Certificates are tricky things. Because these certificates can be used to validate users from other networks, the operating system has be really sure the certificate is valid before it can trust it. With Windows 2000, that means performing a check to ensure that certificates are valid and that they have a valid certification path. Figure 9.3 shows in flowchart form the way Windows checks the certificate.

The fact that certificates need to be checked indicates they can also be invalid. These certificates are deemed to be invalid or are not trusted for a variety of reasons, including the following:

- The start and/or the expiration dates have expired.
- The certificate format does not conform to the X.509 version 3 standard for digital certificates.
- The information contained in the certificate fields is improper or it is not complete.
- In some cases, the certificate's digital thumbprint and signature may fail the integrity check. This indicates that the certificate may have been tampered with or it has been corrupted.
- The certificate, for whatever reason, has been listed as revoked in a published certificate revocation list.
- The issuing CA is not in either a trusted certification hierarchy or a CTL.
- The root CA for the certification path is not in the trusted root certification authorities store.
- The certificate is invalid because it is not permitted for the intended use as specified in a CTL.

FIGURE 9.3 Certificate validation process

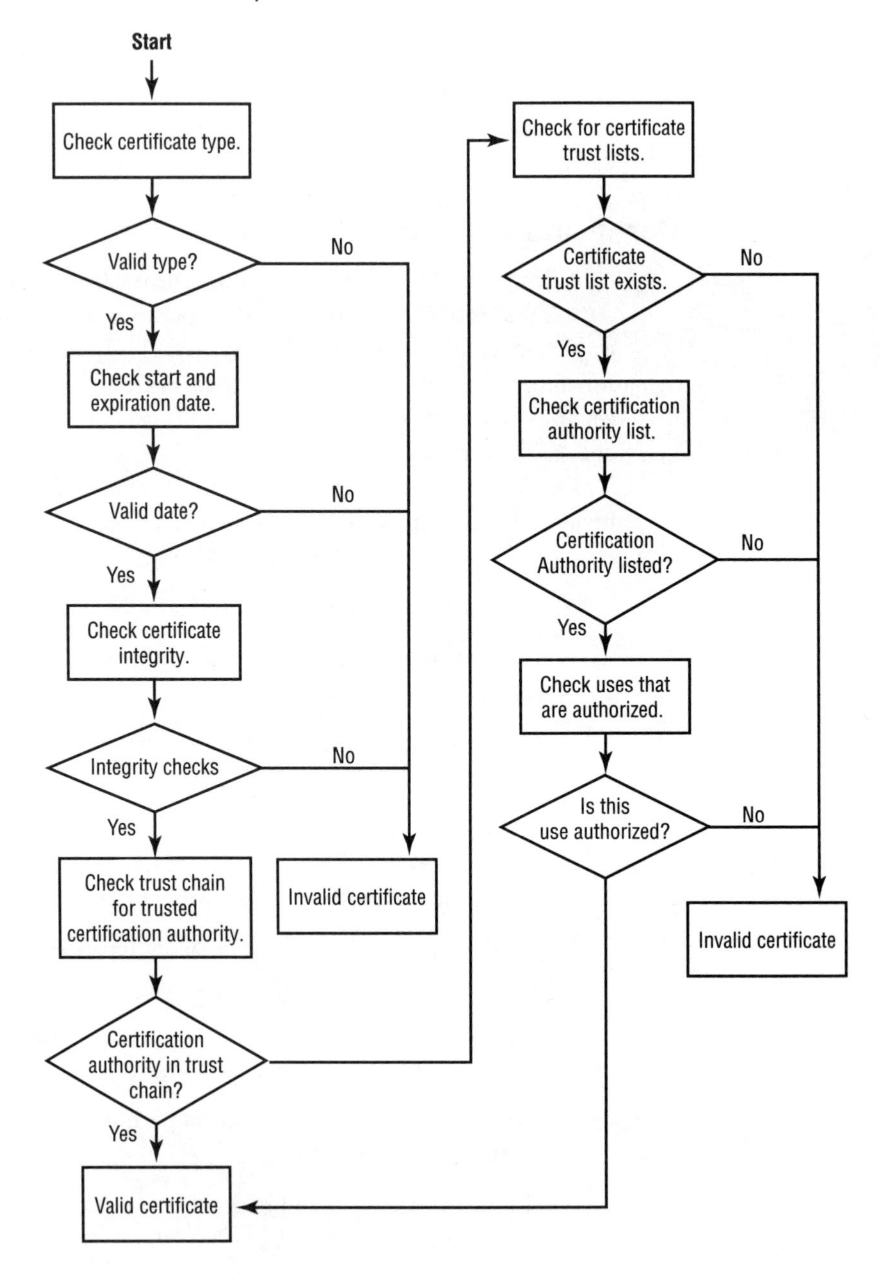

Certificate Types

Earlier in the chapter, we briefly discussed the fact that there could be different types of certificates, but we didn't take the time to explore those types. Table 9.1 outlines the types of certificates and the roles they fulfill.

TABLE 9.1 Types of Certificates

Certificate Type	The Role of the Issued Certificate
Administrator	The administrator certificate is used for authenticating clients and for the encrypted file system (EFS), secure mail, for certificate trust list (CTL) signing, and finally for code signing.
Authenticated session	The authenticated session certificate is used to authenticate clients.
Basic EFS	The basic EFS certificate is used for EFS operations.
CEP encryption (offline request)	The CEP encryption certificate is used to allow Cisco Systems routers to obtain IPSec authentication certificates from a Windows 2000 CA.
Code signing	The code signing certificate is used in code signing operations.
Computer	The computer certificate is used to authenticate clients and servers.
Domain controller	The domain controller certificate is used for authenticating domain controllers. When an enterprise CA is installed, this certificate type is installed automatically on domain controllers so that public key operations are supported. These are required when domain controllers are supporting Certificate Services.

TABLE 9.1 Types of Certificates *(continued)*

Certificate Type	The Role of the Issued Certificate
EFS Recovery Agent	The EFS recovery agent certificate is used for EFS encrypted-data recovery operations.
Enrollment agent	The enrollment agent certificate is used for authenticating administrators that are requesting certificates for smart card users.
Enrollment agent (computer)	The enrollment age certificate is used by authenticating services that request certificates on behalf of other computers.
Exchange enrollment agent (offline request)	The Exchange enrollment agent certificate is used for authenticating Microsoft Exchange Server administrators who are requesting certificates for secure mail users.
Exchange signature only (offline request)	The Exchange signature only certificate is used by Exchange Server for client authentication and secure mail. This certificate is used for signing only.
Exchange user (offline request)	The exchange user certificate is used by Exchange Server to authenticate clients and for secure mail. It is used for both signing and confidentiality of mail.
IPSec	The IPSec certificate is used for IPSec authentication.
IPSec (offline request)	The IPSec offline request certificate is also used for IPSec authentication.
Root certification authority	As its name implies, the root certification authority is used for root CA installation operations. It is important to note that this certificate template cannot be issued from a CA and it is only used when installing root CAs.

TABLE 9.1 Types of Certificates *(continued)*

Certificate Type	The Role of the Issued Certificate
Router (offline request)	The router certificate is used for authentication of routers.
Smart card logon	The smart card logon certificate is used for client authentication and it is also used when logging on with a smart card.
Smart card user	The smart card user certificate is used for client authentication; it is also used for secure mail, and it is used when logging on with a smart card.
Subordinate certification authority (offline request)	The subordinate certificate authority is used to issue certificates to be used by subordinate CAs.
Trust list signing	The trust list signing certificate is used to sign CTLs.
User	The user certificates are used for client authentication, EFS, and secure mail. With secure mail, these certificates are used for both signing and confidentiality of the mail.
User signature only	The user signature only certificates are used for client authentication and are used for secure mail. As the name implies, they are used for signing purposes only.
Web server (offline request)	The Web server certificates are used for authentication to a Web server.

There are several different types of certificate templates that are provided by default to handle online or offline requests. The Online certificate templates are designed to be used to give certificates to requestors that currently have Windows 2000 accounts. These accounts must support getting the certificates directly from an enterprise CA. There are other certificate templates that work with offline requests. These are used to give certificates to requestors that do not currently have a Windows 2000 account or that have an account that does not support getting certificates directly from an enterprise CA.

For example, if a user that had a Windows 2000 user account needed a certificate, the certificate would be issued using the identification information obtained from the Windows 2000 user account. If the request, on the other hand, is offline, then the request has to include things like the requestor's identification information.

Certificate Database

Are some of you out there grumbling about where this information is stored? You are probably thinking that this is just another darn database to take care of. You are right. As a matter of fact, the certificate database is responsible for recording all certificate transactions. The database is tasked with tracking all of the certificate requests and it must record whether the requests were granted or denied. The database also records information about the issued certificate. This includes things like the serial number and the expiration date. The database can provide a complete audit trail for each certificate from the time it was requested to the time it expired. The database also flags and tracks certificates that have been revoked by CA administrators.

Just like your other transactional databases, the certificate database includes certificate log files, which record all certificate transactions. By default, the certificate database and the certificate log files are installed at `<Drive:>\WINNT\System32\CertLog`.

At the time you install the CA, you have the option of choosing another location to install either the database or the logs, including storing the database and log files separately on different drives.

Administering the CA

The Certification Authority console is an MMC snap-in. You can use the snap-in to perform these administrative tasks on multiple CAs:

- Start and stop the CA
- Back up and restore the CA
- Change the exit and policy modules

- View the CA certificate
- Install or reinstall a CA certificate for the CA
- Set security permissions and delegate administrative control for the CA
- Revoke the certificates
- View or modify the certificate revocation list (CRL) distribution points
- Schedule and publish CRLs
- Configure the types of certificates that are to be issued by the CA
- View the information about certificates that have been issued
- View the information about certificates that have been revoked
- View pending certificate requests
- Approve or deny pending certificate requests
- View failed certificate requests
- Renew the CA's certificate

Key Life

It has been mentioned several times in this chapter that certificates do expire, so they do have a *key life*. Like most things in computer communication, the different types of certificates have different times to live. Table 9.2 gives an example of the time to live of some of the certificates.

The certificate life cycle described in Table 9.2 is only an example. Your certificate life cycle will most likely be different in a variety of ways. Some of the ways can include things like the length of certificate lifetimes, key lengths, and key lifetimes.

TABLE 9.2 Certificate Life Spans

Purpose of Certificate	Certificate Life	Private Key Life
Stand-alone root CA (4,096-bit key)	20 years	This key should be renewed at least every 10 years to ensure that intermediate CA certificates can be issued with lifetimes of 10 years. This key should be renewed by using a new key at least every 20 years.
Stand-alone intermediate CA for all certificates except smart card certificates (3,072-bit key)	10 years	This key should be renewed at least every 5 years to ensure that child issuing CAs can be issued for a full 5 years. This key should be renewed by using a new key at least every 10 years.
Enterprise issuing CA for all certificates except smart card certificates (2,048-bit key)	5 years	This key should be renewed at least every 3 years to ensure that Web server certificates can be issued for a full 2 years. This key should be renewed by using a new key at least every 5 years.
Enterprise issuing CA 2 for smart card certificates (2,048-bit key)	5 years	This key should be renewed at least every 4 years to ensure that certificates can be issued for a full year. This key should be renewed by using a new key at least every 5 years.
Enterprise issuing CA 3 for all other certificates besides smart cards, secure mail, and secure browser certificates (2,048-bit key)	5 years	This key should be renewed at least every 4 years to ensure that certificates can be issued for a full year. This key should be renewed by using a new key at least every 5 years.

TABLE 9.2 Certificate Life Spans *(continued)*

Purpose of Certificate	Certificate Life	Private Key Life
Secure mail and secure browser certificates	2 years	This key should be renewed by using a new key at least every year.
Smart card certificates (1,024-bit key)	2 years	This key should be renewed by using a new key at least every year.
Administrator certificates (1,024-bit key)	2 years	This key should be renewed by using a new key at least every year.
Secure Web server certificates (1,024-bit key)	2 years	This key should be renewed by using a new key at least every year.
Business partners' users certificates for an extranet (512-bit key)	1 year	This key should be renewed by using a new key at least every six months.

If you paid particularly close attention to the table, you noticed that everything listed, except the Business Partners users certificates, would be issued by the Windows 2000 CAs. The partners' CAs are trusted in the extranet domain because of CTLs. In this case, stand-alone CAs are being used to manage the lifetimes of the CA where necessary. By renewing the certificates with new keys, the time the keys are used is limited, which reduces the risk of compromise.

The deeper the certification hierarchy, the shorter the certificate lifetimes become. Plan your certificate life cycles to avoid short certificate lifetimes and certificate renewal cycles.

Design Scenario: Certificate Fallout

When you come into the meeting, running just a little late as usual, you find that discussion is revolving around network bandwidth, again. As the conversation goes on, and on, and on, you begin to drift off, and then the topic turns to the ways the bandwidth is being used. As your network has grown and as the company has acquired different divisions, the PKI has never been changed or updated.

One of the suggestions that you can make is to create some subordinate certificate authorities in the outlying reaches of your company. Doing that, and limiting the amount of time that certificates can be valid, will help cut down on some of the bandwidth problems.

Kerberos Authentication

Kerberos v5 is not the newest thing to come along in authentication protocols, even though the people at Microsoft would like you to think that it is. Actually, Kerberos v5 has been used for years in the Unix world. With Windows 2000, however, Kerberos is the mainstay of the native mode implementation.

Why Use Kerberos Authentication?

Think about what the developers of Windows 2000 were trying to do. They were trying to come up with a true, open-platform, enterprise solution for a network operating system. When you start to analyze what that means, you come up with the fact that our forest should be able to work with other directory trees and even work with partners that may not be using Windows 2000. Therefore, there had to be some sort of security standard that could be implemented on the Windows 2000 side, and also implemented without too much of a problem on the partner side of the fence. The goal, again, was seamless access to resources across enterprise network boundaries.

So, now we come to security considerations. The old domain model wasn't going to cut it, so there had to be something else out there that was better. They came up with implementing the Kerberos protocol. Kerberos originated at Massachusetts Institute of Technology more than a decade ago. The first public release of the protocol was Kerberos version 4. Kerberos 4 was put under some wide industry scrutiny, and was found to be okay, but not great. At that time, it was kind of back to the drawing board where the authors reviewed the protocol, enhanced the protocol, and released Kerberos version 5. Kerberos 5 has not been standardized, yet it is on a standards track with the IETF. The implementation of the protocol in Windows 2000 closely follows the specification defined in Internet RFC 1510. In addition, the mechanism and format for passing security tokens in Kerberos messages follows the specification defined in Internet RFC 1964.

Besides using the basic Kerberos protocol, Windows 2000 implements extensions that allow initial authentication using public key certificates rather than conventional shared secret keys. This gives the flexibility to allow the protocol to support interactive logon with a smart card. The extensions for public key authentication are based on a draft specification submitted to the IETF working group by a number of third parties with interests in public key technology.

So, why switch to Kerberos? Well, it is more flexible and efficient than NTLM, and more secure. The benefits gained by using Kerberos authentication are laid out in Table 9.3

TABLE 9.3 Benefits of Kerberos v5

Benefit	Explanation
Faster connections with Kerberos	Without Kerberos, an application server must connect to a domain controller in order to authenticate each client. With Kerberos, the server can authenticate the client by examining credentials presented by the client. Clients can obtain credentials for a particular server once and reuse them throughout an entire network logon session.
Mutual authentication	NTLM authentication was designed for a network environment in which servers were assumed to be genuine. The Kerberos protocol does not make that assumption. With Kerberos, parties at both ends of a network connection can know that the party on the other end is who the party claims to be.

TABLE 9.3 Benefits of Kerberos v5 *(continued)*

Benefit	Explanation
Delegated authentication	When certain Windows services run, they impersonate a client when it is accessing resources. In many cases, a service can complete its work for the client by just accessing the resources on the local computer. Both NTLM and Kerberos can provide the information that a service needs to impersonate its client locally. However, things change when another computer is involved. Some distributed applications are designed so that the front-end service must impersonate clients when connecting to back-end services on other computers. In this case, the Kerberos protocol has a proxy mechanism that allows a service to impersonate its client when connecting to other services. That type of functionality is not available with NTLM.
Simplified trust management	In Windows 2000, mutual authentication with the Kerberos protocol is benefited by the fact that the trust between the security authorities is, by default, two-way and transitive. Networks with multiple domains no longer require a complex web of explicit trust relationships. Instead, the many domains of a large network can be organized in a tree of transitive mutual trust. Credentials issued by the security authority for any domain are accepted everywhere in the tree. This is also the case if more than one tree is involved; in that case, credentials issued by a domain in any tree are accepted throughout the forest.

How Does the Kerberos Protocol Work?

The Kerberos authentication protocol provides a mechanism for mutual authentication between a client and a server, or between one server and another, before a network connection is opened between them. The protocol assumes that initial transactions between clients and servers take place on an open network where most computers are not physically secure, and packets traveling along the wire can be monitored and modified at will. The assumed environment, in other words, is very much like today's Internet, where an attacker can easily pose as either a client or a server, and can readily eavesdrop on or tamper with communications between legitimate clients and servers.

Kerberos Basics

The Kerberos protocol works with an authentication technique that involves *shared secrets*. The basic idea here is really quite simple: If a secret is known by only two people, then either person can verify the identity of the other by confirming that the other person knows the secret. This is kind of a cyber take-off on the secret handshake we used to use as kids.

Let's look at it this way. Suppose you have some information to transmit to another company. Now this is super secret stuff, so you want to make sure that the information only goes to the recipient and the recipient wants to make sure the information comes from you. So, the two of you decide to take a look at the situation. You decide that the best way of making sure that all communication between the two of you is secure is to include a password in the message. So you mutually agree on the password of TopSeCRet! In this case, if you send a message and the password is included in the message, the recipient will know the message comes from you and all will be well. Except. What happens if someone sniffs the network in hopes of spotting a password? In that case, someone may spot that and recognize it as a password. So now the problem becomes how to make sure the message is really from your friend, when your friend has to send you the password without revealing it. Here, Kerberos would solve the problem with secret key cryptography.

With secret key cryptography, rather than sharing a password, you would share a key, and this key would verify one another's identity. For this key thing to work, the single key, or *authenticator*, must be capable of both encryption and decryption. In other words, it must be symmetric. One party proves knowledge of the key by encrypting data, the other by decrypting it. It is kind of like the decoder rings we used to play with when we were just kids, only this time it is on steroids!

Key Distribution

You have probably spotted the potential problem already. Where in the world does the original key come from, and how do both parties get a copy? If we are talking about people, we can just stop down at the local hardware store and get some keys made up. That method has some inherent flaws if we are dealing with a client program that is running on a workstation and a service that is running on a network server. There is also the further problem that the client workstation will want to talk to many servers and will need keys for each of them. Likewise, the service will talk to many clients and will need keys for each of them as well. If each client needs to have a key for every service, and each service needs one for every client, key distribution could quickly become a tough problem to solve. And the need to store and protect so many keys on so many computers would present an enormous security risk.

Kerberos has three parts: a client, a server, and a trusted third party to mediate between them. The trusted intermediary in the protocol is known as the *Key Distribution Center (KDC)*. The KDC is a lot like the CA described earlier in the chapter. It is a service that runs on a physically secure server. It maintains a database with account information for all security principals in its *realm*, which is the Kerberos equivalent of a Windows 2000 domain. The KDC's job is to store a cryptographic key known only to the security principal (the client) and the KDC. This key is used in exchanges between the security principal and the KDC and is known as a *long-term key*. In most implementations of the protocol, it is derived from a user's logon password.

So, now you have a client that wants to talk to a server. To kick off the process, the client asks the KDC, and the KDC distributes a unique, short-term *session key* for the two parties to use while they authenticate each other. The server's copy of the session key is encrypted in the server's long-term key. The client's copy of the session key is encrypted in the client's long-term key. Take a look at Figure 9.4.

FIGURE 9.4 Kerberos authentication process

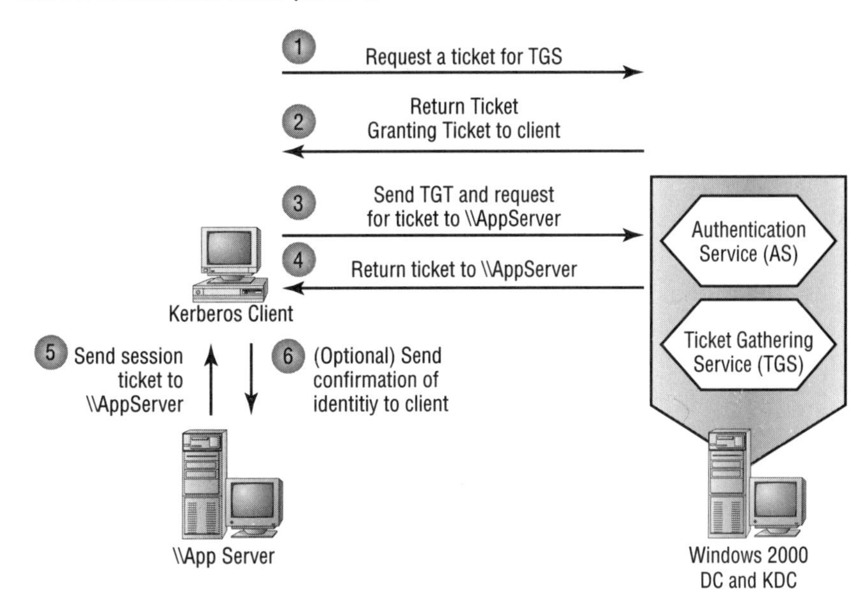

So, here is the way it works. The client asks the KDC for a ticket, making use of the *Authentication Service (AS)*. The AS sends a ticket back to the client, and the client uses this ticket, called the ticket granting ticket or TGT, to ask the KDC for a ticket to use the server—in this case `\\AppServer`. The request is handled by the *Ticket-Granting Service (TGS)* and the TGS returns a ticket to the Kerberos client. At that point the client can present the ticket to the server, and the server can optionally send a confirmation back with its identity to the client.

I don't know about you, but when I first looked at this scenario, it looked like the KDC was working too hard. Why the double effort? Why not just have the AS simply issue a ticket for the target server? Well, that would work, but the user would have to issue a password for every new server/service connection. Issuing the TGT with a very short lifespan gives users a valid ticket for the TGS, which issues the target server tickets, and the user only has to enter a password at logon.

Another benefit gained by using session tickets is that the server does not have to store the session key that it uses in communicating with this client. It is the client's responsibility to hold a ticket for the server in its credentials cache and present the ticket each time it wants access to the server. Whenever the server receives a session ticket from a client, it can use its secret key to decrypt the ticket and extract the session key. When the server no longer needs the session key, it can discard it.

Finally, the client does not need to go back to the KDC each time it wants access to this particular server. Session tickets can be reused. As a precaution against the possibility that someone might steal a copy of a ticket, session tickets have an expiration time, specified by the KDC in the ticket's data structure. How long a ticket is valid depends on Kerberos policy for the domain. Typically, tickets are good for no longer than eight hours, about the length of a normal logon session. When the user logs off, the credentials cache is flushed and all session tickets—as well as all session keys—are destroyed.

Authentication across Domain Boundaries

This breaks down to the fact that the KDC provides two different types of services. The first is an authentication service whose job it is to issue Ticket Granting Tickets. Then there is the ticket-granting service. That service is the one that issues the session tickets. Because of this division, Kerberos can operate across domain boundaries. In other words, a client can get a TGT from the authentication service in one domain, and then take that TGT to get a session ticket from a ticket-granting service in another domain.

One of the advantages of being an MCT is that we sometimes get to sit in on beta exams for Microsoft. Now beta exams are wonderful things. Not only do you get a price break on exams, but you also get to see more than the usual number of questions. Why is this being brought up here?? Well, we both took the beta for the Active Directory Design exam and you would be surprised how the boundaries can be blurred between security and design. Not that we are suggesting that you consider this a hint.... We would never do that. You do have your highlighter out, don't you?

When it comes to seeing how cross-domain authentication works, there are basically two scenarios. One scenario has two domains and the other has more than two. Figure 9.5 shows two domains.

FIGURE 9.5 Cross-domain Kerberos authentication

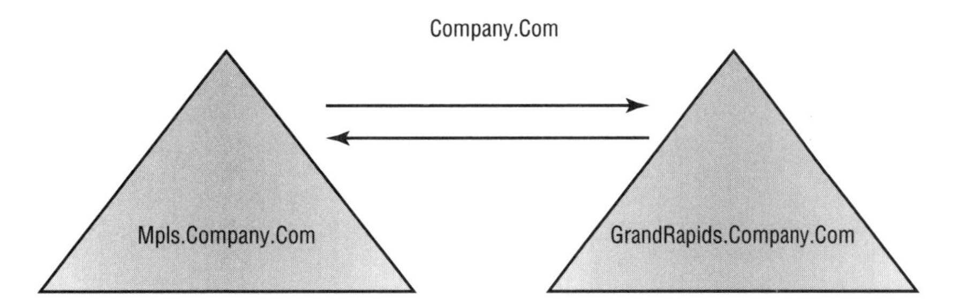

Let's start with the simplest case: a network with only two domains, `Mpls.Company.Com` and `GrandRapids.Company.Com`. Let's say that the administrators of these domains are members of the same organization. Now, if they want to allow authentication across domain boundaries, they can accomplish this simply by sharing an inter-domain key. Now that sounds like some top-secret, high-level security kind of stuff, but it's not. In Windows 2000, this happens automatically when two domains establish a trust relationship. So, once this trust relationship is accomplished, the ticket-granting service of each domain is registered as a security principal with the other domain's KDC. Because of this, the ticket-granting service in each domain can treat the ticket-granting service in the other domain as just another service—something for which properly authenticated clients can request and receive session tickets.

So, let's assume that a user with an account in `Mpls` wants access to a server with an account in `GrandRapids`. If this were the case, the Kerberos client on the user's workstation would send a request for a session ticket to the ticket-granting service in `Mpls`. The ticket-granting service in `Mpls` sees that the server this user wants to access is not a security principal in its domain. The server then replies by sending the client a *referral ticket*. The referral ticket is just a TGT that has been encrypted with the inter-domain key that the KDC in `Mpls` has shared with the KDC in `GrandRapids`. The requesting client then uses that referral ticket to prepare a second request for a session ticket. This is necessary because the request will be going to the ticket-granting service in the remote server's account domain of `GrandRapids`. The ticket-granting service in GrandRapids uses its copy of the inter-domain key to decrypt the referral ticket. If decryption is successful, it sends the client a session ticket to the desired server in its domain. Voila, someone from Minneapolis can now access a resource in Grand Rapids, Michigan.

What if your network looks like the diagram in Figure 9.6?

FIGURE 9.6 Kerberos authentication with more than two domains

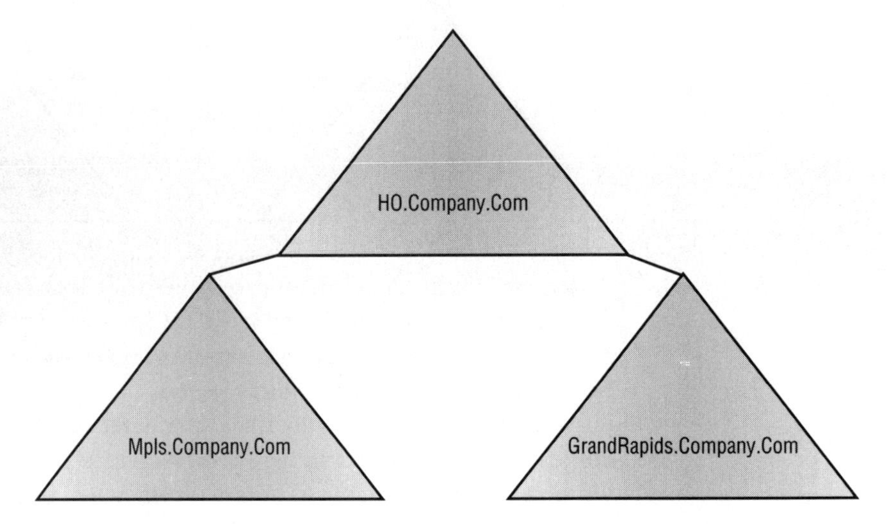

Obviously, the referral process could be much more complicated on networks with more than two domains. The Kerberos protocol solves the problem by making direct links unnecessary. A client in one domain can get a ticket to a server in another domain by traveling a referral path through one or more intermediate domains.

Let's take an example of a network with three domains: Mpls, GrandRapids, and HO. The KDC in Mpls does not share an inter-domain key with the KDC in GrandRapids, but both Mpls and GrandRapids do share inter-domain keys with HO. This is your basic star configuration. Now when a user with an account in Mpls wants access to a server with an account in GrandRapids, the referral path begins at the KDC for the user's account domain, Mpls. It has to pass through an intermediate domain, HO, and then ends up at the KDC for the server's account domain, GrandRapids. The client must send its request for a session ticket three times, to three different KDCs. Here is the way it breaks down:

1. The client asks the KDC in `Mpls` to give it a ticket to the server in `GrandRapids`.

   The KDC for `Mpls` sends the client a referral ticket to the KDC for `HO`. This ticket is encrypted in the inter-domain key `Mpls` shares with `HO`.

2. The client then asks the KDC for `HO` to give it a ticket to the server in `GrandRapids`.

   The KDC for `HO` sends the client a referral ticket to the KDC for `GrandRapids`. This ticket is encrypted in the inter-domain key `HO` shares with `GrandRapids`.

3. The client finally asks the KDC for `GrandRapids` to give it a ticket to the server in `GrandRapids`.

   The KDC for `GrandRapids` finally sends back a ticket for the server.

Now that you know how it works, wouldn't you like to know how to make it work? It all starts with the KDC.

Defining the Key Distribution Center

Windows 2000 implements the *Key Distribution Center* (KDC) as a domain service. It uses the domain's Active Directory as its account database and gets some information about users from the Global Catalog.

As shown in the graphics above, implementing the Kerberos protocol requires a KDC. The KDC is really a single process that provides two services:

Authentication Service (AS) This service issues *ticket-granting tickets (TGTs)* good for admission to the ticket-granting service in its domain. Before network clients can get tickets for services, they must get an initial TGT from the authentication service in the user's account domain.

Ticket-Granting Service (TGS) This service issues tickets good for admission to other services in its domain or to the ticket-granting service of a trusted domain. When clients want access to a service, they must contact the ticket-granting service in the service's account domain, present a

TGT, and ask for a ticket. If the client does not have a TGT good for admission to that ticket-granting service, it must get one through a referral process that begins at the ticket-granting service in the user's account domain and ends at the ticket-granting service in the service's account domain.

Now, here is the good part. Kerberos is already working, so there isn't an extra service to install. As a matter of fact, the KDC is located on every domain controller, as is the Active Directory service. The domain controller's Local Security Authority (LSA) starts both of these services automatically and they run in the process space of the LSA. Neither service can be stopped. Windows 2000 ensures availability of these services by allowing each domain to have several domain controllers, all peers. Any domain controller can accept authentication requests and ticket-granting requests addressed to the domain's KDC.

Just so you know, the security principal name used by the KDC for a Windows 2000 domain is *krbtgt*. This isn't some name that a Microsoft programmer dreamt up after one too many cans of Mountain Dew. It is specified by RFC 1510. An account for this security principal is created automatically when a new domain is created. The account cannot be deleted, nor can the name be changed. A password is assigned to the account automatically and is changed on a regular schedule, as are the passwords assigned to domain trust accounts. The password for the KDC's account is used to derive a secret key for encrypting and decrypting the TGTs that it issues. The password for a domain trust account is used to derive an inter-realm key for encrypting referral tickets.

All instances of the KDC within a domain use the domain account for the security principal krbtgt. Clients address messages to a domain's KDC by including the service principal name, *krbtgt*, and the name of the domain. Both items of information are also used in tickets to identify the issuing authority.

If you are one of those people who really love to drill down into this stuff, you can get more information on name forms and addressing conventions by reading RFC 1510.

Account Database

The next thing that is required for Kerberos to operate is somewhere to store its information. That would be the account database. With Windows 2000, the integration with ADS provides that data store. The KDC can get all the information it needs about each of the security principals from the Active Directory. Each security principal is in the Active Directory as an account object. The encryption key is then used to communicate with a user, with a computer, or with a service. It is stored as an attribute of that security principal's account object.

As you know from your previous studies, only domain controllers can be Active Directory servers. Each domain controller keeps a writable copy of the directory. That means that accounts can be created, passwords reset, and group membership modified at any domain controller. The changes that are made to one replica of the directory are automatically propagated to all other replicas. It is important to note that Windows 2000 does not implement the Kerberos replication protocol. Instead, it replicates the information store for Active Directory using a proprietary multimaster replication protocol over a secure channel between replication partners.

The physical storage of all account data is managed by the *Directory System Agent (DSA)*. The DSA is a protected process that is integrated with the LSA on the domain controller. That way, clients of the directory service are never given direct access to the data store. Any client that wants access to directory information must use one of the supported DSA Active Directory Service Interfaces (ADSI) to connect to the DSA and then search for, read, and write directory objects and their attributes.

This all happens transparently to the end user. I can just imagine some administrative assistant calling, wondering why they can't access the ADSI.

Remember that Kerberos is not the only security protocol at work here. For example, requests to access an object or attribute in the directory are subject to validation by Windows 2000 access control mechanisms. Just like files and folder objects in the Windows NT File System (NTFS), objects in Active Directory are protected by Access Control Lists (ACLs) that specify who can access the object and in what way. Unlike files and folders, however, Active Directory objects have an ACL for each of their attributes. Thus attributes for sensitive account information can be protected by more restrictive permissions than those granted for other attributes of the account.

How is the password handled? This, of course, could be considered some of the most sensitive information about an account. The account object's password attribute stores the encryption key that is derived from the password. It does not store the password itself. Having this key, however, is just as useful to an intruder. To protect against compromise, access to the account object's password attribute is given only to the account holder. That means just what it says—no one else has access, not even administrators. Only processes that come complete with the Trusted Computer Base privilege are allowed to read or change password information.

Now, if someone were really determined to gain access to the network, they could steal a backup tape and try to get the password information that way. To put a stop to an offline attack by someone with access to a domain controller's backup tape, an account object's password attribute is protected by a second encryption using a *system key*. This encryption key can be stored on removable media with some of the other keys we have talked about in this chapter, so that it can be safeguarded separately. Administrators are given the option to choose where the system key is stored and which of several algorithms is used to encrypt password attributes.

Kerberos Policy

Is there any way to control what Kerberos does and how it does it? Well, in Windows 2000, the Kerberos policy is defined at the domain level and implemented by the domain's KDC. Kerberos policy is stored in Active Directory as a subset of the attributes of domain security policy. By default, policy options can be set only by members of the Domain Administrators group.

The policies that can be defined for Kerberos are shown in Table 9.4.

TABLE 9.4 Kerberos Policies

Kerberos Policy	What It Means
Maximum user ticket lifetime	The *user ticket* is a ticket-granting ticket (TGT). The lifetime settings are measured in hours and the default is 10 hours.
Maximum lifetime that a user ticket can be renewed	This setting is measured in days. The default is set for 7 days.

TABLE 9.4 Kerberos Policies *(continued)*

Kerberos Policy	What It Means
Maximum service ticket lifetime	A *service ticket* is a session ticket. These settings are measured in minutes. The setting has to be greater than 10 minutes and it also has to be less than the setting for *Maximum user ticket lifetime*. The default is set to 10 hours, or 600 minutes.
Maximum tolerance for synchronization of computer clocks	Again, the settings are measured in minutes. The default is 5 minutes.
Enforce user logon restrictions	By default, this option in enabled, which means the KDC validates every request for a session ticket by examining user rights policy on the target computer to verify that the user has the right either to *Log on locally* or to *Access this computer from network*. The only reason the verification is optional is because the extra step takes time and may slow network access to services.

Delegation of Authentication

Now, the default Kerberos policy for a domain permits delegated authentication by allowing forwardable tickets. That aspect of policy need not apply to all users or all computers. There may be people in the organization who you simply do not want to have access to resources in other areas. If that is the case, you can set an attribute of an individual user account to disable forwarding of that user's credentials by any server. An attribute of an individual computer's account can be set to disable forwarding of credentials from any user. In both cases, delegation can be disabled by creating a policy to apply to all users or all computers in an organizational unit within the domain.

Kerberos Security Support Provider

When the Kerberos authentication protocol is implemented, it is implemented as a *security support provider (SSP)*. This is a dynamic-link library (DLL) supplied with the operating system. Windows 2000 also includes an SSP for NTLM authentication to maintain backward compatibility with NT 4 during the upgrade. By default, both are loaded by the LSA on a Windows 2000 computer when the system boots. Either SSP may be used to authenticate network logons and client/server connections. Which one is used depends on the capabilities of the computer on the other side of the connection. The Kerberos SSP is always the first choice.

After the LSA establishes a security context for a user, another instance of the Kerberos SSP may be needed. In this case, a process running in the user's security context to support the signing and sealing of messages loads it.

So how is Kerberos actually used? Here are some of the ways in which the Kerberos protocol can be used for authentication:

- Authentication for intranet authentication to Internet Information Server
- Authentication for print spooler services
- Authentication for LDAP queries to Active Directory
- Authentication for distributed file system (dfs) management and referrals
- Authentication for certificate requests to the Microsoft Certificate Server for domain users and computers
- Authentication for IPSec host-to-host security authority authentication
- Authentication for reservation requests for network Quality of Service
- Authentication for remote server or workstation management using authenticated RPC

Kerberos is a protocol for authentication, not authorization. It verifies that security principals *are* who they say they are. It does not determine which files and other objects security principals may access, or how they may access them. These decisions are left to whatever access control mechanism may be available on the system. The protocol assists by providing a field for authorization data in Kerberos tickets, but it does not specify the form of the data or how servers should use it.

How the KDC Prepares Authorization Data

It is up to the KDC to provide the means necessary for a user to be authenticated to a resource. But that doesn't mean that the user is authorized to use the resource. Surely, this communication process must include some information for authorization. It does. It works this way. When Kerberos is used for authentication, a list of SIDs identifying a security principal and the principal's group membership is transported to the local computer as part of the session ticket. The authorization data is gathered in two separate steps. The first step takes place when the KDC in a Windows 2000 domain prepares a TGT. The second step is accomplished when the KDC prepares a session ticket for a server in the domain.

So, when a user requests a TGT, the KDC in the user's account domain requests information from the domain's Active Directory. The user's account record includes an attribute for the user's SID as well as an attribute with SIDs for any domain security groups to which the user belongs. This is the list of SIDs that are returned to the KDC, and this list is placed in the TGT's authorization data field. In a multiple-domain environment, the KDC also queries the Global Catalog for any universal groups that include the user or one of the user's domain security groups. If any are found, their SIDs are added to the list in the TGT's authorization data field.

Now, when the user requests a session ticket for a server, the KDC in the server's domain copies the contents of the TGT's authorization data field to the session ticket's authorization data field. If the server's domain is different from the user's account domain, the KDC queries Active Directory in order to find out whether any security groups in the local domain include the user or one of the user's security groups. If any are found, their SIDs are added to the list in the session ticket's authorization data field.

How Services Use Authorization Data

In Windows 2000, services act in their own security contexts only when accessing resources on their own behalf. For the most part, this is just when they are doing their own housekeeping—you know, things like accessing configuration data stored in registry keys, binding to communications ports, and completing other tasks not related to work for a particular client. When a service does do something for a client, it impersonates the client, acting in the client's security context. This means that in addition to identifying clients, Windows 2000 services must also take on some of their characteristics.

When a service sets up housekeeping on a computer running Windows 2000, it starts by gaining access to its own credentials. This means it needs the secret key for the account under which the service runs. The service then binds to a communications port, for example, where it listens for messages from prospective clients.

When a client requests a connection and presents a session ticket, the service asks the Kerberos to verify the client's credentials, passing the client's session ticket along with a handle to the service's secret key. Kerberos verifies the ticket's authenticity, opens it, and passes the contents of the authorization data field to its parent process, the LSA. If the data includes a list of SIDs, the LSA uses them to build an access token representing the user on the local system. In addition, the LSA queries its own database to determine if the user or one of the user's security groups is a member of a security group created on the local system. If any are found, the LSA adds those SIDs to the access token. The LSA then confirms to the calling service that the client's identity has been authenticated, enclosing a reference to the client's access token.

Once confirmation has been received, the service completes its connection with the client and attaches the client's access token to an impersonation thread. When the impersonation thread needs access to an object, it presents the client's token. The operating system performs an access check by comparing SIDs in the token to SIDs in the object's ACL. If it finds a match, it checks to see that the entry in the ACL grants the level of access requested by the thread. If it does, the thread is allowed access. Otherwise, access is denied.

Design Scenario: Why Can't We Use It?

You have a customer who really wants to be able to provide Kerberos authentication across a multiple tree forest. But he also has a problem. He has heard about Kerberos from his Microsoft sales rep and this has become sort of a tech-weenie-wannabe mantra with him. He keeps asking if Kerberos has been configured yet, has Kerberos been configured yet... and you keep telling him *no*.

He finally get so frustrated with you that he calls your boss and begins to rant and rave. It seems that he is accusing you of not doing what he wants, when he wants, and how he wants. Now, this person has been before the boss already. As a matter of fact, there have been several meetings trying to decide if your company is going to fire him as a client, so the boss is very familiar with the network infrastructure. After the client slows down enough to pause for a breath, the boss asks about the Rapid City, South Dakota office. How is it doing? The client starts to warm up, because now he is talking about his business. After a while, he pauses for another breath, and your boss asks if he is ready to upgrade those five servers to Windows 2000 yet? The client says no, he can't do that just yet, because there is this legacy application that won't run on Windows 2000.

After the client gets those words out of his mouth, there is a pause, then a meek "oh." Problem solved. As soon as Rapid City is deployed to Windows 2000, Kerberos can be in place all over the network.

Clear-Text Passwords

Are they still around? My gosh, enough has been written about *clear-text passwords* to fill several books. Why in the world would anyone use a clear-text password? Well, why in the world would anyone use things like POP3, FTP, Telnet, HTTP, IMAP, or even SMTP? Nearly every nonproprietary IP service that is not specifically designed to provide authentication and encryption services transmits data as clear text.

So what is the problem? I mean really, what kind of person would sit around all day waiting for the stray password to cross on the wire? This is especially true for a password that only works for a POP3 account, or even something to do with FTP. Come on, how valuable can that be?

Think about it. Both Novell and Microsoft are harping on the concept of single sign-on, where one password will get you access to the entire network. Well, just in case you have been living in a cave for the last dozen years, single sign-on of sorts has been around for years. This is the type of single sign-on where a user has the same password for everything. Basically, that requires the end users to re-enter their password a dozen times, but never checks if the passwords for all the different applications are the same. So, people routinely use the same password for all their accounts. That means if you have one of their passwords, even if it is to an AOL account or an unsecured off-site POP3 account, you may have the keys to their kingdom.

Again, who would do this? Pretty much anyone with a PC *can* do this. Some people think packet sniffers cost thousands of dollars. They can, but some don't. If you are familiar with Linux or Unix, you know there are capable packet sniffers for an Ethernet network available for the price of a download. There are even sniffers that will run on Windows 9x or NT machines, and these you can use for two weeks for free.

Network analyzers or packet sniffers operate as passive devices, meaning that they do not need to transmit any data on the network in order to monitor traffic. There are some analyzers that do transmit traffic in an effort to find a management station, but it is not a requirement. In fact, an analyzer does not even need a valid network address. This means that a network analyzer can be monitoring your network and you would have no means of detecting its presence without tracing cables and counting switch and hub ports.

What does an analyzer do? Figure 9.7 shows a packet decode of an authentication session initializing.

FIGURE 9.7 The decoding of a packet that was part of an authentication session initializing

No.	Source	Destination	Layer	Summary	Error	Size	Interpacket Time	Absolute Time
3	0000E82F772A	0020AF247F25	tcp	Port:1067 ---> POP3 SYN		64	323 µs	8:58:38 PM
4	0020AF247F25	0000E82F772A	tcp	Port:POP3 ---> 1067 ACK SYN		64	203 µs	8:58:38 PM
5	0000E82F772A	0020AF247F25	tcp	Port:1067 ---> POP3 ACK		64	372 µs	8:58:38 PM
6	0020AF247F25	0000E82F772A	tcp	Port:POP3 ---> 1067 ACK PUSH		97	49 ms	8:58:38 PM
7	0000E82F772A	0020AF247F25	tcp	Port:1067 ---> POP3 ACK		64	192 ms	8:58:38 PM
8	0000E82F772A	0020AF247F25	tcp	Port:1067 ---> POP3 ACK PUSH		71	326 ms	8:58:38 PM
9	0020AF247F25	0000E82F772A	tcp	Port:POP3 ---> 1067 ACK PUSH		77	7 ms	8:58:38 PM
10	0000E82F772A	0020AF247F25	tcp	Port:1067 ---> POP3 ACK		64	162 ms	8:58:39 PM

```
 0: 00 20 AF 24 7F 25 00 00 E8 2F 77 2A 08 00 45 00 |. .$.%.../w*..E.
10: 00 35 87 05 40 00 80 06 EF CC C0 A8 01 3C C0 A8 |.5..@........<..
20: 01 64 04 2B 00 6E 00 BF 06 D2 00 0D 0D 56 50 18 |.d.+.n.......VP.
30: 22 11 DC 54 00 00 55 53 45 52 20 62 67 61 74 65 |"..T..USER bgate
40: 73 0D 0A                                        |s..
```

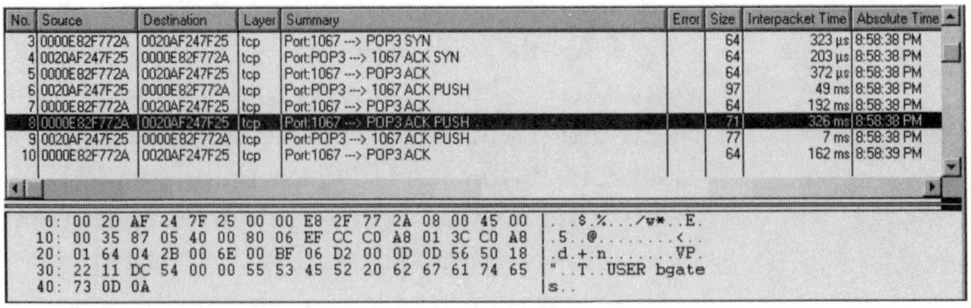

Once the session has been initialized, you can see in Figure 9.8 the POP3 server accepting the logon name.

FIGURE 9.8 POP3 server accepting logon name

No.	Source	Destination	Layer	Summary	Error	Size	Interpacket Time	Absolute Time
6	0020AF247F25	0000E82F772A	tcp	Port:POP3 ---> 1067 ACK PUSH		97	49 ms	8:58:38 PM
7	0000E82F772A	0020AF247F25	tcp	Port:1067 ---> POP3 ACK		64	192 ms	8:58:38 PM
8	0000E82F772A	0020AF247F25	tcp	Port:1067 ---> POP3 ACK PUSH		71	326 ms	8:58:38 PM
9	0020AF247F25	0000E82F772A	tcp	Port:POP3 ---> 1067 ACK PUSH		77	7 ms	8:58:38 PM
10	0000E82F772A	0020AF247F25	tcp	Port:1067 ---> POP3 ACK		64	162 ms	8:58:39 PM
11	0000E82F772A	0020AF247F25	tcp	Port:1067 ---> POP3 ACK PUSH		74	326 ms	8:58:39 PM
12	0020AF247F25	0000E82F772A	tcp	Port:POP3 ---> 1067 ACK PUSH		91	920 µs	8:58:39 PM
13	0000E82F772A	0020AF247F25	tcp	Port:1067 ---> POP3 ACK		64	172 ms	8:58:39 PM

```
 0: 00 00 E8 2F 77 2A 00 20 AF 24 7F 25 08 00 45 00 |.../w*. .$.%..E.
10: 00 3B 1C 00 40 00 20 06 BA CC C0 A8 01 64 C0 A8 |.;..@. ......d..
20: 01 3C 00 6E 04 2B 00 0D 0D 56 00 BF 06 DF 50 18 |.<.n.+...V....P.
30: 22 2B D3 06 00 00 2B 4F 4B 20 75 73 65 72 20 61 |"+....+OK user a
40: 63 63 65 70 74 65 64 0D 0A                      |ccepted..
```

Now that the logon name has been accepted, the next set of commands sent by the POP3 mail client is the PASS command. This is used to send the password string. Any text that follows the command is the password for the user attempting to authenticate into the system. If you look closely at Figure 9.9, you will see the password is plainly visible.

FIGURE 9.9 POP3 client sending the password

No.	Source	Destination	Layer	Summary	Error	Size	Interpacket Time	Absolute Time
6	0020AF247F25	0000E82F772A	tcp	Port:POP3 ---> 1067 ACK PUSH		97	49 ms	8:58:38 PM
7	0000E82F772A	0020AF247F25	tcp	Port:1067 ---> POP3 ACK		64	192 ms	8:58:38 PM
8	0000E82F772A	0020AF247F25	tcp	Port:1067 ---> POP3 ACK PUSH		71	326 ms	8:58:38 PM
9	0020AF247F25	0000E82F772A	tcp	Port:POP3 ---> 1067 ACK PUSH		77	7 ms	8:58:38 PM
10	0000E82F772A	0020AF247F25	tcp	Port:1067 ---> POP3 ACK		64	162 ms	8:58:39 PM
11	0000E82F772A	0020AF247F25	tcp	Port:1067 ---> POP3 ACK PUSH		74	326 ms	8:58:39 PM
12	0020AF247F25	0000E82F772A	tcp	Port:POP3 ---> 1067 ACK PUSH		91	920 µs	8:58:39 PM
13	0000E82F772A	0020AF247F25	tcp	Port:1067 ---> POP3 ACK		64	172 ms	8:58:39 PM

```
 0: 00 20 AF 24 7F 25 00 00 E8 2F 77 2A 08 00 45 00 |. .$.%.../w*..E.
10: 00 38 89 05 40 00 80 06 ED C9 C0 A8 01 3C C0 A8 |.8..@........<..
20: 01 64 04 2B 00 6E 00 BF 06 DF 00 0D 0D 69 50 18 |.d.+.n.......iP.
30: 21 FE B8 5E 00 00 50 41 53 53 20 6D 69 63 72 6F |!..^..PASS micro
40: 24 6F 66 74 0D 0A                               |$oft..
```

Finally we see the server's response to the authentication attempt. This is Figure 9.10. Notice the server has accepted the logon name and password combination. We now know that this is a valid authentication session and that we have a legitimate logon name and password combination.

FIGURE 9.10 The POP3 server accepting the authentication attempt

No.	Source	Destination	Layer	Summary	Error	Size	Interpacket Time	Absolute Time
6	0020AF247F25	0000E82F772A	tcp	Port:POP3 ---> 1067 ACK PUSH		97	49 ms	8:58:38 PM
7	0000E82F772A	0020AF247F25	tcp	Port:1067 ---> POP3 ACK		64	192 ms	8:58:38 PM
8	0000E82F772A	0020AF247F25	tcp	Port:1067 ---> POP3 ACK PUSH		71	326 ms	8:58:38 PM
9	0020AF247F25	0000E82F772A	tcp	Port:POP3 ---> 1067 ACK PUSH		77	7 ms	8:58:38 PM
10	0000E82F772A	0020AF247F25	tcp	Port:1067 ---> POP3 ACK		64	162 ms	8:58:39 PM
11	0000E82F772A	0020AF247F25	tcp	Port:1067 ---> POP3 ACK PUSH		74	326 ms	8:58:39 PM
12	0020AF247F25	0000E82F772A	tcp	Port:POP3 ---> 1067 ACK PUSH		91	920 µs	8:58:39 PM
13	0000E82F772A	0020AF247F25	tcp	Port:1067 ---> POP3 ACK		64	172 ms	8:58:39 PM

```
 0: 00 00 E8 2F 77 2A 00 20 AF 24 7F 25 08 00 45 00 |.../w*. .$.%..E.
10: 00 49 1D 00 40 00 20 06 B9 BE C0 A8 01 64 C0 A8 |.I..@. ......d..
20: 01 3C 00 6E 04 2B 00 0D 0D 69 00 BF 06 EF 50 18 |.<.n.+...i....P.
30: 22 1B 40 E3 00 00 2B 4F 4B 20 57 65 6C 63 6F 6D |".@...+OK Welcom
40: 65 20 6F 6E 20 62 6F 61 72 64 20 42 69 6C 6C 20 |e on board Bill
50: 47 61 74 65 73 0D 0A                            |Gates..
```

Yeah, but doesn't the analyzer have to be loaded on a server somewhere? Not really. It can be any workstation or host on the network. It is possible for an attacker to load the software onto a system they have already compromised. By doing this, the attacker does not even need to be in the building. They can be somewhere else, and let the system do the work for them. In order for a network analyzer to capture a communications session, it has to be connected somewhere along the session's path. This could be on the network at some point between the system initializing the session and the destination system. This could also be accomplished by compromising one of the systems at either end of the session. This means the attacker cannot capture your network traffic over the Internet from a remote location. The attack must come from some sort of probe or analyzer within your network.

How do you stop it? Well, define your organization security policy to eliminate transmission of clear-text passwords on any network and develop a strategy to enable single sign-on or protect password transmission.

Digest Authentication

Plain text passwords are part of what is referred to as *basic authentication*. Now, basic authentication is a part of the HTTP version 1.0 standard, so it makes sense that most browsers support this authentication method. It grants access to Web pages after users have transmitted their Windows 2000 user names and passwords. However, a user must enter the correct user name and password before access is granted. As you have seen above, these user passwords are transmitted in plain text, so someone who "sniffs" communications between the Web browser and the Web server can intercept them easily.

For enterprise Web Enrollment Support pages, basic authentication is enabled to ensure that all browsers have access to the Web pages. Because sending passwords as plain text presents a security risk, you might want to turn off basic authentication or turn on digest authentication.

Beyond basic authentication, you have digest authentication, which is the latest *World Wide Web Consortium (W3C)* authentication standard. Digest authentication offers clear advantages over the basic authentication standard. While digest authentication offers the same features as basic authentication, it transmits the authentication credentials a different way. The authentication credentials go through a one-way process that is referred to as *hashing*. The result of this process is called a hash, or *message digest*. The message digest cannot be decrypted and it doesn't pass the passwords across the wire. Digest authentication provides organizations with a way to offer standard clients more secure and higher-performing authentication to their Web sites.

Because digest authentication is a challenge/response mechanism like the authentication that is integrated in Windows 2000, passwords are not sent unencrypted. That means if you have an intranet site and you need to support only Internet Explorer, you can use the Internet Information Services console, which is an MMC snap-in, to configure security for CertSrv and CertControl. That turns basic authentication off and prevents passwords from being transmitted as plain text. If you need to support other browsers, you can configure security for CertSrv and CertControl to require secure channels with the *Secure Sockets Layer (SSL)* and *Transport Layer Security (TLS)* protocols. With secure channels, passwords that are sent for basic authentication are encrypted.

If you turn on integrated Windows authentication, basic authentication, and digest authentication, it makes sense that there is a pecking order. In this case, authentication is done in the following order:

1. Integrated Windows authentication
2. Digest authentication
3. Basic authentication

The highest-ranked authentication method that is supported by browsers is used to authenticate users. If anonymous access is turned on, authenticated access is used only when NTFS file protection security has been configured to control access for Web site resources.

Smart Cards

Recently, we went to a geek convention. You know the type: Everyone running around with funny-looking badges hanging around their necks in the eternal quest for free stuff. This was truly our kind of place.

This could be considered an editorial comment—or the same as an aside—from Gary Govanus: "This makes the fourth or fifth book Bob King and I have co-authored together. I have known and respected Bob for more years than I care to admit to. One of the things that I admire most about Bob is his ability to scam free stuff. If you look at the front piece of this book, or at any of our Exam Notes books from the NT 4 days, you will notice Bob thanking this computer manufacturer or that manufacturer for providing equipment for his lab. You will also notice the lack of that brash commercialism on my behalf. Actually, that sounds very moralistic doesn't it? In reality it boils down to his ability to scam free stuff and my ability to find ways to lease and buy stuff."

Anyway, when we checked in, our name cards this year were smart cards. Cards the size of credit cards that have a small chip embedded in the card. To register to win free stuff, all you had to do was pass the card over to one of the people in the booth and they would place the card in a reader and the information was automatically added to their Palm device. It was cool. It worked well, until they tried to use the same devices to keep track of who went into each session. Someone forgot to the do the math. Five hundred people going through a door controlled by two people using the Palm device at an average interaction of 20 seconds is not going to fit in a 15-minute window between sessions. Sorry. It causes backups and grumbling.

Another recent experience with smart cards turned out a lot better. Gary Govanus and his wife took a cruise. When they checked in before boarding the ship, they were presented a smart card. To buy anything on the ship, all they had to do was present the smart card; when leaving the ship, present the smart card; when returning to the ship, present the smart card. Because the cruise line had enough people to handle the biggest lines, the entire thing went very smoothly. Smart cards are definitely one of the waves of the future. How can you use them in a network environment?

In standard Kerberos logons, users initially prove to the KDC that they are who they say they are by showing that they know a secret known only to the user and the KDC. This shared secret is a cryptographic key derived from the user's password. It is used only during the AS Exchange. The exchange works like this:

- The client encrypts pre-authentication data
- The KDC decrypts pre-authentication data
- The KDC encrypts the logon session key
- The client decrypts the logon session key

The same key is used for both encryption and decryption. For this reason, shared secret keys are said to be *symmetric*.

To support smart card logons, Windows 2000 uses a public key extension to the Kerberos protocol's initial AS Exchange. In this case, public key cryptography is *asymmetric*. Two different keys are needed. One of the keys is used to encrypt, the other key is used to decrypt. Together, the keys needed to perform both operations make up a private/public key pair. The private key is known only to the owner of the pair and is never shared. The public key can be made available to anyone with whom the owner wishes to share confidential information.

It works like this. A user goes up to a PC and inserts the smart card into a reader. All appropriate logon information is stored on that card. When a smart card is used in place of a password, a private/public key pair stored on the user's smart card is substituted for the shared secret key derived from the user's password. In the public key extension to the Kerberos protocol, the initial AS Exchange is modified so that the KDC encrypts the user's logon session key with the public half of the user's key pair. The client decrypts the logon session key with the private half of the pair.

So, now the user has inserted a smart card into a card reader attached to the computer. When computers with Windows 2000 are configured for smart card logon, a card insertion event sends a signal, just as the key combination Ctrl+Alt+Del does on computers configured for password logon. In response, `Winlogon` displays a Logon Information Dialog. In this case, the user types just one item of information, a Personal Identification Number (PIN).

The user's logon information is sent to the LSA, just as it does with a password logon. The LSA uses the PIN to access the smart card, which stores the user's private key and an X.509 v3 certificate containing the public half of the key pair. All cryptographic operations that use these keys take place on the smart card.

The Kerberos on the client computer sends the user's public key certificate to the KDC as pre-authentication data in its initial authentication request. The KDC validates the certificate, extracts the public key, and uses it to encrypt a logon session key. It returns the encrypted logon session key, along with a TGT, in its reply to the client. If the client is in possession of the private half of the key pair, it will be able to use the private key to decrypt the logon session key. Both the client and the KDC then use the logon session key in all further communications with one another. No other deviation from the standard protocol is necessary.

If you are interested in which types of smart cards are compatible with Windows 2000, see the Windows 2000 Hardware Compatibility List.

NTLM

Backward compatibility is the thing. It always make a great deal of sense, especially when you are introducing a new NOS, to make sure that the new NOS works really well with the old NOS. Otherwise you (and your customers) have some very serious issues. In the case of Windows 2000, the problem arose with security protocols. Basically, the Windows 2000 model is going to center around Kerberos v5. Meanwhile, the Windows NTLM protocol was the default for authentication in Microsoft Windows NT version 4. For the sake of backward compatibility, NTLM is retained in Windows 2000 to make life easier working with clients and servers that are running Windows NT version 4 and earlier. It is also used to authenticate logons to stand-alone computers that are running Windows 2000.

Remember, the Kerberos protocol is still the protocol of choice in Windows 2000—when there *is* a choice. Computers running Microsoft Windows 3.11, Windows 95, Windows 98, or Windows NT 4 must use the NTLM protocol for network authentication in Windows 2000 domains. Computers with Windows 2000 use NTLM when they are authenticating to servers that are running Windows NT 4 and when they are requesting access to resources in Windows NT 4 domains.

Kerberos is so preferred that once all of a network's clients are set up to use Kerberos, administrators will be able to turn off NTLM authentication. According to Microsoft, this is a good thing because Kerberos provides more efficiency and flexibility than NTLM authentication, as well as more security. Microsoft also points out other benefits that Kerberos offers over NTLM.

As we have already seen, Kerberos lets a client verify a server's identity. NTLM simply assumes that every server is genuine, while Kerberos lets both client and server ensure that the other party is genuine. Besides the two-way verification, with Kerberos the server need not connect to a domain controller to authenticate a client. The client can simply be authenticated based on the credentials it presents.

By default, Windows 2000 Server's mutual authentication provides two-way, transitive trust between security authorities. As a result, rather than requiring a maze of complicated trust relationships, domain networks can be organized in a tree of mutually trusting relationships. Network credentials issued in any tree will be accepted in all the forest's trees.

NTLM and Kerberos both allow a service to impersonate its client locally when necessary. But, unlike NTLM, Kerberos provides a proxy mechanism that lets a service impersonate a client while connecting to back-end services on other computers.

Finally, Microsoft has implemented the Kerberos v5 protocol in Windows 2000 Server according to standards-track specifications recommended to the Internet Engineering Task Force. By working from the same basis as other networks using Kerberos v5, Windows 2000 Server provides for cross-platform compatibility with these other networks.

The bottom line is that NTLM will be there when you need it, but as soon as the last NT box or Windows 9x workstation has been upgraded to Windows 2000, you will want to shut it off.

RADIUS

Ever since the beginning of the chapter we have been talking about how to authenticate users that are accessing resources off your network, from your network. What happens if you want to introduce hosts that are running non-Windows operating systems? Or, what happens if you need to provide dial-up connectivity to remote or traveling users?

This is where the *Remote Authentication Dial-in User Service (RADIUS)* comes into play. RADIUS is an industry standard protocol that provides authorization, authentication, and accounting services for distributed dial-up networks. RADIUS is made up of a client and server piece. Table 9.5 highlights the components and the functions.

TABLE 9.5 RADIUS Components and Functions

Component	Function
RADIUS client	The RADIUS client is a remote access server that receives RADIUS authentication requests and forwards them to a RADIUS authentication server. When acting as a client, Windows 2000 can also forward account information to a RADIUS accounting server.
RADIUS server	The RADIUS server is an Internet Authentication Service (IAS) server that provides RADIUS Authentication. As a RADIUS server, Windows 2000 gets authentication and accounting information from RADIUS clients. It then verifies the potential clients, and stores the accounts information in a log files. A RADIUS server must run on an IIS server.

So basically, if you have an IAS server up and working, you have your very own RADIUS system configured. As far as the clients go, they are configured from within the IAS MMC. Take a look at Figure 9.11. To get here, you start with Start ➤ Programs ➤ Administrative Tools ➤ Internet Authentication Service. Once there, simply highlight Clients, and use a right mouse button to choose New Client.

FIGURE 9.11 Configuring a RADIUS client

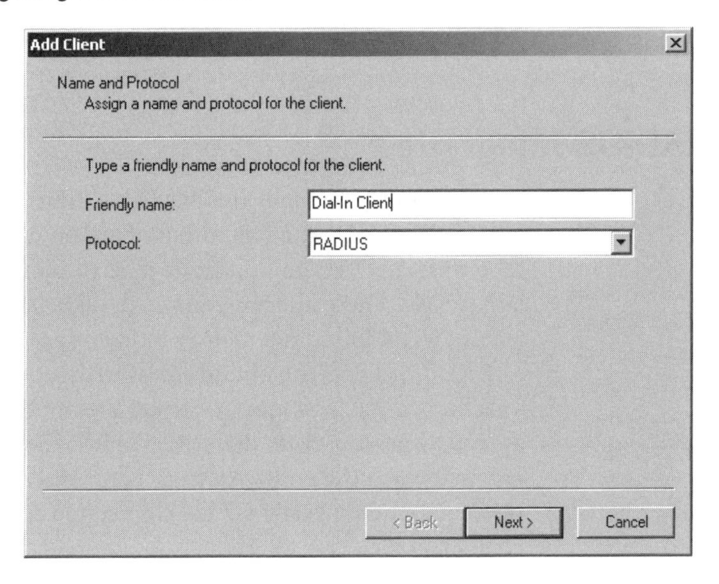

After giving your new client a name and clicking next, you can define the client computer by entering either an IP address or a DNS name. Once you have verified the address, you can add your shared secret. Look at Figure 9.12 to see the just about finished product.

FIGURE 9.12 New RADIUS client defined

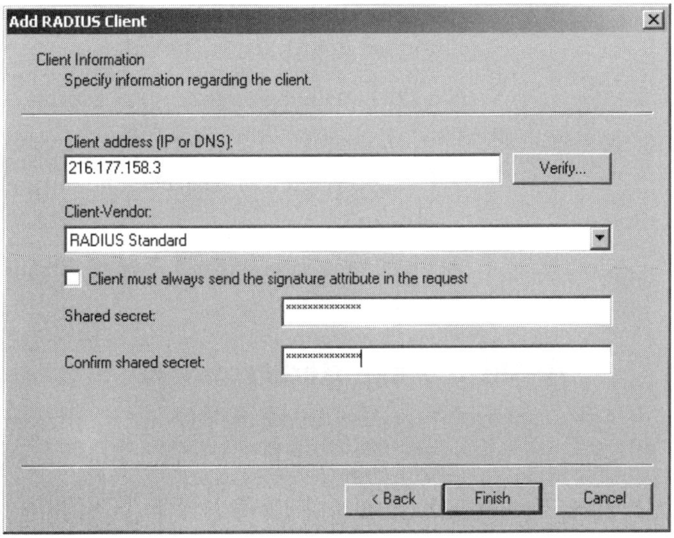

Add RADIUS Client

Client Information

Specify information regarding the client.

Client address (IP or DNS):

216.177.158.3

Verify...

Client-Vendor:

RADIUS Standard

Client must always send the signature attribute in the request

Shared secret:

Confirm shared secret:

< Back

Finish

Cancel

The shared secret doesn't have to be something magical. It can be just a series of letters and numbers, as long as both parts of the communication can agree.

RADIUS Integration

RADIUS is exceptionally flexible. With a minimal amount of work, RADIUS is capable of supporting hundreds of remote access clients. If you spend some time with RADIUS and optimize it, that number can grow to exceptionally large levels. There are constraints, though. Things like local network segments, WAN links, and dial-up modem speeds can slow things down.

RADIUS clients can obtain access to the corporate intranet by using either a dial-up configuration or a Virtual Private Network. Dial-up connections are used when the client dials directly into the corporate modem pool. VPNs are used when the remote access client establishes connections through the Internet and then gets a virtual connection to the organization's remote access servers.

You should start thinking about using RADIUS with dial-up if any (or all) of the following is true:

- You have decided that having users access your intranet from over the Internet (i.e., through a portal in your Web page) is an unacceptable risk.
- You have decided to use Caller ID or a callback function.
- The cost of providing telephone lines, modems, and multiport communication devices is not an issue.

You can consider using the VPN aspects of RADIUS when the following are true:

- Using the Internet to access the intranet-based resources is an acceptable risk.
- The connection to the Internet will support the number of remote access clients.

RADIUS Supported Protocols

RADIUS clients make use of several different communications transport protocols. All these protocols are *Routing and Remote Access Service*

(RRAS) based. Some protocols may be required for some tasks, and others may be required for others. The protocols that are supported by the RRAS based RADIUS clients are shown in Table 9.6.

TABLE 9.6 RADIUS and RRAS Protocols

Protocol	Provides
TCP/IP	TCP/IP provides access to Web-based applications, File Transfer Protocol (FTP) servers, or other applications that are part of the TCP/IP suite.
NWLink	NWLink provides access to NetWare-based services.
AppleTalk	AppleTalk provides access to AppleTalk Remote Access Protocol.

RADIUS Design Tips

As you begin to design your RADIUS implementation, there are a couple of things to keep in mind. On the client side:

- Do you have enough phone lines, modems, and asynchronous ports to handle the incoming traffic?
- Do you have sufficient numbers of Point-to-Point Tunneling Protocol (PPTP) or the Layer 2 Tunneling Protocol (L2TP) ports to handle the number of VPN connections you expect?
- Have the appropriate user accounts been granted remote access?
- Do you have remote access policy restrictions in place?

For the RADIUS client-to-server connections, make sure you include things like support for WAN communications, as well as dial-up. So, make sure these are in place:

- A stable high-speed connection between the RADIUS clients and servers
- Redundant IP routed paths between the RADIUS clients and servers

RADIUS Authentication Protocols

At this stage of the process, we have connectivity between the RADIUS client and the RADIUS server. What we don't have is authentication. Authentication is really important in this case, because we are about to grant a remote user access to our network. That can be a scary thought. Here is someone coming in from the outside, trying to access our systems, and we are going to make it easy on them!

There are special authentication protocols supported by RADIUS. Table 9.7 lists the protocols and when to choose each.

TABLE 9.7 The Use of RADIUS Authentication Protocols

Use	When
MS-CHAP	Use MS-CHAP when providing encrypted authentication for Windows 95, Windows 98, or NT 4.
MS-CHAP v2	Use MS-CHAP V2 when providing encrypted authentication support for Windows 2000.
EAP-TLS	Use EAP-TLS when providing support for a smart card authentication. You can also it use when the RRAS-based remote access server is a member of a Windows 2000–based mixed or native domain. Finally, it can be considered when the cost of adding a smart card reader to each remote access client is not prohibitive.
CHAP	Use CHAP when providing encrypted authentication support for remote access clients that use a diversity of operating systems. You may also use CHAP when the business goals require encrypted authentication.
SPAP	Use SPAP when you are providing encrypted authentication support for remote access clients that use Shiva LAN Rover software.
PAP	Use PAP when you are providing unencrypted authentication and when remote access clients support no other protocol.

RADIUS Encryption Methods

In addition to authentication protocols, RADIUS also supports several different encryption methods.

MPPE

MPPE is the *Microsoft Point-to-Point Encryption* method. As the name implies, this encrypts data for Point-to-Point Protocol (PPP) or PPTP connections. In the United States, the version of Windows 2000 that you are using is either 40-bit or 128-bit encryption. Outside of the United States, Windows 2000 only supports 40-bit encryption.

MPPE works for you if the following apply:

- You are using *Microsoft Challenge Handshake Authentication Protocol (MS–CHAP)*, MS–CHAP v2, or *Extensible Authentication Protocol–Transport Level Security (EAP–TLS)* authentication protocols.
- User authentication is used but there is no machine certificate infrastructure in place.

IPSec

The Internet Protocol Security (IPSec) encrypts data within an L2TP-based connection. In the United States and Canada, this supports the 40-bit *Data Encryption Standard (DES)*, 56-bit DES, or *Triple DES (3DES)* encryption. If you are using Windows 2000 in another country, you get the 40- and 56-bit versions of DES. With IPSec, authentication is carried out using machine-based certificates. This reduces the ability of an unauthorized computer to impersonate an authorized user.

IPSec is the encryption method of choice if you are using these:

- L2TP Tunneling
- A machine certificate infrastructure

Windows 2000 and RADIUS

RADIUS is a network service that is integrated into Windows 2000. This is a plus for the administrator, because it does help to cut down on network management.

RRAS Integration

By integrating RRAS and RADIUS, the management of remote access servers has been centralized. With the integration of RRAS and RADIUS, both the administration of remote access policies and the logging of authentication success or failure can be centralized.

If you use redundant RADIUS-based authentication and accounting servers, the integration of RRAS and RADIUS allows RRAS designs to provide higher availability and load balancing.

RADIUS Management

The security of the RADIUS implementation is determined by the way the design allows access to intranet resources. RADIUS security can do this in the following ways:

- It can use IPSec and VPN tunnels for encryption of transmissions between RADIUS clients and servers
- It can do it by using authentication protocols that will encrypt the authentication credentials
- It can do it by using other encryption methods such as MPPE or IPSec to encrypt data
- It can do it by using remote access configuration to restrict access to resources located on the remote access server
- It can do it by using remote access policies to restrict remote user access

Secure Sockets Layer/Transport Layer Security (SSL/TLS)

Here is a term you haven't come across yet: *Secure Channel*. Secure Channel is a security support provider. It supports a suite of four related security protocols: Secure Sockets Layer 2 and 3, the Transport Layer Security 1, and Private Communications Technology 1. PCT is one of those protocols that is available—it is just not recommended!

Design Scenario: How to Connect Two Offices, Without Really Trying

You have been brought in to consult for a company that has a problem. The CEO calls you in and wants some answers. She has just completed acquisition of a very small 25-person company on the other side of the country. The new company is running Windows 2000, as is the home office. She needs this company to be able to access the home office network, but she does not want to pay the exorbitant costs to install and maintain a leased line all across the country. She is particularly perplexed because she can see their Web page and they can see hers, so why in the world can't they get access to the network?

At this point, you begin to make some notes, and start to explain the features and benefits of a Virtual Private Network. You explain how you will be able to link the two offices together securely without leasing a phone line, just using the Internet. It is another victory for the folks in the white hats!

All four of these protocols provide authentication through the use of certificates and secure communications making use of a variety of possible cipher suites. Each of these rely on digital certificates, usually providing authentication and secure communications over the Internet. SSL is used typically with *Secure HyperText Transfer Protocol (S–HTTP or HTTPS).*

The SSL client and server work together to institute a secure communication channel. This link is established through a handshake procedure that starts with the exchange of random values. Once the client has received the server's random value, it will create a Pre–Master Secret. Since the Pre–Master Secret must be secure, it is encrypted with the server's public key. The client receives this key from the server's certificate.

Once the Pre–Master Secret has been exchanged, now the client and the server can create a shared Master Secret.

The Master Secret is used to create two keys that the client and the server share. This first secret is used in a hashing algorithm. The second secret is called the *Write Key*. Here the client and server use the value in an encryption algorithm.

TLS is really SSL with an attitude. It makes use of a more powerful algorithm in creation of the Master Key. In addition, TLS is a standard, where SSL is not. Finally, at a programming level, TLS has many more alert messages available in case of problems.

Summary

Well, we have certainly jumped in with both feet to look at the security protocols. First, we started out with the "simplest" implementation, dealing with certificates. We looked at the various types of certificates and the different kinds of certificate servers. Once we had the certificate basics down, we began to examine the cornerstone of Windows 2000 security, Kerberos v 5. Kerberos has a lot of flexibility to it, so it took us a while to figure out how everything worked and how the certificates move from one domain to another.

After the discussion of Kerberos, we took a look at some WAN types of authentication, with things like clear-text passwords and digest authentication. Since neither of those are going to be a security administrator's answer to anything, we then looked at what would happen if your users used smart cards. Great technology, but there is all that extra hardware involved.

At this point we had the corporate network pretty well under control, but we hadn't dealt with the security protocol for the remote users. In this case, by configuring IAS, you immediately have the opportunity to use RADIUS and RRAS. We closed out the chapter with a brief discussion of using SSL/TSL to enhance the security of your Web pages. That is a lot of material, isn't it? Remember that we are not even done with the objective. You still have Chapter 10 to get through before we can put this objective to bed.

Key Terms

Before you take the exam, be certain you are familiar with the following terms:

asymmetric

Authentication Service (AS)

authenticator

basic authentication

certification hierarchy

certificate trust lists (CTLs)

certificate revocation list (CRL)

clear-text passwords

Data Encryption Standard (DES)

Directory System Agent (DSA)

enterprise certification authorities (CAs)

enterprise root certificate authorities

enterprise subordinate certificate authorities

Extensible Authentication Protocol–Transport Level Security (EAP–TLS)

hashing

issuing CA

Kerberos v5

key distribution center (KDC)

key life

krbtgt

long-term key

message digest

Microsoft Challenge Handshake Authentication Protocol (MS–CHAP)

Microsoft Point-to-Point Encryption (MPPE)

native mode

referral ticket

Remote Authentication Dial-in User Service (RADIUS)

Routing and Remote Access Service (RRAS)

Secure HyperText Transfer Protocol (S–HTTP)

Secure Sockets Layer (SSL)

security support provider (SSP)

session key

shared secrets

stand-alone root certificate authorities

stand-alone subordinate certificate authorities

ticket-granting service (TGS)

ticket-granting tickets (TGTs)

Transport Layer Security (TLS)

Triple DES (3DES)

World Wide Web Consortium (W3C)

Review Questions

1. Which of the following is usually the top-level certificate authority in your PKI?

   A. Stand-alone subordinate certificate authority

   B. Enterprise subordinate certificate authority

   C. Enterprise root certificate authority

   D. Stand-alone root certificate authority

   E. Master root certificate authority

2. Windows 2000 supports a hierarchical CA trust model using:

   A. CALs

   B. CTLs

   C. CAAs

   D. CTAs

   E. CSSs

3. What is an Authenticated Session Certificate type used for?

   A. Authenticating clients.

   B. It is used to enroll Cisco routers for IPSec authentication certificates.

   C. It is used for code signing operations.

   D. It is used for EFS operations.

4. By default, where are the certificate database and the certificate log files installed?

   A. `<Drive:>\WINNT\System32\certificates`

   B. `<Drive:>\WINNT\authority`

   C. `<Drive:>\WINNT\log`

   D. `<Drive:>\WINNT\System32\CertLog`

5. Two of the following are RADIUS supported protocols. Pick them.

   A. IPX

   B. TCP/IP

   C. NWLink

   D. NFS

   E. SPX

   F. Telnet

6. How does Windows 2000 implement the key distribution center (KDC)?

   A. As a domain service

   B. As a site policy

   C. As an organizational unit policy

   D. As a tree policy

   E. As an application running in a separate organizational unit

7. The Kerberos protocol relies heavily on an authentication technique involving:

   A. Randomly generated strings of numbers and letters

   B. 52-bit encrypted password

   C. 40-bit encryption

   D. Triple secret keys

   E. Shared secrets

8. Digest authentication offers the same features as basic authentication, but it involves a different way of transmitting the authentication credentials. The authentication credentials pass through a one-way process often referred to as:

   A. Trashing

   B. Hocking

   C. Hashing

   D. Encrypting

   E. Disk caching

9. To support smart card logons, Windows 2000 implements a public key extension to the Kerberos protocol's initial AS Exchange. In contrast to how shared secret keys work, public key cryptography is known as:

   A. Asynchronous

   B. Synchronous

   C. Triple DES

   D. Asymmetric

   E. Symmetric

10. RADIUS authentication protocols include:

    A. MS–CHAP v2

    B. Plain text

    C. Digest mode

    D. TCP/IP

    E. NWLink

Answers to Review Questions

1. C. The top-level certificate authority is usually the enterprise root certificate authority.

2. B. Windows 2000 supports a hierarchical CA trust model and makes use of *certificate trust lists (CTLs)*.

3. A. An Authenticated Session Certificate is used for authenticating clients.

4. D. By default, the certificate database and the certificate log files are installed in `<Drive:>\WINNT\System32\CertLog`.

5. B, C. RADIUS support both TCP/IP and NWLink as transport protocols.

6. A. Windows 2000 implements the key distribution center (KDC) as a domain service.

7. E. The Kerberos protocol relies heavily on an authentication technique involving shared secrets.

8. C. Digest authentication offers the same features as basic authentication, but it involves a different way of transmitting the authentication credentials. The authentication credentials pass through a one-way process often referred to as hashing.

9. D. To support smart card logons, Windows 2000 implements a public key extension to the Kerberos protocol's initial AS Exchange. In contrast to how shared secret keys work, public key cryptography is asymmetric.

10. A. MS–CHAP v2 is one of the RADIUS Authentication Protocols.

The Multinational Conglomerate

You should give yourself 10 minutes to review this case study, diagram as needed, and complete the questions for this testlet. Be sure to read each question carefully. While the company may not have changed, its circumstances change in each chapter.

Background

Your consulting firm has been hired to assist in the Windows 2000 migration and integration for a company based in Minneapolis, Minnesota. Until the start of this year, the company had 1,000 employees, all based throughout the Twin Cities of Minneapolis and St. Paul. Just before the end of the year, the owner of your company purchased two companies of roughly the same size that will need to be connected to the enterprise network. The total number of users when the project is completed is estimated at 3,500. In addition, each of these companies comes with various strategic partners that will need to access the information on your enterprise network. The companies that have been acquired are located in Athens, Greece, and in Orlando, Florida.

The three companies can now be considered one, and the preparation for the Windows 2000 rollout is in full swing. At this time, the company is examining various methods of rolling out security across the network. The Windows 2000 network is made up of a forest with three domains.

Current System

Minneapolis Located on the shores of beautiful Lake Calhoun, the company occupies a sprawling campus that includes four floors in a six-story building. Since the merger, the Lake Calhoun facility has become a model of efficiency. Besides being linked to all of the other offices, everyone is beginning to take the notion of an enterprise network seriously.

All of the floors are connected to the Windows 2000 network. The Minneapolis location is a domain in the tree. The network has removed the last vestiges of its old Windows NT BDC systems and has finally made the switch to native mode. Active Directory Services have been deployed to the main campus and the rollout is complete in the branch offices. The desktop and laptop rollout, company-wide, took longer than expected, but it is now completed. The CEO wants to know what the IT team is doing to make sure that everyone within the company can access resources all over the tree, and to protect the network while making dial-up connections available. Finally, there is the matter of the Web page. This company is going to be taking registrations for the download of a new product, and the CIO and CEO want to make sure that the information is safe. In addition, the CEO is concerned that some of the managers are carrying around information vital to the company. She wants to make sure that when executives connect to the company network from their laptops, things are secure.

Orlando The Orlando office is a domain in the corporate tree. It has some valuable resources that need to be made available to the rest of company, particularly the folks in Athens. In addition, there are some things that need to be worked out so that people in Orlando can get complete access to Minneapolis. Now that the last of Windows NT is out the door, it is time to begin getting down and dirty and talking bits and bytes.

Athens The Athens office is now fully staffed at 2,300. The location has discovered that the business is doing well, and the extra folks are justified. The office has been upgraded to Windows 2000 servers and Athens is now its own domain in the tree.

Athens has always been ahead of the curve. They have already rolled out their new 1,500 hosts, replacing all the old computers. All the replacement machines, and all the machines for the new people, are running Windows 2000 Professional.

Problem Statement

Now that the company is in native mode, the CIO wants to make sure that the company is making best use of the available security protocols.

Envisioned System

Now that the three locations are working together and communicating, the CEO wants to make sure that it is done securely. She still wants the Digital Nervous System, but she understands there are other things that have to come first. There are several issues that the CEO wants addressed. One of these is, how can the company switch to a certificate-based authentication system?

Also, the employees of the company are constantly moving throughout the location. The company envisions kiosks that are set up for people to log on for a few moments to perform a task, and then move on to another area. The logon should be simple and straightforward, but most of all it should be quick.

The Web site should make use of protocols that allow users to register in confidence that their information is not available to any 16-year-old kid who can download a sniffer.

Problem Statement

The issues that you are going to have to contend with include which protocols to use, how to make logons fast and easier from any location in the company, how to protect the privacy of people you have never met, and how to secure the remote communications.

Questions

1. Which protocols should you be looking at?

   A. TCP/IP

   B. Kerberos

   C. RADIUS

   D. FTP

   E. Telnet

   F. SSL/TLS

2. What can you do about the kiosks?

   A. Because you are using a domain model, as long as you have unique names within the domain, there should not be a problem.

   B. Train users in the proper use of passwords.

   C. Kerberos will take care of everything.

   D. Install smart cards.

   E. Use TLS to access the network.

3. How do you handle the problem of the remote users?

   A. Make sure the laptop is running Windows 2000 Professional.

   B. Make sure the dial-up connections are made only from hotel rooms with approved communication channels.

   C. Institute RADIUS.

   D. Configure each system to create a VPN when accessing the network.

4. How can you make sure that the people who are registering on your Web page are not transmitting their information using clear text?

   A. Institute digest authentication.

   B. Use Kerberos.

   C. Use RADIUS.

   D. Use SSL/TLS.

Answers

1. B, C, F. The proper configuration of the Kerberos protocol will help people gain access across the domain boundaries. All trust relationships between domains are transitive. Implementing RADIUS will help provide access for those people outside the company attempting to connect remotely and SSL/TLC will solve the Web server problem.

2. D. In this case, because we are working with a fictional company, and fictional companies have all the money in the world, smart cards are the answer. They do make accessing kiosk workstations exceptionally simple, and provide a way of auditing users and controlling logon names and passwords.

3. A, C, D. If you configure your network so that people can either access the network directly using RADIUS or access it through a VPN, you will be providing secure communications.

4. D. Make sure your Web designers make use of SSL/TLS on any page where information is being entered.

An Integration and Authentication Strategy

MICROSOFT EXAM OBJECTIVES COVERED IN THIS CHAPTER:

✓ **Design an authentication strategy.**

- Select authentication methods. Methods include certificate-based authentication, Kerberos authentication, clear-text passwords, digest authentication, smart cards, NTLM, RADIUS, and SSL.
- Design an authentication strategy for integration with other systems.

I will bet that, when you read that objective, you thought you were seeing double, didn't you? Actually, we just decided to split the objective up over two different chapters. You can look at it this way. In Chapter 9, we were taking a high-level overview, and now we are about to get more granular.

In Chapter 9, we spent a lot of time discussing some of the security protocols that can be put to work in the Windows 2000 environment. Part of that chapter, and parts of others, have discussed the differences between *authorization* and *authentication*. In this chapter, we are concerned only with the authentication protocols, how they can be put to use in a Windows 2000 network and in scenarios where the Windows 2000 network needs to communicate with other, non-Windows-based networks. We are going to start the chapter with a discussion of nontraditional ways that users on networks need to communicate.

Now, part of the premise of this book is that there are some people who will read the entire book, and there are other people who will just pick up the book and turn right to the objective they need help with. So, after talking about nontraditional connections, we are going to continue by doing a brief review of the authentication protocols and how they work. Then we are going to determine how these protocols may be used in environments that are not heterogeneous. For those of you who would like a buzzword for nonheterogeneous environments, the appropriate phrase is *single sign-on*. Once that is finished, we will complete the chapter with a review and move on to Chapter 11, "Enhancing Security Using Public Keys," where we look at security group strategies.

Defining Your Network

When networking first started, a long, long time ago in a land far away, one of the toughest sales for IS managers to their superiors was, "Why in the world would we need that?" Now, most of us cannot imagine trying to run a business without networked computers. The Bill Gates dream of a computer on every desktop and a computer in every house is becoming more and more of reality. It used to be you could prove how technologically savvy you were by your intimate knowledge of the Internet. Now, people in their 80s are routinely downloading and uploading files without the least understanding of FTP. After a recent trip to a computer superstore, it became obvious that just having a network in your home is no more of an oddity than having a two-car garage. Heck, there are dozens of products for the Small Office Home Office (SOHO) user to network computers. The advent of cable modems has made it easier for the average person to take advantage of the speed a direct connection offers, and the hardware vendors now have switches available so any Tom, Dick, or Mary can network their computer and the kids' computer and use a single connection to the Internet.

So, for most organizations, remembering back to the days of stand-alone computers is not easy. Network-based communications are quickly becoming the backbone of commerce and communications. And increasingly, the idea of "networked computers" means computers that are securely linked to one another, and to the Internet. It is a short leap from computers that are networked and hooked to the Internet, to networks that are networked and hooked to the Internet.

So, what we are trying to do with the Windows 2000 Server operating system is to let your businesses build or enhance existing services that take better advantage of internal networks and the Internet. Large enterprises can use Windows 2000 networking services within their existing networks to automate daily management tasks, increase network efficiency, and provide richer and more secure communication services to their employees and partners.

Why Can't We Say No and Mean It?

It has always been a contention of ours that the major problem IS people have is the inability to say *no*. Actually, we do say *no*, we just don't stick to it. How many times have you said (or heard someone say), "No, that absolutely cannot be done—positively not"? Now, if they were to shut up then, things would be fine. Unfortunately, they continue with, "But, if I were to do it, I would do it this way..." and that is where things go to heck in a handbasket! Can't you just see the CEO of a Fortune 50 company telling the CIO that she wants to securely link two independent networks so that users on both sides can access resources of the other. "No, that absolutely cannot be done...". And now we all have more work to do.

Networks Linking Together

As businesses grow in the 21st century, you are well aware of the increasing demands on your network. It seems that every day, large companies are announcing reorganization efforts that cause far-flung departments to consolidate. Partnerships are announced and these partner relationships are more closely integrated than ever before. Suddenly, it is your responsibility to connect isolated networks. As the need for communication increases, suddenly it is mandatory that the company link a satellite office to the company network. And, with the consolidation and integration, it might become important to create a new network for the finance department and protect the links to prevent unauthorized access to data as well as improve performance during month-end processes. The way organizations use networks continues to evolve. For example, companies are starting to benefit from connecting partner information systems to better manage inventories.

So how can a company leverage its investment in Windows 2000 to connect networks together? Some of the necessary tools have been mentioned in previous chapters and some will be covered in depth later in the book, but it all boils down to the fact that smaller businesses need to do it inexpensively. Larger companies, meanwhile, need to maintain complex and diverse networks that require advanced capabilities. And many companies are examining how to use the Internet to link company networks together while encrypting communications and controlling what can be accessed through the secured links. With Windows 2000 Server, you can connect networks over private LAN and WAN interfaces or through encrypted *Virtual Private Networking* (VPN) technologies.

So, in this chapter we are going to look at ways that Windows 2000 Server offers benefits for businesses of all sizes by letting them achieve the following:

- Link remote branch offices to a private network
- Connect inter-office networks
- Connect business partner networks
- Provide flexible connections with the right level of security

Linking Remote Branch Offices

Earlier in the book, we discussed the different kinds of offices that can provide challenges for network administration. One of the most common challenges facing small or large businesses is the case of the remote office. Many businesses have one or more remote office locations where there is a smaller network. Many of the applications and services are duplicated, and there usually seems to be an information bottleneck getting the necessary data from one location to another. By connecting those networks, companies can operate more effectively. There are several ways these improvements are manifested. First of all, if there are employees who travel between offices, these people can now get to their own files and resources. Because the networks are linked, the bottleneck is opened and the information flows better and that streamlines the business processes. In cases where bandwidth is not an issue, companies can implement new tools, like videoconferencing to provide for real-time collaboration without the hassles of traveling.

For example, remember back in the earlier chapter, when we talked about Jenny, the queen of Caribou Coffee? Here is a food service chain that can link intra-store communication with the headquarters network to monitor sales and track inventory. This allows the chain to order and deliver the right supplies on time to minimize overstock costs without running out of required ingredients. Headquarters staff could also communicate in real-time with store managers through e-mail or videoconferencing to keep operations running smoothly. This helps the entire operation. If you have ever been to a Caribou coffee or a Starbucks, you know that they violate about every established rule of restaurant management ever taught in Business 101. Think about it. When you are in business school, you are taught to maximize the efficiency of every square foot of your retail space. In addition, one of the keys to running a successful restaurant is customer turnover. During busy times, your staff has to walk a very fine line between making the restaurant comfortable and welcoming, and yet making sure the table clears out as soon as the patrons are finished so staff can move the next group of people in. Coffeehouses everywhere are violating those rules. Whoever heard of a fireplace in an establishment of less than 1,000 square feet? How about sitting areas that rival a living room so you can sit and chat and relax and even read while drinking your coffee. They encourage you to linger! What is up with that??

One of the ways they can do it is with just-in-time product ordering. Since the restaurant is small, it is a great benefit not to have to dedicate large amounts of space to storage. Because the home office knows how much to send based on yesterday's sales (or even sales up-to-the-minute today), the store can replace only what it has used and keep the on-hand surplus to a minimum. Gone are the days of having to order supplies for an entire week. These smaller stores can link offices by running *Routing and Remote Access Services (RRAS)* on servers used for other purposes. This can help keep equipment costs low. If the load gets high, links or CPUs can be added to keep pace with demand, or you can expand to a second server later.

On a larger scale, a multinational corporation could use Windows 2000 RRAS to link its domestic retail offices to the private network over domestic leased lines. International offices could be connected inexpensively and securely over the Internet using Windows 2000 standards-based VPN technology. This way the network infrastructure is optimized to meet budget needs and provide the necessary connectivity for more efficient business operations.

Larger companies can also benefit from the cost savings of using the routing services in their branch offices. Because the routing service supports standard protocols, it works with the special purpose routers that exist in the corporate network.

Connecting LANs or Inter-Office Networks

It used to be that an "enterprise network" or a WAN was just a backbone linking a bunch of LANs. With the advent of TCP/IP and the design of Active Directory sites, we can establish some new guidelines. In Micro-speak, an Active Directory site is a group of subnets connected to a high-speed dependable link. In order for the IS department to keep that link high-speed and dependable, there has to be some way to manage traffic congestion. In addition, they are going to have to minimize the impact of network faults, and isolate sensitive departmental traffic. Companies have simply rezoned the division of the network into subnets that are linked together and form the backbone of the business.

Linking subnets means the use of routers and routing protocols. In previous versions of Windows NT, there were some areas where the operating system may not have shined. Configuring routing was one of them. That has definitely improved with Windows 2000. It can be used in smaller-scale networks to run the routing services on existing servers. In larger networks, Windows 2000 Server can complement the special purpose routers in the core of the campus network by providing connections to departmental networks.

Connecting Business Partners

The logical leap from being more efficient by linking corporate subnets to being more efficient by linking enterprise networks was a short one. In the past, the concept has always been there. The security technology had just never kept pace. Today, companies are discovering that they can work more efficiently with partners by connecting their networks to conduct transactions in real time. This lets teams across two or more companies work together more effectively. Windows 2000 Server has gone a long way to improving the platform for creating these types of connections.

For example, a company may want to publish a subset of business applications for partners to access through secured dynamic Web pages. Say your company is the number one producer of widgets. Your widgets are so popular that your customers are installing thousands of them every day. They could install tens of thousands of them a day, but there is a communication problem. The problem manifests itself like this: The people in your customer's purchasing department are overworked. Besides ordering for every other department in the corporation, they have to check the on-hand inventory of widgets that go into their Super D' Duper Vertical Ferblitzer. So, in addition to everything else they have to do, they have to get the inventory and see how many widgets they need. Then, they have to call your sales office and try to reach the number-one widget salesperson on the planet. This is no easy task. Once the two people get together, the order is placed and written up, and the salesperson starts it on its way to manufacturing. This is a great system. It has worked well for the past 50 years. Unfortunately, the system is holding both companies back. By making a subset of the ordering applications available to your partner, their purchasing guru can order the widgets online and avoid the hassle. If both companies were really efficient and had some Visual Basic or SQL programmers, they could probably develop an automatic interface that would determine how many widgets the manufacturer needed, and enter the order automatically. The whole thing could take place without the input of the purchasing guru or the number-one widget salesperson on the planet. They could be busy doing lunch, and the widget supply would not slow down. This is an example of the inventory database needing to be connected with the supplier's systems for just-in-time delivery, by linking the databases through Microsoft SQL Server–based queries.

Another example is the efficient use of contractors. Now, in today's business world, contractors are wonderful things. They are disposable employees. In addition, contractors can come in and handle specialized projects that your permanent staff is not geared up for. They may have the niche expertise that many companies need once in a while and no company needs full time. There are also times when you don't need just one contractor—you need a team of contractors from different companies to collaborate to solve your business problem. By linking the contracting companies into your company network, these virtual teams can share files, printers, plotters, and videoconferencing tools to solve many of your problems without even being on site. If they don't have to come on site, you are not paying travel, per diem, rental cars, hotels, and entertainment. Those are things that go right to the bottom line.

To meet these business goals, you must have an operating system that is capable of hosting secured Web pages, or a system that can link networks with the security to control where traffic goes and what can go inside them. Those types of solutions mean using some of the security protocols and techniques mentioned in Chapter 9: things like a *Public Key Infrastructure* for cross-platform security and *Secure Socket Layer (SSL)* for secured Web pages.

You also have to have a way to manage and control firewalls. With the use of security policies in the Active Directory service, Windows 2000 is a flexible enough platform to develop the firewall solutions and central management of firewall policies. As was mentioned in earlier chapters, these solutions inspect the traffic coming in to keep viruses out. In addition, firewalls monitor the information that is being accessed. Windows 2000 can handle the routing services needed to link through clear and secure connections with *static routes* and packet filters to control where traffic goes. Once the connection has been made, Active Directory will let you manage access controls to the services used by applying centrally managed authentication and access control policies. When you get these policies configured, your network will be open for e-business without compromising the security or control of your information.

Remote Office Connections

When you cut through all the smoke and mirrors, there are just two major methods of connecting remote offices to the company network. One way is to use a dedicated connection. This usually includes things like a dial-up connection or, if higher bandwidth is needed, you are looking at leased private lines. Depending on distance, desired performance, cost, and other factors, these work well. In other cases, it might be more cost effective to link these networks through the Internet. As we mentioned in Chapter 9, you can use the *Internet Authentication Service (IAS)* and RRAS, to connect branch offices and private networks using either method.

To move traffic between networks, the Windows 2000 system lets you define manually configured *static routes*, or you can use the standards-based routing protocols that are included. Windows 2000 Server supports *RIP* for basic IP and IPX routing, and it includes support for *Open Shortest Path First (OSPF),* for enterprise routing. The system adds support for *Internet Group Management Protocol (IGMP)* version 2 so that multiple PCs can share a single multicast video broadcast stream to reduce traffic on the network link.

A routing protocol is only as good as its infrastructure. In this case, there is native support for a variety of network media, including *asynchronous transfer mode (ATM),* T1, *frame relay, X.25,* dial-up, *ISDN, DSL,* cable modem, and satellite. This lets you choose the right connection for your business. If your company is headquartered in some out-of-the-way places (like ours), you also have the flexibility to change your infrastructure of choice when new technologies become available. You can also choose the level of communications protection to suit your security needs. Where companies are confident of the link privacy, communications between networks can be done in the clear. When security is important and legacy protocols (such as IPX/SPX) or multicast protocols (including important routing protocols) are required, Windows 2000 Server connects networks and encrypts traffic using *Layer 2 Tunneling Protocol (L2TP)* with *IPSec.* If static routes with IP-only and unicast-only traffic are what you need, you can choose IPSec Tunnel Mode alone.

Connecting Telecommuters and Remote Employees

We have said it before and we will say it again. One of the biggest challenges for an IT staff is the traveling or remote user. These people may be telecommuting, traveling, or working permanently from a satellite location. They still need to stay connected to the company network. All the IT staff has to do is find the best solution to let employees work anytime and anywhere, just as if they were directly connected to the company network. Now, in many cases, there have been solutions available in the past to do this. Unfortunately, many of them were written for computer people and not for real people. When you let these nomad employees work in a consistent way, regardless of their location, it can aid productivity, improve internal communications, and increase an organization's responsiveness to customers.

If you are tasked with making this happen, you can configure Windows 2000 so mobile users can connect directly to the company network through their own dial-up connection or ISDN line. Or, they can connect securely through most Internet connections using Virtual Private Networking (VPN). If you institute VPNs, information transmitted will use IPSec, and be encrypted. Anyone on the Internet who is trying to sniff your communication will be thwarted.

So, what kinds of protocols are available to make this happen?

Design Study: Get a Clue!

In this design study, we are going to take a somewhat different approach. We are going to examine a company that could make good use of the Internet and Virtual Private Networks, but doesn't.

Now, I am sure that most of you feel there must be only about three businesses in the world that have been in operation for over a year that don't have some kind of dot-something presence. In actuality, there are hundreds of thousands of companies that don't use the Internet to its full potential. Let's take a look at a small company in Minnesota that should be using the Internet, but doesn't.

The worst part of this study is that the owner of this business *knows* he should be making more use of the Internet. The company is a small, privately held consulting company. The principal travels all over the country plying his trade and has his trips usually scheduled six weeks in advance, but cancellations do occur. He is Web-savvy, though he is not the type to design and implement a Web page. His artistically creative skills are nonexistent. His creativity tends to be more written/verbal than artistic. He does have access to a multitude of resources that could design and maintain the Web page for him, so he cannot even use that as an excuse. Another sort of valid excuse would be that he could not find the registered DNS name he wanted, but that wouldn't fly either, since he has several DNS names registered, and makes use of one of them for e-mail on a regular basis. He even has his very own e-mail server that is accessible from the network. The corporate network is heterogeneous, consisting of Linux, NetWare, NT 4, and Windows 2000, so hardware and OS support can't be used as an excuse either.

In doing an analysis of this company, we come to the conclusion that the customer could be using the Internet to make it easier for his clients to check his schedule and schedule his time. The Web site could also be used to disseminate information on new offerings the company has, as well as to sell some of the adjunct materials the company has produced.

From an information side, the company founder is always whining that he can only get e-mail from his network when he is out of town. He would love to be able to log on to his network and make use of resources in his office from far-flung locations, but he has simply never gotten around to installing a VPN for his office. It is on his list of things to do…and has been for months. What do you think the client should do?

See, Govanus! Get off the dime and get the Web page created and the VPN installed. Enough of this *do-as-I-say, not-as-I-do* stuff!

Authentication Protocols

In Chapter 9 we talked about the various security protocols that were available in Windows 2000. Over the next few chapters, we are going to spend increasing amounts of time talking about these protocols and what best practices should be used when instituting them. Also in the previous chapter, we explained the difference between authentication protocols and authorization protocols. Windows 2000 supports all of these network security protocols because each protocol provides either compatibility for existing clients or some kind of more effective or improved security mechanisms, or else provides interoperability features for heterogeneous networks like the Internet. There are many authentication protocols in use in corporate networks today, and the Windows 2000 architecture does not limit which protocols can be supported. One security protocol to fit all needs would be simpler, but network configurations from small-office networks to large-scale Internet content providers do not share the same security requirements. Customers need to have choices of how to integrate new security technology, such as dynamic passwords or public-key cryptography, into their computing environment.

Now, we are not programmers here, and every time we start talking about protocols or *application programming interfaces (APIs),* we can just feel your eyes start to glaze over. We will try to keep this away from the bit and byte level, but some of that may just work its way in. You should know that Windows 2000 makes use of general-purpose Win32 security APIs. The operating system uses these APIs to isolate supported applications from the details of different security protocols available. Higher-level application interfaces provided by authenticated RPC and DCOM provide abstractions based on interface parameters to use security services. There, now you programming types have had a little something thrown your way!

To review, the Windows 2000 security infrastructure supports these primary security protocols:

Windows NT LAN Manager (NTLM) authentication protocol *The Windows NT LAN Manager (NTLM)* is used by Windows NT 4 and previous versions of Windows NT. NTLM will continue to be supported and used for pass-through network authentication, remote file access, and authenticated RPC connections to earlier versions of Windows NT.

When you start looking at ways to use these protocols, remember that if NT is present in a domain, NTLM must be used.

The Kerberos version 5 authentication protocol Kerberos version 5 replaces NTLM as the primary security protocol for access to resources within or across Windows 2000 domains. Kerberos was discussed in detail in Chapter 9, "Choosing an Authentication Strategy," so we will not take your time to tout its benefits here. If you have questions, check out the previous chapter.

When you think of Kerberos, think of Windows 2000. Notice we said that Kerberos v5 is the primary security protocol for access to resources within or across Windows 2000 domains. It is also used for cross-platform authentication. Make sure that you differentiate Kerberos from NTLM in your mind before taking the exam.

Distributed Password Authentication (DPA) This is the shared-secret authentication protocol used by some of the largest Internet membership organizations, such as MSN and CompuServe. *Distributed Password Authentication (DPA)* is part of *Microsoft Commercial Internet System (MCIS)* services and is specifically designed for users to use the same Internet membership password to connect to any number of Internet sites that are part of the same membership organization. The Internet content servers use the MCIS authentication service as a back-end Internet service, and users can connect to multiple sites without reentering their passwords.

Public-key–based protocols These provide privacy and reliability over the Internet. SSL is the de facto standard today for connections between Internet browsers and Internet information servers. This protocol, which uses Public Key Certificates to authenticate clients and servers, depends on a Public Key Infrastructure for widespread use. We will take an in-depth look at the PKI in Chapter 11, "Enhancing Security Using Public Keys."

Now, any chapter on protocols would not be complete without a graphic showing how the operating system architecture supports the protocols that are implemented. We understand that most of the graphics are totally confusing and don't mean much of anything to anyone, but for fear of losing our highly prized "Author Status" for not fulfilling a requirement, here is that graphic. The diagram in Figure 10.1 shows how Windows 2000 can support all these different protocols using the *Security Support Provider Interface (SSPI)*.

FIGURE 10.1 Operating system architecture for multiple authentication services

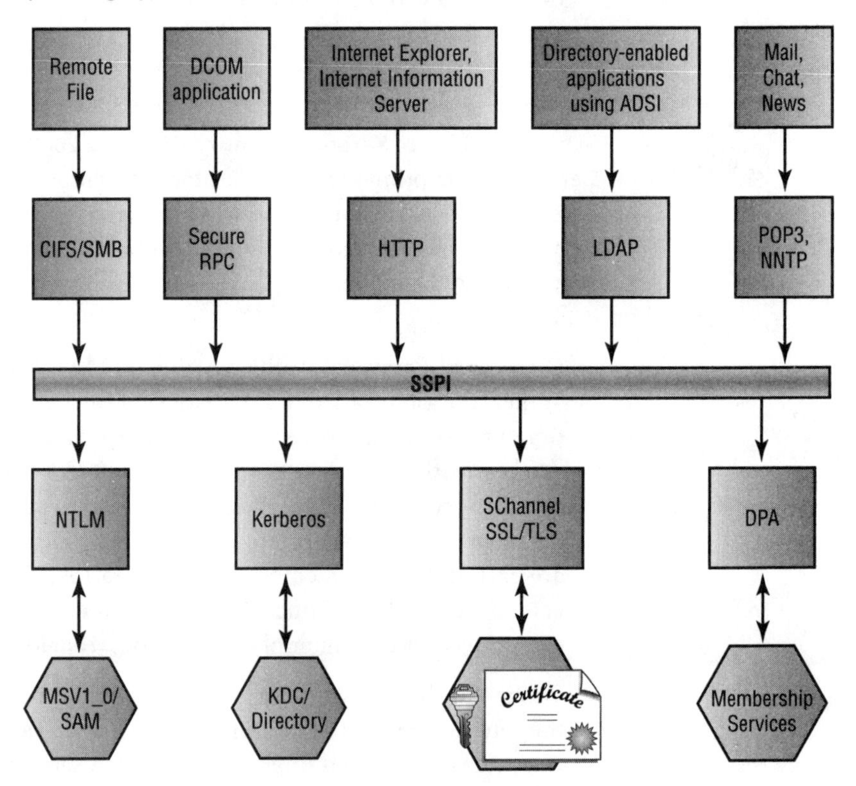

As you can see, the SSPI is used by many common applications and system services, including Internet Explorer (IE) and Internet Information Server (IIS). It serves to isolate the application-level protocols from security protocols used for network authentication.

This separation is required because security providers use different credentials to authenticate the user. These credentials can be either shared-secret or Public Key certificates. The security protocols then interact with different authentication services and account information stores:

NTLM security provider This uses the MSV1_0 authentication service and NetLogon service on a domain controller for client authentication and authorization information. If NTLM is in place on a Windows 2000 network, it is there because you are looking at backward compatibility with previous versions of Windows NT.

Kerberos security provider This connects to an online *key distribution center (KDC)* and the Active Directory account store for session tickets.

DPA This uses the MCIS security services for membership authentication and server-specific access information.

Secure channel services These are based on Public Key Certificates issued by trusted Certificate Authorities; they do not require an online authentication server.

Kerberos Authentication

As we discussed in the last chapter, the foundation or the cross-platform, single sign-on computing model is Kerberos v5. Kerberos defines an encrypted field in session tickets to carry Authorization Data, but the use of that field is left up to the applications. Windows 2000 uses the Authorization Data in Kerberos tickets to carry Windows Security IDs representing the user and group membership. The Kerberos security provider on the server-side of a connection uses the Authorization Data to build a Windows *security access token* representing the user on that particular system. The server follows the Windows security model of impersonating the client. In other words, the server uses the access token that represents the client before attempting to access local resources that may be protected by *access control lists (ACLs)*. This delegation of authentication is supported using *proxy* and *forwarding* flags in session tickets. Windows 2000 uses the delegation feature to allow servers to obtain another session ticket to connect to remote servers on behalf of the client. In this way, any client that authenticates to a Windows 2000 server can get a session ticket that will authenticate it to other remote servers. These remote servers can be on the enterprise network, or part of an interconnected series of privately owned networks.

In this way, Kerberos is implemented for a variety of systems and is used to provide a single authentication service in a distributed network. Kerberos interoperability can be defined by the following characteristics:

- It is a common authentication protocol that can be used to identify the end user or a service by principal name in a network connection.
- It has the ability to define trust relationships between Kerberos realms and to generate ticket referral requests between realms.
- It supports implementations that support the Interoperability Requirements defined in RFC 1510 that deal with encryption, checksum algorithms, mutual authentication, and other ticket options.
- It provides support for *Kerberos version 5* security token formats for context establishment and per-message exchange as defined by the IETF Common Authentication Technology working group.

The whole reason behind the Kerberos ticket is to authenticate the user's identity. That is not all Kerberos can be used for; for example, the protocol may carry additional authorization information that might be managed on the local system for access control.

One of the nice things about standards is that there are so many of them. Each standard usually has several pieces that allow for some tweaking by the final implementer. In the case of Kerberos, the Microsoft implementation of the protocol provides support for some of the interoperability characteristics that are sufficient to provide for identity-based authentication. In addition, Microsoft also integrated authorization data in the form of Windows 2000 group memberships into the Kerberos tickets. This gives Kerberos the ability to convey access control information to Windows 2000 services. The basis for representation of the authorization data is in the Windows Security IDs.

One of the ways that Windows NT security was perceived to be lacking was in the area of services. Many of the services required an account, and many of the accounts had default passwords. Therefore, a hole was created. With Windows 2000, the services still have service accounts. These accounts are defined in the Active Directory, which also defines the shared secret used by the KDC to encrypt session tickets. In that way, clients attempting to connect to Windows 2000 services obtain session tickets to the target server from the KDC in the domain where the service account is defined. The Kerberos security provider supporting a Windows 2000 service expects to find Authorization Data in the session tickets that are used to build a security access token. In this case, the Windows 2000 service impersonates the security context of the client, based on the Authorization Data provided in the session ticket.

When you start talking about cross-platform access, you have to remember this is usually a two-way street. In other words, not only are Windows 2000 clients accessing resources on non–Windows 2000 networks, but there are clients that come into the Windows 2000 network from the outside. In this scenario, the clients must obtain the initial Kerberos *ticket-granting ticket (TGT)* tickets from KDCs on the non–Windows 2000 systems. The non–Windows 2000 system will then use the Kerberos referral mechanism to request a session ticket from the KDC in the Windows 2000 Service domain.

Now, not all Kerberos is created equal. Some Kerberos is newer than others. Of course, as a protocol, each implementation of Kerberos can be handled slightly differently. For example, suppose the referral ticket is created as part of the inter-realm trust relationship between the KDCs. If the ticket request originates from an MIT Kerberos authentication service, it is not likely to contain authorization data. When session tickets do not contain authorization data, the Kerberos security provider on Windows 2000 tries to use the principal name in the ticket and create a security access token for a designated user account or use a default account defined for this purpose.

We will look at cross-platform referral in more detail later in this chapter.

Private/Public Keys

Another extension to the Kerberos protocol that is supported in Windows 2000 is authentication based on private/public-key pairs in addition to shared-secret keys. The *public-key authentication extensions* allow clients to request an initial TGT, using a private key, while the KDC verifies the request using the public key obtained from an X.509 certificate stored in the User object in the Active Directory.

The user's certificate could be issued by a third-party Certificate Authority, such as VeriSign's Digital IDs, or could be issued by the Microsoft Certificate Server in Windows 2000.

After the initial private-key authentication, standard Kerberos protocols for obtaining session tickets are used to connect to network services.

The public-key authentication extensions to the Kerberos protocol provide a foundation for network authentication, using smart card technology. Windows 2000 allows users to log on to a workstation by using a smart card.

Windows 2000 and Internet Security

Internet security is a really a complex issue. You not only have to make your Web presence available to anyone and everyone, you have to protect it from attack. If you are one of the millions who believe strongly in e-business, and you want to take people's money over the Web, your headaches are compounded. How do you securely take and store someone's credit card number? This is another case where public-key cryptography is the security technology that enables strong security for enterprise and Internet communications. In the case of the Internet, the security technologies include a Certificate Server, a secure channel security provider that implements SSL/TLS protocols; the *Secure Electronic Transaction (SET) secure payment protocol* for credit card transactions; and *CryptoAPI* components for certificate management and administration.

Here is another one of those fascinating protocol layouts that are just about impossible to comprehend. We told you before, the Authors Union makes us include them. In Figure 10.2, you see the components of the Microsoft public-key security infrastructure.

FIGURE 10.2 Components of the public-key security infrastructure

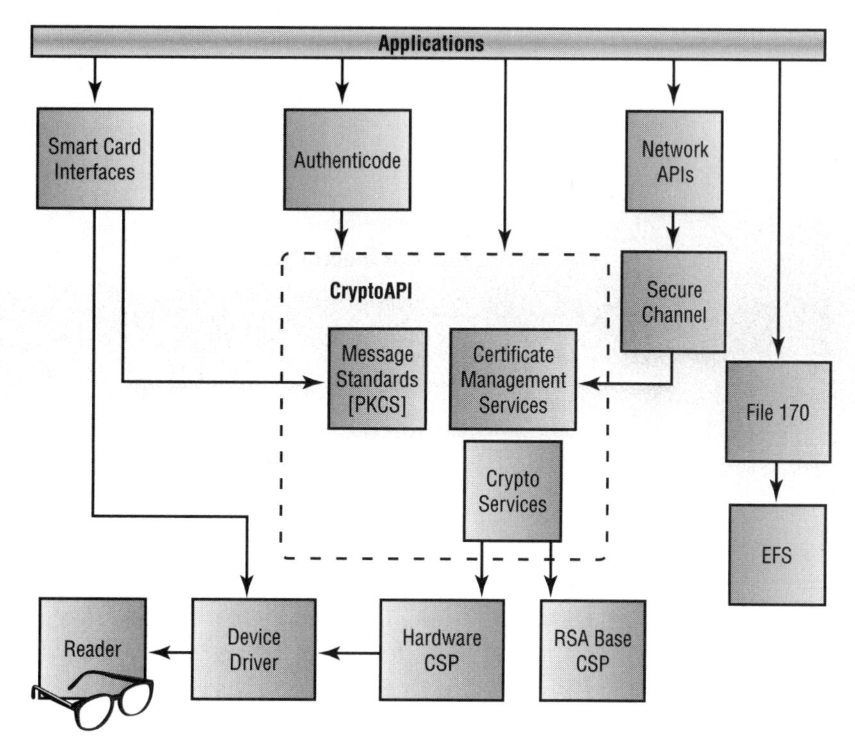

Most of these components are not new, and certainly not just Microsoft. The Microsoft Internet security infrastructure is actually based on industry standards for public-key security. These include support for RSA Public Key Cipher, X.509 certificate formats, and *Public Key Certificate Services (PKCS)* standards.

Many of these components were first released in Windows NT 4. These components include:

- The CryptoAPI. The CryptoAPI comes with programmer support for key generation and exchange. In addition you can use digital signatures, and data encryption.
- CryptoAPI also supports X.509 certificates and PKCS. PKCS was released in Service Pack 3 for Windows NT 4 and is used by Internet Explorer 4 and Windows 2000.

- There is also the Secure Channel implementation of the Secure Sockets Layer (SSL) version 2, version 3 client-side support, and Private Communications Technology (PCT) version 1 public-key security protocols.
- There is also Authenticode, a Microsoft developed solution, that uses digital signatures to verify the integrity of software downloaded from the Internet and identification of the software publisher.

The Microsoft Internet security infrastructure builds on these components to provide the functionality to support public-key security. The new features of the Microsoft Internet security infrastructure for Windows 2000 Distributed Security Services include:

- Client Authentication with SSL 3 based on Public Key Certificates
- Certificate Server for issuing certificates to Windows 2000 domain accounts

Last chapter, we touched on the Secure Socket Layer and Transport Layer Security. These are public-key-based security protocols implemented by the Secure Channel (Schannel) security provider. Internet browsers and servers use these security protocols to provide for mutual authentication. That means they check for message integrity and maintain confidentiality.

Since a perfectly good system has been designed to provide authentication between servers, why re-invent the wheel? In the case of the client to server authentication, why not use the same process as server authentication? So, here the server verifies the cryptographic signatures on the client's certificate, and any intermediate CA certificates, to a known or trusted root CA. Once the identity of the client is verified through certificate verification (client authentication), the application server needs to establish a security context with appropriate access rights defined for the client. The access control information determines what resources the client is allowed to use on this server. In the Windows 2000 security architecture, access control is defined by the group memberships and user accounts and the privileges defined in the security access token.

As we showed above, the public-key client authentication uses the information in the client's certificate to map to local access control information. This mapping determines what authorization the client has to access resources on the server system.

For more involved situations, Windows 2000 provides support for client authentication by implementing a security service that uses the Active Directory to map certificate information to existing Windows accounts. The mapping can be performed using a search of the certificate subject name in the Windows directory or by searching for directory properties that identify the client certificate. Because this is integrated in Active Directory, no separate database is required to define the access rights associated with Public Key Certificates. The access control information is maintained by the group membership stored in the Windows directory. This also means that no special administration tools are required. You just use the common Windows Directory Service administration tools and grant access rights by adding Windows users to groups.

What about the person who needs to access resources on a Windows 2000 network, but does not have a domain account? Here, the support for Public Key Certificate authentication in Windows 2000 allows client applications to connect to secure services on behalf of users who do not have a Windows 2000 domain account. These users are authenticated based on a Public Key Certificate issued by a trusted Certificate Authority. The certificate can then be granted access to Windows 2000 resources. Using the Directory Service administration tools allows administrators, or delegated authorities, to associate one or more external users to an existing Windows 2000 account for access control. The Subject name in the X.509 version 3 certificate is used to identify the external user that is associated with the account. In this way, businesses can share information securely to selected individuals from other organizations without having to create a lot of special Windows 2000 accounts. This is called a many-to-one mapping of certificates.

Client authentication of external users still requires the system administrator to configure the Certificate Authority for the external user's certificates as a trusted CA. This prevents someone with a certificate issued by an unknown authority from authenticating to the system as someone else.

Microsoft Certificate Server

There are several different ways these certificates can be provided. Your company can go out and enlist the aid of a third-party vendor, or you can use the *Microsoft Certificate Server*, which is included with Windows 2000 and IIS 4. The certificate server is designed to provide flexible services for issuing and managing certificates for applications using public-key cryptography. The Certificate Server can perform the management role to provide secure communications across the Internet, or any other nonsecure network. In addition, you can customize the Microsoft Certificate Server so that it will support the application requirements of different organizations.

It works this way. The Certificate Server receives requests for new certificates over transports such as RPC, HTTP, or e-mail. Each request is checked against custom or site-specific policies, sets optional properties of the certificate to be issued, and issues the certificate. The certificate server also allows administrators to add elements to a *Certificate Revocation List (CRL)*, and publish a signed CRL on a regular basis.

The policy module for the Certificate Server uses network authentication of certificate requests to issue certificates to users with Windows 2000 domain accounts. This policy module may be changed if there are specific needs of the issuing organization. Since the Certificate Server generates the certificates using a standard X.509 format, they can be used to authenticate servers and clients using either the TLS or SSL protocols.

Certificates on a Net

Certificates can be used on either a corporate intranet or on the Internet. Here, servers that may already be in place, such as the Microsoft Internet Information Server, can perform client authentication for secure communications using certificates generated by the Certificate Server. Certificate Server can also generate server certificates used by IIS and other Web servers to provide server authentication to assure clients (browsers) that they are communicating with the right place.

Access for Trusted Partners

We have talked time again about the Internet-based enterprises that are already doing business with customers and partners over the Internet. This includes things like resellers, suppliers, distributors, and basically any Tom, Dick or Mary. Anyone who is part of an extended business may need to connect to your corporate intranets and access important company information. Employees and representatives in the field increasingly use local access to public networks, and then connect to remote corporate information sources.

Because inter-business distributed computing is not limited to a single architecture, the security technology can not limit the way people access information. It is up to you to make sure that Windows 2000 integrates support for the security protocols and user models that fit application or business needs. What are some of the options that you can use to manage and support these inter-business relationships?

- One way of doing it is to create user accounts for business partners to access corporate information services. In this way, you can integrate Windows 2000 security with the Active Directory and make management of these accounts easier. As you know by now, we are all for easier. You can also create Organizational Units to be used to group related accounts by partner, supplier, or other business relationship. To really simplify your management life, administration of these accounts can be delegated to the people in the organization who manage these partner relationships. This can take you out of the loop completely. Virtual Private Networks can then be established between organizations. This will ensure that network traffic carried over any public network is encrypted. Also, by using this approach, your company's business partners can use remote access services to get to your corporate information in the same way as any other remote employee. If you need to provide access to databases or just grant access to information repositories, these can all be controlled with Windows 2000 access control.

- You can also use domain trust relationships as another tool for establishing cross-business relationships. Since Active Directory provides much flexibility in the management of a tree of hierarchical domains, and since the Windows 2000 domain names are integrated with DNS naming, Internet routing of information between two domains is relatively easy to configure. If the business relationship is not a two-way street, the domain trust can be used as one way to configure client/server applications that also have the privacy features necessary to communicate over the Internet. As far as accessing information or shared resources, users can use either Kerberos or public-key authentication protocols.

- If you have Internet security problems, your organization can use the Microsoft Internet security infrastructure. Here, your company would issue Public Key Certificates to specific partners who need to access specific information resources. Instead of creating a user account or defining a domain trust relationship, certificates can be used as a way of providing user identification and authorization.

Single Sign-On

Single Sign-on (SSO) is a service that users have been demanding for years. It basically allows enterprise network users to access all authorized network resources on the basis of a single interactive logon with a username and password. This authentication is performed when they initially access the network. The problem has always been to try to figure out a way to authenticate a user to, say, a NetWare network, an AS/400, a mainframe, and a Unix host with one simple sign-on.

Kerberos and SSL to the rescue! SSO is provided natively in Windows 2000 using the built-in Kerberos and Secure Sockets Layer protocols. These protocols can also provide standards-based SSO within mixed networks. Microsoft SNA Server further extends this capability to mainframe environments by means of their proprietary protocols. Homogeneous Windows 2000–based networks enjoy the most easily managed, most seamless SSO capability.

SSO Introduction

As we mentioned above, single sign-on (SSO) is simply the ability of a user to prove her identity to a network one time. After the authentication has occurred, the user will have access to all authorized network resources without any additional work on her part. The network resources in question can range from printers and other hardware, to applications, to files and other data, all of which may be spread throughout an enterprise on servers of various types that may be running different operating systems. Here again, the challenges come in when you do not have a homogeneous network. As soon as you put a resource on the network based on another platform, you could have authentication problems.

So, you are probably asking yourself, "What does this all mean for me?" SSO will provide the following benefits:

- First, there is simpler administration. The primary barrier to adoption for most SSO implementations is that they are operating system–specific and add to the administrator's burden by requiring SSO-specific administrative tasks, using SSO-specific tools. However, under Windows 2000, SSO-related tasks are performed transparently as part of normal maintenance, using the same tools that are used for other administrative tasks.

- There is better administrative control. Since all network management information, including all SSO-specific information, is stored in the Active Directory, there is a single, authoritative listing of each user's rights and privileges. This allows the administrator to change a user's privileges in a single location and know that the results will propagate network-wide.

- You can also improve user productivity. Users are no longer bogged down by multiple logons. They are no longer required to remember multiple passwords in order to access network resources. The Help desk personnel will love you, because they will need to field fewer requests for forgotten passwords.

- There is better network security. Users will no longer use Post-it notes to write down their passwords. All SSO methods provide secure authentication and provide a basis for encrypting the user's session with the network resource. Since information about a user account is stored in one place, the Active Directory, if you have to disable a user account, you will know that it is fully disabled.

- Finally, there is the consolidation of those heterogeneous networks we talked about before. By joining these diverse networks, the administrative efforts can be consolidated. That means that the administrative best practices and corporate security policies are being consistently enforced.

SSO and Windows 2000 Domains

Within Windows 2000 domains, SSO is provided by means of the Kerberos authentication protocol. As you know, when a user logs on, the user authenticates to a KDC, which provides an initial ticket called a ticket-granting ticket (TGT). When the user needs to use a network resource, his user session presents the TGT to the domain controller and requests a ticket for the particular resource, called a *service ticket* or a *session ticket (ST)*. He presents the ST to the resource, which grants access.

One of the problems with previous Kerberos implementations was that the protocol was separate from the operating system rather than a part of it. In other words, the Kerberos software operated on top of the operating system's normal security architecture rather than as a part of it. This meant that any SSO-specific information was stored separately from other system information. You, the administrator, were forced to learn an additional set of administrative tools just to manage the SSO infrastructure.

Since Kerberos is an inherent part of the Windows 2000 security architecture, SSO-related information is stored in the Active Directory along with all other information about network objects. The Kerberos model is integrated into the Windows 2000 domain model—meaning you don't have to learn special tools. You can administer the network using the MMC that you know and love!

SSO in a Multiple Domain Environment

Before we can provide cross-domain authentication, the domain controllers in a multiple domain environment have to "meet" each other and swap tickets. The trust relationships between domains in effect introduce the domain controllers. Since the domain controllers are also the Kerberos KDCs, the servers can authenticate each other.

So, it works like this. Check out Figure 10.3 below. When a user in one domain needs access to a resource in a trusting domain, the user's domain controller services his request for a ticket by making a cross-realm referral to the domain controller that owns the resource. This remote domain controller trusts the referral because it comes from a source it knows, and it issues a ticket to the user. Now you know why, by default, all domains within a Windows 2000 domain tree trust each other and accept referrals from each other. Forests in Windows 2000 do not trust each other by default, but trust relationships can easily be established between them. See Figure 10.3.

FIGURE 10.3 Cross-realm Kerberos referrals

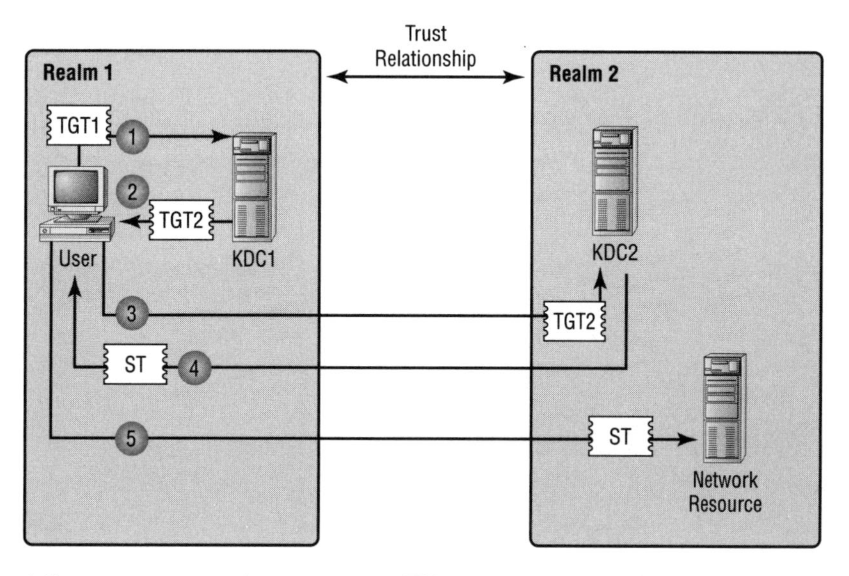

1. User wants to use network resource: presents TGT and requests service ticket.
2. KDC1 can't provide ticket to resource because it is in another realm, provides TGT to KDC2 instead.
3. User session presents TGT to KDC2.
4. KDC2 returns service ticket to resource.
5. User presents ticket and is granted access.

This is another reason why the people at Microsoft keep touting the benefits of a homogeneous Windows 2000–based network. The administrator never has to perform SSO-specific administrative tasks. Instead, SSO functions are a part of the administrative tasks that you already perform. For example, the administrator never has to establish the cryptographic keys that the user and domain controller share. When a user account is created, the shared keys are transparently generated as part of the process of creating the account, and are securely disseminated where needed. Similarly, when the administrator establishes trust relationships between domains, the keys needed to effect cross-realm referrals are transparently generated and securely exchanged.

Like always, administrative tasks are carried out using the Microsoft Management Console (MMC). All SSO administrative functions are carried out via MMC snap-ins like the Certificate Services, shown Figure 10.4.

FIGURE 10.4 Active Directory Manager snap-in

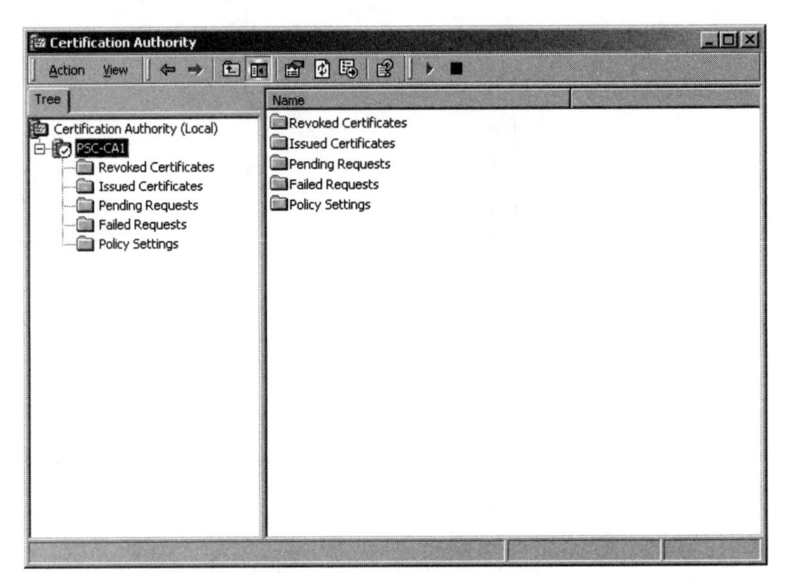

As we mentioned earlier in this chapter, Kerberos, like most protocols, can be extended, based on your desired implementation. In Microsoft's implementation of Kerberos, the use of these extensions enables the tickets to carry authorization information. Most Kerberos implementations carry only authentication information, so, after using the ticket to establish the user's identity, the network resource must consult a local database to determine what the user is allowed to do. This means that someone, usually the network administration team, has to construct and maintain these databases. You may translate that last sentence to mean more work for you! However, in Windows 2000, none of these local databases is needed. All authorization information is centrally stored within the Active Directory, and when a user requests a ticket, Windows 2000 packages the information within the Kerberos ticket in the form of a Security Access Token (SAT).

A side benefit for using Kerberos is that there can be a significant improvement in network performance. After all, you have removed the domain controller as a bottleneck in authenticating users to network resources. In most network authentication protocols, the network's security authority must provide authentication for every use of a network resource. For example, in previous versions of Microsoft Windows NT operating system, a domain controller had to vouch for a user's identity every time the user wanted to use a printer, even if it was the same printer that user had accessed just minutes before. This can obviously slow things down at the domain controller, not to mention increasing the amount of unnecessary network traffic.

This bottleneck elimination is shown below in Figure 10.5. When a user needs access to a network resource for the first time, his user session asks the domain controller for a ticket. The domain controller's sole participation in the use of the resource is to issue the ticket to the user's session. When the user subsequently wants to use the same resource, the domain controller is not involved at all, because the tickets are reusable until they expire. Tickets are stored in a local cache that is part of the security architecture's protected storage, and when one is needed, the user's session simply retrieves the ticket from the cache and presents it to the resource.

There are other ways to improve on network performance. One of these ways is to make better use of trust relationships between the domains in an Active Directory tree. By default, all domains within a tree trust each other. In some networks, this may not be a problem. The chain of cross-realm referrals follows the structure of the domain tree, and if the tree is simple and straightforward, things may not need to be tweaked. However, things are rarely simple and straightforward. If you are working in a complex tree like the one shown in Figure 10.6, many referrals could be needed for a user to obtain a ticket to use a resource on a widely separated domain. However, if there is frequent access to resources in a particular domain, a shortcut trust allows two domains to establish a direct referral between them, regardless of the way the domain tree is laid out.

FIGURE 10.5 Bottleneck elimination

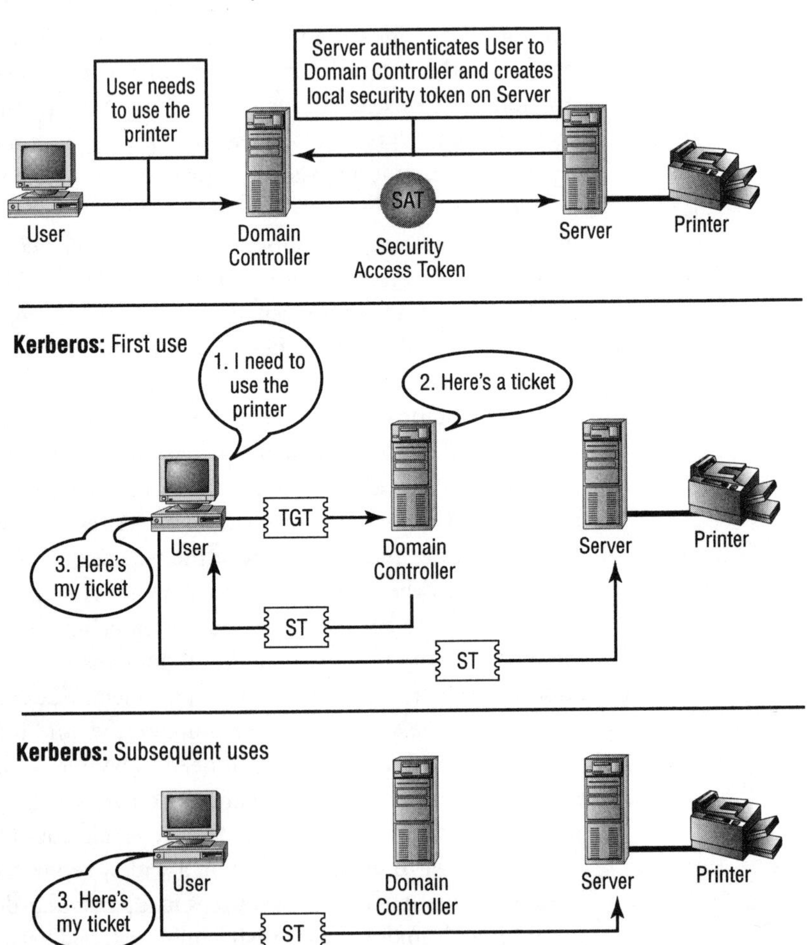

FIGURE 10.6 Example of shortcut trusts

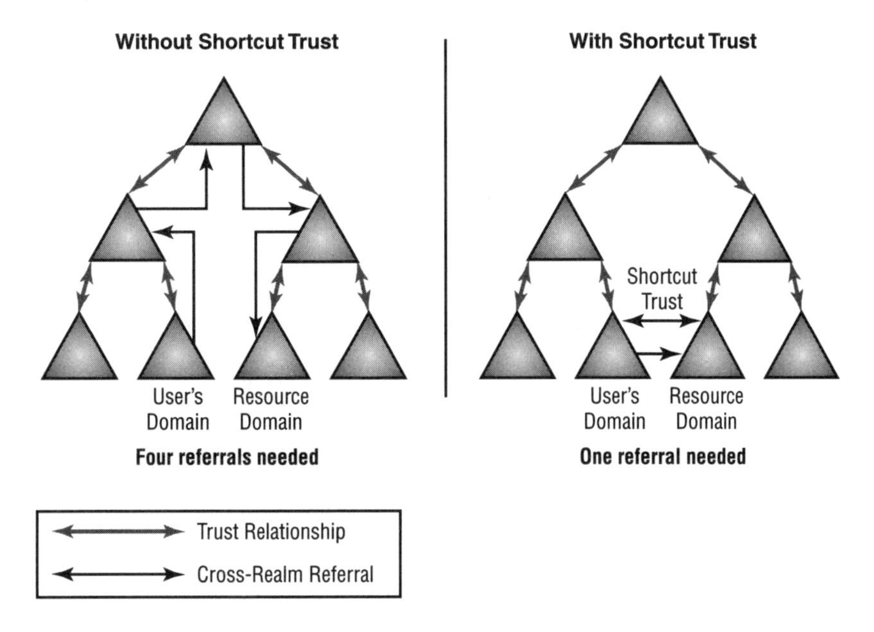

So, you have given yourself some new tools to use in allowing users access to your network from the outside. For example:

- You have mutual authentication. Both the user and the network resource can verify they are not talking to an imposter.
- *Internet Protocol Security (IPSec)* allows encryption of user sessions.
- Kerberos tickets can be delegated, allowing for improved auditing and control in multi-layered applications. A multi-layered application is an application where a user requests a server from the user interface, the interface passes the request on to the middle tier, and the middle tier generates database commands to fulfill the request.

SSO in Normal Networks

As much as Microsoft would love for all companies to have a completely Windows 2000–based network, the chances of that happening are not very great. There are just too many alternatives. If your network is like most, you use the best operating system to do the job at hand. That may be Windows 2000, it may be NT, it may be NetWare, or it may be Unix. So, Microsoft had to provide the flexibility to support SSO within a network comprising a variety of vendors' platforms. This was done with its support for standards-based authentication protocols and Microsoft gateway products. As you can see in Figure 10.7, Kerberos provides just part of the puzzle.

FIGURE 10.7 SSO in a real network

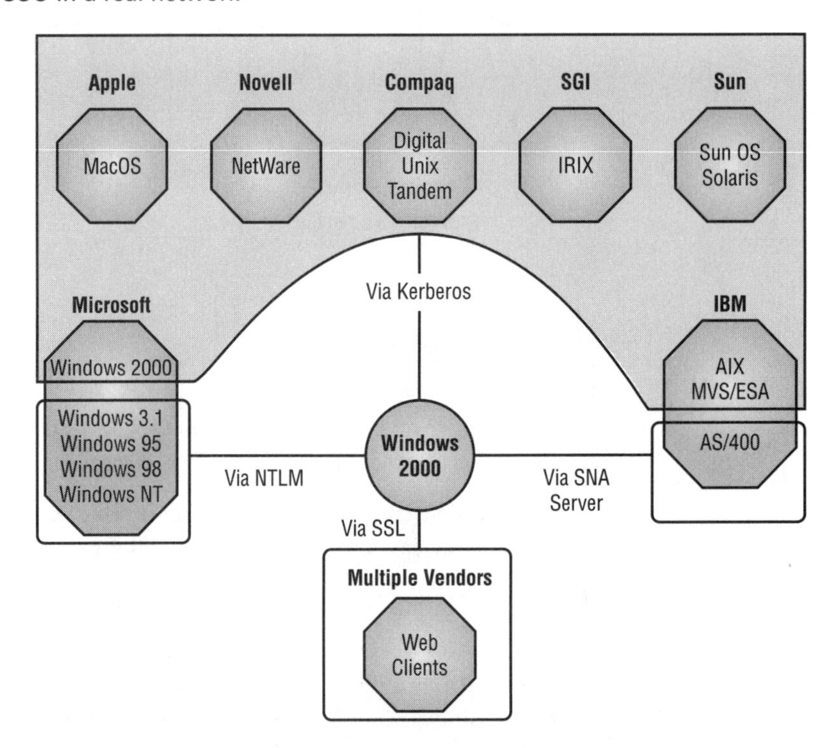

Before SSO, if you had a mixed network, you often found yourself providing duplicate resources for different network segments. Now, enterprises can share existing resources between all users of the network, rather than having to continually redo work that has already been done. In a model similar to the Internet, users can easily navigate through the corporate network without needing to know when they have crossed the boundary from one platform to another. Security is improved by providing for mutual authentication of clients and servers, and by removing the temptation for users to write down their multiple passwords.

How can you make it work? One of the ways is with the introduction of some third-party tools. For example, by using something like CyberSafe's TrustBroker, you can provide SSO between Windows 2000 and networks running the MacOS, AIX, Digital Unix, HP-UX, IRIX, Netware, Solaris, SunOS, Tandem, and MVS/ESA operating systems.

Network Integration

Just like in a homogeneous Windows network, the process starts by establishing a trust relationship between Windows 2000 and the disparate network. In this case, we will be using Kerberos is simplify the process. Once the administrator has established a trust relationship between the KDCs in the different realms, the tickets can be provided for cross-realm referrals. The administrator of Windows 2000 sets up a user account in the usual way, to which the incoming users will be mapped. Once this has been done, the rights and privileges of incoming users are managed the same old way, via their Windows 2000–based user accounts, using the same administrative tools as are used for native Windows 2000 users.

When a user on the other system needs to access a network resource in the Windows 2000 domain, his user session requests a ticket for the resource. The KDC, seeing that the resource lies in the Windows 2000 domain, refers the user to the Windows 2000 domain controller and vouches for his identity. The Windows 2000 domain controller then maps the user's identity to the corresponding Windows 2000 user account and issues the ticket to the user, who presents the ticket to the resource. For a Windows 2000 user who needs to use a resource in the other system, the process happens in reverse, although the administrative procedures that are used on the other system will vary.

Obviously, there is going to be some extra overhead here. For example, when trust is established in a mixed environment, the administrator must manually synchronize keys between the Windows 2000 domain controller and the other system's KDC. Likewise, there is the loss of having a single set of administrative tools and a single repository of SSO-related information. Instead, there is at best a single set of tools for each platform, and a single repository of SSO-related information for each platform. However, the ability to allow seamless sharing of resources is clearly a boon to enterprise customers, and any time you can keep the customers happy, your life is made easier.

SSO for Improved Security

One of the side benefits of using Kerberos is that you can get operating systems to share a common authentication protocol. Usually, when user IDs and passwords are exchanged between different platforms, they are sent as plain text. However, Kerberos tickets are encrypted. This provides a mechanism for securely exchanging authentication information. Also, because the Kerberos ticket contains cryptographic key information, it provides a secure key exchange medium for establishing encrypted sessions between the platforms.

Finally, the trust relationship between KDCs, as the channel through which all user authentication information is exchanged, provides a simple and effective way to control resource sharing. For example, if two departments in a company, one running under Windows 2000 and one running under another system, allow resource sharing via Kerberos-based SSO, it is easy to temporarily disallow the sharing simply by removing the trust relationship. It is not necessary to locate all of the affected user IDs and disable each account.

SSL and SSO

Earlier in the chapter, we mentioned SSL. When we talked about SSL, it was to highlight the way people access your corporate Web page. That is not the only way it can be used, because not all enterprise computer users enter a network by means of network-to-network connections. Some people have to be different, meaning that you must also support users who access your corporate network through intranets. These users can include people who are mobile users and who access the corporate network via the Internet. Or it could be your corporate partners who need access to the corporate intranet. SSO, in this case, can be provided for these customers via the Secure Sockets Layer (SSL) security protocol.

Any of the administrative tasks needed to provide SSO via SSL are performed via MMC snap-ins like the Active Directory Users and Computers, Certificate Services Manager, and IIS Manager. Look at Figure 10.8 to see what I mean.

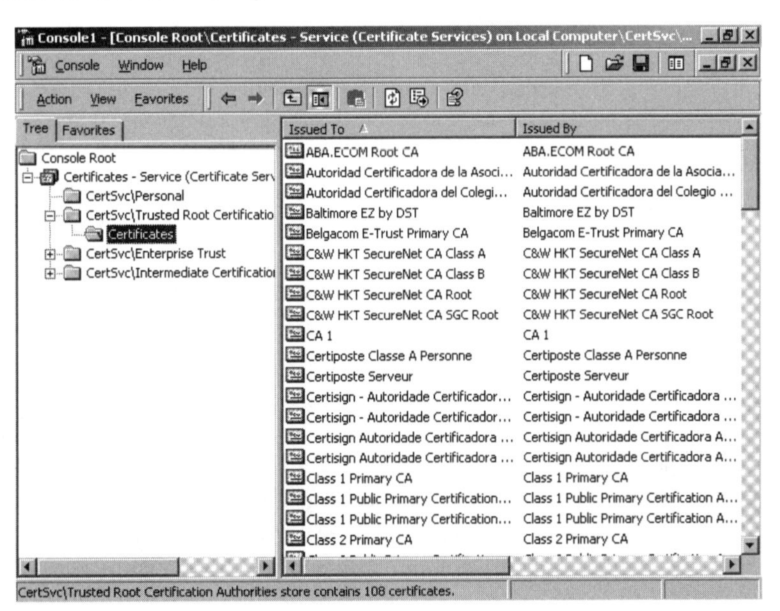

FIGURE 10.8 Certificate Services Manager

So by using SSL, administrators can specify of the way IIS decides whether certificates can be used only to authenticate to the Web server, or whether they can be the basis of a full network logon. As an Administrator, you can associate individual certificates with individual user accounts, or you can state that all certificates from a particular CA map to a single guest account. Finally, you can decide to enable the use of certificates issued by an external CA within your implementation or establish the enterprise as its own CA.

SSL Security

Even with the use of certificate management, how can access control be managed? Just a few sentences ago, we said that an administrator could assign a certificate to a guest account, which seems to bypass the whole process. So, if digital certificates are used for the initial authentication of the user, doesn't the control point for access to network resources remain the user account? Yes, so after authenticating the user, Windows 2000 maps the certificate to the appropriate user account and uses the user's normal security credentials to access network resources. This eliminates the need to keep multiple copies of the user's privileges synchronized.

Session security is improved because of the encryption provided by the SSL protocol implementation. This allows an IT Team to determine the preferred level of encryption for Web-based network access, and to establish it when the session begins.

To comply with U.S. export law, Windows 2000 provides a North American version and an International version of its SSL implementation. The North American version provides 40-bit and128-bit versions of the RC2 and RC4 cryptoalgorithms; 512-, 768-, and 1024-bit version of RSA; and 56-bit DES encryption. The International version provides 40-bit RC2 and RC4, and 512-bit RSA encryption.

Finally, digital certificates whose private keys have been compromised, or whose owners no longer require access to network resources, can be marked as revoked via Certificate Services. The network consults the Certificate Revocation List and refuses to authenticate certificates that are authentic but not valid. This enables administrators to be sure that terminated employees, hackers, and thieves cannot gain access to the network.

Summary

When someone starts talking about connecting enterprises and granting access to users from other areas, they are talking about an SSO capability. Users are happier when barriers are removed between them and the resources they are authorized to use. Networks can be managed with fewer administrators because of the consolidation of management information. Network security is improved by the use of secure authentication protocols and the elimination of the most common threat to network security: users writing down their passwords.

Your Windows 2000 network comes with many of the tools necessary to make this happen right out of the box. It uses Kerberos and SSL protocols, which help ensure interoperability with other vendors' implementations.

Design Study: So How Do I Do This Anyway?

As you saw in the last case study, there are a variety of excuses why companies are not on the Internet. Most of the reasons are excuses rather than reasons. In most instances, you can examine a company and spot several different instances where that company could benefit from an Internet presence. We have talked about the Internet basics, like just having a registered DNS name and e-mail. More and more customers are going to the Web first and to the store later. It is much easier to buy something from a store thousands of miles away that has an Internet presence than to get up, get in the car, drive to a store, and shop. As this book is being written, unemployment in the United States is very low. Most retail stores and service organizations are competing for what few bodies there are who want to work that hard, work those hours, for that level of pay. Because of the poor response to staffing, the people that are working are overworked. They may be forced to work terribly long hours, or work in departments where they have little or no background. In some cases, one or two people are covering the areas normally assigned to four or more. Customer service, which in many retail stores has never been incredibly high, is suffering even more. In this day and age of the Internet, it is simply more convenient for customers to shop online than ever before. If your company is not part of that, you are missing out.

Key Terms

Before you take the exam, be certain you are familiar with the following terms:

access control lists (ACLs)

application programming interfaces (APIs)

asynchronous transfer mode (ATM)

authentication

authorization

Certificate Revocation List (CRL)

CryptoAPI

Distributed Password Authentication (DPA)

DSL

forwarding

frame relay

Internet Authentication Service (IAS)

Internet Group Management Protocol (IGMP)

IPSec

ISDN

Kerberos version 5

key distribution center (KDC)

Layer 2 Tunneling Protocol (L2TP)

Microsoft Certificate Server

Microsoft Commercial Internet System (MCIS)

Open Shortest Path First (OSPF)

proxy

public-key authentication extensions

Public Key Infrastructure

Public Key Certificate Services (PKCS)

RIP

Routing and Remote Access Services (RRAS)

SAP

Secure Socket Layer (SSL)

security access token

Security Support Provider Interface (SSPI)

Secure Electronic Transaction (SET) secure payment protocol

service ticket (ST)

session ticket (ST)

single sign-on

static routes

ticket-granting ticket (TGT)

virtual private networking

Windows NT LAN Manager (NTLM)

X.25

Review Questions

1. How does Kerberos use a TGT?

   A. A TGT is given to a system when it first starts the authorization process.

   B. A TGT is given to a user when it first starts the authentication process.

   C. A TGT is only given to KDCs.

   D. A TGT is only granted in an SNA environment.

2. Layer 2 Tunneling Protocol (L2TP) is a part of what?

   A. HTML

   B. PKI

   C. Kerberos

   D. CyptoAPI

   E. IPSec

3. Kerberos version 5 is inherently part of:

   A. Windows 2000 domains

   B. NetWare 3.X systems

   C. Windows 98 systems

   D. Windows 3.X systems

4. Which of the following describes Distributed Password Authentication (DPA)?

   A. A PKI certificate implementation

   B. Solely an NT 4 implementation

   C. A shared-secret authentication protocol

   D. Only used with smart cards

5. Kerberos v5 is a(n) ____________ protocol that may allow applications to provide ________________ services.

   A. Authorization, authentication

   B. PKI, DPMA

   C. SSL, TLS

   D. Authentication, authorization

   E. TLS, SSL

6. Microsoft Certificate Server is provided with:

   A. Windows 2000

   B. IAS

   C. RRAS

   D. Proxy server

   E. Exchange 2000

7. A Certificate Revocation List (CRL) can be modified by:

   A. Kerberos

   B. DPMA

   C. PKI

   D. The CA

   E. Network administrators

8. Where does SNA Server work?

   A. An open systems environment

   B. In conjunction with proprietary security protocols

   C. With IIS

   D. IPSec

9. Which of the following is true about shortcut trusts?

   A. Can only work in NT 4 networks

   B. Are established by default

   C. Are created between OUs

   D. Must be manually defined between Windows 2000 domains

   E. Work to put copies of the MMC on your desktop

10. Why would you want to delegate Kerberos tickets?

    A. To allow for improved auditing and control in multi-layered applications

    B. To allow for authorization across platforms

    C. To increase the CRL

    D. To interact with NetWare and Unix systems

Answers to Review Questions

1. B. A user is given a ticket-granting ticket after the user has been authenticated by providing a valid user name and password combination, or valid smart card logon. The ticket-granting ticket is then used in place of the user name password combination, or smart card logon, for all subsequent authentication.

2. E. When you see the acronym L2TP, think of IP Security and Virtual Private Networks.

3. A. Kerberos is the default security protocol in Windows 2000 domains.

4. C. DPA is a shared-secret authentication protocol.

5. D. Kerberos is an authentication protocol that has the flexibility to allow applications to provide authorization capabilities.

6. A. Certificate Server is provided with Windows 2000.

7. E. A Certificate Revocation List can be maintained by the network administration team.

8. B. SNA Server works in conjunction with proprietary security protocols that allow it to interact with mainframes.

9. D. A shortcut trust must be manually configured between Windows 2000 domains.

10. A. Kerberos tickets can be delegated, allowing for improved auditing and control in multi-layered applications.

The Multinational Conglomerate

You should give yourself 10 minutes to review this case study, diagram as needed, and complete the questions for this testlet. Be sure to read each question carefully. Although the company may not have changed, its circumstances change in each chapter.

Background

Your consulting firm has been hired to assist in the Windows 2000 migration and integration for a company based in Minneapolis, Minnesota. Until the start of this year, the company had 1,000 employees, all based throughout the Twin Cities of Minneapolis and St. Paul. Just before the end of the year, the owner of your company purchased two companies of roughly the same size, which will need to be connected to the enterprise network. The total number of users when the project is completed is estimated at 3,500. In addition, each of these companies comes with various strategic partners that will need to access the information on your enterprise network. The companies that have been acquired are located in Athens, Greece, and in Orlando, Florida.

The three companies can now be considered one, and the Windows 2000 rollout is in full swing. At this time, the company is examining various methods of providing access to the network, specifically to some special clients. There is also the problem of a new application the company is working with. This application is based in the Unix world, and therefore some areas of the company are going to have to have Unix workstations attached to the Windows 2000 network. These people will still need to access resources on the corporate network.

The Windows 2000 network is made up of a forest with three domains.

Current System

Minneapolis Located on the shores of beautiful Lake Calhoun, the company occupies a sprawling campus that includes four floors in a six-story building. Since the merger, the Lake Calhoun facility has become a model of efficiency. Besides being linked to all of the other offices, everyone is beginning to take the notion of an enterprise network seriously.

All of the floors are connected to the Windows 2000 network. The Minneapolis location is a domain in the tree. Active Directory Services have been deployed to the main campus and the rollout is complete in the branch offices. The desktop and laptop rollout company-wide took longer than expected, but it is now completed. The CEO wants to know what the IT team is doing to make sure that everyone within the company can access resources all over the tree, as well as protect the network.

The corporate network was so impressive that it helped this company snag a very large contract with a very large customer. This contract could put the company on the map. However, with every silver lining, there is a dark cloud. In this case, the dark cloud is that the customer wants to be able to access the online inventory system on your network, as well as share information directly with several new Unix hosts that are currently being installed.

The Unix workstation will all be headquartered in Minneapolis for the time being. To simplify matters, an organizational unit is going to be created to house these machines.

Orlando The Orlando office is a domain in the corporate tree. It has some valuable resources that need to be made available to the rest of company, particularly the folks in Athens.

The new contract may have a long-term effect on Orlando. Current corporate strategy calls for the new contract to be managed in Minneapolis for the first year, and then moved to Orlando after that. Given this strategy, Orlando will make use of their ability to access information in Minneapolis, but several people in the office will need to access the customer's network to work on design issues and planning issues.

Athens The Athens office is now fully staffed at 2,300. The location has discovered that the business is doing well, and the extra folks are justified. The office has been upgraded to Windows 2000 servers and Athens is now its own domain in the tree.

Athens has always been ahead of the curve. When the new contract was announced, Athens' manufacturing geared up for the task, and can now handle that stage. Because the customer wants to be able to look at all the stages of inventory, the customer will need to be able to access the Athens facility as well as Minneapolis and Orlando.

Customer The customer has a Windows 2000 network. The customer and our IS department have decided to link the two forests.

The communication between the trees is established, and now all that remains is to design the layout of the Kerberos infrastructure and the domain trust relationships.

Problem Statement

Provide access for the new client to all areas of the network that they need, while remaining invisible in other areas. Make sure our company also has access to their network to access the resources we need. Insure integration of the new Unix workstations into the network, giving the Unix systems access to resources on the Windows 2000 network.

The issues that you are going to have to contend with include which protocols to use, and how to design the network so that access to KDCs is easy and painless. You must also provide your Unix hosts with access to resources, and ensure that users can authenticate into the customer's network.

Envisioned System

CEO As the new network was designed, the CEO is looking closely at the IS department and saying things like, "Okay people, you wanted the Windows 2000 network because of its flexibility and you now have it. This is where the rubber hits the road. Prove you can make this network do the things you said it can do."

CFO The CFO said, "You know, we are still paying the bills for this rollout. While it looks like our overall cost of operation will drop, it is still a large price to absorb. This contract was awarded on a bid basis. While we did have preferred vendor status, we still had to bid this close. The bidding was designed around the functionality that the IS team said it could provide. Please do not come back and tell me that you need more money for improvements to the network to make this work."

Orlando General Manager "My people need to have access to the information for our newfound friends; how soon can you get me that? Right now, e-mail is just not cutting it. We need to have real-time access and we need to have it now!"

Athens General Manager “We’re ready. We just need to give them access to our network. That shouldn’t be a problem. We do need to have some increased access to the new team in Orlando though. Those Unix hosts need to share information with a lot of different areas.”

Questions

1. Which protocols should you be looking at?

   A. TCP/IP

   B. Kerberos

   C. RADIUS

   D. FTP

   E. Telnet

   F. SSL/TLS

2. What can you do about the Unix hosts?

   A. Because you are using a domain model, as long as you have unique names within the domain, there should not be a problem.

   B. Train users in the proper use of passwords.

   C. Kerberos will take care of everything.

   D. Install smart cards.

   E. Use TLS to access the network.

   F. Install the Unix systems as a separate subnet and install a KDC for the subnet.

3. How do you handle the problem of the new customer accessing the network?

   A. Make sure the new customer can dial in to your network.

   B. Find out more about their network. Help them institute Kerberos.

   C. Institute RADIUS.

   D. Configure each network to create a VPN between routers.

   E. Make sure all the KDCs talk to one another and share keys.

4. This question is a drag and drop question. The columns on the left represent the different locations and their KDCs. Some of the locations are domains, and others are subnets that are sites. On the right is a series of connectors indicating one-way communication and two-way communication. Please drag the locations on the left and drop in the type of trust relationships that you will have to configure manually.

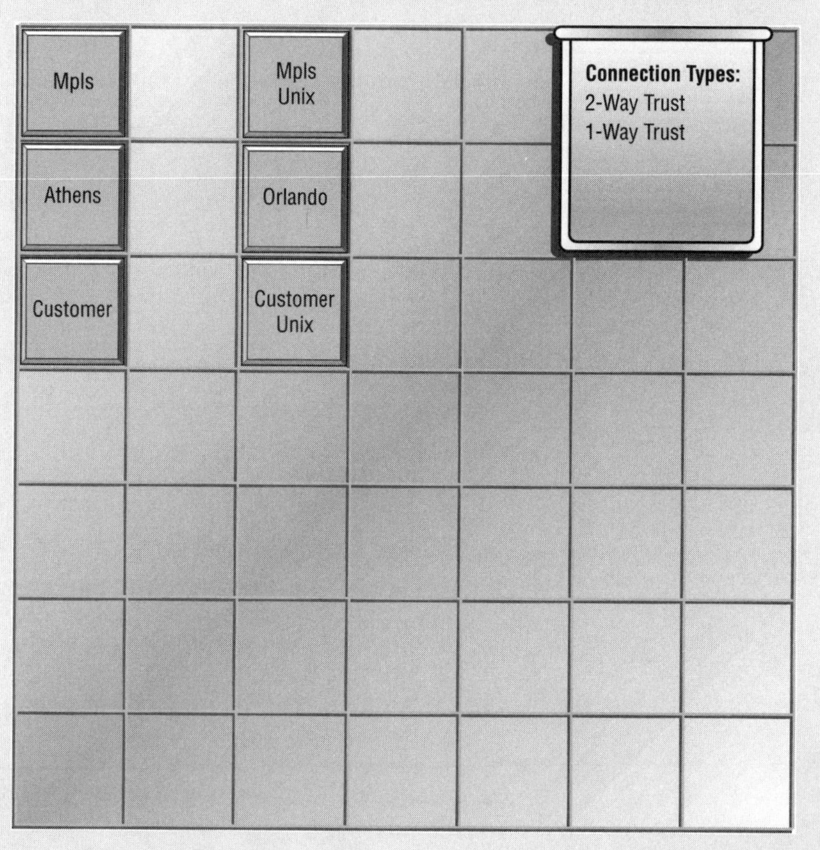

5. This is another drag and drop question. The columns on the left represent different locations and their KDCs. On the right, there is a series of connectors indicating one-way and two-way communications. Please drag the locations on the left and then drop in where keys are going to have to be exchanged.

Mpls

Mpls Unix

Athens

Orlando

Customer

Customer Unix

Connection Types:
2-Way Trust
1-Way Trust

Answers

1. B, F. This implementation has Kerberos and perhaps SSL/TLS written all over it. What you are primarily interested in is getting authentication to various networks. We can work on the authorization in another chapter! Kerberos will be the prime way to provide that authentication. In some cases, SSL may also be useful.

2. C and F. In this case, integration of Unix would probably be simplest if you "segregated" the Unix workstations on their own subnet. Once that has been done, you can simplify the process to provide a KDC to supply tickets for the Unix workstations and have the two KDCs exchange information. You will also have to use a third-party tool to effect this solution.

3. B, D, E. As envisioned, these networks will need constant connections. VPNs seem to be the answer to that problem. But you will also have to authenticate the remote users, and your users will have to authenticate to their network; therefore, all the KDCs will have to be able to communicate.

4.

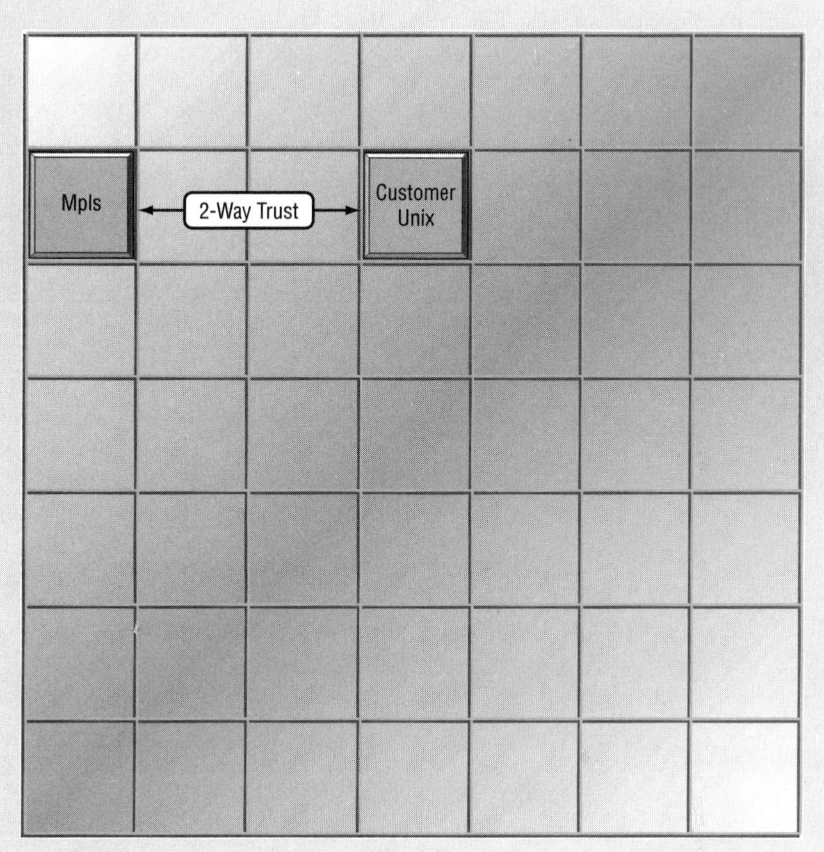

In this case, at the very least, there needs to be a two-way trust created between Minneapolis and the customer site. The customer site is also going to need to access Athens quickly, so you may want to create a shortcut trust relationship. All other trust relationships are created by default. The only relationship that has to be created manually is Minneapolis to the customer site.

5.

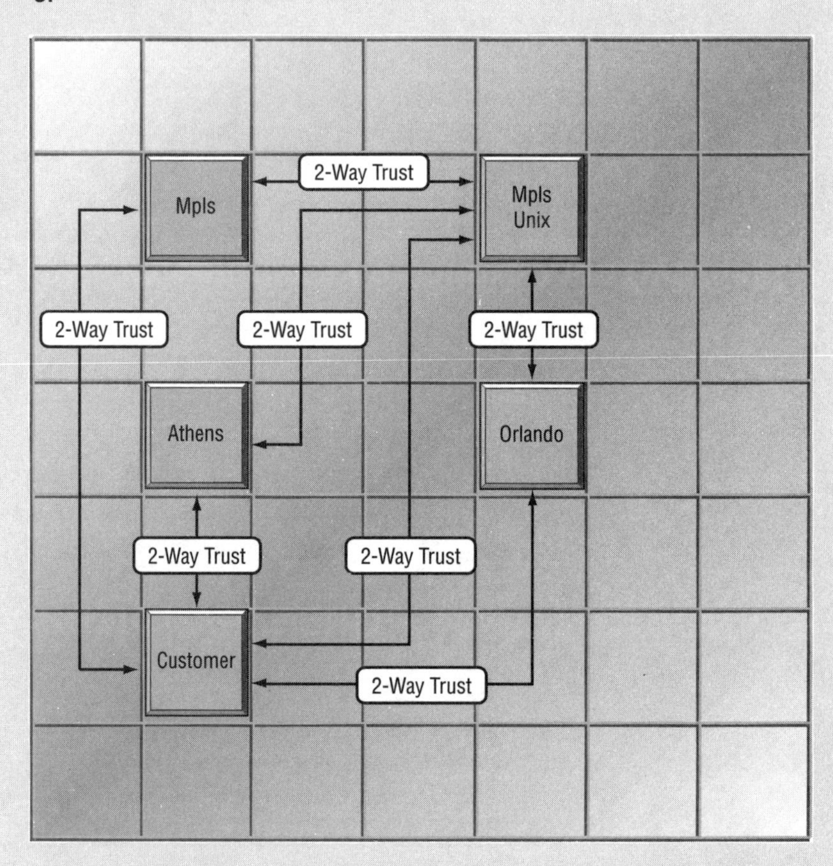

In this case, the customer and the Unix section should exchange keys with everyone. The internal network of the Minneapolis, Orlando, and Athens offices will not have to be manually configured. There should be a two-way connector between Customer and Orlando.

Enhancing Security Using Public Keys

MICROSOFT EXAM OBJECTIVES COVERED IN THIS CHAPTER:

✓ **Design a Public Key Infrastructure.**

- Design Certificate Authority (CA) hierarchies.
- Identify certificate server roles.
- Manage certificates.
- Integrate with third-party CAs.
- Map certificates.

We have talked about Kerberos and certificates several times during this book, and we have even hinted at ways to distribute certificate servers, but we have never come close to really delving into the topic. That is the purpose of this chapter. As you begin your security design over a large network, care needs to be taken to make sure that certificates are available and the certificate servers can provide them on a timely basis. So, in this chapter, we will do a brief review, and then get into designing the Certificate Authority (CA) hierarchies. Once the hierarchies are laid out, we can look at a map of the network and decide which of our servers we want to make into certificate servers. Once that is completed, we will have the ability to distribute certificates, but we will need a way to manage them, integrate them into a security scheme that might contain other vendors, and then find a way to map certificates to various resources. So, once again, there is a large job ahead of us.

Yep, we know. Some of the following information may sound familiar. That is because not everyone goes through this book page-by-page, line-by-line, like you do. Some folks just skip around from one area to another as the need arises. So, this brief review is for them. Then we will get into how to make it work properly.

Just give us a few minutes. If you already know this stuff from previous chapters, you can skip it, but this section will present a brief overview of the Public Key Infrastructure (PKI) features and tools in Windows 2000.

How PKI Works

As you should know by now, a PKI is based on *certificates*. A certificate is nothing more than a digitally signed statement that contains a *public key* and the name of the subject. As you might guess, there can be multiple types of names in the certificate. After all, each object in the Active Directory can be known by a variety of names, so they all have to be represented. Your certificate may have a directory name, an e-mail name, and Domain Name Service (DNS) name. By digitally signing the certificate, the *certification authority* verifies that the *private key* associated with the public key in the certificate is in the possession of the subject named in the certificate. The CA is, in effect, giving its blessing to the object and saying that this object is what it says it is.

A certification authority can come from a variety of sources. You may decide to create and manage your own. Or, you may use a third-party company. Either way, the CA issues a trusted user a certificate containing a public key. This certificate can be freely distributed. The public key can be used to encrypt data that can only be decrypted using an associated private key, which is also provided to the user. The user keeps the private key secure, so that no one else has access to it. The private key can be used to create a digital signature that can be confirmed by the public key. Now, keep in mind, this all happens in the background. In most cases, the end user is not even aware that it is happening.

By now you have a public key and a private key. That is the foundation of public key cryptography. In other words, there are two keys and these two keys are related. One key can be passed openly and freely between parties or published in a public repository. That is why it is called the public key. The other key must remain private.

Not all public keys are created equal. There are different kinds of public key algorithms, each with its own characteristics. This means that it is not always possible to substitute one algorithm for another. If two algorithms can perform the same function, the detailed mechanism by which that result is obtained varies.

With public key cryptography, the two keys are used in sequence. If the public key is used first, followed by the private key, then this is a key exchange operation. If the private key is used first, followed by the public key, this is a digital signature operation. In Windows 2000, PKI processes information in a way that simultaneously identifies and authenticates the source. It makes identity interception very difficult and prevents masquerading and data manipulation.

Prerequisites for Implementing PKI

Earlier in the book, we talked about how to plan a PKI. Like all things involved in Windows 2000, this requires planning and experimentation through pilot programs. Some features of Windows 2000 can be deployed immediately. These include things like the Encrypting File System (EFS) and IP Security (IPSec). In each case, their own certificates are provided without anything special done by the network administrator. Other security features that you may want to deploy may require a hierarchy of Certificate Authorities (CAs). Hopefully, by this point in the process you have completed the planning.

If your system reflects a typical CA hierarchy, it may have a three- or four-level architecture. As far as the "best practices" are concerned, it is a good idea to have one root CA and have the root CA be offline. If that is the base, you will need a second level of CAs to actually implement the certificate policy. This level should also be offline. The third level includes the actual issuing CAs. In this scenario, you can have either internal or external CAs. A local certifying authority, such as your IT department, can be left in charge of internal network authentication and data integrity. In the case of Internet transactions and software signing, your network might require some form of third-party certificates in order to establish public credibility. This third party would be considered a cryptographic service provider.

So now you are tasked with selecting your CA. Be sure to give some careful thought to who or what is going to be your *cryptographic service provider (CSP)*. The CSP is the software or hardware piece that provides the actual encryption services for your CA. If the CSP is software based, it will be the part of the puzzle that generates the key pair. That is just a fancy way of saying a public key and a private key. If the CSP is hardware based, it might be something like a smart card CSP. In that case, it might instruct a piece of hardware to generate the key pair.

Like anything with computing, whenever you are talking bigger and better, you are talking more money. In this case, greater security means more money. Not only will you suffer the expense for additional hardware but you will also pay in CPU cycles devoted to encryption. Greater security is not always cost effective, but it is available when needed.

For extreme levels of security, consider hardware CSP for CAs and smart cards for users.

Designing Your Public Key Infrastructure

As you may have guessed, this is not quite as simple as installing another service. It requires some level of detail to make sure the finished system will do what you want it to do. So, what do you want it to do? Since you are going to be issuing all of these certificates, how are they going to be used? Let's begin by identifying the certificate requirements before we make plans on how to distribute them.

Identify Your Certificate Requirements

So, what applications are you going to be using that are going to require digital certificates? Are you looking at secure e-mail, providing access to users who may not be coming into your network with Active Directory authentication, or providing secure Web services? As you can see, you start by identifying all the uses for certificates that you can think of. This includes what users, computers, and services will require certificates, and what types of certificates you intend to issue.

Then you can decide what service you are going to use to deploy these certificates. Are you going to go with Microsoft Certificate Services, or are you looking at obtaining other certificate services to support your public key needs? Once you have identified the categories of users, computers, and services that will need certificates, then you can determine the following information for each category:

- Name or description of the category
- Why are the certificates needed?

- How many users, computers, or services will need the certificates?
- Where are the users, computers, and services located?

Once all these things have been identified, you can start to figure out how you will provide certificate services to support your organization. Obviously, the certificate services you decide to deploy are going to be determined by the types of certificates that are going to be issued, as well as the number of entities that need certificates, and finally, where all these groups are located.

Now that you know what you are going to use certificates for, how can you distribute them? Well, certificate distribution is done in a hierarchical form.

Certification Authority Hierarchies

The statement has been made that this is usually done in a three- or four-layer design. The unusual thing about it is that half of those levels are not even attached to the network.

Microsoft Exam Objectives

Design a Public Key Infrastructure.

- Design Certificate Authority (CA) hierarchies.

As we have seen in previous chapters, the Windows 2000 Public Key Infrastructure supports a hierarchical CA trust model, called the *certification hierarchy*. In a very small network, a certification hierarchy may consist of a single CA. However, in a more complex environment, the hierarchy will contain several CAs that have clearly defined parent-child relationships. Figure 11.1 shows some of the ways you can define CA hierarchies.

FIGURE 11.1 Certification hierarchies

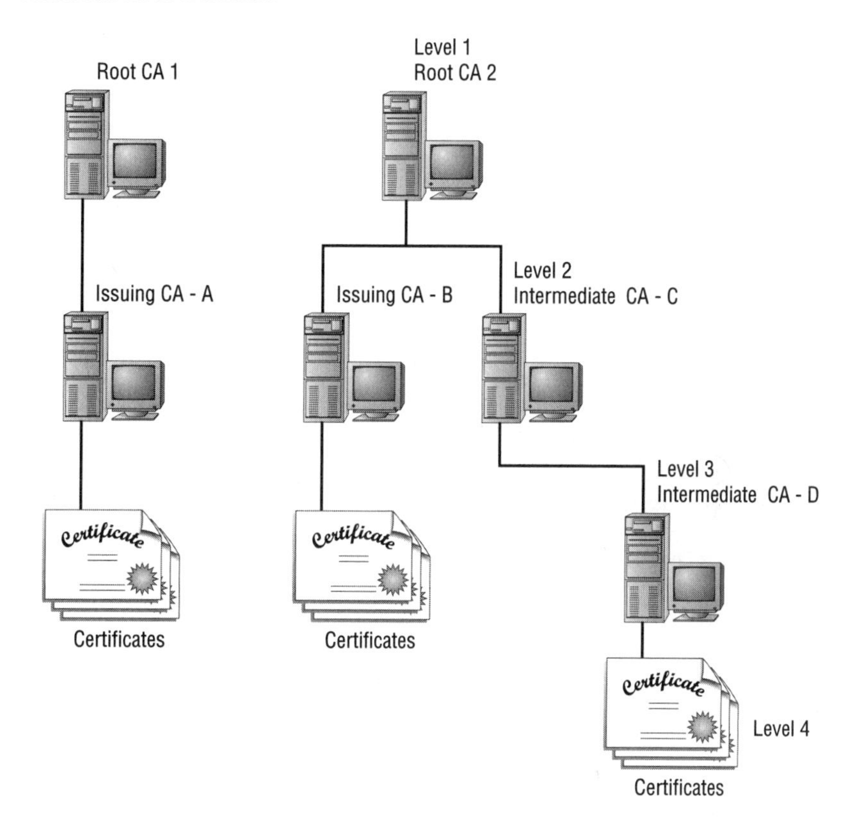

Don't feel like you are locked into either of these two methods. You can get creative and deploy multiple CA hierarchies in any way that will meet your needs. Some things never change, though. For example, the CA at the top of the hierarchy is always called a *root CA*. In addition, the root CAs are always *self-certified* by using a self-signed CA certificate. Since the root CAs are, by definition, the most trusted CAs in the organization, it is recommended that they have the highest security applied to them. This usually translates into having the root CA be a stand-alone system, locked away in a safe somewhere. Notice, the suggestion for the root CA is that it not even be in your computer room! When you begin to work with your design, remember, there is no requirement that all CAs in an enterprise share a common top-level CA parent or root. As a matter of fact, there may be several different top-level parents. It all depends on the needs of your organization.

Even though the trust for CAs does depend on each individual domain's CA trust policy, each and every CA in the trust hierarchy can be in a different domain.

Child CAs are called *subordinate CAs*. The parent CAs certify subordinate CAs. A parent CA certifies the subordinate CA by giving and signing the subordinate CA's certificate. As you learned above, the subordinate CA can be either an intermediate CA or it can be an issuing CA. Any *intermediate CA* will be tasked with issuing certificates only to its assigned subordinate CAs. Intermediate CAs may also be stand-alone systems, away from the network. Since an *issuing CA* issues certificates to users, computers, or services, it must be attached to the network.

As you can tell, there is no be-all and end-all suggestion or restriction as to how deep the certification hierarchy can be. In most cases a three-level certification hierarchy (root CA, intermediate CA, and issuing CA) will meet most needs.

Certification Path

When you look at the certification hierarchy, you are also examining a trust chain that is called the *certification path*. The certification path goes from the certificate all the way back to the root CA. If you think about it, you will see that it is a logical progression, like that shown in Figure 11.2.

FIGURE 11.2 Trusted certification path

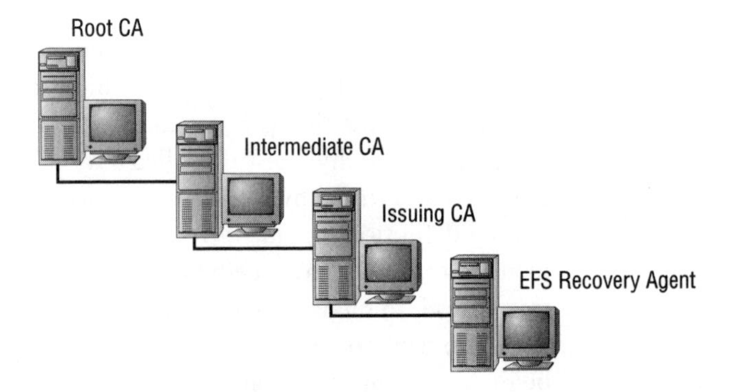

Let's look at the example of the EFS Recovery agent. In the diagram, you see that an EFS Recovery Agent certificate was issued by the issuing CA. Therefore there is a certification path that reaches to the root CA. The EFS

Recovery Agent certificate is trusted simply because the certificate for the root CA is in the Trusted Root Certification Authorities store.

As you have seen, the certification path is designed to link every certificate in the chain all the way back up to the root CA. All the certificates that have a valid certification path back up to any of the root certificates that are in the Trusted Root Certification Authorities store are trusted. This trust extends to all the purposes that are listed in the certificate. What happens if the root CA's certificate that provides for the certification path is not in the Trusted Root Certification Authorities store? In that case, the certification path is not trusted. That relationship remains until the certificate of the root CA has been added to the Trusted Root Certification Authorities store.

Before the Microsoft CryptoAPI will trust a certificate, it has to validate the certification path. The validation goes from the certificate all the way back to the certificate of the root CA. Each step along the way, the CryptoAPI checks each certificate in the path. Remember that each certificate contains information about the parent CA that issued the certificate. This way, the CryptoAPI can retrieve the certificate of each parent CA in the path, no matter whether the certificate comes from either the Intermediate Certification Authorities store or the Trusted Root Certification Authorities stores (if the certificates are present in the stores), or even from an online location (such as an HTTP or LDAP address) that is specified in the certificate. If CryptoAPI finds that there is a problem with one of the certificates in the path, or if it cannot actually find a certificate, it does not trust the certification path. Basically, the CryptoAPI just walks back up the certification trail to make sure every authority is still happy with the final outcome.

When CryptoAPI gets one of the subordinate CA certificates that requires certificate path validation, and if the certificate is not located in the Intermediate Certification Authorities store, the API will store the certificate in the Intermediate Certification Authorities store and hold that certificate for future reference. What about the computers that operate offline? In the case of laptop computers that are used by mobile users, you might actually have to import subordinate CA certificates into the Intermediate Certification Authorities store to make sure that non–root CA certificates are available to actually validate certification paths.

Design Scenario: Small Company

You have gone out to a small company that has need of certificate services. There are enough traveling users going and coming that it would be nice to have the added benefit of making sure users are who they say they are. The GM of the company has been to a Windows 2000 class and has heard that in order to use certificate services, you need a minimum of three servers, two of which are not even attached to the network. Now, with the cost of the licenses alone for Windows 2000, that makes things a little prohibitive. The GM is not currently a happy camper.

You explain to the GM that, in large networks, that is the goal. In a small network, however, you can get by with a single server solution. It is not advisable, because you would like at least the root CA to be protected, but it can be done.

Certificate Server Roles

Earlier in the chapter, we talked about the different ways the CA servers could be deployed. There are specific server roles that these CA servers can take, and it is important to know when to use each type of server.

Microsoft Exam Objectives

Design a Public Key Infrastructure.

- Identify certificate server roles.

Windows 2000 Types of Certification Authorities

Windows 2000 Server and Certificate Services support two types of CAs: enterprise CAs and stand-alone CAs. A root CA or a subordinate CA can be installed as either an enterprise CA or a stand-alone CA. Because there are some gotchas with deployment, it is important for you to know when to use an enterprise CA and when to use a stand-alone CA. The distinction is pretty straightforward, so test writers may not have a difficult time with the information.

Enterprise Certification Authorities

When you think of *enterprise CAs*, think of the Active Directory and Windows 2000. Enterprise CAs are a part of the Active Directory. The enterprise CAs are designed to publish certificates and CRLs to the Active Directory. Enterprise CAs use the certificate template information, user account information, and security group information that is stored in Active Directory to either approve or deny the actual certificate requests. If a certificate request is going to be approved, the requestor must have Enroll permissions that are granted by the security ACLs of the certificate template for the specific certificate type that was requested. When a certificate is finally issued, the enterprise CA will use the information that is in the certificate template to generate a certificate that contains the appropriate attributes for that specific certificate.

Not surprisingly, Microsoft recommends that you install most issuing CAs as enterprise CAs. This will let you gain the benefits of the integration with Active Directory. These benefits include automated certificate approval and automatic computer certificate enrollment. Remember also that only enterprise CAs can issue certificates that can be used for logging on with smart cards. This is the case because this process does require that smart card certificates be mapped automatically to the user accounts in Active Directory.

Stand-Alone Certification Authorities

Stand-alone CAs, on the other hand, do not require Active Directory. They also do not use certificate templates. For stand-alone CAs, any information that is needed about the requested certificate type has to be included in the actual certificate request. An example would be the Web Enrollment Support pages that are installed for stand-alone CAs. These pages will support requests that come in for a wide variety of certificate types.

How are these requests handled? Well, all certificate requests that come into a stand-alone CA are held in an area called the Pending Queue until the CA administrator actually approves them. As an administrator, you can configure stand-alone CAs to go ahead and issue certificates automatically, whenever they are requested, but this adds a significant security risk and usually is not considered to be a great idea.

What if you do want to automate certificate requests for stand-alone CAs? In that case, you may consider developing some custom policy modules that will securely approve or deny certificate requests, based on your criteria. For example, you may decide to develop a custom policy module that will automatically grant certificates to any authenticated requestor based on the security information about the requestor that is stored in a legacy database or even in a third-party directory service. While stand-alone CAs cannot issue certificates to be used for the smart card logon process, they can give out other types of certificates that can be used for smart cards. One example would be the way you can use the Web Enrollment Support pages for a stand-alone CA to issue secure mail and secure Web browser certificates that will interact with a requestor's smart cards.

By default, stand-alone CAs publish CRLs to the following location: <Drive:>\WINNT\System32\Certsrv\Certenroll where <Drive:>\ is the letter of the disk drive where the CA is installed.

Here again, you will have to do a cost benefit analysis because the use of stand-alone CAs in situations requiring high-volume issuing will usually incur a higher administrative cost; this is simply because the administrators must devote time and energy to manually reviewing, approving or denying each certificate request. Therefore, you should consider using stand-alone issuing CAs primarily with public key security applications on extranets and on the Internet. They should be used when users do not have Windows 2000 accounts and the volume of certificates to be issued and managed is relatively low.

If your network is using some form of third-party directory service, or when Active Directory is not available, you have to install stand-alone CAs. Stand-alone CAs can give you more flexibility for planning and managing the certificate life cycle by using root CAs and intermediate CAs.

So, when you pay the big bucks for the privilege of locking yourself in a little room for hours at a time, remember that when Active Directory is present, use *enterprise*. If you are dealing with the public in a Web environment and AD is not present, go with a stand-alone. Also, remember how much more work a stand-alone is!

Design Scenario: What to Use?

You are faced with a mixed environment of NT servers and Windows 2000 servers, and even some NetWare boxes thrown in. What type of certificate server would you use and why?

You would be forced into using a stand-alone certificate server, simply because you are not to the point of having Active Directory over the entire network.

Basic Security Requirements for Certificates

What determines whether certificates will help to provide a *safe* or *secure* computing environment? Well, there are several basic factors that can affect overall security when you use certificates. When you have the certificates defined that you intend to use, you can then define the specific requirements for the following factors shown in Table 11.1.

TABLE 11.1 Sample Certificate Factors

Factor	Settings
Private key length	User certificates are usually given 1,024-bit keys and root CAs are usually given 4,096-bit keys.
Storage and management requirements of special private key	In this case, an example would be the storage on smart cards and the fact that they have non-exportable keys.
Cryptographic algorithms used with certificates	It is recommended that you stick with the default algorithms.
Certificate, private key, and renewal cycle lifetimes	The lifetime of certificates is usually determined by certificate type, specific security requirements, and standard practices common in your industry. Government regulations may also have an impact.

Determining Which Certificate Types to Issue

After you have laid out what your certificates are going to look like, you can then go through and identify each of the types of certificates you will need to issue. Obviously, the types of certificates you issue will depend a lot on the types of certificate services that you are going to deploy as well as all the security requirements you have specified in your security plan. You can decide to issue several different certificate types that will meet the needs of multiple users and that will also meet the different security requirements you have defined.

For example, for your enterprise CAs, you can issue different types based on the certificate templates and the account privileges that will be needed in each of your Windows 2000 domains. Then, the infrastructure can be configured so each enterprise CA will be assigned to issue a specific set of certificate types. In Table 11.2 we will take a look at the types of certificate templates provided and what they are supposed to do.

TABLE 11.2 Windows 2000 Certificate Templates and What They Are Used For

Windows 2000 Certificate template name	Template Purposes	The template is Issued to
Administrator	This template is used to sign code, to sign Microsoft trust lists, for EFS, for secure e-mail, and for client authentication.	Users
Certification authority	This template is used for all purposes.	Computers
ClientAuth	This template is used for client authentication during unauthenticated sessions.	Users
CodeSigning	This template is used for signing code.	Users

TABLE 11.2 Windows 2000 Certificate Templates and What They Are Used For *(continued)*

Windows 2000 Certificate template name	Template Purposes	The template is Issued to
CTLSigning	This template is used for signing Microsoft trust lists.	Users
Domain Controller	This template is used for client authentication and server authentication.	Computers
EFS	This template is used for the Encrypting File System.	Users
EFSRecovery	This template is used for file recovery.	Users
EnrollmentAgent	This template is used for certificate request agents.	Users
IPSECIntermediateOffline	This template is used for IP Security.	Computers
IPSECIntermediateOnline	This template is used for IP Security.	Computers
MachineEnrollment-Agent	This template is used for certificate request agents.	Computers
Machine	This template is used for client authentication as well as server authentication.	Computers
OfflineRouter	This template is used for client authentication.	Computers and routers
SmartcardLogon	This template is used for client authentication.	Users

TABLE 11.2 Windows 2000 Certificate Templates and What They Are Used For *(continued)*

Windows 2000 Certificate template name	Template Purposes	The template is Issued to
SmartcardUser	This template is used for client authentication as well as secure e-mail.	Users
SubCA	This template is used for all purposes.	Computers
User	This template is used for the Encrypting File System. It is also used for secure e-mail and also for client authentication.	Users
UserSignature	This template is used for secure e-mail, and also for client authentication.	Users
WebServer	This template is used for server authentication.	Computers
CEP Encryption	This template is used for the certificate request agent.	Routers
Exchange Enrollment Agent (Offline Request)	This template is used for the certificate request agent.	Users
Exchange User	This template is used for secure e-mail as well as client authentication.	Users
Exchange User Signature	This template is used for secure e-mail as well as client authentication.	Users

If you are using stand-alone CAs, you can specify certificate uses in the certificate request. Table 11.2 describes only the templates that are available if you are using Windows 2000. If you are thinking of using a third-party product, then the specific features and functions of each third-party product determine the services provided.

Certificate Policies and Certification Authority Practices

As we have just seen, you can use Microsoft Certificate Services or other certificate services to create certificates for your organization. However, before deploying these different types of certificates, you are going to have to define the *certificate policies* and *certificate practice statements (CPSs)* for your organization. A certificate policy just tells folks what a certificate should be used for, and the liability assumed by the CA for this use. A certificate practice statement, on the other hand, specifies the practices that the CA employs to manage the certificates it issues. The certificate policy statement is a document that describes how the certificate policy will be implemented in your CA organization. The policy may specify, for example, that the private key cannot be exported.

Certificate Policies

When you lay out your certificate infrastructure, be sure to keep your mind on the following things:

- Your basic certificate policy includes things like how users are going to be authenticated to the CA.
- Certificate policy describes how legal issues will be handled. This can include liability issues or anything else that might arise if the CA is attacked and becomes compromised or even if it is used for what are deemed wrong purposes.
- It may define what the certificate can be used for.
- It may define things like the private key management requirements. This would include policies like requiring storage on smart cards.
- It may define whether the private key can or cannot be exported.
- It may define the requirements for the users of the certificates. This can include things like the process users must go through in case their private keys are lost or stolen.

- It may define the requirements put in place for certificate enrollment and for certificate renewal.
- It may define the lifetime of the certificate.
- It may define which cryptographic algorithms are going to be used.
- It may define the minimum length of the public key and of the private key pairs.

Certificate Practices Statements (CPS)

The certificate practice statement, on the other hand, has to look at the big picture. In this case, it may have to cover several certificate policies. Since each CPS deals with a specific CA, it should be kept in mind that the CPS for a child CA can also refer back to the CPS of the parent for shared information. A CPS should cover the following:

- Ways to provide positive identification of the CA. This positive identification may comprise the name of the CA, its DNS name, or just which server it resides on.
- The policy could include which certificate policies the CA is implementing and what certificate types are being issued.
- The policies, the procedures, and the processes that go into issue and renewal of the various types of certificates.
- The different cryptographic algorithms, the CSP, and even the key length that is used for the CA certificate.
- The CA certificate lifetime.
- How the physical, network, and procedural security of the CA has been determined.
- The lifetime of each type of certificate issued by the CA.
- The various policies that are in place for revoking different types of certificates. This can include the normal conditions for certificate revocation, such as employee termination or misuse of security privileges granted to a member of the domain admins group.
- The various policies put in place for the certificate revocation lists (CRLs). These would include the CRL distribution points and publishing intervals of each CRL.
- The defined policy for renewing the CA's certificate before it expires.

Certificate Management

When you have decided the types of certificates you are going to issue and how you are going to use them, there are still some management pieces that need to be placed in effect.

Microsoft Exam Objectives

Design a Public Key Infrastructure.

- Manage certificates.

The first thing we should look at when it comes to managing these certificates is how long are they going to be around. This is called the *certificate life cycle.*

Define Certificate Life Cycles

When you designed your PKI, you should have determined how long the certificates were going to remain in effect. At times, it becomes confusing trying to figure out exactly what is part of the life cycle and what isn't. To refresh your memory, the certificate life cycle includes the following events:

- Certificates issued by CAs
- When the CAs are installed and what certificates are issued to them
- Certificates revoked (as necessary)
- CA certificates renewed before they expire

You normally define the certificate life cycle to require periodic renewal of issued certificates. Issued certificates expire at the end of their lifetime and can be renewed in a cycle until revoked or expired, or until an issuing CA is unavailable. Each CA can issue certificates through several certificate renewal cycles until the CA approaches the end of its lifetime. At that time, the CA would either be retired because its keys are no longer useful, or the CA would be renewed with a new key pair.

Your certificate life cycles should be designed to meet your business goals and security requirements. The life cycles you choose depend on many different things, including those shown in Table 11.3.

TABLE 11.3 Certificate Life Cycle Criteria

Criterion for the Certificate Life Cycle	Why This Is Important
The length of the private keys for CAs and for issued certificates	It should be a policy that longer keys support longer certificate lifetimes as well as longer key lifetimes.
The security that is provided by the CSP	Typically, if you are using a hardware-based CSP, it is more difficult to attack and compromise than a software-based CSP. Since this is the case, you can justify the support for longer certificate lifetimes and even longer key lifetimes.
The type and the strength of the technology that is used for the cryptographic operations	Some well known cryptographic services or technologies provide stronger security. They also support a stronger set of cryptographic algorithms.
The security that is provided for the CAs and their private keys	Basically, the more physically secure the CA and its private key, the longer the CA lifetime can be.
The security that is provided for the issued certificates and their private keys	Say that private keys are stored on a smart card. This can be considered more secure than the case of private keys that are stored as files on local hard disks. After all, smart cards cannot be coerced to export the private key.

TABLE 11.3 Certificate Life Cycle Criteria *(continued)*

Criterion for the Certificate Life Cycle	Why This Is Important
The risk of attack	Simply put, the risk of attack depends on how secure you have made your network. This, in turn, depends on how valuable the network resources protected by the CA trust chain are deemed to be. Another factor would be how expensive you have made the cost of starting an attack.
How much you can trust the users who are using the certificates	This is pretty straightforward: the lower the level of trust, the shorter the life cycles and the shorter the key lifetimes. An example would be temporary users. You know that you are going to trust temporary users less than normal business users. In that case, you would issue temporary users' certificates that had shorter lifetimes. You can also require that there be stricter controls in place for the renewal of temporary users' certificates.
What is the amount of administrative effort that you are willing to devote to the renewal of certificates or the renewal of a CA?	One of the ways that you can reduce the administrative effort required to renew CAs is by specifying long, safe lifetimes for your certification trust hierarchies.

Now, don't just set these values to anything that jumps into your head. Take time to give careful consideration to how long you want CAs, the issued certificates, and even the keys to be trusted. It is a conundrum, because the longer the certificates and private keys are valid, the greater the risk and the greater the potential for a security compromise. The shorter they are valid, the more work for the system or the more work for you!

There is some flexibility built into the process. The decisions you make today are not carved in stone. If, after you define a life cycle, you decide you need to change it, you can. You can always go in and change it later by renewing CAs, certificates, or keys at different periods than you originally specified. For example, if you later decide that the lifetime of the root CA places the CA at risk of compromise, you can then change it.

What Are the Certificate Enrollment and Renewal Processes?

Another part of certificate management is the definition of the certificate enrollment and renewal process. Here you want to define the certificate enrollment and renewal processes that you will use for your organization. If you are using the Microsoft Certificate Services, it supports the following certificate enrollment and renewal methods:

- Interactive certificate requests with the Certificate Request wizard are supported for users of Windows 2000, as well as computers and services only.
- Windows 2000 computer certificates can be defined as automatic certificate requests using the Automatic Certificate Request setup wizard.
- Most Web clients can use the interactive certificate requests from the Microsoft Certificate Services Web pages.
- You can use smart card enrollment with the Smart Card Enrollment Station.
- If you use the Microsoft Enrollment control, you can create custom certificate enrollments and renewals.

Again, this is not a "one size fits all" kind of decision. The certificate enrollment and renewal process that you choose can be configured for the users and computers for which you intend to provide services. For example, you can use the Certificate Request wizard only for Windows 2000 clients. If there are Web-based clients, you can use Web-based enrollment and renewal services for most clients with Web browsers.

How Does Certificate Revocation Work?

Once you have made arrangements to give the certificates out, how do you ever get them back? Earlier, we talked about the different life cycles of some of these certificates. These life cycles can be extensive, sometimes up to a year. What happens if your circumstances change, or if you need to set up ways of revoking certificates? This is called a *certificate revocation policy*. The certificate revocation policies for your company should look a lot like the certification policy. It should include policies for revoking certificates and policies for *certificate revocation lists (CRLs)*.

Certificate Revocation Policy

Your certificate revocation policy specifies the circumstances that justify revoking a certificate. For example, you can specify that certificates must be revoked when employees are terminated or transferred to other business units. Another prime example would be if you sever business relationships with a formerly trusted partner. Other reasons for revoking a certificate would be if users misuse their security privileges or a smart card is lost, thus compromising the private key. For computer certificates, you can specify that certificates must be revoked if the computer is replaced or permanently removed from service, or if the key is compromised.

Certificate Revocation Lists Policy

Your CRL policies specify where you will distribute CRLs and the publishing schedule for CRLs. For example, you can specify that certain CRLs will be distributed to commonly used public folders and Web pages, as well as to Active Directory. You can also specify that certain CRLs be published daily instead of using the default weekly publication.

Managing Maintenance Strategies

Every company has a disaster recovery plan. How formal that plan is depends on a multitude of factors. In some IT departments, unfortunately, the disaster recovery plan consists of making sure the IT staff knows where the best employment search engines are located on the Web. Most companies, however, will have some plan in place for a variety of disasters. If you institute a PKI, you will have to revisit that plan to make sure the special circumstances presented are covered. In this section we are going to offer some hints to help you define your maintenance and disaster recovery strategies for CAs. Maintenance and disaster recovery strategies look a lot like the maintenance and disaster recovery policies you have in place for other data. It includes:

- The different types of backups that you will perform to protect the CAs
- The schedule that you will use for conducting the backups of the CAs
- The policies that are in-place for restoring CAs
- The policies concerning the use of the EFS recovery agents
- The policies that surround the recovery of secure mail

Developing Recovery Plans

If you have a plan in place to back up your certificates, you should have a plan to help restore CAs if certificate services fail or CAs are compromised. Like all things involved with a backup, don't take the software's word on the fact that it is working. Make sure you test the recovery plans to ensure that they work as intended, and train several levels of your staff in how to use the recovery plans.

Recovery plans should include things like the following:

- The set of recovery procedures and the checklists that administrators will be required to follow. Be specific.
- What are the recovery toolkits that are available?
- Define contingency plans for different occurrences.

I may have mentioned Williams' Law before. If not, Williams' Law states that the skill level of any network administrator is in direct proportion to her level of paranoia. The really skilled network folks are the ones who are really paranoid. They know things will fail. So, they prepare for it.

Failed Certification Authority

Like most things in computing, problems with CAs can come from a variety of sources. After all, CA failure can be caused by a server hard drive failure, a network adapter that has failed, or even a server motherboard failure.

Basic troubleshooting tools should help you locate and correct some of the problems with the CA server. Replacing a failed network adapter or a failed motherboard can restore certificate services quickly.

The problems get a little more complicated if a hard disk has failed. Here, you would start by replacing the hard disk and reinstalling and restoring the server. That should restore the CA.

Compromised Certification Authority

What happens when a CA has been compromised? This gets a little more tricky. First of all, you must start by revoking the CA's certificate. When you revoke the CA's certificate, you invalidate the CA and all of its subordinate CAs. You also invalidate all the certificates that have been issued by the CA and even all of its subordinate CAs. If you discover a compromised CA, you should perform the following activities as soon as possible:

- Start by revoking the compromised CA's certificate. If the CA has recently been renewed, then you will have to revoke all of the CA's certificates. That may be required if other related keys have been compromised.
- You may also have to publish a new CRL. This CRL will contain the revoked CA certificate. Since client applications can actually store the CRL until it expires, you will not see the newly published CRL until the old one expires.
- You will also have to remove the compromised CA certificates from Trusted Root Certification Authorities stores and from any affected CTLs.
- You will have to notify all the users and administrators that have been affected and tell them that the certificates that were issued by the affected CAs are being revoked.
- Fix the hole. This means you will have to repair whatever led to the compromise in the first place.

Certification Authority Trust Hierarchies

As we mentioned earlier, a good CA strategy will have at least three levels, and two of those levels will be offline. So, before you can deploy a Windows 2000 PKI, you need to define the CA trust strategies you want to use in your organization. With Windows 2000, you can establish trust for CAs using hierarchical CA trust chains and certificate trust lists.

Why Use Hierarchies?

Like most things hierarchical, your PKI will contain multiple CAs that have clearly defined parent-child relationships. The subordinate CAs, otherwise known as the children, are certified by the parent CA–issued certificates. When this certification occurs, it binds the CA's public key to its identity.

We should get the terminology down. Let's start at the top. As we have mentioned before, the CA that is located at the top of the hierarchy is the root CA. Any CAs that are located below the root are referred to as subordinate CAs. In Windows 2000, placing its certificate in your Trusted Root Certification Authorities store trusts a root CA. When you trust the root, you are in effect trusting every subordinate authority in the entire hierarchy. This is the case unless a subordinate authority has, for some reason, had its certificate revoked by the issuing CA or if it should happen to have an expired certificate. In other words, any root CA is a very important point of trust in an organization. It should be secured and maintained accordingly.

Why should you deploy multiple subordinate CAs?

Usage As we have shown, these certificates can be issued for a number of reasons, like secure e-mail or network authentication. Therefore, the issuing policy for these uses may be unique, and separation provides a basis for administering these policies. That means it should be easier on you and your staff to keep track of which CA is doing what.

Organizational divisions Again, we have shown that there are different policies used for issuing certificates. Again, you create subordinate CAs to both separate and administer these policies. For example, the policy given to the research and development organization may be completely different than the policies implemented for the word processing department.

Geographic divisions It is not uncommon for organizations to have entities at multiple physical locations. It may be that network connectivity between these sites may dictate a requirement that calls for multiple subordinate CAs to meet viable usability standards. Why send traffic across the WAN when you can get the information locally?

Benefits for the administrative team include the following:

- The CA environment can be configured so that it provides balance between both security and usability. For example, if we were dealing with a root CA, we would want to use special-purpose cryptographic hardware. You would want the root CA to be maintained in a locked vault, and it should be operated in offline mode. If we were talking about an issuing CA, this same setup would be overly expensive, and make the CA impossible to use. With a hierarchy, you can have it both ways.
- You must have the ability to frequently renew keys and renew the certificates for those intermediate and issuing CAs that are at high risk for compromise. This should be done without requiring the established root trust relationship to change. Your policy for some CAs may require a new certificate yearly, where in other areas the renewal would have to take place monthly.
- You should be able to simply turn off a section of the CA hierarchy. This process should not affect the established root trust relationships or anything else in the rest of the hierarchy. For example, if the CA was serving a part of the company that was going to be reorganized, it may no longer be necessary.
- Because this can become such an important part of your infrastructure, you will want to distribute the certificate load and make provisions for redundant services.

Design Scenario: Compromised Certificate

Somehow, one of the disks that you were using to pass out certificates from the enterprise root CA to the intermediate CA and from the intermediate CA to the issuing CA has been lost. People have been searching high and low for the darn thing and cannot find it. During the disaster recovery meeting, the question was asked, "What do we do now?"

Basically, you are being asked how to proceed. What is the first step in recovering from this catastrophe? The first step is to revoke (or cancel, if you will) the lost certificate. Once that is done, it is time to start reissuing certificates, using a more foolproof method this time.

Certification Authority Best Practices

Previously, you defined your CA trust strategies. Before you deploy, it might be a good idea to make sure that your plan follows the suggestions below:

- The depth of CA trust hierarchy should be no deeper than four levels. These levels are made up of the root CA, intermediate CA, issuing CA, and the issued certificates.
- If you want to pass the buck, you can configure your network so third-party CAs can form all or part of the CA trust hierarchies. If you decide to put your career in the hands of strangers, make sure the third-party CAs will do everything you want by testing your proposed configuration in the lab.
- Remember that not everything is compatible with Windows 2000. In this case, some of the third-party products might require some other type of CA trust models and those may not work with the rooted CA hierarchies. Windows 2000 and most commercial CAs do, however, support rooted CA hierarchies.

Certificate Trust Lists

A *certificate trust list*, as the name implies, is just a list made up of self-signed certificates for the CAs whose certificates are to be trusted by your organization. Think of it as an enterprise network buddy list. A certificate trust list gives the administrator the ability to control the purpose and validation periods of all of the certificates that have been issued by external certification authorities.

As you have seen previously, there can be multiple certificate trust lists in existence for any particular site. The uses of certificates for a domain or organizational unit can vary, so you should create certificate trust lists that mirror these uses. You will also want to assign a particular certificate trust list to a particular Group Policy object.

If you do that, when you apply the Group Policy object to a site, domain, or OU, the corresponding computers inherit the policy. The computers that have inherited the policy will then trust the CAs in the certificate trust list. You can even place the root CAs into the Group Policy. You may want to use certificate trust lists because they are more convenient than using Group Policy simply because they expire.

PKI Integration

Like most forms of integration, you simply want this one to work. Like most forms of integration, it may not be that easy.

Microsoft Exam Objectives

Design a Public Key Infrastructure.

- Integrate with third-party CAs.

In a perfect world, your Public Key Infrastructure would be just that: an infrastructure. Everyone's CAs would issue a suite of interoperable certificates that were based on a standard certificate request protocol. Applications relying on certificates would then evaluate them in a consistent way and there would be no question anywhere in the process.

Like most things in computing, the term *standard* is rather ambiguous. Everyone has his own interpretation of the standard, and each interpretation is different. Even though each manufacturer is following the standard, each manufacturer implements the standard in its own way, and that can cause issues. So, basically, the industry has yet to achieve a high level of interoperability. The question, then, is when is it realistic to expect it all to "just work." As more applications take advantage of PK-based technology, relatively seamless interoperability is achievable. Today, SSL/TLS and S/MIME work well across multiple vendor products.

For everything that works well, there have to be some areas of opportunity for you to prove your stuff. That means there are still implementations that don't work well. These usually involve implementations that cross products in the newer and lower-use applications such as code signing and digitally signed forms. To make matters worse, there are no current means to compare something simple like names in two different language encodings. Unicode, for example, allows accented characters to be encoded in multiple equivalent forms.

Taken in perspective, these kinds of problems are attributable to the relative immaturity of PK-based technology. Moving into the future, there are at least two forces that have been identified that will drive interoperability:

- A predicted growing dependence on PK-based systems
- The greater emphasis on standards

Some PKI Internet Standards

Have you ever been involved with developing standards for use on the Internet? Don't think this is a facetious question, because it is not. Just because you may be a network administrator working for a small company in the middle of nowhere, doesn't mean you can't be heard. Anyone can participate in the standards process. That is part of the beauty of the Internet. It is also part of the problem. You see, standards take *forever* to evolve. Standards are defined by Requests for Comment (RFCs) and anyone can comment. Many of those "anyones" are truly industry leaders and visionaries with a complete understanding of the process and the problem to be addressed. Other people who comment have no clue about what the heck they are talking about, but they can still comment. Each comment is taken seriously (usually) and discussed and acted upon. Anyone who has ever been involved in creating a policy statement for a major corporation can understand the frustration. There are hundreds of meetings, many of them discussing the same things ad infinitum; until you get so frustrated you want to pull your hair out. Now, imagine that instead of having a dozen people in the meeting, you have a thousand. And instead of having designated times to meet, the entire process is done by e-mail. Ughhhh! So, the historic problem with standards is that major software companies would like to wait for the standards, but they are already taking heat for not getting product out the door. So, product deployment outpaces the collaborative process.

Another challenge with standards is similar to the challenge you face with any deployment. There is no way that a standard can predict every application's requirements and the interrelated dependencies. Even the most rigorous standards tend to get watered down once they are implemented.

PKI Scenarios

When we start looking at the way PKIs interface, it breaks down into two major scenarios involving Windows 2000 and third-party PKIs. The first scenario concerns using both the Windows 2000 PKI and a third-party PKI in a Windows 2000 environment; and the second scenario involves using a third-party PKI exclusively in a Windows 2000 environment.

Third-Party PKI with Windows 2000 PKI

The first scenario involves use of both the Windows 2000 PKI and a third-party PKI. Let's assume, in this case, that your company already has a third party PKI in place when you decide to upgrade to Windows 2000. Now, you would like to use not only your current solution, but also make use of the Windows 2000 PKI for applications like secure Web access. This scenario, theoretically, could go the other way too. Imagine that your company has already deployed Windows 2000 and its PKI and you have a sudden need of a third-party solution for a specialized purpose.

Let's take a look at those features of Windows 2000 that can be used with third-party PKI products.

Encrypting File System

A third-party CA should be able to issue certificates for use by the Encrypting File System (EFS) if the certificate contains the enhanced key usage extension for EFS and the Microsoft RSA Base cryptographic service provider (CSP) is used to manage the associated private key. Using a certificate issued by a third-party CA can be accomplished either by using the Microsoft RSA Base CSP to generate the public/private key pair or by importing the certificate and private key using the Public Key Cryptography Standards #12 (PKCS#12) file format.

Certificate Mapping

As we mentioned above, certificate mapping is where a certificate issued by a third-party CA can be associated with a Windows 2000 user account stored in Active Directory. Software such as Microsoft Internet Explorer and Internet Information Services (IIS) can be used to authenticate a user (connecting to a Web server over the public Internet using a protocol like Secure Sockets Layer) to an account stored in Active Directory based on name information in a certificate.

The account that the certificate maps to is used to determine the user's access rights on the server. This is an extremely powerful feature for Web-based applications and third-party CAs because it combines strong authentication using public key technology with the native authorization model of Windows 2000. For example, to enable extranet and remote access scenarios without requiring the application and certificate to manage access rights, administrators can use certificates from partner companies and map the certificates to accounts in the Active Directory service.

Trusted CA Root Policy

Trust of a third-party CA can be established using Group Policy. An administrator can specify CA trust for collections of computers and users and apply that policy without having to configure each computer individually. A third-party CA root certificate can be automatically distributed to all computers and users in a domain, site, or organizational unit to support both outsourced PKIs as well as extranet scenarios.

Certificate Trust Lists

Certificate trust lists (CTLs) are used to certify other PKIs without requiring the creation and management of cross-certificates. A CTL is simply a list of hashes of CA root certificates that is digitally signed by a trusted administrator. CTLs are created and applied using Group Policy and have two additional properties that make them useful in extranet scenarios. First, CTLs have validity periods and CTLs have usages that limit the purposes for which a given CA is trusted. Hence, CTLs make it possible to establish a trust relationship with a partner or customer based on the other company's CA certificate without having to issue certificates to the other company's employees and without having to change application behavior.

Third-Party PKI without the Windows 2000 PKI

What about the company that is exclusively using a PKI other than the integrated PKI provided with Windows 2000? This includes companies with an existing third-party PKI wishing to upgrade their computing environment to Windows 2000 as well as companies wishing to install a new third-party PKI in an existing Windows 2000 domain environment.

In this case, Microsoft tells you that you are pretty much on your own. If you want to use a third-party solution, then it is up to you to check with the vendor and make sure that the PKI is Windows 2000 compatible. You can start by checking for the Windows 2000–compatible logo. Third-party products can receive a Windows 2000–compatible logo to signify how well it interoperates with Windows 2000 features, including Active Directory and the security infrastructure.

Certificate Mapping

When we spoke about the management of certificates and the best way of handling disaster recovery in the case of a compromised certificate, we mentioned that you would have to notify all the affected users. How in the world would you ever do that?

Microsoft Exam Objectives

Design a Public Key Infrastructure.

- Map certificates.

There are several ways you can use certificate mapping. First, you can use certificate mapping for controlling access to network resources for domain user accounts. You also can use certificate mapping to control access to Web site resources.

Certificate Mapping and Domain User Accounts

To map user certificates to individual accounts, you use the Active Directory Users and Computers console. These mapped certificates are then used to authenticate users during the Kerberos authentication process. That means that these authenticated users are then granted all of the rights and permissions for user accounts based on the ownership of valid certificates. For your information, the smart card logon certificates are viewed as a special type of mapped certificate. During the smart card logon process, the system maps the smart card certificates to the users' accounts automatically.

Before you can map certificates, you have to point to the Active Directory Users and Computers console, and then click View and Advanced Features. To map certificates, right-click a user account, and then click Name Mappings. When the Security Identity Mapping dialog box appears, click Add to import the certificates that you want to map to the user account. You can map multiple certificates to a user account.

You should remember that you can map certificates only to individual user accounts. They cannot be mapped to security groups. If you map certificates that are not stored on smart cards, you may be limiting user flexibility. Users can log on only to the mapped user account from the computer where the private key is located, unless roaming profiles are being used.

Summary

In this chapter we took a closer look at the Public Key Infrastructure. We reviewed how each of the server types should be implemented, and when, and then looked at how to design and manage the actual keys. We also looked at how Windows 2000 and third-party implementations of PKI would work and play well together.

This chapter should be one of your priorities on your list of things to study. Questions on PKI and when to use the different types of root servers have been cropping up all over. It is just a word to the wise.

You still have some more things to do before moving on to Chapter 12, "Building a DNS/SNMP Security Solution." We have been known to tease a little, so we will tell you that the next chapter has to do with designing a secure DNS and SNMP solution. The end is in sight! A few more chapters and you will be ready for the security exam. Time now, though, to work those pesky key terms and review questions.

Key Terms

Before you take the exam, be certain you are familiar with the following terms:

certificates

certificate life cycle

certificate policies

certificate practice statements (CPSs)

certificate revocation lists (CRLs)

certificate revocation policy

certificate trust list

certification authority

certification path

cryptographic service provider (CSP)

enterprise CA

intermediate CA

issuing CA

private key

public key

root CA

stand-alone CA

subordinate CA

Review Questions

1. In a PKI, the certificate authority is responsible for:
    A. A variable length string of letters and numbers
    B. Digitally signing the certificates
    C. Making sure communications with the Internet are secure
    D. Monitoring the CPS

2. In a PKI, which entity verifies that the private key associated with the public key in the certificate is in the possession of the subject named in the certificate?
    A. CRL
    B. CA
    C. CPS
    D. Enterprise root
    E. Stand-alone root

3. How many levels are there in a typical CA hierarchy?
    A. 1
    B. 1 or 2
    C. 2 or 3
    D. 3 or 4

4. What is a CSP?
    A. Cycles per second squared
    B. Certificate service provider
    C. Cryptographic service provider
    D. Certificate service provider
    E. Certificate sensatory provider

5. What is another term for certification path?

   A. Trust chain

   B. Root CA

   C. Subordinate CA

   D. Intermediate CA

6. Which certification service must have the Active Directory?

   A. Microsoft Designed Certificate Authority (MDCA)

   B. Enterprise root CA

   C. Stand-alone root CA

   D. Issuing CA

   E. Mapped Certificate to an Organizational Unit

7. What is one of the things you can specify in the certificate life cycle criteria?

   A. Placement of the root CA

   B. Assignment of the issuing CA to the Organizational Unit

   C. Length of the private key

   D. Length of the public key given out by the root CA

8. In a typical deployment, what is the length of the certificates?

   A. Root CA keys are 1,024 bits and user certificates are 2,048 bits

   B. Root CA keys are 2,048 bits and user certificates are 2,048 bits

   C. Root CA keys are 4,096 bits and user certificates are 2,048 bits

   D. Root CA keys are 1,024 bits and user certificates are 4,096 bits

   E. Root CA keys are 4,096 bits and user certificates are 1,024 bits

9. Besides Microsoft, name two companies that utilize a rooted hierarchy design for a PKI.

   A. VeriSign

   B. Netscape

   C. Entrust

   D. PGP

Answers to Review Questions

1. B. The certificate authority (CA) is responsible for digitally signing the certificates.

2. B. It is up to the CA to verify that the public key and private key are actually in the possession of the subject named in the certificate.

3. D. Typically, there are three or four levels in a CA hierarchy. One or two of these machines may be offline.

4. C. The CSP is a cryptographic service provider (CSP). The CSP is the software or hardware that provides encryption services for your CA.

5. A. A certification path can also be called a trust chain.

6. B. The enterprise CA must have Active Directory.

7. C. One of the things that can be provided in the certificate life cycle criteria is the length of the private key.

8. E. In a typical deployment, user certificates have 1,024-bit keys and root CAs have 4,096-bit keys.

9. A, B. Both VeriSign and Netscape utilize a rooted hierarchy.

CASE STUDY

The Multinational Conglomerate

You should give yourself 10 minutes to review this case study, diagram as needed, and complete the questions for this testlet. Be sure to read each question carefully. While the company may not have changed, its circumstances change in each chapter.

Background

Your consulting firm has been hired to assist in the Windows 2000 migration and integration for a company based in Minneapolis, Minnesota. Until the start of this year, the company had 1,000 employees, all based throughout the Twin Cities of Minneapolis and St. Paul. Just before the end of the year, the owner of your company purchased two companies of roughly the same size that will need to be connected to the enterprise network. The total number of users when the project is completed is estimated at 3,500. In addition, each of these companies comes with various strategic partners that will need to access the information on your enterprise network. The companies that have been acquired are located in Athens, Greece, and in Orlando, Florida.

The three companies can now be considered one, and the Windows 2000 rollout is in full swing. At this time the company is beginning to implement a PKI. The Windows 2000 network is made up of a forest with three domains.

Current System

Minneapolis Located on the shores of beautiful Lake Calhoun, the company occupies a sprawling campus that includes four floors in a six-story building. Since the merger, the Lake Calhoun facility has become a model of efficiency. Besides being linked to all of the other offices, everyone is beginning to take the notion of an enterprise network seriously.

All of the floors are connected to the Windows 2000 network. The Minneapolis location is a domain in the tree. Active Directory services have been deployed to the main campus and the rollout is complete in the branch offices. The desktop and laptop rollout company-wide took longer than expected, but it is now completed. The CEO wants to know what the IT team is doing to make sure that everyone within the company can access resources all over the tree, as well as protect the network.

The corporate network was so impressive it helped this company snag a very large contract with a very large customer. This contract could put the company on the map. However, with every silver lining, there is a dark cloud. In this case, the dark cloud is that the customer wants to be able to access the online inventory system on your network, as well as share information directly with several new Unix hosts that are currently being installed. The customer is using Windows 2000 exclusively in their network.

Before migrating to Windows 2000, the company made use of the certificate services provided by Entrust. This certificate service is still in place.

Orlando The Orlando office is a domain in the corporate tree. It has some valuable resources that need to be made available to the rest of the company, particularly the folks in Athens.

The new contract may have a long-term effect on Orlando. Current corporate strategy calls for the new contract to be managed in Minneapolis for the first year, and then moved to Orlando after that. Given this strategy, Orlando will make use of their ability to access information in Minneapolis, but several people in the office will need to access the customer's network to work on design issues and planning issues.

Before migrating to Windows 2000, this unit made use of certificate services provided by Netscape. This certificate service is still in place.

Athens The Athens office is now fully staffed at 2,300. The management has discovered that the business is doing well, and the extra folks are justified. The office has been upgraded to Windows 2000 servers and Athens is now its own domain in the tree.

Athens has always been ahead of the curve. When the new contract was announced, Athens manufacturing geared up for the task, and can now handle that stage. Because the customer wants to be able to look at all the stages of inventory, the customer will need to be able to access the Athens facility as well as Minneapolis and Orlando.

Before migrating to Windows 2000, this unit did not use a certificate service. It has since begun to institute the Windows 2000 certificate service.

It has created an offline enterprise CA, an offline intermediate CA, and is just now adding an online issuing CA.

Customer The customer has a Windows 2000 network. The customer and our IS department have decided to link the two forests.

The communication between the trees is established; now, the next step is to provide certificates where necessary. The customer has a fully implemented PKI and is using a third-party service such as Netscape, Verisign, or Entrust.

Problem Statement

Provide a unified approach to certificate services. Decisions to be made include number, type, and locations of root CAs; number, type, and location of intermediate CAs; number, type, and location of issuing CAs; and which service to use.

Envisioned System

CEO As the new network is designed, the CEO is looking closely at the IS department and saying things like, "Okay people, you wanted the Windows 2000 network because of its flexibility and you now have it. This is where the rubber hits the road. Prove you can make this network do the things you said it can do!"

CFO "You know, we are still paying the bills for this rollout. Although it looks like our overall cost of operation will drop, it is still a large price to absorb. In addition, there still seems to be some confusion over who can do what, where, and when with something called certificates. What gives?"

Orlando General Manager "We really do have to get this certificate thing ironed out quickly. I have a good friend who works with Entrust. When would you like her to fly up and give you a presentation?"

Athens General Manager "We're ready. We just have to start issuing the certificates and we are set to go."

Questions

1. Which services should you be looking at?

   A. Entrust

   B. Netscape

   C. VeriSign

   D. None

2. How many root CAs should this implementation use?

   A. 5

   B. 3

   C. 1

   D. None

3. How many issuing CAs would you have?

   A. 1

   B. 3

   C. 5

   D. Not enough information

4. Where would the PKI be administered from?

   A. Minneapolis

   B. Orlando

   C. Athens

   D. Not enough information

Answers

1. D. Because everything is Windows 2000, you really do not have to go out of house to provide a PKI. You can stick with just using the Windows 2000 implementation.

2. B. Now, the key word in this question is *should*. It would make administrative sense to put an enterprise CA at each of the three sites. That way, each site's IT department would be responsible for its own PKI. However, you could also take the approach that since a root has already been established in Athens, you could let them manage the root and the PKI and just issue certificates to intermediate CAs in both Minneapolis and Orlando. In this case, we will go with one CA at each of the three sites.

3. B. You would have three issuing CAs, one in each location.

4. D. You really do not have enough information to make that decision. It could be administered from any of the locations.

Building a DNS/SNMP Security Solution

MICROSOFT EXAM OBJECTIVES COVERED IN THIS CHAPTER:

✓ **Design Windows 2000 network services security.**

- Design Windows 2000 DNS security.
- Design Windows 2000 SNMP security.

Before you can do anything on the network, you have to be authenticated. Before you can be authenticated, you have to be able to locate a domain controller. In Windows 2000, that means everything starts with *Domain Name System (DNS)*.

Locating a Domain Name Controller

Check out Figure 12.1. This is basic networking. As you can see, the client starts the process by looking in cache. If it doesn't find anything there, it then moves on to sending a DNS Lookup query to a DNS server to find domain controllers in the subnet of the client. Then, DNS starts by trying to find the closest domain controller in the client's subnet. After the client locates a domain controller, it establishes communication by using Lightweight Directory Access Protocol (LDAP) to gain access to Active Directory.

Now the negotiation takes place. The domain controller works with the client to determine if it is in the proper site to provide authentication. If it is, great; this means that the domain controller is in the *optimal site*. If not, the domain controller sends back information to the client so the client can try again. So, now the client has located one of the domain controllers. The domain controller entry is then cached. If the domain controller is judged not to be in the optimal site, the client will flush its cache after 15 minutes, thus discarding the cache's entry. The client will then attempt to locate a domain controller that is in the same site as the client.

FIGURE 12.1 How a client locates a domain controller

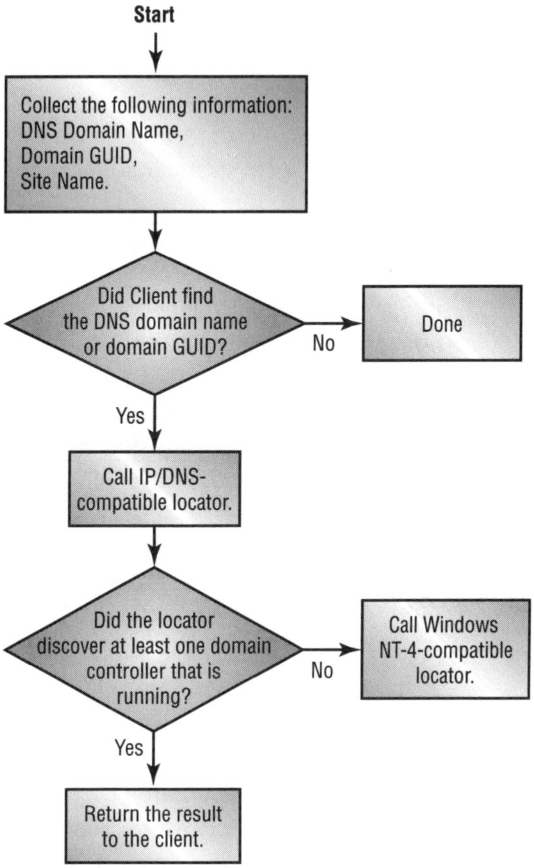

Start

Collect the following information:
DNS Domain Name,
Domain GUID,
Site Name.

Did Client find the DNS domain name or domain GUID?

No

Done

Yes

Call IP/DNS-compatible locator.

Did the locator discover at least one domain controller that is running?

No

Call Windows NT-4-compatible locator.

Yes

Return the result to the client.

Once the client has located the domain controller, it can go ahead and establish the logon and authentication credentials. If Windows 2000 deems it necessary, it will go ahead and set up a secure channel. After all this has been accomplished, the client is ready to get on with life and perform the normal queries and search for information contained in the directory.

The client has to establish an LDAP connection to a domain controller to just establish a logon. The logon process, as you know, goes through the Security Accounts Manager. The client is authenticated through the DSA, and the client account is verified. The information is passed through the Security Accounts Manager to the DSA, the database layer, and finally to the database in the ESE. Therefore, there are a number of different areas where things can go wrong. In order for you to be able to effectively troubleshoot this, you have to be able to identify and diagnose problems that might occur in any of these different areas. Finally, the client can log on to the network. It all started with DNS. Besides logons, any time any one of your clients wants to access a resource by name, it uses DNS. Without DNS, your network is in a world of hurt. This would be a good time to make sure that the DNS servers were secure, and more importantly, the DNS structure was tamperproof.

But what about *Simple Network Management Protocol (SNMP)*? How secure does that have to be? Well, the whole point of SNMP is to gather information on your network. It checks the status of resources—who is doing what where, what services are performing how, and a plethora of other information. Now, if you think about it, if SNMP can get into your network and find out where things are, there should be ways of making sure that only SNMP is getting that information. That is what we will be talking about in this chapter.

Windows 2000 and DNS

As mentioned above, DNS plays a significant role in the operation of your Windows 2000 network. In addition, it is not just any type of DNS that plays a role, but dynamic DNS—and there is a difference!

When you install Windows 2000 Server, the installation wizard goes out and checks your network for the presence of a DNS server that will work with a Windows 2000 Active Directory network. If it finds one, all is well. Otherwise, you may have to configure the new Windows 2000 server to be a DNS server too.

Microsoft Exam Objectives

Design Windows 2000 network services security.

- Design Windows 2000 DNS security.

What exactly is the installer looking for? Does it have to be another Windows 2000 server running DNS? In a word, no. Windows 2000 should be happy with any DNS server implementation supporting *Service Location Resource Records (SRV RRs),* as described in Internet draft RFC 2782, "A DNS RR for specifying the location of services (DNS SRV)." Dynamic Updates in the Domain Name System (DNS Update, RFC 2136) is sufficient to provide the name service for Windows 2000–based computers. However, since the Microsoft-provided version of DNS is designed to fully take advantage of the Windows 2000 Active Directory service, it is the recommended DNS server. There are some advantages to using the Windows 2000 version of DNS server, over and above the integration with Active Directory. For example, while conventional DNS servers use single-master replication, Windows 2000 DNS can be integrated into Active Directory service, so that it uses the Windows 2000 multimaster replication engine. In this way, network managers can simplify system administration by not having to maintain a separate replication topology for DNS.

Another reason for using the Microsoft version of DNS server is compatibility. Like anything IP, there are areas of the protocol that can be vendor-specific. This can cause certain unexpected quirks to show up at the most inopportune time. If you switch over to Microsoft DNS, you can save headaches later.

Before we can look at all the new features of DNS, it is important to make sure that you have all the basics covered. So, what we are going to do is a brief review of DNS for those people just beginning to work with it, or for those people who have worked with it for years, but always considered it Pure Computer Magic (PCM). Once we have completed the review, we will get into the new features.

Windows 2000 Name Service

The way Microsoft talks about name service, you almost expect to hear trumpets go off. A name service is just what the title says. It is the way that you decide to name objects on your network so they can be located again. Contrary to the way Windows 2000 tries to name computers when it is installed, the naming is usually user friendly. The official definition of DNS says that it is, by design, a highly reliable, hierarchical, distributed, and scalable database. In Windows 2000 networks, clients use DNS for name resolution and service location, including locating domain controllers for logon.

Now, the key phrase in the paragraph above is "in Windows 2000 networks." If your network hasn't completely switched over yet, you need to look at backward compatibility issues. For backward compatibility, when Windows 2000 first came out, clients running previous versions of Windows (Windows NT 3.5 and 3.51, Windows NT 4, Windows 95, and Windows 98) had to rely on NetBIOS. NetBIOS can use NBNS (WINS), broadcast, or flat `LMHOSTS` files for name resolution. In particular, the NetBIOS name service is used for domain controller location.

Since DNS as implemented in Windows 2000 is *Windows Internet Name Services (WINS)*–aware, a combination of both DNS and WINS can be used in a mixed environment to locate various network services and resources. Windows NT 4–based clients can register themselves in Windows 2000 WINS, and Windows 2000–based clients can register in Windows NT 4 WINS.

DNS Fundamentals

So, how does it work? In the section above, we said that the Domain Name System is a hierarchical distributed database. It is also a set of protocols that define things like:

- How to query and make changes to the database
- How to replicate the information among different DNS servers
- The makeup of the database

History of DNS

DNS has been evolving for years. It all started when the Internet was still relatively small and people simply got tired of constantly updating `HOSTS` files every time a new resource appeared on the Internet. You see, DNS began in the early days of the Internet when the Internet was a small network established by the United States Department of Defense for research purposes. The host names of the computers in this network were managed through the use of a single `HOSTS` file located on a centrally administered server. Each site that needed to resolve host names on the network downloaded this file. It soon became obvious that if the Internet were to get any bigger, there had to be a better way. This better way should offer things like scalability, distributed and decentralized administration, and the support for different kinds of data types.

The Domain Name System (DNS) was introduced in 1984. With DNS, the various host names reside in a database that is distributed among many servers. This distribution decreases the load on any one server and provides the ability to administer this naming system on a per-partition basis. DNS supports hierarchical names. This, in turn, provides for the registration of different types of data that extend beyond the *host name to IP address* mapping used in the HOSTS files. Because the DNS database is being distributed, it has no size limits and performance does not degrade much when adding more servers.

DNS was originally based on RFC 882 (Domain names: Concepts and Facilities) and RFC 883 (Domain Names: Implementation and Specification). These were replaced by RFC 1034 (Domain Names: Concepts and Facilities), and RFC 1035 (Domain Names: Implementation and Specification). The most popular implementation of DNS—Berkeley Internet Name Domain (BIND)—was originally developed for the 4.3 BSD Unix operating system.

Windows 2000 uses a new version of DNS. For those of you who love to take advantage of free (and for the most part really boring) reading material, the RFCs used in this version are 1034, 1035, 1886, 1995, 1996, 2136, 2308, and 2782.

DNS Structure

As we mentioned, the Domain Name System is a hierarchical and distributed database that contains various types of data. This data includes host names and domain names. The names in the DNS database form a hierarchical tree structure called the *domain name space.*

DNS Domain Names

You would have had to be living under a rock for the last five years not to have used a DNS name, or at least come into contact with one. Here in the United States, they are all over newspaper ads, billboards, yellow page ads, business cards, clothing, tattoos, everything. Well, maybe not tattoos, but you get the picture. Domain names consist of individual labels separated by dots. For example: homedomain.persistent-image.com.

There can be different types of names. A *Fully Qualified Domain Name (FQDN)*, for example, uniquely identifies the host's location within the DNS hierarchical tree. It does this by specifying a list of names that are separated by dots that show the way from the referenced host to the root. Figure 12.2 shows an example of a DNS tree with a host called *mycomputer* within the *persistent-image.com.* domain. The fully qualified domain name for this host would be *mycomputer.persistent-image.com.*

FIGURE 12.2 DNS tree example

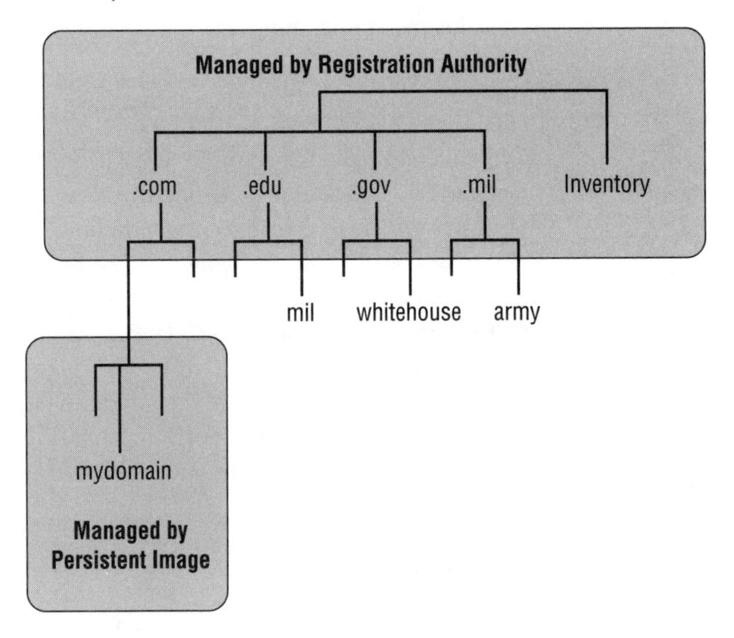

DNS and Internet

A Name Registration Authority on the Internet manages the Internet Domain Name System. This body is responsible for managing the top-level domains that are assigned by organization and country. The domain names follow the International Standard 3166. The existing abbreviations, which are reserved for use by organizations, as well as the two-letter abbreviations used for countries, are well known to most of us. These are dot coms, or the .com, .net, .org, .gov, .uk, .us, .ca, and .edu names that we are all familiar with.

Resource Records

Once most of us get by the familiar FQDN, the DNS database becomes something of a mystery. A DNS database is just like every database on any system anywhere. It is made up a bunch of records. Each record has different properties and each property has different values. Think of a database we are all familiar with, a phone book. In the case of a phone book, there are thousands of records. Each record is made up of three properties: name, address, and phone number. Each property then has different values. To continue the example, if you looked up the name "Gary Govanus," it might have the value in the address property of "123 Main Street" and the value of the phone number property of "123-456-7890."

The records in a DNS database are called *resource records (RRs)*. Each RR identifies a resource within the DNS database. There are several different types of RRs in DNS.

Table 12.1 provides some information on structure of common RRs. This is by no means a list of *all* the resource records.

TABLE 12.1 Sample Resource Records

Description	Type	Data
Start of Authority	SOA	The SOA contains the owner name, the primary name server's DNS name, the serial number, the refresh interval, the retry interval, the expire time, and the minimum TTL.
Host	A	The host name contains the owner name or the host DNS name, and the host IP address.
Name server	NS	The NS record contains the owner name, as well as the name server DNS name.
Mail exchanger	MX	The MX record contains the owner name, the mail exchange server DNS name, a preference number, and any canonical names.
Canonical name	CNAME	The CNAME record contains the owner name (alias name), and a host DNS name.

Putting "Distributed" in the Distributed Database

DNS databases can be partitioned into multiple *zones*. A zone is simply a section of the DNS database that contains the resource records with the owner names that belong to the contiguous portion of the DNS namespace, usually for administrative purposes. These zone files are also maintained on DNS servers. Any DNS server can be configured to host lots of different zones, or it can be configured so that it is just used for lookup and it may not host any zones.

Each zone is anchored in a specific domain name. That domain name can be referred to as the zone's registered domain name. A zone simply contains information about all names that end with the zone's registered domain name—for example, all the names that are handled by persistent-image.com. A DNS server is considered to be *authoritative* for a name if it loads the zone containing that name—again, in our example, persistent-image.com. So, for example, the DNS name of our company is persistent-image.com. Somewhere out there is a DNS server for the .com domain that has all the information on the name persistent-image.com. But we aren't satisfied: Our company has two locations, one in Grand Rapids, Michigan, and one in Apple Valley, Minnesota. So, we can further break down our domain name to Minnesota.persistent-image.com and Michigan.persistent-image.com. Each DNS zone would handle management responsibilities for the hosts in those zones. One server in Minnesota and one server in Michigan would contain the database for the respective zones. Since this would load and manage DNS for that zone, it is the authoritative DNS server for that zone. Each server would have its own database called a zone file. Like all good databases, these are filled with records.

The first record in any zone file is a Start of Authority (SOA) RR. The SOA RR specifies the primary DNS name server that is going to be used for that zone and as an entity that will be processing any updates for the zone.

Names within one zone can also be delegated to another zone or even multiple zones. The delegation process is one of just assigning responsibility for a portion of a DNS namespace to a different entity—a different organization, a different department, or even a workgroup within your company. In technical terms, delegating just means giving the authority over certain portions of your DNS namespace to other zones. The NS record that specifies the delegated zone and the DNS name of the server authoritative for that zone represents such delegation. The process of delegating authority so that it passes across multiple zones was part of the original design of DNS. Here are some of the reasons it is important:

- There can be a need to delegate management of a DNS domain to a number of organizations or departments within a company or an organization. Location may be a deciding factor, as may be the number of hosts.
- There can be a need to distribute the administrative load of maintaining one large DNS database. This load can be spread among multiple name servers. This will improve the name resolution performance as well as help to create a fault tolerance for DNS.
- There may be the need to allow for hosts' organizational affiliations by including them in appropriate domains.

The NS RRs make delegation easier by identifying the DNS servers for each of the new zones. These records will appear in all forward and reverse lookup zones. Whenever a DNS server needs to cross a delegation, it can refer to the NS RRs for DNS servers in the target zone.

Now, unless you are already familiar with DNS, you may be reading those last several paragraphs and saying, "Huh?? What the heck does that mean?" So let's put it in action.

Let's go back in time and say that you and I are the creators of DNS. We are responsible for designing the whole thing. Now, this is a pretty awesome task, but we realize that it is just database stuff, so we don't let it scare the heck out of us. And, being the forward thinkers that we are, we recognize that the Internet is going to become the hottest thing since the wheel and we also realize that keeping track of DNS names for every Tom, Dick, and Mary is going to be a task that we want no part of. That just sounds like too much darn work.

So, we look around the table. This was supposed to be a committee meeting, and there were supposed to be eight people at the meeting. You are I are the only two that showed up, so we get to make all the decisions. We decide that we are going to "distribute" the database. That means that we can partition it, or divide it up, and give other people the responsibility for those partitions. So, looking around the empty seats, we decide that we are going to be responsible for the top level of the database. Our server will know where all the other top-level servers are. We decide that we can handle taking care of a couple of hundred different records without a problem. Now it is time to start dividing up the database. So, we start by assigning names. First of all, we anticipate that when the Internet takes off, there are going to be lots of commercial entities that will want to be part of it, so we will create a .com extension and assign it to one of our missing counterparts. After that, we do the same things for government (.gov), education (.edu), organizations (.org), United Kingdom (.UK), Germany (.DE), etc., until we are all out of top levels. As we are talking about this, we kind of unintentionally start talking about zoning off the world, and the name sticks. So we have created our top-level zones. You and I have the responsibility for the highest level. We have designated all these domain zones, and assigned them to various locations.

Just about this time, one of our harried colleagues comes rushing into the room, apologizing profusely for being late. We smile benignly and explain that, in her absence, she has been assigned to manage the .com zone. Lots of luck and my goodness aren't you going to be busy? She spends some time talking with us, and decides that this zone idea is a good one. Rather than keep track of all those hosts of all those companies that are going to have .com addresses, she decides to take the zone theory one step further. In her case, she decides that each company that applies for a DNS name will have the ability to create and manage its own zone, and therefore, she won't have as much work as we thought.

So, that is how the zone theory works. From the root level (designated by a period or "."), each zone is divided into domains. Each domain can then be subdivided into other zones, if the network infrastructure or corporate business practices demand it. For example, in Figure 12.3, the management of the domain persistent-image.com. is delegated across two zones, persistent-image.com. and homedomain.persistent-image.com.

FIGURE 12.3 Examples of DNS zones

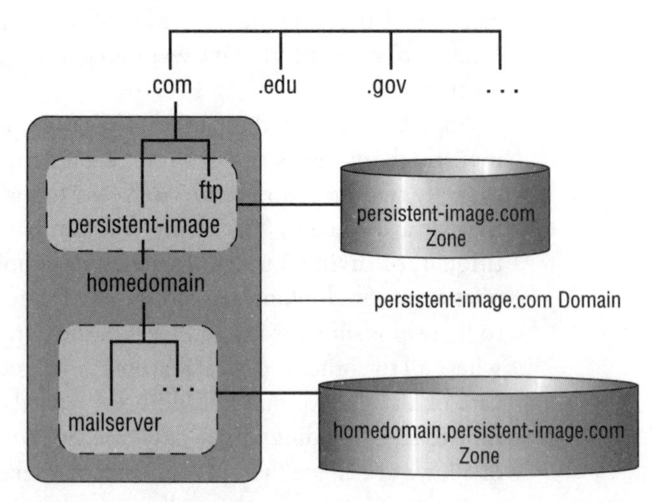

DNS Database Replication

As you witnessed in the graphic above, many times there are multiple zones representing the same portion of the namespace. Keeping track of these can be two types of nameservers:

- Primary
- Secondary

A primary name server is any name server to which all updates for the records that belong to that zone are made. A *secondary name server* is a read-only copy of the primary name server. The changes made to the primary name server are then replicated to the secondary name server file.

In addition, a name server can host multiple zones. It follows then that a name server can be primary name server for one zone (it has the master copy of the zone file) and secondary name server for another zone (it gets a read-only copy of the zone file).

When zone files are copied to multiple name servers, this is called *zone transfer*. Zone transfer is done by just copying the zone file information from the master server to the secondary server.

So, to review, the *master server* is the source of the zone information. The master server can be either a primary or secondary. If the master is a primary, then the zone transfer obviously comes directly from the source. If the master server is secondary, the file received from the master server by means of a zone transfer is a copy of a copy of the read-only zone file.

How do the servers know when it is time to initiate a zone transfer? It is started in one of the two following ways:

- The master server can start the process by sending a *notification* (RFC 1996) to the secondary server(s) of a change in the zone.
- When the secondary server's DNS service starts up or if the secondary server's *refresh interval* has expired (by default it is set to 15 minutes in the SOA RR for Microsoft DNS), it will ask the master server for the changes.

Once that transfer starts, it is completed in one of two ways. The first is called a *full zone transfer (AXFR)*. A full zone transfer replicates the entire zone file. The second way is called an *incremental zone transfer (IXFR)*. This method replicates only the changed records of the zone.

Locating a Host by Querying the DNS Database

There are only two ways that DNS can be queried. The query can be sent from a client otherwise known as a *resolver* to a DNS server, called a *name server*, or between two name servers.

A query is merely a request for records of a specified type with a specified name. For example, a query can request all host RRs with a particular name. A common query comes whenever someone types `www.sybex.com` in his browser. Somehow the browser has to resolve that request to an actual IP address.

There are two types of queries that can be made:

- Recursive
- Iterative

A *recursive* query is one that forces a DNS server to respond to a request with either a failure or a successful response. Resolvers are the ones that typically make recursive queries. With a recursive query, the DNS server that has been contacted is in charge of the request. It must contact any other DNS servers it needs to be able to resolve the request. When it finally receives a successful response from another DNS server(s), it can then send the response back to the client. This type of recursive query is typical for a resolver querying a name server and for a name server querying its forwarder. A forwarder is just a fancy name given to another name server that is configured to handle the requests that are forwarded to it.

When a DNS server processes a recursive query and a query cannot be resolved from its sources or from local zone files, the query must then be escalated to a root DNS server. Each of the standards-based implementations of DNS includes a cache file (or root server hints) that contains entries for root servers of the Internet domains.

The latest version of the named cache file can be downloaded from InterNIC at `ftp://rs.internic.net/domain/named.cache`.

An *iterative query*, on the other hand, is one in which the name server is expected to provide the best information it has, based on what that server knows from either its local zone files or from caching. If a name server doesn't have any way to answer the query, it simply sends back a negative response. A non-forwarding DNS server will make this type of query as it tries to locate names that reside outside of its local domain(s). It may have to ask a number of DNS servers in an attempt to resolve the name.

FIGURE 12.4 An example of recursive and iterative queries

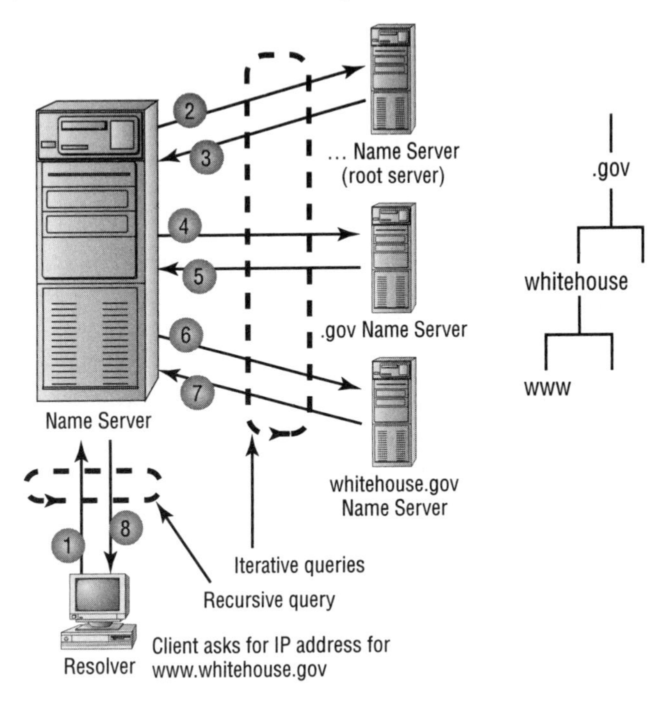

Figure 12.4 shows an example of both types of queries. Based on this figure, the following queries are used to determine the IP address for the Web site at the White House, `www.whitehouse.gov`:

- You will notice in Step 1 that there is a recursive query for `www.whitehouse.gov`, looking for an A type resource record (A RR).
- You should also see the iterative query for `www.whitehouse.gov` (A RR) next to the root name server in Steps 2 and 3.
- Then there is the referral to the gov name server (NS RRs, for gov); for simplicity, iterative A queries by the DNS server (on the left) to resolve the IP addresses of the Host names of the name servers returned by other DNS servers have been omitted. This is shown in Steps 4 and 5.
- Iterative query for `www.whitehouse.gov` (A RR).

- Referral to the whitehouse.gov name server (NS RR, for white-house.gov).
- Iterative query for `www.whitehouse.gov` (A RR) in Steps 6 and 7.
- Answer from whitehouse.gov server (`www.whitehouse.gov`'s IP address)
- Answer from local DNS server to Resolver (`www.whitehouse.gov`'s IP address) in Step 8.

Updating the DNS Database

Because the RRs in the zone files are subject to changes, they must be updated. In the earlier versions of DNS, this was done manually, by making entries using a wizard or by updating text files. The way the updates were handled depended on the version and type of DNS you were using. Because these were manual updates, they were referred to as *static updates*. With the newer implementations of DNS, there is support for both static and dynamic updates of the DNS database. Windows 2000 integrates that dynamic updating into its version of DNS.

Windows 2000 DNS

As we mentioned above, the new DNS is much different than the old DNS. With the Windows 2000 implementation, the differences include:

- It is integrated with Active Directory service.
- It supports incremental zone transfer (IXFR).
- It supports dynamic updates and secure dynamic updates.
- It supports Unicode character support.
- It supports the enhanced domain locator.
- It supports the enhanced caching resolver service.
- It supports the enhanced DNS manager.

DNS/Active Directory Integration

Because of backward compatibility issues, the Windows 2000 implementation of DNS has to make allowances for static entries and administrator configuration of DNS zone file replication. If, however, you are bothered with the backward compatibility issue, you have the option of using the Active Directory services as the data storage and replication engine. With this approach, the following happens:

- DNS replication is performed by Active Directory service. In that way, there is no need to configure another separate replication topology for your DNS servers.
- With the Active Directory service replication, you can have per-property replication.
- With Active Directory service, replication is more secure.
- With Active Directory maintaining the database, a primary DNS server is no longer the single point of failure.

The Active Directory Service Storage Model

When we start talking name space, there has to be somewhere for the information to be stored. If it is stored in Active Directory, DNS information is another object to be managed by the directory. In this case, DNS information is stored as a service object and there are two types of service class objects that pertain to DNS. They are the DnsZone object and the DnsNode object.

If DNS is integrated into the Active Directory, each DNS zone becomes an Active Directory service container object (DnsZone). The DnsZone object contains a DnsNode leaf object for every unique name that resides within that zone. The DnsNode object will also have a DnsRecord, which is a multi-valued attribute. These attributes will have a value for every record that is associated with the specified object's name.

DNS Replication

Since DNS zone information is now stored in Active Directory service, whenever an update is made to a DNS server, it simply writes the data to Active Directory and continues performing its usual functions. Active Directory service is now responsible for replicating the data to other domain controllers. The DNS servers running on other Domain Controllers (DCs) will poll the updates from the Directory Service (DS).

One of the benefits of using the Active Directory service is the multimaster replication model. In this case, DNS updates will be written to any DS integrated DNS server. That means that the data will be replicated across all of the domain controllers. This multimaster replication system, however, does have some gotchas that you should be aware of.

Because there is the ability to write to Active Directory service from multiple domain controllers at the same time, there can be a conflicting situation where the changes are made to the same object on two different DNS servers. When the conflict is resolved, it will be in favor of the last update made to the object. This determination is based on the timestamps of each of the updates. However, until it is resolved, there could be some interesting moments. The same rule can be applied if two or more hosts that have the same name are created on two or more DNS servers. Until the conflict is resolved and the DNS server that contains the invalid update polls the valid data from the Directory Services, it is possible that any requests for the same object made to two different DNS servers will be pointed to different locations. This is why the Active Directory database is called *loosely consistent*.

Zone Conversions

It is possible to change any type of existing DNS zone to any other type. There are some issues surrounding the primary zone conversions.

If a DS-integrated zone is converted to an original (non-DS-integrated) primary zone file, the DNS server that will be loading the new primary zone must become the single primary of the zone for the update. Therefore, any converted zone has to be deleted from Active Directory service (namely from all DC databases previously authoritative for this zone) so that the outdated or incorrect information is not being replicated.

Zone Access

Because DNS is integrated into Active Directory service, it can take advantage of secure dynamic DNS updates. The Active Directory maintains the Access Control Lists (ACL) that specify the groups or users who are allowed to change the AD-integrated zones.

Only Windows 2000 DNS server supports secure dynamic updates for the DS-integrated zones. Windows 2000 implementation provides even finer granularity, allowing per-name ACL specification.

Incremental Zone Transfer

As we said earlier in the chapter, one of the problems the old DNS had was that anytime a database needed to be updated, the name server that received the update received a lot of information it already had. That was a large waste of bandwidth and time. In dynamic DNS, the database is going to be changing frequently. Therefore, the problems would have gotten worse, not better.

To reduce this latency in sending out the changes to a DNS database, there is now a way that actively notifies name servers of the change. This is accomplished by the NOTIFY extension of the DNS. The NOTIFY packet, which is sent by a Master server, does not contain any zone changes information. It merely notifies the other servers that some changes have been made to a zone and that a zone transfer needs to be initiated. When the zone transfer is initiated, it can be an incremental transfer (IXFR), which is more efficient. It transfers only the changed portion(s) of the zone.

The IXFR protocol is defined in RFC 1995.

Static vs. Dynamic Updates

In a conventional DNS implementation, if a host had to be added to the system, the network administrator had to edit the appropriate zone file manually. Remember, the Domain Name System was not originally designed for today's networks. It was, however, designed to support queries of a statically configured database. In other words, while the data was expected to change, those changes were not expected to happen very often, and all of the updates were made as edits to a zone's primary master file.

This system became a hindrance with the advent of dynamic, automated IP addressing using DHCP and related protocols. With DHCP, a host could have a valid DNS name, but its IP address might change every time it was brought online. This, in effect, rendered manual updating of DNS information insufficient and unusable. After all, no system administrator can be expected to keep up with dynamic address assignments in even a medium size network environment. So, it was clear that automatic assignment of addresses had to be integrated with dynamic DNS updates.

The Dynamic Update capability is defined in RFC 2136.

Now, think about the task the designers were taking on here. Let's assume that we are talking about moving a server that contains the Web site for `www.acmecomputerandbarsupply.com` from one subnet to another. This could be as simple as moving it from one computer room on one floor to the computer room on another floor. In the past, this would be a major undertaking. You would have to manually assign the computer a new IP address, change the IP address in DNS, and wait for that change to replicate.

In this case, using dynamic DNS, you move the computer, plug it in, and it goes out and gets a new IP address from DHCP. The DHCP then registers this address with DNS, which moves things along with incremental zone transfers. It is a much more efficient mechanism and one that means much less work for the system administrator.

How Does the Update Work?

The update sequence works this way:

- A client starts by issuing a Start of Authority (SOA) query. Through this query it locates the primary DNS server and zone authoritative for the record it needs to register.
- The client first checks to see if the DNS name is already registered. It does this by sending an assertion to the DNS server that it has located. If the registration does not already exist, the client will then send the dynamic update package that will register the record.
- If the update, for whatever reason, fails, the client will then attempt to register the record with some other primary DNS server. This assumes that the authoritative zone is a multimaster zone. If all the primary DNS servers fail to process the dynamic update, the system will wait, and the process will be repeated after 5 minutes. If, for whatever reason, the process fails again, it will try again after another 10 minutes. If registration still fails, the system will wait for 50 minutes and the whole process will be started over.

Dynamically Updating DNS Records

So far, we have had a pretty good overview of how DNS used to work, and how dynamic DNS is supposed to work. Please understand that this chapter is not designed to be a DNS primer giving you all the ins and outs of dynamic DNS and how to implement it in a Windows 2000 environment. This is to give you the understanding you need to see what the heck is going on in the background so you can make some security decisions. Therefore, do not take this chapter as the gospel according to DNS.

We are not going to be talking about a lot of the material you will need to institute DNS in a mixed environment. Before implementing dynamic DNS on a wide scale, be sure to do more research.

What we have covered so far is that every computer running Windows 2000 will attempt to register its A and its PTR records. The service that generates these DNS dynamic updates is not DNS, as you might think. It really is the DHCP client. This is true even if the client machine has a static IP address, because the DHCP client service runs on every machine even if it is not configured as a DHCP client.

The way dynamic update actually works is different depending on the type of client network adapter engaging in the dynamic update process. Now, when we say network adapter, we are not talking 3-Com or Intel here. We are talking about things like a straight DHCP client, a statically configured DHCP client, and a RAS client.

DHCP Clients

When you start up a Windows 2000 DHCP client, the client negotiates the dynamic update procedure with the DHCP server it finds. The DHCP client will always start by proposing that it update the A resource record and let the DHCP server update the PTR resource record. Now, what the DHCP server does with this information depends on the way it is configured. For example, it can be configured to disable "Perform dynamic updates," or to enable "Update DNS server according to client request," which is the default setting. It can also be configured to "Always update forward and reverse lookups." If the DHCP server is configured to "Always update forward and reverse lookups," it will update both A and PTR RRs itself, regardless of the DHCP client's request. If the DHCP server is configured to disable "Perform dynamic updates," the DHCP client will attempt to update both A and PTR RRs itself.

Remember, this is in a pure Windows 2000 dynamic DNS environment. We are trying to get an idea of how dynamic DNS works so we can secure it. Obviously, there are other scenarios that involve DNS running on other operating systems, which will make this process more difficult.

Statically Configured Client

What happens when we are dealing with a statically configured client? In this case, the statically configured client does not even communicate with the DHCP server. It dynamically updates both the A and the PTR RRs every time it boots up or makes any major changes. Those changes are things like its IP address or its per-adapter domain name.

RAS Clients

A RAS client works the same way as a statically configured client. There is no interaction that occurs between the client and the DHCP server. The client is the system responsible for updating both A and PTR RRs. The RAS client will also clean up after itself. It will attempt to delete both records before it closes the connection. The records will remain stale if that update fails for some reason. The records also remain stale if the phone line or the connection goes down unexpectedly. In these cases it is up to a RAS server to attempt to deregister the corresponding PTR record.

Secure Dynamic Updates

So, what are some of the built-in protections for this process? First of all, the Directory Service zones may be configured to use a secure dynamic update. In this case, Access Control Lists (ACLs) specify the list of groups or users allowed to update resource records in such zones. The Windows 2000 DNS implementation of the secure dynamic update is based on providing security services independently of the underlying security mechanism, and separates the security services into the following processes:

- The establishment of a security context generated by the passing of security tokens.
- Once a security context has been established, it has a finite lifetime. During this lifetime, it is used to either create or verify transaction signatures on the messages that are sent between the two parties.

The sequence of events in the secure dynamic update process is shown in Figure 12.5.

FIGURE 12.5 Secure dynamic update process

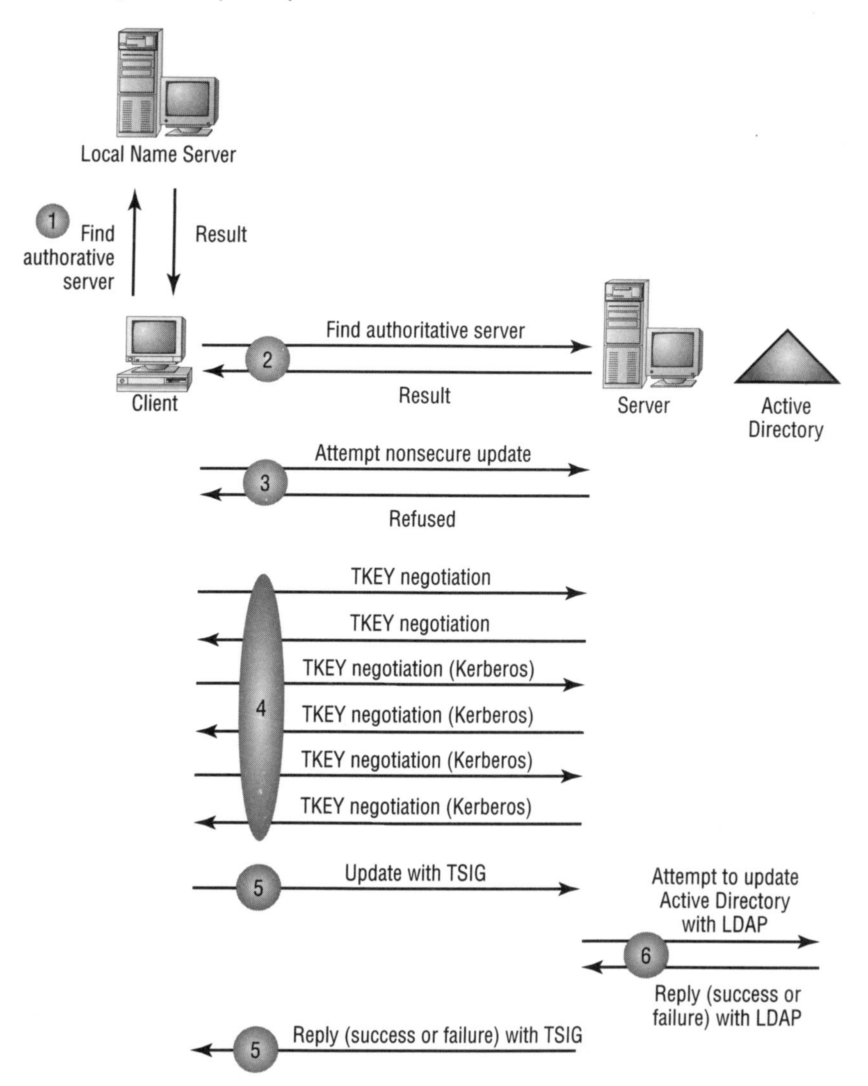

Let's break down what is actually happening here, step by step.

In Step 1, the client asks the local name server which server is authoritative for the name the client wants to update. At that point the local name server should respond with the location of the authoritative server.

In Step 2, the client sends its inquiry off to the authoritative server. This inquiry is just to verify that the server is authoritative for the name it is attempting to update, and the server should confirm it.

In Step 3, the client will try a nonsecure update, and the server should refuse it.

This attempt at a nonsecure update is only the case because the server is configured for only secure updates. Had the server been configured for nonsecure dynamic update for the appropriate zone rather than secure dynamic update, the server would have instead attempted to make the update.

In Step 4, the client and server begin to negotiate. The negotiation starts with the exchange of one or more security tokens. The number will depend on the underlying security provider. This is done using the *TKEY* resource record to transfer security tokens between the client and the server.

First, the client and server have to negotiate an underlying security mechanism. With the Windows 2000 dynamic update clients and servers, the original proposal is to use Kerberos. In this case, assuming both machines are Windows 2000, they would agree on using Kerberos. Next, they verify each other's identity using Kerberos.

Now, the security context has been established. This context will be used to create and verify all the transaction signatures on all the messages that pass between the client and server.

Now that security has been established, we move to Step 5. Here, the client gets down to business and sends the signed dynamic update request off to the server. At this point, the client and server are using the *TSIG* resource record.

Now, Active Directory has to be taken care of. In Step 6, the server will attempt to make the update to Active Directory. Whether or not it can will depend on whether the client has the proper permissions to make the update and if all of the prerequisites are satisfied.

In Step 7, the server sends a reply telling the client whether it was able to make the update. This reply is signed with the TSIG key. If the client receives a *spoofed* reply (meaning the reply appears to have come from another destination), it throws it away and waits for a signed response from the server.

Secure Dynamic Update Policies

How does a client attempt a dynamic update on the DNS server? It can be configured to use one of several approaches:

- First of all, it can try a nonsecure dynamic update. If that fails, it can then try to negotiate a secure dynamic update. This is the default configuration.
- The client can be configured so that it always negotiates a secure dynamic update.
- The client can be configured so that it can attempt only a nonsecure dynamic update.

The default approach allows a client to register with DNS servers even if they are not capable of the secure dynamic update. The default setting is changed through the registry.

Controlling Update Access to Zones and Names

As we said before, access to the secure DNS names and zones is controlled through the Active Directory and through the ACLs. These ACLs can be specified for either an entire zone or they can be modified to suit some specific names. The way Windows 2000 is set up, by default, any user that is authenticated can create the A or PTR RRs in any zone. But once an owner name has been created (regardless of type of record), only the users or the groups that are specified in the ACL for that name, and that have *write* permission, are able to modify the records corresponding to that name. While this approach is preferred, there are some situations that will need to be considered separately.

DNS Update of a Proxy Group

In a mixed environment, a DHCP server can be configured so that it will dynamically register A and PTR records for non-Windows-2000-level clients. This situation can cause outdated or stale records. Say, for example, a DHCP server performs a secure dynamic update on a name. Like it or not, the DHCP server now becomes the owner of that name. That means that only that DHCP server can update the name. This can cause problems in a few cases. Try this on for size: Your network is configured with several DHCP servers. When the client firstcomputer.acmecomputerservicesand-barsupply.com registered, the server DHCP_SRVR_1 handled the registration. If DHCP_SRVR_1 went down, its DHCP server, DHCP_SRVR_2, would replace it. The backup server would then try to update the name. It would not be able to update the name because it did not own it. In a similar example, suppose DHCP_SRVR_1 added an object for the name firstcomputer.acmecomputerservicesandbarsupply.com, and then the administrator upgraded the host firstcomputer.acmecomputerservicesandbarsupply.com to Windows 2000. Since the firstcomputer.acmecomputerservicesandbar-supply.com host did not own the name, it would not be able to update its own name.

To solve this problem, the developers of Windows 2000 introduced a new group called "DNS Update Proxy." Any object that is created by the members of this group have no security. The first user that is not a member of the DNS Update Proxy group that "touches" a name becomes its owner. So, if every DHCP server registering A records for pre–Windows 2000 clients is a member of the DNSUpdateProxy, the problem is eliminated. This special group is configured through the Active Directory manager.

While this may be a great solution, it does introduce security holes. For example, any DNS name that is registered by the computer that is running the DHCP service is nonsecure. Let's take it one step further and imagine that a DHCP server (that is, a member of the DNSUpdateProxy group) is installed on a domain controller. In this case all SRV, A, and CNAME records registered by netlogon for that DC are not secure and are subject to compromise. To minimize the problem, don't install a DHCP server on a DC.

DNS Admins Group

If you are working for a large enterprise, your DNS configuration could have multiple zones. It would be wonderful if there could be a way for the administration of these zones to be distributed. There is a way. Now, by default, the DNS Admins group has been given full control for all the zones and all the records in a Windows 2000 domain in which it is specified. For a user to be able to work with the zones in a specific Windows 2000 domain, the user (or a group the user belongs to) has to be listed in the DNS Admins group. That is the default.

To do this, you would create several groups, giving them really catchy names like Zone1Admins, and Zone2Admins, and so forth. Then the ACL for each zone will contain the appropriate Zone Admins group and that group will be given full control. At the same time all these groups with the catchy names will be included in the DNS Admins group. The DNS Admins group should only have read permission. Since a zone's ACL always contains the DNS Admins group, all users enlisted in the Zone1Admins and Zone2Admins will have read permission for any of the zones in the Domain.

The DNS Admins group is configurable through the Active Directory Users and Computers manager.

Reserving Names

Another problem that may arise in a highly secure environment is the fact that any authenticated user may create a new name in a zone. To solve this problem, the default ACL can be changed so that the creation of any object in a specific zone can only be done by certain groups or by certain users. The *Per-name* granularity of ACLs provides yet another way to solve this problem. Here, an administrator can reserve a name in a zone. That can leave the rest of the zone open for creation of the new objects by all the other authenticated users. To do this, the administrator just needs to create a record for the reserved name and then set the list of groups or users in the ACL. Then only the users listed in the ACL will be able to register another record under the reserved name.

So, now that we have looked at DNS and DHCP, how about Simple Network Management Protocol?

Design Scenario: The Case of the Cautious Client

One of your better clients is thinking about upgrading his Windows NT network with Windows 2000. He has heard through the grapevine that the new version of DNS does not work flawlessly with older versions, like the version of BIND he has running on a Unix box. For the past several weeks his company has been planning dozens of moves and adds that will reconfigure many of the hosts and intranet Web servers on the network. He is concerned that when the moves and adds are completed, the locations of the intranet servers may not be configured right in the DNS database.

Your customer is also concerned because the company has recently hired some new IT personnel. These people are straight out of school and have no experience. He would like them to get experience at the desktop first, and he is concerned that they can screw up the DNS system. He asks for your advice.

After you listen to the comments, you suggest that the moves and adds wait until after the Windows 2000 rollout is complete. Once dynamic DNS is in place, many of his concerns will evaporate because the system will handle the client registrations. In addition, you can configure DNS security to make sure that only the appropriate staff members can add or move servers on the network.

Simple Network Management Protocol (SNMP) Security

Many of you may have a high-level understanding of SNMP. This would be the type of understanding that says, "I know our network uses it, but I am not really sure how it works." In most cases, we don't really have to know how it works, as long as it does its work.

Microsoft Exam Objectives

Design Windows 2000 network services security.

- Design Windows 2000 SNMP security.

In this section, we are going to take a look under the hood to see how this thing actually functions so we can figure out how to secure it.

What Is SNMP?

Like many things in computing, the name SNMP says it all. Simple Network Management Protocol helps you manage your network by giving you more information about your network. SNMP-compliant devices on your network keep track of various things that they do. These "things" can be starting up, shutting down, printing a job, sending an e-mail, or any one of a myriad of other tasks. The information about these events is sent to a designated SNMP manager. The SNMP manager, like all good managers everywhere, takes the information, digests the information, and sends it to the administration team in some usable form. That form make take the shape of a report, an alert, an e-mail, or even a page.

SNMP is a network management standard traditionally used with TCP/IP networks. Recently, advances have been made so that it could work with Internetwork Packet Exchange (IPX) networks.

As we said, SNMP provides a method of managing network nodes from a centrally located host. These nodes can include things like servers, workstations, routers, bridges, and hubs. These "nodes" can be hardware based or even software service based. No matter what type the node is, SNMP performs its management services by using systems and agents. As shown in Figure 12.6, the local host, which happens to be running network management software, is called an SNMP manager. The network nodes that are managed are called SNMP *agents*.

FIGURE 12.6 Distributed architecture of SNMP

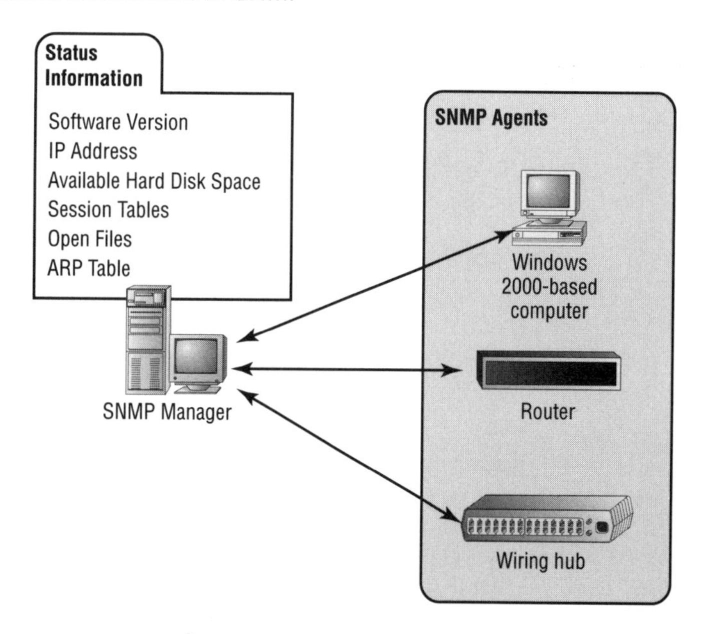

SNMP provides network management, and network management, in turn, allows the administration team to do a better job of resource management and auditing. Some of the uses of SNMP are laid out in Table 12.2.

TABLE 12.2 Uses of SNMP

Use	Example
To configure remote devices	You can use SNMP to configure information so that it can be sent to each networked host from a centrally located management system.
To monitor different levels of network performance	In this case, you can track things like the speed of processing or the network throughput. You can also collect information about the success or failure of data transmissions.
To detect network faults or to detect inappropriate access	You can configure things called trigger alarms to work on network devices. These alarms will alert you when specific events occur. When an alarm is triggered, the device forwards an event message to the management system. Common alarm types of events include things like the shutdown or restart of a device, or the detection of a link failure on a router or an attempt at inappropriate access.
To audit network usage	In this case, you can monitor the way the network is being used and identify things like user or group access or the types of usage for network devices or services. This information can be used in a variety of ways. One way would be to generate direct billing of individual or group accounts. You could also use this to plan ahead and to justify current network costs or planned expenditures.

How does SNMP work with Windows 2000? Well, SNMP is a 32-bit service that works with computers that are running either TCP/IP or the IPX protocols. On Windows 2000 Professional, it is optional. It can be installed after either TCP/IP or IPX have been configured.

SNMP Architecture

We said above that SNMP uses a distributed architecture of management systems and agents. The following sections discuss the role of each component, including the objects and messages used to store and retrieve managed information.

We showed above that there are two distinct pieces of the SNMP management system, the SNMP management console (also known as the SNMP manager) and the SNMP agent. The SNMP management console is a host that collects information from SNMP agents. The SNMP management console may or may not be running on a computer that has SNMP agents installed. The SNMP manager can request the following information from managed computers (SNMP agents):

- Information about the network protocol identification and statistics.
- Information about the dynamic identification of any devices attached to the network. This is a process that is referred to as *discovery*.
- Information about the hardware and software configuration.
- Information about the device performance and usage.
- Information about the device error and event messages.
- Information about the program and application usage.

Now it is up to the SNMP agents to provide the SNMP management systems with any information about the activities that occur at the Internet Protocol (IP) network layer. The agents must also respond to the management system requests for information. Any computer that is running SNMP agent software, such as the Windows 2000 SNMP Service, is an SNMP agent. The SNMP agent service can be configured to determine what statistics are to be tracked and what management systems are authorized to request information.

It is important to keep in mind that agents are very much like the people who work in your office. For the most part, agents do not originate messages to management. Agents only respond to messages. Now, there are exceptions. One of these exceptions is an alarm message that has been triggered by a specific event. In SNMP-speak an alarm message is known as a *trap message*. A *trap* is an event like a system reboot or an illegal attempt at access on an agent computer. These traps and trap messages provide a very crude form of security by just notifying the management system any time such an event occurs. It could be described as almost tattle-tale security.

Management Information Base

How does the manager know what types of information the agent can provide, and how does the agent know what the manager is going to be looking for? It is all a matter of databases. In the case of SNMP, these are referred to a *Management Information Base (MIB)*. A MIB is a container of objects. Each of these objects represents a specific type of information. This collection contains all of the information that is required by the specific management system. For example, one MIB object might represent the number of active sessions that are currently running on a particular agent; another MIB object may represent the amount of available hard drive space on another agent. Any and all of the information that a management system might possibly request from an agent has to be stored in the appropriate MIBs.

A MIB defines values for each object it contains:

- The object name and its identifier.
- What is the defined data type?
- A description of the object.
- For complex data types, there may be an index method. This is usually described as a multidimensional array, or perhaps as tabular data.
- Read/write permissions.

In addition, each object in a MIB has a unique identifier that includes the following information:

- The type (counter, string, gauge, or address)
- The access level (read or read/write)
- Any size restriction
- Any range information

Any device manufacturer (or any programmer) can define its own MIB. Whether those MIBs work properly or not depends on if the management console can recognize the information in the MIB. The Windows 2000 SNMP service supports the Internet MIB II, LAN Manager MIB II, Host Resources MIB, and Microsoft proprietary MIBs.

SNMP Messages

Agents and management systems can use SNMP messages to inspect objects or to communicate information about the managed objects. These SNMP messages are sent via the User Datagram Protocol (UDP). IP is used to route messages between the management system and host. IPX can also be used.

When an SNMP manager sends a request to a device, the agent receives the request and gets the information from the MIBs. The agent then sends the requested information back to the SNMP manager. Think of this as a normal process around our office. The boss sends out a memo and says that she wants to know what we did all last week. We check our MIB (our Exchange calendar) and compile the information and send it back to the manager. In the case of a network, an SNMP agent will send information at these times:

- When it is asked
- When a trap event occurs

To carry our boss/employee analogy further, there really aren't too many different types of communications we receive from our boss. You know what I mean—they fall into the "do this," "did you do this?" "thanks for doing this," and "why didn't you do this?" category. With SNMP, the number of commands it uses to communicate is just about as limited. To perform all these tasks, the management system and agent programs use the messages shown in Table 12.3.

TABLE 12.3 SNMP Messages

Message	Purpose
GET	The basic SNMP request message. Sent by a management system, it requests information about a single MIB entry on an agent—for example, the amount of free drive space.
GET-NEXT	An extended type of request message that can be used to browse the entire hierarchy of management objects. When it processes a GET-NEXT request for a particular object, the agent returns the identity and value of the object that logically follows the previous information that was sent. The GET-NEXT request is useful mostly for dynamic tables, such as an internal IP route table.

TABLE 12.3 SNMP Messages *(continued)*

Message	Purpose
SET	A message that can be used to send and assign an updated MIB value to the agent when write access is permitted.
GET-BULK	A request that the data transferred by the agent be as large as possible within the given restraints of message size. This minimizes the number of protocol exchanges required to retrieve a large amount of management information.
NOTIFY	Also called a trap message, NOTIFY is an unsolicited message that is sent by an agent to a management system when the agent detects a certain type of event. For example, a trap message might be sent when a system restart occurs. The management system that receives the trap message is referred to as the *trap destination*.

By default, UDP port 161 is used to listen for SNMP messages and port 162 is used to listen for SNMP traps. You can change these port settings by configuring the local Services file.

SNMP Communication

The example illustrated in Figure 12.7 shows how management systems and agents communicate information.

FIGURE 12.7 SNMP manager and agent communication

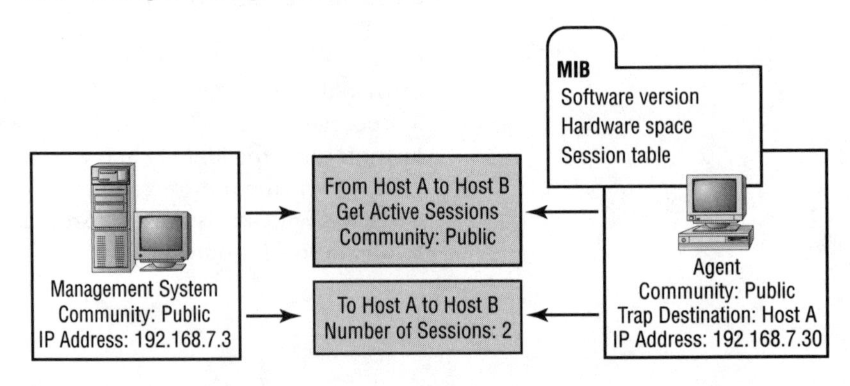

So, the communication process works like this:

1. A management system forms an SNMP message. This message contains a GET, as well as the name of the community to which the management system belongs, and the destination of the message—the agent's IP address (192.168.7.30).
2. The SNMP message is forwarded to the agent.
3. The agent receives the message and decodes it. The community name (Public) is deemed acceptable.
4. The SNMP service makes a call to the appropriate subagent. In this way it retrieves the session information that has been requested by the MIB.
5. The agent takes the session information from the subagent and creates a return message that contains the requested information and the destination address—the management system's IP address (192.168.7.3).
6. The SNMP message is sent to the management system.

SNMP Security

The security that comes with most SNMP services is rather basic. SNMP security is based on the use of community names and authentication traps. When you configure your network, you can restrict SNMP communications for the agent and allow it to communicate with only a set list of SNMP management systems. These management systems form the basis for communities.

Traps

Traps messages can also do some very limited security checking. When traps are configured, the SNMP service generates messages when specific events occur. For example, an agent can be configured to initiate an authentication trap if a request for information is sent by a management system the agent doesn't recognize. In this case, a message from such a management system is then sent to a trap destination. This destination is specified explicitly in the SNMP service configuration.

These trap destinations are made up of the host name and the IP address or IPX address of the management system. The trap destination must be a host that is running SNMP management software—otherwise the information would simply go to cyberspace. While these trap destinations are configured by the administrator, the actual events that generate a trap message are defined by the agent.

You can configure trap destinations by using the Traps tab in the Microsoft SNMP Properties dialog box. This is shown in Figure 12.8.

FIGURE 12.8 SNMP trap properties

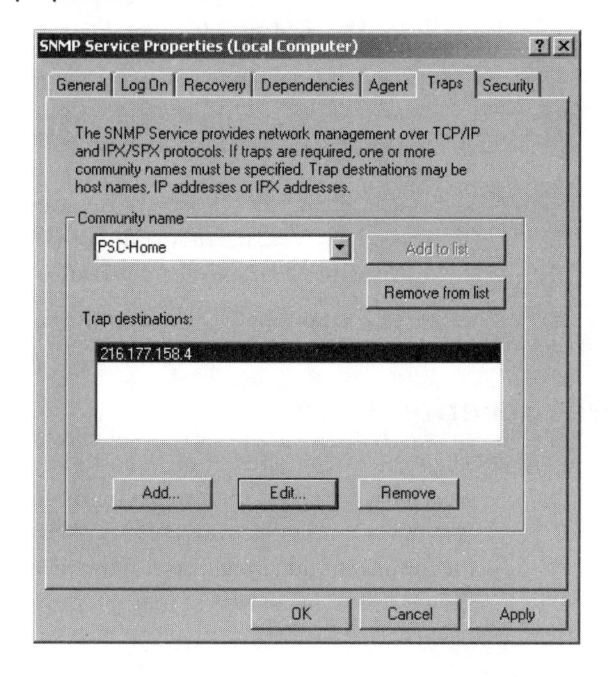

Communities

Every SNMP management host and agent belongs to what is called an SNMP community. An SNMP community is nothing more than a collection of hosts grouped together for administrative purposes. There is no real mystery or magic here. You may group computers together as communities that bypass Organizational Unit or Site boundaries. For example, all computers on the network that you want to monitor when they come up or are shut down could be part of one community. What we are trying to say is that there is no relationship between community names and domain names or even workgroup names. A community name is simply a password that is shared by the

SNMP management consoles and its managed computers. It is your responsibility as a system administrator to set hard-to-guess community names when you install the SNMP service.

To see what we mean, take a look at Figure 12.9. Agent1 can respond to SNMP requests from and can send traps to Manager2 because they are both members of the Public2 community. Agent2, Agent3, and Agent4 can respond to SNMP requests from and can send traps to Manager1 because they are all members of the (default) Public community.

FIGURE 12.9 Example of SNMP communities

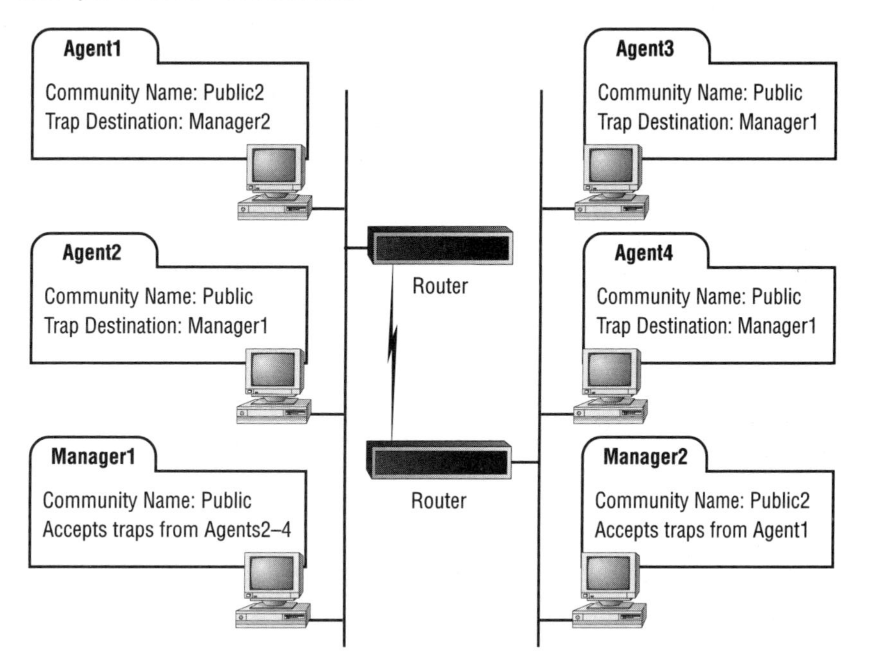

When an SNMP agent receives a message, the only way it can know if the message is valid is to check the community name. The community name that is contained in the packet is verified against the agent's list. After the name is verified, the request is evaluated against the agent's list of permissions for that community. The types of permissions that can be granted are shown in Table 12.4.

TABLE 12.4 SNMP Access Permissions

Permission	Purpose
None	The SNMP agent doesn't process the request. If the agent receives an SNMP message from a management system in this community, it discards the request and then it generates an authentication trap.
Notify	This is the same as None.
Read Only	The agent doesn't process SET requests from this community. It will process only GET, GET-NEXT, and GET-BULK requests. The agent will discard any SET requests from any manager systems in this community and it will generate an authentication trap.
Read Create	The SNMP agent will process or create all requests from this community. It processes SET, GET, GET-NEXT, and GET-BULK requests, including SET requests that require the addition of a new object to a MIB table.
Read Write	Currently this is identical to Read Create.

These community permissions are configured by using the SNMP Security tab of the Microsoft SNMP Properties dialog box. This is shown in Figure 12.10.

FIGURE 12.10 SNMP service properties

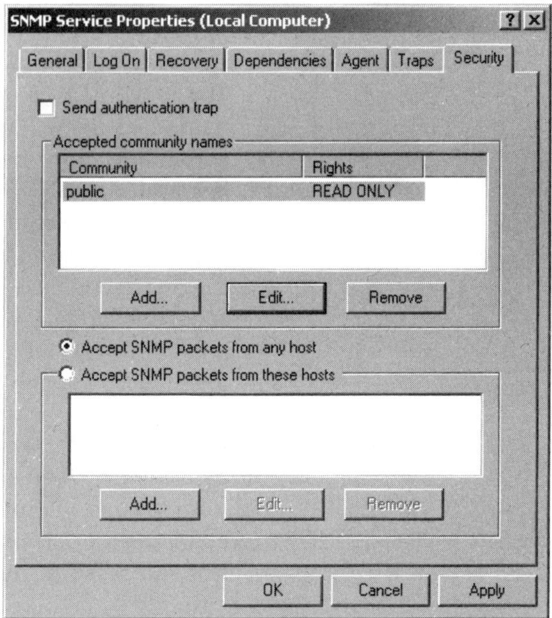

Community names are sent across the network as plain text. Since this is true, it is obvious that the use of SNMP community names represents a potential security risk. For more information about configuring SNMP for IP security, see the next section, "Configuring SNMP Security Options."

Configuring SNMP Security Options

As you can see, on its own, SNMP is not the most secure thing on your network. There are some things you can do to help configure and enable SNMP security. Let's start by looking at Table 12.5.

TABLE 12.5 Setting SNMP Security Options

Suggestion	Purpose
Accepted Community Names	The SNMP service needs at least one community name. The name Public is generally accepted as the community name because it is the common name that is found in all SNMP implementations. As the person responsible for configuring SNMP, you can delete or change the community name or add different names. If the SNMP agent gets a request from a community that is not on this list, it will generate an authentication trap. If there are no community names defined, the SNMP agent will deny any and all incoming SNMP requests.
Permissions	In this case, you can select a permission level that will determine how an agent processes SNMP requests from the various communities. For example, you can configure the permission level to block the SNMP agent from processing any request from a specific community.
Accept SNMP Packets from Any Host	Here, the source host and a list of acceptable hosts refer to the source SNMP management system and the list of other acceptable management systems. When this option is enabled, no SNMP packets are rejected on the basis of the name or address of the source host or on the basis of the list of acceptable hosts. This option is enabled by default.
Only Accept SNMP Packets from These Hosts	If you choose to select this option, it will provide very limited security. When the option is enabled, only SNMP packets received from the hosts on a list of acceptable hosts are accepted. The SNMP agent rejects messages from other hosts and sends an authentication trap. Limiting access to hosts on a list provides a higher level of security than limiting access to specific communities because a community name can encompass a large group of hosts.

TABLE 12.5 Setting SNMP Security Options *(continued)*

Suggestion	Purpose
Send Authentication Traps	When an SNMP agent receives a request that does not contain a valid community name, or the host that is sending the message is not on the list of acceptable hosts, the agent can send an authentication trap message to one or more trap destinations (management systems). The trap message indicates that the SNMP request failed authentication. This is a default setting.

Other Considerations Before Implementing SNMP

Here are some other things you may do to take advantage of the SNMP service securely.

Changing SNMP Port Settings

SNMP uses the default UDP port 161 for general SNMP messages and UDP port 162 for SNMP trap messages. If these ports are being used by another protocol or service, you can change the settings by modifying the local Services file on the agent. The Services file is located in `\%SystemRoot%\System32\Drivers\Etc.`

There is no file name extension. You can use any text-based editor to modify the file. The management system must also be configured to listen and send on the new ports.

Another thing to consider before changing port addresses is the importance of updating IP Security policy after configuring IP Security to encrypt SNMP messages on the default ports.

If you have previously configured IP security to encrypt SNMP messages on the default ports, you must also update the IP Security policy with the new port settings. Otherwise, communication can be erroneously blocked or SNMP communications might not be secured.

Securing SNMP Messages with IP Security

If you want to use IPSec to protect SNMP messages, you have to configure all the SNMP-enabled systems to use IPSec, or the communications will fail. If you can't configure all SNMP-enabled systems to use IPSec, you have to configure the IPSec policies of the systems that are SNMP-enabled so that they can send plain text information. However, this somewhat defeats the idea of trying to secure messages because all communications will be unsecured.

IP Security does not automatically encrypt the SNMP protocol. You must create filter specifications in the appropriate IP filter list for traffic between the management systems and SNMP agents. The filter specification must include two sets of settings.

The first set of filter specifications are for typical SNMP traffic (SNMP messages) between the management system and the SNMP agents:

- Mirrored: enabled
- Protocol Type: TCP
- Source and Destination Ports: 161
- Mirrored: enabled
- Protocol Type: UDP
- Source and Destination Ports: 161

The second set of filter specifications are for SNMP trap messages sent to the management system from the SNMP agents:

- Mirrored: enabled
- Protocol Type: TCP
- Source and Destination Ports: 162
- Mirrored: enabled
- Protocol Type: UDP
- Source and Destination Ports: 162

For additional information about creating filter specifications, see Windows 2000 Help.

Design Scenario: SNMP

One of your customers has just completed reading a book on SNMP and she is expressing her concern. It appears that their network makes extensive use of SNMP and she is concerned that all of the information is flying around the network using plain text. Her network makes extensive use of Virtual Private Networks; therefore, many of the hosts are currently using IPSec. She looks to you for advice.

At this point, you tell her that she can increase her SNMP security by utilizing the IPSec already on the network. You can show her how to configure SNMP to take advantage of the tunneling capabilities to keep the communication channel secure.

In addition, you point out, she may want to look at changing port numbers on some of the applications to move away from the well-known ports used by default.

Summary

In this chapter we took a look at how DHCP works with DNS and how to secure DNS. In addition, we explored SNMP. We found out how SNMP works, took a look at the basic security provided with it, and then saw how it could be secured using IPSec and filters. All and all, we did an awful lot in this chapter. Now is time to take a look at Remote Installation and Terminal Services Security.

Key Terms

Before you take the exam, be certain you are familiar with the following terms:

Domain Name System (DNS)

full zone transfer (AXFR)

incremental zone transfer (IXFR)

resource records (RRs)

TKEY

TSIG

Windows Internet Name Services (WINS)

zone transfer

Review Questions

1. When a client computer sends a query out to a DNS server, looking for another host, this is called a:

   A. DNS Search

   B. DNS Question

   C. DNS Lookup

   D. DNS Index

2. When Windows 2000 Server is first installed on a network, it looks for a DNS server that can handle a particular type of record. That type of record is:

   A. Start of Authority (SOA)

   B. Service Location Resource Records (SRV RRs)

   C. Mail Exchanger (MX)

   D. None of the above

3. Windows 2000 uses DNS for these two reasons:

   A. Name resolution

   B. WINS resolution

   C. Dynamic allocation of IP addresses

   D. Service location

4. Which protocol registers a host with dynamic DNS?

   A. DNS

   B. DHCP

   C. UDP

   D. TCP

   E. IP

5. The two types of hosts in an SNMP system are called:
   A. Client
   B. Server
   C. Agent
   D. Manager
   E. Boss
   F. Worker

6. MIBs are proprietary and must be approved by the IEEE before they can be released. Is this true or false?
   A. True
   B. False

7. What is a group of hosts that communicate with a particular SNMP manager about a particular event called?
   A. cluster
   B. community
   C. gaggle
   D. covey
   E. site

8. SNMP information can only be transmitted across the network in plain text.
   A. True
   B. False

9. A community is a type of SNMP security.
   A. True
   B. False

10. With dynamic DNS, there are two kinds of replication. These are:

A. Full

B. Partial

C. Incremental

D. Mail Exchanger

Answers to Review Questions

1. C. It is called a DNS lookup.

2. B. When the first server is installed in a Windows 2000 network, it is looking for a DNS server that supports Service Location Resource Records (SRV RRs).

3. A, D. Windows 2000 and the Active Directory use DNS for name resolution and service locations.

4. B. DHCP handles the client registration with dynamic DNS.

5. C, D. There is the SNMP agent and the SNMP manager.

6. B. MIBs can be written by anyone.

7. B. A community is a group of hosts that communicates with a particular SNMP manager about a particular event.

8. B. You can configure SNMP to use IPSec, so the information is encrypted.

9. A. A community is the most rudimentary type of SNMP security.

10. A, C. Dynamic DNS can either replicate the complete database or do an incremental replication.

The Multinational Conglomerate

You should give yourself 10 minutes to review this case study, diagram as needed, and complete the questions for this testlet. Be sure to read each question carefully. While the company may not have changed, its circumstances change in each chapter.

Background

Your consulting firm has been hired to assist in the Windows 2000 migration and integration for a company based in Minneapolis, Minnesota. The company has been using the Active Directory and has a DNS namespace of acme-computerwarehouse.com. Until the start of this year, the company had 1,000 employees, all based throughout the Twin Cities of Minneapolis and St. Paul. Just before the end of the year, the owner of your company purchased two companies of roughly the same size that will need to be connected to the enterprise network. The total number of users when the project is completed is estimated at 3,500. In addition, each of these companies comes with various strategic partners that will need to access the information on your enterprise network. The companies that have been acquired are located in Athens, Greece, and in Orlando, Florida.

The three companies can now be considered one, and the Windows 2000 rollout is in full swing. The Windows 2000 network is made up of a forest with three domains.

Up until now, the network has been using the latest version of BIND DNS to make sure it was backwardly compatible with the older systems on the network. Since the rollout is all but completed, it is time to switch the DNS over to Windows 2000 and to make sure it is secure.

In addition, the company is beginning to implement SNMP, but is concerned about security.

Current System

Minneapolis Located on the shores of beautiful Lake Calhoun, the company occupies a sprawling campus that includes four floors in a six-story building. Since the merger, the Lake Calhoun facility has become a model of efficiency. Besides being linked to all of the other offices, everyone is beginning to take the notion of an enterprise network seriously.

All of the floors are connected to the Windows 2000 network. The Minneapolis location is a domain in the tree. Active Directory Services have been deployed to the main campus and the rollout is complete in the branch offices. The desktop and laptop rollout company wide took longer than expected, but it is now completed. The CEO wants to know what the IT team is doing to make sure that everyone within the company can access resources all over the tree, as well as protect the network.

The corporate network was so impressive it helped this company snag a very large contract with a very large customer. This contract could put the company on the map. With every silver lining, there is a dark cloud. In this case, the dark cloud is that the customer wants to be able to access the online inventory system on your network, as well as share information directly with several new Unix hosts that are currently being installed. The customer is using Windows 2000 exclusively in its network.

At the present time, the customer is able to access most of the hosts on the network using the current DNS system. The management team wants to make sure that trend continues.

Orlando The Orlando office is a domain in the corporate tree. It has some valuable resources that need to be made available to the rest of company, particularly the folks in Athens.

The new contract may have a long-term effect on Orlando. Current corporate strategy calls for the new contract to be managed in Minneapolis for the first year, and then moved to Orlando after that. Given this strategy, Orlando will make use of their ability to access information in Minneapolis, but several people in the office will need to access the customers network to work on design issues and planning issues.

At this time, this domain has already has its own namespace: Orlando.acmecomputerwarehouse.com.

Athens The Athens office is now fully staffed at 2,300. Management has discovered that the business is doing well, and the extra folks are justified. The office has been upgraded to Windows 2000 servers and Athens is now its own domain in the tree.

Athens has always been ahead of the curve. When the new contract was announced, Athens' manufacturing geared up for the task, and can now handle that stage. Because the customer wants to be able to look at all the stages of inventory, the customer will need to be able to access the Athens facility as well as Minneapolis and Orlando.

At this time, this domain already has its own namespace of Athens.acme-computerwarehouse.com.

Customer The customer has a Windows 2000 network. The customer and our IS department have decided to link the two forests.

The communication between the trees is established, and now the next step is to provide certificates where necessary. The customer has a fully implemented PKI.

Problem Statement

Provide a unified approach to DNS and SNMP, including number, type, and locations of DNS servers, and number, type, and location of SNMP communities.

Envisioned System

CEO As the new network was designed, the CEO is looking closely at the IS department and saying things like, "Okay, people, you wanted the Windows 2000 network because of its flexibility and you now have it. This is where the rubber hits the road. Prove you can make this network do the things you said it can do."

CFO "Things are really working out nicely. I do wish we had more information from the outlying offices on network usage, but we will take things one-step at a time. You say the next part of the project can be completed without any expenditure of funds? I am all for that!"

CIO "You know, I didn't say 'without any expenditure of funds.' I said, 'without any expenditure of additional funds that were not already budgeted.' There is a big difference. I agree with the CFO; I would like to see more information on the network, but primarily I am looking for things like bandwidth usage statistics. I am also looking for a way to isolate the information by domain and get proactive information about incorrect logons."

Orlando General Manager "We are getting ready to re-subnet our network. I have already dispatched someone to start figuring out which DNS servers we will have to impact."

Athens General Manager "You know, we have noticed some weird stuff going on out here with the network. I hear from my IS person that there may be someone trying to break in, but right now, we don't have a way of knowing. Can you help?"

Questions

1. What features of Windows 2000 DNS will be most beneficial in the scenario described above?

   A. AD integration

   B. Iterative queries

   C. Incremental zone transfer (IXFR)

   D. Dynamic update and secure dynamic update

   E. Unicode character support

   F. Enhanced caching resolver service

2. When SNMP is configured, what is the minimum number of communities that should be defined?

   A. One.

   B. Three.

   C. Five.

   D. Six.

   E. Not enough information is provided to make a determination.

3. If you wanted to make sure the SNMP communications were secure, what protocols would have to be present?

A. IPX

B. DHCP

C. FTP

D. IPSec

E. DNS

Answers

1. A, C, D. In this scenario, the features that this company will use the most will be the integration with Active Directory, the ability to use incremental zone transfers and dynamic updates, and secure dynamic updates.

2. B. The CIO said that he wanted information broken down by domain. Given that information, you would need to create three communities—one for each of the domains.

3. D. You would have to make sure that IPSec was present and properly configured.

Designing Remote Services Security

MICROSOFT EXAM OBJECTIVES COVERED IN THIS CHAPTER:

✓ **Design Windows 2000 network services security.**

- Design Windows 2000 DNS security.
- Design Windows 2000 Remote Installation Services (RIS) security.
- Design Windows 2000 SNMP security.
- Design Windows 2000 Terminal Services security.

In the last chapter, we covered half of this objective, on DNS and SNMP security. In this one, we are going to focus on making sure that *Remote Installation Services (RIS)* and Terminal Services are secure.

Potentially, one of the largest tasks of any major rollout is upgrading the desktop. The task of upgrading all the workstations on a network can be daunting, especially if you have several thousand to do. Most of us would do just about anything to minimize the number of times we have to click through an installation. By using RIS, you can install Windows 2000 Professional on client computers throughout the network from a central location.

While all security functions are vital, Terminal Services takes on special meaning. After all, you are opening up your network to the outside world on purpose. You are making it possible for people to access the front door of your network. Now, it is up to you to make sure the doors are locked and they can't get in.

Obviously, both of these services need to have some type of protection built in. Let's take a look at how best to secure each of these services.

Understanding Remote Installation

I suppose this section could be subtitled, "Let's Be Nice to Desktop Support." Think about what their lives must be like. In large companies, they may be tasked with installing and configuring dozens of Windows 2000 Professional workstations each and every week. Think how tedious that would get—just click, click, click, wait, click, click, click, wait, every day, all day. That would be enough to make you crazy.

Microsoft Exam Objectives

Design Windows 2000 network services security.

- Design Windows 2000 Remote Installation Services (RIS) security.

Well, there is a much more efficient method of deploying Windows 2000 Professional, and that is to use Remote Installation Services (RIS). RIS can be used if you have configured a Windows 2000 Server or a Windows 2000 Advanced Server to store the images and if the computers on the network support remote booting, or use a RIS remote boot disk. What this means to the desktop support group is that they can bring the new computers into the staging area, plug them into the network, remote boot them, and Windows 2000 Professional will be magically installed just the way they want it, without a lot of click, click, click, and wait. Management loves the concept because they see all that click, click, click, and wait time as an inappropriate use of a long-term human asset. That translates from management speak into, "It sure looks like the IT folks are goofing off again!"

In addition to the timesaving, RIS also offers a few other benefits. For example, with RIS you don't have to have hardware-specific images. RIS will detect plug and play hardware during setup. You can also use RIS to support recovery of the operating system and computer in the event the computer fails.

RIS will also retain security settings after restarting the destination computer and, because RIS allows people to be more efficient, it reduces the total cost of ownership.

Installing RIS

We said that before it can be used, RIS has to be installed. As with the installation of any new service, there are some prerequisites that have to be met. Most of these prerequisites are commonsense things that have to do with the stress you are about to put on the server.

Prerequisites

When you configure your RIS server, it can be either a domain controller or a member server. There are some other services that have to be present before RIS will function. These are included in Table 13.1.

TABLE 13.1 RIS Prerequisite Services

Network Service	RIS Function
Domain Name System (DNS)	RIS needs a DNS server for locating the directory service.
DHCP	Client computers need DHCP so they can receive an IP address.
Active Directory directory services	RIS needs Active Directory in Windows 2000 for locating existing client computers as well as existing RIS servers.

Now, there are some other things that have to happen. For example, RIS has to be installed on a volume that is shared over the network.

This is a kind of *duh*. If the volumes were not shared, you could access them, but it would be a real pain, wouldn't it?

Not only must the volume be shared, but also it cannot be on the same drive that is running Windows 2000 Server or Windows 2000 Advanced Server. The drive must be large, because it has to hold the RIS software and all the Windows 2000 Professional images. The volume must be formatted in NTFS.

Setting Up RIS

Once all the prerequisites have been met, you can kick off the Remote Install Services Setup wizard. This is done as part of the Add/Remove Programs in Control Panel. It is shown in Figure 13.1.

FIGURE 13.1 Configure Remote Installation Services Add/Remove Windows Components

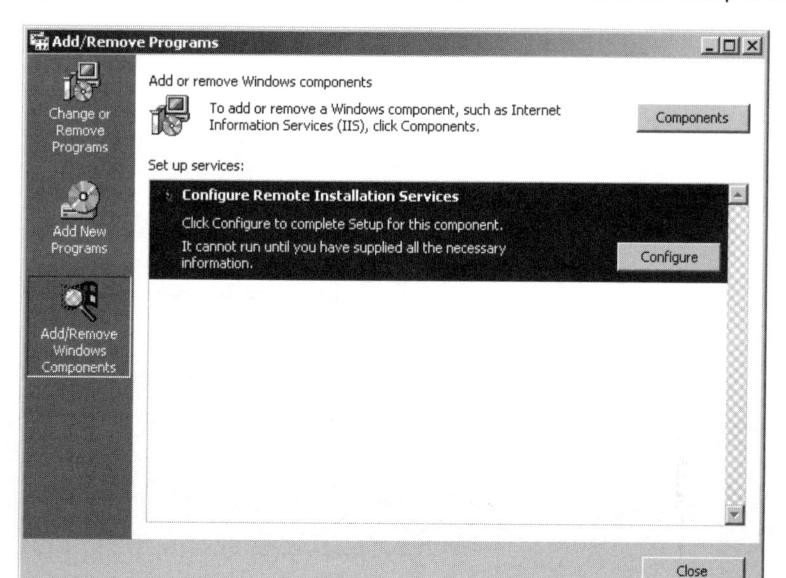

The Wizard installs the RIS software, copies the Windows 2000 Professional Installation files to the server and configures the Client Installation Wizard screens that will appear during a remote installation. In addition, the session will add various files that have an extension of *SIF (Setup Information File)*. If you are familiar with a similar remote installation concept from the NT 4 days, think of the old `Unattend.txt` files. The `.SIF` files perform the same task.

As you can see in Figure 13.2, the wizard will not let you put the remote installation files on the boot partition.

FIGURE 13.2 Remote Installation Services Setup wizard, default folder location

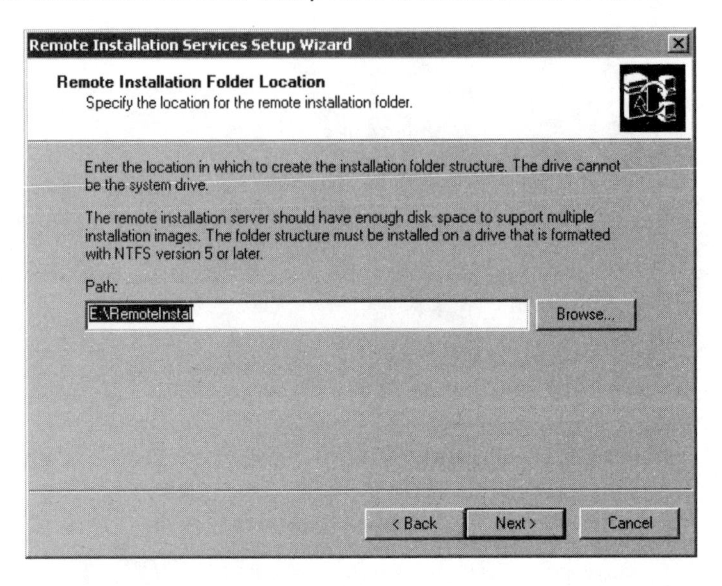

The next screen is where the RIS security actually starts. As you can see from Figure 13.3, when you work with client support, the default is to not respond to client support. If I choose to respond to client computers requesting service, I also have the choice of, "Do not respond to unknown client computers."

FIGURE 13.3 Initial setting of client support

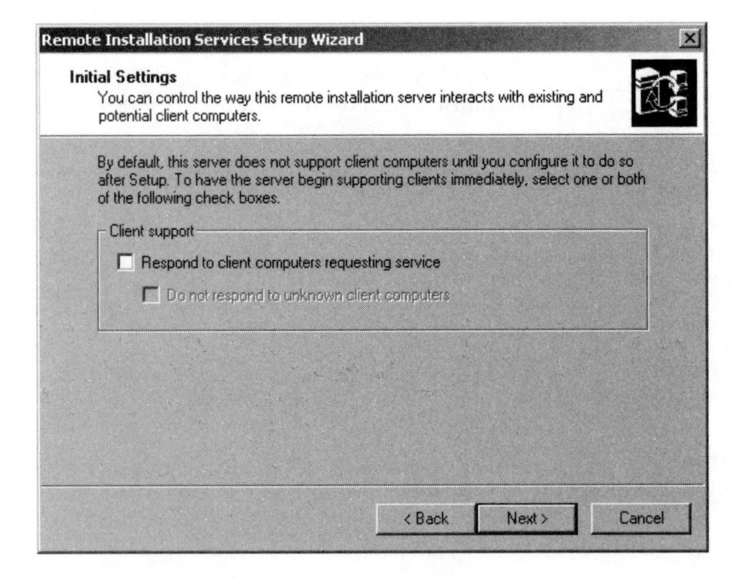

Why would you want to not respond to an unknown client computer? If you check this box, you are actually making some more work for yourself. Before you can install Windows 2000 Professional, you have to create a computer account for the client to be installed. In some ways, this is a good idea. If this box is not selected, then anyone who can reach the server can receive an operating system installation, provided that the user has adequate permissions.

There may also be a compatibility issue with some remote-boot applications. If you don't select the check-box and you are using some other company's remote boot/installation program on the network, clients may not be able to reach the other program. When you select this check-box, you ensure that only clients with registered computer accounts will use RIS.

When the RIS installation is ready to copy files, it will prompt you for your Windows 2000 Professional CD. In this case, not any CD will do. It has to be the full version, not just a CD that contains the upgrade.

When the installation is complete, you configure RIS by using the server's computer object in the Active Directory Users and Computer snap-in. Start by going into the proper domain, go into either domain controllers or computers, highlight the computer, and right-click for properties. At that point, choose the Remote Install tab and you should see the configuration screen shown in Figure 13.4.

FIGURE 13.4 Remote installation properties

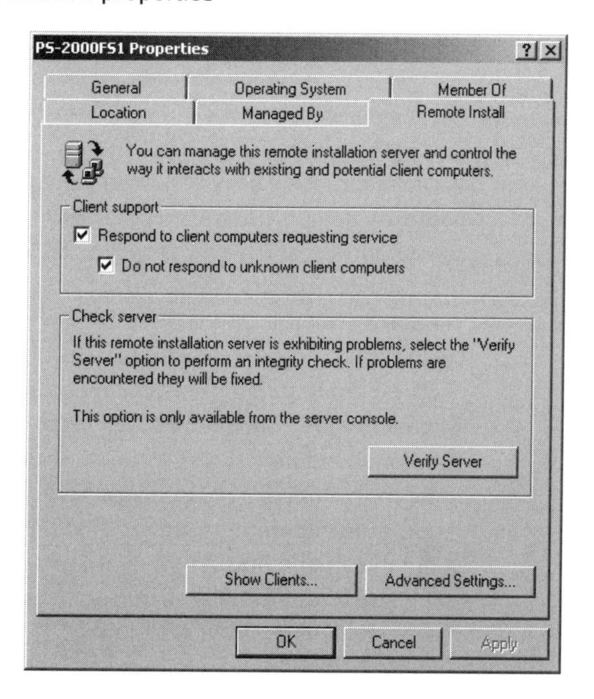

Now, notice on the graphic above that there is an Advanced Settings tab. Those kinds of tabs always enthrall us, so let's take a look at the kinds of things we can do with them. Check out Figure 13.5, and you begin to see some of the other security options you have available.

FIGURE 13.5 Advanced Settings

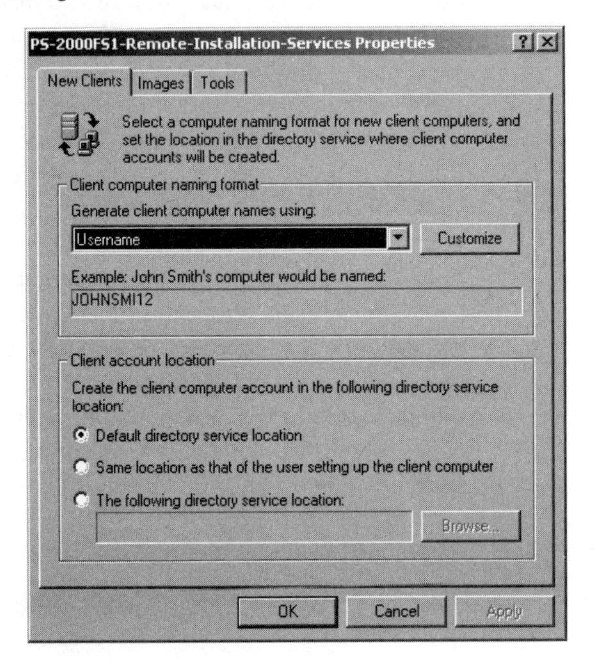

As you can see, in this case, the advanced settings may not do much for us in the realm of security. They do provide a way of defining the computer name, by default using the username. There are other selections, all using some iteration of the username, the MAC address, and an incremental number. You can specify where the client account will be located, what images you have available and if there are any tools available for working with the clients.

These tools are a unique enhancement. These tools come not from Microsoft, but from other *independent software vendors (ISVs)* and *original equipment manufacturers (OEMs)*. This gives you the opportunity to make these tools available to users and administrators for use prior to the installation of the operating system. This is especially handy when dealing with computers that come in with blank hard disks. These tools can also be used to update things like the client's system BIOS. The tools are installed using the external setup program supplied with the tool.

RIS and Group Policies

At this point, the server side is all set and ready to accept requests from clients for the operating system installation. That would be wonderful if you could completely trust clients to make all the right decisions in how you want the new systems configured. You know that you can control the systems once they are installed into an AD container, through the use of group policies. Well, there are some group policy settings that can be put into place to control how the computers are configured in the first place.

Now, I am not sure if you have the same problem, but even though we have been working with Microsoft Management Consoles (MMCs) for awhile, they are still somewhat of a mystery and a maze, so forgive us if we get a little granular here. To start the process, start up a new MMC by choosing Start ➢ Run and then typing ***MMC*** and clicking OK. At this point, we need to add the Group Policy snap-in, so from the Console menu way up at the top, click Add/Remove Snap-In. This brings up the Add/Remove Snap-In window; click Add again, which will bring up the Add Standalone Snap-In menu. In the Snap-In window (the one on the left) scroll down until you see Group Policy. Click Group Policy to highlight it and choose Add. At this point you can choose whether you want the Group Policy stored in Active Directory or on the local computer. Since we are just doing this for demonstration purposes, and because we are exceptionally lazy, we will leave it at the default of *local computer*. Click Finish at the bottom of the screen. Click Close to shut down the Add Standalone Snap-In window and click OK to close the Add/Remove Snap-In window. At this point, your screen should look something like Figure 13.6.

FIGURE 13.6 MMC console with the Local Computer Policy expanded

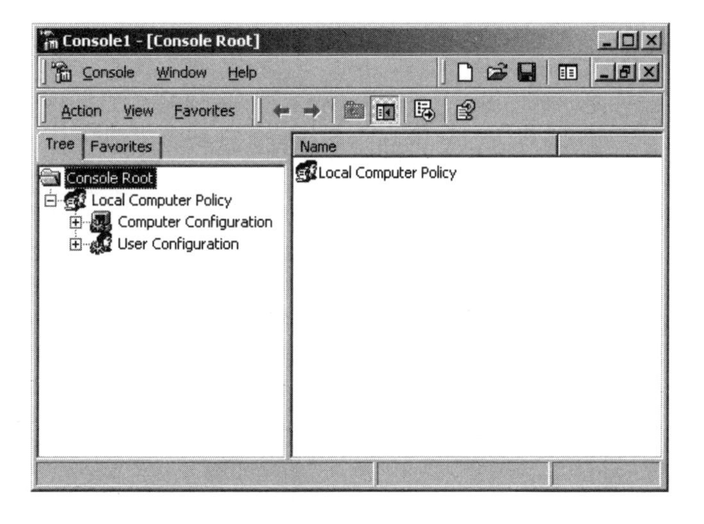

So, now we have to find where the remote installation policy is configured. Remember, your screen may not look exactly like ours, depending on whether you chose to configure the policy for the local computer or not. Anyway, open User Configuration ➤ Windows Settings ➤ Remote Installation Services and then double-click Choice Options in the right-hand pane. Finally, you will get to the Choice Options Properties Policy tab shown in Figure 13.7.

FIGURE 13.7 Choice Options Properties Policy tab

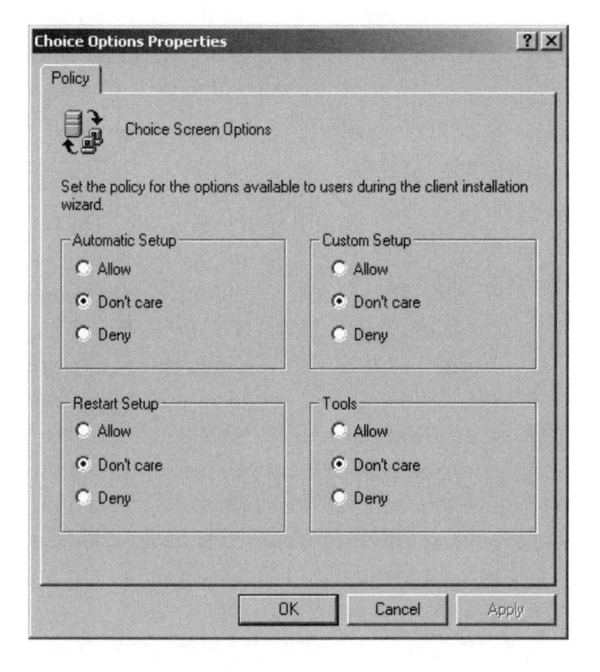

With this setup policy, you can choose to *allow*, *deny*, or *don't care* on the options defined in Table 13.2.

TABLE 13.2 Remote Installation Services Group Policy Options

Option	Description
Automatic setup	With automatic setup most of the options will be configured by the administrator. The user will not be offered any client installation wizard choices.

TABLE 13.2 Remote Installation Services Group Policy Options *(continued)*

Option	Description
Custom setup	This provides the ability to supply a unique name for this computer and also to specify where the computer account will be created within Active Directory.
Restart a previous setup attempt	This selection restarts an operating installation attempt if it fails prior to completion.
Tools	This selection accesses tools from the client installation wizard.

The choice to *allow*, *deny*, or *don't care* affects each choice above. The definition is shown in Table 13.3.

TABLE 13.3 Selection Definition

Option	Description
Allow	Choosing *allow* will offer this installation option to users to whom this policy applies.
Don't care	Choosing *don't care* will accept the policy settings of the parent container.
Deny	Choosing *deny* will prevent users affected by this policy from accessing that installation option within the client installation wizard.

RIS Group Policy Notes

There are some things that should be kept in mind when using RIS Group Policy objects:

- The default setting is *don't care*.
- The default display option for users of a client computer is the automatic setup.

- It can take up to eight hours for the security settings that have been set on a domain controller through Group Policy within the Active Directory Users and Computers console to take effect for the defined user or group accounts.

What about on the client side? Well, the client computer has to meet the following prerequisites:

- It has to be a PXE-enabled personal computer with revision of .99c or later, or it has to have a network card that will work with a remote installation floppy.
- The computer BIOS has to be configured so the load boot order goes to the network card boot before it gets to the hard disk.

When the client computer boots, attaches to the RIS server, and loads Windows 2000 Professional, it will be ready to ship to its new owner. At that time, the new owner can turn the computer on and logon. That is when the computer will be named, using information you provided as part of the RIS configuration. When the users chooses Automatic Setup for their new computer, the computer account object (CAO) is created in active directory. The default naming format for the computer is the user name of the account that has been type in the Client Installation Wizard (CIW), followed by an incremental number. For example, by default, if JHIBBARD@myplace.com logged on to the computer, the computer account would be JHIBBARD1. These can be customized. When all is said and done, you have a client computer with the operating system installed. If you have played your group policy cards right, when the user logs on to the network, the group policy can either assign applications or publish applications, so the user has a fully functional computer.

Terminal Services

Now, this is a rather tricky section, simply because so much information is available on Terminal Services. I mean, we could do an entire book on Terminal Services. For this book, however, we are interested primarily in how to secure Terminal Services, not necessarily how to install and administer it. That is important certainly, but in this case, we just want to look at the security of the service.

Microsoft Exam Objectives

Design Windows 2000 network services security.

- Design Windows 2000 Terminal Services security.

So, at this point we can only assume that you have Terminal Services successfully installed, or are at least thinking about installing it. You know that you can install Terminal Services at the time of installation or later. Before we get too far into this, let's do a high level overview of Terminal Services so, even if you never want to install it, you will at least have an idea about why Microsoft thinks you should know this stuff.

Terminal Services Basics

Terminal Services was introduced back in the Windows NT 4 days. It was a separate product. With Windows 2000, Terminal Services is integrated into the operating system on all Windows 2000 servers. Terminal Services brings multi-user capability to Windows. This is something that Unix people have had for years, so if you are familiar with Unix, the concept will not be too strange. In this case, you have a single large server that will serve many terminals. It is almost like we are going back to the days of the mainframe, when everyone had dumb terminals on their desks.

When users connect to Terminal Services, they are using the resources of the server itself. Usually, as you know, when a user requests a resource from a server, the resource is pushed down to the workstation and any processing takes place there. With Terminal Services, everything is done using the power of the server.

Each user that connects get his or her own Windows Terminal Services session and each session is completely isolated from other sessions on the same server. If one user has a session that crashes, that will not effect any of the other sessions running off the same server.

Windows 2000 Terminal Services supports a wide variety of machines that can connect and run as a terminal. For example, you can use diskless display stations running Windows CE in memory, to Windows 95/98 Workstations to Windows 2000 Servers. Since the terminal is only responsible for the console functions, almost anything that has a keyboard, mouse, and display can connect.

Remote Access

Terminal Services can be used for the mobile user who needs to be able to access network intensive or processor intensive applications over connections as slow as a dial-up. Since the local machine is basically getting only screen refreshes and taking care of the keystroke buffer, response time is enhanced.

In addition, Terminal Services can also be configured to allow the administration team to do remote administration of the network. In this way it serves two purposes.

Terminal Services Best Practices

If you have already installed Terminal Services, you know there are some "words to the wise" that you should heed before trying to make this system work. First of all, be very cognizant of what it is that you are asking the Terminal Services server to do. It is going to be doing the processing for several (maybe dozens?) of different sessions all at the same time. Most of the applications that are going to be loaded on this server are going to be network intensive, processor intensive, and memory intensive. If you look at the business requirements of this piece of equipment, it should not be a shock that this server should not be an old 486 out of the closet. It should be a heavy-duty server, with a very fast, powerful processor and lots of memory. In addition, this server potentially could have an awful lot to do just being a Terminal Services server. It would not do to have this computer also be a domain controller that is responsible for authentication and authorization.

Since users are going to be accessing applications and information off this machine just as though they were sitting at the keyboard, there is a potential for data loss due to end user mistakes. Therefore, every precaution should be taken to make sure that the users can only go where they are supposed to. This calls for extensive permissions and group policies, which calls for NTFS partitions. NTFS will provide greater security for users in a multisession environment who are accessing the same data structure.

Terminal Services also has a command structure all of its own. When you are shutting down a Terminal Services server, remember that you could be shutting down dozens of sessions. It is best to let Terminal Services handle the shutdown for you by using the `tsshutdn` command instead of the Shut Down option on the Start menu. This will shut down the server in a controlled manner. The Shut Down option on the Start menu does not notify users before ending user sessions and is not recommended. Ending a user's session without warning can result in loss of data at the client.

When you start thinking about how this server is going to be used, the licensing issues alone are staggering. If you have looked over any of Microsoft's information on Terminal Services, you know that about 50% of it revolves around licensing. Everything else kind of takes a backseat. Licensing is handled with a *license server*. Make sure this is backed up regularly. Backing up your license server regularly protects data from accidental loss due to hardware or storage failure. You should also create a duplicate copy of the data on your hard disk and then archive the data on another storage device such as a hard disk or tape. In the event that the original data on your hard disk is accidentally erased or overwritten, or becomes inaccessible because of a hard disk failure, you can easily restore the data from the archived copy. Redundancy, especially in a mission critical server like a Terminal Services unit, is key.

Program Installation

When using Terminal Services, installing applications is not as easy as clicking Start ➤ Run ➤ Setup.exe. You should make use of the Add/Remove Programs options in Control Panel to install applications on the Terminal Services server. With this method, you can install programs for multisession use.

Once Terminal Services have been enabled and applications have been installed, this machine becomes very much like a Unix box. Many people will tell you that once you have installed Unix and applications, there is no reason to shut the computer off. If a process hangs, you can simply kill it. The same is true here. Do not switch Terminal Services on and off as part of basic troubleshooting. Terminal Services installs programs for use in a multisession environment. Programs that were installed while Terminal Services was installed might not work correctly when Terminal Services is turned off. You should reinstall all programs for use without Terminal Services if you decide to remove the component.

Not all applications are created equally. Some work better with Terminal Services than others. For that reason, make sure you check for application compatibility scripts before installing programs for use with Terminal Services. Many commonly used programs (read Microsoft) have been tested for compatibility. Some programs require minor changes to the installation. Scripts are available for these programs and must be run after the program installation is complete. Scripts are located in the systemroot in `\Application Compatibility Scripts\Install`.

User Management

Another area that the system administrator has to pay close attention to is in the management of users. Start by coming up with a set of groups that are specific to Terminal Services. Obviously, maintaining users through groups is easier and less time-consuming than managing individual users. Having specific sets of groups set aside for Terminal Services helps in the troubleshooting process, also.

Along those same lines, while you are creating profiles, have profiles that are specific to Terminal Services. For example, one common profile is for logging into Terminal Services. Many of the common options that are stored in profiles, such as screensavers and animated menu effects, are not desirable when using Terminal Services because they create so much unnecessary traffic. Assigning a specific profile allows users to get the most out of the system they are working with without expending additional server resources. When you create these profiles, make sure they are mandatory. Use a mandatory Terminal Services profile that is created to suit the needs of all of the different types of clients and that provides the best server performance. Be aware that 16-bit computers and Windows-based terminals might not support some screen resolutions.

Some clients will look at the Terminal Services server as their 24-hour window to the network. They will try to set up one session and then just leave it open for hours. You can prevent this by setting time limits. Setting limits on the duration of client connections may irritate a few people, but most will benefit because it can improve server performance. You can set the limits on how long a session lasts, how long a disconnected session is allowed to remain active on the server, and the time allowed for a session to remain connected, yet idle.

If you have people that only need to access a certain application off the server, make sure that you use the *Starting program* option. The *Starting program* option will allow you to specify a program to start when the session connects.

To make connecting to Terminal Services easier, you can supply users with preconfigured connections. Collections of connections can also be made either for different departments within your organization or for different job titles. Preconfigured connections are created using Client Connection Manager.

Terminal Services Security

The best way to approach Terminal Services security is to look at some of the features of the service that can be used to secure it. There are two feature levels that we have broken this into—manageability and security. Gosh, this feels almost like a features and benefits sales pitch. But it's not. It should be considered more of a listing of some of the management features that can be used to your benefit. The easiest way of listing these is in table form, so take a look at the manageability features in Table 13.4.

TABLE 13.4 The Manageability Features of Terminal Services

Feature	Description
Session remote control	With session remote control support, persons can either view or control another Terminal Services session. Keyboard input, mouse movements, and display graphics are shared between two Terminal Services sessions, giving a support person the ability to diagnose and resolve configuration problems, as well as train the user remotely. This feature is particularly useful for organizations with branch offices.

TABLE 13.4 The Manageability Features of Terminal Services *(continued)*

Feature	Description
Network load	With network load balancing, Terminal Services clients connect to the least-busy member of a group of servers running Terminal Services.
Windows-based terminals	Based on a custom implementation of the Windows CE operating system and the Remote Desktop Protocol (RDP), Windows-based terminals are available from a variety of manufacturers.
Client Connection Manager	Administrators and users can set up predefined connections to servers for either a single program or full desktop access. Client Connection Manager creates an icon on the client desktop for single-click connectivity to one or more Terminal Services servers. Administrators who want to provide a single program across the computing environment can create a connection and distribute that connection along with the Terminal Services client software.
Terminal Services licensing	Terminal Services licensing allows system administrators and their purchasing offices to track clients and their associated licenses.
Distributed file system (Dfs) support	Distributed file system (Dfs) support allows users to connect to a Dfs share, and allows administrators to host a Dfs share from a Terminal Services server.
Terminal Services Manager	Administrators can use Terminal Services Manager to look at and manage Terminal Services sessions, users, and processes on Windows 2000 servers.

TABLE 13.4 The Manageability Features of Terminal Services *(continued)*

Feature	Description
Terminal Services Configuration	Terminal Services Connection Configuration can be used to create, modify, and delete both sessions and sets of sessions on a Windows 2000 server and access server settings.
Integration with Windows 2000 Server Local Users and Groups and Active Directory Users and Computers	Administrators can create accounts for Terminal Services users the same way they create accounts for Windows 2000 Server users. Extra fields are available for specifying information specific to Terminal Services. This includes things like the Terminal Services Profile Path and Home Directory.
Integration with Windows 2000 Server System Monitor	Integration with Windows 2000 Server System Monitor enables administrators to monitor Terminal Services system performance, including tracking processor use, memory allocation, and paged memory usage and swapping per-user session.
Messaging support	Administrators can alert users to important information, such as system shutdowns, upgrades, or new programs.
Remote administration	Any user that has both administrative privileges and access to the Terminal Services administrative utilities can remotely manage all aspects of a server that is running Terminal Services.
Configurable session timeout	Administrators can reduce server resource usage by configuring session time-outs. Administrators can determine the length of an active session and how long a session can remain idle on the server before it is terminated.

Now let's take a look at the security features of Terminal Services in Table 13.5.

TABLE 13.5 Terminal Services Security Features

Feature	Description
Encryption	The multiple encryption levels allow administrators to encrypt all or some of the data transmitted between the Windows 2000 Server and Terminal Services clients at three levels (low, medium, or high), depending on security needs. In addition, the Terminal Services logon process includes *change password, unlock desktop,* and *unlock screensaver* features. The encrypted logon process helps ensure secure transfer of user name and password. Terminal Services supports both 40-bit and 128-bit encryption (available only in the U.S. and Canada) between server and client.
Limit logon attempts and connection time	Administrators can limit the connection time of an individual or group, and can limit the number of user logon tries. These constraints help prevent unauthorized server access.

Configuring Terminal Services

If you already have Terminal Services installed, you know that it is configured using Terminal Services Configuration. When you open Terminal Services Configuration, you will see that there is one connection that has automatically been configured. This connection is called the RDP-TCP connection. Usually, this is the only connection that has to be configured to allow clients to use the Terminal Services server. For Terminal Services servers, there is only one *Remote Desktop Protocol (RDP)* connection that can be configured for each network adapter.

Pay close attention to the protocols necessary to run Terminal Services. It runs with TCP/IP and RDP. This may come up again, sometime when you are locked in a little room with money on the line!

There are times when you will want to reconfigure the properties of the RDP-TCP connection, such as when you want to limit the amount of time client sessions can remain active on the server, when you want to set protection levels for encryption, or when you want to allow permissions for your users and groups. Some of these connection properties can be configured on a per-user basis with the Terminal Services extension to Local Users and Groups. In this case, you can decide to set different session time limits for different users. Using Terminal Services Configuration, you can also set the session time limits on a per-connection basis. This means that the same time limit will apply to all users who log on to the server using that connection.

You can use Terminal Services Configuration to change settings that apply to the Terminal Services server. These are settings for temporary folders, the default connection security, and to enable or to disable Internet Connector licensing.

Terminal Services Configuration can be used to configure connections for Citrix ICA-based clients. Citrix is an ISV that produces a product that is Terminal Services with an attitude. For more information on Citrix products, check out `www.citrix.com`.

Since we have said that there are certain settings you can use to enhance the security of your Terminal Services sessions, we should look at each of them. We will explore things like these:

- Encryption levels
- The use of remote control
- How to configure session limits
- How to manage permissions on connections
- How to manage drive, printer, and device mappings

Determining the Level of Encryption

Data encryption protects your data by encrypting it while it is being transported over the communications link between the client and the server. Microsoft suggests that you enable encryption whenever there is a risk of a sniffer on the link between server and client. When you think about it, that is a pretty broad statement. If we were talking about using Terminal Services to provide access to a critical application across an intranet, there would still be some threat from sniffing. So, it is time to go back to the early chapters of the book and reread the sections on Risk Analysis.

Terminal Services provides multilevel encryption support, so, after you have completed your Risk Analysis, you can decide the level of security that is right for your organization. All levels of security use the RSA RC4 encryption.

With Terminal Services, there are three levels of encryption available. These are summarized in Table 13.6.

TABLE 13.6 Terminal Services Encryption

Level of Encryption	Description
Low	This level provides security for all data that is sent from the client to the server by using either a 56-bit or 40-bit key. A Windows 2000 Terminal Services server uses a 56-bit key when Windows 2000 clients connect to it, and a 40-bit key when earlier versions connect.
Medium	This level secures data sent in both directions (from the client to the server and from the server to the client) by using either a 56-bit or a 40-bit key. A Windows 2000 Terminal Services server uses a 56-bit key when Windows 2000 clients connect to it, and a 40-bit key when earlier versions of the client connect. Use medium encryption if you want to secure sensitive data as it travels over the network to display on remote clients.
High	If you are located in the United States or Canada, you have the option to select the high level. High encryption affects all data sent in both directions, but encrypts using the nonexportable 128-bit key.

Using Remote Control

If you have installed or are planning to install Terminal Services, one of the things you are going to want to do as an administrator is to keep track of how people are using the service. With remote control, you can do that and more. For example, you can monitor the actions of a client logged on to a Terminal Services server by remotely controlling the user's session from another session. Now, remote control monitoring comes in a variety of flavors. You can start by just observing and watching what parts of the server are being accessed. If the user ends up getting in trouble, you can take over and actively control another session.

If you choose to actively control a session, you will be able to input keyboard and mouse actions to the session. If you opt to do this, for your own sake, make sure a message is displayed on the client session asking permission to view or take part in the session before the session is remotely controlled.

There are some other things you need to be aware of before configuring remote control. These are:

- Remote control can be configured on a per-user basis using the Terminal Services Extension to Local Users and Groups and Active Directory Users and Computers.
- The console session cannot remotely control another session, and a client session cannot remotely control the console session.
- The computer used for your session must be capable of supporting the video resolution used at the remotely controlled client session. Otherwise, the operation fails.

Configuring Session Limits

As we said earlier, when you plan your Terminal Services installation, it would be a good idea to take into account the user who establishes a connection and wants to leave it open forever. This is an obvious security risk! Determine how you want to limit the amount of time a connection can be active, disconnected, and idle (session without client activity) before they are removed from the server. Sessions that remain running for an indefinite period of time use valuable system resources, as well as leaving an open portal to your network. When the predetermined session limit is reached, you can choose to either disconnect the user from the session or simply end the session. A user who is disconnected can reconnect to the same session at a later time. However, when a session ends, it is permanently deleted from the server and any running applications are forced to shut down. That can result in a loss of data at the client.

When you configure session limits with Terminal Services Configuration, those limits apply to all sessions using the connection to log on to the server. If you want to become more granular, session limits can be configured on a per-user basis by using the Terminal Services Extension to Local Users and Groups and Active Directory Users and Computers.

Broken Connections

A connection can be broken by a request, by a connection error, or when the active or idle session limit is reached.

Reconnecting to a Disconnected Session

A Terminal Services server will allow you to reconnect to a disconnected session from any computer. However, as an administrator, you can restrict users and allow them to reconnect only from the computer where the session originated. This option is only good for clients that provide a serial number when connecting.

Managing Permissions on Connections

Just like file system permissions, Terminal Services server permissions are used to define how users and groups can access a Terminal Services server, allowing the administrator to secure the server. The TCP/IP connection that is automatically installed with Terminal Services comes with its own set of default permissions. You can go in and modify these default permissions simply by setting different permissions for different users or groups. These can be adjusted to fit the requirements of your particular organization. As you would imagine, you must have administrative privileges to manage the connection permissions.

The Terminal Services default permissions are shown in Table 13.7. So what do these permissions mean and how do they work?

TABLE 13.7 Default Terminal Services Permissions

Group Name	Permission Description
System	Full control
Administrators	Full control
Users	User access
Guests	Guest access

Permissions are not limited to users. You can add any user, group, or computer in your network to Terminal Services permissions lists. If your server belongs to a domain, you can also add user accounts and global groups from both the local domain and trusted domains. Let's look at what each permission will allow a user to do.

Full Control

As the name implies, full control is the god- or goddess-like permissions for Terminal Services. Full control allows these permissions:

- You can get information about a session.
- You can modify the connection parameters.
- You can reset a session.
- You can go in and remotely control another user's session.
- You can log on to a session on the server.
- You can log off a user from a session.
- You can send a message to another user's session.
- You can connect to another session.
- You can disconnect a session.
- You can make use of virtual channels, which provides access from a server program to client devices.

User Access

We start limiting access when you go to user access. User access allows users these permissions:

- They can log on to a session on the server.
- They can get information about a session.
- They can send messages to other user sessions.
- They can connect to another session.

Guest Access

Guest access is obviously very limited. Guest access allows users a single permission:

- A guest can log on to a session on the server.

There are additional permissions available to use to control connection access. Those will be covered in the next section.

Controlling Connection Access

Use the permissions provided for Terminal Services to control how users and groups get to the server. You can change the standard permissions to keep individual users and groups from doing certain things, like logging off a user from a session or even ending sessions. You manage permissions from Terminal Services Configuration. You must have been granted administrative privileges to set permissions. As you saw in the section above, by default, there are three levels of permissions: full control, user access, and guest access. These permissions are shown in Table 13.8.

TABLE 13.8 Connection Access Permissions

Permission	Allows You to Do This
Set information	To configure connection properties.
Query information	To query sessions and servers for information.
Reset	To end a session. This can result in loss of data at the client.

TABLE 13.8 Connection Access Permissions *(continued)*

Permission	Allows You to Do This
Remote control	To view or actively control another user's session.
Logon	To log on to a session on the server.
Logoff	To log off a user from a session. This can result in loss of data at the client.
Virtual channels	To use virtual channels.
Message	To send a message to another user's sessions.
Connect	To connect to another session.
Disconnect	To disconnect a session.

Managing Drive, Printer, and Device Mappings for Clients

Because client sessions can set up multiple data channels that go between the client and server, users can map to their local devices, which include drives and printers. The drive and printer mappings that are set during a client session are only temporary and are not available the next time the user logs on. If you would like to make them permanent, you can, by specifying that client mappings are automatically restored whenever the user logs on. This would be helpful if, for example, you had a group of salespeople all accessing the same Terminal Services connection. You know that they are all going to need to access the same data storage areas each time they log in. On the other hand, there may be resources that users can use in the office that you do not want them to be able to use remotely.

Settings for client drive, printer, and device mappings configured in Terminal Services Configuration apply to all client sessions on the server. If you want to specify client settings on a per-user basis, use the Terminal Services extensions to Local Users and Groups or Active Directory Users and Computers.

There are other ways of configuring security. One is to use a profile, in this case using the Terminal Services Profile.

Using Terminal Services Profile

By using the Terminal Services Profile, you can create a profile that will be used to apply to a user during the user's Terminal sessions. The Terminal Services Profile can be used for things like restricting access to applications by removing them from the user's Start menu.

Terminal Services Home Directory

You can define the path to a home directory to be used during the Terminal sessions. This directory can either be a local directory or it can be on a network share.

Allow Logon to Terminal Services

You can define on a per-user basis whether the user will have access to Terminal Services. If this option is left disabled, the user is not allowed to log on to any Terminal Services servers.

Terminal Services and Firewalls

Obviously, your Terminal Services server is going to have to be accessible to the outside world. That means it will normally reside in your screened subnet or DMZ. Somehow, you have got to be able to provide access to that server through the firewall.

Terminal Services Access Over Wide Area Network

When you plan your installation, check with the firewall folks and determine if filters have been implemented on the routers or firewalls that would prevent clients from remotely gaining access to a Terminal Services server. Check to make sure that the Remote Desktop Protocol (RDP) port (port 3389) is not blocked at the firewall and that access to specific corporate segments is not limited to Internet Protocol (IP) or Internetwork Packet

Exchange (IPX) network addresses. If these blocks are in place and remote connections are blocked, Terminal Services will not work.

Terminal Services Access to Network Services

There will be occasions when you will want to provide your customers or your suppliers with access to applications or data from your network. You might even decide that the Internet is the easiest way for end users to gain access to Terminal Services. If you plan to make servers available over the Internet, you will need to look closely at the security implications.

If your organization uses a firewall, you will have to determine if it is a packet-level or application-level firewall. Packet-level firewalls are easier to configure for new protocols. If your organization uses an application-level firewall, check to see if the vendor has defined a filter for the RDP; if not, contact the vendor and ask them to create a filter.

Design Scenario: When To Use Terminal Services

It is a beautiful day as you are driving to one of your least favorite clients. You just know that somehow this upcoming contact is going to ruin your whole day and set your mood off for all the really nice people you are going to meet. It is especially galling that you have to start the day here. It is not that you resent the fact that your first call of this beautiful day is to go sit in a stuffy old meeting room and listen to these people haggle. You hate doing that any time, but today, it is really a sin.

When you get to the client site, you sit talking to the CIO and she informs you the meeting has been cancelled. The CEO decided that after meeting with the CIO, there just wasn't enough information to make a decision. Score one point for their side. The CIO looks at you and says, "You know, looking at this beautiful day from my window just isn't going to cut it. There is a coffee shop downstairs with tables out on the sidewalk, why don't we continue this discussion down there?" Life is definitely looking up!

When you finally get your coffee and the discussion starts, you find that the CEO has come to the CIO with a problem. It seems the company is going to investigate installing this business-critical application that has to be accessed by all the salespeople. Since most of the salespeople are out on the road, this could prove to be a problem. The original suggestion was to install a Citrix server in the server room and run the application from that platform. Preliminary estimates indicate that while Citrix is an exceptional product, the cost of over $15,000 is prohibitive to do what they want to do, especially to start.

The CIO had thought of simply setting up something like Symantec's PC AnyWhere, but the IS Department tested that out and it was really slow. The CIO comes to you and asks what they can do to solve the problem without breaking the bank.

You suggest setting up a server to run Terminal Services. You point out that there are some hardware investments that will have to be made, but some of the services can be installed on equipment that is currently in place. You also point out that the product can be secured so that salespeople can get access to one area of the network while other users can be configured to access other points. You also mention that the company's firewalls can be configured to allow the communication through. Since the company is already moving to Windows 2000, the original cash outlay will be minimal.

The CIO thinks that is a wonderful idea and asks if you would like to handle the configuration. You set another meeting for the next Wednesday to discuss the details, and leave a happy person. You know, maybe this day will not turn out too badly after all.

Summary

After all we have been through, this must seem like a really short chapter. It does have some very hot topics in it, and topics that are going to plague security for a long time to come. Think about what we have talked about. First of all, we discussed RIS. Now, if remote installation is not configured properly, you could be propagating security problems every time someone created a new workstation.

As far as Terminal Services goes, you are inviting people to use your network resources from the outside world. You are making it easy for them to get access to your network. That, obviously, has got to be thought out carefully and tested extensively before implementation.

Well, we have two more chapters left. You are close to ready to take the exam. Now, if you are like us, you are sitting there thinking, okay, I have this material down, but can I remember the stuff that was covered in the first five chapters!

Key Terms

Before you take the exam, be certain you are familiar with the following terms:

independent software vendors (ISVs)

license server

original equipment manufacturers (OEMs)

Remote Desktop Protocol (RDP)

Remote Installation Services (RIS)

SIF (Setup Information File)

Review Questions

1. When you install Terminal Services, what are the two protocols that have to be present to communicate between the client and the server?

   A. TCP/IP

   B. IPX

   C. SPX

   D. RDP

   E. ARF

2. If you are running Terminal Services on a screened subnet, which port needs to be opened for RDP?

   A. 1677

   B. 7100

   C. 25

   D. 8080

   E. 3389

   F. 6345

3. After you install RIS, you notice that there are several files on your server that have an extension of SIF. Why are they there?

   A. SIF files are the answer files that Remote Installation Services use.

   B. SIF files are temporary files used as part of the RIS installation process. They can be deleted.

   C. SIF files are actually system log files that are generated during the installation process.

   D. SIF files are the executables for Windows 2000 Professional, similar to the CAB files from Windows 95/98.

4. Which of the following are prerequisites to installing RIS?

   A. Domain Name System (DNS)

   B. File Transfer Protocol (FTP)

   C. Dynamic Host Configuration Protocol (DHCP)

   D. Internet Packet Exchange Protocol (IPX)

   E. Active Directory directory services

5. You are attempting to install RIS on a Windows 2000 Advanced Server and you seem to be having some problems. The installation wizard will not let you install into the `c:\Services\Win32\RISINSTAL` folder. What would be the most likely problem?

   A. Your hard disk is full.

   B. Your volume is formatted with NTFS.

   C. Your volume is formatted with FAT32.

   D. Your system files are on that volume.

   E. Your system files are not on that volume.

6. Which products can be installed with RIS? Choose all that apply.

   A. Windows 2000 Server

   B. Windows 2000 Advanced Server

   C. Windows 2000 Cluster Server

   D. Windows 2000 Professional

   E. Windows NT 4 Server

   F. Windows NT 4 Workstation

   G. Windows NT 3.51 Server

   H. Windows NT 3.51 Workstation

   I. All of the above

7. Your company has an application-level firewall and you want to install Terminal Services. What should you do?

   A. Check to see if the firewall manufacturer has a filter for the RDP. If not, ask the manufacturer to create one.

   B. Switch to a packet-level firewall.

   C. Move the Terminal Services server on the outside of the firewall.

   D. Nothing.

8. By default, what access permissions does the Guest access have in Terminal Services?

   A. Log on to a session on the server

   B. Query information about a session

   C. Send messages to other user sessions

   D. Connect to another session

9. By default, what access permissions does User access provide?

   A. Log on to a session on the server

   B. Query information about a session

   C. Send messages to other user sessions

   D. Connect to another session

10. Which of the following are not default groups for Terminal Services?

   A. Domain admins

   B. Administrators

   C. Local administrators

   D. System

   E. Everyone

   F. Users

   G. Guests

   H. Power users

Answers to Review Questions

1. A, D. Terminal Services needs both the Remote Desktop Protocol (RDP) and TCP/IP.

2. E. You would have to open up port 3389.

3. A. SIF files are the answer files that Remote Installation Services uses to complete a workstation installation.

4. A, C, E. Having the Domain Name System present, having a Dynamic Host Configuration Protocol server present, and having Active Directory installed are prerequisites to installing RIS.

5. D. RIS cannot be installed on any volume that contains the Windows 2000 system files.

6. D. RIS will only handle the installation of Windows 2000 Professional.

7. A. Check to make sure the application-level firewall has a filter for RDP. If it doesn't, ask the firewall manufacturer to create one. Since this is necessary for a Windows product, the manufacturer may actually listen.

8. A. Guest access just lets the user log on to a session on the server.

9. A, B, C, D. By default the user access has all of these permissions.

10. B, D, F, G. There are four default groups: Administrators, System, Users, and Guests.

The Multinational Conglomerate

You should give yourself 10 minutes to review this case study, diagram as needed, and complete the questions for this testlet. Be sure to read each question carefully. While the company may not have changed, its circumstances change in each chapter.

Background

Your consulting firm has been hired to assist in the Windows 2000 migration and integration for a company based in Minneapolis, Minnesota. Until the start of this year, the company had 1,000 employees, all based throughout the Twin Cities of Minneapolis and St. Paul. Just before the end of the year, the owner of your company purchased two companies of roughly the same size, which will need to be connected to the enterprise network. The total number of users when the project is completed is estimated at 3,500. In addition, each of these companies comes with various strategic partners that will need to access the information on your enterprise network. The companies that have been acquired are located in Athens, Greece, and in Orlando, Florida.

The company is now beginning to look at ways of dealing with remote users and small, local sales offices.

Current System

Minneapolis Located on the shores of beautiful Lake Calhoun, the company occupies a sprawling campus that includes four floors in a six-story building. Since the merger, the Lake Calhoun facility has become a model of efficiency. Besides being linked to all of the other offices, everyone is beginning to take the notion of an enterprise network seriously.

All of the floors are connected to the Windows 2000 network. The Minneapolis location is a domain in the tree. Active Directory Services have been deployed to the main campus and the rollout is complete in the branch offices. The desktop rollout is just getting underway. IT is predicting that after all is said and done, 2,000 new Windows 2000 Professional desktops are going to be needed in Minneapolis in less than a month. They must all be configured the same way.

The corporate network was so impressive it helped this company snag a very large contract with a very large customer. This customer has suddenly started to make some demands. It wants your company to establish local offices to service its account in several locations worldwide. These offices would house 5 to 10 people, and the way it looks now, each office would have its own Windows 2000 servers and a router to the Internet.

Orlando The Orlando office is a domain in the corporate tree. It has some valuable resources that need to be made available to the rest of company, particularly the folks in Athens.

The large contract had a long-term effect on Orlando. Current corporate strategy calls for the new contract to be managed in Minneapolis for the first year, and then moved to Orlando after that. At this point it is mandatory that all offices have access to a business-critical application that is run from Minneapolis.

Athens The Athens office is now fully staffed at 2,300. Management has discovered that the business is doing well, and the extra folks are justified. The office has been upgraded to Windows 2000 servers and Athens is now its own domain in the tree.

Athens has always been ahead of the curve. When the new contract was announced, Athens' manufacturing geared up for the task, and can now handle that stage. Because the customer wants to be able to look at all the stages of inventory, the customer will need to be able to access the application from the Athens facility as well as from Minneapolis and Orlando.

Problem Statement

Provide access to certain applications on the network for the local offices. In addition, be sure to have a way for remote users to access the applications necessary to perform their tasks.

Envisioned System

Overview Several of the management team have input on this project, including the CEO, the CFO, the General Managers of the Orlando office, and the General Manager of the Athens Office. At this stage, we have also begun to hear from the Sales Manager.

CEO As the new network was designed, the CEO is looking closely at the IS department and saying things like, "Okay, people, you wanted the Windows 2000 network because of its flexibility and now you have it. This is where the rubber hits the road. Prove you can make this network do the things you said it can do."

CFO The CFO said, "You know, we are still paying the bills for this rollout. While it looks like our overall cost of operation will drop, it is still a large price to absorb. We are now looking at taking a hit for all of these local offices. Make sure that you do everything in your power to maintain costs, while providing all the resources those people need to keep the customer happy. It is especially important that everyone in Orlando and Athens that needs access to the Minneapolis business application gets access. Also, try to keep the overtime to a minimum on the desktop rollout."

Orlando General Manager "Sure, I get this project dumped in my lap. Now my budget is going to take the hit for connecting to all these local offices. The costs of leased lines alone will rival my payroll, and I have a hefty payroll! Surely there has got to be a better way?"

Athens General Manager "Why are you talking to me about this? This appears to be a problem for Orlando."

Corporate Sales Manager "Cool. How long have you been having these meetings? Why wasn't I invited? Can we do this over lunch? Oh, and by the way, computer guy, how can my salespeople get information from the network when they are on the road? They keep calling and I have to look it up for them. It's not a problem in the winter, but it is spring and all my clients like to play golf, so I may not be available too much, you know what I mean?"

Questions

1. What type of solutions are you looking at?
   - **A.** Proxy Server
   - **B.** Terminal Services
   - **C.** Pass-through VPN
   - **D.** Router-to-Router VPN
   - **E.** Remote Access VPN
   - **F.** Remote Installation Services

2. Where could the Terminal Services servers be located?
   - **A.** Minneapolis
   - **B.** Orlando
   - **C.** Athens
   - **D.** At each remote office
   - **E.** At each remote salesperson's home

3. If the Terminal Services servers are installed in Minneapolis, where should they be placed?
   - **A.** In front of the firewall for easy access.
   - **B.** Behind the first firewall, but in front of the second firewall.
   - **C.** Behind the second firewall.
   - **D.** Only on the intranet.
   - **E.** There is not enough information to make that determination.

4. What protocols can be used for the Terminal Services?
   - **A.** TCP/IP
   - **B.** L2TP
   - **C.** PPTP
   - **D.** RDP
   - **E.** MS-CHAP

Answers

1. B, F. In this scenario, you would be looking at creating a Terminal Services server in Minneapolis for the business-critical application. To aid in the rollout of the 2,000 workstations, you would need to have RIS installed.

2. A, B, C. Depending on the need, Terminal Services servers could be installed in the three primary locations to make access from the outside easier.

3. B. In your heart-of-hearts, you wanted the answer to be *E*, didn't you? And in the real world, you would have been correct. Here, in the testing world, you have to go with B. The Terminal Services server should sit between the firewalls in the screened subnet or DMZ.

4. A, D. Terminal Services requires IP and RDP.

Providing Secure Access at the Network Level

MICROSOFT EXAM OBJECTIVES COVERED IN THIS CHAPTER:

✓ **Provide secure access to public networks from a private network.**

✓ **Provide external users with secure access to private network resources.**

✓ **Provide secure access between private networks.**

- Provide secure access within a LAN.
- Provide secure access with a WAN.
- Provide secure access across a public network.

✓ **Design Windows 2000 security for remote access users.**

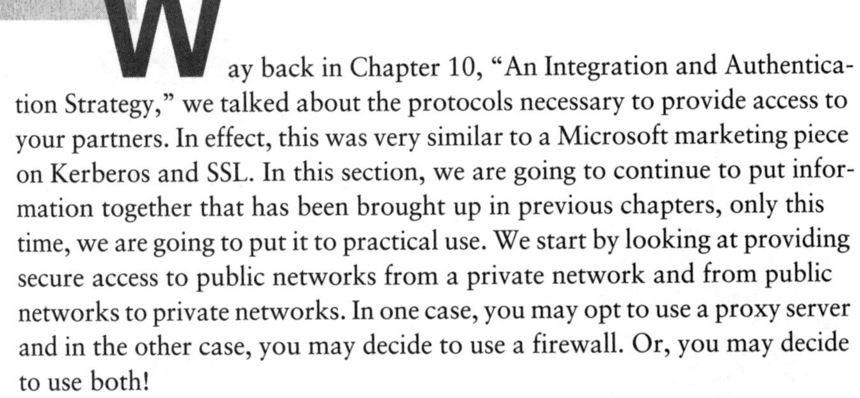

Way back in Chapter 10, "An Integration and Authentication Strategy," we talked about the protocols necessary to provide access to your partners. In effect, this was very similar to a Microsoft marketing piece on Kerberos and SSL. In this section, we are going to continue to put information together that has been brought up in previous chapters, only this time, we are going to put it to practical use. We start by looking at providing secure access to public networks from a private network and from public networks to private networks. In one case, you may opt to use a proxy server and in the other case, you may decide to use a firewall. Or, you may decide to use both!

Next, we are going to look at providing secure access between private networks. The trick is defining what is a private network? Is a private network within a LAN, with a WAN, or across a public network? Each of the three scenarios will be looked at in detail.

In this chapter there is going to be lots of material on proxy servers, firewalls, and VPNs.

Access to Public Networks from a Private Network

Earlier in the book, we quoted some pretty shocking statistics about Internet abuse in private companies. Over 90% of the companies surveyed said that they had been or were being abused by employees misusing their Internet privileges. If you are a network administrator, sooner or later someone is going to ask you to do something about it. After all, you and the entire

IS team do manage the connection to the Internet, don't you? Therefore you should be able to be the porn-police in your spare time!

Microsoft Exam Objective

Provide secure access to public networks from a private network.

Proxy Server Basics

One way that you can protect yourself and your company is with the use of a *proxy server*. Now, some people confuse a proxy server with a firewall. As a matter of fact, some large companies had been hawking a proxy server as a firewall, but according to the latest word we heard from Microsoft, the company is now saying it really isn't. Take a look at Figure 14.1.

FIGURE 14.1 Diagram of a proxy server

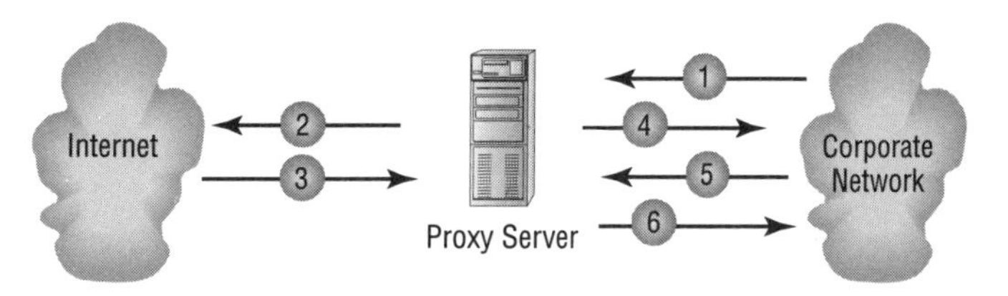

For an explanation, let's start with the fact that this drawing is way oversimplified. In the request for services indicated by the number 1, let's assume that a workstation on the corporate network wants to go out to `www.Microsoft.com` to check out its home page. In step 1, the host sends the request to the proxy server. The proxy server looks at the request and decides if it can service the request out of cache. If it can't (we will come to that part a little later), the proxy server makes a note of the IP address of the requesting workstation. It then reconfigures the packet so the proxy server's IP address is in the return address. Once that has been done, the proxy server forwards the request to `www.Microsoft.com`, as shown in step 2. In step 3, `Microsoft.com` returns the Web page to the proxy server, and the proxy server caches it (stores it in memory) and then it passes the Web page back to the requesting workstation in step 4. At this point the proxy server is acting like an intermediary.

The true beauty of the system comes the next time another workstation wants to go to www.Microsoft.com, as in step 5. Instead of having to go through all the gyrations that it went through the first time, this time, the proxy server (as in step 6) simply returns the Web page it has in memory, speeding up the response time for the client. In this example, the proxy server is a true Web accelerator. As a matter of fact, many companies use what is called a *reverse proxy server*. Let us show you what we are talking about in Figure 14.2.

FIGURE 14.2 Diagram of reverse proxy server

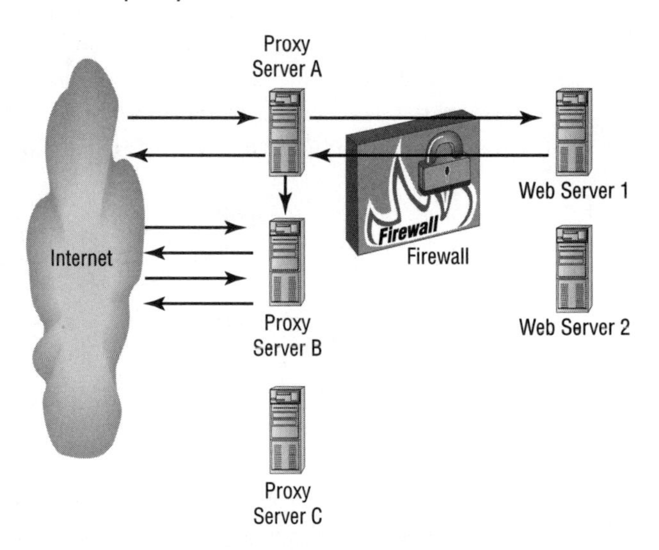

In this case, the scenario has been complicated a little bit with the addition of the firewall. The first thing you will probably notice is that the proxy servers are on the outside of the firewall. Their placement can be on either side of the firewall, but for the sake of argument, we will leave them as part of the cold cruel world on the outside of the wall.

So, you are running a *very* popular Web site and you can't keep up with the traffic. In this case, we have configured three proxy servers to help out two Web servers. When one of the proxy servers gets a request for a Web page, it gets the page from the Web server and caches it. The proxy server may be configured to pass the Web page along to its brethren, as shown in

Figure 14.2. Now that the Web page is stored in cache on two servers, both servers can respond to requests for the page, speeding up the process.

This is a very high-level overview of how and why proxy servers work!

Proxy Servers and Security

While proxy servers traditionally are not considered firewalls, they do have some similar functions. For example, a proxy server examines every packet going out of the network. It also resends the packet after adding its address to it. So, the communicant on the other side of the proxy server thinks all communications are coming directly from the proxy server.

Most proxy servers, usually with the use of some third-party software, can also provide some type of censoring function. If your server is using any one of a dozen programs for example, and it finds that there is a request from the inside of the network going to a prohibited site, it will short circuit the request. The requestor will get a message back saying the request could not be fulfilled.

Some non-Microsoft implementations that include a proxy server's function can also be used in a type of address translation function. Since all communication from the public network passes through the proxy server, and since the proxy server knows all the addresses on the inside of the public network, there is no real reason for the private addresses to be *real* registered IP addresses. This is why many of the networks that you may run across will have a 10.x.x.x or a 192.168.x.x address. These addresses are designated as private addresses: they are not assigned to any sites, so they can be used in a NAT environment.

FYI:10.x.x.x and 192.168.x.x are not the only private addresses. There are others.

Figure 14.3 shows you what we mean.

FIGURE 14.3 A design implementing a form of address translation at the Proxy Server

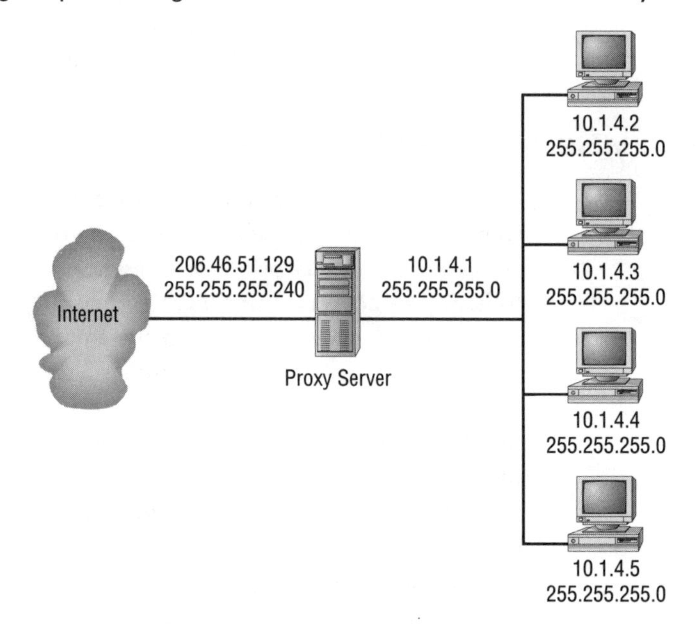

Here, you see the proxy server is all that is standing between the private network and the public network. The proxy server has two network cards, each with its own IP address. The 206.46.51.129, subnet mask 255.255.255.240, is a valid, registered, IP address that points to that host. All the addresses on the private network are made up. The proxy server shields those addresses from the outside world. The benefit in this case is that you do not have to pay for or manage multitudes of registered IP addresses. One (or a few, depending on the size of your company) is plenty, and all the addresses in the private side of the house are made up.

In this case, the proxy server is protecting the hosts on the private network by shielding the true IP addresses from the outside world. It is also serving to ensure that the access from the private network to the public network is secure.

Proxy Servers and Auditing

Another way that you can ensure the security of the private network and communications going out to the Internet is by auditing what happens to the proxy server. Obviously, the proxy server would represent a single point of failure. Since there would be concern about compromise, you could audit the success or failure of logons or other specific events.

It should be reiterated that proxy servers are *not* firewalls. They do perform some of the same functions, but not with the same thoroughness or same results. We will be talking more about firewalls later in this chapter.

Design Scenario: When to Proxy

One of your customers comes to you looking for advice. It seems the company has somewhat of a dilemma. When you do your exploration of the problem, you discover that this is a small company. Each and every day, employees are accessing the same few Web sites. In addition, the company has a limited class C IP addressing scheme and it is getting ready to add on several dozen new employees. Each of these employees will need access to the Internet, but the company does not want to apply for another class C address and go through the hassle of addressing dozens of machines. In addition, since these employees will be new and will be temporary, the CIO wants to make sure that the sites they visit on the Internet are approved. The CIO knows he is asking a lot, but surely there has to be a way to do this?

In this implementation, a proxy server is the perfect solution. A proxy server will save all the Web pages that are accessed frequently and provide them whenever asked. This way, your users will not have to go all over the Internet looking for them. It should speed things up. By instituting this form of address translation, you may make use of the limited addresses you already have, and still provide IP addresses for all the new folks. Finally, by instituting something like a censoring program in addition to the proxy server, all the needs will be met.

Virtual Private Networking

When you look at the Microsoft exam objectives at the beginning of the chapter, you will notice that at least four of the topics listed can be solved with a Virtual Private Network. You can provide external users with secure access to private network resources. You can use a VPN to provide secure access between private networks by using it to provide secure access with a WAN and to provide secure access across a public network. If it seems like a pretty handy tool, it can be.

We have been talking around the subject for a while, so let's explain what a VPN is, and how it actually works. We will start with taking an overview of VPNs and then move into specifics.

VPN Overview

As implied previously, a *virtual private network (VPN)* is simply a private network that has been extended across a shared network or across a public network like the Internet. In a nutshell, you are using the Internet for your very own private purposes. With a VPN, you can send data between two computers across the aforementioned shared or public network in a way that is very similar to a point-to-point private link. When you actually configure and create the VPN, you are doing what is known as virtual private networking.

The goal of a VPN is to simulate a regular network connection. Now, to do that, or to create a virtual point-to-point link, any data that is transmitted is encapsulated. This encapsulation requires that there be a header, and that the header provide all the routing information necessary to allow the packet to travel across the shared or public network and reach its destination. To create the virtual private network hookup, the data that is being sent has to be encrypted. Once the packets are encrypted, any of the packets intercepted along the way would be indecipherable without the encryption keys. So this link is known as a VPN connection.

Take a look at Figure 14.4, which shows, in theory, how a VPN simulates the point-to-point link.

Now, VPN connections are very flexible things. As a matter of fact, we have a friend who works for a company in Provo, Utah. Unfortunately, he lives in Salt Lake City, about 45 miles away. Anytime he can, he tries to avoid the drive and work from home instead. Using a VPN allows users who are working away from the office to be able to get a remote access connection to a server using the infrastructure that is provided by a public network. From the user's point of view, the VPN is just a simple point-to-point connection between the computer (also known as the VPN client) and the server (otherwise known as the VPN server). The infrastructure of the shared network just doesn't matter because it looks as if the data is sent over a dedicated line. In other words, it is so seamless that the end user doesn't notice much of a difference.

FIGURE 14.4 Virtual Private Network (VPN)

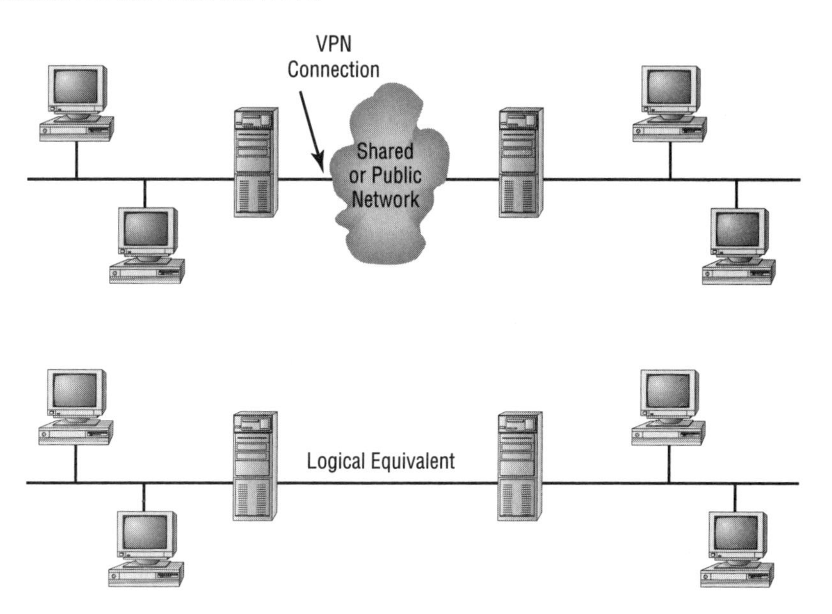

Now, before we get too carried away here, it is prudent to point out that all this encryption stuff does add overhead to the process. If you are working off a cable modem or DSL, the overhead may not be noticeable. If you have a dial-up connection using a modem that is not the fastest one on the market, you will notice the difference. As a system administrator, you have the peace of mind to know the data going across the public network is encrypted. You will also have the hassle of knowing your users are going to whine about the speed of the connection.

Now CIOs have picked up on this and have figured out that these VPN connections can also be used by their organizations to provide for routed connections between remote offices. They can also be used to work with other organizations over the Internet while keeping their communications secure. This means that the VPN connection is logically operating as a dedicated WAN link, without the cost. So, what the company is doing is creating a VPN so that the company can trade long distance dial-up or leased lines for local dial-up or leased lines to an Internet service provider (ISP). Again, you are looking at cost savings going right to the bottom line—might even mean a raise for the person who suggests it!

Elements of a VPN Connection

The VPN is not a Microsoft Windows 2000 invention. Microsoft just provided the framework in the operating system, something many other companies charge extra for. To put together a *VPN connection*, the following components need to be provided. They are illustrated in Figure 14.5.

VPN server The VPN server is the computer that will accept the VPN connections from VPN clients. A *VPN server* can also provide VPN connections between routers.

VPN client. The *VPN client* is the computer that starts the VPN connection that ends up at the VPN server. The client can be either an individual computer that gets a remote VPN connection or a router that gets a router-to-router connection. These VPN clients can be running Windows NT version 4, Windows 2000, Windows 95, and Windows 98. Each of these operating systems can be configured to create remote access connections to a Windows 2000–based VPN server. Router-to-router connections can be made by Microsoft Windows 2000 Server– and Windows NT 4 Server–based computers running Routing and Remote Access service (RRAS). When you get right down to it, these VPN clients can be any *Point-to-Point Tunneling Protocol (PPTP)* client or *Layer 2 Tunneling Protocol (L2TP)* client using IPSec.

Tunnel The *tunnel* is that part of the connection where the data is encapsulated.

VPN connection The *VPN connection* is that part of the connection where the data is encrypted. The data must be both encrypted and encapsulated along the same part of the connection for the connection to be considered a secure VPN connections.

So you know, you can create a tunnel and send the data through the tunnel without encryption. This is not considered a VPN connection because, by definition, the private data must be sent across a shared or public network in an encrypted form. Since the data is in an easily readable form, this is not considered a VPN.

Tunneling protocols The *tunneling protocols* are the communication standards that are used to manage the tunnels and to encapsulate the data. Windows 2000 uses PPTP and L2TP.

Tunneled data The *tunneled data* is data usually sent across the private point-to-point link.

Transit network The transit network is the shared or public network that is crossed by the encapsulated data. For Windows 2000, the *transit network* is always an IP internetwork. The transit network can be the Internet or some other private IP-based intranet, like AT&T Worldnet.

FIGURE 14.5 Components of a VPN connection

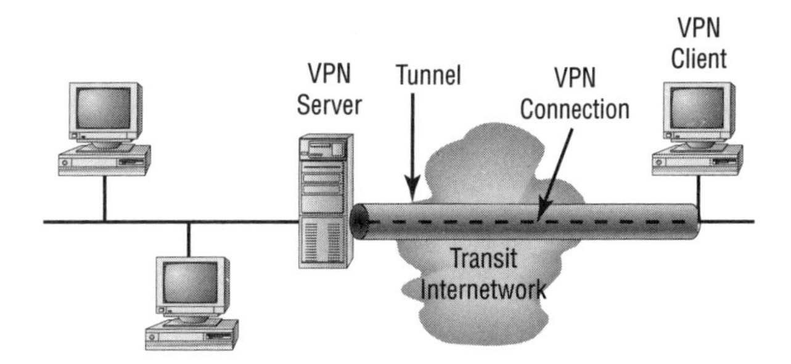

VPN Connection Types

So, how do you go about creating the VPN connection? Actually, it is very much like setting up a point-to-point dial-up networking connection and a demand-dial routing procedure. As we said earlier, there are just two types of VPN connections that we have to deal with: the remote access VPN connection and the router-to-router VPN connection.

Remote Access VPN Connection

A remote access connection is made by a client, which is usually a single-user computer. This client uses the connection to connect to the private network. The VPN server, on the other hand, is put in place to provide the access to all of the resources of the server or even to the network that the VPN server is attached too. All of the packets that are sent across the VPN connection come from the remote access client. In the parlance of the Microsoft objective writers, this would be to "provide external users with secure access to private network resources."

Microsoft Exam Objective

Provide external users with secure access to private network resources.

So, why is it judged to be secure? Well, the remote access client has to authenticate itself to the remote access server. To be sure the authentication is mutually agreed upon, the server also has to authenticate itself to the client. Now all that is very descriptive, but also somewhat confusing. Here is what it all means.

Say you have a job that is similar to ours—you are a traveling instructor. We travel all over the country at the drop of a hat. To be truthful, we travel all over the country at the drop of a check, but you get the point. Now, while we are toiling away in Lower East Duluth, Minnesota, we need to access information from our network. In this case, we would hook our trusty laptops up to a phone, and dial into our nationwide Internet Service Provider. Once we were connected to the ISP, we would use the VPN client to establish a session with the VPN server. In this case, the laptop would authenticate itself to the server and the server would authenticate itself to the laptop. Once the authentication was completed, we would have complete access to the network resources.

Router-to-Router VPN Connection

The router-to-router VPN connection is made between two routers and it will connect two portions of a private network. In this scenario, the VPN server has to provide a routed connection to the network to which the other

VPN server is attached. On a router-to-router connection, packets that are sent from either router across the connection do not start at either of the routers.

Now, in this case, differentiation is getting somewhat challenging. Let's call the router that is initiating the connection the VPN client. In this case, the client has to authenticate itself to the other system. Since we already have a VPN client, this server must be considered the VPN server. Again, for mutual authentication, the VPN server will authenticate itself to the VPN client.

Although this is all good information, it isn't really given to real world scenarios. In this case, we can be talking about two scenarios: LAN segment to LAN segment, or between WAN segments. So, when we look at these, we are looking at two objectives—provide secure access within a LAN, and provide secure access with a WAN.

Microsoft Exam Objectives

Provide secure access between private networks.

- Provide secure access within a LAN.
- Provide secure access with a WAN.
- Provide secure access across a public network.

Here is how it works. For the LAN scenario, let's look at a case that a friend of ours dealt with. Nick used to be a consultant in New York City. He received a call one day to come out and bid a project that called for the linking of two network segments. In each case, the network segments were small, with a minimum number of users on each segment. The two segments were even very close together, probably less than 200 yards apart. Nick was thinking that this task was going to be a piece of cake, until he showed up on the client site. When he got there, he found that the two segments were about 200 yards apart, as the pigeon flew. The segments were in different towers of the World Trade Center. The two offices were close enough so occupants of one could see the occupants of the other, but as far as networking was concerned, they were miles apart. In this case, Nick could set up access between the two network segments using a public internetwork as an intermediary much more easily than he could have arranged for a cable to be run between the two buildings.

In the second case, assume that the corporate home office is in Chicago. In addition, there is a very tiny satellite office in St. Louis. Both offices are hooked to the Internet and the St. Louis office really wants to share information with the Chicago office. In this case, both these sites have routers that are capable of establishing a VPN. Now, whenever someone on the St. Louis network wants to access a resource in Chicago, the router in St. Louis calls the router in Chicago and authenticates itself. The Chicago router authenticates itself to the St. Louis router and you have a VPN.

The Properties of VPN Connections

The VPN connections that will be using PPTP and L2TP over Internet Protocol Security (IPSec) have the following things in common. First of all, the information sent across the VPN is encapsulated. Secondly, to make sure all the parties are who they say they are, the client and the server use some form of authentication. Thirdly, the data sent across the VPN link is encrypted. Finally, there has to be some mutually agreeable way to handle the assignment of IP addresses. Let's take a closer look at each of the properties.

Encapsulation

As we have seen earlier, in order to use VPN technology, it must have a way of encapsulating the private data with a header that allows the data to travel across the public network. If you are not comfortable with the term encapsulating or *encapsulation*, think of it this way. If we were talking about snail-mail here, the data packet would be the letter inside an envelope. If the packet were encapsulated, you would simply take the envelope and letter, add a note to it, put it inside a larger envelope, address that envelope, and mail it.

Authentication

Since there is a two-sided communication, authentication for the VPN connections can take two forms:

User authentication In order for the VPN connection to be established, we have seen that the VPN server must authenticate the VPN client that is attempting the connection. This is called *user authentication*. The VPN server also must verify that the VPN client has all of the right permissions.

If mutual authentication is in place, then the VPN client also has to authenticate the VPN server. This process provides protection against masquerading VPN servers. In this case, both parties are simply exchanging the super-secret handshake.

Data authentication and integrity Now that the two machines are convinced they are who they say they are, there has to be a way in place to check the data being sent on the VPN connection. There should be a way of making sure that it originated at the other end of the connection and that someone or something has not modified it in transit. The data may contain a cryptographic checksum based on an encryption key known only to the sender and the receiver. This means that once the two sides have exchanged the super-secret handshake (established *data authentication and integrity*), they can begin exchanging information. As long as all these pieces are in place, you have a secure communication.

Data Encryption

To make sure that the data that travels the public network is really secure, it is encrypted by the sender and decrypted by the machine that receives it. The way the encryption and decryption processes unfold depends on both sides knowing about the common encryption key. In our example, think of a magic decoder ring. As long as you and I both have the same magic decoder ring, our messages make sense.

Because they are encrypted, intercepted packets would be unusable to anyone who does not have the encryption key. The length of the encryption key is a really important security parameter. There are computational techniques around for determining the encryption key, but cracking larger and larger keys requires more and more computing power. If you can, use the largest possible key size.

On the flip side, the more information that is encrypted with the same key, the easier it is to decipher the encrypted data. With some encryption technologies, you can even specify how often the encryption keys will be changed during any individual connection.

Address Allocation

When a VPN server is configured, it has to create what is called a virtual interface. This virtual interface represents the interface on which all VPN connections are made. When a client establishes a connection, the virtual interface is created on the VPN client that represents the virtual interface connected to the server. This creates the point-to-point VPN connection.

These virtual interfaces have to be assigned IP addresses. This is called *address allocation*. It is up to the VPN server to handle the assignment of these addresses. By default, the VPN server gets these addresses for itself and for the clients using the Dynamic Host Configuration Protocol (DHCP). If necessary, a static pool of IP addresses can be defined by a simple IP network ID and a subnet mask.

There are other pieces that must also be put in place. Since this is a network connection, there must be some form of name server assignment. This can include the assignment of domain name system (DNS) and Windows Internet Name Service (WINS) servers. The VPN client obtains the IP addresses of the DNS and WINS servers from the VPN server for the intranet to which the VPN server is attached.

Design Scenario: VPNs

A small company has two offices located on different coasts. Both offices have connections to the Internet, but are currently not linked. There are resources that would be handy for everyone to share, and this would also minimize duplication.

In this case, the company could set up a VPN between routers. In this way, a secure connection would be maintained and the two offices could communicate without having the expense of a leased line.

Intranet-Based VPN Connections

VPNs can be based over the Internet, or over an intranet. We have already looked at ways to connect using the Internet, but there are occasions when the intranet can also be used for remote locations.

Remote Access over an Intranet

On some intranets, the data of a single department is determined to be so sensitive that the entire department's network segment is just physically disconnected from the rest of the intranet. While this certainly protects the department's data, it makes accessing information a virtual nightmare for those users who use the separate network segment.

To solve this problem, you can consider using a VPN connection so the sensitive department's segment can be reconnected to the intranet but separated from the rest of network by a VPN server. The VPN server is not put in place to provide a routed connection between the corporate intranet and the separate network segment. Users on the intranet who have the right permissions can establish a connection with the VPN server and they can gain access to the resources of the protected department's network. Besides, all the communication that goes across the VPN connection is already encrypted for data confidentiality. What about those people who are not in the know? If they do not have the right permissions to establish a VPN connection, the network segment is hidden from view and might as well not even be there.

Network Connections over an Intranet

As we have mentioned earlier, VPNs can also be used to connect two networks over an intranet using a router-to-router VPN connection. This type of VPN connection is necessary when two departments are in separate locations, and when the data they have to share is highly sensitive. For example, the corporate finance department usually has to share information with the human resources department so they can exchange payroll information. If the finance department and the HR department are connected as VPN clients or VPN servers, the users on either network can swap sensitive data.

Hybrid Internet and Intranet VPN Connections

Now, that you have the basics, this gets to the meat of the discussion on allowing trusted partners access to your network. As you have seen, a VPN connection is a tool that can give a secured point-to-point connection. There are some other types of connections: For example, there is the pass-through connection, which is shown in Figure 14.6. The pass-through connection lets a remote access client that is connected to one of the company's intranets gain access to the resources of another company's intranet using the Internet as a backbone. So, in this case, a remote access connection goes through one intranet and over the Internet before it can negotiate to gain access to a second intranet. Barney, sitting in a cube at the Bedrock Quarry, can access data at the Flintstone Rock Crushers Emporium without ever leaving his cube. It is so transparent, Barney doesn't even know something magical is going on.

FIGURE 14.6 Pass-through VPN connection

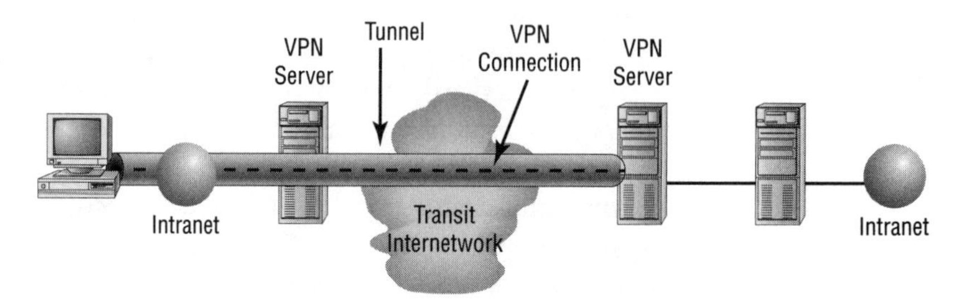

Virtual Private Networking Security

Any time you add a new technology to the network, you are adding more headaches. Ooops, make that more opportunities. Virtual private networking is no exception. It must be managed just like any other network resource, and VPN security issues, particularly with Internet VPN connections, must be addressed carefully. In an earlier chapter, we did a risk assessment. To do a sort of risk assessment lite, let's consider the following questions:

- Where is all of the user account data going to be stored?
- Each of the VPN clients will need an address. How will that address be assigned?
- Which of the users will be allowed to create VPN connections?
- How is the VPN server going to verify the identity of the user that is attempting to establish the VPN connection?
- Is the VPN server going to record all of the VPN activity?
- How is the VPN server going to be managed?

Managing User Accounts

Now, this could be the same type of scenario as "What came first the chicken or the egg?" Where are you going to store information about the user? First of all, it is an administrative nightmare to have separate user accounts on separate servers for the same user and try to keep them all simultaneously current. Because of that, there should be a master account database that is usually defined at a domain controller or on a *Remote Authentication Dial-in User Service (RADIUS)* server. In this way, the VPN server can send the authentication credentials to a centrally located authenticating device. Then, this same user account can be used for both dial-in remote access and for VPN-based remote access.

Managing Addresses and Name Servers

Next, we have the problem of how to assign IP addresses? Any time you assign an IP address, you also have to decide how you can provide the client with DNS or WINS information. The VPN server has to have a group of IP addresses ready and waiting so that it can assign them to the VPN server's virtual interface. The addresses will also go to the VPN clients during the *Internet Protocol Control Protocol (IPCP)* negotiation phase that is an integral part of the establishment of the connection process. The IP address that is assigned to the VPN client is given to the virtual interface of the VPN client. Let's see if we can make that just a little clearer. Although that sentence describes exactly what is happening, just about any other explanation would be clearer.

When a host contacts the VPN server and wants to establish a communication session, the server and the host must come up with a unique way of identifying the session. In this case, the server maintains a virtual address for its connection to the Internet. This is a private address known only to the server and any of the clients it services. When a client comes calling, the server assigns each client its own virtual address. The server has to get these mystical IP addresses from somewhere. When you are using Windows 2000–based VPN servers, it is up to DHCP to assign the IP addresses to the VPN clients. This is the default configuration. If you so desire, you can also configure a pool of static IP addresses. The VPN server must have the address of DNS and WINS servers to give to the client during IPCP negotiation. When the IPCP negotiation phase is complete, the client will have all the information it needs to locate the resources on the network.

VPNs and Firewalls

As we have been discussing VPNs so far, it has almost seemed as if the VPN client just magically connected directly to the VPN server. While having a direct connection between the client and the VPN server is certainly one of the ways that the VPN can be configured, that would leave the VPN server unprotected by a firewall. As you know, a firewall is designed to filter packets by allowing or disallowing the flow of very different types of network traffic. Packet filtering simply means that the firewall examines every IP packet going into or out of your network. By either allowing the packet to continue on into your network, or disallowing the packet, you are using IP packet filtering. This gives you a way to decide what types of IP traffic you are going to allow to cross the firewall.

VPN Servers and Firewalls

When you think about it, there are only two possible ways to use a firewall and a VPN server together. In the first approach, the VPN server is attached directly to the Internet and the firewall is located between the VPN server and the intranet. That is what is shown in Figure 14.7.

FIGURE 14.7 A VPN server in front of the firewall

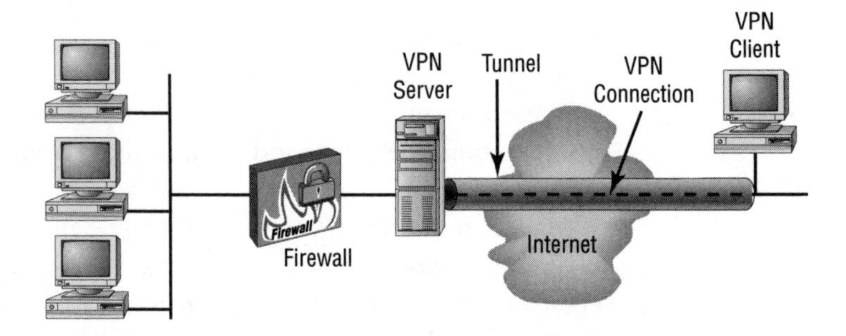

The second implementation would have the firewall attached directly to the Internet and the VPN server would be between the firewall and the intranet.

VPN Server in Front of the Firewall

Let's take a closer look at how this works, including spending some time with the protocols that might be involved. Look closely again at Figure 14.7.

Okay, starting from the far right, you see the VPN client. The VPN client establishes a connection with the VPN server using either L2TP over IPSec or PPTP. In either case, all communication between the VPN server and client is conducted through the tunnel and is encrypted for good measure. Once the VPN server gets the packets, it decrypts the packets and then it needs to transfer them to the firewall. It is going to do this using straight TCP/IP, so the firewall needs to add packet filters to its Internet interface that allow only VPN traffic to and from the IP address of the VPN server's interface on the Internet. Basically, this says the firewall is going to allow traffic to come into the network only from the VPN server.

So, for the inbound traffic, the first stop will be the VPN server. At this point, the tunneled data has to be decrypted by the VPN server. Once the traffic is decrypted, it is forwarded to the firewall, and the firewall employs its filters to allow the traffic to be forwarded to intranet resources.

There is an added benefit to this scenario. Because the only traffic that is crossing the VPN server is traffic generated by authenticated VPN clients, firewall filtering can be used to prevent VPN users from accessing specific intranet resources. When connecting partners to your network, this is one way of controlling what parts of the intranet they can access.

This is also a benefit if you want to control other forms of inbound traffic. After all, the only Internet traffic that is allowed to enter the intranet must pass through the VPN server. This will effectively prevent the sharing of *File Transfer Protocol (FTP)* or Web intranet resources with non-VPN Internet users.

When you are configuring the Internet interface on the VPN server, you will want to configure the following input and output filters using the Routing and Remote Access snap-in.

The Packet Filters to Use with PPTP

You should configure the following input filters with the appropriate filter action set to *Drop all packets except those that meet the criteria below*:

- The destination IP address should be of the VPN server's Internet interface, the subnet mask should be set to 255.255.255.255, and the TCP destination port should be 1723 (0x06BB). This is the filter that allows PPTP tunnel maintenance traffic to move from the PPTP client to the PPTP server.

- The destination IP address should be of the VPN server's Internet interface, the subnet mask should be set to 255.255.255.255, and the IP protocol ID should be 47 (0x2F). This is the filter that allows the PPTP tunneled data to move from the PPTP client to the PPTP server.
- The destination IP address should be of the VPN server's Internet interface, the subnet mask should be set to 255.255.255.255, and the *TCP [established]* source port should be 1723 (0x06BB). This filter will be required only if the VPN server is also acting as a VPN client in a router-to-router VPN connection. When you select *TCP [established],* the traffic is accepted only if the VPN server starts the TCP connection.

You should configure the following output filters with the filter action set to *Drop all packets except those that meet the criteria below*:

- The source IP address should be set to the VPN server's Internet interface, subnet mask should be set to 255.255.255.255, and the TCP source port should be 1723 (0x06BB). This is the filter that allows the PPTP tunnel maintenance traffic to move from the VPN server to the VPN client.
- The source IP address should be set to the VPN server's Internet interface, subnet mask should be set to 255.255.255.255, and IP protocol ID should be set to 47 (0x2F). This is the filter that allows the PPTP tunneled data to move from the VPN server to the VPN client.
- The source IP address should be set to the VPN server's Internet interface, the subnet mask should be set to 255.255.255.255, and the *TCP [established]* destination port should be defined as 1723 (0x06BB). This filter is required only if the VPN server is also acting as a VPN client in a router-to-router VPN connection. When you select *TCP [established],* the traffic is sent only if the VPN server starts the TCP connection.

Packet Filters for L2TP over IPSec

You should configure the following input filters so the filter action is set to *Drop all packets except those that meet the criteria below*:

- Set the destination IP address to the VPN server's Internet interface, the subnet mask should be set to 255.255.255.255, and the UDP destination port should be set to 500 (0x01F4). This is the filter that allows the *Internet Key Exchange (IKE)* traffic to access the VPN server.

- You should configure the destination IP address to the VPN server's Internet interface, the subnet mask should be set to 255.255.255.255, and the UDP destination port should be set to 1701 (0x6A5). This is the filter that allows L2TP traffic to move from the VPN client to the VPN server.

You should configure the following output filters so that the filter action is set to *Drop all packets except those that meet the criteria below*:

- Set the source IP address to that of the VPN server's Internet interface, set the subnet mask to 255.255.255.255, and define the UDP source port for 500 (0x01F4). This is the filter that allows IKE traffic to move from the VPN server.
- Set the source IP address to that of the VPN server's Internet interface, set the subnet mask to 255.255.255.255, and set the UDP source port to 1701 (0x6A5). This is the filter that allows L2TP traffic to move from the VPN server to the VPN client.

Keep an eye on the source and destination port numbers. Notice that there are two ports to worry about for PPTP (47 and 1723) and two ports to worry about for L2TP (500 and 1701). This information might come in handy in ruling out (or in) selections on exam questions.

Design Scenario: VPN Server in Front of the Firewall

One of your longtime customers calls and has a question. She has just changed jobs, and in looking over the network map, she was excited to see that the company was making extensive use of VPNs to handle remote communication and also to handle communication between distant offices. When she looked at a network map, she discovered that the VPN server was on the outside of the firewall. She wondered if that was a mistake and if that defeated the purpose of using this type of technology.

You explained to her that even though the VPN server is in front of the firewall, all communication between the server and its clients is tunneled and encrypted. In this case, VPN server placement is not defeating the purpose of the firewall.

VPN Server behind the Firewall

Now, while the previous method may work, it is not preferred. After all, your main form of communication with the outside world is out there exposed for all to see. Take a look at Figure 14.8. Here, the firewall is all that is connected to the Internet and the VPN server is just another intranet resource that is connected to a *screened subnet.*

FIGURE 14.8 VPN connection with the VPN server located behind the firewall

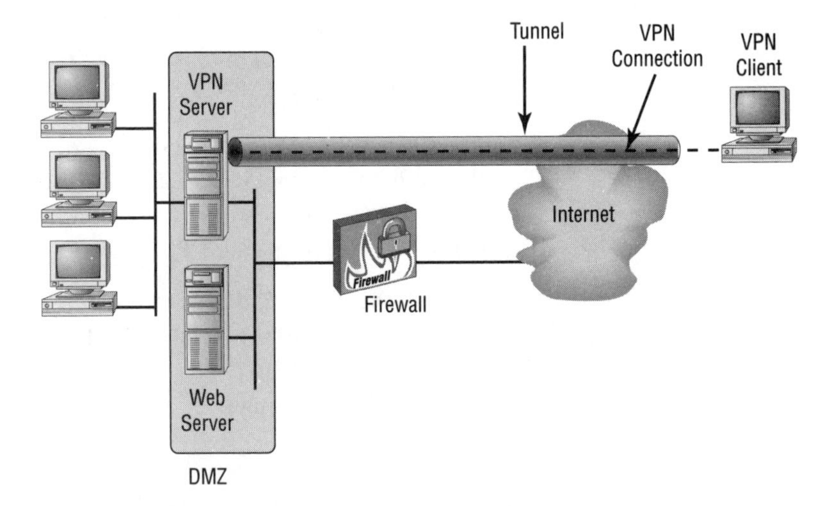

A screened subnet is more commonly referred to as a *demilitarized zone (DMZ)*. The screened subnet is a network segment that just contains resources that have to be available to Internet users. This can include things such as Web servers or FTP servers. The VPN server can have an interface that attaches to the screened subnet and have an interface that attaches to the intranet.

Here, the firewall must be configured so the input and output filters on the Internet interface will let the passing of tunnel maintenance traffic and tunneled data flow through to the VPN server. Any additional filters can also allow the passing of traffic to reach the Web servers, the FTP servers, and any other type of server that resides on the screened subnet.

The firewall will not have the encryption keys for the VPN connections. The firewall can only filter on the plain text headers of the tunneled data. That means that all of the tunneled data will pass through the firewall. In case you are wondering, this is not a security concern. The VPN connection still requires an authentication process, and that process can prevent unauthorized access to go beyond the VPN server.

The following input and output filters should be configured using the IP address for the Internet interface on the firewall.

Packet Filters for PPTP

Configure the following input filters so that the filter action is set to *Drop all packets except those that meet the criteria below*:

- The destination IP address should be set to the VPN server's screened subnet interface and the TCP destination port should be set to 1723 (0x06BB). This filter is what allows the PPTP tunnel maintenance traffic to move from the PPTP client to the PPTP server.
- The destination IP address should be set to the VPN server's screened subnet interface and the IP protocol ID should be set to 47 (0x2F). This is the filter that allows PPTP tunneled data from the PPTP client to the PPTP server.
- The destination IP address should be set to the VPN server's screened subnet interface and the *TCP [established]* source port should be set to 1723 (0x06BB). This is a required filter if the VPN server is acting as a VPN client in a router-to-router VPN connection. When you select *TCP [established]*, the traffic is accepted if the VPN server starts the TCP connection.

You should configure the following output filters with the filter action set to *Drop all packets except those that meet the criteria below*:

- The source IP address should be set to the VPN server's screened subnet interface and TCP source port should be set to 1723 (0x06BB). This is the filter that allows PPTP tunnel maintenance traffic to move from the VPN server to the VPN client.
- The source IP address should be set to the VPN server's screened subnet interface and IP protocol ID should be set to 47 (0x2F). This is the filter that allows PPTP tunneled data to move from the VPN server to the VPN client.

- .The source IP address should be set to the VPN server's screened subnet interface and *TCP [established]* destination port should be set to 1723 (0x06BB). This action is only required if the VPN server is acting as a VPN client in a router-to-router VPN connection. When you select *TCP [established]*, traffic is sent only if the VPN server starts the TCP connection.

Packet Filters for L2TP over IPSec

You should configure the following input filters so that the filter action is set to *Drop all packets except those that meet the criteria below*:

- The destination IP address should be set to the VPN server's screened subnet interface and UDP destination port should be set to 500 (0x01F4). This is the filter that allows the IKE traffic to move to the VPN server.
- The destination IP address should be set to the VPN server's screened subnet interface and IP protocol ID should be set to 50 (0x32). This is the filter that allows the IPSec ESP traffic to move from the VPN client to the VPN server.

You should configure the following output filters so the filter action is set to *Drop all packets except those that meet the criteria below*:

- The source IP address should be set to the VPN server's screened subnet interface and UDP source port should be set to 500 (0x01F4). This is the filter that allows the IKE traffic to move from the VPN server.
- The source IP address should be set to the VPN server's screened subnet interface and IP protocol ID should be set to 50 (0x32). This is the filter that allows the IPSec ESP traffic to move from the VPN server to the VPN client.

There are no filters required for L2TP traffic at the UDP port of 1701. At the firewall, all L2TP traffic including tunnel maintenance and tunneled data is encrypted as an IPSec ESP payload.

Again, notice we are only dealing with a limited number of ports. For PPTP, the ports 47 and 1723, and for L2TP, look for ports 500 and 50. There are several test questions where ports do come up, so you will probably want to be on top of these.

VPNs and NAT

A *network address translator (NAT)* is simply an IP router that has the ability to translate the IP address and TCP/UDP port numbers of packets as they are forwarded. Suppose you are the owner of a small business who wants your employees to be able to connect multiple computers to the Internet. Normally, you would have to obtain a set of public addresses that could be assigned to each computer on your network. With a NAT, however, you do not need to have multiple public addresses. NAT can use private addresses (as documented in RFC 1918) on the private network segment and use the NAT to map the private addresses to one or more public IP addresses as rented from your ISP.

Say your business is using the 10.0.0.0 numbering convention with a subnet mask of 255.0.0.0, and it has been given the public IP address of *w.x.y.z* by your ISP. Here, the NAT will either statically or dynamically map all the private IP addresses used on network 10.0.0.0 (255.0.0.0) to the IP address of *w.x.y.z*.

If the packets are leaving the network, the source IP address and TCP/UDP port numbers are set to *w.x.y.z* and a changed TCP/UDP port number. If the packets are entering the network, the destination IP address and TCP/UDP port numbers are then remapped to the private IP address and original TCP/UDP port number.

By default, NAT keeps track of all this and translates the IP addresses and the TCP/UDP ports. There are many situations where the IP address and the port information are only in the IP and TCP/UDP headers. In these cases, the application protocol is translated transparently. This is the case with the HyperText Transfer Protocol (HTTP) traffic.

Now, there are some applications and protocols that do store the IP address or TCP/UDP port information within their own headers. FTP, for example, stores the dotted decimal representation of IP addresses in the FTP header for the FTP PORT command. In some cases, this can cause a problem if the NAT does not properly translate the IP address within the FTP header. Some other protocols can cause NAT fits because they do not use TCP or UDP headers. These use fields in other headers to identify data streams.

If you have an implementation where the NAT component has to translate and adjust the payload beyond the IP, TCP, and UDP headers, there must be some kind of NAT editor required. The NAT editor will properly modify the nontranslatable payloads so that they can then be forwarded across a NAT. If you are planning on using NAT and a VPN, additional steps must be implemented.

VPN Traffic with Address and Port Mapping

So, now you have a problem if you want to use both a VPN and NAT. The VPN encrypts its information, including the destination and source addresses. NATs need access to those things in order to work. So, for PPTP and L2TP over IPSec tunnels to work over a NAT, the NAT has to be able to map multiple data streams to and from a single IP address.

PPTP Traffic

PPTP traffic is made up of a TCP connection for tunnel maintenance and GRE encapsulation for tunneled data. The TCP connection is not a problem, because it is NAT-translatable. This is true because the source TCP port numbers can be transparently translated. However, the *Generic Routing Encapsulation (GRE)*–encapsulated data is a problem, because it is not NAT-translatable without a NAT editor.

With tunneled data, the tunnel is identified by the source IP address and by the Call ID field, which is in the GRE header. If there are multiple PPTP clients located on the private side of a NAT, and they are all tunneling to the same PPTP server, then all that tunneled traffic has the same source IP address. Since all those PPTP clients are unaware that they are being translated, they could just pick the same Call ID when they are establishing the PPTP tunnel. Given that set of circumstances, it is possible for the tunneled data from the multiple PPTP clients located on the private side of the NAT to have the same source IP address and the same Call ID when translated. The result, as you can imagine, is chaos and confusion.

To be proactive and try to stop this problem before it happens, a NAT editor for PPTP has to be able to monitor the PPTP tunnel creation. It also has to be able to create separate mappings between a private IP address and the

Call ID as used by the PPTP client while mapping to a public IP address and unique Call ID received by the PPTP server on the Internet.

The NAT routing protocol that is used as part of the Routing and Remote Access service contains a PPTP editor that can translate the GRE Call ID. This way, it can distinguish between the multiple PPTP tunnels on the private side of the NAT.

L2TP over IPSec Traffic

If you are going to use NAT, you are not going to use L2TP. It is pretty much that simple. L2TP over IPSec traffic is not translatable by a NAT, because not only does L2TP encrypt the UDP port number, but that value is protected with a cryptographic checksum. Not only does that cause a problem, but L2TP over IPSec is not translatable even with an editor for the following additional reasons:

The Inability to Distinguish Multiple IPSec ESP Data Streams

The ESP header has a field that is called the Security Parameters Index (SPI). Now, the SPI is used with the destination IP address in the plain text IP header and IPSec security protocol (ESP or *Authentication Header (AH)* to identify an IPSec *security association (SA)*.

For outbound traffic that is going from the NAT, the destination IP address does not have to be changed. For inbound traffic, the destination IP address must be mapped to a private IP address. Just as we saw in the case of the PPTP clients, the destination address for inbound traffic of multiple IPSec ESP data streams is the same address. To distinguish one IPSec ESP data stream from another, the destination IP address and SPI would have to be mapped to a private destination IP address and SPI. However, because the ESP Auth trailer has that pesky cryptographic checksum that verifies the ESP header and its payload, the SPI cannot be changed without invalidating the cryptographic checksum. If it were changed, the whole process would do nothing more than cause the packet to be discarded.

The Inability to Change Those TCP and UDP Checksums

In L2TP over IPSec packets, UDP and TCP headers also contain a checksum that includes the source and destination IP address of the plain text IP header. The addresses in the plain text IP header can't be changed because it would invalidate the checksum in the TCP and UDP headers. To compound the problem, the TCP and UDP checksums can't be updated because they are written in the encrypted portion of the ESP payload.

So, why all the talk about what you can't do? You never know when someone may ask you a question about the types of protocols you can use in given situations. If the situation involves a VPN and NAT, you will know that you can rule out L2TP.

The Pass-Through VPN

This section is kind of a throwback to Chapter 10, on providing access to other systems. As a matter of fact, our friend Barney Rubble had a *pass-through VPN* earlier in this chapter. In Chapter 10 we looked at some of the authentication protocols, but we didn't really get into how to physically make the connection. We mentioned a pass-through VPN earlier in this chapter, but we really didn't get into the how's and why's. We will take care of that oversight here. The pass-through VPN lets a remote access client that is hooked up to one company's intranet access resources on another company's intranet while communicating across the Internet. If you follow the logic here, you will see that a remote access VPN connection is passed to one intranet through the Internet and into another intranet.

An example of this would be that Brandice and CJ are playing golf and talking about the synergy between their two companies being just so overpowering. Wouldn't it be wonderful if they could connect the companies' networks so that they could share information? After the 19th hole, both CEOs go back to their respective IS departments and make life wonderful for the IS Managers. CJ calls in Fiona, and Brandice talks with Gillian. Fiona is thrilled to be told to set up an appointment to go see Gillian and start the process to get the networks connected. Meanwhile, Gillian is wondering how in the world she is ever going to pull this off. When Fiona attends the meeting, the first thing they decide they should try to do is establish a VPN connection between the two intranets. In this way, visiting employees can access their own networks for information. Fiona starts the process by connecting a laptop computer to Gillian's intranet; and an intranet IP address configuration is obtained. At this point, Fiona needs to connect to the intranet back at her company. This process can be carried out two ways, all as a precursor of things to come. In the first instance, Fiona can end up using a phone line in the conference room. She can directly dial into a company remote access server to make a dial-up connection to the company intranet. If that isn't feasible, she can dial a local ISP and make a VPN connection to the company intranet.

So (assuming Fiona did not have to resort to dialing in), by using simple VPN technology and the appropriate infrastructure, the employee of one company can create a tunnel across the intranet of another company, jump out to the Internet, and then create another tunnel to another intranet. Why couldn't this be done with a permanent connection? The next question is, how is this done? Well, first we have to start by identifying companies; it will make the following scenario so much easier. Right now we have two people who work for two companies, Fiona and Gillian. Let's say that Fiona works for Carpenter's Woodworking (CWW) and Gillian toils away for Stephenson Saws (SS). (See Figure 14.9.)

FIGURE 14.9 A pass-through connection between companies

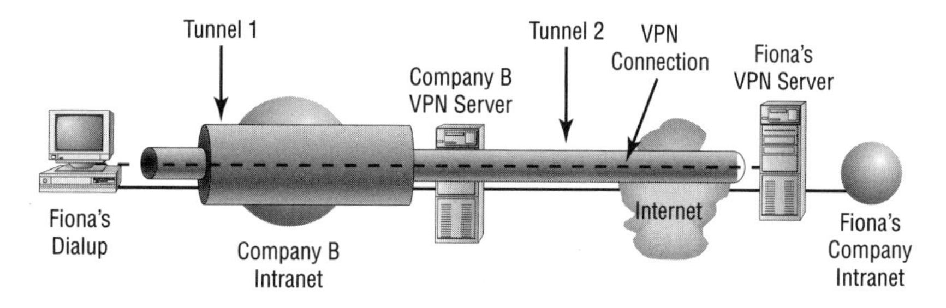

Configuration of the CWW VPN Server

Fiona's company would configure the CWW VPN server so that it would accept a remote access VPN connection from remote clients on the Internet. These would have the appropriate remote access policies and would require strong authentication and encryption. These policies have been discussed in earlier chapters, but if you are still unsure how to do it, check out the Windows 2000 server Help files for information.

Configuration of the SS VPN Server

Gillian's company would have to configure the SS company VPN server as follows:

1. Gillian would have to configure the SS VPN server to accept remote access VPN connections.
2. She would then have to manually configure the IP address pool so that it would contain a range of public IP addresses.
3. Gillian could then create a group in Windows 2000 that would define the user accounts for the visiting employees of other companies that are making the pass-through VPN connections. For example, create the group with the somewhat cryptic name of VPN_PassThrough.
4. Finally, she would create the user account that would be used by the employees of CWW who would be using the pass-through VPN.

If this was a VPN server that was only going to be used for a pass-through VPN for the visiting employees of this business partner, the administrator would then be able to delete the default remote access policy called *Allow access if dial-in permission is enabled* and be able to create a remote access policy called *VPN Pass-Through for Business Partners*. This policy would have the remote access policy permission setting, *Grant remote access permission*, selected. Then the administrator would set the conditions and the profile settings as listed in Tables 14.1 and 14.2.

TABLE 14.1 Remote Access Policy Conditions for Gillian's VPN Server

Conditions	Settings
NAS-Port-Type	Virtual.
Called-Station-ID	This would be the IP address of the VPN server interface that would be accepting VPN connections.
Windows-Groups	As defined above, the group could be named VPN_PassThrough.

TABLE 14.2 Remote Access Policy Profile Settings for Gillian's VPN Server

Profile Settings	Setting
Authentication Tab	Enable Microsoft Encrypted Authentication (MS-CHAP)
Encryption Tab	Select Basic, Strong, or No Encryption

We are making some assumptions here. These remote access policy settings are assuming that you are setting up and managing remote access on a group basis. This is being done by setting the remote access permission on all the user accounts to *Control access through remote access policy*.

Filtering Configuration

So how would you set up the firewall to make sure that Gillian's VPN server is connected to the Internet and is confined to just accepting and forwarding pass-through VPN traffic? She would have to use the Routing and Remote Access Snap-in to configure the following filters.

To Configure Filtering for PPTP

To configure PPTP filtering, you need to do the following:

1. On the intranet interface, set the following input IP filters with the filter action set to *Drop all packets except those that meet the criteria below*:
    - The destination IP address should be set to the VPN server intranet interface, with a subnet mask that should be set to 255.255.255.255, and TCP destination port that should be set to 1723.
    - The destination IP address should be set to the VPN server intranet interface, the subnet mask should be set to 255.255.255.255, and the IP protocol should be set to 47.

2. On the intranet interface, set the following output IP filters with the filter action set to *Drop all packets except those that meet the criteria below*:
   - The source IP address should be set to the VPN server intranet interface, the subnet mask should be set to 255.255.255.255, and the TCP source port should be set to 1723.
   - The source IP address should be set to the VPN server intranet interface, the subnet mask should be set to 255.255.255.255, and the IP protocol should be set to 47.
3. On the Internet interface, you should set the following input IP filters with the filter action set to *Drop all packets except those that meet the criteria below*:
   - The destination IP address and the subnet mask should be set to the public IP address pool, and the TCP source port should be set to 1723.
   - The destination IP address and the subnet mask should be set to the public IP address pool, and the IP protocol should be set to 47.
4. On the Internet interface, you should set the following output IP filters with the filter action set to *Drop all packets except those that meet the criteria below*:
   - The source IP address and the subnet mask should be set to the public IP address pool, and the TCP destination port should be set to 1723.
   - The source IP address and the subnet mask should be set to the public IP address pool, and the IP protocol should be set to 47.

As we mentioned above, take note that in the case of the VPN using PPTP, the port addresses are 1723 and 47.

To Configure L2TP over IPSec Filtering

If Gillian's system was not going to use NAT, she could choose to use L2TP over IPSec for filtering. In this case she would have more work to do to configure the VPN server as follows:

1. On the intranet interface, she would have to configure the following input IP filters with the filter action set to *Drop all packets except those that meet the criteria below*:
   - The destination IP address should be set to the VPN server intranet interface, the subnet mask should be set to 255.255.255.255, and the destination UDP port should be set to 1701.
   - The destination IP address should be set to the VPN server intranet interface, the subnet mask should be set to 255.255.255.255, and the destination UDP port should be set to 500.
2. On the intranet interface, she should configure the following output IP filters with the filter action set to *Drop all packets except those that meet the criteria below*:
   - The source IP address should be set to the VPN server intranet interface, the subnet mask should be set to 255.255.255.255, and the source UDP port should be set to 1701.
   - The source IP address should be set to the VPN server intranet interface, the subnet mask should be set to 255.255.255.255, and the source UDP port should be set to 500.
3. On the Internet interface, she should configure the following input IP filters with the filter action set to *Drop all packets except those that meet the criteria below*:
   - The destination IP address and the subnet mask should be set to the public IP address pool, and the IP protocol should be set to 50.
   - The destination IP address and the subnet mask should be set to the public IP address pool, and the source UDP port should be set to 500.

4. On the Internet interface she should configure the following output IP filters with the filter action set to *Drop all packets except those that meet the criteria below*:
    - The source IP address and the subnet mask should be set to the public IP address pool, and the IP protocol should be set to 50.
    - The source IP address and the subnet mask should be set to the public IP address pool, and the destination UDP port should be set to 500.

In this case, you are looking at three port addresses: 50, 500, and 1701.

Configuration of the VPN Client Computer

Since Gillian did all that work, it is only fair that Fiona be required to do something! In order for her to configure a Windows 2000–based VPN client for PPTP and L2TP over IPSec for a pass-through VPN, Fiona would have to start with the following process.

To Configure a PPTP Connection

1. Creating a VPN connection object that would connect Fiona with the VPN server of Gillian's company:
    - From the General tab, type in the host name or the IP address of the intranet interface of Gillian's VPN server.
    - From the Security tab, choose *Secure my password but not my data*.
    - From the Networking tab, choose *Point-to-Point Tunneling Protocol (PPTP)* as the type of server you are dialing.

2. Creating a VPN connection object that hooks Fiona into the Internet VPN server of her company:

   - From the General tab, enter the host name or the IP address of the Internet interface of Fiona's VPN server.
   - From the Security tab, choose either *Secure my password and data* or *Custom*. If you choose *Custom*, you should also choose the appropriate encryption and authentication options.
   - From the Networking tab, choose *Point-to-Point Tunneling Protocol (PPTP)* as the type of server you are dialing.

To Configure an L2TP over IPSec Connection

1. Creating a VPN connection object that hooks Fiona into the VPN server of Gillian's company:

   - From the General tab, enter the host name or IP address of the intranet interface of Gillian's VPN server.
   - From the Security tab, choose *Secure my password but not my data*.
   - From the Networking tab, choose *Layer 2 Tunneling Protocol (L2TP)* as the type of server into which you are dialing.

2. Creating a VPN connection object that hooks Fiona into the Internet VPN server of her company:

   - From the General tab, enter the host name or IP address of the Internet interface of Fiona's VPN server.
   - From the Security tab, choose either *Secure my password and data* or *Custom*. If you choose *Custom*, you must also choose the appropriate encryption and authentication options.
   - From the Networking tab, choose *Layer 2 Tunneling Protocol (L2TP)* as the type of server you are dialing.

Establishing the Pass-Through VPN Connection

Now that both Gillian and Fiona have gone through all of these gyrations, it would be nice to see some fruits of their labors. Remember, the goal is that after the pass-through VPN connection is made, Fiona can get access to the company intranet resources for as long as she has the VPN connection with the VPN server.

To Create a Pass-Through Connection

Fiona can create a pass-through VPN connection to her company VPN server on the Internet by performing these steps:

1. In the Network and Dial-up Connections folder, she should double-click the connection object that will create the tunnel to Gillian's company's VPN server on the SS company intranet.
2. When she is prompted for her user credentials, she should type in the credentials that correspond to her SS company user account.
3. In the Network and Dial-up Connections folder, she should double-click the connection object that will create the VPN to her company CWW VPN server on the Internet.
4. When she is prompted for her credentials, she should type the credentials corresponding to her CWW corporate account.

Once that is done, Fiona connects to Gillian's network, uses Gillian's VPN server to create a tunnel to her own system, and she is home free.

Design Scenario: Protocol Selection

One of your clients calls and is obviously having a really bad day. He has tried to institute a VPN using L2TP but he just can't seem to get it to work. He has tried just about everything he can think of, and now he wants to try everything you can think of.

You start by digging out your network map and you suddenly come across the problem. The company is using NAT behind the firewall, so no wonder it won't work. Once the company switches to PPTP and gets the editor running, things smooth out and life is good.

Troubleshooting 101 for VPNs

You don't really troubleshoot VPNs. You have to troubleshoot IP connectivity, or you have to troubleshoot remote access and demand-dial connection establishment, routing, and IPSec. So, it may not be as easy as it seems. Let's start the process by taking a look at where problems can occur, and then refer to some common solutions.

Common VPN Problems

According to Microsoft, VPN problems typically fall into the following categories:

- Your connection attempt is rejected, when it really should be accepted.
- Your connection attempt is accepted, when it really should be rejected.
- The user in question can't reach locations beyond the VPN server.
- The user in question can't establish a tunnel.

Keep the following troubleshooting tips close: They may help you to isolate the configuration or infrastructure problem causing these common VPN problems.

The Connection Attempt Is Rejected When It Should Be Accepted

- Try using the Ping command. This should verify that the host name or IP address of the VPN server is at least reachable. If you are using a host name make sure that the host name is being resolved to the correct IP address. If the ping attempt doesn't work, don't panic—packet filtering might be in place and be preventing the delivery of the ICMP messages to or from the VPN server.
- Try to verify that the Routing and Remote Access service is up and running on the VPN server. When in doubt, you may try stopping and starting the service. This follows the troubleshooting premise that rebooting tends to solve about 80% of the world's problems.

- Try to check the remote access VPN connections by verifying that the VPN server is enabled for remote access. For router-to-router VPN connections, verify that the VPN server is enabled for demand-dial routing.
- To check remote access VPN connections, start by verifying that the PPTP and L2TP ports are enabled for inbound remote access. If you are using router-to-router VPN connections, verify that the PPTP and L2TP ports are enabled for inbound and outbound demand-dial connections.
- Make sure to verify that the VPN client and the VPN server as well as a remote access policy are configured to use at least one common authentication method.
- Make sure that both the VPN client and the VPN server have a remote access policy that is configured to use at least one common encryption method.
- Make sure that the parameters of the connection have the appropriate permissions through remote access policies.

In order for the connection to be established, the connection attempt must meet the following criteria:

- It must match every one of the conditions for at least one remote access policy.
- It must be given the remote access permission through the user account (set to *Allow access*), or if the user account has the *Control access through remote access policy* option selected, the remote access permission of the matching remote access policy must have the *Grant remote access permission* option selected.
- They must match all the settings of the profile.
- They must match all the settings of the dial-in properties of the user account.

The properties of the remote access policy profile and the properties of the RAS server both must contain settings for these:

- Multilink
- The bandwidth allocation protocol
- The authentication protocols

If the settings of the profile for the matching remote access policy conflict with the settings of the VPN server, the connection attempt will be rejected.

If you are working with a VPN server that is a member server in a mixed-mode or native-mode Windows 2000 domain, but is configured for Windows 2000 authentication, be sure to check on the following:

- Make sure the RAS and the IAS Servers security group exists. If not, then you will have to create the group and set the group type to *Security* and the group scope to *Domain local.*
- Make sure the RAS and IAS Servers security group has been given the Read permission to the RAS and IAS Servers Access Check object.
- The computer account of the VPN server computer is a member of the RAS and IAS Servers security group. You can use the *netsh ras show registeredserver* command to view the current registration. You can use the *netsh ras add registeredserver* command to register the server in a specified domain.
- If you add or remove the VPN server computer to the RAS and IAS Servers security group, the change does not take effect immediately (due to the way that Windows 2000 caches Active Directory information). For the change to take effect immediately, restart the VPN server computer.
- If you have a problem with remote access VPN connections, make sure that the LAN protocols that are used by the VPN client are enabled for remote access on the VPN server.
- Make sure the PPTP or L2TP ports on the VPN server are not all being used. If necessary, change the number of PPTP to L2TP ports to allow more concurrent connections.
- Check to make sure that the tunneling protocol of the VPN client is in fact supported by the VPN server.

If Your Connection Attempt Is Accepted When It Should Be Rejected

One of the biggest problems comes when a connection is granted and it should have been rejected. When that occurs, you can start with this:

- Checking that the parameters of the connection have not gotten permission through remote access policies.

A connection should be rejected for the following reasons:

- The settings of the connection attempt must be denied remote access permission because of the remote access permission of the user account (with Deny access selected).
- The user account has the *Control access through remote access policy* option selected, and the remote access permission of the first remote access policy that matches the parameters of the connection attempt has the Deny remote access permission selected.

Your User Is Unable to Reach Locations Beyond the VPN Server

This is a setting where the users can access the VPN and establish a connection; they just cannot go anywhere else. To troubleshoot this, start by doing this:

- For remote access VPNs, check to be sure that either the protocol is enabled for routing or the *Entire network* option is selected for LAN protocols being used by the VPN clients.
- For remote access VPNs, check the IP address pools of the VPN server.
  - If the VPN server is configured to use static IP addresses, check that the routes to the range of addresses are actually reachable by the hosts and routers of the intranet. If not, then an IP route must be added to the routers of the intranet.
  - If the VPN server is configured to use DHCP and no DHCP server is available, the VPN server assigns addresses from the Automatic Private IP Addressing (APIPA) address range from 169.254.0.1 through 169.254.255.254. Allocating APIPA addresses for remote access clients works only if the network to which the VPN server is attached is also using APIPA addresses.
  - If the VPN server is using APIPA addresses when a DHCP server is available, verify that the proper adapter is selected from which to obtain DHCP-allocated IP addresses.
- If you are having problems with router-to router VPN connections, check that there are routes on both sides of the router-to-router VPN connection that actually support the two-way exchange of traffic.
  - A router-to-router VPN connection does not automatically create a default route. You will need to create routes on both sides of the router-to-router VPN connection so that traffic can be sent to and from the other side of the router-to-router VPN connection.

    - You can manually add static routes to the routing table, or you can add static routes through routing protocols. For persistent VPN connections, you can enable Open Shortest Path First (OSPF) or Routing Information Protocol (RIP) across the VPN connection. For two-way initiated router-to-router VPN connections, verify that the router-to-router VPN connection is not interpreted by the VPN server as a remote access connection.
    - Check to see if the user name of the calling router's credentials appears under Remote Access Clients in the Routing and Remote Access snap-in. If that is the case, then the VPN server has interpreted the calling router as a remote access client. Check that the user name in the calling router's credentials matches the name of a demand-dial interface on the VPN server.
- Verify that there are no TCP/IP packet filters enabled on the profile properties of the remote access policy being used by the VPN connection.
- For demand-dial VPN connections, check that there are no packet filters on the demand-dial interfaces that would prevent the sending or receiving of traffic.

Unable to Establish Tunnel

If you are unable to establish a tunnel, you should do this:

- Verify that packet filtering is properly configured.
- Check to make sure that the Winsock Proxy client is not currently running on the VPN client.
    - If the Winsock Proxy client is running, the Winsock API calls needed to create tunnels and send tunneled data are intercepted and sent to a configured proxy server, rather than where they were supposed to go.

Troubleshooting Tools

The following tools, which enable you to gather additional information about the source of your VPN problem, are included with Windows 2000.

TABLE 14.3 VPN Troubleshooting Tools Provided with Windows 2000

Tool	Use
Unreachability Reason	If a demand-dial interface can't make a connection, the interface is left in what is called an unreachable state. You can right-click in the interface, and then you can select *Unreachability reason* to get more information about why the interface was unable to connect.
Event Logging	On the Event Logging tab in the properties of a VPN server, there are four levels of logging. Start by selecting *Log the maximum amount of information*, and then try the connection again. When the connection fails, go back and check the system event log for events logged during the connection process. After you are done viewing remote access events, be sure to change the logging level back to *Log errors and warnings* option on the Event logging tab. This will help to conserve system resources.
Tracing	Tracing goes through and records the sequence of programming functions that are called during a process to a file. If you enable tracing for remote access and VPN components and then try the connection again, you can view the traced information. Once again, be sure to reset the tracing settings back to their default values to conserve system resources.

TABLE 14.3 VPN Troubleshooting Tools Provided with Windows 2000 *(continued)*

Tool	Use
Network Monitor	If you use Network Monitor, you can view the traffic sent between a VPN server and VPN client during the VPN connection process and during data transfer. You cannot interpret the encrypted portions of VPN traffic with Network Monitor. The proper interpretation of the remote access and VPN traffic with Network Monitor requires an in-depth understanding of PPP, PPTP, IPSec, and other protocols. Network Monitor captures can be saved as files and sent to Microsoft support for analysis.

Designing Security for Remote Access Users

You know, this is really an odd, kind of out-of-place objective, because we have been handling it in several different locations. We talked about remote access users when we talked about RAS servers and Security baselines back in Chapter 7; we talked about them again in Chapter 8 when we looked at how and why you might configure EFS; in Chapter 9 we mentioned remote users when we talked about different kinds of authentication methods; and in Chapter 13 we talked about how remote users could access applications over a Terminal Server connection. Now they want us to talk about designing Windows 2000 security for remote access users. We are going to do that in the spirit of the rest of this chapter, basically having a remote access user access the private network via a VPN connection.

Microsoft Exam Objective

Design Windows 2000 security for remote access users.

Basically, there are three ways to administer remote access permissions and connection settings. Those three ways are to administer the access by the user account, to administer the access using a policy in a Windows 2000 native-mode domain, and to administer the access using a policy in a Windows 2000 mixed-mode domain.

Administering Access by the User Account

In this model, the remote access permissions come from the tab of the same name on the Dial-in tab for the user account in the Active Directory. This is where you can enable or disable remote access permission on a per-user basis simply by setting the remote access permission to either *Allow access* or *Deny access*. Therefore, the remote access permission setting on the user account determines whether remote access permission is allowed or denied. Check out Figure 14.10 to see what we mean.

FIGURE 14.10 Remote access permission granted on a per-user basis in the Active Directory

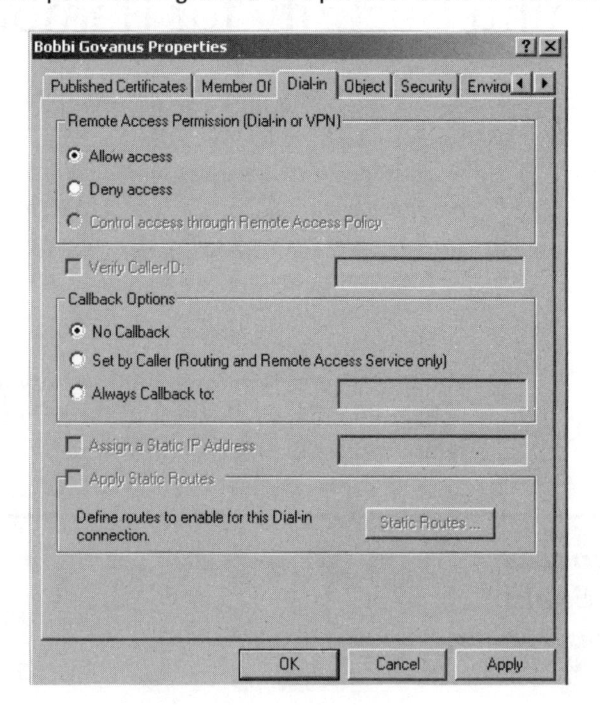

You can also allow or disallow access on a per-group basis. This is done by creating a remote access policy using the Windows-Group condition. If you are providing access this way, only the members of the group who have the remote access permission set to *Allow access* will be granted access.

If you want to make sure that some users cannot access your VPN, you can simply deny access on a per-group basis. This can be done regardless of the user account's remote access permission setting. Here, you start by setting up a remote access policy using the Windows-Group condition. In order to make sure that access will not be allowed, within the profile properties you specify a connection constraint that cannot be met. The easiest way to do this is by creating a bogus phone number. Enabling the *Restrict dial-in to this number only* dial-in constraint, and typing a number that does not correspond to any dial-in number being used by the server, will do this.

Access by Policy in a Windows 2000 Native-Mode DomainHere, the remote access permission on every user account is set to *Control access through remote access policy*. Therefore, the remote access permission setting on the remote access policy determines whether remote access permission is allowed or denied. Take a look at Figure 14.11. This will show what we mean.

FIGURE 14.11 Remote access policy setting

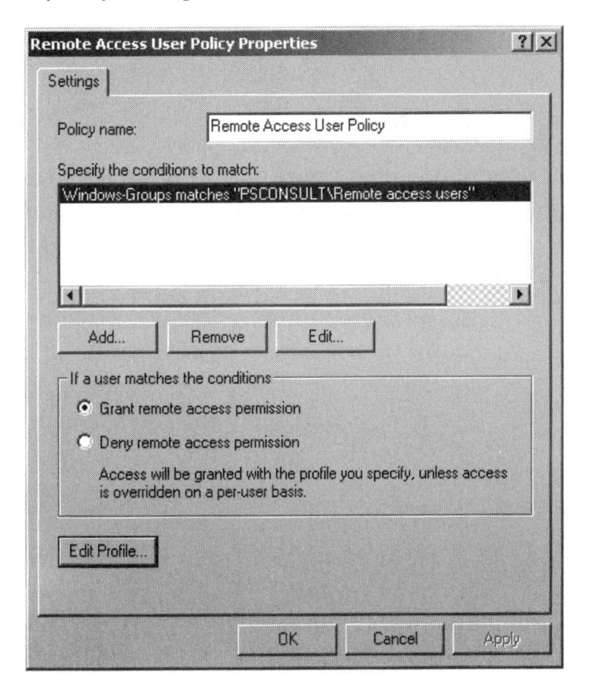

You can allow access on a per-group basis by creating a remote access policy using the Windows-Group condition and by setting the remote access permission on the remote access policy to *Grant remote access permission.* You can deny access on a per-group basis by creating a remote access policy using the Windows-Group condition and by setting the remote access permission on the remote access policy to *Deny remote access permission.*

Access by Policy in a Windows 2000 Mixed-Mode Domain

In this model, the remote access permission on every user account is set to Allow access and the default remote access policy called Allow access if dial-in permission is enabled is deleted. On a remote access server running Windows 2000 that is a member of a Windows 2000 mixed-mode domain, the Control access through remote access policy remote access permission setting on the user account is not available.

You can allow access on a per-group basis by creating a remote access policy using the Windows-Group condition. You can deny access on a per-group basis by creating a remote access policy using the Windows-Group condition. However, within the profile properties, you must specify a connection constraint that cannot be met. Enabling the *Restrict dial-in to this number only* dial-in constraint and typing a number that does not correspond to any dial-in number being used by the server will do this.

Managing Authentication

One of the questions you will have to answer before configuring a VPN server is, what is going to provide the authentication services? The VPN server can be configured to use either Windows or RADIUS as an authentication provider. If you decide on Windows, then the user credentials that are sent by users attempting VPN connections are handled using the typical Windows authentication techniques.

On the other hand, if you choose RADIUS, the user credentials and all of the information about the connection request are sent as RADIUS request messages directed to a RADIUS server. In this case, the RADIUS server gets a user-connection request from the server and authenticates the request by using its authentication database. In addition to the *yes* or *no* response given to the authentication request, the RADIUS server can also inform the VPN server of any other connection parameters that may pertain to this user. They can include things like the maximum allowable session time, a static IP address assignment, or something similar.

Summary

In previous chapters we covered the methodology behind using some of these tools, but this chapter helps you get down to the basics. We talked about when and where to use a proxy server and how firewalls can be used. We also spent an extended period of time with VPNs. There was a reason for the amount of time dedicated to each feature. Proxy servers were not stressed on the exam we took. Firewalls were covered, but usually in a manner that suggested how to use them and what it would take to get various components to operate through firewalls. If you have read this chapter, you know that we put a good deal of emphasis on the protocols that are used with VPNs and firewalls and how they are configured.

Well, there is only one more chapter in your studies. It seems like it has been a millennium ago that we were talking about business plans and business needs, doesn't it. Chapter 15 is going to cover the final set of objectives on designing SMB solutions and we will spend some time with IPSec. The quest is almost over. Hang in there for just a little longer!

Key Terms

Before you take the exam, be certain you are familiar with the following terms:

address allocation

Authentication Header (AH)

data authentication and integrity

demilitarized zone (DMZ)

encapsulation

File Transfer Protocol (FTP)

Generic Routing Encapsulation (GRE)

Internet Key Exchange (IKE)

Internet Protocol Control Protocol (IPCP)

Layer 2 Tunneling Protocol (L2TP)

network address translator (NAT)

pass-through VPN

Point-to-Point Tunneling Protocol (PPTP)

proxy server

Remote Authentication Dial-in User Service (RADIUS)

reverse proxy server

screened subnet

security association (SA)

transit network

tunnel

tunneled data

tunneling protocols

user authentication

virtual private network (VPN)

VPN client

VPN connection

VPN server

Review Questions

1. Which of the following is true about a proxy server?

   A. It is the same as a firewall.

   B. It tries to answer requests for Internet Web pages from cache.

   C. It checks the destination of every packet that goes out or comes in through the proxy server.

   D. It can only be used to handle requests going from the private network to the Internet.

   E. It cannot be used with L2TP.

2. What is the function of a reverse proxy server?

   A. It handles requests from the private network going to the Internet.

   B. It handles requests from the private network to the firewall.

   C. It acts as a mail forwarding agent.

   D. It handles requests from the Internet that may need to go to a Web Server.

   E. None of the above.

3. What is the definition of a virtual private network?

   A. A VPN connects two network segments using leased lines.

   B. A VPN connects two network segments using a dial-up connection.

   C. A VPN can only be used with services like ATM networks or AT&T Worldnet Services.

   D. A VPN is any wireless implementation.

   E. A VPN is the extension of a private network that encompasses links across shared or public networks like the Internet.

4. What is the goal of a VPN?
   - A. To make remote connections to the corporate network faster
   - B. To simulate a secure private LAN connection
   - C. To transfer e-mail securely
   - D. To lay the groundwork for voice over IP

5. Which of the following are components of a VPN?
   - A. VPN server
   - B. VPN client
   - C. Tunnel
   - D. VPN connection
   - E. All of the above

6. Which of the following are tunneling protocols?
   - A. TCP/IP
   - B. PPTP
   - C. L2TP
   - D. FTP
   - E. Encapsulation

7. What are the two types of VPNs?
   - A. The remote access VPN connection and the router-to-router VPN connection
   - B. The pass-through VPN and the firewall
   - C. Proxy servers and firewalls
   - D. VPN clients and VPN servers

8. How is data transferred over a VPN?

    A. Tunneled

    B. Plain text

    C. Encapsulated

    D. Decrypted

9. If you were configuring a firewall to packet filter for a VPN Server that is using PPTP, which ports would you have to leave open?

    A. 1723

    B. 47

    C. 1677

    D. 7100

    E. 50

10. If you were configuring a firewall to work with L2TP and a VPN, which ports would you be concerned about?

    A. 1723

    B. 1701

    C. 500

    D. 50.

    E. 1700

Answers to Review Questions

1. B, C. A proxy server examines all packets leaving or entering the private network, and also tries to handle any request for Web pages from cache.

2. D. A reverse proxy server handles requests from the Internet. It will maintain a copy of the Web page in cache and provide that when asked. Otherwise, it requests information from the Web server.

3. E. A virtual private network (VPN) is simply the extension of a private network that encompasses links across shared or public networks like the Internet.

4. B. The goal of a VPN is to simulate a secure private LAN connection.

5. E. All of the above are components of a VPN.

6. B, C. PPTP and L2TP are the tunneling protocols provided with Windows 2000.

7. A. The two types of VPNs are the remote access VPN connection and the router-to-router VPN connection.

8. C. VPN technology provides a way of encapsulating private data with a header that allows the data to traverse the transit internetwork.

9. A, B. With PPTP, you have to have access to ports 1723 and 47.

10. B, C, D. L2TP uses ports 1701, 500, and 50.

The Multinational Conglomerate

You should give yourself 10 minutes to review this case study, diagram as needed, and complete the questions for this testlet. Be sure to read each question carefully. Although the company may not have changed, its circumstances change in each chapter.

Background

Your consulting firm has been hired to assist in the Windows 2000 migration and integration for a company based in Minneapolis, Minnesota. Until the start of this year, the company had 1,000 employees, all based throughout the Twin Cities of Minneapolis and St. Paul. Just before the end of the year, the owner of your company purchased two companies of roughly the same size, which will need to be connected to the enterprise network. The total number of users when the project is completed is estimated at 3,500. In addition, each of these companies comes with various strategic partners that will need to access the information on your enterprise network. The companies that have been acquired are located in Athens, Greece, and in Orlando, Florida.

The company is now beginning to look at ways of dealing with remote users and small, local sales offices.

Current System

Minneapolis Located on the shores of beautiful Lake Calhoun, the company occupies a sprawling campus that includes four floors in a six-story building. Since the merger, the Lake Calhoun facility has become a model of efficiency. Besides being linked to all of the other offices, everyone is beginning to take the notion of an enterprise network seriously.

All of the floors are connected to the Windows 2000 network. The Minneapolis location is a domain in the tree. Active Directory Services have been deployed to the main campus and the rollout is complete in the branch offices. The desktop and laptop rollout company-wide took longer than expected, but it is now completed. The CEO wants to know what the IT team is doing to make sure that everyone within the company can access resources all over the tree, and what the IT team is doing to protect the network.

The corporate network was so impressive, it helped this company snag a very large contract with a very large customer. This customer has suddenly started to make some demands. It wants your company to establish local offices to service its account in several locations worldwide. These offices would house 5 to 10 people, and the way it looks now, each office would have its own Windows 2000 servers and a router to the Internet.

Orlando The Orlando office is a domain in the corporate tree. It has some valuable resources that need to be made available to the rest of company, particularly to the folks in Athens.

The large contract had a long-term effect on Orlando. Current corporate strategy calls for the new contract to be managed in Minneapolis for the first year, and then moved to Orlando after that. In this case, all the local offices will need to access the Orlando domain.

Athens The Athens office is now fully staffed at 2,300. Management has discovered that the business is doing well, and the extra folks are justified. The office has been upgraded to Windows 2000 servers and Athens is now its own domain in the tree.

Athens has always been ahead of the curve. When the new contract was announced, Athens' manufacturing geared up for the task, and can now handle that stage. Because the customer wants to be able to look at all the stages of inventory, the customer will need to be able to access the Athens facility as well as Minneapolis and Orlando.

Problem Statement

Provide access to all areas of the network for the local offices. In addition, be sure to have a way for remote users to access the network.

Envisioned System

Overview Several of the management team have input on this project, including the CEO, the CFO, the general manager of the Orlando office, and the general manager of the Athens Office. At this stage, we have also begun to hear from the sales manager.

CEO As the new network was designed, the CEO is looking closely at the IS department and saying things like, "Okay, people, you wanted the Windows 2000 network because of its flexibility and you now have it. This is where the rubber hits the road. Prove you can make this network do the things you said it can do."

CFO The CFO said, "You know, we are still paying the bills for this rollout. While it looks like our overall cost of operation will drop, it is still a large price to absorb. We are now looking at taking a hit for all of these local offices. Make sure that you do everything in your power to maintain costs, while providing all the resources those people need to keep the customer happy."

Orlando General Manager "Sure, I get this project dumped in my lap. Now, my budget is going to take the hit for connecting to all these local offices. The costs of leased lines alone will rival my payroll, and I have a hefty payroll! Surely there has got to be a better way?"

Athens General Manager "Why are you talking to me about this? This appears to be a problem for Orlando."

Corporate Sales Manager "Cool. How long have you been having these meetings? Why wasn't I invited? Can we do this over lunch? Oh, and by the way, computer guy, how can my sales people get information from the network when they are on the road? They keep calling and I have to look it up for them. It's not a problem in the winter, but it is spring and all my clients like to play golf, so I may not be available too much, you know what I mean?

Questions

1. What type of a solution are you looking at?

A. Proxy server

B. Firewall

C. Pass-through VPN

D. Router-to-router VPN

E. Remote access VPN

2. Where would the VPN servers be located?
   - A. Minneapolis
   - B. Orlando
   - C. Athens
   - D. At each remote office
   - E. At each remote salesperson's home

3. How many VPN servers will have to be installed in Orlando?
   - A. At least one.
   - B. Two.
   - C. One for every two remote offices.
   - D. One for every remote office.
   - E. There is not enough information to make that determination.

4. What tunneling protocols can be used for the VPN?
   - A. TCP/IP
   - B. L2TP
   - C. PPTP
   - D. PPP
   - E. MS-CHAP

5. What would you do to take care of client access?
   - A. Install NDS.
   - B. Contact Verisign.
   - C. Use the regular Windows 2000 network accounts.
   - D. Authentication is handled at the client, so this is not an issue.

Answers

1. D, E. In this scenario, you would be looking at creating a router-to-router VPN so the remote offices could connect to the home network, and you would also be looking at a remote access VPN for the remote salespeople.

2. B, D. The main VPN server would be placed in Orlando, since that is where the project will be handled. After that, there would be a VPN server in each of the remote offices.

3. A. In your heart-of-hearts you wanted the answer to be E, didn't you? And in the real world, you would have been correct. Here, in the testing world, you have to go with A. A VPN server can serve multiple roles: it can be part of router-to-router connections and also part of remote access connections.

4. B, C. As long as the networks are not using NAT, you can use either L2TP or PPTP for your tunneling protocols.

5. C. In this case, you would make use of regular accounts in the Active Directory.

Securing Communication Channels

MICROSOFT EXAM OBJECTIVES COVERED IN THIS CHAPTER:

✓ **Design an SMB-signing solution.**

✓ **Design an IPSec solution.**

- Design an IPSec encryption scheme.
- Design an IPSec management strategy.
- Design negotiation policies.
- Design security policies.
- Design IP filters.
- Define security levels.

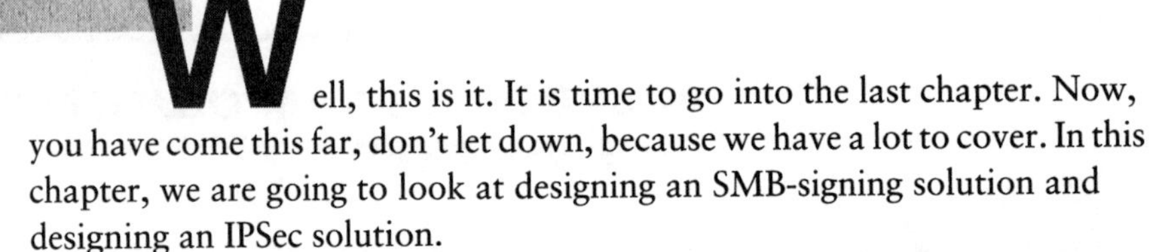

Well, this is it. It is time to go into the last chapter. Now, you have come this far, don't let down, because we have a lot to cover. In this chapter, we are going to look at designing an SMB-signing solution and designing an IPSec solution.

Now don't get concerned because the number of objectives seems to have blossomed in this chapter. As a matter of fact, a lot of this information will be review from previous chapters. Chapter 14, "Providing Secure Access at the Network Level," did an adequate job of showing you how IPSec can be used as part of a Virtual Private Network. There are other uses for IPSec, so we will review some of that material, as well as throw in some new stuff, just to keep you on your toes. The first objective is completely new, however. We have not seen the Server Message Blocks (SMB) acronym before. As a matter of fact, this whole chapter can almost be considered a carryover from Chapter 14, because we are still talking about interoperability here.

SMBs

Just imagine that you were one of the programmers of Windows 2000 Server and Advanced Server and you had to make sure that everything was backwardly compatible with previous versions of the operating system. One of the places that you would start ensuring things were compatible would be at the file system level. Now, Windows 2000 network file sharing is based on the traditional Microsoft networking mechanism of something called *Server Message Blocks (SMB)*. According to the Windows 2000 Server Operations Guide Glossary, SMB is a "file-sharing protocol designed to allow networked computers to transparently access files that reside on remote systems over a variety of networks. The SMB protocol defines a series of commands that pass information between computers. SMB uses four message types: session control, file, printer, and message." So, another way of providing cross platform support for NetWare or Unix systems is enabling SMB.

Microsoft Exam Objective

Design an SMB-signing solution.

Enabling SMB should not be taken lightly. According to Microsoft, there is a 10% to 15% performance hit. In addition, if you are using SMB with Unix, you have two options for security: workgroup level and Windows NT 4 domain level security. That means that SMB (at least as far as Unix is concerned) is not compatible with Active Directory and will cause you to postpone your conversion to native mode. We are going to be taking a quick look at setting up SMBs with both Unix and with NetWare, but first, in keeping with every other chapter in this book, we will do a brief review!

File System Basics

Obviously, sharing information across platforms has been done for years. With the release of an add-on product called Microsoft Windows NT *Services for Unix (SFU)*, sharing information with Unix no longer requires a third-party piece of software. So, while Windows NT–based systems use SMBs, Unix systems use *Network File System (NFS)* to share files across networks. Obviously, we have an incompatibility here that must be resolved. It is up to the SFU product to resolve the differences between SMB and NFS.

Network File System

When NFS was created, it was designed to run as a broadcast protocol using *User Datagram Protocol (UDP)*. If you remember back to your TCP/IP classes, UDP is an unreliable, connectionless protocol, which created some performance and network traffic issues for those systems that were intending to implement large amounts of NFS networking. As NFS evolved, it was changed to make use of TCP, and now many of the modern clients and servers support this iteration. *But*, there are still a lot of implementations that remain stuck back in the UDP days—and to be compatible, the default SFU mechanism and other NFS implementations in Windows 2000 is UDP.

To be honest, performance of NFS file transfers to and from a Windows 2000 server is pretty poor compared to most third-party SMB implementations. These implementations range in cost from free to pretty expensive. In the past, the main problem with SMB implementations has been the issue of service packs. It seems that every time Microsoft would come out with a new service pack, it would goof up the third-party SMB software.

So, when is the best time to implement an NFS solution? If you are working in an environment where large files are going to be copied back and forth between a Unix System and a Windows 2000 system, NFS is not going to make your life wonderful. That may be the time to work with the add-on product SFU. If, on the other hand, your business needs call for transparent access to Unix resources residing on Unix servers, NFS is the way to go.

Server Message Block

NFS is not the only way that SMBs are used. When you start talking about SMBs, you also have to look at other platforms, like NetWare. We will come back to Unix in a minute, but let's take a look at how Microsoft is handling communicating with a "legacy" implementation like NetWare.

The first thing you are going to notice is that *Gateway Service for NetWare (GSNW)* has not gone away. As a matter of fact, GSNW is designed to act as a bridge that goes between the server message block (SMB) protocol that is used by the Windows 2000 network and the *NetWare Core Protocol (NCP)* that is used by the NetWare network. When this gateway is put in place, the network clients that are running Microsoft client software can access NetWare files and printers without having to run the NetWare client software locally. If you look at Figure 15.1, you will see an example of a file gateway configuration.

FIGURE 15.1 Gateway Service for NetWare configuration

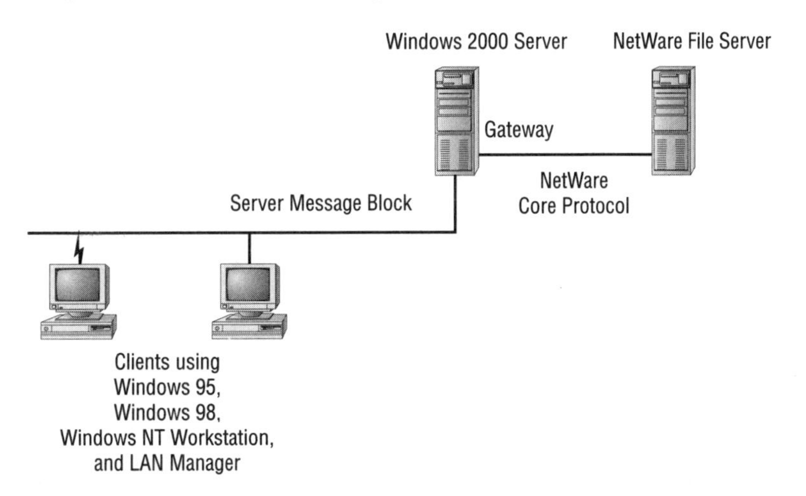

To provide file access, the server that is designated as the gateway remaps one of its own drives to point to the NetWare volume and then share that drive with all the other appropriate Microsoft clients. The file gateway makes use of a NetWare account that is set up on the computer running Windows 2000 Server that will allow it to create a valid licensed connection to the NetWare server. This connection simply appears on the Windows 2000 Server as a redirected drive. When this drive is shared, it becomes just like any other shared resource on the Windows 2000 Server.

For example, suppose you are working in a mixed environment and your users need to access information from a NetWare server called Fred. There is a volume on the Fred server called `DATA` and on the `DATA` volume there is a folder called `STUFF`. This is where your users need to go to access their information. In this case, you will have to create a gateway that goes from the Windows 2000 computer that we are going to call Wilma and point it to the NetWare folder `\\FRED\DATA\STUFF`. Now, Wilma will have to be running the Gateway Service for NetWare. So, when you activate the gateway, you will specify `\\FRED\DATA\STUFF` as the NetWare resource, and then you specify the share name for Microsoft clients. That share name would be something like `Nw_Stuff`. The Microsoft clients would just refer to this resource as `\\Wilma\Nw_Stuff`.

Now, after the gateway connection has been established, it can only be disconnected if the Windows 2000 server is shut off, if the administrator goes in and disconnects the shared resource, or if the administrator decides to disable the gateway. There is one other way, and that would be if a network problem somehow prevented access to the NetWare server. For your information, simply logging off the Windows 2000 server does not disconnect the gateway.

SMB Signing and Performance

In the scenario above, what is the performance hit? Obviously, there is going to be some. Because requests from Microsoft networking clients are processed through the gateway, access is slower than direct access from the client to the NetWare network. If performance is an issue, then clients that require frequent access to NetWare resources should run Windows 2000 Professional with Client Services for NetWare, or Windows 95 and Windows 98 with their NetWare client software, to achieve higher performance.

By tweaking the registry, you can configure SMB to use signing, where each packet is signed for and every packet must be verified. In order to change the registry, do the following:

1. Run Registry Editor (`Regedt32.exe`).
2. From the `HKEY_LOCAL_MACHINE` subtree, go to the following key:

   `\System\CurrentControlSet\Services\LanManServer\Parameters`
3. Double-click each of the following two values and change the Data value from 0 (disable) to 1 (enable):
   - EnableSecuritySignature
   - RequireSecuritySignature

   In both cases, the default is 0 (disable).
4. Click OK and then quit Registry Editor.
5. Shut down and restart Windows 2000.

Perform the following steps to configure SMB signing on a workstation:

1. Run Registry Editor (Regedt32.exe).
2. From the `HKEY_LOCAL_MACHINE` subtree, go to the following key:

   `\System\CurrentControlSet\Services\lanmanworkstation\`
   `Parameters`

3. Double-click each of the following two values and change the Data value from 0 (disable) to 1 (enable):

   - EnableSecuritySignature
   - RequireSecuritySignature

   In both cases, the default is 0 (disable).

4. Click OK and then quit Registry Editor.
5. Shut down and restart Windows 2000.

What about with Unix? The biggest issue that the SMB-on-Unix has to deal with is the Windows 2000 security model. As we mentioned above, when you talk Unix, you are talking either workgroup-level security or Windows NT 4 domain-level security.

When you are talking about workgroup security, you are talking about all the same problems that workgroups had in an enterprise environment: You know, all those things that make peer-to-peer networks such a joy to work with; like the difficulty managing the systems that seems to grow every time someone joins the workgroup or the very limited options for managing security. Don't get me wrong, workgroups have a place in a small environment, where the workgroup is easy to set up and easy to understand. Workgroups are also wonderful because they are cheap; if you are using SMB with Unix, take a look at a freeware SMB server called Samba, which is available for just about every Unix platform. There are other commercial workgroup SMB servers that tend to be more Windows-like and easier to set up and administer than Samba, but as you add utility, you also add cost.

If you like, check out one of the Windows NT 4 domain SMB servers that are available from several Unix vendors. All of these are based on AT&T's initial port to Unix of Microsoft's technology. Each is limited to running on the platform for which it was designed and each has slight difference because, in most cases, the port from AT&T required some tweaking. All SMB servers can be either a Primary Domain Controller or a Backup Domain Controller in a Windows NT 4 domain, but all will have some problems dealing with the Windows 2000 security model. These servers, being based on the Windows NT 4 security model, will force you to stay in mixed mode.

The advantage of SMB domain server over workgroup servers is that they all look and feel exactly like a Windows NT 4 server. The familiar administration tools are used to manage them and the servers and shares look exactly like a Windows NT server to your users, eliminating training and user-interface issues. These servers also have an advantage over the NFS solution. They are faster at file transfers, especially when handling larger files.

Now that you know the pluses and minuses of SMBs and how they can affect cross-platform communication, let's take a look at IP Security.

Design Scenario: Drat! Foiled Again

One of your customers called yesterday, just after you walked out the door. She left you a kind of cryptic message that you weren't really sure you understood. She mentioned something about a snafu being able to hold up the switch to native mode on their Windows 2000 network and they wanted to know why. Now, you have worked with this company and others, and you know only too well how small- to medium-size snafus can have potentially devastating effects on even the most carefully laid out projects.

You called your customer back and she said that yesterday, she had been in a meeting with some of the IT folks and they were talking this strange IT language. All she got out of it was written on a small scrap of paper. She said her notes, sketchy as they were, included the phrases *Unix*, *snafu*, *SMB*, *NT domain*, and *not going to native mode*. All she wanted was some sort of a translation.

You pondered for a minute, and suddenly it struck you. You explained that what the IT people were really saying was this: Since the network made use of Unix hosts, Services for Unix (SFU, not snafu) was installed. That meant the system needed to work with SMB to impersonate an NT4 BDC. Since that was the case, the company had opted to remain with Windows NT domain security, rather than really complicate things by going to workgroup security. Thus, the network could not migrate to Windows 2000 native mode.

Once you got done explaining, the client laughed and said, "Now I know how they feel sitting through a business meeting."

IP Security Protocol

I think we started talking about *Internet Protocol Security (IPSec)* somewhere back in the first chapter. It is about time we got around to covering it in depth. IPSec is a set of industry-standard, cryptography-based protection services and protocols. IPSec protects all protocols in the TCP/IP protocol suite and Internet communications using *Layer 2 Tunneling Protocol (L2TP)*. Now that we know what the definition is, it is time to get serious in finding out how it works. The remainder of this chapter will cover designing an IPSec solution and all of the subobjectives listed below.

Microsoft Exam Objectives

Design an IPSec solution.

- Design an IPSec encryption scheme.
- Design an IPSec management strategy.
- Design negotiation policies.
- Design security policies.
- Design IP filters.
- Define security levels.

We have been talking about Internet Protocol Security (IPSec) enough so you know its purpose is to encrypt data as that data makes its way between two computers. By encrypting the data, it is protecting it from unwanted and unexpected modification and will prevent anyone from being able to even read it if it were to be intercepted on the network.

IPSec basically is one of the first lines of defense against any type of attack, whether it is internal, from the private network, or from an external source. It is true that most network security strategies have become centered on stopping attacks from outside of your organization's network. However, there is a ton of sensitive information that can be lost by internal attacks that sniff the data as it crosses the network. Most data just is not protected when it travels across the network, so employees, other supporting staff members, or even visitors may be able to plug into your network and copy data and take it away to analyze it later. These people could also start a network-level attack against other computers on your network. Firewalls cannot offer any protection against a threat from inside the network. Since something has to be done, using IPSec will offer significantly greater security for your network data.

IP Security is a service that allows administrators to monitor network traffic—they can examine addresses and even apply different types of security methods to the IP data packet. All this can be done regardless of where the data has originated. By using *IP filtering*, IPSec will examines all the IP packets for addresses, ports, and transport protocols. It then takes this information and compares it to rules that are contained in local or group policies that are designed to tell IP Security to either ignore or secure specific packets. All this can be done by using the addressing and protocol information.

IP Security can be broken down into six components:

- First there is the IP Security (IPSec) driver that is used to monitor, filter, and secure the traffic.
- *The Internet Security Association Key Management Protocol (ISAKMP/Oakley)* key exchange and management services are put into place to oversee the security negotiations that go on between hosts. ISAKMP/Oakley will also provide keys for use with the appropriate security algorithms.
- There is also the Policy Agent. It is up to the policy agent to look for the appropriate policies and deliver these policies to the IPSec driver and ISAKMP.
- Another piece of the puzzle is the IP Security Policy and all of the security associations that are gathered from those policies. These are the pieces that are used to define the security environment in which the two hosts must finally communicate.
- Earlier, we saw that the security association API will provide the actual programming interface that will be used between the IPSec driver, ISAKMP, and the Policy Agent.
- The final pieces are the management tools that are used to create the policies, keep track of the IP Security statistics, and create and log the appropriate IP Security events.

So, what is the process that IPSec uses to determine how to handle a packet? The process goes like this:

1. First it is determined that an IP packet really does match one of the IP filters that have been defined as part of an IP Security policy.
2. This IP Security policy can have several different types of security method. It is up to the IPSec driver to determine which method is going to be used to secure the packet. So, the IPSec driver will request that ISAKMP help by negotiating the security method and the appropriate security key.
3. ISAKMP handles the negotiations and determines the security method and sends that method, along with a security key, to the IPSec driver.
4. At this point, the security method and the security key become the IPSec *security association (SA)*. The IPSec driver takes this information and stores this SA in its database.
5. Now, both communicating hosts need to decide if there is going to be secure or unsecure IP traffic. Both communicating partners need to know about and store the SA.

Now the question is, what are these mysterious security methods the IPSec driver applies to an IP packet? To make matters somewhat simpler, there are just two security methods that can be used. These methods can be used either separately or together. The two methods handle the data and the address integrity through keyed hashing and/or data integrity plus confidentiality through encryption.

In order for any of this to work, the two computers in question must agree on what is going to happen and how. That means that when the data packets are encrypted as they cross the wire, there must be an SA between the two computers that are involved in the communication. The administrator has to first define how these two machines will trust each other. Once that has been determined, then it must be specified how the computers are going to secure their traffic. All of the pieces of this configuration are contained in an IPSec policy that has been created by the administrator and has been applied on the local computer or by using a Group Policy in Active Directory. We will look at the Group Policy objects for IPSec a little later in this chapter.

IPSec Encryption and Management

Designing an IPSec implementation is like most other projects. The first time you look at it, it can be somewhat overwhelming, but if you break it down in chunks, it gets easier. Let's start at the beginning.

Microsoft Exam Objectives

Design an IPSec solution.

- Design an IPSec encryption scheme.
- Design an IPSec management strategy.

As you know by now, when you think of encryption, you can think of locking up something valuable in a safety deposit box and sticking the key in your pocket. If anyone wants to get into the safety deposit box, they have to have your key, or they have to figure out a way to get one that is just like it. Well, the same is true when we start looking at encrypting data. Here, the data is encrypted using a key that is in the form of an algorithm. This algorithm takes the data and renders it unreadable to anyone who does not have knowledge of the key. These data encryption keys are determined when the two systems connect. This is part of the negotiation process that we will discuss later. Because communication is a two-way street, the use of data encryption can be initiated by your computer or by the server you are connecting to.

The availability of IPSec encryption features in Windows 2000 is subject to United States export regulations, and may also be subject to your local and national regulations.

IPSec Basics

The whole purpose of IPSec is to make data so difficult to decrypt that an attacker will give up because it is either too hard or just impossible to interpret. Usually, making things very difficult is enough to cause the attacker to go play somewhere else. In any case, there is the combination of the algorithm and a key that is used to secure this information. The higher level of security is achieved by using the complex cryptography-based algorithms and keys. When we are talking about IPSec, the algorithm is the mathematical process the information is put through to make it secure; the key, on the other hand, is the secret code or a number that is required to read, modify, or verify the secured data.

Here are some of the things that IPSec uses to protect your information.

Automatic Key Management

We have discussed different types of keys and different types of key management throughout this book. With IPSec, key management can be automatic. The first thing that has to be done with the key is to have it generated.

Key Generation

Before two computers can communicate securely, they have to be able to agree on a key. Now, this is not as simple as it sounds. At first blush, you might think that one computer would generate the key and send it to the other, and communication would start. That would work, as long as there was some guarantee that the key would not be intercepted. The two computers just have to determine and use the same, shared key. To make the process somewhat more challenging, this should be done without sending that key across the network where it could possibly be sniffed. To accomplish this, IPSec uses the *Diffie-Hellman* algorithm to enable this key exchange, and to provide the key material for any of the other encryption keys.

The two computers start the Diffie-Hellman process. The computers will then have to exchange an intermediate result publicly and securely. This is done using authentication. Neither computer can ever send the actual key. However, by using the shared information that comes from the intermediate exchange, each computer can generate an identical secret key. Then, to make sure this stays really secure, it is up to expert users to change the default key that is exchanged and to alter data encryption key settings.

Key Lengths

The longer the key, the more possible combinations there are. Every time the length of a key is incremented by just one bit, the number of possible keys doubles. As the number of possible keys grows, it becomes exponentially more difficult to break or decipher the key. The IPSec Security negotiation that goes on between these two computers generates two kinds of shared secret keys. There are master keys and there are session keys. Master keys are long, usually either 768 bits or 1,024 bits long. The master keys are then used as the source from which the session keys are derived. Session keys come from the master keys in a standard way. There is one session key allowed for each encryption and integrity algorithm.

Dynamic Rekeying

To make the communication even more secure, IPSec can be configured to automatically generate new keys during the course of a communication. In this case, even if an attacker had compromised a single key, she could not obtain the entire communication. In addition, the default keying intervals can be changed.

IPSec Protocols

When you decide to use IPSec, you can choose between one of two different protocols. They are the *Authentication Headers (AH)* or *Encapsulating Security Payloads (ESP)*. Each of the protocols can be used to provide security for different purposes. These purposes can be generically broken down into data integrity, authentication, confidentiality, nonrepudiation, and anti-replay/anti-spoofing. Let's take a quick look at them one at a time.

Integrity

Earlier in the book, we laid out some of the dangers of sniffers. They really are easy to obtain and you would be amazed at what you can see and do as information crosses the wire. Data *integrity* is what protects information from any type of unauthorized modification while it is on the wire. This makes sure that the information that has been received is exactly the same information that was sent. This is done by making use of mathematical hash functions to mark, or "sign," each and every packet. The receiving computer is responsible for checking the signature before it opens the packet. If the signature has been changed, it means the packet has been changed. That means the packet will be discarded to guard against a possible network attack. The Authentication Headers provide this authentication, integrity, and anti-replay protection for the IP header and for the entire data payload that is carried in the packet. The process means that the data is readable while it travels the wire, but it is protected from modification during the time it is being transported.

Authentication

Another problem that arises could be called the how-do-I-know-you-are-who-you-say-you-are syndrome. It is up to *authentication* to verify the origin and also verify the integrity of each message by making sure of the genuine identity of each of the computers that is part of the communication process. Without this strong authentication, any unknown computer can be suspect, and that can include any information it sends. There are multiple types of authentication that may be listed in each policy. This to ensure that some form of common authentication method is found for Windows 2000 domain members, as well as for any computers that are not running Windows 2000, and even for remote computers. Both AH and ESP assure the sender and the receiver that only they are sending and receiving the IP packets. The AH provides authentication, integrity, and anti-replay protection for both the IP header and the data payload that is carried in the packet. Again, the IP header and all the data are readable while on the wire, but they are protected from modification during transport through the network infrastructure.

Confidentiality

Confidentiality makes sure that the data is given only to its intended recipients. When it is put in place, the Encapsulating Security Payload (ESP) format of IPSec packets is used. With ESP, the packet data is encrypted before it is transmitted. This makes sure that the data cannot be read while it is being transmitted. This is true even if the packet is sniffed or intercepted by a potential attacker. Only the computer that has the shared, secret key is able to open, read or change the data. The United States Data Encryption Standard (*DES*) algorithms, DES and 3DES, are used to make sure the security negotiations and the exchange of data are confidential.

Cipher Block Chaining (CBC), on the other hand, is used to disguise patterns of identical blocks of data that may occur within a certain packet. CBC does not increase the size of the data after it has been encrypted. The reason this is important is that repeated encryption patterns can actually compromise security by providing a clue that the attacker can use to try to discover the encryption key. An Initialization Vector, which is a fancy name for an initial random number, is used as the first random block to encrypt and decrypt a block of data. These different random blocks are then used with the secret key to encrypt each block. This makes sure that identical sets of unsecured data are changed into unique sets of encrypted data.

Nonrepudiation

Nonrepudiation is the process that make sure the sender of a message is the only person who could have sent the message; this also means that the sender cannot deny having sent the message. Think of it as instant credibility.

Anti-replay

Anti-replay can be called replay prevention. Anti-replay is designed to make sure that each IP packet is unique. Therefore any message that has been captured by an attacker can't be reused or replayed in an attempt to establish a session. Both AH and ESP formats provide sequence numbers in each packet, which are checked when the packet is received. Thus the receiver knows that the packets were not captured in the past and then retransmitted by an attacker.

Data Encryption

Only ESP provides data confidentiality through data encryption of the contents of the IP packet. ESP does provide an option to provide both integrity and authenticity, but not the privacy that is similar to what AH provides. ESP is not able to protect the IP header from modifications, whereas AH can protect at least the address information in the IP header. ESP can be used alone or in combination with AH. So, when you configure IPSec on your network, start by figuring out what role you want IPSec to play. If you are ensuring that only authorized users are allowed to communicate with a specific server using a predetermined protocol, you can configure Authentication Headers. If AH cannot be used by the client, communication will not take place.

If you want the actual data flow to be encrypted, configure IPSec filter actions to use ESP. This will ensure that all data that matches the filter list and that is transmitted between the client and the server will be encrypted. The bottom line is that it is up to you to determine how best to use these tools.

IPSec Policies

Now that we know how we *want* the two computers to communicate, it is up to the computers to figure out how to communicate that way. Like all good communications, this will involve some negotiations.

Now when communication starts, the IP Security (IPSec) Policy's negotiation policy can either allow or disallow unsecured traffic. If two computers that support IPSec communicate with each other, they establish security associations that are determined through negotiation of the Internet Security Association and Key Management Protocol (ISAKMP) and IPSec Policy rules. If either of two computers does not support IPSec, they must communicate without security. This is called a *soft association*. Clients that are based on earlier versions of Windows do not support IPSec communication and cannot communicate unless soft associations are permitted.

Microsoft Exam Objectives

Design an IPSec solution.

- Design negotiation policies.
- Design security policies.

So, what is to negotiate? Obviously, if we have two computers that are IPSec aware, communication should proceed smoothly. Let's take a look at two other types of scenarios, things like an IPSec computer trying to initiate the communication with a non-IPSec computer, or a non-IPSec computer trying to start things off. You can depend on the default negotiations described here, or you can configure your own negotiation policies, described in the "IPSec Custom Policies" section later in the chapter.

IPSec-Aware Computers Trying to Communicate with Non–IPSec-Aware Computers

In the first case, we have a computer that has been configured with IPSec trying to initiate communication with a computer that is not configured to use IPSec. The communication process would go something like this:

1. The initiating computer sends an ISAKMP request to the non-IPSec-aware computer and receives a "destination unreachable" response back from the responding computer. This is because the non-IPSec-aware computer cannot send or receive ISAKMP messages using UDP port 500. The ISAKMP message gets to the client, but the client does not "understand" the packet.
2. The initiating computer tries this four times.
3. The IPSec policy can allow for unsecured communications. This is called making a "soft association" with the remote computer. A soft association tells the IPSec driver to use no security between the two addresses and sets the security operation for that security association to *None*. This setting allows unsecured packets to be transmitted across the wire.

It should be interesting to see that the ISAKMP communication takes place at UDP port 500. That would be one of the ports you would have to look at to allow communication through your firewall, and it would also be something relatively easy for the test writers to pick up on.

Non–IPSec-Aware Computer Trying to Communicate with IPSec-Aware Computer

In the second case, the computer that is not IPSec-aware is starting the communication. Obviously, the communication is not going to start at UDP port 500.

1. The non-IPSec computer initiates communication by sending an unsecured packet to the IPSec-aware computer. The IPSec-aware computer contains rules for responding as well as initiating, as stated above. If the inbound packets match an IP filter, the associated filter actions are followed. The IPSec computer sends an ISAKMP request for security association negotiation to the non–IPSec-aware computer. The IPSec computer can raise the security level if possible, but the non–IPSec-aware computer cannot do so.

2. The responding IPSec-aware computer attempts to negotiate four times, but the initiator cannot reply to any of the attempts.

3. The IPSec-aware computer then checks its security policy to set up a soft association if allowed, or it ignores the incoming insecure packets. If the policy does not allow unsecured communication, the IPSec computer can only communicate with other IPSec computers. The more tightly secured the communications are, the more resource intensive the communication becomes. If the policy does allow unsecured communication, soft associations are allowable. This is less secure and less resource intensive.

So, how can you configure two computers that have IPSec implemented to communicate with each other?

IPSec Communication Modes

Take a look at Figure 15.2; you can see that IPSec communication can happen in one of two ways.

FIGURE 15.2 IPSec communication modes

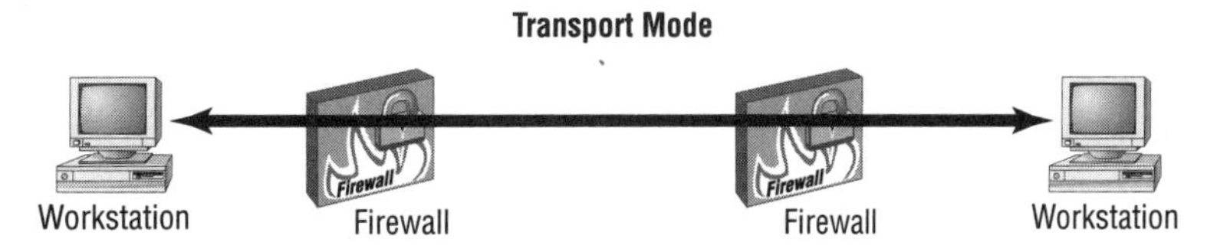

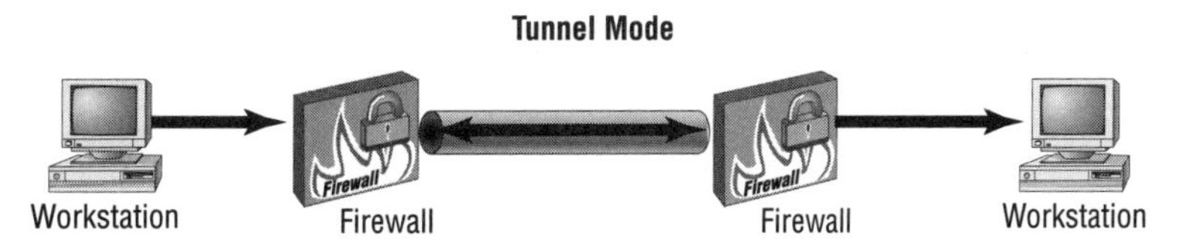

Transport Mode

First of all, the communication can go from end-point to end-point. This is called *transport mode*. In transport mode, we want to ensure that the information moving between your computer and my computer is encrypted and authenticated, so IPSec is configured to work between the two systems. In this case, all traffic that meets an IPSec filter is encrypted between the client and the server computer. This method is usually performed on the LAN by defining a common IPSec policy between the two end-point systems. Transport mode is used in the following cases:

- Communications are taking place between two hosts on the same private network.
- Communications are taking place between two hosts and do not cross a firewall that is performing Network Address Translation (NAT).

If you remember back from Chapter 14, "Providing Secure Access at the Network Level," IPSec cannot pass through NAT because the fields that are translated are included in the IPSec protected fields.

Tunnel Mode

IPSec encrypts all traffic transmitted between the client and server systems as it traverses between the two end-points of the tunnel. Data is decrypted when it reaches the end-point nearest the destination computer. *Tunnel mode* is used in the following cases:

- You only need encryption of data over an insecure portion of a network. For example, if two partner organizations want to encrypt data between their offices on the Internet, it may be configured to only encrypt between the firewall computers at each office.

IPSec Group Policies

Depending on the size and complexity of your organization and its IPSec needs, defining IPSec group policies could be extremely simple, or it could be a project by itself. Windows 2000 does have some predefined IPSec policies that may meet your organization's needs. In addition, you always have the opportunity to design your own using an MMC. We will call those policies custom policies.

Predefined IPSec Policies

You can get to the predefined IPSec Policies by opening a Microsoft Management Console and adding in the Group Policy Snap-in. We chose to do it for the local computer. After selecting *finish*, click OK enough times to get back to the actual MMC with the Local Computer Policy snap-in in place. Open the Local Computer Policy ➤ Computer Configuration ➤ Windows Settings ➤ Security Settings ➤ IP Security Policies on Local Machine. When you get to this point, your screen should look like Figure 15.3.

FIGURE 15.3 IPSec MMC with predefined policies

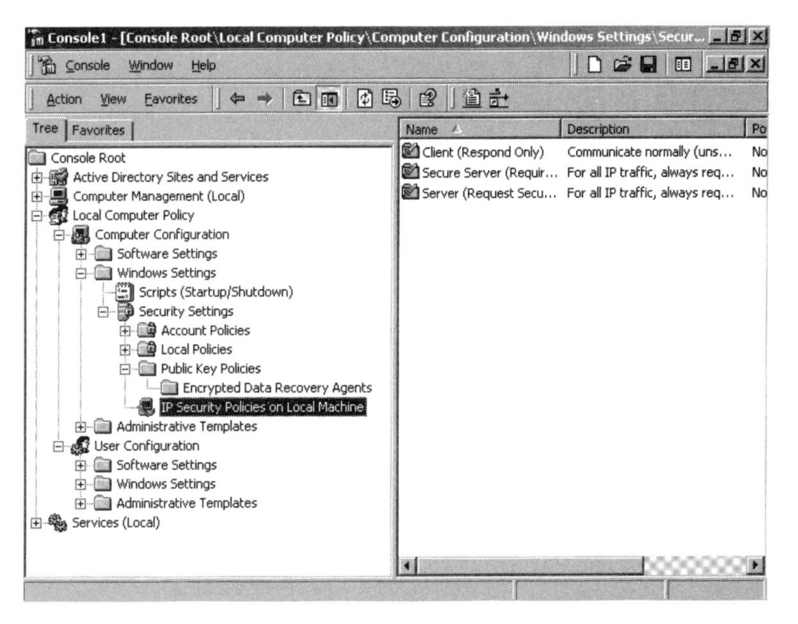

Once you get there, you will see that there are three predefined and disabled policies. These policies are defined in Table 15.1.

TABLE 15.1 Predefined IPSec Security Policies

Policy	Purpose	Used For
Client (Respond Only)	This policy is usually assigned to the domain group security policy to ensure all computers can respond as needed to requests for secure communications. The client will not initiate a request to use IPSec for transmission of data, but will enter a negotiation for Internet Key Exchange (IKE) when requested. If you require IPSec protection on a network, it is a good idea to assign this IPSec policy at the domain level.	Computers
Secure Server (Require Security)	This policy is assigned to ensure that outgoing communication never falls back to unsecured if negotiations fail or if the other computer is not IPSec-capable. Even communication with domain controllers is negotiated and secured. This policy is most appropriate when a predefined data stream must be encrypted. Due to the strictness of this policy, you may need to add exemptions for special traffic types such as SNMP traffic.	Highest Security Servers
Server (Request Security)	This policy is assigned to servers that will communicate with both Windows 2000 and non–Windows 2000 clients. If the client can use IPSec, all defined communication will use IPSec. If the client does not support IPSec, communication can occur using standard data transmissions. This policy is most appropriate when in a mixed network where both Windows 2000 and non–Windows 2000 clients will communicate with the server	Secure Servers

IPSec Custom Policies

It would be wonderful if everything fit into the three predefined policies, but since we don't live in a cookie cutter world, the chances of your organization getting by using just those three policies may be remote. So let's take a look at how to create custom policies.

This section is going to encompass the last three subobjectives, but it will not necessarily be neat and clean and segmented perfectly. In this case there is a lot of overlap, so just be aware as you look this stuff over, you will be getting a lot of bang for your buck!

Microsoft Exam Objectives

Design an IPSec solution.

- Design security policies.
- Design IP filters.
- Define security levels.

Start at the Beginning

Now we are going to review somewhat. We are going to go way back in the book to where we were originally setting security levels for different types of data. We formed a committee and then sat down and tried to decide what the cost would be to the organization if certain resources were lost, altered, or stolen. In addition, we viewed this from a variety of perspectives: How much would it affect the operation of the company over the short term, intermediate term, and long term? How much time and money would it cost to return the company to "normal" operations?

This is not rocket science. You simply start out by making a list of secure objects. Any object that does not appear to be the focus of security concerns should still be examined, because you want to make sure that the object does not create a backdoor access to other secured objects.

Once you get your list of assets, rate them as high, medium, or low in terms of their impact on the organization should they be compromised. Take a look at Table 15.2 to see the kind of thing we are talking about.

TABLE 15.2 Determining Impact Level for Different Data Types

Type of data	Impact level
Accounting	High
Customer list	High
Research data	High
Marketing plan	Medium
Human resource resume tracking	Medium
Prospects	Low
Parking permits	Low

We did say to do this at a committee level. This is not because we love committee meetings. The exact opposite is the case. It is because you will need to get a variety of input on these security levels. For example, the Customer list may have very little impact on the life of the security guard, but would obviously be critical to the workings of the sales manager.

Defining the IPSec Policies

So, now you take the information and lay out a diagram of communication flow. For example, if accounting data has a high security level, then you will probably want communications between the server that contains the accounting information and the accounting workstations to be run using IPSec. So now you have to define the IPSec policy.

An IPSec policy has three main components:

- IP Security rules
- IP filter lists
- IP filter actions

IPSec Policy Configuration

To start this off, let's go back to the IPSec MMC that we created a few pages ago, and take a look at the most secure setting, *Secure Server (Require Security)*. When we got back into the MMC, we double-clicked Secure Server (Require Security) and opened the window shown in Figure 15.4.

FIGURE 15.4 Secure Server (Require Security)

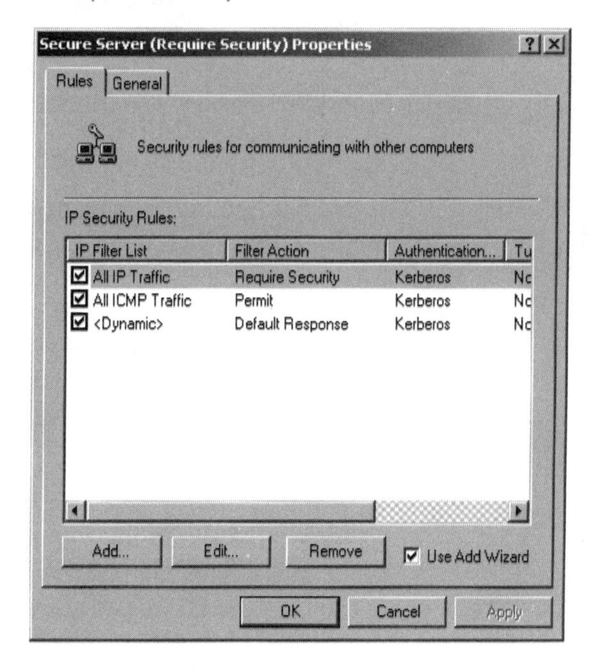

As you can see, there are two tabs: Rules and General. Rules are applied to computers that match the criteria specified in a filter list. The IP filter list contains source and destination IP addresses. Now, before you start to hyperventilate thinking about all the IP addresses you would have to add to this list, the source or destination can either be an IP address or a network ID. That may not be much of a comfort, but we try.

You are probably wondering about what this is going to do to things like DHCP. Well, implementing IPSec can have some impact on the way certain services interact with client computers. For example, if you think about what you have already learned about IPSec and what you already know about things like DHCP and DNS, you will recognize this can be a problem. If you have a server that is set to Secure Server (Require Security) and it is also running DHCP, that means that each client has to be running IPSec or the server will ignore any inbound request. The server ignores the inbound request aimed at the DHCP service, and the client does not get an IP address. See where that could be an issue?

When communication is coming from a machine that has been identified as a participant, the filter action that is specific for that connection will be applied. An example of this would be the All IP Traffic filter list, which includes all computers that communicate with the server via TCP/IP. Any instructions in the filter action associated with the ALL IP Traffic filter will be applied. If, on the Rules tab shown in Figure 15.5, you were to highlight All IP Traffic and click Edit, you would get the screen shown in the graphic below.

FIGURE 15.5 Edit Rules Property All IP Traffic

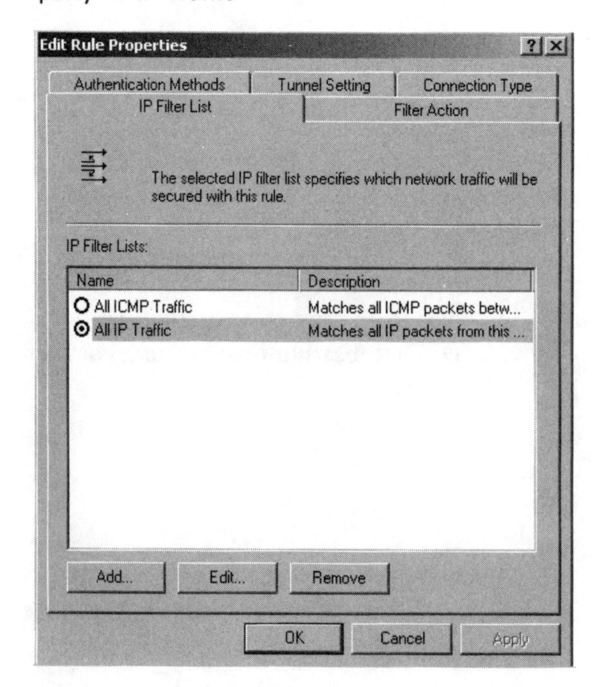

This graphic is an intermediate step to where we really want to go, which is on to the Filter Action tab. Click on that, and your screen should look like Figure 15.6.

FIGURE 15.6 Filter Action tab

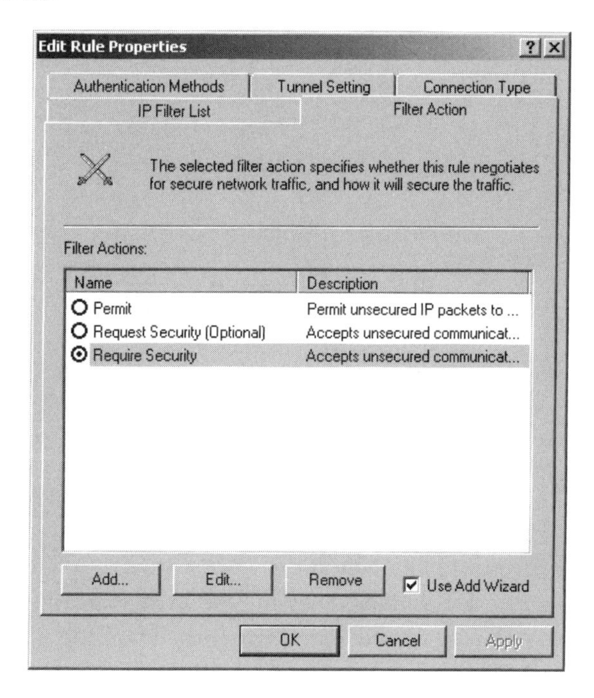

As expected, in this case our filter action requires security. Any communication with this device has to be handled with IPSec. If you wonder what happens when you choose Require Security, click on Edit and you will see all the negotiation choices we discussed earlier in the chapter, including DES and 3DES. To get an idea of what it looks like, if you are not sitting in front of a Windows 2000 Advanced Server, take a look at the screen shot in Figure 15.7.

FIGURE 15.7 Require Security Properties

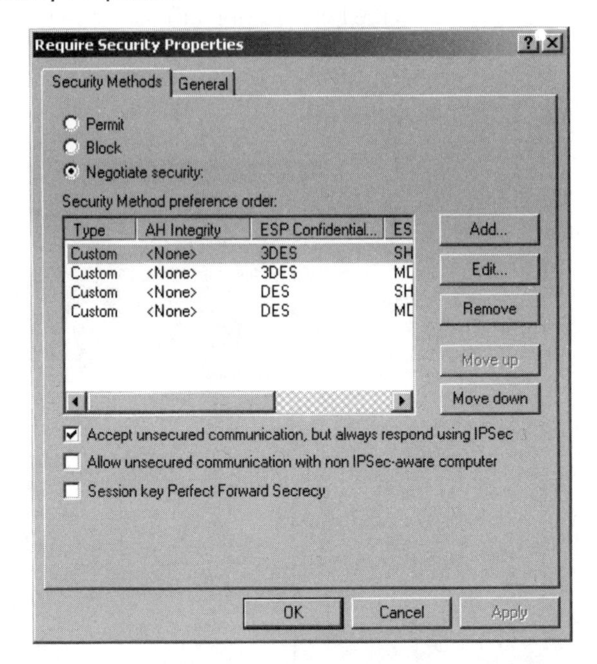

Filter actions, as you can see, are used to define the types of security and the methods by which security is established. The primary methods of security establishment are shown in Table 15.3.

TABLE 15.3 Methods of Security Establishment

Method	Impact
Permit	Blocks negotiation for IP security. This is the appropriate choice if you never want to secure traffic to which this rule applies.
Block	This action blocks all traffic from computers specified in the IP filter list.
Negotiate	Allows the computer to use a list of security methods to determine security levels for the communication. This list is in descending order of preference. If the Negotiate security action is selected, both computers must be able to come to an agreement regarding the security parameters included in the list. The entries are processed sequentially in the order of preference. The first method the two systems have in common is enacted.

Now, if you are really observant, you have noticed that there are three check-boxes on the bottom of the dialog box. These check-boxes represent the following choices:

Accept unsecured communication, but always respond using IPSec Allows unsecured communication initiated by another computer but requires the computers to which this policy applies to always use secure communication when replying or initiating.

Allow unsecured communication with non-IPSec-aware computers Allows unsecured communications to or from another computer. This is used if the computers in the IP filter list are not IPSec enabled. If negotiation for security fails, this will disable IPSec for all communication to which this rule applies.

Session Key Perfect Forward Secrecy Ensures that session keys or keying material are not reused. Selecting *Session Key Perfect Forward Secrecy* also ensures that new Diffie-Hellman exchanges will take place after the session key lifetimes have expired.

There are a few more tabs we should look at before we finish. Figure 15.8 shows the next tab, for Authentication Methods.

FIGURE 15.8 Authentication Methods configuration tab

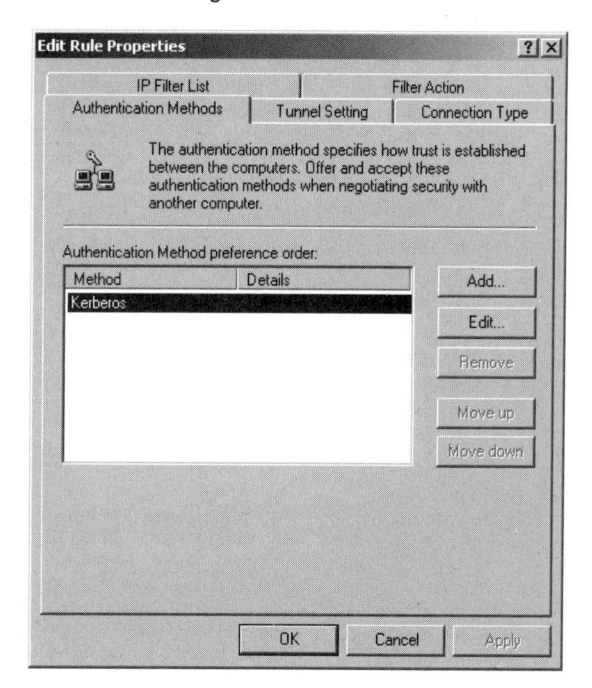

By default, Kerberos is the default authentication method. You can include other methods in the list, and each will be processed in descending order. Clicking Add will give you the opportunity to add additional methods.

Had you clicked the Tunnel tab, you would have seen the screen shown in Figure 15.9.

FIGURE 15.9 Tunnel Setting tab

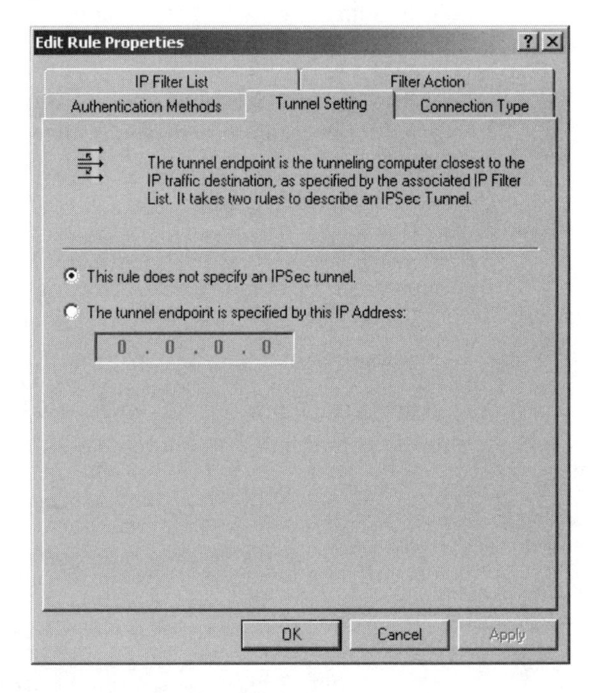

You would need to use the Tunnel setting if the end-point for the filter is a tunnel end-point. Click the Connection Type tab to apply the rule to all network connections, Local Area Network (LAN), or Remote Access. The Connection Type tab is shown in Figure 15.10.

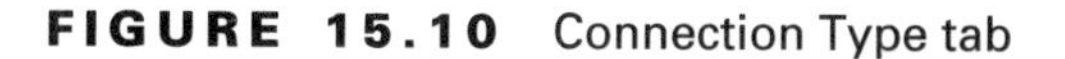

FIGURE 15.10 Connection Type tab

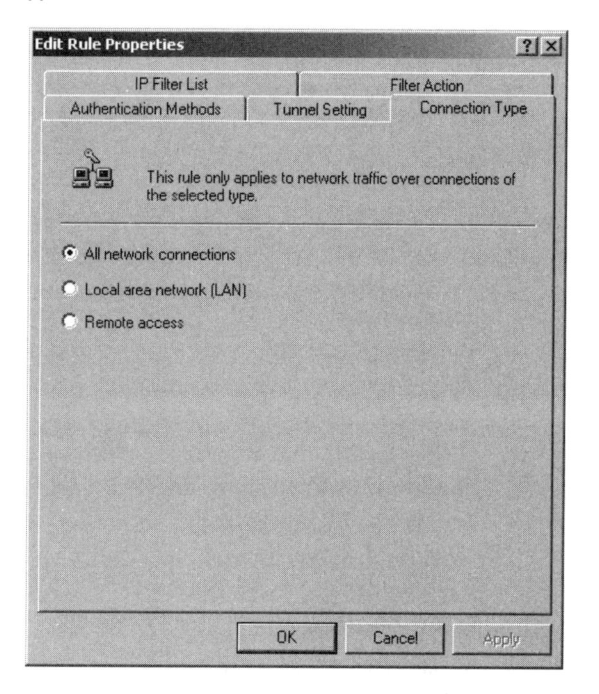

IPSec Best Practices

Some of these may map to the objectives, and some may not. You didn't buy this book just to pass the test—you probably wanted more out of it, didn't you? We will call this part a brief value add! These are some of the IPSec Best Practices that Microsoft suggests.

To start, let's look at IKE. The *Internet Key Exchange (IKE)* uses encryption to make sure the security negotiations are really secure. It also uses the IPSec component of TCP/IP to encrypt the application data packets. IKE has to be able to use at least DES encryption to secure the negotiations.

When you define your IPSec policies, you are given the ability to chose a strong encryption algorithm, *3DES*. Triple DES is more secure because it uses a longer key length than DES. As we have seen before, a longer key length makes for higher security. Like all policies, this one will be received by all computers to which the policy is assigned. However, not all of those computers may be able to implement it. Windows 2000 computers have to have the High Encryption Pack installed to use the 3DES algorithm. If a computer receives a 3DES setting from the policy, but does not have the High Encryption Pack installed, then the 3DES setting in encryption policy is reset to take advantage of the weaker DES.

IP Filter Lists

As we mentioned above, creating an IP filter list could turn into a job and a half. When you start defining your filters, start by using the general filters. Assign the general filter to a group of computers with just one filter. For example, try using Any IP address or an IP subnet address, rather than specifying a specific computer's source and destination IP address. Once this has been done, test it to make sure the results you receive are the results you wanted.

Remember that when you define any filters, do it in a way that gives you the opportunity to group and secure traffic coming from and going to related segments of your network. As always, test, test, and test before there is any final implementation.

Filter Actions

What should you do if you need to stop communications with a group or unauthorized computers? It this case, you can make sure that the security is not negotiated for data that is deemed to be nonessential. The same should be true when peers are not IPSec-enabled. Be sure to make use of the filter actions like packet blocking *(Block)* or by using the pass-through policies *(Permit)*.

If you decide that you need to define some custom security settings, set only the ESP confidentiality selection to *None*. This should be done when it is up to a higher-layer protocol to provide data encryption.

If you are dealing with a remote communication scenario (including IPSec tunneling), you will want to define a list of security methods. These methods should specify high levels of security, using things like 3DES only. It should also define short key lifetimes, and also Perfect Forward Secrecy for the master and session keys. This will help protect against a variety of known key attacks.

Remote Access Communications

To continue with our discussion of remote access communications, let's take a look at L2TP. If your network is going to be using L2TP for remote access, the list of authentication methods should be configured to contain certificates, as well as at least one computer-level public key certificate. This certificate must be configured on each peer computer. If you want, you can configure your Windows 2000 domain controllers so that they will auto-enroll the domain members with a certificate authority.

In order to protect against network attacks on a remote access server, you should make sure to activate the predefined filter action, *Require Security*. You should also be sure to be very careful when you are enabling *Allow unsecured communication with non-IPSec-aware computers* and *Accept unsecured communication but always respond using IPSec*. Allowing unsecured communications can cause some unexpected security problems.

When you are configuring the IP filter list that will be used for the remote access server, do not set the filters to *My IP Address*. In many cases, these types of computers will usually have multiple interfaces and several different IP addresses. If you do mistakenly set the filter to *My IP Address*, IPSec will try to enforce that filter on all of the network interfaces installed on that server. In order to bypass this problem, configure the filter to the IP address of the interface that sends and receives just the traffic you want to secure.

SNMP

If a particular server or host will be running the SNMP service, you have to add a rule that will prevent the SNMP messages from being blocked:

- To make sure that the SNMP packets can get through, you should configure the IP filter list to specify both the source and destination addresses of the SNMP management systems and all the agents. The Protocol type should be set to UDP, to and from ports 161 and 162. This will require two filters: one for UDP, to and from port 161, and the other for UDP, to and from port 162.

- The filter action should be set to *Permit*. This will block negotiation for security and pass through any traffic that matches the IP filter list.

Internet Access Points

An Internet access point can be a security gateway, a firewall, a proxy server, a router, or really any server that gives the intranet access to the outside world. For security purposes, there is some special filtering that should be enabled to make sure that the packets that are secured with IPSec are not rejected. At a minimum, you should define the following inbound and outbound filters for the Internet portal:

Inbound Filters

This is the set of filters that define what can come into your network from the public network.

- IP Protocol ID of 51 (0x33) for inbound IPSec Authentication Header traffic.
- IP Protocol ID of 50 (0x32) for inbound IPSec Encapsulating Security Protocol traffic. UDP port 500 (0x1F4) for inbound ISAKMP/Oakley negotiation traffic.

Outbound Filters

These are the filters that define what kinds of packets can leave the private network for the public network.

- IP Protocol ID of 51 (0x33) for outbound IPSec Authentication Header traffic.
- IP Protocol ID of 50 (0x32) for outbound IPSec Encapsulating Security Protocol traffic. UDP port 500 (0x1F4) for outbound ISAKMP/Oakley negotiation traffic.

DHCP, DNS, and WINS Services; Domain Controllers

When you decide to use a server that has IPSec enabled to also provide things like DHCP, DNS, WINS, or even as a domain controller, you need to make sure that any and all of the clients are also IPSec-capable. Otherwise, secure negotiation will probably fail, access to the network resource will be blocked, and your phone will ring.

DNS

Suppose you want to specify a particular DNS name in an IP filter list. If your DNS servers are not IPSec-enabled, you will have to come up with a special policy setting—otherwise, IPSec and even the other services on the server may not be able to resolve the DNS computer name to a valid IP address.

You will have to define the IP filter list so that it will exempt traffic between the computer and the DNS server from requiring IPSec:

- Set the Source address to My IP address.
- Set the Destination address to the IP address of your DNS server.
- Enable Mirrored to automatically create the inbound filter.
- Configure the protocol settings, From this Port and To this Port, to the port which your DNS server has been configured to use for traffic. It is generally port 53.

Set the filter action to Permit. This will make sure that the DNS traffic passes through and security will never be negotiated for any traffic that matches this IP filter list.

Design Scenario: Dang, It Used To Work Just Fine!

You were sitting at your desk, minding your own business and thinking about how wonderful things were going to be over the holiday weekend. You didn't get stuck on call, there were no major projects, and it looked like, for once, you were not going to be needed. You might actually get to enjoy the three-day weekend like a normal person.

You were interrupted from your daydream by the phone. Someone called up and said they were having a difficult time locating things on the network. You asked, "like what?" and were surprised to note that the intranet server had suddenly disappeared. About that time, one of your partners walked in scratching her head and asked if you had done anything to the DHCP server. You asked why, and she said that she had been configuring a laptop, had put a network card into it and booted it up, but it couldn't get an IP address. Everything looked okay, so she tried assigning the system a static address and suddenly she could ping the rest of the network, but she could not get to the intranet Web server.

Then you were perplexed, so you opened up the Web browser on your system, and sure enough, you couldn't find it either. Hmm. Curious. You tried to ping the IP address of the server and that worked just fine. You then tried putting in the IP address as the URL instead of the host name, and that worked just fine.

More people started calling and couldn't find other things on the network. As they described what they were doing, it should have worked just fine; you went out and made a DNS request, the IP address was returned, and life was good...wait a minute, what about the DNS server? You went out to a command prompt and pinged the DNS server by address and it was there. When you used the host name, it was not found. No problem, you checked the DNS server, and sure enough the service was up, and there were people who could access the server. What the heck was going on here?

Just about that time, the IT cowboy comes in. This is the person who is famous for institute now and test later. Every department has one. He is smiling to himself and singing a little tune. When you ask why the heck he is so dang chipper, he tells you he has just configured an IPSec configuration that will protect all sorts of information. After you ask a few questions, he mentions Secure Server and the IP address of the server running DNS and DHCP, and now things start to make sense. When he secured the server, all those hosts not configured to use IPSec were left out in the cold. Once again, you patiently explain the proper testing procedures, while you are on your way to fix the problem.

Summary

In this chapter, we spent some time talking about the way that Windows 2000 works and plays well with other file systems, and how these different file systems interact with Server Message Blocks, or SMB. These can work with Apple systems, Novell systems, and Unix machines.

Then we looked at the different ways you can configure IP Security to maintain secure communications between hosts on the same network and by setting up a tunnel between hosts on different networks. When you think of all the options you have to configure IPSec on your network, you can see how difficult it would make the life of an intruder. Keep in mind, as you begin to institute these IPSec policies, one wrong click and all of a sudden the rest of the system may not recognize a key resource on your network. It is always a very good idea to test, test, and test an implementation before putting it into production. This is certainly a very valid suggestion when talking about IPSec.

Key Terms

Before you take the exam, be certain you are familiar with the following terms:

anti-replay

3DES

Authentication Headers (AH)

DES

Diffie-Hellman

Encapsulating Security Payloads (ESP)

Gateway Service for NetWare (GSNW)

Internet Key Exchange (IKE)

Internet Protocol Security (IPSec)

Internet Security Association Key Management Protocol (ISAKMP/Oakley)

IP filtering

Layer 2 Tunneling Protocol (L2TP)

NetWare Core Protocol (NCP)

Network File System (NFS)

nonrepudiation

Secure Server (Require Security)

security association (SA)

Server (Request Security)

Server Message Blocks (SMB)

Services for Unix (SFU)

Session Key Perfect Forward Secrecy

transport mode

tunnel mode

User Datagram Protocol (UDP)

Review Questions

1. If you are using SMB with Unix, you have two methods of implementing security. What are they?

   A. Active Directory

   B. Workgroup-level security

   C. GPOs

   D. Windows NT 4 domain-level security

2. Which file system is used by Unix systems?

   A. NTFS

   B. FAT32

   C. NFS

   D. NCP

   E. DES

3. How do you configure SMB signing?

   A. Through the Group Policy object snap-in to MMC

   B. Through a wizard

   C. Editing the registry

   D. From the tools menu of Control Panel

   E. Using a Unix-based management tool

4. What does IPSec use to encapsulate all the protocols in the TCP/IP protocol suite?

   A. DES

   B. ESP

   C. 3DES

   D. AH

   E. L2TP

   F. FTP

5. In IPSec, what is it that monitors, filters, and secures traffic?

   A. DES

   B. IPSec driver

   C. AH

   D. ESP

   E. TCP

   F. IP

6. What part of IPSec oversees security negotiations between hosts and provides keys for use with security algorithms?

   A. DES

   B. Diffie-Hellman

   C. IEK

   D. IKE

   E. ISA

   F. ISAKMP

7. What provides the interface between the IPSec driver and the Policy Agent?

   A. SA

   B. 3DES

   C. AH

   D. ESP

   E. PES

   F. AARP

8. Name the two IPSec packet formats.

   A. SA

   B. 2DES

   C. AH

   D. ESP

   E. PES

   F. AARP

9. Which of the two packet formats in IPSec can ensure confidentiality of data?

   A. SA

   B. 3DES

   C. AH

   D. ESP

   E. PEZ

   F. AARP

10. What is nonrepudiation?

    A. It means anyone could have sent the message.

    B. It means that only computers on a particular sub-net could have sent the message.

    C. It means the message is totally invalid and should be discarded.

    D. It ensures that the sender of the message is the only person who could have sent the message.

Answers to Review Questions

1. B, D. With SMB and Unix, the two methods you have of implementing security are workgroup-level and Windows NT 4 domain-level security.

2. C. Unix systems use Network File System (NFS).

3. C. By tweaking the registry, you can configure SMB to use signing.

4. E. IPSec protects all protocols in the TCP/IP protocol suite and Internet communications using the Layer 2 Tunneling Protocol (L2TP).

5. B. The IP Security (IPSec) driver monitors, filters, and secures traffic.

6. F. The Internet Security Association Key Management Protocol (ISAKMP/Oakley) key exchange and management services oversee security negotiations between hosts, and provide keys for use with security algorithms.

7. A. The security association (SA) API provides the interface between the IPSec driver, ISAKMP, and the Policy Agent.

8. C, D. The two IPSec protocols are Authentication Headers (AH) and Encapsulating Security Payloads (ESP).

9. D. Confidentiality ensures that data is disclosed only to intended recipients. When it is selected, the Encapsulating Security Payload (ESP) format of IPSec packets is used. Packet data is encrypted before transmission, ensuring that the data cannot be read during transmission, even if the packet is monitored or intercepted by an attacker.

10. D. Nonrepudiation ensures that the sender of a message is the only person who could have sent the message.

The Multinational Conglomerate

You should give yourself 10 minutes to review this case study, diagram as needed, and complete the questions for this scenario. Be sure to read each question carefully. While the company may not have changed, its circumstances change in each chapter.

Background

Your consulting firm has been hired to assist in the Windows 2000 migration and integration for a company based in Minneapolis, Minnesota. Until the start of this year, the company had 1,000 employees, all based throughout the Twin Cities of Minneapolis and St. Paul. Just before the end of the year, the owner of your company purchased two companies of roughly the same size that will need to be connected to the enterprise network. The total number of users when the project is completed is estimated at 3,500. In addition, each of these companies comes with various strategic partners that will need to access the information on your enterprise network. The companies that have been acquired are located in Athens, Greece, and in Orlando, Florida.

The company is now beginning to look at ways of dealing with remote users and small, local sales offices.

Current System

Minneapolis Located on the shores of beautiful Lake Calhoun, the company occupies a sprawling campus that includes four floors in a six-story building. Since the merger, the Lake Calhoun facility has become a model of efficiency. Besides being linked to all of the other offices, everyone is beginning to take the notion of an enterprise network seriously.

All of the floors are connected to the Windows 2000 network. The Minneapolis location is a domain in the tree. Active Directory Services have been deployed to the main campus and the rollout is complete in the branch offices. The desktop and laptop rollout company-wide took longer than expected, but it is now completed. The CEO wants to know what the IT team is doing to make sure that everyone within the company can access resources all over the tree, as well as protect the network.

The corporate network was so impressive it helped this company snag a very large contract with a very large customer. This customer has suddenly started to make some demands. It wants your company to establish local offices to service its account in several locations worldwide. These offices would house 5 to 10 people and the way it looks now, each office would have its own Windows 2000 servers and a router to the Internet.

Orlando The Orlando office is a domain in the corporate tree. It has some valuable resources that need to be made available to the rest of company, particularly the folks in Athens.

The large contract had a long-term effect on Orlando. Current corporate strategy calls for the new contract to be managed in Minneapolis for the first year, and then moved to Orlando after that. In this case, all the local offices will have to access to Orlando domain.

Athens The Athens office is now fully staffed at 2,300. The location has discovered that the business is doing well, and the extra folks are justified. The office has been upgraded to Windows 2000 servers and Athens is now its own domain in the tree.

Athens has always been ahead of the curve. When the new contract was announced, Athens' manufacturing geared up for the task, and can now handle that stage. Because the customer wants to be able to look at all the stages of inventory, the customer will need to be able to access the Athens facility as well as Minneapolis and Orlando.

Problem Statement

Provide access to all areas of the network for the local offices. In addition, be sure to have a way for remote users to access the network.

Envisioned System

Overview Several of the management team have input on this project, including the CEO, the CFO, the general managers of the Orlando office, and the general manager of the Athens office. At this stage, we have also begun to hear from the sales manager.

CEO As the new network was designed, the CEO was looking closely at the IS department and saying things like, "Okay people, you wanted the Windows 2000 network because of its flexibility and you now have it. This is where the rubber hits the road. Prove you can make this network do the things you said it can do."

CFO "You know, we are still paying the bills for this rollout. While it looks like our overall cost of operation will drop, it is still a large price to absorb. We are now looking at taking a hit for all of these local offices. Make sure that you do everything in your power to maintain costs, while providing all the resources those people need to keep the customer happy."

Orlando General Manager "Sure, I get this project dumped in my lap. Now my budget is going to take the hit for connecting to all these local offices. The costs of leased lines alone will rival my payroll, and I have a hefty payroll! Surely there has got to be a better way?"

Athens General Manager "Why are you talking to me about this? This appears to be a problem for Orlando."

Corporate Sales Manager "Cool. How long have you been having these meetings? Why wasn't I invited? Can we do this over lunch? Oh, and by the way, computer guy, how can my salespeople get information from the network when they are on the road? They keep calling and I have to look it up for them. It's not a problem in the winter, but it is spring and all my clients like to play golf, so I may not be available too much, you know what I mean?"

Questions

1. In Chapter 14, you created a router-to-router VPN. What type of IPSec communication mode is that?

A. IPSec tunneling

B. IPSec transport

C. 3DES VPN

D. Kerberos VPN

E. Remote Access VPN

2. If you wanted to set up tunneling where the servers had to establish a secure connection, how could you do that?

   A. IPSec Policy object

   B. GTO

   C. AH

   D. ESP

   E. At each remote salesperson's home

3. Which of the common security protocols is the default for IPSec?

   A. TCP/IP

   B. PKI

   C. Kerberos

   D. FTP

   E. SNMP

4. Which of the following services cannot be used at all with IPSec?

   A. TCP/IP

   B. L2TP

   C. DNS

   D. DHCP

   E. MS-CHAP

   F. NAT

Answers

1. A. Because the communication is going between two routers over a public network and because it does not involve the end-points in the communications, it would be tunneling.

2. A. You would do it by creating an IPSec Policy object and selecting Secure Server. You could then define tunnel connections between the servers.

3. C. Kerberos is the default security protocol.

4. F. IPSec cannot be used in conjunction with NAT.

Practice Exam

This practice exam takes into account the content of all the review questions in this book. This exam includes 40 review questions and two case studies. Where the case studies at the end of each chapter more or less tried to concentrate on the subject matter of the chapter at hand, these practice exam case studies might include a mixture of topics from several different chapters. This, of course, is the real-life administrator's job: to take into account factors from several different sources and then make a design decision that best meets the business and computing needs of the enterprise at hand.

Review Questions

1. Which of the following is not a task in the Implementation phase?

   A. Evaluation

   B. Test pilot design

   C. Installation

   D. Configuration

2. Select the four design criteria.

   A. Functionality

   B. Effect

   C. Timeliness

   D. Security

   E. Availability

   F. Efficiency

   G. Performance

3. Which of the following is the type of project where actions are determined by the goal of solving a particular business problem?

   A. User-centric

   B. Server-centric

   C. Customer-focused

   D. Workstation-focused

4. Which of the following correctly ranks corporate entities from the top level to the bottom level of the management pyramid?

   A. Staff, middle management, senior management, board of directors, chairman of the board, and shareholders

   B. Shareholders, chairman of the board, board of directors, senior management, middle management, and staff

   C. Chairman of the board, board of directors, shareholders, senior management, middle management, and staff

   D. Senior management, middle management, chairman of the board, board of directors, shareholders, and staff

   E. Senior management, chairman of the board, board of directors, middle management, staff, and shareholders

   F. Shareholders, staff, middle management, senior management, board of directors, and chairman of the board

5. Which of the following is not a type of end user?

   A. External authenticated user

   B. Regular user

   C. Network user

   D. Roaming user

6. Which of the following is a suite of protocols that allow secure, encrypted communication between two computers over an insecure network?

   A. Encryption File System

   B. IP Security

   C. Public Key Encryption

   D. Symmetric Key Encryption

7. Which stage of the decision-making process is concerned with gaining a deeper understanding of the security problem?

   A. Stage 1, problem realization

   B. Stage 3, search for information

   C. Stage 5, evaluation of alternatives

   D. Stage 7, selling the alternative

8. Which of the configurations below is the best for a small business that requires access to the Internet, but not much of an Internet presence?

   A. Bastion host

   B. Three-pronged screened subnet

   C. Mid-ground screened subnet

   D. None of the above

9. Which of the following is not one of the four steps for assessing and managing risks?

   A. Identify risks

   B. Quantify risks

   C. Plan for risks

   D. Solve risks

10. Which of the following is not one of the three ways to do threat assessment?

    A. Tiger team approach

    B. Past threat review

    C. Corporate think tank

    D. System security engineering process

11. Which of the following should be included in the software inventory?

    A. Applications

    B. Version numbers

    C. DLLs

    D. All of the above

12. The logical organization documentation of your network would include which of the following?

    A. Name and address resolution methods

    B. Network card type

    C. OS version

    D. None of the above

13. What is the first step when documenting the bandwidth and performance of a network?

    A. Look for high peak traffic times

    B. Look for low peak traffic times

    C. Create a baseline

    D. Interview users

14. Which of the migration goals makes sure that the users' access to data, resources, and applications is maintained during the migration process?

    A. Minimum disruption to the production environment

    B. Increase mean time between failures

    C. Maintain system performance

    D. Maximize the number of quick wins

15. Domain B is a resource domain that trusts Domain A. After the upgrade, you want to mirror this relationship. Which of the following will do that?

    A. Restructuring resource domains into organizational units

    B. Upgrading the resource domain within the existing forest

    C. Upgrading a resource domain as a tree in a new forest

    D. None of the above

16. Which of the following encryptions uses two keys?

    A. Symmetric Key Encryption

    B. Planar Key Encryption

    C. Public Key Encryption

    D. Sign-on Encryption

17. Which of the following is not a reason to restructure your domain?

    A. You do not like your current domain structure.

    B. You like most of the structure and can do a two-phase migration.

    C. You feel you cannot manage the migration without impacting the production environment.

    D. You need to create more domains due to the user limitation.

18. Which of the following is the most secure method of authentication?

    A. Single sign-on

    B. Random password

    C. Smart card

    D. Cryptic ID

19. Which of the following must be used to authenticate Windows 9x and NT 4 Servers?

    A. Kerberos

    B. NTLM

    C. Clear text

    D. NTFS

20. Which user members have different access control permissions in Windows 2000 than they did in Windows NT?

    A. Everyone and Users

    B. Power users

    C. Administrators

    D. All are the same

21. How often is recovery agent information for an EFS encrypted file refreshed?

    A. Every hour

    B. Every file system operation

    C. Every time the file is closed

    D. Every 600 seconds

22. Which of the following is not true concerning encrypted (EFS) files?

A. Users should not store sensitive data on servers that might be physically at risk.

B. Remote servers must be designated as trusted for delegation.

C. Data is encrypted when it is transmitted over the network.

D. Encrypted files are not accessible to Macintosh clients.

23. What is the upper limit on the number of groups a user can be in?

A. 250

B. 500

C. 750

D. 1,000

24. Which of the following is not a type of certification authority you can create using Microsoft's Certificate Services?

A. Dependent certificate authorities

B. Enterprise subordinate certificate authorities

C. Stand-alone root certificate authorities

D. Enterprise root certificate authorities

25. By default, the certificate database and log files are installed in which directory?

A. `\WINNT\System\Certificates`

B. `\WINNT\System32\CertLog`

C. `\WINNT\System32\Logs`

D. `\WINNT\System\Certs`

26. Which of the following authentication methods passes the authentication credential through a one-way process called hashing?

A. Basic authentication

B. Kerberos v5

C. SSL

D. Digest authentication

27. Identify the two major methods of connecting remote offices to the company network.

A. Dedicated connection

B. Internet

C. Intranet

D. SSL

28. Which of the following is used by NTLM for authentication service?

A. MSV1_0

B. KDC

C. MCIS

D. TCA

29. Which of the following SSL versions is not included in the International version?

A. 40-bit RC2

B. 128-bit RC2

C. 40-bit RC4

D. 512-bit RSA

30. What must the Microsoft CryptoAPI do before it can trust a certificate?

A. Encrypt the root CA

B. Validate the certification path

C. Decrypt the certificate

D. All of the above

31. A certificate practice statement (CPS) describes how requirements of the certificate policy are implemented in which of the following contexts?

A. Operating policies

B. System architecture

C. Physical security

D. All of the above

32. Which of the following components is not part of a VPN connection?

A. VPN server

B. WAN link

C. Tunneling protocols

D. Transit internetwork

33. How can you deny access on a per-group basis that overrides the user account's remote access permission setting?

A. Create a remote access policy and select the Deny check-box.

B. Create a remote access policy and select *Override user permission*.

C. Create a remote access policy and specify a connection constraint that cannot be met.

D. You can't. Group policies cannot override user permission settings.

34. Why can't L2TP be used for VPN traffic when using a NAT?

A. L2TP encrypts the UDP port number.

B. The Generic Routing Encapsulation cannot be translated, even with an editor.

C. The TCP connection is not NAT translatable.

D. The Call ID is not reachable by the editor.

35. Which of the following is one of the resource records found in the DNS database?

A. SOP

B. CX

C. SNA

D. CNAME

36. Which of the following two-zone transfer types does Windows 2000 support?

A. AXFR

B. DXFR

C. IXFR

D. NXFR

37. What default Terminal Services permissions does a User group have?

A. Full control

B. Change

C. User access

D. No access

38. Which of the following protocols can be used by Terminal Services to configure connections for Citrix ICA–based clients?

A. IPX/SPX

B. NetBIOS

C. TCP/IP

D. Asynchronous

E. All of the above

F. None of the above

39. Where do you configure SMB to use signing?

A. Server manager

B. Registry

C. Network manager

D. User manager for domains

40. Which of the protocols below is used by IPSec?

A. ESP

B. AMP

C. AC3

D. HA

Answers to Review Questions

1. A. The three tasks in the Implementation phase are test pilot design, installation, and configuration. This puts the new system or process in place.

2. A, D, E, G. The four design criteria are functionality, security, availability, and performance. These four items should be uppermost in your mind as you begin to analyze your company's business model.

3. C. A customer-focused project is one where the project actions are determined by the goal of solving a particular business problem rather than for the sake of interesting technology.

4. B. The top of the pyramid is the shareholders. This level is followed by the chairman of the board, the board, senior management, middle management, and finally staff.

5. C. The identified end user types include the external authenticated, Internet, regular, roaming, and traveling users.

6. B. Windows 2000 incorporates Internet Protocol Security (IPSec) for data protection of network traffic. It forms the basis of a Virtual Private Network.

7. B. It is important to search for information about the security problem. This can involve both the internal and external environment.

8. A. The bastion host is less expensive and requires less configuration. The screened subnets place all Internet-accessible resources in a separate network segment.

9. D. A, B, and C are correct. The fourth step is *Monitor and manage risks*. This step leads back to step one, *Identify risks*.

10. B. A, C, and D are the three ways of doing a threat assessment. Option B can be an important part of the assessment, but is only one part.

11. D. All of the items above should be included. In addition, the date and time stamp of the data should also be recorded.

12. A. The logical organization documentation includes name and address resolution methods, and the existence and configuration of the services used.

13. C. It is important to create a baseline that uses various times during the day and various days during the week. Without a baseline, changes cannot be evaluated for impact.

14. A. Plans need to be in place to make sure that users' access to data, resources, and applications, as well as a familiar environment, is maintained during and after the migration.

15. C. To mirror the old relationship, you could upgrade the resource domain and make it a tree in a new forest. The tree would then be linked to Domain A using an explicit one-way trust.

16. C. Public key encryption consists of two keys: the public and private keys. Either key can encrypt data that can be decrypted by the other key.

17. D. A, B, and C are the main reasons why you would restructure your domain. Restructuring normally reduces the number of domains since the user limitation in NT 4 has been overcome in Windows 2000.

18. C. The smart card is used instead of a password for interactive logon. It has other security uses as well.

19. B. Windows 2000 maintains compatibility with NT Server 4 and Windows 9x machines by using the NTLM authentication protocol.

20. A. The members of the Everyone and Users groups have read-only permission to most parts of the system and read/write permission only in their own profile folders.

21. B. The recovery agent information is updated every time the file system performs an operation on the file. This can include opening the file, copying the file, and closing the file.

22. C. Files transmitted over the network are not encrypted by EFS. If this is a concern, IPSec must be implemented to provide for encryption between the encrypted storage areas.

23. D. Microsoft indicates that the upper limit on group membership is 1,000 groups. This includes universal, global, domain local, and local computer groups.

24. A. The four types of certification authorities are Enterprise root certificate, enterprise subordinate certificate, stand-alone root certificate, and stand-alone subordinate certificate authorities.

25. B. The certificate database includes log files, which record all certificate transactions. The database that stores the certificates and the log files themselves are placed in the `\WINNT\System32\CertLog` directory, by default.

26. D. The latest World Wide Web Consortium authentication standard is digest authentication. The authentication credential is passed through a one-way process called hashing. The result (called a hash or message digest) cannot be decrypted and doesn't send passwords across the wire.

27. A, B. There are just two major methods of connecting remote offices to the company network: the dedicated connections (dial-up, leased lines) and through the Internet (IAS and RRAS).

28. A. The NTLM security provider uses the MSV1_0 authentication service and NetLogon service on a domain controller for client authentication and authorization information.

29. B. To comply with U.S. export law, Windows 2000 does not include the 128-bit RC2 encryption version in the International SSL implementation.

30. B. Microsoft CryptoAPI must validate the certification path from the certificate to the certificate of the root CA by checking each certificate in the path.

31. D. A CPS specifies the practices that the CA employs to manage the certificates it issues. For example, a certificate policy might specify that the private key cannot be exported, so the CPS describes how this is accomplished by the PKI you deploy.

32. B. A WAN link normally is used to connect two segments of an intranet. It is not a component of a VPN connection.

33. C. To deny access with a Windows-Group condition, the profile properties must specify a connections constraint that cannot be met. For example, select *Restrict dial-in to this number only*, and then enter a phone number that does not exist on the server.

34. A. L2TP encrypts the UDP port number and its value is protected with a cryptographic checksum. Additionally, L2TP cannot be used due to its inability to distinguish multiple IPSec ESP data streams and its inability to change TCP and UDP checksums.

35. D. The CNAME resource record identifies aliases for the host name. This allows the database to identify one host with multiple names. All aliases would be resolved to the same IP address as the first name.

36. A, C. Windows 2000 supports both full zone transfer (AXFR) and incremental zone transfer (IXFR). Windows NT 4 supported only full zone transfer.

37. C. User access permissions are the default setting for the User group. The Administrators and Systems groups have full control, while the Guests group has Guest access.

38. E. IPX/SPX, NetBIOS, asynchronous, and TCP/IP transport protocols can be used when the Citrix ICA protocol and Citrix ICA–based client software are added to the system.

39. B. Changing the registry in the `\System\CurrentControlSet\Services\LanManServer\Parameters` will enable packet signing. The two values are *EnableSecuritySignature* and *RequireSecuritySignature*.

40. A. The two protocols that can be used are Authentication Headers (AH) and Encapsulation Security Payloads (ESP). Each of the protocols can be used to provide security for different purposes.

Case Study 1: Update and Security

You should give yourself 10 minutes to review this case study, diagram as needed, and complete the questions for this testlet.

Background

You have been hired to review a company's current operations, including security, and to help identify the best upgrade path for Windows 2000. The company is headquartered in Las Vegas, and has branches in White Plains (NY) and Anaheim (CA). Each location is a separate network, and no site has Internet access at this point. Communications between the locations is done using 56K modems, on an as needed basis. This worked quite well when the company first started and had just two people in each branch office, but now that the offices have expanded, the modems are too slow. Communication must be improved and centralized data sharing put in place.

Current System

Las Vegas There are 200 employees in the main office. The main office is located close to a major interstate and includes both office space and warehouse space for the distribution center. Most of the employees (125) work in the distribution center, processing orders.

The company owns the building and has three NT 4 servers. One server is for authentication and the other two servers are used for printing and applications. The major application is the customer order application. Customers phone associates, who use the application to take and process the order. Once the order is complete and verified, in the Las Vegas communication flow the application sends a shipping notice to the distribution center, and generates a charge slip in accounting. All transactions are contained in a SQL database using Microsoft's SQL 7.

White Plains and Anaheim Orders received at the branch offices are sent via modem to the ordering department at the end of the day for input into the main system. The branch offices are running the same major application, but since they do not have full communications with the main system, the orders must be combined and batched. All ordered items for the day submitted from Anaheim or White Plains are sent from Las Vegas first thing the next morning to the appropriate branch office. The ordered items are then separated and the individual orders are sent to the customer.

Problem Statement

The current system was put into operation when the company first started eight years ago. The order volume has been increasing slowly each year until the current year when it doubled in the first five months. You have been asked to review the company and help determine how to increase communication and decrease the duplication of effort.

Envisioned System

During your meeting with the owner of the company, you were told that the company must become unified in order processing and shipping. Each branch must be able to communicate with the main office in a timely manner. The owner just installed a cable modem at her home and she wants her company to be able to take advantage of the possibilities of the Internet. She also feels that it is important to have the latest version of software.

Security

The life of this company is the ordering and shipping of their product. Any communication between machines must be secure and protected. The orders contain customer information, including credit card numbers. The owner stressed how important it is to protect this information.

Availability

Orders are taken 24 hours a day and seven days a week. The distribution center is staffed between 7:00 A.M. and 8:00 P.M. PST Monday through Friday, and from 8:00 A.M. until 6:00 P.M. on Saturday. This means that the order system must be available at all times.

Maintainability

The biggest problem here is that while the company has grown, the IT department has not. There are only three people in the IT department at the main office. Each branch office has one person responsible for the computers. The owner has expressed a willingness to hire additional people, if needed, to maintain the system. She wants your opinion at the end of the study on what type of personnel will be needed for the new system. The other concern is that when the system becomes integrated, and available 24x7, there will be a need for 24x7 maintenance. The owner is a bit concerned about the cost of such maintenance.

Funding

The owner has agreed to your normal review fee. The owner is willing to "do what it takes" to make the system more viable, especially since the order volume is continuing to increase. She wants cost estimates for equipment and other items included in your final report.

Questions

1. What is the first step that should be taken to determine how to make the system more viable and improve communications?

   A. Technology review

   B. Up-version the NT Server 4 machines to Windows 2000

   C. Upgrade the application software to the latest version

   D. Perform the risk assessment

2. You have started the risk assessment for communications between sites. The owner is concerned that using passwords and IDs alone is not secure enough since Windows often stores passwords. What Windows 2000 security feature might calm the owner?

   A. SSL

   B. Kerberos v5

   C. Smart cards

   D. Encryption

3. Reorder the actions on the right into the Risk Assessment Plan on the left. Include each substep under the appropriate step.

Risk Assessment Plan	Actions
	Step: Quantify risks
	Substep: Assign a cost to each risk
	Step: Identify risks
	Substep: Assign a priority to each risk
	Substep: Determine tolerance levels
	Step: Monitor and manage risks
	Step: Plan for risks
	Substep: Assign a probability to each risk

4. Connect the ordering and processing elements to show how better communication would affect the current ordering and fulfillment system among the three sites. You might not need to use all the elements shown; you may need to use some elements more than once.

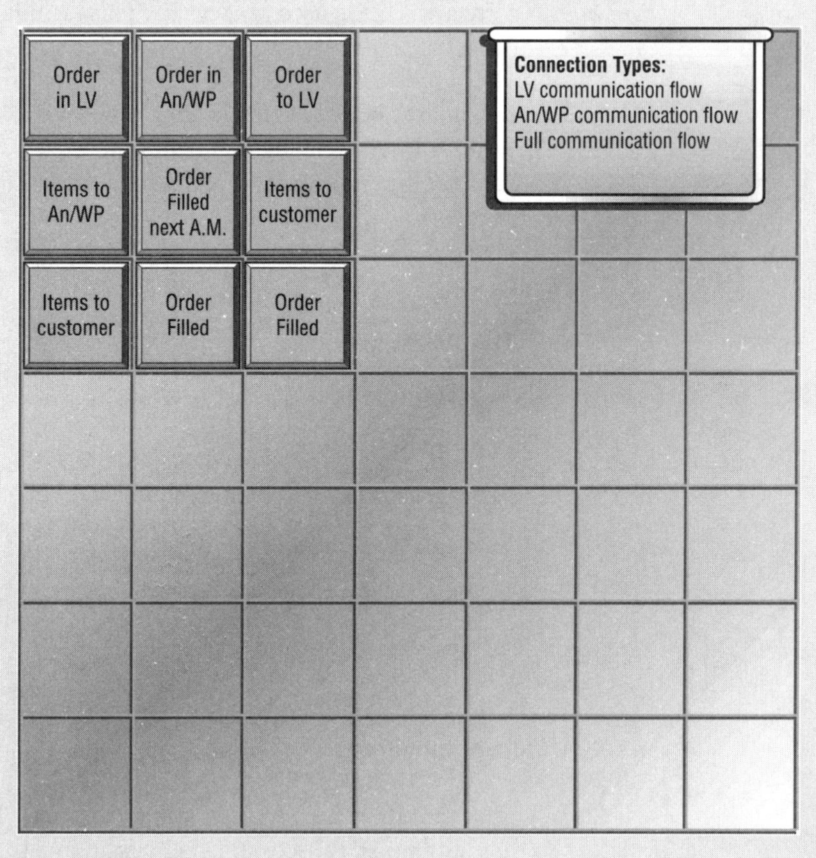

Answers

1. A. Before you can start taking action concerning communication and upgrading to Windows 2000, you need to know what equipment and software is being used at each site. This includes how the equipment is being used.

2. C. Smart cards are supported by Windows 2000. Smart cards can be used for interactive logon in addition to passwords and include the capacity for cryptography and secure storage for private keys and certificates.

3.

Risk Assessment Plan

Step: Identify risks

Step: Quantify risks

Substep: Determine tolerance levels

Substep: Assign a probability to each risk

Substep: Assign a cost to each risk

Substep: Assign a priority to each risk

Step: Plan for risks

Step: Monitor and manage risks

There are four main steps in risk assessment. The Quantify step has four additional substeps that help make sure that resources are applied to the most damaging risks first. It is important to realize that this process is ongoing.

4.

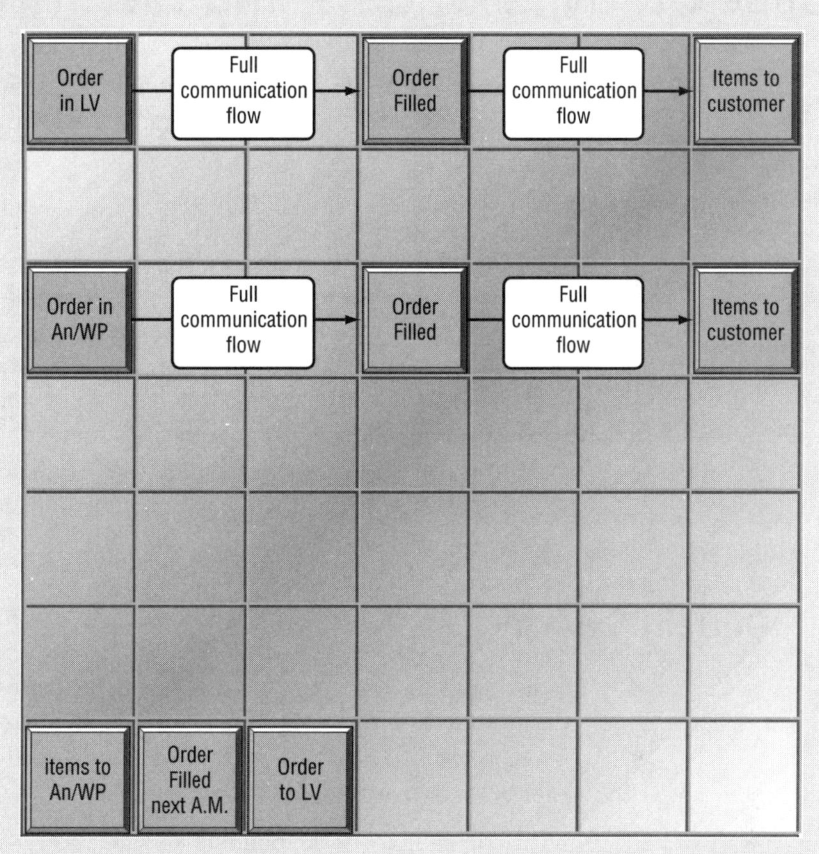

If the communications are interconnected between the sites, the order process will be the same no matter the location. The current system has some definite redundancies due to the need to ship the items back to the remote sites before they can be sent to the customer.

Case Study 2: Update and Security

You should give yourself 10 minutes to review this case study, diagram as needed, and complete the questions for this testlet.

Background

You have been hired to review a company's current operations, including security, and to help identify the best upgrade path for Windows 2000. The company is headquartered in Las Vegas, and has branches in White Plains (NY) and Anaheim (CA). Each location is a separate network, and no site has Internet access at this point. Communications between the locations is done using 56K modems, on an as needed basis. This worked quite well when the company first started and had only two people in each branch office, but now that the offices have expanded, the modems are too slow. Communication must be improved and centralized data sharing put in place.

Current System

Las Vegas There are 200 employees in the main office. The main office is located close to a major interstate and includes both office space and warehouse space for the distribution center. Most of the employees (125) work in the distribution center, processing orders.

The company owns the building and has three NT 4 servers. One server is for authentication and the other two servers are used for printing and applications. The major application is the customer order application. Customers phone associates, who use the application to take and process the orders. Once the order is complete and verified, the application sends a shipping notice to the distribution center, and generates a charge slip in accounting. All transactions are contained in a SQL database using Microsoft's SQL 7. You have verified that the software is compatible with Windows 2000.

White Plains and Anaheim Orders received at the branch offices are sent via modem to the ordering department at the end of the day for input into the main system. The branch offices are running the same major application, but since they do not have full communications with the main system, the orders must be combined and batched. All ordered items for the day submitted are sent first thing the next morning to the appropriate branch office. The ordered items are then separated and the individual orders are sent to the customer.

Problem Statement

The current system was put into operation when the company first started eight years ago. The order volume has been increasing slowly each year until the current year when it doubled in the first five months. You have been asked to review the company and help determine how to increase communication and decrease the duplication of effort.

Envisioned System

During your meeting with the owner of the company you were told that the company must become unified in order processing and shipping. Each branch must be able to communicate with the main office in a timely manner.

Security

The life of this company is the ordering and shipping of their product. Any communication between machines must be secure and protected. The orders contain sensitive customer information, including credit card numbers. Security is still one of the most important concerns of the owner.

Availability

Orders are taken 24 hours a day and seven days a week. The distribution center is staffed between 7:00 A.M. and 8:00 P.M. PST Monday through Friday, and from 8:00 A.M. until 6:00 P.M. on Saturday. This means that the order system must be available at all times.

Maintainability

There are now five people in the IT department at the main office. Each branch office has two people responsible for the system.

Funding

The owner was again very impressed with your suggestions and design of the VPN and other communication systems. She is enthusiastic about the savings and increase in customer service. Some employees in White Plains and Anaheim have expressed concern about the possible reduction of staff dedicated to order shipping. All servers have been upgraded to Windows 2000.

Questions

1. You have the chance now to restructure the three domains shown below. Connect the domains to reflect their current organization, and then connect them to show how you suggest restructuring them.

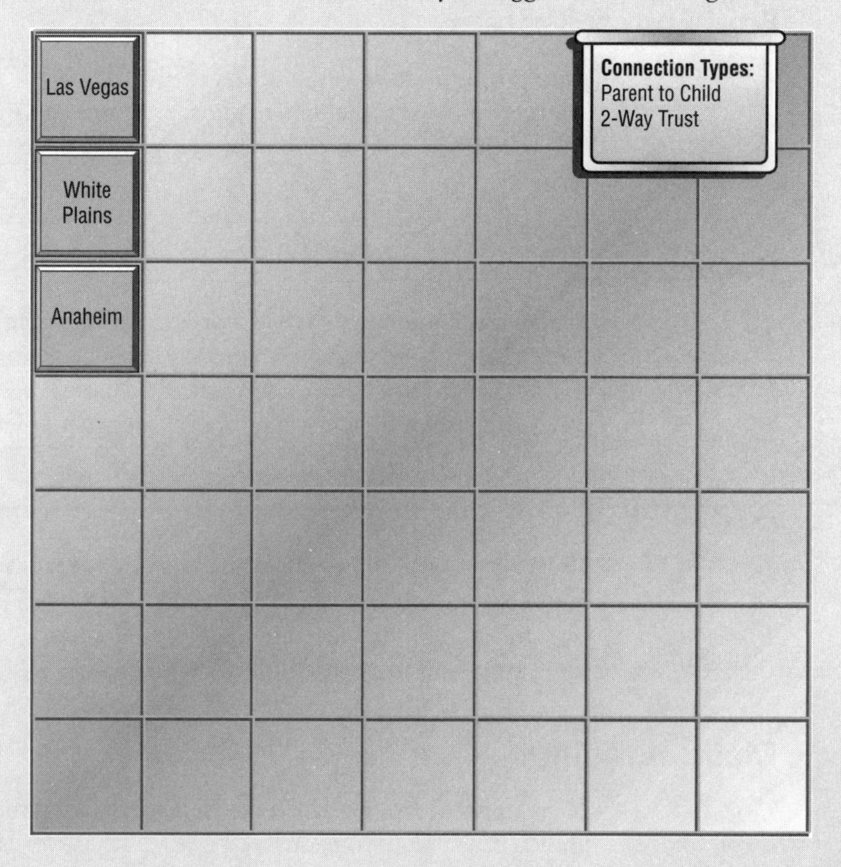

2. What is the final operational mode state of a Windows 2000 domain?

   A. Mixed

   B. Final

   C. Native

   D. Complete

3. Which domain cannot be changed after it has been created?

   A. Parent

   B. Root

   C. Child

   D. Master

4. Place the following SID components in the correct order (hierarchical convention).

Component Hierarchy	Components
	Revision number
	RID
	Domain ID
	Assigning authority

Answers

1.

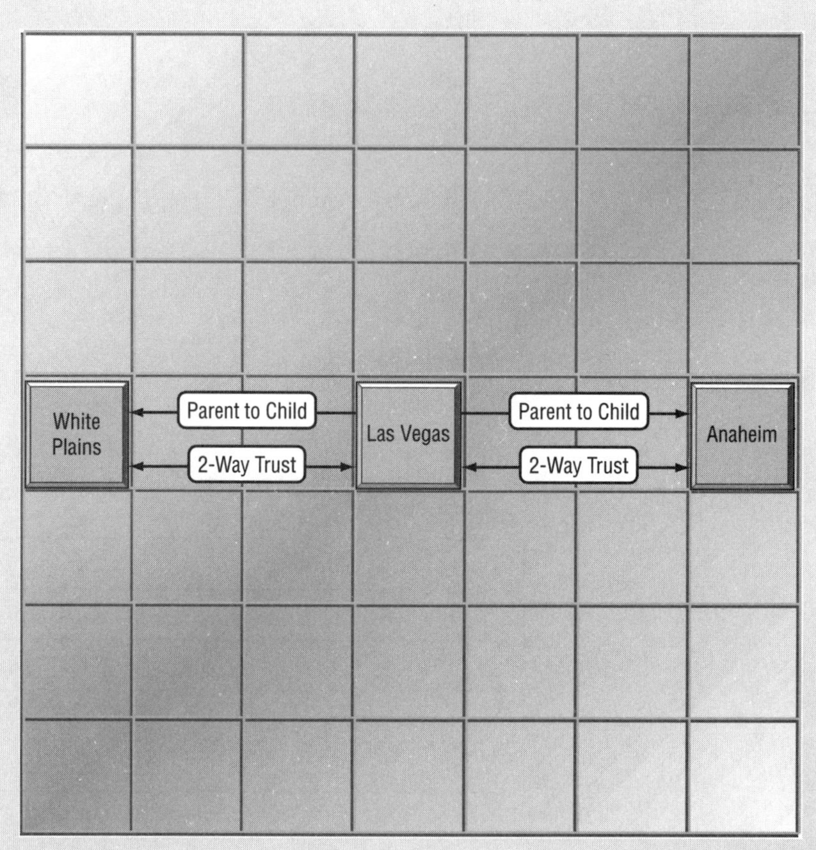

The old structure required two-way trusts between all domains. Thus, each domain required its own administrative personnel. This created a large amount of redundancy. The suggested solution above sets each area in its own organizational unit. The grand majority of administrative detail will be done at the main office in Las Vegas. This will permit the technicians at the other sites to dedicate more time to the equipment and less time to network administration. This design also shows the dependency of the children organizational units to the parent as the actual corporate environment exists.

2. C. Native mode can be done after all domain controllers in the network have been upgraded to Windows 2000. Once native mode has been set, it cannot be undone.

3. B. The root domain is the first domain in the forest. Once it has been created, it cannot be changed. Other domains that are created are called child domains.

4.

Component Hierarchy

Revision number

Assigning authority

Domain ID

RID

The components of the SID follow a hierarchical convention. The first piece is the revision number of the SID, followed by the piece that identifies which authority actually assigned the SID to the object. The third piece identifies the controllers' domain, and the final part is the RID that uniquely identifies the security principal relative to the issuing authority.

Glossary

Account Operator Windows NT Server operator who manages user accounts. In Windows 2000, Account Operators can manage users, groups, and computers in the Active Directory.

account policies Windows 2000 policies used to determine password and logon requirements. Account policies are set through the Microsoft Management Console (MMC) Local Computer Policy snap-in.

anti-replay Prevents acceptance of a packet that has been captured and later resent.

asymmetric policy Provides different security services for inbound and outbound packets between two hosts.

auditing Refers to the system's ability to detect, track, and log breaches in security.

audit policy A Windows 2000 policy that tracks the success or failure of specified security events. Audit policies are set through *Local Computer Policy.*

Authentication Headers (AH) A field that immediately follows the IP header in an IP datagram and provides authentication, integrity, and anti-replay checking for the entire datagram.

authenticator A way for one party to prove that another party has access to and knows a secret key. In Kerberos, for example, the authenticator will include things like timestamps. The authenticator is also encrypted with the session key issued by the Key Distribution Center (KDC).

Authenticode A cryptographic feature of Microsoft Internet Explorer that makes it possible to determine who has published a piece of software and to make sure that that software has not changed since publication.

availability Assures information and communications services will be ready for use when expected.

AXFR Type of DNS zone transfer; AXFR replicates the entire zone.

bandwidth utilization On a network, the way the transmission capacity of a communications channel is being used.

basic authentication An authentication protocol supported by Microsoft Internet Explorer. There is no encryption in this protocol.

bastion host Any computer that must be secure because it is accessible from the Internet and exposed to attack. It can be a gateway between an inside network and an outside network.

certificate life cycle You normally define the certificate life cycle to require periodic renewal of issued certificates. Issued certificates expire at the end of their lifetime and can be renewed in a cycle until revoked or expired, or until an issuing certification authority is unavailable.

certificate practice statement (CPS) Specifies the practices that the certification authority employs to issue and manage certificates to meet your certificate policies.

certificate policy States your organization's requirements for certificates, such as public key lengths, certificate lifetimes, and uses for certificates.

certificate revocation list (CRL) A digitally signed list of certificates that are no longer valid.

certificate revocation policy Specifies the circumstances that justify revoking a certificate.

certificate trust list A signed list of root certification authority certificates that an administrator considers reputable for designated purposes, such as client authentication or secure e-mail. See also *certificate*, *certification authority*, *root certificate*, and *root certification authority*.

certification hierarchy A model of trust for certificates in which certification paths are created through the establishment of parent-child relationships between certification authorities. See also *certification authority* and *certification path*.

centralized administration Network management provided by a small group of individuals.

CGI Common Gateway Interface; CGI is the method that Web servers use to allow interaction between servers and programs.

change-management The process of planning, tracking, and controlling changes to network software, hardware, and microcode.

clear-text passwords Passwords that are not encrypted before being sent over the network.

code authentication This strategy requires that code downloaded from the Internet be signed with the digital signature of a trusted software publisher.

communication flow Managed information movement from one entity to another.

computer local groups Security groups specific to a computer and not recognized elsewhere in the domain.

data confidentiality Users who do not have proper permissions to data cannot see the data.

data encryption standard (DES)
Definition 1: An unclassified crypto algorithm adopted by the National Bureau of Standards for public use.
Definition 2: A cryptographic algorithm for the protection of unclassified data, published in Federal Information Processing Standard (FIPS) 46. The DES, which was approved by the National Institute of Standards and Technology (NIST), is intended for public and government use.

data integrity The property that data meets an *a priori* expectation of quality.

decryption The process of taking encrypted data and making it readable again.

delegation of control wizard A wizard used to distribute precise elements of the administrator's control over resources to others.

Diffie-Hellman algorithm One of the most widely-used secure algorithms to provide for key exchange. The two parties exchange key information. Windows 2000 will provide additional protection by using a hash function encryption. The parties never exchange the actual key; however, after their exchange of the key information, each is able to generate the identical shared key. At no time is the actual key ever exchanged.

Directory Service Access Event Both the directory information source and the service that make the information available and usable. A directory service enables the user to find an object, given any one of its attributes. When an object is accessed, it is a Directory Service Access Event.

Directory System Agent (DSA) The process that manages and provides access to stored directory information.

distributed administration Network management provided by a large group of individuals. Each group is responsible for different areas of network administration.

distributed security Distributed password-based authentication that provides a single, secure user interaction for both dial-up connectivity and applications across multiple servers and sites.

domain architecture When used in relation to Windows 2000 and Active Directory, a domain is a collection of computers that has been defined by the administrator of a Windows 2000 Server network. These computers share a common directory database. When looked at from the perspective of DNS, a domain is any tree or subtree within the DNS namespace. DNS domains are not the same as Windows 2000 domains and should not be confused with the Windows 2000 and Active Directory networking domain model.

domain credentials User name and password or smart card logon.

domain local group A Windows 2000 group that is only available when a domain is in native mode. This group can contain members from anywhere in the Windows 2000 forest, or from members that reside in trusted forests, or even in a trusted Windows NT domain. Domain local groups can only be used to grant permissions to resources within the domain in which they exist. In most cases, the domain local groups are used to gather security principals from across the forest to control access to resources within a specific native mode domain.

domain restructure As part of the migration process, domain restructure can result in any number of outcomes. Typically the result is some rationalization of the current domain structure with fewer larger domains.

domain upgrade Upgrading a domain from an earlier operating system version to Windows 2000.

empty recovery policy A recovery policy remains, but all of the recovery agent certificates have been deleted.

Encapsulating Security Payloads (ESP) A mechanism to provide confidentiality and integrity protection to IP datagrams.

encryption The process of translating data into code that is not easily accessible; done to increase security. Once data has been encrypted, a user must have a password or key to decrypt the data.

enterprise certification authorities A certification authority that is completely integrated with Active Directory.

enterprise root certificate authorities The most trusted certification authority (CA). This is also at the top of the certification hierarchy. The enterprise root CA has a self-signed certificate. It is also called the root authority.

enterprise subordinate certificate authorities The next level of a trusted certification authority (CA), which is at the second or third layer of a certification hierarchy. The enterprise subordinate CA has a certificate from the root authority.

Extensible Authentication Protocol-Transport Level Security (EAP-TLS) An extension to PPP that allows for arbitrary authentication mechanisms to be employed for the validation of a PPP connection.

file encryption key (FEK) A symmetric bulk encryption key.

firewall A system or combination of systems that enforces a boundary between two or more networks. A gateway that limits access between networks in accordance with local security policy. The typical firewall is an inexpensive micro-based Unix box kept clean of critical data, with many modems and public network ports on it, but just one carefully watched connection back to the rest of the private network.

Gateway Service for NetWare (GSNW) A service that allows Microsoft clients to access NetWare networks.

global group A group that is used in its own domain, in member servers and workstations of the domain, and in trusting domains. In all those places a global group is used for the granting of rights and permissions. A global group can become a member of local groups. Global groups can contain user accounts only from its own domain.

Group Policy An administration tool that can be used to define and control how programs, network resources, and the operating system operate for users and computers. In Active Directory, Group Policy is applied to users or computers on the basis of their membership in sites, domains, or organizational units.

hashing A result that is obtained from applying a one-way mathematical function called a message digest function to an arbitrary amount of data. This can also be called a *hash function* or a *hash algorithm*.

independent software vendors (ISVs) A third-party software developer; an individual or an organization that independently creates computer software.

intruder detection Pertaining to techniques that attempt to detect intrusion into a computer or network by observation of actions, security logs, or audit data. Break-in (or attempted break-in) detection, either manual or via software expert systems that operate on logs or other information available on the network.

Internet Key Exchange (IKE) The protocol that establishes the security association as well as the shared keys that are necessary for two parties to communicate using Internet Protocol Security.

Internet Protocol Security (IPSec) A set of protection services and protocols. IPSec can be used to protect all the protocols in the TCP/IP protocol suite as well as communication over the Internet using L2TP.

Internet Security Association Key Management Protocol (ISAKMP/Oakley) A protocol for the secure exchange of key material in IPSec.

IP filtering Decision criteria based on the source or destination address of an IP Packet.

issuing CA The CA giving out the certificate.

IXFR Incremental zone transfer, which replicates only the changed records of the zone file.

Kerberos v5 A method of authentication that is used to verify the identity of a user or of a host. In Windows 2000, the Kerberos v5 protocol is the default authentication service. IPSec uses the Kerberos protocol for authentication.

key distribution center A privileged process that is running as a network service on all domain controllers. It supplies session tickets and temporary session keys that are used in the Kerberos authentication protocol. The KDC uses Active Directory to manage different types of account information like passwords for user accounts.

key life A policy that determines how long a key may remain in circulation.

krbtgt The security principal name used by the Key Distribution Center in all Windows 2000 domains.

LAN emulation (LANE) A group of protocols that will allow Ethernet and Token Ring LANs to work with an ATM network. LANE allows LAN- and ATM-attached stations to connect.

Layer 2 Tunneling Protocol (L2TP) A tunneling protocol that encapsulates PPP frames that can then be sent over IP, X.25, frame relay, or ATM networks.

license service A server in Terminal Services that manages all the client licenses. This includes tracking the licenses that have been issued to client computers or terminals.

management by empowerment A management philosophy that gives the employees the power to make decisions necessary to complete their projects.

master and slave DNS servers A relationship between two DNS servers that contain copies of the same zone. In this relationship, one of the copies is directly replicated from the other. The source of this replication is called the master server, and the destination of the replication is called the slave server. Each master server may have one or more slaves and every slave may have one or more masters. The same DNS server may be both the master and the slave server at the same time.

message digest The result that is obtained by applying a one-way mathematical formula called a message digest function to a set of data. In this way, if you are given a change to the input data, the resulting value in the message digest will change. The message digest can also be called a hash.

micromanagement A management philosophy that has the manager watching every move an employee makes.

Microsoft Challenge Handshake Authentication Protocol (MS-CHAP) An authentication method that is used for PPP connections. It is similar to CHAP.

Microsoft Point-to-Point Encryption (MPPE) A 128/40-bit encryption algorithm using RSA RC4. MPPE provides for packet security between the client and the tunnel server and is useful where IPSec is not available. The 40-bit version addresses localization issues based on current export restrictions. MPPE is compatible with Network Address Translation.

mixed mode Allows for compatibility between Windows 2000 domain controllers and Windows NT backup domain controllers in a domain. Mixed mode does not support the universal and nested group enhancements that are available in Windows 2000. The domain mode can be changed to native mode only after all Windows NT domain controllers are either removed from the domain or upgraded to Windows 2000.

native mode All domain controllers within a domain are Windows 2000 domain controllers and native mode operation has been enabled.

Network Control Protocol (NCP) A protocol from the PPP protocol suite that is used to negotiate the parameters of LAN protocols such as TCP/IP or IPX.

Network File System (NFS) The file system used in Unix implementations.

nonrepudiation Nonrepudiation gives assurances that any one of the parties involved in a communication cannot falsely deny that the communication occurred.

NTLM authentication protocol An authentication protocol that was used in previous versions of Windows NT. It is a challenge/response authentication protocol. The protocol continues to be supported in Windows 2000.

original equipment manufacturer (OEM) The original maker of a piece of equipment.

pass-through authentication Secure channels are used to authenticate Windows 2000 and Windows NT computer accounts and to authenticate user accounts when a remote user connects to a network resource and the user account exists in a trusted domain.

PC/SC smart card specification This is the standard for smart cards and smart card readers. It is published by the PC/SC Workgroup, which is a consortium of industry-leading computer software and hardware manufacturers.

personal identification number The code that is used to protect smart cards from misuse. The PIN is similar to a password and should be known only to the owner of the card.

public key encryption Type of cryptography in which the encryption process is publicly available and unprotected, but in which a part of the decryption key is protected so that only a party with knowledge of both parts of the decryption process can decrypt the cipher text.

recovery agent An account that can be used to decrypt a file that has been encrypted by the Encrypting File System (EFS). It is used if the file owner's decryption key is unavailable.

Redundant Array of Independent Disks (RAID) A fault-tolerant disk system. There are six levels that are used to gauge various mixes of performance, reliability, and cost. Windows 2000 provides three of the RAID levels: Level 0 (striping), Level 1 (mirroring), and Level 5 (stripe sets with parity).

referral ticket A ticket-granting ticket that is encrypted with the interdomain key shared by the KDCs with a trust relationship. The ticket-granting service in the trusting domain uses its copy of the interdomain key to decrypt the referral ticket. If decryption is successful, it sends the client a session ticket to the desired server in its domain. The password for a domain trust account is used to derive a Kerberos interdomain key for encrypting and decrypting referral tickets.

Remote Authentication Dial-in User Service (RADIUS) A security authentication system used by many Internet Service Providers (ISPs). A user connects to the ISP and enters a username and password. This information is verified by a RADIUS server, which then authorizes access to the ISP system.

Remote Desktop Protocol (RDP) Client/Server protocol used to connect to Microsoft Terminal Services server.

Remote Installation Services (RIS) An optional component of Windows 2000 that remotely installs Windows 2000 Professional. It installs operating systems on remote boot–enabled client computers by connecting the computer to the network, starting the client computer, and logging on with a valid user account.

Resource Record A record stored in the DNS database. All resource records have the same format that includes NAME, TYPE, CLASS, TTL, RDLENGTH, and RDATA that depends on TYPE and CLASS of the resource record. A set of resource records builds up a DNS zone.

risk contingency strategy A study of vulnerabilities, threats, likelihood, loss or impact, and theoretical effectiveness of security measures. The process of evaluating threats and vulnerabilities, known and postulated, to determine expected loss and establish the degree of acceptability to system operations.

risk contingency trigger An event that indicates a risk has become a reality.

risk management strategy The total process to identify, control, and minimize the impact of uncertain events. The objective of the risk management program is to reduce risk and obtain and maintain DAA (Designated Approving Authority) approval.

screened subnet model This area is a network that permits access from the Internet into a private network, while still maintaining the security of the private network. In this area go all of the servers that have any Internet exposed interfaces. This is also known as a DMZ.

Secure/Multipurpose Internet Mail Extensions (S/MIME) An extension of MIME to support secure electronic mail.

security analysis A study of network resources to determine level of risk and level of protection.

Security Association (SA) The parameters that define the services and methods necessary to protect IPSec.

security baseline The current level of network security.

security group The unit that is used to administer permissions for users and other domain objects.

security risk The likelihood that a network resource will be attacked.

security templates A way of representing a security configuration that can then be applied to a local computer or imported into a Group Policy object in Active Directory. When the security template has been imported into a Group Policy object, Group Policy processes the template and then makes the corresponding changes to the members of that Group Policy object. Members of the GPO can be users or computers.

Server Message Block (SMB) A file-sharing protocol that is designed to allow computers to access files that reside on remote systems over a variety of networks.

Services for Unix (SFU) Special services added to a Windows 2000 environment to enhance the integration of Unix hosts.

session key A key used during a session for encryption and decryption. Session keys are used with algorithms where the same key is used for both encryption and decryption.

Session Key Perfect Forward Secrecy An option of the IPSec policy that determines how a new key is generated. Enabling PFS ensures that a key used to protect a transmission cannot be used to generate any additional keys. In addition, the keying material for that key cannot be used to generate any new keys. Session Key PFS does not require a re-authentication and therefore uses less resources than Master Key PFS. When Session Key PFS is enabled, a new key exchange is performed to accumulate new key material before the new session key is generated.

Server-Gated Cryptography (SGC) Used by financial institutions to transmit private documents via the Internet.

smart card A credit card–sized device that is used with a PIN number to enable certificate-based authentication and single sign-on.

symmetric key encryption An encryption algorithm that requires the same secret key to be used for both encryption and decryption. Often called secret key encryption.

ticket-granting service A service provided by the Key Distribution Center (KDC).

ticket-granting tickets A credential given to a user by the Key Distribution Center (KDC) when the user logs on. The user then has to present the TGT to the KDC whenever requesting session tickets for access to services. It is sometimes called a user ticket.

time to live (TTL) A timer value included in TCP/IP packets that determine the effective life of the packet.

TKEY A resource record specified in the IETF Internet–Draft "Secret Key Establishment for DNS (TKEY RR)" as the vehicle to transfer security tokens between the client and the server and to establish secret keys to use with the TSIG resource record.

transitive trust The two-way trust relationship that exists between Windows 2000 domains in a domain tree or forest. It can also exist between trees in a forest, or even between forests.

Transport Layer Security (TLS) A standard protocol that provides for secure Web communications on the Internet or intranets. By using TLS clients can authenticate servers or, optionally, servers to authenticate clients. TLS provides a secure channel by encrypting all communications.

transport mode End-to-end IPSec communication mode.

TSIG A resource record specified in the IETF Internet–Draft "Secret Key Transaction Signatures for DNS (TSIG)" to send and verify signature-protected messages.

Tunnel mode One of the two modes available in IPSec, tunnel mode is usually used between two routers or firewalls.

two-factor authentication policy An authentication policy requiring two forms of identification before accessing a network, for example a policy requiring a smart card and a personal identification number to log on.

User Datagram Protocol (UDP) A TCP protocol that provides connectionless service that does not guarantee delivery or correct sequencing of delivered packets.

World Wide Web Consortium Created in October 1994 to lead the World Wide Web to its full potential by developing common protocols that promote its evolution and ensure its interoperability.

Zone Transfer The replication of the zone information from master server to slave server.

Index

Note to the Reader: Throughout this index **boldfaced** page numbers indicate primary discussions of a topic. *Italicized* page numbers indicate illustrations.

A

B

C

D

E

F

G

H

I

J

K

L

M

N

O

P

Q

R

S

T

U

V

W

X

Z

W

X

Z

MCSE: Windows 2000 Network Security Design Study Guide Exam 70-220

OBJECTIVE	PAGE
Analyzing Business Requirements	
Analyze the existing and planned business models. • Anlalyze the company model and the geographical scope. Models include regional, national, international, subsidiary, and branch offices. • Analyze company processes. Processes include information flow, communication flow, service and product life cycles, and decision-making.	12, 19
Analyze the existing and planned organizational structures. Considerations include management model; company organization; vendor, partner, and customer relationships; and acquisition plans. I	54
Analyze factors that influence company strategies. • Identify company priorities. • Identify the projected growth and growth strategy. • Identify relevant laws and regulations. • Identify the company's tolerance for risk. • Identify the total cost of operations.	70, 163
Analyze business and security requirements for the end user.	95, 105
Analyze the structure of IT management. Considerations include type of administration, such as centralized or decentralized; funding model; outsourcing; decision-making process; and change-management process.	95, 105
Analyze the current physical model and information security model. • Analyze internal and external security risks.	153
Analyzing Technical Requirements	
Evaluate the company's existing and planned technical environment. • Analyze company size and user and resource distribution. • Assess the available connectivity between the geographic location of work sites and remote sites. • Assess the net available bandwidth. • Analyze performance requirements. • Analyze the method of accessing data and systems. • Analyze network roles and responsibilities. Roles include administrative, user, service, resource ownership, and application.	201, 209, 215, 220, 224
Analyze the impact of the security design on the existing and planned technical environment. • Assess existing systems and applications. • Identify existing and planned upgrades and rollouts. • Analyze technical support structure. • Analyze existing and planned network and systems management.	258, 266, 272, 279, 283